Oxford Dictionary of

Word

Origins

SECOND EDITION

Edited by JULIA CRESSWELL

Julia Cresswell is an experienced author and language researcher, having worked on the fourth edition of the *Shorter Oxford English Dictionary*. She has also authored *Naming Your Baby: The Definitive Dictionary of First Names* and *The Cat's Pyjamas: The Penguin Book of Clichés*.

OXFORD
UNIVERSITY PRESS

Great Clarendon Street, Oxford OX2 6DP

Oxford University Press is a department of the University of Oxford.
It furthers the University's objective of excellence in research,
scholarship, and education by publishing worldwide in

Oxford New York

Auckland Cape Town Dar es Salaam Hong Kong Karachi
Kuala Lumpur Madrid Melbourne Mexico City Nairobi
New Delhi Shanghai Taipei Toronto

With offices in

Argentina Austria Brazil Chile Czech Republic
France Greece Guatemala Hungary Italy Japan Poland
Portugal Singapore South Korea Switzerland Thailand
Turkey Ukraine Vietnam

Oxford is a registered trade mark of Oxford University Press
in the UK and in certain other countries

Published in the United States
by Oxford University Press Inc., New York

© Oxford University Press 2002, 2004, 2009, 2010
First published 2002
First issued as an Oxford University Press paperback 2004
Second edition published 2009, issued as an Oxford University Press paperback 2010

The moral rights of the author have been asserted
Database right Oxford University Press (maker)

British Library Cataloguing in Publication Data

Data available

Library of Congress Cataloging in Publication Data

Data available

Typeset by SPI Publisher Services, Pondicherry, India
Printed in Great Britain
on acid-free paper by
Clays Ltd., St Ives plc

ISBN 978-0-19-954793-7

10 9 8 7 6 5

Contents

Abbreviations

To save space the following abbreviations have been used to show the periods in which words are used.

OE stands for Old English, used up to *c*.1149
ME stands for Middle English used *c*.1150–*c*.1350
LME stands for Late Middle English used *c*.1350–1500

Thereafter, date ranges are given by century, proceeded by E, M, or L standing for Early (up to the 29th year) Middle (30–69) and Late (70–99), so that a word labelled [E17th] would have come into use between 1600 and 1629; one labelled [M18th] between 1730 and 1769; and one labelled [L19th] between 1870 and 1899.

Introduction

It is well established that English has an unusually large vocabulary. This is partly because its history has exposed the language to an unusually large number of influences, and partly because it has never been slow to borrow from any language it meets. Although there are borrowings from many exotic languages, the majority of words in English have come from one of the large number of languages that belong to the Indo-European group, as English itself does. This is the dominant family of languages in Europe and Western Asia, all of which are descended from a hypothetical language called Proto-Indo-European. Who the original Indo-Europeans were we do not know. The majority of scholars would probably say that they were a people living somewhere in the region of the Black Sea approximately 6000 years ago, but views vary widely both as to when and where they lived. What we do know is that their language spread, changing all the while. How and why it spread are again hotly debated, but speakers of the language group spread as far east as western China, south into India, and west as far as Ireland, before the languages were exported to other continents at a later date.

It may seem impossible that Irish, English, Greek, Persian, and Hindi are all related, but they are indeed all descended from Proto-Indo-European. The secret behind discovering the links lies in the study of early forms of the languages and of the way in which sounds change in language, combined with careful comparison of the languages. Of these, the most important for our purposes is sound change. The way that a language is pronounced is constantly changing, although we may not be aware of it. Today we are lucky, because we have sound recordings stretching back over 100 years, and can hear for ourselves how odd someone speaking only 50 years ago sounds today. We are so used to the idea of a standard written language that it is easy to forget how much variation there is in the sounds of the spoken English we hear today. Those who want to check this out for themselves will find the British Library website has an excellent collection of recordings.

The brain has an extraordinary ability to recognize the same words in the widely different sounds of English spoken, say, in Mumbai, Melbourne, Alabama, and Glasgow. Over time which of these varying sounds becomes the generally accepted one varies. This is the key to one of the ways sounds in speech change—there is constant variety all around us, but we can usually ignore it. If what we think of as the standard form changes, it can eventually lead to a change in the written form. Speakers of English English can hear for themselves how this process works. One of the changes that is taking place in English at the moment is a change in the sound written 'th'. 'Th' is actually the symbol for two closely related sounds—that in *think* and that in *bothered*. More and more people are pronouncing the first of these as *fink* and the second as *bovvered*. This is not a sudden change. It was recorded in London in the 19th century, spread slowly through the 20th, but became much more common in the last quarter of that century. It is possible that in the future it will become the dominant form (although not inevitable) and then a sound change will have happened. Although on paper the change from 'th' to 'v' or 'f' may seem great, in fact, if you say the sounds you will find that the only significant difference is the position of the lower lip, and the resulting slight change in the position of the tongue. This is an important point; sound changes are not arbitrary, but go to a sound made in a neighbouring part of the mouth.

By comparing old written forms of the language we are able to reconstruct what changes have taken place in the past and so establish the relationships between Indo-European languages. This enables us to show, for instance, that Germanic languages (including English) and Latin once shared a common ancestor, and that our word 'tooth' and the Latin word behind 'dentist' were once the same. By comparing all the available vocabulary it was possible to establish the rules of how different sounds correspond in the two languages, and it was found that 'd' regularly appears as 't' in English, and Latin 't' regularly appears as th. Thus Latin **dentem** (which gives us dentist) corresponds to **tooth** in English. Likewise, since Latin 'p' regularly appears as 'f', **pedem**, Latin for foot, and source of pedestrian, appears as **foot** in English. Working in this way, it has been possible to establish the relationships between the surviving languages, and go some way towards reconstructing lost ones.

Modern English emerges from this history with a vastly enriched vocabulary because it is a blend of more than one branch of the Indo-European family. The basic structure and the vocabulary of the language belongs to the Germanic branch, the family of languages spoken throughout north-west Europe. This was introduced to the British Isles when the Anglo-Saxons became the dominant group after the Romans left in the 5th century AD. Even then, the Anglo-Saxon language, known as Old English, was already a mixture of different dialects as different tribes settled different areas leading to regional variations, which can still be traced in the language today. From the end of the 8th century the British Isles were subject to increasingly frequent Viking raids, which led to large tracts of the country being settled by Scandinavian speakers of Old Norse, and eventually, with Canute (*d*.1035), to a Scandinavian ruler. These invasions had a profound influence on the language, adding to the vocabulary providing both basic words such as 'she' and enriching the stock of words by duplicating vocabulary. For instance, shirt and skirt are basically the same Germanic word, but because they are both available they can be used much more precisely than the original one word, which seems to have been a catch-all term for a long garment.

After the Scandinavians, their relatives who had settled in France invaded in 1066. Norman is simply a form of 'North man' or Viking, but the Scandinavians who had settled in Normandy had largely abandoned their Germanic language and adopted the local form of French. This belonged to a different branch of the Indo-European family, the Romance languages that developed from the language of Rome, Latin. With the Norman conquest, Old English, which had had a flourishing and sophisticated literature, largely disappeared from the written record for a couple of generations, to be replaced by Latin and French, and became the language of the uneducated, a situation that tends to lead to rapid change. When the language re-emerged, it had changed into Middle English and acquired large elements of French and Latin vocabulary. Most of the Old English words were still there, although often in much more restricted senses, but people were able to express themselves much more precisely. Throughout the Middle Ages the vocabulary continued to expand, mainly with Latin-based words, for Latin was the language of learning well into the 17th and 18th centuries, but also with words adopted from classical Greek and from trade relationships, particularly with the Dutch. By about 1500 the language had become Early Modern English, but since these changes are largely to do with the structure of the language rather than vocabulary, they need not concern us. Much the same process has continued up until modern times. Latin and Greek continued to be important sources of new words, particularly in the sciences, and changing and expanding trade had brought words into the language from an ever-widening pool of other languages.

The importance of Latin as a source means that it is necessary to consider some of the peculiarities of the language. Latin is an inflected language—that is to say, the relationship between words is mainly indicated by the endings. Old English had been inflected, but in modern English most of the inflections have been lost, although we still put an 's' on the end of words to show they are plural, and in verbs the 's' that distinguishes 'he eats' from 'I eat' still survives. Instead we rely on word order: 'Man bites dog' is very different from 'Dog bites man'. In Latin the three words could be in any order, but the ending of the words would show who was the biter and who bitten. Another peculiarity of Latin is that the middle of the word often adds or changes sounds from the basic form (the stem) in the inflected form. Thus 'the king' is *rex*, but 'of the king' is *regis*. This makes the language hard work for those learning it at school, but gave little trouble to the native speakers, any more than we have problems recognizing that 'won't' is the same as 'will not'. There are always good historical reasons for these sound changes, if you know where to look. In the case of *rex* and *regis* the difference is mainly one of spelling. If you spell *rex regs*, you can tell that the 'x' rather than 'g' is simply a running together of the two final sounds. This affects us in that words in other languages tend to be taken from the inflected forms of the Latin. In the case of the *rex*, we use the word 'regal' for kingly, incorporating the 'g' of the inflected form. In the earlier example above of the relationship between the Latin and English words for 'foot' it was necessary to cheat, for the basic form of foot in Latin is *pes*, the 'd' only appears in the inflected forms. As a result, in this book in entries for words from Latin it may not always be obvious where some of the sounds incorporated have come from. However, rather than fill the space with material explaining the Latin forms it has been decided to ask the reader to take the Latin inflected forms on trust. They can always be checked in one of the larger Oxford dictionaries of current English which include them in the etymologies. Another small point worth mentioning about Latin is that the letters 'i' and 'j' and the letters 'u' and 'v' were interchangeable in written forms, their pronunciation varying in time and in different areas. This explains some rather strange-looking spellings in the source words (similarly the development of Old English words is easier to understand if you know that the letters 'ge' were pronounced as if the 'g' was a 'y').

This is not the only way that considerations of space have affected the contents of the book. With such a vast vocabulary to choose from, only a small proportion could be included. Priority has gone to words with interesting history, rather than choosing to use the core vocabulary of the language. This is because the history of many Old English words is frankly rather dull; a word like 'hand' has changed its spelling from *hond* to hand, but otherwise all you can say about it is that it is a Germanic word and has relatives in other Germanic languages. Similarly some Latin roots have hardly changed in English either in form or sense. 'Placid' comes from Latin *placidus* and there is little more to say about it. Hand has been left out of the book, placid is mentioned in passing as one of a group of more interesting words that descend from the same root word.

The dates given in this book are based on those of the *Oxford English Dictionary* and its files. They are the first recorded dates, but it must be remembered that we are dependent on what has survived, and someone having spotted it and reported it. The record is full of gaps; for instance the word 'marzipan' is recorded once in 1542, again in 1583, and 1657 and then disappears until the 19th century, although there is no reason to think that the product does. 'Mend' is thought to be a shortening of 'amend', but is actually recorded slightly earlier than the longer form. Similarly, 'journalist' is recorded earlier than the 'journal' from which the job description comes. The study of word histories is very much dependent on what chance has handed down to us. This is why the majority of dates given for words are expressed only in terms of date ranges rather than exact dates.

Julia Cresswell

Wordbuilding

Many of the words in this book, particularly those from Greek and Latin, are made up of elements, known as combining forms or prefixes and suffixes, that alter the basic sense of the root word. Some of the more common are listed below with their usual meanings.

a- 1. With Greek roots (an- in front of a vowel) from Greek for 'not' means: not (atheist); without (anaemic) 2. With Old English roots means: to(wards) (aback); in a state of (aflutter); on (afoot); in (nowadays)

ab- From Latin for 'from, by, with' means: from (abduct)

ad- In Latin means 'to', used for motion (advance); change (adulterate); addition (adjunct)

be- In words from Old English, from 'by', means: all over (bespatter); thoroughly (bewilder); covered with (bejewelled); turns adjectives and nouns into verbs (befriend)

com- From Latin *cum*, 'with', sometimes appears as co-, col, cor or con depending on the sound following it, means: with (combine); together (compact); altogether (commemorate)

de- 1. From Latin for 'off, from', used for: down, away (descend); completely (denude) 2. From Latin *dis-* used for 'not, un-, apart', changed to de- in French, used for: removal (de-ice); undoing the action of something (deactivate)

di- 1. From Greek *dis* 'twice' means: twice, two, double mainly in technical words (dichromatic); in chemistry etc. with two atoms (dioxide) 2. From Latin: an alternative to *dis-* (*see below*)

dia- From the Greek for 'through', means: through (diaphanous); across (diameter); apart (dialysis)

dis- From Latin *dis-* used for 'not, un-, apart' means: not, un- (disadvantaged); used to reverse an action (disown); to remove or deprive of something (dismember); to separate or expel (disbar)

dys- Greek equivalent of *dis-*, means: bad (dysentery); difficult (dyspepia)

en-, em- 1. French form of Latin *in-*, means: put into (embed); in, into (ensnare); make, bring into a state (encrust); make more so (enliven) 2. From Greek equivalent of Latin *in-* means: within (empathy)

-en Old English, makes nouns and adjectives into verbs (deepen); makes adjectives from nouns (woollen)

ex- 1. From Latin *ex* 'out of', means: out (exclude); thoroughly (exterminate); cause to be in a state (exasperate); indicates a former state (ex-husband); removes from a state (excommunicate) 2. The Greek equivalent of the Latin, means: out (exodus)

for- From Old English, used to modify the sense of a word in the following ways: to make it more intense (forlorn); to prohibit (forbid); to show neglect (forget); to show renunciation or abstention (forgo, forgive)

fore- From Old English, means: in front of (foreshorten); before in time (forebode, forefathers); in front (forecourt, forebrain)

hyper- From Greek *huper* 'over, beyond' means: over, above, beyond (hypersonic); exceedingly, more than normal (hypersensitive); in electronic media used for complex structure as in hypertext

in- 1. From Latin *in* 'in', or English in, can also appear as il- im- ir- depending on sound following, used for: in, towards, within (inborn, influx) 2. From Latin *in* 'not', can also appear as il- im- ir- depending on sound following, used for: not (infertile), without (inequality)

non- From Latin *non* 'not', means: not involved in (non-aggression); not of the kind or way described (non-conformist); not of the importance implied (non-issue); not needing or causing (non-iron, non-skid); not having or being (non-human)

para- 1. From Greek *para* 'beside, alteration from' meaning: beside, alongside (parallel); beyond, different but with similarities (paramilitary) 2. From French and Italian, meaning: protecting (against) (parachute, parasol)

pen- From Latin *paene* 'almost' used in this sense (peninsula, penultimate)

per- From Latin *per-* 'through, by means of', means: through, all over (perforate); completely (perfect)

poly- From Greek *polus* 'much, many', means: much, many (polygon, polychrome)

pro- 1. From Latin *pro* 'in front of, on behalf of, for, instead of, because of', means: supporting (pro-choice); moving to, out or away (proceed) 2. From Greek *pro* 'before', meaning: before in time or place (proactive)

re- From Latin *re-* 'back, again', means: again, once more (reactivate); in response (react); against (resist); behind, after (remain); back, away, down (recede); more, again (refine)

semi- From Latin *semi-* 'half' meaning: half (semi-circular); almost (semi-darkness); partly (semi-detached)

sub- From Latin *sub* 'under, close to', changing to suc-, suf-, sug-, sup-, or sus- when influenced by a following sound, means: at a lower level (subalpine); lower or smaller (subordinate, subaltern); secondary (sublet, subdivision)

trans- From Latin *trans* 'across', means: across, to the other side of (transatlantic); through (transparent); to another state (transform)

un- 1. Old English, meaning: not (unrepeatable); the reverse of (unhappy); a lack of (unrest) 2. Old English, having much the same sense as 1. but from a different source, meaning: reversal (untie); separation, reduction (unmask, unman); release (unhand).

aardvaark *see* SOUTH AFRICAN WORD PANEL

abacus [LME] The abacus that we know today, with rows of wires along which slide beads, is an ancient object used by the Babylonians, Greeks, and Romans and is still found in many parts of the world. The earliest abacus was probably a board covered with sand, on which a clerk could draw figures and then rub them out again, and this was the original meaning in English. The word was borrowed from Latin, but came from Greek *abax* 'board, slab, plate', and probably ultimately from Hebrew *ābāq* 'dust'.

abandon *see* BAN

abase *see* BASE

abate, abattoir *see* BATED

abbot [OE] This comes from Aramaic 'abbā 'father' introduced through its use in the Bible.

abbreviate *see* BRIEF

abdicate [M16th] This is from Latin *abdicare* 'to renounce' from *ab-* 'away, from' and *dicare* 'declare'. Examples of the sense 'give up sovereignty' date from the early 18th century.

abduct *see* DUCT

aberrant *see* ERRANT

abet [LME] If you abet someone these days you are very likely to be up to no good, but this was not always the case. Since the late 18th century the word has mainly been found as **aid and abet**, 'to help and encourage someone in some wrongdoing', but in its early use to abet someone was simply to urge them to do something, not necessarily bad. It comes from the Old French word *abeter*, which could also mean 'to encourage a hound to bite'. BAIT [ME] has a similar root.

abhor [LME] Abhor literally means something that makes you shudder. It comes from Latin *ab-* 'away from' and *horrere* 'to shudder with fright', also the basis of *HORROR. In Shakespeare's day abhor could also mean 'to cause horror': 'It does abhor me now I speak the word' (*Othello*).

abject *see* JET

able [LME] In the past able had the senses 'easy to use' and 'suitable' as well as the more familiar sense 'having the qualifications or means' to do something. It comes from Latin *habilis* 'handy' from *habere* 'to hold'. The jargon term **abled**, as in *differently abled* was formed in the 1980s from **disabled** [L16th], from able with the negative *dis-* in front.

abominable [ME] People used to think that abominable came from Latin *ab-* 'away from' and *homo* 'human being', and so literally meant 'inhuman or beastly'. Consequently, until the 17th century it was frequently spelt *abhominable*, a spelling found in Shakespeare. In fact, the word comes from Latin *abominari*, meaning 'to regard something as a bad omen', and is related to **omen** [L16th] and **ominous** [L16th]. **Abominable Snowman** is another name for the Himalayan Yeti. The name was brought back by the Royal Geographical Society expedition mounted in 1921 to Mount Everest, which found mysterious footprints in the snow. Abominable Snowman is a translation of Tibetan *Meetoh Gangmi*, the name the Sherpa porters gave to the animal responsible for the tracks. **Yeti** is from Tibetan *yeh-the* 'little man-like animal'.

aborigine [M19th] This is a shortening of the 16th-century plural *aborigines* 'original inhabitants', which in classical times referred to the early people of Italy and Greece. The word comes from the Latin phrase *ab origine* 'from the beginning'. Now both Aborigines and **Aboriginals** are standard plural forms when referring to Australian Aboriginal people, a specialized use which dates from the 1820s.

abortive [ME] The early use of abortive, from Latin *aboriri* 'to miscarry' from *oriri* 'be born', was for a stillborn child or animal. **Abortion** is also mid 16th century.

abound *see* WATER

abracadabra [L17th] These days abracadabra is just a fun word said by magicians as they do a trick, but formerly it was much more serious—a magic word that was supposed to be a charm against fever and was often engraved on an amulet worn around the neck. Abracadabra was written so that it formed a triangle, beginning with 'A' on the first line, 'AB' on the second, and so on. It ultimately goes back to ancient times, first recorded in a Latin poem of the 2nd century AD. *See also* **presto** at PRESTIGE

abrupt [M16th] The Latin source of this word was *abrumpere* 'broken off, steep', from *rumpere* 'to break'. In the past, abrupt could be used as a noun meaning 'abyss' (Milton *Paradise Lost*: 'Upborn with indefatigable wings Over the vast abrupt').

abscess *see* CEDE

abseil [1930s] This is from the German verb *abseilen*, from *ab* 'down' and *seil* 'rope'.

absolve *see* SOLVE

abstract [ME] The Latin source of abstract, meant literally 'drawn away' and is from *abstrahere*, from the elements *ab-* 'from' and *trahere* 'draw off'. The use in art dates from the mid 19th century. *Trahere* is found in many English words including: **attract** [LME] with *ad* 'to'; **portrait** [M16th],

something drawn; **protract** [M16th] with *pro* 'out'; **retract** [LME] and **retreat** [LME] both drawing back; and words listed at *TRAIN.

absurd [M16th] One sense of the Latin word *absurdus* was 'out of tune', and in the past absurd was occasionally used with this meaning. From this Latin sense it developed the meaning 'out of harmony with reason, irrational'. The term **Theatre of the Absurd**, describing drama by writers such as Samuel Beckett (1906–1989), Eugène Ionesco (1904–1994), and Harold Pinter (1930–2008), was coined by the critic Martin Esslin (1918–2002) in 1961.

abuse *see* USUAL

abut [LME] Abut 'have a common boundary' is from Anglo-Latin *abuttare*, from *a-* (from Latin *ad* 'to, at') and Old French *but* 'end'.

abysmal [M17th] The original literal sense of abysmal was 'very deep', and people did not start using it to describe something utterly appalling, 'the pits', until the beginning of the early 19th century. The word shares a source with **abyss** [LME] Greek *abussos* 'bottomless'.

academy [LME] An academy today is a place of learning or culture. It is fitting, then, that the word originated with one of the most influential scholars who ever lived, the Greek philosopher Plato. During the 4th century BC he taught in a garden in Athens called the *Akadēmeia*, which was named after an ancient hero called Akadēmos. It gave its name to the school Plato founded, the Academy. *See also* OSCAR

a cappella *see* CHAPEL

acceleration [LME] This comes from Latin *accelerare* 'hasten', which was formed from *celer* 'quick'.

accent [LME] English distinguishes the different parts or syllables of a word by stressing one of them, but the ancient Greeks pronounced them with a distinct difference in musical pitch. Syllables marked with a **grave accent** (for example *à*, from Latin *gravis* 'heavy, serious') were spoken at a comparatively low pitch, those with an **acute** (*á*, from Latin *acutus* 'sharp, high') at a higher pitch, and those with a **circumflex** (*â*, from Latin *circumflexus*, 'bent around') began at the higher pitch and descended during the pronunciation of the syllable. This gives some explanation of why the root of accent is Latin *cantus* 'song', which was a direct translation of the Greek word *prosōidia* (source of **prosody** [LME] 'versification'). Quite a few languages (technically known as 'tonal' languages) still have this musical way of speaking, among them Chinese and Swedish.

accept *see* CAPABLE

access *see* CEDE

accident [LME] An accident was originally 'an event, something that happens', not necessarily a mishap. It came into English via Old French, ultimately from Latin *cadere*, meaning 'to fall', which also gave us words such as **cadaver** [LME] 'someone fallen', *CHANCE, **decay** [LME] 'fall away', **incident** [LME] 'fall upon' so 'happen'; and **occasion** [LME]. The idea of an event 'falling' remains in the English word **befall** [OE]. Later the meaning of accident evolved into 'something that happens by chance', as in the phrase **a happy accident**. By the 17th century the modern meaning had become established in the language. The full form of the proverb **accidents will happen**, which dates from the early 19th century, is **accidents will happen in the best-regulated families**. According to Mr Micawber in Charles Dickens's *David Copperfield* (1850): 'Accidents will occur in the best-regulated families; and in families not regulated by... the influence of Woman, in the lofty character of Wife, they must be expected with confidence, and must be borne with philosophy.' *See also* ADVENTURE

acclaim *see* CLAIM

accolade [E17th] The Provençal word *acolada* is the source of accolade. This literally meant an embrace or a clasping around the neck, and described the gesture of a friendly hug that was sometimes made when knighting someone, as an early alternative to a stroke on the shoulder with the flat of a sword. The ultimate root of the Provençal word is Latin *collum* 'neck', from which we also get **collar** [ME].

accommodate [M16th] The source of accommodate is Latin *accommodare* 'make fitting, fit one thing to another', formed from *commodus* 'fit'. It came into English with the basic Latin sense, and through the idea of finding something that fitted someone's needs, had developed the sense of 'provide lodgings for' by the early 18th century. Latin *commodus* is also the base of **commode** [M18th] something 'fit, convenient', and originally used of a chest of drawers before becoming a seat containing a chamber pot in the early 19th century and of **commodity** [LME] originally something useful.

accompany *see* COMPANION

accord, accordion *see* CHORD

account *see* COUNT

accrue *see* CRESCENT

accumulate *see* CLOUD

accurate *see* CURATE

ace [ME] An ace was originally the side of a dice marked with one spot. The word comes from Latin *as*, meaning 'unit'. Since an ace is the card with the highest value in many card games, the word often suggests excellence. This gave us the ace as a wartime fighter pilot who brought down many enemy aircraft, extended to anyone who excels at something. An **ace up your sleeve** (or in American English **an ace in the hole**) is a secret resource ready to use when you need it. A cheating card player might well hide an ace up their sleeve to use at an opportune moment. To **hold all the aces** is to have all the advantages, from a winning hand in a card game. To be **within an ace** of doing something is to be on the verge of doing it. This is from the ace as one and thus a tiny amount.

acerbic [M19th] This is from Latin *acerbus* 'sour-tasting'.

ache [OE] The word ache is a good example of the way that English spelling and pronunciation have developed and in many cases have diverged from each other. The noun comes from Old English and used to be pronounced 'aitch' (like the letter H), whereas the verb was originally spelled *ake* and pronounced the way ache is today. Around 1700, people started pronouncing the noun like the verb. The spelling of the noun has survived, but the word is said in the way the verb (*ake*) used to be. The modern spelling is largely due to Dr Johnson, who mistakenly assumed that the word came from Greek *akhos* 'pain'. Other pairs of words that have survived into modern English with *k*-for-the-verb and *ch*-for-the-noun spellings include **speak** and **speech** and **break** and **breach**.

achieve [ME] The early sense was 'complete successfully', from Old French *achever* 'come or bring to a head', from the phrase *a chief* 'to a head'.

acid [E17th] Acid originally meant 'sour-tasting' and came from Latin *acidus*. The term seems to have been introduced by the scientist Francis Bacon, who in 1626 described sorrel as 'a cold and acid herb'. The chemical sense developed at the end of that century because most common acids taste sour. The **acid test** was originally a method of testing for gold using nitric acid. An object made of gold will show no sign of corrosion if immersed in nitric acid, unlike one made of another metal. By the late 19th century the expression had come to mean any situation that proves a person's or thing's quality. The Australian expression **put the acid on**, meaning 'to extract a loan or favour from', comes from acid test—the would-be borrower is seen as 'testing' their victim for resistance or

weakness. **Acrid** [E18th] is from the related Latin *acer* 'sharp, pungent' with spelling influenced by acid.

acme [L16th] In Greek *akmē* meant 'point' or 'pinnacle, highest point'. Its use in English dates from the late 15th century, although for the next hundred years or so it was consciously used as a Greek word and written in Greek letters. For many people their first exposure to the word comes from the 'Looney Tunes' cartoons featuring the Roadrunner and Wile E. Coyote, where the characters buy products from the Acme company. 'Acme' was a real brand name for various US firms in the last two decades of the 19th century, chosen in part because the word comes near the top of any alphabetical list of suppliers. **Acne** [M19th] the skin condition, has a similar root. The idea is that all those red pimples are little points sticking up from someone's face.

acne *see* ACME

acolyte [ME] English acolyte is from ecclesiastical Latin *acolytus*, from Greek *akolouthos* 'follower'.

acorn [OE] An Old English word, related to **acre** [OE] and meaning 'fruit of the open land or forest'. It was later applied to any fruit, then subsequently restricted to the most important fruit produced by the forest, the acorn. The spelling of the word, originally *aecern*, evolved into its modern form because people thought the word must have something to do with OAK and CORN.

acquaint *see* QUAINT

acquiesce [E17th] There is a notion of peacefully leaving an argument unspoken in *acquiesce* which comes from Latin *acquiescere*, from *ad-* 'at' and *quiescere* 'to rest'.

acquire [LME] This is from Latin *acquirere* 'get in addition' from *ad-* 'to' and *quaerere* 'seek'. The late Middle English spelling was *acquere*, the change is an example of the many words which

acerbic   ache   achieve   acid   acme   acne

developed new spellings around 1600 to make them look more like their Latin originals, evidence of early, if misplaced, interest in word histories.

acquit *see* QUIT

acre *see* ACORN

acrid *see* ACID

acrobat [E19th] The earliest acrobats were tightrope walkers, which explains why the word derives from Greek *akrobatos*, meaning 'walking on tiptoe'. The *akro-* part of *akrobatos* meant 'tip, end, or summit' and is found in several other English words. The **acropolis** [M17th] of a Greek city, most famously Athens, was the fortified part, which was usually built on a hill. **Acrophobia** [L19th] is fear of heights. An **acronym** [M20th] is a word such as *laser* or *Aids* formed from the initial letters of other words, and an **acrostic** [L16th] is a poem or puzzle in which the first letters in each line form a word or words.

acronym, acrophobia *see* ACROBAT

acropolis *see* ACROBAT, POLICE

across [ME] Early use was as an adverb meaning 'in the form of a *CROSS'; the word comes from Old French *a croix, en croix* 'in or on a cross'.

acrostic *see* ACROBAT

actor [LME] An actor was originally simply 'a doer', usually an agent or an administrator; the theatrical sense dates from the 16th century. Like **act** [LME] it comes from Latin *actus* 'thing done', which comes from *agere* 'to do, drive'. This is the basis of other English words such as **agenda** [E17th] 'things to be done'; **agent** [LME] 'someone or thing who does things'; **agile** [LME] 'able to do things'; **agitate** [LME] originally meaning 'drive away'; **ambiguous** [E16th] 'drive in both ways', a word, which appears to have been coined by the English scholar and statesman Sir Thomas More (1478–1535), originally in the sense 'indistinct, obscure'; **transaction**

[LME] 'something driven across or through' and many more. **Actuality** [LME] originally had the sense 'activity'; from Old French *actualite* from *actualis* 'active, practical'. The modern French word **actualité** (usually meaning 'news') is sometimes used in English to mean 'truth', a sense not found in French as in: 'When asked why the company had not been advised to include the potential military use, he [Alan Clark] said it was our old friend economical . . . with the *actualité*' (*Independent* 10 November 1992).

actualité, actuality *see* ACTOR

actuary [M16th] An actuary started out as the name for a clerk or registrar of a court; the source is Latin *actuarius* 'bookkeeper', from *actus* 'event' (*see* *ACTOR). The current use in insurance contexts dates from the mid 19th century.

acumen [L16th] Acumen is an adoption of a Latin word meaning 'sharpness, point', from *acuere* 'sharpen'.

acute *see* ACCENT

adamant [OE] The Greek word *adamas*, originally meaning 'invincible or untameable', came to be applied to the hardest metal or stone and to diamond, the hardest naturally occurring substance. Via Latin it was the source not only of adamant but also of *DIAMOND. In Old English adamant was the name given to a legendary rock so hard that it was believed to be impenetrable. Early medieval Latin writers mistakenly explained the word as coming from *adamare* 'take a liking to' and associated *adamant* with the lodestone or magnet which 'takes a liking' to iron, and the word passed into modern languages with this confusion of meaning. The modern use, with its notion of unyielding conviction, is much more recent, probably dating from the 1930s.

adder [OE] One of the words Anglo-Saxons used for a snake was *naedre*, which became *nadder* in medieval times. At some point during the 14th or 15th century the

acquit   acre   acrid   acrobat   acronym

word managed to lose its initial *n*, as people heard 'a nadder' and misinterpreted this as 'an adder'. A northern dialect form *nedder* still exists. A similar process of 'wrong division' took place with words such as *APRON and umpire (*see* *PAIR), and the opposite can happen too, as with, for example, *NEWT and *NICKNAME. In time adder became the term for a specific poisonous snake, also known as the *VIPER. The same change nearly happened to the word **aunt** [ME] (which comes from Latin *amitia* 'aunt'), for between the 13th and 17th centuries 'mine aunt' can appear as 'my naunt'. In France this change has happened: the word was *ante* in Old French, but is now *tante* through the running together of *ta* 'your' and *ante*. *See also* DEAF.

addict *see* VERDICT

addle [ME] An addled egg is rotten and produces no chick, whereas if your brain is addled you are confused. Originally a rotten egg was described as an *addle egg* from Old English *addle,* liquid mud or dung, the sort of stuff you might come across in a farmyard, and which came to describe rotten eggs because of their smell.

address [ME] This was first used in the senses 'set upright' and 'guide, direct', which developed into 'write directions for delivery on' and 'direct spoken words to'. The source is Latin *ad-* 'towards' and *directus* 'put straight'. **Direction** [E16th] shares the same source.

adequate *see* EQUAL

adjacent *see* EASY

adjourn [ME] Now adjourn suggests 'break off (until a later time)', but the early sense was 'summon someone to appear on a particular day'. It comes from Old French *ajorner,* from the phrase *a jorn (nome)* 'to an (appointed) day'.

adjust [E17th] The notion of 'bringing in close proximity' is present in adjust. The source was the obsolete French verb *adjuster,* from Old French *ajoster* 'to approximate', based on Latin *ad-* 'to' and

juxta 'near', source of words such as **joust** [ME] originally to 'bring near to join battle' and **juxtapose** [M19th] 'place near'.

adjutant [E17th] An *adjutant* was originally an 'assistant, helper'; the origin is Latin *adjutant-* 'being of service to', from *adjuvare* 'assist'. The term now usually describes an officer assisting a senior officer with administrative matters.

admiral [ME] The first recorded meaning of admiral refers to an emir or Muslim commander, and the word ultimately comes from Arabic *amir* 'commander'. The Arabic word was used in various titles of rank, such as *amir-al-bahr* ('commander of the sea') and *amir-al-ma* ('commander of the water'). Christian scholars, not realizing that *-al-* simply meant 'of the', thought that *amir-al* was a single word meaning 'commander', and accordingly anglicized it as admiral. The modern maritime use comes from the office of 'Amir of the Sea', created by the Arabs in Spain and Sicily and later adopted by the Genoese, the French and, in the form 'Amyrel of the Se' or 'admyrall of the navy', by the English under Edward III. From around 1500 the word admiral on its own has been used as the naval term.

admiration *see* MIRACLE

admit *see* PERMIT

admonish *see* MONITOR

ado *see* AFFAIR

adolescent [LME] Both adolescent and **adult** [M16th] come from Latin *adolescere,* 'to grow to maturity'. The root of the Latin word is *alescere* 'to grow up', which in turn derives from *alere* 'to nourish or give food to', so the idea of coming to maturity is closely related to the idea of feeding yourself up. *See also* ALIMONY

adopt *see* OPTION

adore [LME] The semantic strands of 'worship' and 'spoken prayer' are interwoven in adore, which came from Latin

addict addle address adequate adjacent

adorare 'to worship'. The **adorable** came into use in the early 17th century meaning 'worthy of divine worship'; the current meaning 'lovable, inspiring great affection' dates from the early 18th century.

adroit [M17th] This is an adoption from French, from the phrase *à droit* 'according to right', 'properly'.

adult *see* ADOLESCENT

advent *see* ADVENTURE

adventure [ME] The meaning of adventure has changed over the centuries. In the Middle Ages it meant 'anything that happens by chance' or 'chance, fortune, or luck', and came from Latin *advenire* 'to arrive'. Gradually the idea of 'risk or danger' became a stronger element and later evolved into 'a dangerous or hazardous undertaking', and still later into 'an exciting incident that happens to someone'. *Compare* ACCIDENT. Related words are **advent** [OE] 'coming, arrival' and **adventitious** [E17th] originally describing something happening by chance. *See also* REVENUE

adverse *see* VERSE

advertisement [LME] Latin *advertere* 'turn towards' is the base of **advertise** [LME] and advertisement. Advertisement was originally 'a statement calling attention to something'; it started to be abbreviated to **advert** in the mid 19th century. If you do something **inadvertently** [M17th] then you have not turned your mind towards it. *VERSE is related.

advice [ME] Advice is from Old French *avis*, based on Latin *videre* 'to see'. The original sense was 'a way of looking at something', 'a judgement', which led later to 'an opinion given'. **Supervise** [LME] 'to over see' and words at *VISION are from the same root.

advocaat [1930s] This word for a liqueur made of eggs, sugar, and brandy, is an adoption of the Dutch word for 'advocate': it

was originally considered 'a lawyer's drink', and this was the meaning of the full form in Dutch: *advocatenborrel*. **Advocate** [ME] comes from Latin *advocare* 'to call to one's aid'.

aegis [E17th] An aegis was originally a piece of armour or a shield, especially that of a god. The word came into English via Latin from Greek *aigis* 'shield of Zeus'. It is now often used in the phrase **under the aegis of** meaning 'under the protection of'.

aeon [M17th] This entered English via ecclesiastical Latin from Greek *aiōn* 'age' and is usually used in the plural in phrases such as **aeons ago**.

aerial *see* AIR

aerobic *see* AIR

aeronaut *see* ASTERISK, NAUSEA

aeroplane [L19th] An aeroplane is literally an 'air wanderer'. Coined in the late 19th century, the word is from French *aéro-* 'air' and Greek *-planos* 'wandering', and so the short form **plane** has the less-than-reassuring meaning of 'wanderer'. *See also* PLAIN, PLANET

aesthetic [L18th] The early sense was 'relating to perception by the senses'; the source is Greek *aisthētikos*, from *aisthēta* 'material things'. This was opposed to things that were thinkable, in other words, immaterial things. The sense 'concerned with beauty' was coined in German in the mid 18th century, and adopted into English in the early 19th century, but its use was controversial until much later in the century. **Aesthete** was formed on the pattern of pairs such as *athlete*, *athletic*.

affair [ME] This is from Old French *à faire* 'to do'. The history of the English word **ado** is parallel to that of affair. It comes from Old Norse *at* and *do*. This parallel between *at do* and *to do* can be seen in the sense that 'fuss' is apparent in the phrases **without more ado** and **what a to do!**

adroit adult advent adventure adverse

affidavit [M16th] A legal term from medieval Latin, *affidavit* means literally 'he has stated on oath'.

affiliate [E17th] We talk about parent companies, so why not child companies? This is literally what an affiliated company is. The first meaning of affiliate was 'to adopt as a son', and the word ultimately came from Latin *filius* 'son', from which we also get **filial** [LME]. By the mid 18th century affiliate was being used to mean 'to adopt as a subordinate member of a society or company'.

affinity *see* PARAFFIN

afflict [LME] The early senses of afflict were 'deject' and 'humiliate'; the word comes from Latin *afflictare* 'knock about, harass'. **Inflict** [M16th] originally had the same meaning and comes from Latin *infligere* 'to strike against'.

affluent [LME] From Latin *affluere* 'flow towards', affluent was originally used to describe water either flowing towards a place or flowing freely without any restriction. It later came to mean 'abundant' and then 'wealthy', a meaning which dates from the mid 18th century. Related words, all based on Latin *fluere* 'to flow' are **fluent** [L16th] and **fluid** [LME]; **flume** [ME] originally a stream; **flux** [LME] a state of flowing; **effluent** [LME] something that flows out; and **superfluous** [LME] 'overflowing'.

afford [OE] Old English *forthian* 'to further' lies behind afford. The original sense was 'accomplish', later coming to mean 'be in a position to do'. The association with wealth is recorded from late Middle English.

affray [ME] Although an affray is now a disturbance of the peace caused by fighting in a public place, its first meaning was 'alarm, fright or terror' or 'frighten'. Its root is the old Norman French word *afrayer*, which also gives us **afraid** [ME].

affront *see* CONFRONT

aficionado [M19th] This started out as a term for a devotee of bullfighting. It is a Spanish word meaning 'amateur', now used to describe any ardent follower of an activity. Examples of this extended usage date from the 1880s. *Compare* AMATEUR

afraid *see* AFFRAY

aftermath [LME] The aftermath was originally the crop of new grass that springs up after a field has been mown in early summer. John Buchan (1874–1940), the Scottish writer of adventure stories such as *The Thirty-Nine Steps*, wrote about 'Meadowland from which an aftermath of hay had lately been taken'. *Math* was an old word meaning 'a mowing'. The modern meaning of **aftermath** developed in the 19th century.

aga *see* SAGA

agenda, agent *see* ACTOR

agglomerate [L17th] Latin *glomus* 'ball' is at the core of agglomerate which comes from the Latin verb *agglomerare* 'add to'.

agglutinate *see* GLUE

aggregate *see* CONGREGATE

aggression *see* PROGRESS

aghast [LME] Gast (originally *gaestan*) was an Old English word meaning 'frighten or terrify'. It was still being used in this sense in Shakespeare's day: 'Or whether gasted by the noise I made, Full suddenly he fled' (*King Lear*). This gave rise to *agast*, which had the same meaning. The spelling **aghast** (probably influenced by the spelling of *GHOST) was originally Scottish but became generally used after 1700. **Ghastly** [ME] comes from the same word. The sense 'objectionable' dates from the mid 19th century.

agile, agitate *see* ACTOR

agnostic [M19th] This word was actually invented by a specific person and then successfully entered the language. It was coined by the Victorian biologist Thomas Huxley (1825–95) to describe his own beliefs: he did not believe in God but did not think one could say for sure that God did not exist. Before Huxley devised agnostic there was no word for such a religious position. He is said to have first used it in 1869 at a party held in Clapham, London, prior to the formation of the Metaphysical Society. Huxley formed the word from the Greek *a-* 'not' and *gnostos* 'known'.

agog [M16th] If you are agog you are now very eager to hear or see something, but originally you were having fun. The word comes from Old French *en gogues*, 'in mirth, in a merry mood'. The French-coined 1960s phrase **a gogo**, meaning 'galore', comes from the same root.

a gogo *see* AGOG

agony [LME] Agony referred originally only to mental anguish. It came into English via late Latin from Greek *agōnia*, from *agōn* 'contest' (the base, too, of **agonize** [L16th]). The Greek sense development moved from struggle for victory in the games, to any struggle, to mental struggle specifically (such as the torment of Christ in the Garden of Gethsemane). The extension in English to an idea of 'physical' suffering dates from the early 17th century. Greek *agōn* is also the source of the dramatic **protagonist** [L17th] from Greek *proto-* 'first' and *a agōnistes* 'actor, contestant' and at the root of **antagonist** [L16th] from *anti-* 'against' and *agōnízesthai* 'struggle'.

agoraphobia [E19th] Agoraphobia is literally 'fear of the market place', from Greek *agora* 'a market place' and the English suffix *-phobia* (from Greek *phobos* 'fear'). In ancient Greece an *agora* was a public open space used for markets and assemblies.

agree [LME] When we agree to something, there is a core notion of trying to please; the word is from Old French *agreer*, based on Latin *ad-* 'to' and *gratus* 'pleasing'. It took over a hundred years after the phrase 'to agree' first appeared in the writings of

Chaucer for its opposite, **disagree**, to appear in writing during the 1490s.

agriculture *see* AIR

aid [LME] This comes via Old French from Latin *adjuvare*, from *ad-* 'towards' and *juvare* 'to help'.

aikido *see* JAPANESE WORD PANEL

aim [ME] Aim has the basic notion of evaluation before a direction is taken. It comes via French from the Latin verb *aestimare* meaning 'assess, estimate'.

air [ME] **1** The main modern sense of air, 'the invisible gaseous substance surrounding the earth' entered English via Old French and Latin from Greek *aēr*. **Aerial** [L16th], meaning 'a rod or wire by which signals are transmitted or received' and 'existing or happening in the air', comes from the same source, along with the Italian word **aria** [E18th]. **Aerobic** [L19th] is from *aēr* combined with Greek *bios* 'live'. **2** The senses of air 'an impression or manner' and 'a condescending manner' (as in *she gave herself airs*) are probably from a completely different word, Old French *aire* 'site, disposition', which derives from Latin *ager* 'field', the root of English words such as **agriculture** [LME]. **Airy-fairy** [M19th] 'impractical and foolishly idealistic', was originally used to mean 'delicate or light as a fairy'. The English poet Alfred, Lord Tennyson (1809–1892), in his poem 'Lilian' (1830), described the subject as 'Airy, fairy Lilian, Flitting, fairy Lilian'. *See also* GAS

aisle [LME] The early spellings *ele*, *ile* are from Old French *ele*, from Latin *ala* 'wing'. The spelling change in the 17th century was due to confusion with isle (*see* ISLAND); the word was also influenced by French *aile* 'wing'.

ajar [L17th] In this strange word *a-* 'on' is prefixed to obsolete *char*, which in Old English was *cerr*, meaning 'a turn, return'.

akimbo [LME] You might think that the odd-looking word akimbo, 'with hands on the hips and elbows turned outwards',

agog   a gogo   agony   agoraphobia   agree

derives from some exotic language. In fact it appeared in medieval English in the form *in kenebowe* or *a kembow* and was probably an alteration of an Old Norse phrase meaning 'bent in a curve, like a horseshoe'.

à la carte *see* FRENCH WORD PANEL

alack *see* ALAS

alarm [LME] Alarm started out as an exclamation meaning 'to arms!'; it stems from Old French *alarme*, from the Italian phrase *all' arme!* 'to arms!'. The spelling **alarum** existed in English in early times because of the way the 'r' was rolled when pronouncing the word; this form became restricted specifically to the peal of a warning bell or clock. The original exclamation as a call to arms, is seen in the phrase **alarums and excursions**, a stage direction found in Shakespeare's *Henry VI* and *Richard III*.

alas [ME] This expression of dismay is from Old French *a las*, *a lasse*, from *a* 'ah' and *las(se)*, from Latin *lassus* 'weary'. Late Middle English **alack** is a comparable exclamation, from *a* 'ah!' and *lak* 'lack'. It originally expressed dissatisfaction and the notion 'shame that it should be the case'; this came to convey regret or surprise, as in **alack-a-day**.

albatross [L17th] The spelling of albatross was influenced by Latin *albus*, 'white'. The large white seabird was originally called the *alcatras*, a name which was also applied to other water birds such as the pelican (who gave their name to the prison-island of Alcatraz in San Francisco Bay) and came from Spanish and Portuguese *alcatraz*, from Arabic *al-gattās* 'the diver'. In golf an albatross is a score of three under par at a hole (*see* BIRD). Albatross sometimes carries with it an idea of misfortune and burdensome guilt: this alludes to Coleridge's *Ancient Mariner* (1798), in which an albatross is shot by the mariner, bringing disaster on the rest of the crew and long-lasting guilt to him.

albino *see* ALBUM

Albion [OE] A poetic or literary name for Britain or England which today is particularly associated with the names of soccer teams such as West Bromwich Albion and Brighton and Hove Albion. Albion probably derives from Latin *albus* meaning 'white', and alludes to the white cliffs of Dover. *See also* PERFIDY

album [E17th] The Latin word *albus* 'white' was originally used as a noun meaning 'a white (or rather blank) marble tablet' on which public notices were written. Brought into English as album, the word has subsequently been used to describe various blank books used for compiling a collection of items, such as stamps or photographs, and in the 1950s became applied to a collection of recorded pieces of music. Other *alb-* words with an element of whiteness in their meaning include **albino** [L18th], **albumen** [L16th], the white of the egg, and *ALBION. *See also* AUBURN, CANDID

albumen *see* ALBUM

alchemy *see* CHEMICAL

alcohol [M16th] Arabic *al-kuhl* gave us the modern English word alcohol, but there were several changes in meaning along the way. *Al* in Arabic means 'the', and *al-kuhl* means 'the kohl', referring to a powder used as eye make-up. By extension, the term was applied to a fine powder and then to a liquid essence or spirit obtained by distillation.

alcove [L16th] French *alcôve* is the source of alcove, from Spanish *alcoba*, from Arabic *al-kubba* 'the vault'.

al dente *see* ITALIAN WORD PANEL

ale *see* BEER

alert [L16th] This comes from the Italian military phrase *all' erta*, 'on the lookout' or, more literally, 'to the watchtower'. It was originally a military term in English too, before it acquired its more general meaning. Alert was first used as an adverb, so you could say that the later expression **on the alert** strictly means 'on the on the lookout'.

à la carte   alack   alarm   alas   albatross

algebra [LME] Bone-setting does not seem to have much to do with mathematics, but there is a connection in the word algebra. It comes from the Arabic *al-jabr* 'the reunion of broken parts', used specifically to refer to the surgical treatment of fractures and to bone-setting. Algebra was used in this meaning in English in the 16th century. The mathematical sense comes from the title of a 9th-century Arabic book *ilm al-jabr wa'l-mukabala*, 'the science of restoring what is missing and equating like with like', written by the mathematician al-Kwarizmi (*c*.790–*c*.840).

algorithm [L17th] Algorithm initially meant the Arabic or decimal notation of numbers; it is a variant, influenced by Greek *arithmos* 'number', of Middle English *algorism* which came via Old French from medieval Latin *algorismus*. The Arabic source, *al-kwārizmī* 'the man of Kwārizm' (now Khiva), was an alternative name for the 9th-century mathematician Ab Ja'far Muhammad ibn Msa, author of widely translated works on algebra and arithmetic.

alias [LME] A Latin word, alias means literally 'at another time, otherwise'. The term **aliasing** has been taken up in specialist fields such as computing for the use of an alternative name referring to a file etc, and telecommunications for misidentification of a signal frequency, introducing distortion or error.

alibi [ME] Alibi is recorded from the late 17th century, as an adverb in the sense 'elsewhere', and was originally a Latin word with the same meaning and spelling. A typical example of its use comes from John Arbuthnot's *History of John Bull* (1727): 'The prisoner had little to say in his defence; he endeavoured to prove himself Alibi.' The noun use, 'a piece of evidence that a person was somewhere else when a crime was committed', dates from the 18th century. The weakened sense of 'excuse' is early 20th century.

alien [ME] The word came via Old French from Latin *alienus* 'belonging to another', from *alius* 'other'. It was initially used for foreigners, but since the 1950s has mostly been used for beings from another planet. From the same base is early 16th-century **alienate** and **alienation** [LME]. The theatrical phrase **alienation effect** dates from the 1940s and is a translation of German *Verfremdungseffekt*.

alimentary *see* ALIMONY

alimony [E17th] Today alimony means 'provision for a husband or wife after divorce' (what is usually called **maintenance** in Britain). Originally, though, in the early 17th century, it simply meant 'nourishment or means of subsistence'. It comes from Latin *alere* 'nourish', which is the root of words such as *ADOLESCENT, **alimentary** [LME] and **coalesce** [M16th] 'grow up, nourish together'.

alive *see* LIVE

alkali [LME] The chemistry term alkali is from medieval Latin, from Arabic *al-kalī* 'calcined ashes' referring to the plants from which alkalis were made. Early 19th-century **alkaloid** (a class of compounds including morphine, quinine, and strychnine) was coined in German from *alkali*.

all [OE] A little Old English word found in a host of popular phrases. Although associated with the Second World War, **the all-clear** dates from the very beginning of the 20th century. It refers to a signal such as a siren that indicates enemy aircraft have left the area, making it safe to come out into the open from bomb shelters or other places of refuge. **All animals are equal, but some animals are more equal than others** comes from George Orwell's *Animal Farm* (1945) a satire in which the animals take over the farm, only to find the pigs become even worse masters. **All done with mirrors** means 'achieved by trickery or illusion'. One of the earliest examples of the phrase comes from a 1908 play by G.K. Chesterton (1874–1936) called *Magic*, about a conjuror working out how an effect might be created, but it probably goes back to 19th-century magicians. **All human life is there** was an advertising slogan used by British tabloid

algebra   algorithm   alias   alibi   alien

newspaper the *News of the World* in the 1950s. The phrase had been used earlier by the novelist Henry James (1843–1916) in *The Madonna of the Future* (1879). A maker of statuettes says of his wares, 'Cats and monkeys—monkeys and cats—all human life is there!' The first things to be described as **all-singing, all-dancing** were film musicals. Posters for *Broadway Melody* (1929) carried the slogan 'All Talking All Singing All Dancing'. These days something 'all-singing, all-dancing' is generally an advanced computer or other gadget. The proverb **all good things must come to an end** dates back to the 15th century, usually in the form 'All things must come to (or have) an end'. The inclusion of the word 'good' in the proverb appears to be a 20th-century development. The other 'all' proverb, **all's well that ends well**, is even older and was first recorded in the 14th century as 'If the end is well, then is all well'.

allegory [LME] An allegory is basically speaking about one thing in terms of another, and comes from Greek *allos* 'other' and *-agoria* 'speaking'.

allergy [E20th] There is a notion of something 'alien' present in allergy which comes from German *Allergie*, from Greek *allos* 'other'. It was formed on the pattern of German *Energie* 'energy'.

alleviate *see* ELEVATE

alligator [L16th] The English word alligator comes from two Spanish words *el lagarto*, 'the lizard'. The first record of its use is from an account of his travels written by 16th-century English adventurer Job Hortop. He was press-ganged to sail to the Americas on a slaving voyage when he was only a teenager, and wrote vividly of the strange animals he encountered, among them the alligator.

alliteration *see* LETTER

allocation *see* LOCAL

allow [ME] This was originally used to mean 'commend, sanction' and 'assign as a right'. Both meanings were adopted from

Old French *alouer* in about 1300. The source was Latin *allaudare* 'to praise', reinforced by medieval Latin *allocare* 'to place'.

alloy *see* ALLY

allude [LME] Allude is from Latin *alludere* 'play with', from *ad-* 'towards' and *ludere* 'to play'.

ally [ME] Latin *alligere* 'combine together', formed from *ad-* 'to(gether)' and *ligare* 'bind' developed into two closely related words in Old French: *alier* which became ally in English, and *aloyer* which became **alloy** [L16th]. *Ligare* is also hidden in **furl** [L16th] which comes from French *ferler*, from *ferm* 'firm' and *lier* 'bind'; **league** [LME] a binding together; and **oblige** [ME] originally meaning 'bind by oath'.

alma mater [M17th] This phrase, used with reference to a university or college once attended, first had the general sense 'someone or something providing nourishment'; in Latin the literal meaning is 'bounteous, nourishing mother'. It was a title given by the Romans to several goddesses but in particular to Ceres and Cybele, both representing fostering mother-figures. **Alumnus** [M17th] is related, being Latin for 'nursling, pupil', from *alere* 'nourish', source of *alma*.

alms [OE] Old English *ælmesse* comes from Christian Latin *eleemosyna*, from Greek *eleēmosunē* 'compassion'; based on *eleos* 'mercy'. The 's' therefore was not originally a plural ending, and people wrote about 'an alms' until the middle of the 16th century.

aloe [OE] Old English *alewe* was used for the fragrant resin or heartwood of certain oriental trees; it came via Latin from Greek *aloē*. The emollient **aloe vera** is a term from the early 20th century and is modern Latin, literally 'true aloe', probably in contrast to the American agave, which closely resembles aloe vera.

aloft [ME] Aloft is from Old Norse *á lopt*, from *á* 'in, on, to' and *lopt* 'air'.

allegory   allergy   alleviate   alligator

aloof [M16th] Aloof was originally a nautical term for an order to steer a ship as close as possible towards the wind. It literally means 'to windward', *loof* (or **luff** [LME]) being an old term meaning 'windward direction'. The idea was that keeping the bow of the ship close to the wind kept it clear of the shore.

alphabet [E16th] The first two letters of the Greek alphabet are *alpha* and *beta*. In Greek these two letters were combined to make the word *alphabētos*, which was taken as a name for all 24 letters of the Greek alphabet as a whole, just as English-speaking children are taught their **ABC**.

Al-Qaeda *see* ARABIC PANEL

already *see* YIDDISH WORD PANEL

altar *see* ALTITUDE

alter [LME] If you alter something you change it to something else. The word comes via French from Latin *alter* 'other', also found in **alternative** [M16th]. It also lies behind **altruism** [M19th] which is from Italian *altrui* 'somebody else', from Latin *alteri huic* 'to this other'.

altitude [LME] Altitude is from Latin *altitudo*, from *altus* 'high'. The latter is also the source of **altar** [OE], a raised structure for worship, **enhance** [ME], originally 'make higher'; **exalt** [LME], with *ex-* 'out, upwards'; and **haughty** [M16th], from *altus* via French *haut*.

alto *see* ITALIAN WORD PANEL

altruism *see* ALTER

alumnus *see* ALMA MATER

amass *see* MASS

amateur [L18th] An amateur does something for love rather than for money. Borrowed from French in the 18th century, and ultimately from Latin *amator* 'lover', it was originally used to describe a person who loves or is fond of something. Later on it came to be used of a person who practises

an art or sport as a hobby, rather than professionally, and also of someone who is inept at a particular activity. *Compare* AFICIONADO

amaze *see* MAZE

Amazon [LME] In Greek legend the Amazons were a race of female warriors who were supposed to exist in the unexplored regions of the north. The word Amazon is Greek for 'without a breast', referring to the story that the women cut off their right breasts in order to draw their bows more easily. Nowadays an Amazon is any tall, strong, or athletic woman. The River Amazon was given its name by European explorers because of stories that a race of female warriors lived on its banks.

ambassador *see* EMBASSY

amber [LME] Amber comes from Arabic *'anbar*, which also meant 'ambergris' a wax-like substance used in the manufacture of perfume that originates as a secretion of the sperm whale. *See also* ELECTRICITY. Much more appealing is **amber nectar**, which was popularized as an advertising slogan for Fosters lager from 1986. It goes back much further than that, though, and has been a slang term for beer since the 1890s, especially in Australia.

ambidextrous [M17th] As anyone left-handed knows, we live in a right-handed world. The bias towards right-handedness is present in the language too. While the positive word *DEXTEROUS or 'skilful, good with the hands' comes from the Latin for 'right-handed', the rather more negative *SINISTER comes from the Latin for 'left-handed'. And if you are ambidextrous, it is as though you have got two right hands: the word is from Latin *ambi* 'both, on both sides' and *dexter* 'right, right-handed'. At one time ambidextrous could also be used to mean 'double-dealing, trying to please both sides', as in 'a little, dirty, pimping, pettifogging, ambidextrous fellow' (Laurence Sterne, 1768).

ambient *see* AMBITION

ambiguous *see* ACTOR

ambition [ME] Ambition comes from Latin *ambire*, literally meaning 'to go round or go about' (also the source of late 16th-century **ambient**), but with the more specific sense of 'to go round canvassing for votes'. From this developed the idea of eagerly seeking honour or advancement.

amble *see* AMBULANCE

ambrosia [M16th] This came into English via Latin from the Greek word which meant 'elixir of life', from *ambrotos* 'immortal'. Ambrosia in classical mythology was the food of the gods.

ambulance [E19th] First used in the Crimean War, an ambulance was originally a mobile temporary hospital—a field hospital—that followed an army from place to place. The term was later applied to a wagon or cart used for carrying wounded soldiers off the battlefield, which in turn led to its modern meaning. Ambulance comes from the French *hôpital ambulant*, literally 'walking hospital': the root is Latin *ambulare*, 'to walk', which gave us words such as **alley** [LME], **amble** [ME], and early 17th-century **ambulate** (a formal way of saying 'walk'). **Ambulance chaser** is a wry nickname for a lawyer. The first example of the term, from 1897, tells us that 'In New York City there is a style of lawyers known to the profession as "ambulance chasers", because they are on hand wherever there is a railway wreck, or a street-car collision...with...their offers of professional services.'

ambush [ME] Ambush is from Old French *embusche*, based on late Latin *inboscare* from 'in' and *boscus* 'wood' also source of **bush** [ME] and **bosky** [L16th]. It also gave French *bouquet* 'clump of trees', which entered English meaning 'bunch of flowers'. The use of bouquet for the aroma from wine dates from the mid 19th century.

amen [OE] This comes via ecclesiastical Latin, from Hebrew *'āmēn* 'truth, certainty', used to express agreement, and adopted in the Septuagint as a solemn expression of belief or affirmation.

amend *see* MEND

amenity [LME] Amenity goes back to Latin *amoenus* 'pleasant'.

amethyst [ME] It was traditionally believed that putting an amethyst in your drink could prevent you getting drunk, through an association of the colour of the stone and the colour of red wine. The word comes from the Greek *amethustos*, meaning 'not drunken'.

amicable *see* ENEMY

ammunition [L16th] This comes from obsolete French *amunition*, which was formed by misunderstanding where the division came in *la munition* 'the munition' (*compare* words at *ADDER). At first the word referred to stores of all kinds. **Munitions** [LME] show the division in the right place.

amnesty [L16th] This comes via Latin from Greek *amnēstia* 'forgetfulness' (which shares a root with **amnesia** [L18th]), a meaning found in early use in English.

amok [M17th] If someone **runs amok** they rush about behaving uncontrollably and disruptively. The word amok comes via Portuguese from a Malay word *amuk* meaning 'fighting furiously' or 'rushing in a frenzy'. It was first used in English in the 17th century, referring to a Malay person in a murderous frenzy after taking opium.

amount *see* MOUNTAIN

ampersand [M19th] A corruption of 'and per se and', an old phrase that used to be chanted by schoolchildren as a way of learning the character &. *Per se* is Latin for 'by itself', so the phrase can be translated '& by itself is *and*'. The word is recorded from the mid 19th century, while the symbol itself is based on a Roman shorthand symbol for Latin *et* 'and'.

amphibian [M17th] Amphibians live both in water and on land, and it is the idea of 'living in both' that gives us the word, which comes from Greek *amphi* 'both' (also found in **amphitheatre** [LME] from *amphi* 'on both sides' and *theatron* 'place for beholding') and *bios* 'life', source of words such as **biology** [E19th] and **antibiotic** [M19th]. Before it was applied specifically to frogs, toads, and newts, amphibian simply meant 'having two modes of existence, of doubtful nature'.

amphitheatre *see* AMPHIBIAN

ample [LME] This is an adoption of a French word, from Latin *amplus* 'large, capacious, abundant'.

amputate [M16th] This is from the Latin verb *amputare* 'lop off', based on *putare* 'to prune'.

amuse [LME] In its early senses amuse had more to do with deception than entertainment or humour. Dating from the late 15th century and coming from an Old French word meaning 'to stare stupidly' (also the source of to *MUSE), it originally meant 'to delude or deceive'. In the 17th and 18th centuries to amuse someone usually meant to divert their attention in order to mislead them. In military use it meant to divert the attention of the enemy away from what you really intend to do, so Lord Nelson, wrote in 1796: 'It is natural to suppose their Fleet was to amuse ours whilst they cross from Leghorn.' **We are not amused** is associated with Queen Victoria (1819–1901). It is first recorded in *Notebooks of a Spinster Lady* (1919) by Caroline Holland—Victoria is supposed to have made the stern put-down in 1900 to a man who had made an inappropriate joke. There is no firm evidence that she said it, though, and her biographer Stanley Weintraub (*b.* 1929) claimed that 'she was often amused'.

anachronism [M17th] An anachronism, something which is wrongly placed in a particular period, comes from Greek *anakhronismos*, from *ana-* 'backwards or against' and *khronos* 'time'. The latter is the source of other time-related words such as

chronicle [ME], **chronometer** [M18th] a 'time measurer', **chronological** [M16th], and **synchronize** [E17th] 'to make the same time'. *See also* CHRONIC

anagram [L16th] A word or phrase formed by rearranging the letters of another, anagram goes back to Greek *ana-* 'back, anew' and *gramma* 'letter'.

analgesia *see* NOSTALGIA

analysis *see* PARALYSIS

anarchy *see* ARC

anathema [E16th] An ecclesiastical Latin word for an 'excommunicated person, excommunication', anathema comes from the Greek word meaning 'thing dedicated', later coming to mean 'thing devoted to evil, accursed thing'.

anatomy [LME] At first anatomy was not just the study of the structure of the human body, it was specifically the practice of cutting up human bodies to learn about them. The word came into English from Greek *anatomia*, from *ana-* 'up' and *tomia* 'cutting'. Anatomy used also to be applied to a skeleton, and in this meaning it was commonly found in the contracted form **atomy**, as in 'His sides ... looked just like an atomy, ribs and all' (J. Fenimore Cooper, 1863).

ancestor *see* CEDE

ancillary [M17th] Now meaning 'supporting' or 'subordinate', ancillary comes from Latin *ancilla* 'maidservant'.

Andalusia *see* VANDAL

anecdote [L17th] This is from Greek *anekdota* 'things unpublished'. The word came to be used for any short story as a result of its use by Byzantine historian Procopius (*c.*500–*c.*562) for his *Anekdota* or 'Unpublished Memoirs' (also known as *The Secret History*) of the Emperor Justinian, which were tales of the private life of the court.

amphitheatre ample amputate amuse

angel [OE] Angels are to be found in the traditions of Christianity, Judaism, Islam, and other religions. They are messengers from God, and the word angel comes ultimately from Greek *angelos* 'messenger'. An angel was also the name given to an old English gold coin (known in full as the **angel-noble**) minted between the reigns of Edward IV and Charles I and stamped with the image of the Archangel Michael slaying a dragon. To be **on the side of the angels** is to be on the side of what is right. In a speech given at Oxford in 1864 the British statesman Benjamin Disraeli (1804–1881) referred to the controversy that was then raging about Charles Darwin's book *On the Origin of Species*, saying: 'Is man an ape or an angel? . . . I am on the side of the angels.' The plant **angelica** [E16th] is the 'angelic herb' because it was believed to work against poison and disease. *See also* ANGLE

anger [ME] Anger is from Old Norse *angr* 'grief', *angra* 'to vex'. Original use was in the Old Norse senses; current senses date from late Middle English.

angina [M16th] The Latin word *angere*, 'to choke, squeeze, or strangle', is the source of a number of English words. The most obvious is perhaps angina, which originally meant quinsy (an inflammation of the throat) and later referred to **angina pectoris**, a heart condition characterized by a feeling of suffocation and severe pain. Nervous tension can produce feelings of tightness in the throat and chest, which explains why *angere* is indirectly the root of **anguish** [ME] and **anxiety** [E16th].

angle [OE] The angle meaning 'the space between two intersecting lines' and the one meaning 'to fish with a rod and line', or 'to prompt someone to offer something' are different words. The first comes from Latin *angulus* 'corner' and the second is an Old English word from ancient Germanic roots. The **Angles** were a people who migrated to England from Germany during the 5th century and founded kingdoms in the Midlands and East Anglia, eventually giving their name to England and the English. They came from the district of *Angul*, on the long, curved peninsula that is now called Schleswig-Holstein, and are thought to have got their name because the area was shaped like a fish hook—angle is also an old name for a hook. The **ankle** [OE], the bend in the leg, goes back to the same Indo-European root as angle.

anglophile *see* PHILATELY

angst *see* GERMAN WORD PANEL

anguish *see* ANGINA

animal [ME] Animals are so called simply because they breathe. The word, used as an adjective in English before the noun became established, originally described any living being, as opposed to something inanimate. Its source is the Latin word *animalis*, 'having the breath of life', from *anima* 'air, breath, life'. As a noun, the word was hardly used in England before the end of the 16th century—the older **beast** [ME] from Latin *besta* was the usual term—and does not appear in the King James Bible of 1611. **Animate** [LME] is also from *anima*. *See also* MESMERIZE

anime *see* JAPANESE WORD PANEL

ankle *see* ANGLE

annals *see* ANNUAL

annex [LME] This is from Latin *annectere* 'connect', made up of the elements *ad-* 'to' and *nectere* 'tie, fasten'.

annihilate [LME] Hidden in the middle of annihilate is the Latin word *nihil*, meaning 'nothing', which is at the heart of the English word's meaning. Deriving in the 14th century from the Latin *annihilatus* 'reduced to nothing', it was first used as an adjective with the meaning 'destroyed or annulled'. *Nihil* is also the source of **nil** [M16th].

anniversary *see* ANNUAL

announce [LME] The base of announce is Latin *nuntius* 'messenger' (also the base of **nuncio** [E16th] a papal ambassador).

angel anger angina angle anglophile angst

From the same root come **annunciation** [ME] 'act of announcing'; **denounce** [ME] with *de-* having a negative sense; **pronounce** [LME] from *pro-* 'out, forth'; **renounce** [LME] from *re-* (expressing reversal); and **enunciate** [M16th] 'announce clearly' from *e-* (a variant of *ex-*) 'out'.

annoy [ME] Annoy originally has a much stronger sense than the modern one. It came into English from Old French *anoier*, but was based on Latin *in odio*, from the phrase *mihi in odio est*, 'it is hateful to me'.

annual [LME] This comes via Old French from late Latin *annualis*, based on Latin *annus* 'year'. The notion of a 'yearbook' recording events of the past year, arose in the late 17th century. From the same word we get **annals** [M16th] from Latin *annales* (*libri*) 'yearly (books)' giving a historical record of the events throughout each year; **anniversary** [ME] 'returning yearly'; **annuity** [LME] something paid 'yearly'; **perennial** [M17th] '[lasting] through the year'; and the Latin phrases **annus horribilis** 'year of disasters' and **annus mirabilis** 'wonderful year'.

annul [LME] Introduced into English via Old French from late Latin *annullare*, annul is based on the Latin elements *ad-* 'to' and *nullum* 'nothing', the source also of **null** [LME].

annunciation *see* ANNOUNCE

anodyne [M16th] Introduced via Latin from Greek *anōdunos* 'painless', the base elements of anodyne are *an-* 'without' and *odunē* 'pain'.

anoint *see* UNCTION

anorak [1920s] The anorak comes from Greenland, where the Inupiaq language of the Inuit gave us the word for a hooded waterproof jacket. The shabby anoraks traditionally worn by trainspotters and others with unfashionable preoccupations led to such people being known as anoraks from the early 1980s.

anorexia [L16th] This is based on Greek *an-* 'without' and *orexis* 'appetite'.

answer *see* SWEAR

ant [OE] The dialect word **emmet** for an ant, used since the 1970s as a Cornish term for a tourist, is like *ant*, from Old English *æmete*. **Antsy**, dating from the mid 19th century, is probably from the phrase **have ants in one's pants;** it means 'agitated', 'restless'.

antagonist *see* AGONY

ante The expression **up the ante**, meaning 'to increase what is at stake', comes from the world of card games and gambling. *Ante* is a Latin word meaning 'before' and is a component of English words such as **anteroom** [M18th] and **antenatal** [E19th]. **Ante** was first used in English by American players of card games in the early 19th century for a stake put up by a player to start the betting before drawing the cards. 'Upping' (or 'raising') the ante is putting up a higher stake than your opponent in order to put more pressure on them.

antecedent *see* CEDE

antediluvian *see* DELUGE

antelope [LME] Before 17th-century zoologists gave the name to a fast-running horned animal, an **antelope** was a fierce mythical creature with long serrated horns that was believed to live on the banks of the River Euphrates and was often depicted in heraldic designs. It was said to be able to use its saw-like horns to cut down trees. Although the word came into English via Old French and medieval Latin from Greek *antholops*, the origin and meaning of the Greek word is a mystery.

antenatal *see* ANTE

antenna [M17th] On old Mediterranean sailing ships certain types of triangular sail, called lateen sails, were supported by long yards or poles at an angle of 45 degrees to the mast, which reminded the ancients of an insect's antennae. The Latin word

annoy annual annul annunciation anodyne

antenna was an alteration of *antemna* 'sailyard', and was used by writers to translate the Greek *keraioi* 'horns of insects'. When Marconi and others developed radio in the 1890s the word was quickly taken up, along with aerial (*see* *AIR), to refer to a rod or wire by which signals were received.

ante-room *see* ANTE

anthology [M17th] An anthology is literally a collection of flowers. The Greek word *anthologia* (from *anthos* 'flower', source also of the botanical **anther** [E18th], and *logia* 'collection') was applied to a collection of the 'flowers' of verse, poems by various authors that had been chosen as being especially fine. Writing in 1580, the French essayist Montaigne uses the same metaphor: 'It could be said of me that in this book I have only made up a bunch of other men's flowers, providing of my own only the string that ties them together.' *See also* POSY

anthracite [L16th] Originally an anthracite was a gem described by Pliny as resembling coals. The word is from Greek *anthrakitēs*, from *anthrax, anthrak-* 'coal' or 'carbuncle' (meaning both a red gem like a glowing coal, and a swelling that looks like one). The same word is the source of the disease **anthrax** [LME] which causes black lesions in humans. **Carbuncle** [ME] itself keeps the same image, coming from Latin *carbunculus* 'small coal' from *carbo* 'coal, charcoal', the source of words such as **carbon** [L18th].

anthrax *see* ANTHRACITE

anthropology *see* PHILATELY

antibiotic *see* AMPHIBIAN

anticipation *see* CAPABLE

antics *see* ANTIQUITY

antidote [LME] An antidote is 'something given against' the effects of a poison; it has come via Latin from Greek *antidoton* 'given against'.

antipodes [LME] Think of a person standing on the other side of the world, exactly opposite the point on the Earth's surface where you are standing. The soles of their feet are facing the soles of your feet. This is the idea behind the word **Antipodes**, which came via French or Latin from the Greek word *antipous*, meaning 'having the feet opposite'. Writing in 1398, John de Trevisa described the Antipodes who lived in Ethiopia as 'men that have their feet against our feet'.

antiquity [ME] This word comes from Latin *antiquitas*, from *antiquus* 'old, former' developed from *ante* 'before' (*see* *ANTE). **Antics** [E16th] is from the same source by way of Italian *antico* 'antique', used to mean *GROTESQUE, and as a term for the grinning faces carved on architecture fashionable at the time. From this it came to be used for grotesque behaviour.

antirrhinum *see* RHINOCEROS

anvil [OE] An anvil is something to strike on. In Old English the spelling was *anfilte*, from the Germanic base of *on* and a verb meaning 'beat'.

anxiety *see* ANGINA

aorta *see* ARTERY

apart, apartment *see* PART

apathy *see* PATHETIC

ape [OE] Until *MONKEY came into the language in the 16th century, the Old English word **ape** applied also to monkeys. The verb use 'to imitate unthinkingly' was formed when 'ape' still meant 'monkey', and was suggested by the way that monkeys sometimes mimic human actions. The expression **go ape** is often thought to be a reference to the 1933 film *King Kong*, in which a giant ape-like monster goes on the rampage through New York, but the phrase is not recorded until quite a bit later: US newspaper reports from 1954 and 1955 both say that 'go ape' is current teen slang. The cruder version **go ape shit** is recorded from 1951.

ante-room anthology anthracite anthrax

aperture [LME] This is from Latin *apertura* from *aperire* 'to open'.

apex [E17th] Apex is Latin for 'peak, tip'.

aphrodisiac [E18th] The name Aphrodite for the goddess of beauty, fertility, and sexual love in Greek mythology lies behind aphrodisiac.

aplomb *see* PLUMB

apology [M16th] Used in legal contexts at first, an apology was a formal defence against an accusation; it goes back to Greek *apologia* 'a speech in one's own defence'.

apostle [OE] Old English *apostol* comes via ecclesiastical Latin from Greek *apostolos* 'messenger' (*compare* *ANGEL). The bird known as an **apostlebird** is named from the supposed habit of these birds of going about in flocks of twelve, drawing on an association with the twelve chief disciples of Christ.

apostrophe [M16th] Now a punctuation mark, apostrophe originally referred to the omission of one or more letters; it comes via late Latin from Greek *apostrophos* 'accent of elision', from *apostrephein* 'turn away'.

apothecary *see* BOUTIQUE

appal [ME] Like *ABHOR, appal has its origin in the physical effect of being horrified. Old French *apalir* meant both 'to grow pale' and 'to make pale', and these senses were carried over into the English word in the 14th century. As shock or disgust can make the colour drain from your face, appal soon acquired its current meaning.

apparatus [E17th] This is a Latin word, from *apparare* 'make ready for', from *parare* 'make ready'. Other words going back to *parare* include **disparate** [LME], 'prepared apart'; **pare** [ME]; **prepare** [LME] 'prepare in advance'; and **separate** [LME] from *se-* 'apart' and *parare*.

appeal [ME] Recorded first in legal contexts, appeal comes via Old French from Latin *appellare* 'to address, accost, call

upon'. **Peal** [LME] is a shortening of appeal, perhaps from the call to prayers of a ringing bell. The base of appeal is Latin *pellere* 'to drive', found also in **compel** 'drive together'; **dispel** 'drive apart'; **expel** 'drive out'; **impel** 'drive towards'; and **impulsive**; **propel** 'drive forwards'; **repel** 'drive back', all Late Middle English. It is also the source of the **pulse** [ME] that you can feel on your wrist and is related to **push** [ME]. The other kind of **pulse**, an edible seed, is a different word, which comes via Old French from Latin *puls* 'porridge of meal or pulse', related to the sources of both *POLLEN and *POWDER.

appease *see* PEACE

appendage *see* PENTHOUSE

appendix [M16th] The appendix is a tube-shaped sac attached to the lower end of the large intestine. The word comes directly from Latin and is based on *appendere* 'to hang on', the source of other English words such as **append** [LME], and **appendage** [M17th]. It is first recorded in the sense 'section of extra matter at the end of a book or document', the anatomy term appears early in the 17th century.

appetite [ME] 'Seeking' and 'desire' are involved in appetite, which comes via Old French from Latin *appetitus* 'desire for', from *appetere* 'seek after'.

applaud *see* PLAUDIT

apple [OE] Originally the Old English word apple could be used to describe any fruit. The **forbidden fruit** eaten by Adam and Eve in the Garden of Eden is generally thought of as an apple, and pictured as such, but the 1611 King James Version of the Bible simply calls it a fruit. The apple is the predominant fruit of northern Europe, and many common phrases involve it. A **rotten apple** (or a **bad apple**) is someone who is a bad influence on the rest of a group, from the idea of a rotten apple spoiling other fruit. The idea can be traced back at least as far as the days of the early printer William Caxton in the 15th century. The **apple of

your eye was once a term for the pupil, which people used to think of as a solid ball. They later applied the expression to anything considered to be similarly delicate and precious. The proverb **an apple a day keeps the doctor away** dates from the 19th century, as does the alternative form 'eat an apple on going to bed, and you'll keep the doctor from earning his bread'. The Australian expression **it's** (*or* **she's**) **apples** means 'everything is fine, there is nothing to worry about'. This derives from *apples and rice* (or *apples and spice*), rhyming slang for 'nice'. Another example of rhyming slang is **apples and pears** for 'stairs'. The city of New York has been known as **the Big Apple** since the 1920s, possibly from the idea that there are many apples on the tree but New York is the biggest. **Applet** [1990s] is an unconnected word, being computer jargon formed from 'application' and the ending for 'little' -let.

appliance [M16th] Until the manufacturer Zanussi introduced its slogan 'The appliance of science' in the 1970s the use of **appliance** to mean 'the application of something' had become rare if not obsolete. This sense was the original one, but had fallen out of use, and appliance generally meant 'a device designed to perform a specific task'. Appliance entered the language much later than **apply** [LME], which is formed from Latin elements *ad-* 'to' and *plicare* 'to fold'.

appraise, appreciate *see* PRICE

apprehend *see* PRISON

apprize *see* PRICE

approach [ME] 'Bringing near' is involved in approach, which is from Old French *aprochier, aprocher*, from ecclesiastical Latin *appropiare* 'draw near'.

appropriate *see* PROPER

apricot [M16th] The Romans called the apricot the *malum praecocum* or 'the apple that ripens early'. The second part of the Latin name, meaning 'early-ripening', is also the root of the word **precocious** [M17th], now used of children but originally used to describe flowers or fruit that blossomed or ripened early. Over the centuries *praecocum* gradually mutated in a multilingual version of Chinese whispers. It passed into Byzantine Greek as *perikokkon*, to Arabic as *al-birquq*, to Spanish *albaricoque*, and to Portuguese *albricoque*. In the 16th century the word was adopted into English from Portuguese in the form *albrecock*. The modern spelling was probably influenced by French *abricot*, and perhaps by Latin *apricus* 'ripe'.

apron [ME] What we now call an apron was known in the Middle Ages as a *naperon*, from Old French *nape* or *nappe* 'tablecloth' (also the source of **napkin** [LME] and its shortening **nappy** [E20th]). Somewhere along the line the initial 'n' got lost, as people heard 'a naperon' and misinterpreted this as 'an apron'. A similar process of 'wrong division' took place with words such as *ADDER.

apt [LME] Originally apt meant 'suited, appropriate'; the source is Latin *aptus* 'fitted', the past participle of *apere* 'fasten'. **Inept** [M16th] is its opposite, the change in the vowel sound having already happened in Latin *ineptus*.

aquamarine [E18th] In Latin *aqua* means 'water' and *marina* means 'of the sea, marine'. Put them together and you get **aquamarine**, a precious stone the blue-green colour of sea water. Other words from *aqua* include **aquarium** [M19th], **aquatic** [LME], and **aqueduct** [M16th], which is combined with Latin *ducere* 'to lead'.

aquiline *see* EAGLE

arc [LME] A number of English words comes from Latin *arcus* 'a bow, arch, or curve', among them arc, **arcade** [L17th], and **arch** [ME]. Arc was originally a term for the path of the sun or other celestial objects from horizon to horizon. Given the shape of a bow for shooting arrows, it

Who put the sugar in your coffee?

While much of the Western world was in the Dark Ages, **Arabic** *culture was making enormous contributions to art, philosophy, science, and medicine. From medieval times merchants brought Arabic words to the West along with new goods and materials, including those household staples coffee and sugar.*

COFFEE derives from Arabic *qahwa*, although the word entered English in the late 16th century via Turkish *kahveh*. Muslims had taken wild plants from Ethiopia and cultivated them in Arabia, from where the drink spread throughout the Arabic world and Turkey, becoming particularly popular in the international metropolis of Constantinople. The word **sugar** has been in English much longer than coffee, coming in the 13th century by way of Old French and Italian from Arabic *sukkar*. **Candy**, the North American term for 'sweets', is another Arabic word, from *qandī* 'candied', or clarified and crystallised by repeated boiling.

Another important commodity was **cotton**, or in Arabic *qutn*, known in Britain by the 14th century. More exotic were **mohair**, which in Arabic was *mukayyar*, literally 'choice, select', and **saffron**, or *za'faran*. A **sequin** was originally a Venetian gold coin whose name came from Arabic *sikka*, 'a die for making coins'. Trade often involves customs and tariffs, so it is no surprise that the word **tariff** itself is from Arabic.

In Arabic *al-* means 'the', which is reflected in the spellings of *ALBATROSS, *ALCOHOL, **alcove**, and *ALGEBRA, and also in many proper names. **Al-Qaeda** means literally 'the base'—a reference to the training camp or base in Afghanistan used by the **mujahideen**, or guerrillas fighting the Russian occupiers, from which the terrorist group developed.

Islam and **Muslim** are both from the same word, *aslama*, meaning 'to submit, surrender', or 'to submit to Allah or God', and both were first recorded in English in the early 17th century. An **ayatollah** is a Shiite religious leader in Iran. The word has been used since around 1950 in English, and many people only became aware of it when Ayatollah Khomeini (1900–1989) led the Iranian revolution in 1979. A much more established word in English is **imam**, the leader of prayers in a mosque, known since the 17th century. The word's root is *amma* 'to lead the way'.

Fatwa was in use in English as early as the 17th century, but it was an obscure and unfamiliar word until 1989, when it suddenly gained new and widespread currency. In this year Ayatollah Khomeini issued a fatwa sentencing the British writer Salman Rushdie (*b.*1947) to death for publishing *The Satanic Verses*, a novel regarded by many Muslims as blasphemous. **Fatwa** is a generic term for any legal decision made by an Islamic religious authority, but, because of the particular way in which the

English-speaking world became familiar with it, the term is sometimes wrongly thought to refer to a death sentence.

Another word often misunderstood by non-Muslims in the West is **jihad**. It is generally taken to mean 'war by Muslims against non-believers', yet this is only a small part of the word's meaning. In Arabic *jihād* literally means 'effort', and expresses the idea of struggle on behalf of God and Islam, of which war is but one small part. The concept is sometimes divided into **lesser jihad**, or struggle against unbelievers or oppressors, and **greater jihad**, a person's spiritual struggle against sin.

See also ELIXIR, GIRAFFE, LEMON, ORANGE, SOFA, ZERO

should not be surprising that **archer** [ME] has the same Latin source. Another meaning of arch, 'chief or principal' (as in **archbishop** [OE] or **arch-enemy** [M16th]), has a different origin, coming from Greek *arkhos* 'a chief or ruler'. This Greek word can also be seen in **anarchy** [M16th], which literally means 'the state of having no ruler', in **architect** [M16th] from *archi* and *tektōn* 'builder', and **archipelago** [E16th] from *archi* and *pelagos* 'sea'. This was originally used as a proper name for the Aegean Sea; the general sense 'group of islands' arose because the Aegean Sea is remarkable for its large numbers of islands.

arcane *see* ARK

arch, archbishop, arch-enemy, archer, archipelago, architect
see ARC

arctic [LME] Arctic ultimately comes from Greek *arktos* 'bear', but not because of the polar bears that live in the northern polar regions. The bear in question is the Great Bear, the constellation Ursa Major, which can always be seen in the north.

area [M16th] Originally a 'space allocated for a specific purpose', area is from Latin, literally 'a vacant piece of level ground'. The historical unit of measurement, the **are**, dating from the late 18th century, came via French from Latin *area*.

arena [E17th] Roman amphitheatres, used for staging gladiatorial combats and other violent spectacles, were strewn with sand to soak up the blood spilled by the wounded and dead combatants. The word for 'sand' in Latin was *harena* or *arena*, and after a time this came to be applied to the whole amphitheatre.

aria *see* AIR

aristocracy [LME] The term originally meant the government of a state by its best citizens, later by the rich and well born, which led, in the mid 17th century, to the sense 'nobility', regardless of the form of government. The origin is Old French *aristocratie*, from Greek *aristokratia*, from *aristos* 'best' and -*kratia* 'power'.

ark [OE] *Aerc* was the Old English word for a chest, from Latin *arca* 'a chest or box'. This developed into ark, as in the **Ark of the Covenant**, the wooden chest in which the tablets of the laws of the ancient Israelites were kept, and the **Holy Ark** in a synagogue, a chest, or cupboard which contained the scrolls of the Torah or Hebrew scriptures. A ship may be thought of as a floating container, hence **Noah's Ark**, the vessel built by Noah to escape the Flood. The Latin word is also the source of **arcane** [M16th], which describes something hidden, concealed, or secret, as if it were shut up in a box, which only a few people can open.

arm [OE] Although they may seem connected, arm meaning 'part of the body' and arm meaning 'a weapon' are different

arcane   arch   archbishop   arch-enemy

words. The former is Old English, while the latter came into medieval English from French and ultimately Latin. It is also found in **armadillo** [L16th], from the Spanish for 'little armed man'; in **armistice** [E18th] from Latin *arma* and *stitium* 'stoppage'; **armour** [ME] and **armature** [M16th], both from Latin *armatura* and both originally meaning armour. **The long arm of the law** is the police force. The phrase was first recorded in *Rob Roy* by Sir Walter Scott (1817) as 'the arm of the law', but the more usual form was 'the strong arm of the law'. The first example of the 'long' form is in Charles Dickens's *The Old Curiosity Shop* of 1841. If something **costs an arm and a leg** it is extremely expensive. The traditional story connects the expression with portrait painting. A pose in which the sitter's arms and legs were all visible might be more difficult to paint, making the portrait more expensive. More likely is that the phrase originates in the idea that a person's arms and legs are very precious to them. It may be an insensitive punning reference to 'lost an arm and a leg', a phrase which was all too common in reports of wartime casualties. There is a similar thought behind the much older expression **give your right arm for** something, meaning 'to want something very much and be willing to pay a high price for it'.

armpit *see* PIT

aroma [ME] A walk past any Indian restaurant will confirm that spices have a definite aroma, and it is 'spice' that was the original meaning of **aroma**. From the 13th century, when the word entered English via Latin from Greek *arōma*, 'spice' was the only meaning, and the modern sense 'a distinctive pleasant smell' did not appear until the beginning of the 19th century.

arrant *see* ERRANT

arrest *see* REST

arrive [ME] Until about 1550 the main meaning of arrive was 'to come ashore or into port after a voyage'. You could also talk about 'arriving' a ship or a group of passengers, meaning to bring them to shore. Only later did the more general sense of 'to reach a destination, come to the end of a journey' develop. Arrive comes from the Old French word *ariver*, ultimately from Latin *ad-* 'to' and *ripa* 'shore' also the source of *RIVER.

arrogant [LME] This comes, via French, from Latin *arrogare* 'to claim for oneself'.

arrow [OE] This is from Old Norse, but is only indirectly the source of the plant called **arrowroot** [L17th]. The tubers of this Caribbean plant were used to absorb poison from arrow wounds. The word is an alteration of Arawak *aru-aru* (literally 'meal of meals') to conform with the more familiar words *arrow* and *root*.

arse [OE] Like *BUM, arse was not originally a rude slang word. It dates back to before 1000 in English, and is connected to various old German and Scandinavian forms that were probably linked to Greek *orros* 'the rump or bottom'. Arse was perfectly respectable until the 17th century. To **go arse over tip** (the original form, rather than **tit**) and **not know your arse from your elbow** are first found in the early 20th century. **My arse!** as a derisive comment is first recorded in the 1920s, though all these expressions are probably older. The American spelling is **ass**, which is nothing to do with **ass** meaning 'donkey'. The latter is from an Old English word that is related to *EASEL and goes back to Latin *asinus*, as in **asinine** [LME] or stupid.
See also WHEAT

arsenic [LME] The chemical element arsenic is a brittle steel-grey substance with many highly poisonous compounds, but its root word means 'gold'. In English the word first referred to a compound of arsenic called arsenic sulphide or yellow orpiment, which was used as a dye and artist's pigment. The word comes from Greek *arsenikon*, from Arabic *az-zarnīk*, the root of which was Persian *zar* 'gold'.

arson [L17th] This was an Anglo-Norman legal term which came from Latin *ardere* 'to burn'.

arsy-versy *see* TOPSY-TURVY

art [ME] Originally art was simply 'skill at doing something'. Its use in the modern sense dates from the early 17th century. The word comes from Latin *ars*, from a base which meant 'to put together, join, or fit'. There are many related words which stress the more practical roots of the word. These include **artefact** [E19th] from Latin *arte factum* 'something made by art'; **artifice** [LME] from the same roots; and **artisan** from the Latin for 'instructed in the arts'. The phrase **art for art's sake** conveys the idea that the chief or only aim of a work of art is the self-expression of the artist who creates it. It was the slogan of the Aesthetic Movement, which flourished in England during the 1880s. The Latin version of the phrase, **ars gratia artis**, is the motto of the film company MGM, and appears around the roaring lion in its famous logo. **Art deco**, was shortened from French *art décoratif* 'decorative art', from the 1925 Exhibition title *Exposition des Arts décoratifs* in Paris. Latin *iners* which gives us **inert** [M17th] and **inertia** [E18th] meant 'unskilled, inactive', and was formed as the opposite of *ars*.

artery [LME] This comes via Latin from Greek *artēria*, probably from *aeirein* 'raise'. Arteries were popularly thought by the ancients (who thought the word was from Greek *aēr* 'air') to be air ducts so they do not contain blood after death. Medieval writers thought they contained an ethereal fluid distinct from that of the veins: this was referred to as *spiritual blood* or **vital spirits**. **Aorta** [M16th] also comes from *aeirein*. It was used by Hippocrates for the branches of the windpipe, and by Aristotle for the great artery.

artesian [M19th] This comes from French *artésien* 'from Artois', a region of north-west France where wells of this type were first made in the 18th century.

artifice, artisan *see* ART

Aryan [LME] This is based on Sanskrit *ārya* 'noble'. Aryan is used by some as an equivalent of the term Indo-European for a language family. In the 19th century, the notion of an Aryan race corresponding to a definite Aryan language became current and was taken up by nationalistic historical and romantic writers. One of these was De Gobineau (1816–82), an anthropologist who linked the idea to a notion of inferiority of certain races. Later the term Aryan race was revived and used as propaganda in Nazi Germany.

asbestos [E17th] In Greek asbestos meant 'unquenchable'. In English it originally referred to a mythical stone that once set alight was impossible to extinguish. This was probably a distorted reference to what happens when cold water is poured on quicklime—it reacts with a lot of heat and fizzing. The word was revived in the 17th century to refer to the fibrous mineral used for making fireproof material.

ascend *see* SCALE

ascetic [M17th] Suggestive of severe self-discipline and abstention from indulgence, *ascetic* is from Greek *askētikos*. The base is *askētēs* 'monk'.

ash [OE] The two meanings of ash, the powder and the tree, started out as two completely different words. In Old English *aesce* or *aexe* referred to the powder, and *aesc* referred to the tree. When something **turns to ashes in your mouth** it becomes bitterly disappointing or worthless. The origins of this phrase can be traced back to John de Mandeville's *Travels*, a 14th-century work claiming to be an account of the author's travels in the East, where there is a description of a legendary fruit known as the Dead Sea fruit, sometimes also called the apple of Sodom. Although the fruit was appetizing to look at, it dissolved into smoke and ashes as soon as anyone tried to eat it The name of **the Ashes**, the cricket competition played roughly every other year between England and Australia comes from a mock obituary notice published in the *Sporting Times* newspaper on

2 September 1882, after the Australians had sensationally beaten the English team at the Oval: 'In Affectionate Remembrance of English Cricket Which Died at the Oval on 29th August, 1882. Deeply lamented by a large circle of sorrowing friends and acquaintances. R.I.P. N.B.—The body will be cremated and the ashes taken to Australia.' During the subsequent 1882–3 Test series in Australia the captain of the English team declared that his mission was to recover the Ashes for England. During the tour a group of women presented him with a wooden urn containing the ashes of a bail or stump, which has since been kept at Lord's Cricket Ground.

asinine *see* ARSE

ask [OE] Like many short but vital words, ask is Old English. Variations of the saying **ask a silly question and you get a silly answer** date back to at least the 13th century. It has a biblical source, 'Answer a fool according to his folly, lest he be wise in his own conceit', from the Book of Proverbs. **A big ask** is a difficult demand to make of someone, a lot to ask. The phrase originates in Australia, where it was first recorded in 1987, but has spread quickly into British English, and is a favourite of sports players, commentators, and writers, as in the example 'If we get four wins we will make the play-offs, but it's a big ask' (*Bolton Evening News*).

asparagus [M16th] The vegetable we know as asparagus was originally called *sparagus* (from medieval Latin), which was soon turned into the more English-sounding **sparrow-grass**. This process is called folk etymology, where people modify the form of an unusual word to make it seem to be derived from familiar ones. Sparrow-grass remained the polite name for the vegetable during the 18th century, with only botanists sticking to the spelling asparagus. As the compiler of a pronunciation dictionary wrote in 1791: '*Sparrow-grass* is so general that *asparagus* has an air of stiffness and pedantry.' It wasn't until the 19th century that asparagus returned into literary and polite use, leaving sparrow-grass to survive as an English dialect form.

aspersion [LME] To engage in **casting aspersions** is almost literally mud-slinging. Aspersion originally meant 'sprinkling water or other liquid on someone', especially in baptism, and came from Latin *spargere* 'to sprinkle' (the root of **disperse** [LME] 'scatter widely', and **intersperse** [M16th] 'sprinkle between'). Sprinkling a person with water developed into the idea of spattering them with something less pleasant, such as mud or dung. This in turn led to the notion of soiling a person's reputation by making false and damaging insinuations against them. *See also* SLUR

aspic [L18th] This jelly gets its name from the French word for a snake which appears in English as '**asp**'—a small southern European viper, which gets its name from Greek. There has been much debate why this should be. The best suggestions is that it is from a French expression *froid comme un aspic* 'as cold as an asp', so that the association is the coldness. Other suggestions are that it is something to do with the colour or patterns in the jellies in the 18th century, or with the shape of the moulds used.

aspire *see* SPIRIT

aspirin [L19th] This was coined in German, from *a(cetylierte) Spir(säur)e* 'acetylated spiraeic acid'; spiraeic acid is an old name for alicylic acid, given its name because it was first isolated from the leaves of the plant *Spiraea ulmaria* (meadowsweet).

ass *see* ARSE

assail *see* SALIENT

assassin [M16th] During the Crusades political and religious leaders were targeted for murder by a fanatical sect of Ismaili Muslims led by Hassan-i-Sabbah, known as the 'Old Man of the Mountains'. Members of the sect were said to prepare themselves for these deeds by smoking or chewing hashish or cannabis, and were accordingly known in

Arabic as *hasīsī*, 'hashish-eaters', which was filtered through French and eventually became our word assassin.

assault *see* SALIENT

assay *see* ESSAY

assess *see* SIZE

asset [M16th] An asset is literally something of which you have enough. It was originally a term used in connection with paying out money from a will, and comes from the old form of the French *assez* 'enough'.

assist *see* CONSIST

assize *see* SIZE

associate *see* SOCIAL

assume [LME] The word comes from Latin *assumere* formed from *ad* 'towards' and *sumere* 'take, take up'. *Sumere* also gives us, from the same period **consume** 'take up together'; **presume** 'take before' hence 'take for granted'; and **resume** 'take back'.

assure *see* SURE

asterisk [LME] The Greeks had two words for 'star', *astēr* and *astron*. They go back to an ancient root that is also the source of the Latin word *stella*, which gave us *STAR itself and also **stellar** [M17th]. An asterisk is a little star, the meaning of its source, Greek *asteriskos*. *Asteriskos* is from *astēr*, which is also the root of *asteroeidēs*, 'star-like'. This entered English in the early 19th century as **asteroid** [E19th], a term coined by the astronomer William Herschel. *Astēr* also gave us our name for the plant **aster** [E18th], which has petals rather like an asterisk. Words beginning with *astro-* come from *astron*. In the Middle Ages **astronomy** [ME] covered not only astronomy but astrology too. The Greek word it descends from meant 'star-arranging'. Rather poetically, an **astronaut** [1920s] is literally a 'star sailor'. The word comes from Greek *astron* 'star' and *nautēs* 'sailor'. It was modelled on **aeronaut** [L18th], a word for a traveller in a hot-air balloon or airship. **Cosmonaut** [1950s], the Russian equivalent of astronaut, literally means 'sailor in the cosmos'. *See also* DISASTER

astonish [E16th] The Old French *estoner*, from Latin *ex-* 'out' and *tonare* 'to thunder' is the source of astonish, the shorter form **stun** [ME], and of **astound** [ME].

astringent *see* STRICT

astrology *see* STAR

astronaut, astronomy *see* ASTERISK

astute [E17th] This is from obsolete French *astut* or Latin *astutus*, from *astus* 'craft'.

asylum [LME] At first an asylum was a 'place of refuge, especially for criminals'; it came via Latin from Greek *asulon* 'refuge', from *a-* 'without', and *sulon* 'right of seizure'. Current senses referring to political refuge or to an institution for the mentally ill, date from the 18th century.

atheist *see* ENTHUSIASM

athlete [LME] In Greek *athlon* meant 'prize', and the word *athlētēs*, from which we get athlete, literally meant 'someone who competes for a prize'. It originally referred to one of the competitors in the physical exercises—such as running, leaping, boxing, and wrestling—that formed part of the public games in ancient Greece and Rome.

atlas [L16th] Atlas was a Titan, or giant, in Greek mythology who was punished for taking part in a rebellion against the gods by being made to bear the weight of the world on his shoulders. He gave his name to the Atlas Mountains in Morocco, which are so high that they were imagined to be holding up the sky. A collection of maps is called an atlas because early atlases were published with an illustration of Atlas bearing the world on his back on the title page. The first person to use the word in this way was probably the map-maker Gerardus Mercator in the

assault assay assess asset assist assize

late 16th century. The **Atlantic Ocean** also gets its name from Atlas. The word **Atlantic** originally referred to the mountains, then to the sea near the west African coast, and later to the whole ocean.

atmosphere [M17th] This word meaning literally 'ball of vapour' is from modern Latin *atmosphaera*, from Greek *atmos* 'vapour' and *sphaira* 'globe'.

atom [LME] Long before scientists were able to prove the existence of atoms, ancient Greek philosophers believed that matter was made up of tiny particles that could not be broken down into anything smaller. The word the Greeks used for this hypothetical particle was *atomos* 'indivisible, that cannot be cut up'. By way of Latin *atomus*, this came into English in the 15th century as atom. The word was used in the early 19th century by the British chemist John Dalton (1766–1844) when he gathered evidence for the existence of these building blocks of matter. A century later the physicist Ernest Rutherford (1871–1937) disproved the theory that the atom could not be divided when he split the atom for the first time in 1919. The term **atom** *BOMB was first recorded in *The Times* on 7 August 1945, the day after the Hiroshima blast. Japan surrendered on 15 August, the date when **the Bomb** first appeared in a headline in *The Times* as 'Victory and the Bomb'. But the English novelist H.G. Wells (1866–1946) was writing about an **atomic bomb** as early as 1914.

atrocious [M17th] Whereas nowadays atrocious tends to describe something such as bad weather or poor English, it used to be a stronger word which referred to great savagery, cruelty, or wickedness, as in Charles Darwin's reference to 'Atrocious acts which can only take place in a slave country' (1845). The source of the word was Latin *atrox* 'fierce or cruel', based on *ater* 'black' and literally meaning 'black-looking'. **Atrocity** [M16th] has not had its sense weakened in the same way.

attach *see* ATTACK

attack [E17th] This is from French *attaquer* (from Italian *attaccare* 'join battle'). The base is an element of Germanic origin shared by **attach** [ME]; 'joining' is a key sense.

attempt *see* TEMPT

attest *see* TESTICLE

attic [L17th] Attic originally referred to an arrangement of small columns at the top of a building. It is from French *attique*, from Latin *Atticus* 'relating to Athens or Attica', from the type of architecture found there. The phrase **attic storey**, used from the mid 18th century, described a low space above the main tall façade, which eventually gave attic the sense 'highest storey of a building'.

attire *see* TYRE

attract *see* ABSTRACT

auburn [LME] The root of our word auburn is Latin *albus*, which actually meant 'white'. Based on this, medieval Latin formed the word *alburnus* 'whitish', which in Old French became *alborne* (or *auborne*) 'yellowish white' and was subsequently adopted into English. In the 16th and 17th centuries it was spelt in a number of different ways, including *abron*, *abrune*, and *abroun*, and these spellings must have put into people's minds the idea that auburn was in fact a kind of brown. Its meaning gradually changed from 'yellowish-white' to 'golden-brown or reddish-brown'. *See also* ALBUM, BAIZE, BROWN

auction [L16th] The way in which bids increase in an auction is embodied in the word's origin, as it comes from Latin *auctio* 'an increase', from *augere* 'to increase', also the source of **augment** [LME] and *AUTHOR.

audacious [M16th] Today audacious means 'willing to take surprisingly bold risks' and 'showing a lack of respect, impudent', but it originally had a more direct sense of 'bold, confident, daring'. The root is Latin *audax* 'bold'.

audience [LME] When people go to the theatre they generally talk about going to 'see' a play, but in former times the usual verb was 'hear'. In keeping with this idea, the oldest meaning of audience is 'hearing, attention to what is spoken'. Audience is based on the Latin word *audire* 'to hear' also found in **audible** [LME], 'able to be heard'. An **auditorium** [E17th], originally a Latin word, was a place for hearing something. Before it meant a trial performance of an actor or singer, **audition** [L16th] was the act of hearing or listening. And an **audit** [LME] was originally a hearing, in particular a judicial hearing of some kind—it was later used as the term for the reading out of a set of accounts, hence the modern meaning.

audio *see* VIEW

augment *see* AUCTION

augur *see* AUSPICIOUS

August *see* OCTOPUS

Auld lang syne *see* SCOTTISH WORD PANEL

Auld Reekie *see* REEK

aunt *see* APRON

au pair *see* FRENCH WORD PANEL

aura [LME] Originally a gentle breeze, aura comes via Latin from a Greek word meaning 'breeze, breath'. Current senses 'distinctive atmosphere', 'emanation', date from the 18th century.

aural *see* EAR

aurora borealis *see* EAST

auspicious [L16th] In Roman times people tried to predict future events by watching the behaviour of animals and birds. An *auspex* was a person who

observed the flight of birds for omens about what to do in important matters. A related word, *auspicium*, meant 'taking omens from birds'. Like *auspex*, it came from *avis* 'bird' and *specere* 'to look', and is the source of **auspice** [M16th]. It was originally used to translate the Roman concept, but later came to mean 'a premonition or forecast, especially of a happy future'. Auspicious accordingly meant 'fortunate or favourable'. If the *auspex*'s omens were favourable, he was seen as the protector of a particular enterprise, hence the expression **under the auspices of**, 'with the help, support, or protection of'. An *auspex* was also known as an *augur* (again, *avis* 'bird' is the root of this word, together with *garrire* 'to talk'). If something **augurs** [LME] well, it is a sign of a good outcome. *See also* AVIATION, INAUGURAL

Australia [16th] Since the days of the ancient Greeks, travellers speculated on the existence of an 'unknown southern land', or in Latin *terra australis incognita*, from *australis* 'of the south'. At first the continent was known as New Holland, and was not officially named Australia until 1824.

author [ME] In medieval English the author of something was the person who originated, invented, or caused it. God was sometimes described as 'the Author of all'. The word came into English via Old French from Latin *augere* 'to increase or originate'. (*See also* *AUCTION.) In time author came to be applied specifically to the composer of a book or other piece of writing. An **authority** [ME] was thus once the originator of something.

autograph *see* PHOTOGRAPH

autopsy [M17th] In an autopsy someone seeks to find out how a person died by seeing the body with their own eyes. An early sense of the word was 'personal observation', and this is the key to the word's origin. It comes from Greek *autoptēs* 'eyewitness', based on *autos* 'self' and *optos* 'seen', which

audience audio augment augur August

Digger dialect

*The English of **Australia** and New Zealand is funny, direct, and informal. TV programmes such as* Neighbours *and films like* Crocodile Dundee *have spread it around the rest of the English-speaking world, with the result that everybody is familiar with expressions such as* arvo *(afternoon) and* barbie *(barbecue).*

AUSTRALASIAN English has been enriched by the hundreds of indigenous languages that pre-dated European settlers, although only about 50 continue as first languages today. The 18th-century journals of the explorer Captain James Cook (1728–79) record **kangaroo** as the animal name used by Aboriginals in what is now North Queensland. The later suggestion that the word actually meant 'I don't understand', given as a reply to an enquiry in English, took people's fancy but seems to be an invented story. In Australia one way of suggesting that someone is mad or eccentric is to say that they have **kangaroos in the top paddock**—a zoological contrast with the traditional British 'bats in the belfry'.

When European settlers first came across the Aboriginal word **budgerigar** for the colourful little native bird they had no idea how they should spell it, and early attempts included *betshiregah*, *budgery garr*, and *budgregore*. The Maori word **kiwi** was first used in English in the 1830s. People started using the bird as the emblem of New Zealand at the end of the 1890s, and New Zealanders have been known as Kiwis since shortly after that.

The **larrikin** is one of the Australian stereotypes—the maverick with an apparent disregard for convention or the boisterous young man. The word could have been brought over from England—it is recorded in Cornish dialect in the 1880s—or based on **Larry**, a form of the man's name Lawrence common in Ireland and the Irish-Australian community.

During the First World War, Australian and New Zealand soldiers were referred to as **diggers**, in the sense 'miner', which was used for gold and opal miners in Australasia. In peacetime, **digger** became a friendly form of address for a man, like **cobber**, which probably came from English dialect *cob* 'to like'. One of the things that friends do together is drink, and as a consequence may **chunder**, or vomit, in the **dunny**. The first is probably from rhyming slang *Chunder Loo* = 'spew'. Chunder Loo of Akim Foo was a cartoon character devised by Norman Lindsay (1879–1969) that appeared in advertisements for Cobra boot polish in the early 20th century. **Dunny**, or 'toilet', was originally a **dunnekin**, an English dialect word from **dung** and **ken**, meaning 'house'.

Australians may refer to a Brit as a **Limey** or a **pom**. The former comes from the rations of lime juice given to Royal Navy seamen to ward off scurvy, while the latter term probably derives from *POMEGRANATE, as a near rhyme for 'immigrant'. The red, sunburnt cheeks of new arrivals may also have reminded people of the fruit. If an Australian or New Zealander tells you to **rattle your dags**, you would be well advised to hurry up. Dags are locks of wool clotted with dung at the rear end of a sheep, which can rattle as they move. The word may be related to **tag**, and goes back to medieval England, when dags were pointed divisions on the edge of a garment that were then fashionable. Today an entertaining or eccentric person can also be called a dag, as can someone who is untidy or dirty-looking, or an awkward adolescent.

Australian bushmen used various women's names for a bundle or 'swag' of personal belongings, but Matilda is the one whose name stuck, especially after 1893 when A.B. 'Banjo' Paterson (1864–1941) wrote his famous song 'Waltzing Matilda'. To **waltz** (or **walk**) **Matilda** is to travel the roads carrying your swag. The other woman's name forever associated with Australia is **Sheila**, an Irish name that has meant 'a girl or woman' since the 1820s.

The **billy** or **billycan** used in the Australian bush was until recently thought to derive from an Aboriginal word for 'water', *billa*, which is also found in **billabong**, a branch of a river forming a backwater. In fact, it is probably from the old Scots word *billy-pot* 'cooking utensil'.

One of Australia's best-loved exports in recent years has been the singer Kylie Minogue. Many of her fans will be unaware that in Western Australia a **kylie** is a boomerang. The word is from the Aboriginal language Nyungar.

See also ANTIPODES, BLUE, DINKUM, LAIRY, MOCKER, PIKE, POSSUM

means that it is related to other English words such as **optic** [LME] and **optician** [L17th].

autumn [LME] We now call the season between summer and winter **autumn**, a word borrowed in the 14th century via Old French from Latin *autumnus*. *HARVEST, an older word, was the usual name for the season until autumn displaced it in the 16th century. Americans call it *FALL, originally a British expression first recorded in 1545 for the season when leaves fall from the trees, which travelled over to the New World with the first colonists.

avalanche [L18th] This word comes from French Alpine dialect word *lavanche* of unknown origin, its current form influenced by the French *avaler* 'to descend'.

avant-garde [LME] This French phrase was originally used in English in its original sense for the vanguard of an army. Use for

those in the vanguard of what is new in the arts dates from the early 20th century.

avast [E17th] This nautical term is from Dutch *hou'vast, houd vast* 'hold fast!'.

avenge *see* REVENGE

avenue *see* REVENUE

average [LME] Originally a shipping term, meaning either the duty payable by the owner of goods about to be shipped or the financial liability for any goods lost or damaged at sea, average came into English in the 15th century from French *avarie* 'damage to a ship or cargo, customs duty'. The ultimate source was Arabic *awar* 'damage to goods'. All this may seem a long way from the modern meaning of average, but the word came to be applied to the fair splitting of the financial liability between the owners of the vessel and the owners of

autumn   avalanche   avant-garde   avast

the cargo, which in time led to the modern senses.

aviation [M19th] The Latin word for 'bird', *avis*, is the root of a number of English words that relate to birds, such as **aviary** [L16th], and **avian** [L19th]. It is also the source of words connected with the idea of flying, such as **aviation** and **aviator**, both 19th-century borrowings of French words. *See also* AUSPICIOUS

avocado [M17th] The name of the avocado in the Aztec language Nahuatl was *ahuacatl*, also the word for 'testicle' and applied to the fruit because of its shape. In the 16th century the Spanish conquerors of Central America adopted this word but converted it into the form *aguacate* and then to the more familiar-sounding *avocado*, the Spanish word for 'a lawyer' (and related to the English advocate, *see* *ADVOCAAT). The word came into English in the mid 17th century.

avuncular *see* UNCLE

awake *see* WATCH

aware [OE] Old English *gewær* has a West Germanic origin and is related to German *gewahr*. An early meaning was 'vigilant, cautious' as well as 'informed'. **Wary** [LME] is from the same root.

awe [OE] The battle plan for the 2003 invasion of Iraq by US-led forces was dubbed **shock and awe**. The phrase was not invented by President George W. Bush or Secretary of Defense Donald Rumsfeld, but came from *Shock and Awe: Achieving Rapid Dominance* (1996), by the US strategic analysts Harlan K. Ullman and James P. Wade. The Old English word awe originally meant 'terror or dread'. Gradually people started to use it to express their feelings for God, thereby introducing the senses of great respect and wonder. Both **awful** [OE] and **awesome** [L16th] have become weaker in meaning over the centuries. Awful was originally used to describe things that caused terror or dread. Other old meanings included 'awe-inspiring' and 'filled with awe'; the modern sense 'extremely bad' dates from the early 19th century. Awesome at first meant 'filled with awe'. It later came to mean 'inspiring awe', and in the 1960s took on the rather weaker meaning of 'overwhelming, remarkable, staggering'. Now it can just mean 'great, excellent', especially in the USA.

awkward [LME] There used to be a word **awk**, based on an Old Norse *afugr*, that meant 'turned the wrong way round'. So awkward meant 'in an awk direction', 'in the wrong direction, in reverse order, upside down'. It could be applied, for instance, to an animal that was on its back and was unable to get up. The meaning 'clumsy or ungainly' developed in the 16th century, followed by other meanings such as 'embarrassing', or 'difficult to deal with'.

axe [OE] Since Anglo-Saxon times an axe has been a tool or weapon, but since the 1950s it has also been a musical instrument. Jazz fans started referring to saxophones as axes, but now an axe is generally an electric guitar. **The axe**, meaning a measure intended to reduce costs, especially by making people redundant, goes back at least to 1922. A person who **has an axe to grind** has a private reason for doing something. The phrase is thought to come from an 18th-century cautionary tale in which a passing stranger takes advantage of a bystander and, by flattering him, tricks him into turning a grindstone to sharpen his axe.

axis [LME] In Latin *axis* means 'axle' or 'pivot'. That is really what an axis is—an imaginary line through a body, around which it rotates, rather like an invisible axle. In the Second World War **the Axis** was the alliance of Germany and Italy, later also including Japan and other countries, which opposed the Allies. The connection with an axis was the idea of the relations between countries forming a 'pivot' around which they revolved. *See also* EVIL.

ayatollah *see* ARABIC WORD PANEL

aviation avocado avuncular awake aware

Bb

babble, babe *see* BABY

Babel [ME] Genesis 11 tells the story of Babel, where God, angered by the arrogance of builders who thought they could reach heaven by erecting a tower, confused their language so that they could no longer understand each other. The word was originally Hebrew for 'Babylon', a name from the Babylonian Akkadian language meaning 'gate of God'. The Bible story led to its use in English in the general sense of 'a confusion of sounds'.

baboon [ME] Baboon was originally used for a carving such as a gargoyle, and probably comes from Old French *baboue* 'muzzle' or 'grimace'. By about 1400 it was being used for the long-snouted monkey.

baby [LME] Both baby and **babe** probably come from the way that the sound *ba* is repeated by very young children. **Babble** [ME] probably came from the same source, along with words such as **mama** [M16th] and **papa** [L17th]. Similar forms are found in many different languages. A person's lover or spouse has been their baby since the middle of the 19th century. The sense 'someone's creation or special concern' dates from later in that century—in 1890 artificial silk was referred to as its inventor's 'new-born baby'. The proverb **don't throw the baby out with the bathwater** is from German. The first known appearance in English is from the Scottish historian and political philosopher Thomas Carlyle (1795–1881), who wrote in 1853 that 'The Germans say, "You must empty out the bathing-tub, but not the baby along with it".' Babe originally just meant 'child', and only later became restricted to a child too

young to walk. Inexperienced people in a situation calling for experience are **babes in the wood**, from characters in an old ballad *The Children in the Wood*, whose wicked uncle wanted to steal their inheritance and abandoned them in a wood. The proverbial phrase **out of the mouths of babes** is used when a precocious child says something unexpectedly appropriate. It has biblical origins, being found in Psalms and the Gospel of Matthew. A babe today is generally an attractive young person. The first babes were men. In the 1870s the youngest member of a class of US military cadets was called the babe, rather like 'the baby of the family'. The term was then used as a friendly form of address between men before it came to mean a sexy girl. See also BIMBO

bacchanal [M16th] This word comes from **Bacchus** (in Greek *Bakkhos*), the god of wine. The association with the **Bacchanalia**, the Roman festival in honour of the god, with its renowned free-flowing wine and licentious behaviour, gave the sense 'drunken revelry or orgy'.

bachelor [ME] The word bachelor was adopted from French in the early Middle Ages. The earliest meaning was 'a young knight serving under another's banner', one who was not old or rich enough to have his own band of followers. The sense 'unmarried man' is known from the late Middle Ages—Geoffrey Chaucer (*c*.1343–1400) wrote in *The Canterbury Tales* that 'bachelors have often pain and woe'.

bacillus *see* BACTERIUM

back [OE] Old English back has been prolific in forming compounds, phrases and popular expressions. If you **get someone's back up** you make them annoyed. The image is that of a cat arching its back when angry or threatened. The idea is recorded as early as 1728: a character in *The Provok'd Husband*, a comic play of that year by John Vanbrugh (*c*.1664–1726) and Colley Cibber (1671–1757), remarks, 'How her back will be up then, when she meets me!' Sir Walter Scott was the first to use **the back of beyond**, in 1816. In Australia the back of beyond is **back o'Bourke**, Bourke being a remote town in New South Wales. In America there have been **backwoods** since the early 18th century. Failure has sent people **back to square one** since the 1950s. This possibly comes from a board game such as Snakes and Ladders, in which the board has some squares that send a player who lands on them back to the beginning or to an earlier position. **Back to the drawing board** does not seem to have been used until the 1940s, though drawing boards themselves have been known by that name from the early 18th century. Andrew Johnson, the 17th president of the USA, gave us the phrase to **take a back seat**. He said in 1868 after the American Civil War that 'in the work of Reconstruction traitors should take back seats'. In the 20th century the car brought with it the **back-seat driver**. By the 1950s the term appears in other contexts: in 1955 *The Times* reported a comment that 'it was contrary to democracy for elected members to consult "pressure groups" and "back-seat drivers" '. *See also* NIMBY

bacon [ME] The word bacon was adopted from French in the 14th century and can be traced back to an ancient German root that links it to *BACK, probably in the sense of the cut of meat. In early use it could mean fresh pork, as well as cured, and could also refer to a pig's carcass. To **bring home the bacon**, 'to supply food or support', first appeared in the USA during the early years of the 20th century. It may have developed from to **save one's bacon** ('to escape danger or difficulty'), an older expression which dates from the mid 17th century.

bacterium [M19th] This modern Latin term is formed from Greek *baktērion* 'little staff'; the first bacteria to be discovered were rod-shaped. The word **bacillus** [L19th], a pathogenic bacterium, also meant 'little rod' in late Latin. *Bacillus* is also behind the French word **debacle**, adopted into English in the early 19th century. It literally means an unbarring and was first used of the breaking of ice or other blockage

in a river and its effects, and then transferred to human behaviour.

bad [ME] Homophobia may lie at the root of the meaning of bad. The word appeared in the 13th century, and at that time had two syllables, like **baddy**. This suggests that it may be a shortening of Old English *bæddel* 'effeminate man, hermaphrodite'. Bad was specifically applied to coins with a reduced content of precious metal. This gives us the **bad penny**, which 'always turns up'. Debased coinage also features in the proverb **bad money drives out good**, also known as Gresham's law, after Queen Elizabeth I's chief financial adviser Sir Thomas Gresham (1519–79). He observed that people tended to hang on to coins of a high intrinsic value, like gold sovereigns, while being happier to spend those of a lower intrinsic worth but equal face value. At the end of the 19th century **bad** underwent a complete reversal of meaning in US black slang, and in the 1920s jazz enthusiasts began to use it as a term of approval—something 'bad' was now 'good'. *Compare with the development of* FUNK, WICKED

badge *see* BADGER

badger [E16th] Badger is probably based on **badge** (a LME word of unknown origin), with reference to the animal's distinctive facial markings. Use as a verb arose in the late 16th century and reflects the popularity at that time of badger-baiting, a pastime where badgers were drawn from their setts by dogs and killed for sport (illegal in the UK since 1830). The alternative name **brock** is a use of the Old English word for badger, one of the few words the Anglo-Saxons adopted from Celtic.

badminton [M19th] The game gets its name from the place in south west England which was the country seat of the Duke of Beaufort. Forms of the game had long existed, and were generally known as **battledore** and **shuttlecock** (the first from the same root at *BAT, the second, originally 'shuttle-cork' from *SHUTTLE and cork). A more competitive version of the old game

bacon   bacterium   bad   badge   badger

was brought back by army officers from India in the 19th century and became a popular game in English country houses.

bag [ME] The origin of bag is uncertain but it may come from an old Scandinavian word. Some phrases in English come from its use to mean a hunter's game bag, such as having something **in the bag**, 'as good as secured'. Another sense, 'a particular interest or distinctive style', as in 'Dance music isn't really my bag', is probably jazz slang of the 1950s. In the sense 'an unattractive woman', bag or **old bag** was originally American, and was first recorded in the 1890s.

bagel *see* YIDDISH WORD PANEL

bail [ME] The spelling **bail** represents several different words. The one meaning 'temporary release of an accused person' came via French from Latin *bajulare*, 'to bear a burden', and is related to **bailiff** [ME], someone who bears the burden of responsibility. The Latin word is also ultimately the source of **bail** (in Britain also spelled **bale**) meaning 'to scoop water out of a boat'. The **bailey** [ME] or outer wall of a castle has a quite different origin, but it is connected with the third bail, a crosspiece on a cricket stump: originally this bail meant the same as bailey. The ultimate origin of both of these appears to be Latin *baculum*, 'a rod or stick' which developed the sense 'palisade' in French. **Bailing out** from an aircraft may be a development of the 'to scoop water' sense. It was at first spelled **bale out**, though, and could come from the idea of letting a bale of straw though a trapdoor in a barn. The first written record dates from 1930. This sort of bale [ME] has the basic idea of something bundled and is related to *BALL.

bait *see* ABET

baize [L16th] Despite being generally green in colour today, **baize**, a material used for covering billiard tables, is from the French word *bai* 'chestnut-coloured', presumably from the original colour of the cloth. *Bai* is also the root of the English word

*BAY [ME], used to describe a brown horse with black mane and tail.

bake [OE] **and batch** [LME] Both words go back to the same Old English root. **Baker's dozen** meaning 'thirteen', arose in the 16th century. It was a traditional bakers' practice to add an extra loaf to every dozen sold to a shopkeeper—this extra, thirteenth loaf was the source of the retailer's profit when the loaves were sold on to customers.

balaclava [L19th] A balaclava was first a type of woollen covering for the head and neck worn by soldiers on active service in the Crimean War (1854), and was named after the village of *Balaclava* in the Crimea.

balance [ME] The original sense of balance was for the sort of scales that statues of Justice are shown holding. The word is based on late Latin *(libra) bilanx* '(balance) with two scale-pans', composed of *bi-* 'twice', 'having two' and *lanx* 'scale-pan'.

balcony [E17th] Balcony is from Italian *balcone*, based on *balco* 'a scaffold' from a Germanic root meaning 'beam'. The English word was pronounced with the stress on the second syllable until about 1825, reflecting the Italian source.

bald [ME] Words related to bald in other northern European languages suggest that its core meaning was 'having a white patch or streak'. This may survive in the phrase **as bald as a coot**. The coot is not actually bald: it has a broad white area on its forehead extending up from the base of its bill. Descriptions of people as being as bald as a coot appear as far back as the 15th century.

balderdash *see* POPPYCOCK

bale *see* BAIL

baleful [OE] This comes from an old Germanic word, bale, meaning 'evil'.

balk *see* BAULK

ball [ME] The spherical ball dates from the early Middle Ages, and comes from an old

Scandinavian word that was the ultimate root of Italian *ballotta*, from which English took **ballot** in the mid 16th century, and also of French *ballon* and Italian *ballone* 'large ball', one of which was the source of *BALLOON. The ball at which people dance is unrelated. It came, in the early 17th century, from French, and goes back to Latin *ballare* 'to dance'. This was also the source of **ballad** [LME] and **ballet** [M17th].

In America a ball game is a baseball match and a ballpark a baseball stadium. These have entered even British English in phrases such as **a whole new ball game**, 'a completely new set of circumstances', **in the (right) ballpark**, 'a particular area or range', and a **ballpark figure** (an approximate figure).

The dancing sense has notably given us **have a ball**, meaning 'enjoy yourself a lot'. This was originally an American expression of the 1930s, but is now used nearly everywhere that English is spoken.

Testicles have been balls since the Middle Ages, but the slang sense 'nonsense' is Victorian. The meaning 'courage, determination' is more recent still, dating only from the 1950s. People often claim that the phrase **cold enough to freeze the balls off a brass monkey** comes from a former naval custom of storing cannonballs on a brass rack or 'monkey'. When the weather was very cold the rack could contract and eject the cannonballs. There are some severe problems with this explanation, though. First, cannonballs were stored on a wooden rack, not a brass one. Second, it would have to be extremely cold to cause sufficient contraction in the metal for this to happen. And third, the earliest recorded versions of the phrase (dating from the 19th century) feature noses and tails rather than balls, suggesting that the reference is to a brass statue of a monkey, and that the 'balls' are testicles rather than cannonballs. *See also* BOLLOCK, COB, EVIL

ballistic [L18th] Two ancient engines of war, a catapult for hurling large stones and a large crossbow firing a spear, were each known as a **ballista**. The Latin source, *ballista*, from Greek *ballein* 'to throw', gave us ballistic. As a technical term this dates

from the 18th century, but it only became widely known in the mid 20th century with the development of the **ballistic missile**, a missile which is initially powered and guided but falls under gravity on to its target. In the 1980s to **go ballistic** began to be used meaning 'to fly into a rage'.

balloon [L16th] The balloon that carries passengers in a basket is older than the one used as a children's toy. In 1782 the brothers Joseph and Jacques Montgolfier built a large balloon from linen and paper and successfully lifted a number of animals, and the following year people, whereas the toy version did not appear until the middle of the next century. The word was adopted from French or Italian in the late 16th century, and originally referred to a large inflatable leather ball used in a game of the same name. It goes back to the same root as *BALL.

The phrase **when the balloon goes up**, 'when the action or trouble begins', has been used in Britain since the 1920s. It may refer to the release of a balloon to mark the beginning of a race. By contrast, to **go down like a lead balloon** is American in origin: **lead balloon** appears as a term meaning 'a failure, a flop' in a comic strip of 1924 in which a man who had been sold dud shares discovered they were 'about to go up as fast as a lead balloon'.

ballot *see* BALL

balsa [E17th] A balsa was originally a kind of South American raft or fishing boat and is an adoption of this Spanish word for 'raft'. Because it was used for rafts the word was transferred to the lightweight wood from a tropical American tree.

ban [OE] In Old English this meant 'to summon by popular proclamation'. The word is Germanic and also passed into French where it had the sense 'proclamation, summons, banishment'. This lies behind **abandon** [LME] based on the Old French phrase *a bandon* 'at one's disposal, under one's jurisdiction'; and **banal** [M18th] which originally related to feudal service and meant 'compulsory'.

ballistic   balloon   ballot   balsa   ban

From this came a notion of 'common to everyone' and so 'ordinary and everyday'. The marriage **banns** [ME] read in church also come from the sense 'proclamation'. **Bandit** [L16th] comes from Italian *bandito* a 'banned person', and **banish** [LME] comes from the same root.

banana [L16th] Africa is the original home of the banana. The word travelled to English through Portuguese and Spanish from Mande, a language group of West Africa, arriving in the 16th century. In the 20th century slang expressions began to appear. American people began to **go bananas** with excitement, anger, or frustration in the 1950s. The **top banana**, 'the most important person in an organization', derives from US theatrical slang. It referred to the comedian with top billing in a show, a use first recorded in 1953 from a US newspaper, which also mentions **second** and **third bananas**. People have been slipping on a **banana skin** since the beginning of the 20th century: the comic writer P.G. Wodehouse (1881–1975) referred in 1934 to 'Treading upon Life's banana skins'. The **banana republic**, a small state, especially in central America, whose economy is almost entirely dependent on its fruit-exporting trade, was referred to as early as 1904.

band [OE] A band in the sense 'a strip of something' comes from the same Germanic root as **bind** [OE] and **bond** [ME]. Bend is a variant found in **bend sinister** [E17th], a broad diagonal stripe from top right to bottom left of a shield, a supposed sign of bastardy. **Bandage** [L16th] and **bandbox** [M17th], now a box for carrying hats, but originally for carrying neckbands, come from this word. In early use a band in the sense 'a group', usually consisted of armed men, robbers, or assassins. The first groups of musicians called a band (in the 17th century) were attached to regiments of the army. **Banner** [ME] is related. A **bandwagon** [M19th] was a wagon used for carrying the band in a parade or procession. The word now occurs more often in phrases such as to **jump on the bandwagon**. This use

developed in America in the late 19th century.

bandit *see* BAN

bang [M16th] This is probably a Scandinavian word, which imitates the sound. The American expression **bang for your buck**, 'value for money, return on your investment', was originally used in the early 1950s of military spending, especially on nuclear weapons. The phrase **bang on**, meaning 'exactly right, excellent', originated in air force slang, and referred to dropping a bomb exactly on target. A nuclear explosion was referred to as the **big bang** in John Osborne's 1957 play *Look Back in Anger*: 'If the big bang does come, and we all get killed off...'. Nowadays the **Big Bang** is more usually the explosion in which the universe originated. It was originally a term of ridicule, used by the scientist Fred Hoyle (1915–2001) in 1950, but is now the standard term for a respectable theory. In 1986 it was also the name given to the major changes in trading on the Stock Exchange introduced that year.

banger Banger has had several slang senses since the beginning of the 1800s. It was first a gross or blatant lie, what we would now call a 'whopper'. It was also a loud or forceful kiss, or a 'smacker', and in US college slang it was a cane or club. The meaning 'sausage' is originally Australian, and was probably suggested by the tendency of fat sausages to 'pop' if not pricked before cooking. The 'old car' sense is surprisingly recent, not being recorded before the 1960s.

banish *see* BAN

bank [ME] The very different uses of bank are all ultimately related. The bank beside a river was adopted from a Scandinavian word in the early Middle Ages, and is related to **bench** [OE]. The earliest use of the bank for a financial institution referred to a money-dealer's counter or table. This came from French or Italian in the late 15th century, but goes back to the same root as the river bank. A bank of oars or of lights

banana band bandit bang banger banish

represents yet another related form. It came into English in the early Middle Ages from French, and originally meant a bench or a platform to speak from. The bench or platform sense is also found in **mountebank** [L16th] for a charlatan, which comes from Italian *monta in banco* 'climb on the bench' referring to the way they attract a crowd, while a **bankrupt** [M16th], originally a *bankrout* takes us back to the 'counter' sense. It is from Italian *banca rotta*, which really means 'a broken bench', referring to the breaking up of the traders business at the counter. The word was altered early on in its history in English, through association with Latin *ruptus* 'broken'. Yet another word from the same source is **banquet** [LME] which comes from the French for 'little bench' and was originally a snack rather than a lavish meal.

banner *see* BAND

banns *see* BAN

banquet *see* BANK

banshee [L17th] A banshee in Irish legend is a female spirit who wails a warning of an imminent death in a house; the word is ultimately from Old Irish *ben síde* 'woman of the fairies'.

banyan [L16th] The Indian fig tree known as a banyan comes via Portuguese, from a Gujarati word for 'a man of the trading caste'. The word originally meant a Hindu merchant, but in the mid 17th century came to be applied by Europeans to one particular tree, the Banyans' Tree, under which traders had built a pagoda.

bar [ME] There are few more functional words than bar. It gives us bars of soap and chocolate, bars serving drinks, bars that we can put criminals behind, and in Britain members of the Bar who can help put them there. The word entered English from French in the early Middle Ages, but beyond that its history is unknown. Its earliest use was for fastening a gate or door. People used it for various kinds of **barrier** [LME], a related word. In a court a bar marked off the area around the judge's seat, where

prisoners were brought to be charged, hence **prisoner at the bar**. At the Inns of Court, where lawyers were trained in England, a bar separated students from those qualified, and a student was 'called to the bar' to become a fully fledged **barrister** [LME]. From this **the Bar** came to mean the whole body of barristers, or the barrister's profession, as early as the 16th century. At this time a bar was also a barrier or counter from which drink was served.

From barring doors and barring a person's way, it took a small step for **bar** to mean 'to prohibit', as in **no holds barred** [M20th], and 'except': **bar none** [E18th] means 'without exception'.

barbarian [ME] The ancient Greeks had a high opinion of themselves and a correspondingly low one of other peoples. They called everyone who did not speak Greek *barbaros* or 'foreign', which is where we get barbarian and related words **barbaric** [LME], **barbarity** [L17th], and **barbarous** [E16th]. The word *barbaros* originally imitated the unintelligible language of foreigners, which to the Greeks just sounded like *ba*, *ba*, *ba*.

barbecue [M17th] This word comes from Spanish *barbacoa*, perhaps from Arawak (West Indies) *barbacoa* which was a 'wooden frame on posts'. Barbecue is used in space in the phrases **barbecue mode** and **barbecue manoeuvre** describing the rotation of a spacecraft to allow the heat of the sun to fall on all sides. *See also* AUSTRALIAN WORD PANEL

barber [ME] The word barber goes back to French *barbe*, 'a beard'. In the 16th and 17th centuries barbers provided lute or guitar music for customers waiting their turn. Some would sing along. This **barber's music** was not always pleasant to listen to, and the term was quite insulting. In America standards seem to have been higher: the term **barbershop** for close-harmony singing is first recorded in the early 20th century.

barge [ME] A barge was originally a small seagoing vessel rather than a flat-bottomed boat for carrying freight. The word is French

banner　banns　banquet　banshee　banyan

and probably comes ultimately from Greek *baris*, which referred to a kind of Egyptian boat used on the Nile. The sense 'move forcefully or roughly' [L19th] refers to the way a heavily laden, unwieldy barge might collide with the bank or other traffic. If you **wouldn't touch something with a bargepole** you refuse to have anything to do with it. The equivalent expression in America says that you **wouldn't touch something with a ten-foot pole**.

baritone *see* ITALIAN WORD PANEL

bark [OE] Dogs have always barked, so it is not surprising that bark is a prehistoric word. If **someone's bark is worse than their bite** they are not as ferocious as they appear. To **bark at the moon** meaning 'to make a fuss with no effect', is first recorded in the 17th century. To **bark up the wrong tree** is from 19th-century America. People have been **barking** or **barking mad** since the 1930s. The bark of a tree is possibly related to the name of the **birch** tree [OE]. **Bark** or **barque** [ME] is also an old-fashioned word for a boat from Latin *barca* 'ship's boat', from which we get **embark** [M16th].

barley *see* BARN

barn [OE] A barn was originally a place for storing **barley** [OE], the word coming from Old English from *bere* 'barley' and *ern* 'house'. In the 1940s barn started to be used in particle physics as a unit of areas. It is apparently from the phrase **as big as a barn door**, a long established measure of size.

barnacle [ME] A barnacle was originally what we would now call a **barnacle goose**. The name appeared in English in the early Middle Ages, but its ultimate origin is unknown. The barnacle goose breeds in the Arctic tundra of Greenland and similar places, but for a long time its place of origin was something of a mystery. People thought it hatched from a type of barnacle that attaches itself to objects floating in the water and has long feathery filaments protruding from its shell, which presumably suggested the notion of plumage. The

shellfish itself started to be called a **barnacle** in the 16th century.

baroque [M18th] A baroque was originally the name of an irregularly shaped pearl, its shape reminiscent of the elaborate detail of the architectural style. The word came via French from Portuguese *barroco*, Spanish *barrueco*, or Italian *barocco* but the ultimate origin is unknown.

barque *see* BARK

barrel [ME] This word goes back to Latin *barillus* 'small cask'. Before refrigerators made domestic life easier, the barrel used for storage was a more familiar object. Various phrases refer back to those earlier days. To **have someone over a barrel** is to have them in a helpless position, at one's mercy. People rescued from drowning would be laid face down over a barrel to help the water drain out of their lungs, and it is possible that the idea of helplessness developed into one of coercion, although the phrase could derive from the idea of someone forced to lie over a barrel to be flogged. If you **scrape the barrel** (or **the bottom of the barrel**) you are reduced to using things or people of the poorest quality because there is nothing else available. Neither of these is recorded until the early 20th century.

barricade [L16th] To **man the barricades** is to stage a protest of a kind particularly associated with France. The word is indeed French, formed from *barrique* 'cask'; The 'day of the barricades' in Paris on 12 May 1588 during the Huguenot Wars was characterized by the use of barrels to build defences and obstruct access; hence the current sense. The French word came ultimately from Spanish *barrica*, and the form *barricado* was formerly used in English as well as barricade, both from the late 16th century.

barrier, barrister *see* BAR

base [ME] There are two different words spelled as 'base' in English. The old-fashioned one meaning 'low, ignoble' comes

baritone   bark   barley   barn   barnacle

from Latin *bassus* 'short', also the source of to **abase** [LME]. The low musical **bass** [LME] and the **bassoon** [E18th] come from the same source. The other base comes, along with **basis** [L16th] and **basic** [M19th], via Latin from Greek *basis*, which meant 'step' and 'pedestal'. Its first English meaning was 'the pedestal of a statue'. **Basement** [M18th] probably comes via archaic Dutch *basement* 'foundation', from Italian *basamento* 'base of a column', from *basis*.

Although **baseball** is primarily an American game the earliest recorded use of the word is actually from Jane Austen in *Northanger Abbey*: 'It was not very wonderful that Catherine . . . should prefer cricket, base ball . . . to books.' Phrases drawn from the US game are familiar elsewhere. A notable example is to **touch base**, 'to briefly make or renew contact with something or somebody'. Other phrases using **base** include to **get to first base**, 'to achieve the first step towards your objective', and **off base**, 'mistaken', though these are still primarily American. *See also* BAT

basilica [M16th] Basilica is a Latin word, literally 'royal palace', based on Greek *basileus* 'king'. This Greek root has also given rise to: the aromatic herb **basil**, the 'royal' herb for its many qualities—one early source even says that it is 'good for the stryking of a se dragon'; and **basilisk** [ME] which has come via Latin from Greek *basiliskos* with the senses 'little king', 'serpent' (specifying a type distinguished by a crown-like spot), and a 'wren' (with a gold crown-like crest). In English a basilisk is either a mythical reptile hatched by a serpent from a cock's egg, or a zoological term for a Central American lizard.

basis, bass, bassoon *see* BASE

bastard [ME] Bastard probably derives from medieval Latin *bastum* 'packsaddle' (a horse's saddle which was adapted for supporting loads); the French equivalent was *fils de bast* or 'packsaddle son'. The reference was to a loose-living mule driver who used a packsaddle for a pillow and the next morning was off to the next town. *See also* BAT

baste *see* LAMBASTE

bat [OE] The nocturnal flying mammal was originally not a bat but a 'back'. The earliest form, adopted in the early Middle Ages from a Scandinavian word, was altered to bat in the 16th century, perhaps influenced by Latin *batta* or *blacta* 'insect that shuns the light'. The creature has inspired numerous expressions. You could be **as blind as a bat** from the 16th century— before then the standard comparison was with a beetle. From the early 20th century you could **have bats in the belfry**, 'be mad', or, in the same vein, be **bats** or **batty**. The first recorded example of **like a bat out of hell**, 'very fast and wildly', is from the *Atlanta Constitution* of 3 February 1914: 'One day we saw an automobile go down the street like a bat out of hell and a few moments later we heard that it hit the last car of a freight train at the grade crossing.' An old-fashioned name for a bat is **flittermouse** [M16th], meaning literally 'flying mouse'. Dutch *vledermuis* and German *Fledermaus* are matching terms in other languages.

The other bat, for hitting a ball, is a word adopted from French in the Old English period, and is related to *BATTERY. If you do something **off your own bat** you are using a cricketing phrase; it originally referred to the score made by a player's own hits, and so 'at your own instigation'. But if you did something **right off the bat**, 'at the very beginning, straight away', you would be taking a term from baseball.

Batman has been a comic character and superhero since 1939. The less glamorous **batman** [M18th] is a British army officer's personal servant. This bat is unrelated to the other two. It came through French from medieval Latin *bastum* 'a packsaddle' (*see* *BASTARD) and originally referred to a man in charge of a *bat-horse*, which carried the luggage of military officers.

batch *see* BAKE

basilica basis bass bassoon bastard baste

bated [ME] A shortened form of **abated** [ME], meaning 'reduced, lessened'. The idea behind the phrase **with bated breath** is that the anxiety or excitement you experience while waiting for something to happen is so great that you almost stop breathing. The word is sometimes spelled **baited**, from a mistaken association with a fisherman's bait. It came from the Old French *abattre* 'to fell', from Latin *ad* 'to, at' and *batt(u)ere* 'to beat' which is also the source of **abattoir**, which to some extent replaced the medieval term **slaughterhouse** in the early 19th century.

bath [OE] The city of **Bath** in the west of England derives its name from its hot springs, where people immersed themselves for health reasons. The city gave its name to the **bath chair** [E19th] in which its invalids were transported. The British order of knighthood, the **Order of the Bath,** has this name because recipients took a bath before being installed—it was a special event. If sports players take **an early bath** they have been sent off by the referee.

bathos [M17th] This is a Greek word and was first recorded in English in the literal Greek sense 'depth'. The literary sense was introduced by Alexander Pope in the early 18th century. He published the *Bathos* in the *Miscellanies* (third volume) in 1728, which was a lively satire giving descriptions of bad authors, identified by initials. **Bathyspere** [1930] for a spherical chamber that can be lowered into the depths of the sea, comes from the same source.

baton [M16th] The original baton was a club or cudgel and came from French, ultimately from Latin *bastum* 'stick'. The baton used to direct an orchestra or choir was first mentioned by the music historian Charles Burney (1726–1814) (father of the novelist Fanny Burney) in 1785. The baton passed from hand to hand in a relay race is first mentioned by that name in 1921. This use gives rise to **pass on the baton**, 'to hand over a particular duty or responsibility', and to **take up** (or **pick up**) **the baton**, 'to accept a duty or responsibility'. The French name of **Baton Rouge**, the capital of Louisiana, means 'Red Stick' in English. It comes from a red-stained Indian boundary marker seen by early French explorers of the area.

battalion, batter *see* BATTLE

battery [ME] The root of battery is Latin *battuere* 'to strike, beat', and originally referred to metal articles shaped with a hammer. The military soon adopted the term to mean a succession of heavy blows inflicted upon the walls of a fortress with artillery, and so it came to have the sense 'a number of pieces of artillery combining in action'. It is this idea of combining to produce a result that is behind the use in electrical batteries. The original electrical battery was a series of Leyden jars, glass jars with layers of metal foil on the outside and inside, used to store electric charge. Benjamin Franklin (1706–1790) mentioned the device in a letter of 1748. Sir Humphry Davy (1778–1829) developed the later **galvanic battery** (named after the Italian physicist Luigi Galvani (1737–98)), using chemical action to produce electric current, and described it in 1801. An electrical battery is a container with one or more cells, and this no doubt prompted the use of the word for a series of cages for laying hens.

battle [ME] Along with **battalion** [L16th], **batter** [ME], and *BATTERY, the word **battle** goes back through French to Latin *battuere* 'to strike, beat', also found in **combat** [M16th] 'fight together'. Battle appears in many phrases. We say that we are **fighting a losing battle** when a struggle is bound to end in failure, or that something that contributes to success is **half the battle**. A fiercely contested fight or dispute is a **battle royal**, which was originally a fight with several combatants.

baulk [OE] The verb baulk (US variant balk) is used with a sense of 'refusal' in phrases such as **baulk at an idea**, or **baulk at doing something**. This notion developed, together with the verb senses 'hesitate' and 'hinder' in late Middle English, through a use of the noun as 'obstacle'. The early spelling of the noun was *balc*, from an Old Norse word for 'partition'. The first English usage was 'unploughed ridge', later 'land left unploughed by mistake', which was then extended to 'blunder, omission'. **Bollards** [ME] originally short posts on a ship's deck or on a quayside, may be related.

bawdy [E16th] Bawdy has gained its sexual overtones, in phrases such as bawdy jokes and bawdy house, from **bawd** [LME] 'a woman in charge of a brothel', a late Middle English word shortened from the now obsolete *bawdstrot*, from Old French *baudestroyt* 'procuress' (from *baude* 'shameless').

bay [ME] Hounds have bayed since the Middle Ages. Like *BARK, the word probably imitates the sound. People can now also **bay for blood**, when they call loudly for someone to be punished. The related phrase **at bay** comes from hunting and means 'cornered, forced to face one's attackers'. It is often used now in **to hold someone at bay**, 'to prevent someone from approaching or having an effect'. The geographical **bay** [LME] can be traced back to Old French *baie*, from Old Spanish *bahia*, but no further. The **bay tree** [LME] came via Old French from Latin *bāca* 'berry', and the type of bay found in a **bay window**, also late Middle English, comes from Old French *baie*, from the verb *baer* 'to gape'. This is also, via *baif* 'open-mouthed' the source of **bevel** [L16th]. *See also* BAIZE

bayonet [L17th] A bayonet first described a kind of short dagger. The origin is based on *Bayonne*, a town in south-west France where these daggers were first made.

bazaar [L16th] A Persian word for 'market' is the ultimate source of bazaar, which came into English from Italian *bazarro* that was in turn borrowed from Turkish.

bead [Old English] The original meaning of bead was 'prayer'. Current meanings of bead come from the use of a rosary, each bead representing a prayer. **Bid** [OE] first found in the sense 'ask, beg' is related.

beam [OE] As well as referring to a piece of wood, beam originally also meant 'a tree', a use that survives in the name of the

hornbeam [L16th], a member of the birch family. Sailors understood a beam to be one of the timbers stretching from side to side of a ship, supporting the deck and holding the vessel together. From there beam came to mean a ship's greatest breadth. This is why you can call someone **broad in the beam**, 'wide in the hips'. A ship that is **on its beam ends** is heeled over on its side, almost capsized, and so if a person is on their beam ends they are in a very bad situation.

The **beam in your eye**, the fault that is greater in yourself than in the person you are finding fault with, comes from the Bible. Matthew contrasts the large beam unseen in someone's own eye with the mote ('speck') noticed in the eye of another. When someone is **way off beam** they are mistaken, on the wrong track. Here they are being likened to an aircraft that has gone astray from the radio beam or signal used to guide it.

'**Beam me up, Scotty**' will forever be associated with the American television series *Star Trek*, as the words with which Captain Kirk asked Lieutenant Commander Scott to 'beam' or transport him from a planet back to the starship USS *Enterprise*. The exact words, however, do not occur in any of the television scripts, although it was later used in the films.

bean [OE] Beans have long been a basic foodstuff. To **spill the beans**, 'to reveal a secret' is an American expression from the early 20th century. **Full of beans**, 'lively, in high spirits', first recorded in the mid 19th century, originally referred to horses. Beans were one of their staple foods and a well-fed horse would be full of energy and vitality. As an insulting term for an accountant, **bean-counter** is another US term, originating in the 1970s. The rather dated bean meaning 'the head' is also originally from the US. It lives on in the close-fitting hat, the **beanie** [1940].

bear [OE] The verb bear comes from Indo-European. Related forms are found in Sanskrit, the ancient language of India, as well as in Latin and Greek. The core meaning is 'to carry'. In English it is related to **bier** [OE], the frame carrying a coffin or

bawdy   bay   bayonet   bazaar   bead   beam

corpse. From early times bear has also been used of mental burdens, of suffering, or toleration. Wise people have encouraged us to **bear and forbear**, 'be patient and endure', since the 16th century, and from the mid 19th century others have told us more briskly to **grin and bear it**.

Bear, the large animal, is a different Old English word that also goes back to ancient times. In Stock Exchange terminology a bear is a person who sells shares hoping to buy them back later at a lower price (the opposite of a *BULL). The use is said to be from a proverb warning against 'selling the bear's skin before one has caught the bear'.

beard [OE] As well as referring to a man's facial hair, beard, which is related to Latin *barba* 'beard', is used of the chin tuft of certain animals, such as a lion and a goat. These uses come together in the phrase to **beard the lion in his den** or **lair**, 'to confront or challenge someone on their own ground'. To invade someone's personal space enough to be able to touch or pull their beard was always an aggressive or provocative act—in 1587 the English sailor and explorer Francis Drake (*c*.1540–96) described his expedition to Cadiz as 'the singeing of the King of Spain's Beard'. In the Middle Ages to **run in someone's beard** was to defy him, and by the 16th century you could simply 'beard someone'. Clearly this stopped being fearsome enough, and lions were introduced in the 18th century.

beast *see* ANIMAL

beat [OE] An Old English word related to *BEETLE in the sense 'heavy mallet'. The **beat generation** was a group of unconventional artists and writers of the 1950s and early 1960s, who valued free self-expression and liked modern jazz. Here the beat probably originally meant 'worn out, exhausted' rather than referring to a musical rhythm. The first people to **beat about the bush** were the 'beaters' who tried to disturb game birds so that they would fly up to be shot at. Beaters beat bushes, but soldiers beat drums. This is the origin of the phrase to **beat a hasty retreat**. To 'beat a retreat' was to sound the drums in a way that signalled

to soldiers that they should withdraw from the battle. The drumming also helped them to retreat in an orderly manner.

beatnik *see* YIDDISH WORD PANEL

beauty [ME] The Latin word *bellus*, 'beautiful', is the root of **beauty**, and also of a **beau** [L17th], and **belle** [E17th]. The idea that **beauty is in the eye of the beholder** is very old indeed, appearing in the works of the ancient Greek poet Theocritus (*fl*.3rd century BC). In English the proverb as we know it today is recorded from the 18th century. The warning that **beauty is only skin-deep** is known from the early 17th century. **The beautiful game** is soccer. The phrase is from the title of the 1973 autobiography by the Brazilian star Pelé, *My Life and the Beautiful Game*.

beck [ME] If you are **at someone's beck and call** you have to be ready to obey their orders immediately. The phrase is known from the 19th century, but **beck** itself is much older, being a Middle English shortening of **beckon**. The northern English word **beck** [ME], meaning a stream or brook, is unconnected, and comes from Old Norse.

bed [OE] The core idea of this Old English word may be 'digging', as if the very first beds were dug-out lairs or hollows. Medieval uses of **to make a bed** refer to the preparation of a sleeping place on the floor of an open hall, one which would not have existed until 'made'. The term **bed and breakfast** first appeared in the late 19th century—in 1910 a 'residential hotel' is recorded offering 'Bed and breakfast from 4/-' (4 shillings or, in modern British currency, 20 pence). In the 1970s the phrase began to describe the financial practice of **bed-and-breakfasting**, in which dealers sell shares late in the day and buy them back early the next morning to gain a tax advantage.

bedlam [LME] The word is a corruption of *Bethlehem*, from the Hospital of St Mary of Bethlehem, also known as Bethlem Royal Hospital, in London—what used to be

beard beast beat beatnik beauty beck

known as an *ASYLUM. In the 17th century **bedlam** became a term for any mental hospital, and from that for any scene of mad confusion.

bee [OE] A form of the word bee is found in almost all the languages that are closely related to English, and the familiar insect has inspired numerous familiar phrases. A worker is **as busy as a bee**, a comparison made from at least the 16th century. People used to describe an obsessive person as having **a head full of bees**, whereas we now say that you **have a bee in your bonnet**. Before close studies of insect behaviour, people believed that bees instinctively take a straight line when returning to the hive. This is the origin of **beeline** [M19th]. If you **make a beeline for** a place, you hurry directly to it. A **spelling bee** is a spelling contest, and a **sewing bee** a gathering for people to do their sewing together. This use, to mean 'a meeting for communal work or amusement', was suggested by the insect's social nature, and is first recorded in the USA in the 1760s.

beech *see* BOOK

beef [ME] We often find that after the Norman Conquest people used French words for an animal's meat and the English word for the animal itself. **Beef** is from French, and *COW and **ox** are native English words, whereas *BULL was adopted from Scandinavian. Beef, meaning 'a complaint' or 'to complain', was originally American, from the mid 19th century. The first person to write of the kind of beef possessed by a muscular man was American writer Herman Melville (1819–91), author of *Moby-Dick*. The British are so well known for eating beef that a French insult for an Englishman is *un rosbif* ('a roast beef'). In English too, **beefeater** [E17th] was originally a term of contempt for a well-fed domestic servant. Now a Beefeater is a Yeoman Warder or Yeoman of the Guard at the Tower of London, a nickname first used in 1671.

beefburger *see* US WORD PANEL

Beelzebub *see* LORD

beer [OE] The ancestor of beer came from a Latin term used in monasteries. Classical Latin *bibere* 'to drink', is also behind **beverage** [ME], **bibulous** [L17th], and **imbibe** [LME]. Although beer appears in Old English, it was not common before the 16th century, the usual word in earlier times being **ale,** which now refers to a drink made without hops. The late 16th-century proverb 'Turkey, heresy, hops, and beer came into England all in one year' reflects the difference. Ale continues to be applied to paler kinds of liquors for which the malt has not been roasted. Some areas still use beer and ale interchangeably. *See also* BIB

beetle [OE] The meaning of the source word for this creature is 'biter', and it is closely related to *BITE. The other word beetle, 'a heavy mallet', is unrelated. It comes ultimately from the ancestor of BEAT, 'to strike'. The Beetle is an affectionate name for a type of small Volkswagen car that was first produced in 1938. The term started as a nickname, and was not officially adopted by the company until the 1960s. A review of the car in *Motor* magazine during 1946 said: 'It has the civilian saloon body on the military chassis with the higher ground clearance, and it looks rather like a beetle on stilts.' **Beetle-browed** means 'having bushy eyebrows'. In Middle English *brow* was always an eyebrow and not the forehead; it has been suggested that the comparison is with the tufted antennae of certain beetles, which may have been called eyebrows in both English and French.

befall *see* ACCIDENT, FALL

behave [LME] Behave is from *be-* 'thoroughly' and *have* in the sense 'have or bear (oneself) in a particular way'; this corresponds to modern German *sich behaben*.

beige [M19th] Beige was first used for a woollen fabric which was usually undyed and unbleached, and then used for things of a similar colour. The immediate source is French, but earlier details are unknown. The colour **greige**—halfway between beige and grey appears in the 1920s.

bee beech beef beefburger Beelzebub beer

belfry [ME] Although you will find bells (as well as *BATS) in a belfry, the Old English word **bell** is not related to **belfry**. A belfry was originally a movable wooden tower used in the Middle Ages by armies besieging a fortification. The word originally had an 'r' not an 'l' in the middle, and came from Old French *berfrei*. The first part probably meant 'to protect' and the second 'peace, protection'. The first belfry associated with a church was a separate bell tower: the word began to be used for a room or storey where the bells were hung in the middle of the 16th century. **Bell** [OE] is a Germanic word. **Saved by the bell** comes from the bell marking the end of a boxing round. **Bells and whistles** for attractive but unnecessary extras, particularly on computers, is an allusion to the bells and whistles of old fairground organs.

belle *see* BEAUTY

bellicose *see* REBEL

belt [OE] An Old English word that can be traced back to Latin *balteus*, 'girdle'. It is unlawful for a boxer to land a punch below his opponent's belt, and people often use the phrase **below the belt** about a critical or unkind remark. Margot Asquith (1864–1945), wife of the Liberal Prime Minister Herbert Asquith (1852–1928), once remarked of another Liberal prime minister, Lloyd George (1863–1945): 'He can't see a belt without hitting below it'. If you take a **belt and braces** approach to something you make doubly sure that nothing will go wrong. The reference is to someone so anxious that their trousers will fall down that they wear both. **Belting** or hitting someone with a belt, is behind the verb sense 'to strike, hit', and probably also the meaning 'to move very fast'. **Belt up**, or 'be quiet', seems to have started life as RAF slang, in the 1930s.

bench *see* BANK

bend [OE] In Old English *bendan* (of Germanic origin) was 'put in bonds' or 'make a bow taut by means of a string', leading to an association with the curved shape of the bow.

bend sinister *see* BAND

benefit [LME] The source of benefit is Latin *benefactum*, 'a good deed', and that was the original meaning in English, in the late Middle Ages. The ordinary modern sense is recorded from the early 16th century. To **give someone the benefit of the doubt** originally meant to give a verdict of not guilty when the evidence was not conclusive.

benevolent [LME] This comes, via Old French, from Latin *bene volent-* 'well wishing'.

bequeath [OE] The Old English form *becwethan* is composed of *be-* 'about' and *cwethan* 'say'; the related **bequest** is Middle English, both reflecting a time when wills were often spoken rather than written. **Quoth**, an old term for 'he/she said' also comes from *cwethan*.

bereave, bereft *see* ROB

berk [E20th] This British slang term for a stupid person is generally regarded as fairly acceptable in polite society, but it has a rude origin. It is an abbreviation of *Berkeley* or *Berkshire Hunt*, rhyming slang for what has increasingly been called, since the 1970s **the C word**. The first written example dates from the late 1920s.

berserk [E19th] A **berserker** was an ancient Norse warrior who fought with wild, uncontrolled ferocity—he went **berserk**. The name came from an old Scandinavian word, *berserkr*, which probably meant 'bear coat' or 'bearskin', a suitably rugged garment for a terrifyingly unhinged Viking. An alternative possibility is that the first element is the equivalent of 'bare', referring to fighting without armour. The phrase to **go berserk** is first recorded in 1896.

berth [E17th] When we **give someone a wide berth**, or stay away from them, we are using a nautical expression. **Berth** shares a root with *BEAR, 'to carry'. Originally, in the early 17th century, it meant 'sea room', or space to turn or manoeuvre. It developed the sense 'a ship's allotted place at a wharf or

belfry belle bellicose belt bench bend bend

dock', and could also mean the place where seamen stowed their chests, then later the space where the sailors themselves slept.

bête noir *see* FRENCH WORD PANEL

betide *see* WOE

betroth *see* PLIGHT

bevel *see* BAY

beverage *see* BEER

bib [L16th] A bib for a baby is recorded from the late 16th century. It probably came from the old word *bib* from Latin *bibere*, meaning 'to drink'. Towards the end of the 17th century adults too were wearing bibs, often as part of an apron. Women could decorate this with a **tucker**, a piece of lace worn round the top of the bodice—'The countrywoman...minds nothing on Sundays so much as her best bib and tucker' (1747). Soon men, too, were described as wearing their **best bib and tucker**, their smartest clothes. *See also* BEER

Bible [Middle English] *Bible* has come via Old French from ecclesiastical Latin *biblia*, from Greek *(ta) biblia* '(the) books'. The singular *biblion* was originally a diminutive of *biblos* 'papyrus, scroll', of Semitic origin. There is a link with the Eastern Mediterranean port of Byblos, which was a major exporter of papyrus to Greece. Words like **bibliography** [E19th] come from the same source.

bibulous *see* BEER

biceps [M17th] This Latin word means literally 'two-headed', from *bi-* 'two' and *-ceps* (from *caput* 'head'), from the fact that the muscle has two points of attachment. Examples of bicep have been found since the 1970s, suggesting that people are beginning to see the word as a plural (*compare* PEA).

bicycle [M19th] The **velocipede** (literally 'rapid foot') was the early form of bicycle, which is formed from *bi-* 'two' and Greek

kuklos 'wheel'. The abbreviation **bike** was not long to follow, in the late 19th century. A **tricycle** as a name for a three-wheeled coach drawn by two horses, dates from the 1820s, with the abbreviation **trike** appearing in the 1880s. **Unicycle**, from *uni-* 'one', was first recorded in the US in the 1860s.

bid *see* BEAD

biddy [E17th] **Old biddy** suggests an interfering or annoying elderly woman, but a biddy was originally 'a chicken'; the origin is unknown. The word was probably influenced by the use of biddy in the US for an Irish maidservant, which arose from the pet form of Bridget, and extended as a general derogatory word for a 'woman' in slang use.

bidet [M17th] Originally in both French and English bidet meant 'pony, small horse'—the link was the way that people sat astride both.

bier *see* BEAR

biff *see* FLIRT

big [ME] Like many small words, big appeared from nowhere. It is first recorded in the early Middle Ages meaning 'strong, powerful', and clear examples referring just to size do not emerge until the 16th century. The sense 'elder' as in **big brother** or **big sister** is first found in the 19th century. In George Orwell's novel *Nineteen Eighty-four* the head of state is called Big Brother, and 'Big Brother is watching you' is the caption on posters showing his face. The novel was published in 1949, and very quickly people started using **Big Brother** to refer to any person or organization exercising total control over people's lives. Various other phrases involving big refer to an important or influential person, such as **big cheese**, which first came into use in American slang during the early 1900s. It almost certainly has no connection with food—the word **cheese** here probably comes from Urdu and Persian *cīz*, which just means 'thing'.

bigot [L16th] A bigot first denoted a superstitious religious hypocrite; the immediate source is French but further than that is not known.

bigwig [E18th] People of importance in the 17th and 18th centuries wore large wigs that covered their heads and came down to their shoulders. These were the original 'big wigs'. In Britain this type of headdress can still be worn by judges, the Lord Chancellor, and the Speaker of the House of Commons. In the 18th century **bigwig** began to refer to the person wearing the wig, and the word has outlived the fashion.

bike *see* BICYCLE

bikini [1940s] In 1946 the USA exploded an atom bomb at Bikini, an atoll in the Marshall Islands in the western Pacific. Not long after, a scanty two-piece swimming costume caused a sensation on the beaches of France. Its effect was so great that the French called it the bikini. The word seems to have appeared first in English in a US newspaper, the *Waterloo Daily Courier*, on 26 June 1947. In an article on swimwear it reports: 'The French, it seems, have a new suit planned that is about twice as wide as a piece of string. It's so explosive that they call it the Bikini.'

bilberry *see* BLUE

bile *see* YELLOW

bill [ME] During the Middle Ages a bill was any written statement or list, an early sense that survives in **a clean bill of health**. The master of a ship about to sail from a port where various infectious diseases were known to be common would be given an official certificate before leaving, to confirm that there was no infection either on board the ship or in the port. *See also* BULLETIN

The Old Bill is British slang for the police, with the first written evidence arriving in the 1950s. The original Old Bill was a cartoon character of the First World War, portrayed as a grumbling Cockney soldier with a walrus moustache. The 'police' meaning may have arisen from subsequent use of the cartoon character, this time wearing police uniform, on posters in a Metropolitan Police recruitment campaign, and then during the Second World War giving advice on wartime security. Police officers before the Second World War often wore 'Old Bill' moustaches, and this could provide another connection.

billabong *see* AUSTRALIAN WORD PANEL

billet [LME] A billet (from Anglo-Norman French *billette*, a little *BILL) was once a short written document. In the mid 17th century, it came to be a 'written order requiring a householder to lodge the bearer of the billet'; this was usually a soldier, hence the current meaning 'temporary lodging for a soldier'. The early sense is preserved in the old-fashioned **billet-doux,** French for 'sweet letter'. *See also* BILLIARDS

billiards [L16th] French *billard*, 'little tree trunk' was originally the name of the cue for the game, but was soon transferred to the game itself. The word is also the source of **billet** [LME] for a thick piece of wood. The French comes from medieval Latin *billa*, *billus* 'branch, trunk', probably from a Celtic root.

billy *see* AUSTRALIAN WORD PANEL

bimbo [E20th] Bimbos in English are young women, but in Italian a *bimbo* is a baby, and in English bimbo was originally an American slang term for a fellow or chap, especially a foolish one. In 1947 P.G. Wodehouse wrote of 'Bimbos who went about the place making passes at innocent girls after discarding their wives'. This meaning is first recorded in 1918, and by the 1920s the modern sense was being used. In the 1980s the word **himbo** was coined to mean 'a male bimbo'. At the same time **bimbette** was coined for a younger bimbo. *Compare* BABE

bind *see* BAND, BOUND

binge [M19th] Binge drinking is generally thought of as a modern problem, but the word **binge** has been around since at least the 1850s. It was originally a dialect term in the English Midlands, first meaning 'to wash or soak', which was taken up by boozy students at Oxford University.

binocular *see* INOCULATE, MONOCLE

biology *see* AMPHIBIAN

bird [OE] The origin of bird is unknown, and there are no parallel forms in any of the languages related to English. Old English *brid* (with the *r* before the *i*) meant only a chick or a nestling: an adult bird was a **fowl**. The form *brid* existed alongside bird in the literary language into the 15th century, but after that it survived only in dialect. Meanwhile fowl stopped being a general term, and it now refers only to specialized groups such as wildfowl and waterfowl. The first record of the proverb **a bird in the hand is worth two in the bush** comes in the mid 15th century. In **birds of a feather flock together**, first recorded a century later, the word 'a' means 'one' or 'the same'.

The British slang use of bird to mean a young woman is associated with the 1960s and 1970s, but goes back as far as the Middle Ages. In those days there was another word bird, also spelled *burd*, that meant a young woman, which people confused with the familiar bird. The Virgin Mary could be described in those days as 'that blissful bird of grace'. The modern use, recorded from the beginning of the 20th century, appears to be something of a revival.

The earliest version of the expression **give someone the bird**, meaning to boo or jeer at them, is **the big bird**, which was used by people working in the theatre in the early 19th century. The big bird referred to was a goose, a bird well known for its aggressive hissing when threatened or annoyed. The booing and hissing of the audience at an actor's poor performance might well have suggested a flock of angry geese.

Bird meaning 'a prison sentence' is a shortening of **birdlime** (*see also* VISCOUS) used in rhyming slang to mean 'time'. So if you were 'doing bird' or 'doing birdlime', you were 'doing time', a sense known from the mid 19th century.

In golf a **birdie** is a score of one stroke under par (*see* PAIR) at a hole. Two under par is an *EAGLE, three under par is an *ALBATROSS or **double eagle**, and one over par is a **bogey** (*see* BOGUS). This scoring

terminology is said to have originated at the end of the 19th century when an American golfer hit a bird with his drive yet still managed to score one under par at the hole—this bird suggested **birdie**, and the other bird names were added to continue the theme.

biscuit [ME] The basic meaning of biscuit is 'twice cooked', coming into English via French from Latin *bis* 'twice' and *coctusi* 'cooked'. The name comes from the original process of making biscuits—they were first baked and then dried out in a slow oven so that they would keep.

bishop [OE] The meaning of Old English *biscop* is literally 'overseer', from Greek *episkopos*, formed from *epi* 'above' and *-skopos* '-looking'.

bit *see* BITE

bitch [OE] Old English *bicce* has a Germanic source. Whether there is a relationship between the English word and French *biche* meaning both 'bitch' and 'fawn' is not known. The derogatory reference to a woman as a 'bitch' arose in late Middle English.

bite [OE] There are words related to bite in many other European languages. Their ancestor also gave us **bit** [OE] and *BITTER, and it probably meant 'to split, to cleave'. To **bite the bullet** now means 'to face up to something unpleasant'. Its origin is said to be in battlefield surgery—that wounded soldiers would be given a bullet to bite on to prevent them from crying out when the pain became unbearable. However, there is no evidence that this ever happened, and surgeons always carried leather straps with them for this purpose. Another phrase involving biting something unusual is to **bite the dust**, 'to be killed or come to an end'. Nowadays people are likely to associate it with Westerns and gunfights, but it is used by the Scottish novelist Tobias Smollett in 1750, and similar expressions such as to **bite the ground** and **bite the sand** are found even earlier. **Man bites dog** is a much-used jokey newspaper

binocular biology bird biscuit bishop bit

headline, which harks back to the quote: 'When a dog bites a man, that is not news, because it happens so often. But if a man bites a dog, that is news.' This was said by the American journalist John B. Bogart (1848–1921).

The bit in computing, a unit of information expressed as either a 0 or 1, is a contraction of **binary digit**. Bit and bite were combined to give **byte**, a group of eight bits.

bitter [OE] Like bit, bitter is related to *BITE. In the phrase **to the bitter end** 'until something is finished, no matter what', is probably not from this word. It derives instead from a nautical term bitter [E17th], meaning the last part of a cable, that goes around the 'bitts' or fastening points for ropes on board ship. The biblical quotation 'her end is bitter as wormwood' may have helped popularize the phrase. Many Englishmen love their pint of bitter. This use seems to have started life as Oxford University slang in the 1850s, when students would talk of 'doing bitters'.

bivouac [E18th] 'A night watch by the whole army' was the original meaning of bivouac. The origin is French, probably from Swiss German *Bîwacht* 'additional guard at night', apparently referring to a citizens' patrol giving support to the ordinary town watch. The word is said to have been introduced into English during the Thirty Years War (1618–48). The abbreviation **bivvy** is recorded from the early 20th century.

bizarre [M17th] This adjective meaning 'strange', 'odd' came into English from French, from Italian *bizzarro* which meant 'angry'. The ultimate origin remains unknown.

black [OE] Since the Middle Ages the word black has had connotations of gloom, foreboding, and anger, and since Shakespeare's time it has been associated with wickedness. It is also a perennially stylish colour, and the **little black dress** has been a byword of fashion from the very beginning of the 20th century. The car manufacturer Henry Ford was not motivated by any of these associations when he said of his Model T Ford, 'Any customer can have a car painted any colour that he wants **so long as it is black**'—nor was he trying to impose uniformity. Black simply dried quicker than any other paint. To **blackball** [L18th] derives from the practice of registering an adverse vote by placing a black ball in a ballot box. **Black sheep** [L18th] comes from the proverb **there is a black sheep in every flock**. Blackguard [E16th] was originally a two-word phrase for a body of attendants or servants, especially menials who were responsible for the kitchen utensils, but the exact significance of the epithet 'black' is uncertain. The sense 'scoundrel, villain' dates from the mid 18th century, and was formerly considered highly offensive.

To **be in someone's black books** is to be out of favour. Since the 15th century various types of official book were known as black books, especially those used to note down misdemeanours and punishments. The relevant books here are probably the black-bound books in which Henry VIII's commissioners recorded accounts of scandals and corruption within the English monasteries in the 1530s. These books provided the evidence to support Henry's plan of breaking with the Pope and the Church of Rome, allowing him to dissolve the monasteries.

Not all things called black are black in colour. An aircraft's **black box**, its flight recorder, for instance, is not. Black here refers to the mystifying nature of the device to anyone but an aeronautical engineer. The first use of black box is as RAF slang for a navigational instrument in an aircraft which allowed the pilot and crew to locate bombing targets in poor visibility. *See also* PLAGUE

blackmail [M16th] Blackmail was originally a form of protection racket. Scottish chiefs in the 16th century exacted a tribute from farmers and small landowners in the border counties of England and Scotland, and along the Highland border. The money was in return for protection or immunity from plunder. The second part of

bitter bivouac bizarre black blackmail

the word means 'tribute, rent' and comes from an old Scandinavian word *mál*, meaning 'speech, agreement'. Black may have been a joke on **white money**, the silver coins in which legitimate rents were paid.

blade [OE] The common senses of Old English *blæd* were 'leaf of a plant' and 'flat section (of an oar, sword, etc.)'; the root is Germanic.

blaeberry *see* BLUE

blame [ME] Blame is from the Old French *blamer*, *blasmer*, from a popular Latin variant of ecclesiastical Latin *blasphemare* 'reproach, revile, blaspheme', from Greek *blasphēmein*, source also of Middle English **blaspheme**.

blancmange [LME] In medieval times a blancmange was a dish of white meat or fish in a cream sauce—the 'dessert' sense seems to have come into use in the middle of the 16th century. The word is from Old French *blanc mangier* and literally means 'white food'. Other words from French *blanc* include **blanch** [ME], **blank** [ME], and **blanket** [ME]. Originally **blanket** referred to undyed (hence 'white') woollen cloth used for clothing. A dampened blanket would sometimes be used to extinguish a fire before going to bed. This is the origin of a **wet blanket**, a term for someone who spoils other people's fun by refusing to join in or by showing disapproval.

bland [LME] In early use bland was 'gentle in manner', from Latin *blandus* 'soft, smooth'. This Latin adjective also forms the base of the Middle English noun **blandishment.**

blank, blanket *see* BLANCMANGE

blaspheme *see* BLAME

blatant [L16th] A word first used by the Elizabethan poet Edmund Spenser (*c*.1552–99) in *The Faerie Queene*, as a description of a thousand-tongued monster, offspring of the three-headed dog Cerberus and the fire-breathing Chimera. Spenser used this monster as a symbol of slander, and called it 'the blatant beast'. He may just have invented the word, or taken it from Scots *blatand* 'bleating'. Blatant was subsequently used to mean 'clamorous, offensive to the ear', and did not take on its modern meaning 'unashamedly conspicuous' until the late 19th century.

blaze [OE] The blaze meaning 'a bright flame' and the one referring to a white streak on a horse's face are probably related, through the idea of shining or brightness. In America the second came to apply to a white mark chipped in a tree to indicate a path or boundary in the mid 17th century. This is where we get to **blaze a trail**, 'to set an example by being the first to do something'. Cricketers and other sportsmen wore a type of brightly coloured, often striped jacket called a **blazer** in the late 19th century. The name came from the brightness of the cloth.

bleak [OE] In Old English this meant 'shining, white' and came from the same Germanic root as **bleach** [OE]. The modern sense 'bare of vegetation' and 'chilly' did not develop until the 16th century.

bless [OE] Old English *blēdsian*, *blētsian* are perhaps based on *blōd* 'blood', the likely original semantic core being 'mark or consecrate with blood'. The history is difficult to trace because there is no equivalent in other Germanic languages. The meaning was influenced by the word's use to translate Latin *benedīcere* 'to praise', 'to worship', and Greek *eulogein* meaning essentially 'speak well of'; these in turn translated Hebrew *brk* 'to bend', in this case 'bend the knee (in praise)'. There is therefore a series of rich associations, pagan, Jewish, and Christian, mixed together in the English words bless and blessing; there is also a later association with *BLISS.

Blighty [E20th] It was British soldiers serving in India who first started calling their homeland Blighty. The word was an alteration of Urdu *bilāyatī* 'foreign,

blade blaeberry blame blancmange bland

European', which came from Arabic *wilāyat* 'country, district'. During the First World War soldiers hoped for a **blighty one**—a wound not too serious but bad enough to get safe passage home.

blimey [L19th] This is a mild expletive but its original unaltered form was *blind me!* or *blame me!* **Gorblimey** is an altered form of *God blind me!*

blind [OE] The original sense was 'unable to see'. The sense of blinds that are hung on windows developed in the early 18th century, and Venetian blinds appear at the end of that century. To **turn a blind eye to**, 'to pretend not to notice', goes back to the Battle of Copenhagen in 1801. The British admiral Horatio Nelson (1758–1805), who was leading the attack against the Danes, had lost the sight in one eye in action several years before. His superior, Sir Hyde Parker (1739–1807), feared that his men would suffer very heavy losses, so hoisted the signal for Nelson to halt his attack and withdraw. Nelson avoided seeing the signal by putting a telescope to his blind eye, and continued the battle. An hour later he was victorious. The *-fold* of **blindfold** is not the fold meaning 'to bend over on itself'. It derives from **fell**, 'to knock or strike over'. The Old English word from which blindfold developed meant 'to strike blind'. By the 16th century people stopped understanding **blindfell**, and substituted the more familiar **fold**. *See also* BUFF

bling [1990s] This term, probably suggested either by the idea of light reflecting off a diamond or by the sound of jewellery clashing together, first appeared in a song by the US rapper B.G. ('Baby Gangsta') in 1999. From there it moved quickly into the mainstream to describe ostentatious jewellery and flashy clothes. Such has been the impact of the word that black slang has been dubbed **Blinglish**.

bliss [OE] This word from a Germanic root is related to **blithe** 'happy'. *BLESS and bliss have influenced each other from an early period, which has meant a gradual semantic distinction between **blitheness** as an earthly lightness of heart and the heavenly bliss of the 'blessed'.

blitz *see* GERMAN WORD PANEL

blizzard *see* US WORD PANEL

block [ME] In the early Middle Ages a block was a log or tree stump. The word came from French *bloc*, which English readopted in a different sense as **bloc**, 'a group of countries that have formed an alliance', in the early 20th century. By the late Middle Ages a block was often a large lump of wood on which chopping, hammering, and beheading were performed. We refer to an executioner's block when we use the phrase to **put your head** (*or* **neck**) **on the block**.

A block of buildings, bounded by four streets, dates from the late 18th century in North America. This use has given rise to numerous popular phrases: the **new kid on the block**, and the person believed to **have been around the block a few times** (to have a lot of experience). It also gave us the **blockbuster**. Although this now means 'a great commercial success', in the 1940s it was a huge aerial bomb capable of destroying a whole block of streets.

Block has meant head, as in to **knock someone's block off**, since the 17th century. In Australia. to **do** or **lose your block** is to lose your temper. *See also* LOGGERHEAD

blonde [LME] Long before it referred to fair-haired women who were *DIZZY or *DUMB, blonde simply meant 'yellow'. *Blond* (m.) or *blonde* (f.) means 'fair-haired' in French, but the word was descended from medieval Latin *blondus* 'yellow'. The adjective was adopted by the English at the end of the 15th century, but the noun use, 'a blonde woman', dates only from the 19th century, since when the desirability of blondes has become almost proverbial. ***Gentlemen Prefer Blondes*** was the title of a 1925 book by Anita Loos, which in 1953 was made into a film starring Marilyn Monroe and Jane Russell, and the album ***Blondes Have More Fun*** was released by Rod Stewart in 1978. *See also* BOMB, DIAMOND

blimey blind bling bliss blitz blizzard

blood [OE] Something so vital to life is bound to play a large part in the language. Blood represents violence, genetic inheritance, and, in **blood, sweat, and tears**, hard work and sacrifice; in 1940 Winston Churchill announced to Parliament that he had 'nothing to offer but blood, toil, tears, and sweat'. Nowadays **bloody** is a relatively mild swear word, but it used to be virtually unprintable. In the 19th century, and well into the 20th, it was on a par with obscene language and caused deep offence. Its use by George Bernard Shaw (1856–1950) in *Pygmalion* (1913), where Eliza Doolittle says, 'Walk! Not bloody likely', caused a sensation, and indeed the play's stage directions mark the word 'Sensation' after the line in question. This reaction probably arose because people thought the word contained a blasphemous reference to the blood of Christ, or was a corruption of **by Our Lady**. In fact the most likely origin lies in the aristocratic rowdies, or 'bloods', of the late 17th and early 18th centuries. Most of the earliest examples, in the second half of the 17th century, involve someone being 'bloody drunk', which probably simply meant 'as drunk as a blood'.

bloom [ME] The early word for 'flower' in English was **blossom**. Old Norse *blóm* 'flower, blossom', was the source of bloom in English, which shares a base with the verb **blow** [OE] 'to burst into flower', now most often met in **overblown** [E17th]. A **bloomer** [L19th] is from the use of blooming for 'bloody' in **blooming error** and is thought to be Australian prison slang. In the 1930s another **bloomer** entered the vocabulary as a name for a type of loaf but it is not clear where from.

bloomers [M19th] Bloomers were first trousers gathered at the ankle and worn with a short skirt; they were named after Mrs Amelia J. Bloomer (1818–94), an American social reformer who advocated wearing this type of clothing. In the late 19th century, bloomers were considered appropriate for activities such as cycling. At the beginning of the 20th century the name started to be applied to loose knee-length knickers and then colloquially, to any knickers.

blossom *see* BLOOM

blouse [E19th] Women did not originally wear blouses. When it first appeared in English the word referred to the blue blouse traditionally worn by French workmen, although where the French got the word from is not known. In the course of the 19th century the word began to apply to various smocks and tunics worn by English farm labourers, and in 1870 came the first reference to a blouse 'for a young lady'. Testimony to the fact that it is now fundamentally a female garment comes in **a big girl's blouse**. In Britain this is an insult for a man regarded as weak, cowardly, or oversensitive.

blow [OE] One of the more colourful phrases involving Old English blow is to **blow hot and cold**, or keep changing your mind, which comes from Aesop's fable of the man and the satyr. A traveller lost in a forest meets a satyr who offers him lodging for the night, promising to lead him safely out of the woods in the morning. On the way to the satyr's home the man blows on his hands. The satyr asks him why he does this, to which he replies, 'My breath warms my cold hands.' At the satyr's home they sit down to eat some steaming hot porridge. The man blows on his first spoonful and again the satyr asks him why. 'The porridge is too hot to eat and my breath will cool it,' he answers. At this the satyr orders him to leave, saying 'I can have nothing to do with a man who can blow hot and cold with the same breath.' *See also* BLOOM, GAFF

blue [ME] The English **blue** and French *bleu* are ultimately the same word, which goes back to ancient Germanic and is related to the *blae-* in **blaeberry** [ME], a Scottish and northern English name for the **bilberry** [L16th]. Blue occurs in a number of phrases, in particular those relating either to depression and melancholy or to the blue of the sky, as in **out of the blue**, 'as a total surprise'. *See also* BOLT. Something occurring **once in a blue moon** is something very rare.

blood bloom bloomers blossom blouse blow

A blue moon sounds fanciful but it is a phenomenon that does occur occasionally, due to large amounts of dust or smoke in the atmosphere. A particularly Australian use of blue is as a humorous nickname for a red-haired person. This is first recorded in 1932, although **bluey** is earlier, from 1906.

Depression or melancholy have always been around, but no one called these feelings **the blues** until the mid 18th century, although people have been feeling blue since as early as the 1580s. **The blues** was a contraction of **blue devils**, which were originally baleful demons punishing sinners. In the 18th century people fancifully imagined them to be behind depression, and later also to be the apparitions seen by alcoholics in delirium tremens. The first printed record of the name of the melancholic music style is in the 'Memphis Blues' of 1912, by the American musician W.C. Handy, who later set up his own music-publishing house and transcribed many traditional blues. Its later development, **rhythm and blues**, appeared in the 1930s.

Obscene or smutty material has been known as blue since the mid 19th century. The link may be the blue gowns that prostitutes used to wear in prison, or the blue pencil traditionally used by censors.

Blue-chip shares are considered to be a reliable investment, though less secure than **gilt-edged** stock (used since the later 19th century for government stock, and earlier to suggest excellent quality). Blue chips are high-value counters used in the game of poker. In America a **blue-collar** worker [M20th] is someone who works in a manual trade, especially in industry, as opposed to a **white-collar** worker [E20th] in the cleaner environment of an office. A **blueprint** [L19th] gets its name from a process in which prints were composed of white lines on a blue ground or of blue lines on a white ground. *See also* MURDER

bluestocking [L17th] During the 17th and 18th centuries men favoured blue worsted stockings for informal daytime wear, but never on formal occasions, when black silk stockings were in order. In about 1750 the botanist and writer Benjamin Stillingfleet was asked to an assembly for literary conversation at Montagu House in London. These gatherings were notable for being attended by women with literary and intellectual tastes. Stillingfleet felt he had to refuse the invitation as he was too poor to afford the formal dress required, but his hostess told him to come as he was, in his informal day clothes. So he turned up in his everyday blue worsted stockings and started a trend. Some sneered at these assemblies, using such terms as **bluestocking assemblies** and **bluestocking ladies**, and an intellectual woman soon became just a **bluestocking**.

bluff [E17th] There are two bluffs in English. The older is the steep cliff. It was originally a nautical adjective meaning 'broad' describing a ship's bows. The origin is not known. In the early 18th century it developed the sense 'surly, abrupt in manner'. The current positive connotation 'direct and good-natured' dates from the early 19th century. The Canadian sense 'grove, clump of trees' dates from the mid 18th century.

The other bluff, from the late 17th century, was first 'to blindfold, hoodwink'. The word was adopted from Dutch *bluffen* 'to brag, boast'. During the mid 19th century poker players in the USA began to use it— when players 'bluffed' in the game they tried to mislead others as to how good their hand of cards really was. The game of poker itself was called bluff. To **call someone's bluff** meant making another player show their hand to reveal that its value was weaker than their heavy betting had suggested. *See also* BUFF

blunder [ME] The original meaning of blunder, 'to move blindly, flounder', gives a clue to its origin. It is likely to be related to *BLIND. Clumsiness was a central part of the word's original meaning, and towards the end of the 15th century was added clumsiness in speech, with the meaning 'to say thoughtlessly, to blurt out'. The modern sense developed in the early 18th century. In his poem 'The Charge of the Light Brigade' (1854), Alfred, Lord Tennyson wrote of one of history's greatest blunders: 'Forward, the Light Brigade! / Was there a man dismayed?

blueprint   bluestocking   bluff   blunder

/ Not though the soldier knew / Some one had blundered.' A **blunderbuss** [M17th] is unrelated, being an alteration of Dutch *donderbus*, literally 'thunder gun'.

blurb [E20th] Not many words are simply made up, but blurb, 'a short description written to promote a book or other product', is one of them. It was invented by the American humorist Gelett Burgess in 1914, although the jacket of one of Burgess's earlier works carried an image of a young lady with the facetious name of 'Miss Blinda Blurb'.

board [OE] It is more difficult to cheat at cards if your hands are clearly visible above the table. This is where the expression **above board** comes from. Board is an old word for table, as well as the planks that make it, and if a card player was playing 'above board' they were showing that they were not trying to cheat. The members of the board that runs a company typically sit round a large table in the boardroom, and it is again the meaning 'table' that gives them their name. *See also* *CABINET.

The expression **across the board** originally comes from horse racing. A bet made 'across the board' is one in which you stake equal amounts of money on the same horse to win a race, to come second, or to finish in the first three. The board here is one on which bookmakers write up the odds. **Go by the board** was originally said at sea of masts and pieces of rigging that fell overboard. The board in this case was the side of the ship, and is used also in **on board**, **overboard** [OE], and **shipboard** [ME].

boatswain *see* COX

bob [LME] Short words are often the hardest to pin down, and this is the case with bob, which has many uses. Some imply 'short'; for example, the hairstyle, which became fashionable in the 1920s. Before that people had used bob for a horse's docked tail, a short bunch of hair or curls, and a short wig, and the bob in **bobcat** [L19th], **bobsleigh** [M19th], and **bobtail** [M16th] also means 'short'.

Another set of uses involves a quick, short movement. People and things **bob up and down**, and boxers **bob and weave**. The British **bob**, 'a shilling', dating from the late 18th century, does not appear to be related to any of these, and its origin remains a mystery.

Bob's your uncle, used to draw attention to the ease with which something can be done, is from the pet form of the name Robert. The Robert in question may have been Lord Salisbury, who in 1887 gave the important post of Chief Secretary for Ireland to his nephew, Arthur Balfour, who was only 39 at the time. The problem with this suggestion is that the earliest recorded examples do not appear until the 1930s, around 50 years after the incident in question. However, we do know that the British **bobby** comes from Sir Robert Peel, British Home Secretary from 1828–30, who established the Metropolitan Police. The old-fashioned term **peelers** for policemen also comes from his name.

bodge *see* BOTCH

bodice [M16th] The original form of bodice was bodies, the plural of **body** [OE]. This referred to an item of clothing for the upper body from the mid 16th century, when the pronunciation of bodies would have been like that of bodice. A similar thing happened with *DICE, which is in origin the plural of die. A **bodice ripper** is a sexy romantic novel with a historical setting, often having a cover featuring a woman with revealingly torn clothes swooning in the arms of a masterful man. The term was not used until the start of the 1980s.

bodkin [ME] The origin is perhaps Celtic linked with Irish *bod*, Welsh *bidog*, and Scottish Gaelic *biodag* 'dagger'. This was the first sense recorded in English and is used by Shakespeare in *Hamlet*: 'When he himself might his quietus make With a bare bodkin'. Another early use was for a sharp instrument for piercing cloth; now, in needlework, a bodkin is, on the contrary, blunt with a large eye for threading tape and other thick threads through material.

blurb   board   boatswain   bob   bodge

body *see* BODICE

Boer *see* BOOR, SOUTH AFRICAN WORD PANEL

boffin [1940s] All that is known for sure about boffin is that it originated in the Second World War as naval slang for an older officer. In 1945 there was the first reference to a person engaged in complex scientific or technical research, when *The Times* wrote of 'A band of scientific men who performed their wartime wonders at Malvern and apparently called themselves "the boffins" '. These days a boffin is any person with great skill or knowledge in a difficult or obscure area. But however clever the dictionary boffins are, they still cannot find the origins of the word. The US slang term **boff**, dating from the 1920s and meaning 'to have sex with', is unrelated. It first meant 'to hit or strike', and arose as an imitation of the sound of a blow.

bog [ME] In Gaelic bog means 'soft', and this is the source of our word. In the slang sense 'toilet', bog was originally **bog-house**, which is recorded as early as 1665. The British Labour Party spin doctor Alistair Campbell caused widespread offence in 2001 when he said that 'The day of the bog-standard comprehensive school is over'. **Bog standard** is first recorded in print as recently as the mid 1960s, although people working in the British motor industry remember it being used a little before this. It may be a reference to bog in the sense 'lavatory', but it is more likely to be an alteration of **box standard**, meaning either 'made in a standard form and packaged in a box' or 'shaped like a box, plainly designed, and without refinements'.

bogey *see* BOGUS, MIND

boggle, bogle *see* MIND

bogus [L18th] Originally an American word, which first appeared meaning an apparatus for making counterfeit coins. The source could have been **tantrabogus**, a New England word for any strange-looking apparatus or object that possibly came from **tantarabobs**, which was brought over by colonists from Devon and meant 'the devil'

or another dialect name for the devil, Bogey, which gave us **bogey** [M19th] and **bogeyman**. In golf a **bogey** is a score of one stroke over par at a hole. Also American is the modern slang sense of bogus, 'bad', which came to a wide audience in the name of the 1991 film comedy *Bill & Ted's Bogus Journey*. It seems to have originated as a term used by young computer hackers in the 1970s for anything useless or incorrect.

bohemian [M19th] The English novelist William Makepeace Thackeray (1811–63) was apparently the first to use bohemian to mean 'a socially unconventional person'. He took it from French *bohémien*, which meant 'a person from Bohemia' (now part of the Czech Republic) and also *GYPSY. Gypsies do not originate in Bohemia but people probably called them Bohemians because that was one route by which they reached western Europe.

boil [ME] Boil in the sense of what hot water does is from Old French *boillir*, based on Latin *bullire* 'to bubble', from *bulla* 'a bubble'. The swelling is unrelated, and was an Old English word.

bold *see* BRAVE

bollard *see* BAULK

bollocks [M18th] Bollocks used to be *ballocks*, and in that spelling they go back to the time of the Anglo-Saxons. The word is related to *BALL, and like many rude words it was perfectly standard English until around the 18th century. It is now used in several colourful expressions. A **bollocking**, or severe telling-off, is more genteelly written as a **rollicking** [M20th], and it is more refined to **make a Horlicks of** [L20th] something than to **make a bollocks of** it. **The dog's bollocks** is a coarse version of expressions like **the bee's knees** or **the cat's pyjamas**, meaning 'an excellent person or thing', which was popularized in the late 1980s by the comic *Viz*.

bolt [OE] In Old English bolt meant 'an arrow'. This is the bolt in **bolt upright**, 'with the back very straight'. Why this comparison was made is not clear—bolts are held more

body Boer boffin bog bogey boggle bogle

or less horizontally to fire, or at least not straight up, which would be dangerous to the archer. To **have shot your bolt**, 'be able to do no more', is also taken from archery. The completely unexpected **bolt from the blue**, on the other hand, is a thunderbolt, a flash of lightning with a simultaneous crash of thunder. Such a bolt coming from a totally clear and unclouded sky would indeed be a shock.

bomb [L17th] In terms of origin, a bomb goes **boom** (LME from a Germanic root)—the word probably goes right back to Greek *bombos* 'booming, humming'. The first bombs, in the late 17th century, are what we would call 'shells'. Soldiers ignited their fuses and fired them from *MORTARS. Before they were dramatically unexpected events or sexy blondes, **bombshells** were originally the casings of such devices. Bombs as we know them came to prominence in the First World War. It was not until after the Second World War, though, that to **go like a bomb** began to be used for 'to go very fast', or **cost a bomb** for 'be very expensive'. *See also* ATOM. A **bombardier** [L16th] gets his name from an early gun called a **bombard** [LME], which came from the same source as bomb.

bombardier *see* BOMB

bombastic [M16th] Although it now means 'high-sounding language with little meaning', **bombast** originally referred to raw cotton or cotton wool used as padding. The source is Old French *bombace*, from medieval Latin *bombax*, an alteration of *bombyx* 'silk'.

bonanza [E19th] Bonanza first referred in the US to success when mining. It is a Spanish word meaning 'fair weather, prosperity', from Latin *bonus* 'good'.

bonce [M19th] This slang word for 'head' was originally a large marble; the origin remains unknown.

bond *see* BAND

bone [OE] This Old English word gives us the phrase **bone idle** which arose in the early 19th century implying *idle through to*

the bone. **Bonfire** [LME] was originally a **bone fire**, on which people burned animal bones. People would collect old animal bones through the year to make a big fire for annual celebrations.

bonk [E20th] Bonk is an imitation of the sound of a solid object striking a hard surface. It first appeared as a verb, meaning 'to shell', in the First World War. The sexual sense does not seem to have been used before the mid 1970s, but has become established, perhaps because people feel it is an acceptable term that is not too rude. The link with **bonkers** [M20th], 'mad', probably comes from the idea of a mad person having been 'bonked' on the head one too many times.

bonnet [LME] A type of soft brimless hat for men was once known as a bonnet. The source is Old French *bonet*, from medieval Latin *abonnis* 'headgear'. In the late 15th century it came to be used for the distinctive type of hat worn by a woman or a child with a brim framing the face and ribbons tied under the chin.

bonny *see* BONUS

bonsai *see* JAPANESE WORD PANEL

bonus [L18th] This was probably originally Stock Exchange slang, coming from Latin *bonus* 'good'. Very recently—too recently to get into most dictionaries—the word **malus** has been recorded for a fine or penalty, based on Latin *malus* 'bad' on the pattern of *bonus*. The French form of *bonus*, *bon* may lie behind the mainly Scottish **bonny** 'good, fair'. **Bounty** [ME] goes back to the same source. *See also* BONANZA

boob [E20th] Boob meaning 'mistake' is an abbreviation of **booby** 'stupid or childish person' in use two centuries earlier and probably derived from Spanish *bobo*, from Latin *balbus* 'stammering'. **Boo-boo** which arose in the 1950s in the US for 'mistake' is from boob, as is the slang term **boob tube** [M20th] for a television. Also American is boob for 'breast'. This is an abbreviation of another booby, a 1930s alteration of dialect

bomb bombardier bombastic bonanza

bubby. There is perhaps a connection with German dialect *Bübbi* 'teat'.

book [OE] The forerunners of the modern book would have been scrolls of papyrus or parchment, or engraved tablets—the first example of what we might recognize as a book came in Roman times. The word book goes back to Old English and has related forms in most of the other northern European languages of the time. Their ancestor was probably a word related to **beech** [OE], which would have been a wood that people used for engraving inscriptions. A **bookmaker** is someone who 'makes a book'. Bookmakers keep a record of bets made with different people, which was originally done in a memorandum book.

boom *see* BOMB

boor [M16th] Before the Norman Conquest a *gebūr* was a peasant or tenant farmer, and is the source of boor, 'a rough and bad-mannered person'. The Normans swept away the Anglo-Saxon social structure, and with it the word, until in the mid 16th century English readopted it from related Dutch and German words meaning a peasant or rustic. Much later, in the 19th century, the Dutch word *boer* gave rise to the **Boer** farmer of southern Africa. The second part of the word is also found in **neighbour**—literally a 'nigh or near boor' and in use in Old English.

bootleg [L19th] The formation of this word is due to the smugglers' practice of concealing bottles inside the long leg part of their boots. The ultimate source of **boot** [ME] is not known.

booty [LME] The original core meaning of booty was 'to distribute'. Victors in war divided the booty stolen from an enemy among themselves. The modern American word meaning 'a person's bottom or buttocks' is unconnected. It is probably an alteration of **botty** [L19th] in the same sense, itself an alteration of **bottom**, an Old English word used for the buttocks since the late 18th century. If someone urges you to **shake your booty**, they want you to dance

energetically. A sexy woman has been **bootylicious** since 1994, although the word was popularized by the single of the same name by Destiny's Child in 2001.

booze [ME] People have been boozing for a long time. The spelling booze dates from the 18th century, but as *bouse* the word entered English in the 13th century, probably from Dutch. We have been going to the **boozer**, or pub, since the 1890s.

bore [OE] There are three words spelt bore in English. The sense 'to make a hole' is Old English. The sense 'a steep-fronted wave caused by the meeting of two tides' may be from Old Norse *bára* 'wave'. It was used in the general sense 'billow, wave' in Middle English, but only in the modern sense since the early 17th century. The bore that is boringly tedious has been with us since the mid 18th century, but the origin of the word is unknown

borough [OE] The early words *burg* and *burh* meant 'a fortress'. Later they became 'a fortified town' and eventually 'town', 'district'. **Burgh** is a Scots form. **Burgher** [M16th] meaning 'inhabitant of a borough' was reinforced by Dutch *burger*, from *burg* 'castle'. **Bourgeois** [L17th] adopted from French (from late Latin *burgus* 'castle') is related. An animal's defensive place, its **burrow** [ME] is a variant of borough.

bosh *see* POPPYCOCK

bosie *see* GOOGLY

bosky *see* AMBUSH

boss *see* DUTCH WORD PANEL

bosun *see* COX

botany [L17th] This comes from the earlier word **botanic** borrowed from French *botanique*, which goes back to Greek *botanē* 'plant'. The explorer Captain James Cook (1728–79), who landed there in 1770, named **Botany Bay** because of the large variety of plants collected there by his companion, Sir Joseph Banks (1743–1820). Later the area became noted from its wool production and

book boom boor bootleg booty booze bore

from the late 19th century botany was used for Australian wool.

botch [LME] The first meaning of botch was simply 'to repair', with no implication of clumsiness or lack of skill. By the early 17th century it seems to have taken on its modern meaning, and Shakespeare's use of the noun in *Macbeth* (*c*.1603) makes this clear: 'To leave no rubs nor botches in the Work.' **Bodge** [M16th] is the same word as **botch**, but always had the negative meaning. The origin of the word is unknown.

bother [L17th] The origins of bother are in Ireland. It is probably related to Irish *bodhaire* 'deafness' and *bodhraim* 'to deafen, annoy'. It is first recorded meaning 'noise, chatter'. In the 18th century emphasis moves to worry, annoyance, and trouble. The word quickly spread out of its Anglo-Irish confines, and in the 19th century appears as a common mild oath in the works of Dickens and Thackeray. The late 1960s gave us **bovver**, 'deliberate troublemaking', which represents a cockney pronunciation of the word. The **bovver boy** (a hooligan or skinhead) wore **bovver boots**, heavy boots with a toe cap and laces. *The Catherine Tate Show*, introduced and popularized the catchphrase **'Am I bovvered?'** in 2004.

bottle [LME] The word bottle goes back to Latin *buttis* 'cask, wineskin', the origin of **butt** [LME] and also of **butler** [ME] originally the man in charge of the wine-cellar. To **have a lot of bottle** and the related phrases to **lose your bottle** and to **bottle out**, meaning 'to lose your nerve', date back to the 1950s. 'Bottle' here may be from rhyming slang **bottle and glass**, 'arse'.

bottom, botty *see* BOOTY

botulism *see* BOWEL

boudoir [L18th] Etymologically, a boudoir is a place where someone sulks. The word was adopted from French in the late 18th century, and literally means 'sulking place', from *bouder* 'to sulk, pout'.

bough *see* BOW

boulevard [M18th] The first boulevards referred to in English were in Paris, in the mid 18th century. They were wide avenues planted with trees, originally on the top of demolished fortifications. The word boulevard then meant 'the horizontal portion of a rampart' in French. It derives from the same German and Dutch word as **bulwark** [LME], and its elements are related to **bole** (ME from Old Norse), 'the stem or trunk of a tree', and *WORK. The French boulevard also gave us the **boulevardier**, a person who frequented the boulevards, and so a wealthy, fashionable socialite, in the late 19th century.

bounce *see* FLIRT

bound [E16th] The word bound meaning to 'leap' and **rebound** [LME] are from French *bondir* 'resound', later 'rebound', which went back to Latin *bombus* 'humming', and is thus related to *BOMB. When a man is described as a **bounder** there is a connection with the slang term bounder for a four-wheeled cab (mid 19th century) which 'bounded' over rough roads causing discomfort. Bound [ME] in the sense **boundary** [E17th] is also from French but its ultimate history is unknown. Bound [ME] in the sense of 'bound for, heading towards' is from an Old Norse word; while bound [LME] in the sense of 'under an obligation' as **in duty bound** is simply a past form of **bind**.

bounty *see* BONUS

bouquet *see* AMBUSH

bourgeois *see* BOROUGH

boutique [M18th] Small shops started being called *boutiques* in French during the mid 18th century. The French word goes back through Latin to Greek *apothēkē* 'a storehouse'. This is ultimately the source of **apothecary** [LME], and of *bodega*, a shop in Spain selling wine. In the 1950s boutique

botch   bother   bottle   bottom   botty

came to be used particularly of a shop selling fashionable clothes. Other small businesses claiming exclusive clienteles began to call themselves boutiques: the **boutique winery** appeared in the United States in the 1970s, and an early mention of a **boutique hotel**, in New York, dates from 1989.

bovver *see* BOTHER

bow [OE] The bow of a ship has nothing to do with a person bowing in respect or a support bowing under pressure. The nautical **bow** [E17th] is in fact related to **bough** [OE], the limb of a tree. Its immediate source, in the later Middle Ages, was German or Dutch. The phrase **a shot across the bows**, 'a warning statement or gesture', has its origins in the world of naval warfare, where it is one which is not intended to hit, but to make ships stop or alter their course. See also *BUXOM. The archer's bow and the act of bending, both Old English, are related and come from Germanic roots. The archer's bow got its name from the shape, which also appears in Old English **rainbow** and **elbow** [OE]. The first part of the latter gives us the old measurement the **ell**, a variable measure, originally the distance from elbow to fingertip, which comes from the Indo-European root that also gives us **ulna** [M16th] for the bone that runs from elbow to wrist.

bowel [ME] Old French *bouel* has given bowel in English, from Latin *botellus* 'little sausage', from *botulus*, source of **botulism** [L19th], a form of food poisoning, adopted from German *Botulismus*, originally 'sausage poisoning'.

bowl *see* BULLETIN

bowser [1920s] This type of tanker used in the fuelling of vehicles such as aircraft or for water, owes its name to a company of oil storage engineers.

box [OE] The box describing a type of container is probably via late Latin *buxis*, from Greek *puxis*, the name of the tree yielding hard timber for making boxes. This Greek word has also given **pyx** [LME], a term used in the Christian Church for a box storing the consecrated bread of the Eucharist. **Boxing Day**, originally the first working day after Christmas Day, was the one on which well-off households traditionally gave presents of money or other things to tradespeople and employees. Such a present was called a **Christmas box**, from the custom of collecting the money in an earthenware box which was broken after the collection had been made and the contents shared out. Pugilistic box [LME] was first in the general sense 'a blow'; the origin is not known. *See also* BOG

boy [ME] A boy was originally 'a male servant'; the origin is obscure. It is apparently identical to East Frisian *boy* 'young gentleman' and may be identical to Dutch *boef* 'knave'. Although boy is used positively and indulgently in phrases such as **that's the boy** and **one of the boys**, the connotation of lower status persisted alongside this in its use as a form of address for summoning and giving orders to slaves or servants. This negative association has connections with the phrase **good ole boy** used to refer to a white male of the southern US portrayed as believing in simple pleasures, but with deep social and racial prejudices (1982 S. B. Flexner *Listening to America 286*: 'A loyal southerner, with all the charm and prejudice the term conveys, has been widely called a *good ole boy* since the mid-1960s'). *See also* TOY

boycott [L19th] In Ireland during the late 19th century the Irish Land League was campaigning for lower rents and land reform. One of its tactics was to ostracize people, refusing to have any dealings with them. In September 1880 a land agent called Captain Charles C. Boycott became one of the first to be shunned in this way and **boycott** was born. Newspapers took up the term immediately and enthusiastically, and other European languages quickly borrowed it. French, for example, has *boycotter*, Dutch has *boycotten*, and German *boycottiren*.

bovver bow bowel bowl bowser box boy

bracelet [LME] Adopted from Old French, from *bras* 'arm', from Latin *bracchium*. Old French had a special word, *brace* for 'both arms, two arms'. This is the source of **brace** [ME] from 'two' as in 'a brace of pheasants', and also for something that clasps, like the brace on teeth, or that supports. **Embrace** [ME], to clasp in both arms, goes back to the same source.

bracket [L16th] This support is apparently via French *braguette* from Spanish *bragueta* 'codpiece, bracket, corbel'. The base is Latin *brāca*, singular of *brācae* 'breeches'; it seems that the architectural bracket may have derived its name from a resemblance to the codpiece of a pair of breeches. An erroneous connection with Latin *bracchium* 'arm' (*see* BRACELET), because of the notion of 'support', seems to have affected the sense development.

braise *see* BRAZIER

bramble *see* BROOM

brand [OE] Something that is **brand new** is really being likened to something hot and glowing from a fire: Shakespeare used the similar phrase *fire-new*. **Brand** existed in Old English in the senses 'burning' and 'a piece of burning wood'. The sense 'mark permanently with a hot iron' gave rise to 'a mark of ownership made by branding', hence the current use 'a type of product manufactured under a particular name'.

brandy *see* DUTCH WORD PANEL

brave [LME] In Old English people with all the attributes of bravery were 'bold'. In the Middle Ages they could also be 'courageous', but it was not until the late 15th century that they became **brave**. The word came through French from Italian or Spanish *bravo* and goes back to Latin *barbarus*, the source of *BARBARIAN. Scots **braw** [L16th] 'fine', **bravado** [M16th], **bravo** [M18th], and **bravura** [M18th] all go back to the same source. The phrase **brave new world** refers to a new or hopeful period of history brought about by major changes in society—usually implying that the changes are in fact undesirable. It is taken from the

title of a satirical novel by Aldous Huxley (1894–1963), published in 1932. Huxley himself borrowed the phrase from a line in Shakespeare's *The Tempest*. Miranda has grown up isolated on an island with her magician father Prospero, the monster Caliban, and some spirits. On first encountering some other humans she exclaims: 'How beauteous mankind is! O brave new world / That has such people in it!'

brawn [ME] Brawn for both muscular strength and pressed potted meat is from Old French *braon* 'fleshy part of the leg', from a Germanic root. A related word is German *Braten* 'roast meat'.

brazier [L17th] The French *braise* 'hot coals, embers' gives us both brazier and to **braise** [M18th], originally to cook something on a brazier. **Braze** [L16th] 'to solder' probably shares the root. **Breeze** [L16th] as in the cinder blocks called breeze blocks also comes from the French.

bread [OE] In Old English bread was not the standard term for the familiar food. That was *LOAF, which has since become restricted to a lump of bread. Bread was such an important part of the diet in the past that it came to stand for food in general. That is why the old translation of the Lord's Prayer says 'Give us this day our **daily bread**'. It also lies behind the word **breadwinner** [E19th] for the person whose income feeds the family and to be **on the breadline** [E20th]. The sense 'money', suggested by the similar use of **dough** [OE], was originally 1930s underworld slang in the USA. People have been writing **bread and butter letters** as a thank you for hospitality since the beginning of the 20th century, initially in the USA, but have **known which side their bread is buttered** since at least the mid 16th.

breeches [ME] Breeches are old-fashioned trousers that are now worn for riding or as part of ceremonial dress. Like *TROUSERS and pants (*see* PANTALOONS), the word is now always plural, but it used to be singular. From Anglo-Saxon times until the 16th century a **breech** was a

bracelet   bracket   braise   bramble   brand

garment covering the groin and thighs, like a loincloth or kilt, still found in the old-fashioned **breech-clout**. A breech was also a person's bottom, a sense which survives in **breech birth**, in which the buttocks or feet of a baby are delivered first. The idea of 'back' or 'end' is also preserved in the breech of a gun, the back part of the barrel.

breeze [M16th] A **breeze** was originally a north or northeast wind, especially a trade wind on the Atlantic seaboard of the West Indies and the Caribbean coast of South America. This is the meaning of the Spanish and Portuguese word *briza* from which **breeze** probably derived in the 16th century. In the following century it began to refer to any gentle wind. *See also* BRAZIER

brekkers *see* RUGBY

breve *see* BRIEF

bric-a-brac [M19th] This comes from French, from the obsolete phrase *à bric et à brac* 'at random'.

brick [LME] English brick is found only from the middle of the 15th century. It was probably introduced by Flemish workmen, for it is a Low German word and Flemings were associated with early brick making. Use of the word was probably reinforced by Old French *brique* 'a form of loaf'. Some French dialects still have the phrase *brique dé pain* 'piece of bread'. The ultimate origin is unknown.

bride [OE] In Old English **bride** was *bryd*. The **bridegroom** had nothing to do with the word groom. The original form was *brydguma*, from *guma* 'man'. This second part was always a slightly poetic word, and by the end of the Middle Ages people would not have recognized it. So they substituted a word they did know. The origin of **bridal** shows that people have always partied at weddings. The word comes from Old English *bryd-ealu* 'wedding feast', from *bryd* 'bride' and *ealu* 'ale-drinking'.

brief [ME] Briefs or underpants, which were first worn in the 1930s, are literally 'shorts'. **Brief** comes from the Latin word *brevis*, meaning 'short', a root shared by **abbreviate** [LME] and the musical note **breve** [LME], which used to mean a short note.

brigadier [L17th] The high-ranking and no doubt respectable brigadier and the lawless **brigand** are related. Both words go back to Italian *brigare* 'to contend, strive'. This gave *brigata* 'a troop, company', from which French took *brigade* and which English adopted as **brigade** in the mid 17th century. French *brigade* also gave us brigadier. Brigand has been around since the late Middle Ages. It came through French from Italian *brigante* 'foot soldier', which is formed from *brigare*. Originally a brigand could be a lightly armed irregular foot soldier, but this use was rare after the 16th century and finally died out.

brilliant [L17th] This is from French *brillant* 'shining' which is probably from Latin *beryllus* 'beryl'. The abbreviation **brill** meaning 'great, wonderful' came into use in the 1980s.

brimstone *see* FIRE

brisk *see* BRUSQUE

Bristol [OE] The city in southwest England, whose name means 'assembly place by the bridge', has been a leading port since the 12th century. Its history is the background to the phrase **shipshape and Bristol fashion**, or 'in good order, neat and clean'. Something in a pleasing or well-ordered state would be described as Bristol fashion because sailors regarded Bristol as a model of prosperity and success. Its importance as a port for the wine trade has given us sherries such as **Bristol Cream**. One of the city's two soccer teams, Bristol City, is the reason that a woman's breasts are sometimes called **bristols**. This is rhyming slang, from Bristol City = titty.

British The Latin word for Britain was *Britannia*, and its inhabitants were the *Brittones*. These words gave English **Britain** and **Briton** during the Anglo-Saxon period, and **Brittany** in northern France—settled by Britons fleeing the Anglo-Saxon invasion. British originally referred to the ancient Britons or their Celtic language; the later inhabitants, descended from Angles, Saxons, Jutes, and Normans, as well as from the native Celtic peoples, were not described as British until the later Middle Ages. *See also* ENGLISH

broach, broccoli, brochette
see BROCHURE

brochure [M18th] Although now associated particularly with holidays, brochure is a French word meaning 'stitching' or 'stitched work'. The connection is that the first brochures were little booklets that were roughly stitched together rather than properly bound. The root, Latin *brocchus* or *broccus* 'projecting [tooth] something that pierces', connects brochure with **broach** [ME] 'to pierce a cask' and **brooch** [ME]. This was originally a variant of broach and meant a skewer (as in **brochette** [LME]) and then an ornamental pin. **Broccoli** [L17th] is from the same source, which became *brocco* 'sprout, shoot, projecting tooth' in Italian, and then broccoli 'little sprouts'.

brock *see* BADGER

brogue *see* SCOTTISH WORD PANEL

bronosaurus, brontophobia *see* PHOBIA

bronze [M17th] Bronze comes via French, from Italian *bronzo*, probably based on Persian *birinj* 'brass'.

brooch *see* BROCHURE

broom [OE] Old English *brōm* was the name of the shrub. Of Germanic origin, it is related to Old English **bramble**. The name was applied to an implement for sweeping in Middle English when it was made of broom, heather, or similar twigs. The history of **brush** [ME] is not so clear, but both the brush for sweeping and the brush as in brushwood come from French and are probably the same word.

brown [OE] In Old English brown simply meant 'dark'. It acquired its modern sense in Middle English. The idea of darkness developed into a further sense of 'gloomy or serious', and this is the sense that occurs in the 16th-century phrase **a brown study**, 'absorbed in one's thoughts'. The use of 'study' is puzzling to us today. It is not a room for working in, but a state of daydreaming or meditation, a meaning long out of use in English. *See also* AUBURN, BAIZE

brush *see* BROOM

brusque [M17th] This has been adopted from the French word meaning 'lively, fierce', from Italian *brusco* 'sour'. **Brisk** [L16th] is probably the same word.

brute [LME] Brute comes from Old French *brut(e)*, from Latin *brūtus* 'dull, stupid'.

bubonic *see* PLAGUE

buccaneer [M17th] A buccaneer was originally a French hunter of wild oxen in South America or the Caribbean who cooked meat on a wooden frame over an open fire. The name for this frame was a *boucan*, a word that came through French from Tupi, a language of the Amazon basin. Later in the same century people began to apply buccaneer to a pirate of the Spanish American coasts, because the hunters changed career.

buck [OE] From the mid 19th century in poker a buck is an article placed as a reminder in front of a player whose turn it is to deal at poker. This is the buck in **to pass the buck**, 'to shift the responsibility to someone else'—to pass the buck is to hand over the responsibility for dealing to the next player. The original buck may have been the handle of a buckhorn knife used as a marker. A related expression is **the buck stops here**. The US President Harry S. Truman had this as a motto on his desk, indicating that the ultimate responsibility

broach broccoli brochette brochure brock

for running the country lay with him. The buckhorn came from Old English. The phrases **buck someone up** and **buck up one's ideas** have a connection with the sharp jerk of the buck's butting movements, while the verb to buck [M19th] seems to have come from the way a buck jumps. Why a US dollar has been known as a buck from the mid 18th century is unclear, but it may have been from the use of buckskins as a medium of exchange particularly among frontiersmen and Native Americans.

buckle [ME] This word for a fastener is from Old French *bocle* 'buckle, boss', from Latin *buccula* 'cheek strap of a helmet'; the base is Latin *bucca* 'cheek'. The verb 'to buckle' as in buckle under a weight or strain is from French *boucler* 'to bulge'.

budge *see* BULLETIN

budgerigar *see* AUSTRALIAN WORD PANEL

budget [LME] When the British Chancellor of the Exchequer holds up the battered case containing details of his budget speech, he may or may not know that he is making a gesture towards the origin of the word. A budget was originally a pouch or wallet. The word came from French in the late Middle Ages, and goes back to Latin *bulga* 'leather sack, bag', from which English also gets **bulge** [ME].

buff [M16th] The word buff originally meant 'a buffalo or other type of wild ox', and **buff leather**, often shortened to simply buff, was leather made from the hide of such an animal. This leather was very strong, with a pale yellowish-beige colour. It was used to make military uniforms, and so soldiers would be described as 'wearing buff' or 'in buff'. The combination of these descriptions and the similarity of the leather's colour to that of a white person's skin led to **in the buff**, 'naked'. **The buff** meaning 'the bare skin' dates from the mid 17th century. The slang sense 'good-looking, fit, and attractive', which appeared in California at the beginning of the 1980s, comes from the idea of 'buffing' or polishing something, originally with a cloth of buffalo leather. Another buff uniform gave rise to the **buff** who is enthusiastic and knowledgeable about a particular subject. The original buffs were, in the words of *The New York Sun* in 1903, 'men and boys whose love of fires, fire-fighting, and firemen is a predominant characteristic'. The volunteer firemen in New York City formerly wore buff.

The buff in the game **blind man's buff** is an old word for 'a blow, a buffet' which survives only in this context. It is not surprising that people want to change the word to something more familiar, and in America the game is called **blind man's bluff**. A **buffet** [ME] was originally a lighter buff. The idea of blows is also found in the **buffer** [M19th] for a shock-absorbing piston. The sense of buffer found in **old buffer** comes from an old dialect word for someone who stuttered or spluttered.

buffoon [M16th] This comes via French and Italian from medieval Latin *buffo* 'a clown'. In the late 16th century a buffoon was a professional jester.

bugger [ME] A bugger was originally a heretic—this was the meaning of Old French *bougre*. The word ultimately comes from *Bulgarus*, which was the Latin term for a Bulgarian, in particular one who belonged to the Orthodox Church, which was regarded by the Roman Catholic Church as heretical. **Bugger** was first used in English in reference to members of a heretical Christian sect based in Albi in southern France in the 12th and 13th centuries, the Albigensians. The sexual use of the term arose in the 16th century from an association of heresy with forbidden sexual practices.

bugle [ME] The early English sense was 'wild ox', hence the compound bugle-horn for the horn of an ox used to give signals, originally during hunting. The word comes via Old French from Latin *būculus*, 'little ox' from *bōs* 'ox'.

bulgar *see* GOO

bulge *see* BUDGET

buckle   budge   budgerigar   budget   buff

bull [OE] Bull goes back to Old Norse. In Stock Exchange terminology a bull is a person who buys shares hoping to sell them at a higher price later, the opposite of a *BEAR. The latter term came first, and it seems likely that bull was invented as a related animal analogy. Nowadays, people might associate bull in the sense 'nonsense' with the rather cruder term **bullshit**, which has been used with the same meaning since the early 20th century. Bull is much older being first recorded in the early 17th century, in the sense 'an expression containing a contradiction in terms or a ludicrous inconsistency'. An **Irish bull** was a fuller name for this. Where this bull comes from is unknown, though the experts are sure it has nothing to do with a **papal bull** (an order or announcement by the pope), which is from medieval Latin *bulla*, 'a sealed document'. The bull of **bulrush** [LME] and **bullfrog** [M18th] probably indicates size and vigour. *See also* BULLETIN

bulldozer [L19th] To bulldoze someone first meant to intimidate them, and a bulldozer was a bully who intimidated others. Early examples often use the spelling **bulldose**, and the reference may have been to a severe 'dose' of flogging. In the 1890s bulldozer seems to have become attached to various devices for pushing things such as piles of earth or snow, and then around 1930 to the heavy tractor we are familiar with.

bullet *see* BULLETIN

bulletin [M17th] The word bulletin derives from Italian *bulletta* meaning 'official warrant or certificate'—something like a passport today. The root is the Italian and medieval Latin word *bulla* 'seal, sealed document', the source of *BILL meaning 'written statement of charges' and of *BULL meaning 'papal edict'. The original Latin meaning of *bulla* was 'bubble', and this is the basis of **bowl** [OE] in the sense 'ball' and ultimately 'basin' and of **budge** [L16th] which comes via French *bouger* 'to stir', from Latin *bullire* 'boil, bubble', **bullet** [E16th] originally a small ball, **bullion** [ME] from the idea of bubbling metal, and **ebullient** [L16th] 'bubbling'.

bullion *see* BULLETIN

bully [M16th] People originally liked bullies. When it came into the English language in the 16th century, probably from an old Dutch word *boele* 'lover', bully was a term of endearment, much like 'sweetheart' or 'darling'. At the end of the 17th century it was being used to mean 'admirable or jolly', and finally the more general sense of 'first-rate' developed. Today this survives only in the expression **bully for you!**, 'well done! good for you!' The usual modern sense dates from the late 17th century, probably from its use as an informal way of addressing a male friend, or referring to a 'lad' or 'one of the boys'. The bully of **bully beef** is a mid 18th-century alteration of French *bouilli* 'boiled'.

bulrush *see* BULL

bulwark *see* BOULEVARD

bum [LME] There are two different words spelled **bum**. To a Brit, the **bum** is their bottom. The origin of this word is unknown. From the Middle Ages until around the 18th century bum in this sense was not regarded as a rude word: Shakespeare used it, and a treatise on surgery could refer to '[pulling] the feathers from the bums of hens or cocks'. The American **bum** [M19th] is a tramp or vagrant. The origin of this one is known—it is probably from **bummer** [M19th], which now chiefly means 'a disappointing or unpleasant situation' but in the USA first referred to a vagrant. It comes from German *bummeln* 'to stroll about'.

The British slang word **bumf** [L19th], meaning 'tedious printed material' was originally **bum fodder**—it first meant 'toilet paper'. The novelist Virginia Woolf wrote in a letter of 1912, 'Is this letter written upon Bumf? It looks like it.'

bump *see* JUMP

bumpkin *see* DUTCH WORD PANEL

bundle [ME] Bundle may come from Old English *byndelle* 'a binding'. In the mid 18th century anatomists and physiologists started using the Old English word 'bundle' for a set of muscle or nerve fibres running in parallel. The phrase **a bundle of nerves** is common in US sources from the 1880s. The phrase to **go a bundle on** someone or something, or be very fond of them, comes from the world of betting and horse racing. Bundle is a slang term for 'a large sum of money', first used in the US around 1880. If a person 'goes a bundle on a horse' they bet a lot of money on it.

bungalow *see* RAJ WORD PANEL

bungee [1930s] A bungee was originally a rubber or eraser, although why has yet to be discovered. In the 1930s the word came to mean an elasticated cord for launching a glider, and by the 1960s the bungee or bungee cord, with a hook at each end, was used for securing articles. By the late 1970s a similar band allowed the development of **bungee jumping**, the sport of jumping from a high place secured by a band round the ankles.

bunk [M19th] A shortening of **bunkum**, which also means 'nonsense' but is now rather dated. Originally also spelled **buncombe**, it refers to Buncombe County in North Carolina, USA. Around 1820 the congressman representing the county mentioned it in an inconsequential speech, just to please his constituents. **Buncombe** immediately became a byword for tedious nonsense. **Bunk** meaning 'a kind of bed' and **bunk** as in **bunk off** are different words, both of unknown origin. *See also* HISTORY

bunny [E17th] The first recorded example of bunny, in 1606, reads, 'Sweet Peg...my honey, my bunny, my duck, my dear'. The word was originally a term of endearment for a person, and was not found as a pet name for a rabbit until late in the 17th century. It is itself a pet form of **bun**, a dialect word for a squirrel or a rabbit. The origin of that word is not known, but it is unlikely to be connected with **bun** 'a small cake', which is also of obscure origin. The 1987 film *Fatal Attraction*, in which Glenn Close's character, rejected by Michael Douglas, boils his child's pet rabbit, gave us the term **bunny boiler** for a woman who acts vengefully after having been spurned by her lover.

bureau [L17th] The French word *bureau* originally meant '*BAIZE', a material that was used for covering writing desks, and probably comes from a form of *buire* 'dark brown'. In the early 18th century bureau entered English both as a writing desk and as an office, a place where writing desks are found. In North America the piece of furniture called a bureau is a chest of drawers rather than a desk. The word is common there in the official titles of some government offices, for example the Federal Bureau of Investigation or FBI.

burger *see* US WORD PANEL

burgh, burgher *see* BOROUGH

burn [OE] The **burn** meaning 'to be on fire' and the Scottish word for a small stream are not connected, although both are Old English. To **burn the midnight oil**, 'to read or work late into the night', and to **burn the candle at both ends**, 'to go to bed late and get up early', both recall the days before gas and electricity, when houses were lit by candles and oil lamps. To **burn your boats** (in Britain also to **burn your bridges**) derives from military campaigns. Burning the boats or bridges that a force used to reach a particular position would mean that they had destroyed any means of escape or retreat: they had no choice but to fight on.

burrow *see* BOROUGH

bursar *see* PURSE

burst *see* BUST

Burton [1940s] To **go for a Burton** first appears in RAF slang in the 1940s, when it was used to mean 'be killed in a crash'. The most plausible explanation is that it was a reference to going for a pint of Burton's beer. Burton upon Trent in Staffordshire, England, was a well-known centre of the brewing industry. Another suggestion is that

bungalow   bungee   bunk   bunny   bureau

it referred to a suit from the British men's clothing firm Burton's, but there is no known record of to 'go for a Burton's suit', as you might expect if this were the origin of the phrase, and 'gone for a pint' is a much more likely euphemism for a young man's sudden death.

bus *see* OMNIBUS

bush *see* AMBUSH, GRAPE

bushel [ME] If a bushel is a measure of capacity, how can you **hide your light under a bushel**? The answer is that the word here is used in an old sense, 'a container used to measure out a bushel'. The origin of the phrase is biblical, from the Gospel of Matthew: 'Neither do men light a candle, and put it under a bushel, but on a candlestick; and it giveth light to all that are in the house.' The word entered English from French and may be Gaulish.

bushido *see* JAPANESE WORD PANEL

business [OE] Old English *bisignis* meant 'anxiety', but the main early sense, which lasted from the Middle Ages down to the 18th century, was 'the state of being busy'. The modern senses began to develop in the later Middle Ages, and the meanings existed happily in parallel for several hundred years. Then people began to feel that a clear distinction needed to be made between simply being busy and having business to attend to. In the early 19th century this resulted in the form **busyness**, the exact equivalent of *bisignis*.

busk [M17th] Busking used to take place not in shopping centres but at sea. The word busk comes from Italian *buscare* or Spanish *buscar*, which both mean 'to seek'. Its earliest use in English was in the nautical sense 'cruise about, tack'. This became extended to mean 'go about selling things', and then, in the middle of the 19th century, 'go about performing'.

bust [M17th] Originally bust referred only to sculpture, usually a piece of sculpture representing a person's head, shoulders, and chest. The term came into English in the 17th century through French from Italian *busto*. The Latin source of the Italian word was *bustum* 'a tomb, sepulchral monument'. When in the early 18th century a living person was described as having a bust, there was usually some comparison with marble or a sculpture. It was not until the later 19th century that the word appeared in the context of dress and fashion, and the measurement of a woman's bosom for clothing sizes. The bust, meaning 'to break' is a mid 18th-century US variant of Old English **burst**.

butcher [ME] The origin of butcher may tell us something about the diet of early Europeans. It goes back to a French *boc* meaning 'male goat' that is probably related to *BUCK 'male deer'. A butcher was originally more a slaughterman than a salesman, and the word very quickly came to refer to a person responsible for the slaughter of many people, a brutal murderer. *See also* SHAMBLES. **Butch** [1940s] for 'masculine' may be a shortening of the word. In the phrase to **have a butcher's**, 'to have a look', **butcher's** is short for **butcher's hook**, rhyming slang for 'a look'. The first known printed example dates from the 1930s.

butler *see* BOTTLE

butt [LME] Butt meaning an end, such as a cigarette stub or the part of a rifle that you hold, is related to Dutch *bot* 'stumpy'. It is the same word as butt for your bottom, a meaning that goes back to medieval England. The word is related to Old English **buttock**. *See also* BOTTLE

butterfly [OE] The word **butter** has been known in Britain since Saxon times. It goes back to Greek *bouturon*, and before that possibly to the Scythians, an ancient people from the area of the Black Sea. The butterfly may get its name from the brimstone butterfly and other yellow or cream-coloured butterflies. The idea of likening a feeling of nervousness to having a butterfly or butterflies in one's stomach dates from the early 20th century, though the exact formulation **butterflies in one's stomach** is

bus bush bushel bushido business busk

not recorded before the 1950s. The boxing strategy of Muhammad Ali was famously described as 'Float like a butterfly, sting like a bee'. The quote first appeared in *The Cassius Clay Story* (1964—Cassius Clay was Ali's original name), and is thought to have been coined by Ali's trainer Drew 'Bundini' Brown. *See also* CHAOS

buxom [ME] Today buxom describes a woman's physical appearance, but originally it would have described her character. From the early Middle Ages and into the 19th century buxom meant 'obedient, compliant' and applied to both sexes. The word comes from the root of *BOW, 'to incline the head or body' and originally 'to bend'. From 'compliant' it moved to 'obliging, amiable', and then in the 16th century it became more active and positive, taking in 'bright, cheerful, lively'. Good spirits depend on good health, and soon a buxom woman was one full of health, vigour, and good temper. And since plumpness has a traditional association with health, she became plump or large-breasted.

buzzard [LME] Old French *busard* is the source, based on Latin *būteō* 'falcon'. The buzzard was considered an inferior kind of hawk which was useless for falconry; this led, apparently, to its use as a derogatory description of an ignorant or stupid person. The force weakened over time and the phrase **old buzzard** may convey nothing more than 'old chap'. In dialect a buzzard is sometimes 'a moth' or 'cockchafer' but this word is based on **buzz**, a late Middle English word based on the sound.

Byronic *see* MAD

byte *see* BITE

butterfly buxom buzzard Byronic byte

cab [E19th] A cab was originally a **cabriolet**, now a car with a roof that folds down but in the mid 18th century a kind of light two-wheeled carriage with a hood, drawn by one horse. The motion of the carriage suggested its name, which is from French *cabriole* 'a goat's leap'—the root is Latin *caper* 'goat'. *See also* CAPER

cabal [L16th] Historically, cabal was a committee of five ministers under Charles II of England (1630–85), whose surnames began with C, A, B, A, and L (Clifford, Arlington, Buckingham, Ashley (Earl of Shaftesbury), and Lauderdale). However, the first recorded use of *cabal* (from French *cabale*) was in reference to the Cabbala, the ancient Jewish tradition of mystical interpretation of the Bible. Medieval Latin *cabala* is the source of several variants of Cabbala, including *Kabbalah* (the preferred modern spelling), *Kabbala*, *Cabala*, and *Qabalah*, based on a rabbinical Hebrew word for 'tradition'.

cabaret [M17th] Samuel Pepys wrote in his diary, 'In most cabaretts in France they have writ upon the walls "*Dieu te regarde*" ['God is watching you'], as a good lesson to be in every man's mind'. He was referring to French inns, which is what the word cabaret meant in the 17th century. The modern sense of an entertainment in a nightclub dates from before the First World War. Cabaret is from the Old French for 'shed'.

cabin *see* CABINET

cabinet [M16th] The modern meaning of 'a piece of furniture' developed from the original sense 'little cabin' or 'small room'. The use for the body of chief ministers who meet to discuss government policy dates from the 17th century. Confidential advisers of the monarch or chief ministers used to hold their meetings in a private room, and in time the term for the room was applied to the politicians themselves. *Compare* BOARD

caboodle [M19th] The caboodle in the expression **the whole caboodle** or **the whole kit and caboodle**, meaning 'the whole lot', is a mysterious word. The phrase was originally **the whole kit**, and later **the whole kit and boodle**. **Boodle** meant 'a lot, a crowd', or 'money', and may be connected to Dutch *boedel*, meaning 'possessions'. *See also* KIT

cacao *see* CHOCOLATE

cacophony [M17th] The word cacophony, meaning 'a harsh discordant combination of sounds', came via French from Greek *kakophonia*. *Kakos* was Greek for 'bad', and *phōnē* meant 'sound'—it is the root of words like **euphonious** (*see* EUPHEMISM), **symphony** [ME] 'harmonious sound', and **telephone** (*see* TELEGRAPH).

cacotopia *see* UTOPIA

cad [L18th] This is a dated term to describe a man who behaves dishonourably towards a woman, and appears to have arisen at the universities as a colloquial insult for a 'man of low, vulgar manners'. It may have originated at Oxford in a contemptuous application to townsmen in the 'town-and-gown' rivalry. Cad, however, once referred to any passenger picked up by the driver of a horse-drawn coach for his personal profit. It is an abbreviation of Scottish **caddie** or its more standard form **cadet**. This term for a younger son comes from French Gascon dialect *capdet*, 'little head' hence 'junior' from Latin *caput* 'head'.

cadaver *see* ACCIDENT

cadence [LME] This has come via Old French from Italian *cadenza*, based on Latin *cadere* 'to fall'. **Cadenza** [M18th] is used as a musical term for a virtuoso solo passage usually inserted near the end of a movement in a concerto or other work. The phrase have a cadenza is used informally in South African English to mean 'be extremely agitated': this is said to be from Danny Kaye's *The Little Fiddle*, a humorous recording made in the 1940s.

cadet *see* CAD

cadge [E17th] The first recorded use of cadge was the English dialect sense 'to carry about'. This was formed from the noun **cadger**, which had existed since the late 15th century and meant, in northern English and Scots, 'a pedlar or dealer who travelled between town and country'. From this developed the verb sense 'to hawk or peddle' and eventually the modern sense, 'to ask for something that you are not strictly entitled to'. **Codger**, meaning an elderly man, is probably a variant of cadger.

Caesar Roman emperors from Augustus (63 BC–AD 14), the first emperor, to Hadrian (AD 76–138) were known by the title Caesar. The word came simply from the name of Julius Caesar (100–44 BC), who was Augustus's predecessor as ruler of Rome. It is the root of both the German **Kaiser** and the Russian **Tsar**, used in the USA for a boss since the mid 19th century, and an officially appointed person in charge of something since the mid 20th. A person who should be above suspicion can be referred to as **Caesar's wife**. According to the Greek biographer Plutarch (*c.*AD 46–120), Julius Caesar's wife Pompeia was accused of adultery. Although he did not believe his wife was guilty, Caesar divorced Pompeia anyway. His justification for this was, 'I thought my wife ought not even to be under suspicion'. A **Caesarian section** is so called because Julius Caesar is supposed to have been delivered by this birth method.

cage *see* JAIL

cahoots [E19th] To be **in cahoots** with someone is to be working in collusion with them. It is an American expression, recorded in the early 19th century in the neutral sense of 'in league or partnership'. Nowadays the expression invariably suggests dishonesty and conspiracy. Where cahoots comes from is uncertain. It might derive from the French word *cahute*, meaning 'a hut or cabin', with the idea of plotting together in an intimate closed environment. Or it may be an alteration of **cohort** (*see* COURTEOUS) based on the notion of a group of people working closely together.

cake [ME] This is a Scandinavian word and the first cakes were small flat bread rolls baked hard on both sides by being turned during the baking process—you can see the idea of a rounded flattened shape surviving in **fishcake** and **potato cake**. The word occurs in many common expressions as something pleasant or desirable. The phrase **cakes and ale**, for example, means 'merrymaking, a good time'. It comes from Shakespeare's *Twelfth Night*, when the roistering Sir Toby Belch says to the puritanical steward Malvolio: 'Dost thou think because thou art virtuous there shall be no more cakes and ale?' The idea behind the saying **you can't have your cake and eat it** is that you cannot enjoy both of two equally desirable but mutually exclusive things. The expression has been around since at least the mid 17th century. **Let them eat cake** is what Marie-Antoinette (1755–93), wife of Louis XVI (1754–93) of France, is alleged to have said on being told that her people had no bread. (The French word she is supposed to have used was *brioche*, not cake.) This story is good, but its authenticity is suspect—Louis XIV's wife is supposed to have said 'Why don't they eat pastry?' in a similar situation.

calamity [LME] This is from Old French *calamite*, from Latin *calamitas* 'damage', 'disaster', 'adversity'. Latin writers thought this was from *calamus* 'straw, corn stalk' linked to damage to crops by bad weather, but this is doubtful.

calcium *see* CHALK

calculate [LME] The Latin word *calculus* meant 'a small pebble', specifically one used on an *ABACUS. This is the base of Latin *calculare* 'to count', from which calculate comes. **Calculator** [LME] first meant a person who calculates, just as a *COMPUTER was a person who computes. **Calculus** has become an English word in its own right, as the name of a branch of mathematics, since the late 17th century.

calibre [M16th] This word, now meaning 'the quality of someone's character or ability' and 'internal diameter or bore of a gun barrel', travelled around the Mediterranean and Middle East before arriving in English during the 16th century. It may have started in Greece, from where the word *kalapous*, 'shoemaker's last', migrated east and became Arabic *qālib*, 'mould for casting metal'. The jump to Italy or Spain and then France produced the spelling **calibre**, and from there it came to England, where it first meant 'social standing or importance'. The sense changes seem to have been from the mould to metal to something for casting bullets, then since the calibre of a gun determines its effectiveness this was interpreted as indicating personal qualities. **Calliper** [L16th], which would have been used for something to measure the diameter of a bullet, is an alteration of calibre.

calix *see* POISON

call [OE] Call appears in Late Old English from an Old Norse root, but **recall** 'call back' does not appear until the late 16th century. To **call the shots** or **call the tune** is to dictate how something should be done. Call the tune is a shortening of **he who pays the piper calls the tune**, only recorded from the late 19th century. Call the shots, not recorded before the 1920s, is from sports and games. In pool to call your shots is to say in advance which ball you intend to hit into which pocket. In target shooting it means to announce which part of the target you are going to hit; if someone else calls the shots you have to aim at the bit they choose.

calligraphy [E17th] This is from Greek *kalligraphia*, from *kallos* 'beauty' and *graphein* 'write'. In **callisthenics** [E19th] (US calisthenics) *kallos* is combined with *sthenos* 'strength'.

calliper *see* CALIBRE

callisthenics *see* CALLIGRAPHY

callous [LME] The Latin source *callosus* means 'hard-skinned', and the word was originally used in this sense. The transference to 'insensitive to others' feelings', which happened in the late 17th century, has a parallel in **thick-skinned**. **Callus** [M16th], for hardened skin, is from the same word.

callow [OE] You would not think of a callow youth as someone who was bald, but that is what Old English *calu* meant. A later use referred to young birds and meant 'not yet able to fly, unfledged'. The idea of fluffy young birds must have put people in mind of the down on a youth's cheek and chin, which led to the present sense 'immature or inexperienced'.

callus *see* CALLOUS

calm [LME] The origin of calm can be traced back to the idea of the heat of the midday sun in a hot climate, when people are indoors and everything is quiet and still. Calm came into English via Italian, Spanish, or Portuguese from Greek *kauma* 'heat of the day', and was perhaps also influenced by Latin *calere* 'to be warm'.

calumny *see* CHALLENGE

camel [OE] Our term for the camel comes from Greek *kamēlos*, which itself probably came from an Arabic or Hebrew word. When it was adopted into Old English it replaced the existing word for the animal, *olfend*. This sounds suspiciously like *ELEPHANT, and it seems that people often got the two animals confused, not being familiar with either. A further confusion is found in **camelopard**, an archaic name for a *GIRAFFE, from Greek *kamelopardalis*, from *kamēlos* 'camel' and *pardalis* 'female panther or leopard'. People thought that a giraffe's spotted skin looked like that of a leopard. *See also* CHAMELEON. It was Alec Issigonis, the designer of the Morris Minor and Mini cars, who said that 'A camel is a horse designed by a committee'.

calibre   calix   call   calligraphy   calliper

camera [L17th] A camera was first a council or legislative chamber in Italy and Spain. The word is borrowed from Latin, where it meant 'vault or chamber', and is also the source of **chamber** [ME]. In legal contexts the Latin phrase **in camera** is used to mean 'in the judge's private chamber' instead of in open court. The photography sense comes from the **camera obscura** (literally 'dark chamber'), a device popular in the 18th century for recording visual images—the first example of the modern sense comes in the 1840s.

camouflage [First World War] This was adopted from French, from *camoufler* 'to disguise', which was originally thieves' slang. It comes from Italian *camuffare* 'to disguise'.

campaign [E17th] Latin *campania* meant 'open countryside' and was based on *campus* 'a field'. It is the source of English campaign, which was originally a tract of open land and is a close relative of French **champagne**, both an area of open country and the winemaking region. The connection between countryside and fighting is that armies tended to spend the winter in a fortress or town, 'taking the field' in summer. Hence the countryside became associated with military manoeuvres. **Camp** [E16th], which is also from Latin *campus* was similarly used in Latin not only to mean 'a field, level ground' but, more specifically, 'an open space for military exercises'—the most famous one was the *Campus Martius*, or Field of Mars, in Rome. This developed into the idea of a place where soldiers are housed. **Campus** itself came into English in the 18th century as the term for university or college grounds. *See also* CHAMPION

can [OE] Nowadays a **can** is a cylindrical metal container, but its ancestor, Old English *cann*, was a general word for any container for liquids. It may come from Latin *canna* (*see* CANNON). If someone **carries the can** they take responsibility for a mistake or misdeed. The origin of this expression is uncertain, but it probably started life as early 20th-century naval slang. One theory is that it refers to the beer can or keg which one sailor carried for all his companions. An early version was to **carry the can back**, which might have referred to returning the empties. In film-making and recording you can talk about something being **in the can** when it has been captured on tape or film to a satisfactory standard. Though videotape and digital recordings are not stored in cans, the older expression has been transferred to them. *See also* WORM, CUNNING, KNOW

canal *see* CANNON

canary [L16th] The canary acquired its name from the Canary Islands, which is where the ancestors of our cage birds originate. The name of the islands comes from Latin *canaria insula*, which meant 'island of dogs' from *canis* 'dog', one of the islands having had a large population of dogs. *Canis* is also the source of **canine** [LME] and **kennel** [ME].

cancel [LME] The early sense was 'obliterate or delete writing by drawing or stamping lines across it', which, in legal contexts, rendered documents void. It is from Old French *canceller*, from Latin *cancellare*, from *cancelli* 'crossbars, grating' describing the shape of the lines.

cancer [OE] The pattern of swollen veins around malignant tumours gave them the name cancer because they looked like the limbs of a crab—*cancer* in Latin. In English **canker** [ME] was the usual form for the disease until the 17th century, when canker became the term for various plant diseases. The medical term **carcinoma** [E18th] comes from *karkinos*, Greek for 'crab'.

candid [M17th] 'The stones came candid forth, the hue of innocence', wrote the poet John Dryden around 1700. He was using the word candid in its original meaning 'white', from Latin *candidus*. Over time the English word developed the senses 'pure and innocent', 'unbiased', and 'free from malice', before finally settling on the meaning 'frank'. **Candour** [LME] has a similar history, its meaning developing from 'whiteness' to the current 'openness and honesty in expression'. *See also* ALBUM.

camera camouflage campaign can canal

These days someone running for office needs to be 'whiter than white'. So did the candidates in Roman times, since the word **candidate**, is also based on *candidus*. A *candidatus* was a white-robed person, as candidates for office were traditionally required to wear a pure white toga or robe, meant to reflect their unstained character.

candle [OE] Old English *candel* came from Latin *candela*, from *candere* 'to be white, shine, glisten' (*compare* CANDID). From the same source comes **chandelier** [M18th] from Old French *chandelier* which also gave Middle English **chandler**, originally a candle maker or seller. A person who **cannot hold a candle to** someone else is nowhere near as good as them. In the past an assistant might stand next to his superior with a candle to provide light to work by, and so the idea of holding a candle to someone became synonymous with helping them as a subordinate or in a menial way. **Not worth the candle** originated as a translation of the French phrase *le jeu ne vaut pas la chandelle*, 'the game is not worth the candle'. The 'game' was a game of cards involving betting, and would not be worth playing if the expense of candles to provide light was more than the expected winnings.

candour *see* CANDID

candy *see* ARABIC WORD PANEL

cane *see* CANNON

canine *see* CANARY, EYE

canister *see* CANNON

canker *see* CANCER

canna *see* CANNON

cannabis *see* CANVAS

cannelloni *see* CANNON

cannibal [M16th] The explorer Christopher Columbus brought back the word cannibal to Europe. On landing in the West Indies he encountered the warlike Caribs, and gained the impression they were cannibals. His interpretation of their name was *Canibales*, which entered English in a translated account of his voyage written in 1553. The Caribs also gave their name to the **Caribbean** sea and region.

cannon [LME] This large heavy piece of artillery derives its name from French *canon*, from Italian *cannone* 'large tube', from *canna* 'cane, reed, tube'. Soldiers have been called **cannon fodder**, no more than material to be used up in war, since the late 19th century—the expression is a translation of German *Kanonenfutter*. Shakespeare did encapsulate a similar idea much earlier, with his phrase 'food for powder' in *Henry IV Part 1*. *Canna* or its Greek equivalent *kanna* is the base of a number of other words in English, as well as giving us the name of the **canna lily** [M17th], which gets its name from the shape of its leaves. Some reflect the use of the plants for making things, some their hollow stems. **Canes** [ME] are basically the same plant. **Canister** [LME] was originally a basket from Latin *canistrum* 'basket for bread, fruit, or flowers', from Greek *kanastron* 'wicker basket', from *kanna*. **Canal** [LME] and **channel** [ME] both come via French from Latin *canalis* 'pipe, groove, channel' from *canna*, and share a source with the Italian pasta **cannelloni** [M19th]. The medical **cannula** [L17th] was originally a 'small reed'; a **canyon** [M19th] is from Spanish *cañón* 'tube' from *canna*.

cannula *see* CANNON

canny *see* UNCANNY

canopy [LME] *Conopeum*, the Latin word from which canopy derives, referred to a mosquito net over a bed. The ultimate source is the Greek word *kōnōps* 'mosquito'.

canteen [M18th] This was originally a type of shop in a barracks or garrison town, selling provisions and liquor to soldiers. The form comes from French *cantine*, from Italian *cantina* 'cellar'. The French had already transferred this to the water bottle soldiers carry with them, and this sense

candle candour candy cane canine canister

came into the language at the same time as the original.

canter [E18th] This word began as a shortened form of **Canterbury pace** or **Canterbury gallop**, the term for the gentle rate at which mounted pilgrims made their way to the shrine of St Thomas à Becket at Canterbury in the Middle Ages. To win something **at a canter** is to do so with the greatest ease. In horse-racing a horse easily wins a race if it is able to run the final stretch cantering rather than galloping.

canticle *see* ENCHANT

canvas [LME] You can smoke **cannabis** [L18th], or, more legally, make canvas out of its fibre. The versatile cannabis plant, also known as **hemp** (ultimately from the same root), gives its name to the fabric, as both come from Latin *cannabis*. To win a race or competition **by a canvas** is to win it very narrowly. The canvas here is the tapered front end of a racing boat, covered with canvas to keep water out. In the early16th century the verb **canvass** meant 'to toss someone in a canvas sheet', as a punishment or as part of a game. Other early meanings included 'to beat' and 'to criticize severely'. This led on to the idea of discussing an issue, and then to proposing something for discussion. Finally, the word acquired the meaning 'to seek support', as in 'to canvass for votes' at an election.

canyon *see* CANNON

cap [OE] We get our word cap from Latin *cappa* 'hood', which may be related to Latin *caput* 'head'. **Cape** [L16th], 'a cloak', also come from *cappa*, while the geographical **cape** [LME] goes back to *caput*. The same source gives us **chaperone** [LME] first recorded as a hood. A person providing protection or cover by accompanying another, dates from the early 18th century. The saying **if the cap fits, wear it** goes back to a dunce's cap, of the kind that poor performers at school had to wear as a mark of disgrace. Americans use the version **if the shoe fits, wear it**. *See also* CHAPEL

capable [M16th] The first recorded sense of this was 'able to take in', physically or mentally. It comes from Latin *capere* 'take or hold' which is found in many other English words including: **accept** [LME] from *ad-* 'to' and *capere*; **anticipation** [LME] 'acting or taking in advance'; **capacity** [LME] 'ability to hold'; **caption** [LME] originally an act of capture; **captive** [LME]; **catch** [ME]; **chase** [ME]; **conceive** [ME] literally 'take together'; **except** [LME] 'take out of'; **incapacity** [E17th] inability to hold; **intercept** [LME] to take between; **perceive** [ME] to hold entirely; *PRINCE; **receive** [ME] 'take back'; **susceptible** [E17th] literally 'that can be taken from below'.

cape *see* CAP

caper [L16th] Two frisky animals are behind the word caper. It was adapted from **capriole**, a movement performed in riding in which the horse leaps from the ground and kicks out with its hind legs. Its origin was Italian *capriola* 'leap', based on Latin *caper* 'goat'. Members of the Victorian underworld seem to have been the first to use the word in the sense 'an illicit or ridiculous activity'. In an 1867 edition of the *London Herald* a policeman is quoted as saying: 'He'll get five years penal for this little caper.' Edible capers are something quite different—the word comes from Greek *kapparis*. *See also* CAB

capillary *see* DISHEVELLED

capital [ME] The first meaning of capital was 'to do with the head or the top of something'. From this evolved such modern meanings as 'the large form of a letter' and 'the chief city or town in a country'. The word goes back to Latin *caput* 'head'. Capital in the financial sense was originally the **capital stock** of a company or trader, their main or original funds. The use as an adjective meaning 'excellent', now old-fashioned, dates from the mid 18th century. The capital of a column comes via French from Latin *capitellum* 'a little head'. To **capitulate** [M16th] is to admit that you are defeated and surrender. When it first entered the language it meant 'to parley or

canter canticle canvas canyon cap capable

draw up terms', having come via French from medieval Latin *capitulare* 'to draw up under headings'. Like capital, its ultimate root is Latin *caput* 'head', source also of *CAP, *CHAPTER, **chief** [ME], and **captain** [LME], both the 'head' of a group of people, and **decapitate** [E17th].

cappuccino *see* ITALIAN WORD PANEL

caprice [M17th] A caprice and hedgehogs seem far apart but if you put the Italian words *capo* 'head' and *riccio* 'hedgehog' together you get the word *capriccio*, or 'hedgehog-head'—a head with the hair standing on end, like a hedgehog's spines. This is what can happen if you are terrified by something, so *capriccio*, the source of English caprice, came to mean 'horror or shuddering'. Over time this eventually became 'a sudden start, a sudden change', perhaps influenced by Italian *CAPER. *Compare* HORROR

capsule *see* CASE

captain *see* CAPITAL

caption, captive *see* CAPABLE

car [LME] The earliest recorded uses of car, dating probably from the 14th century, referred to wheeled vehicles such as carts or wagons. The word came into English from Old French *carre*, based on Latin *carrus* 'two-wheeled vehicle', the source of words such as *CAREER, **cargo** [M17th], **carriage** [LME], **carry** [LME], **charge** [ME], and **chariot** [LME]. From the 16th to the 19th centuries car was mainly used in poetic or literary contexts to suggest a sense of splendour and solemnity. Alfred Lord Tennyson (1809–1892) used it to describe the funeral carriage bearing the body of the Duke of Wellington (1769–1852) at his state funeral: 'And a reverent people behold / The towering car, the sable steeds' ('Ode on the Death of the Duke of Wellington', 1852). The first self-propelled road vehicle was a steam-driven carriage designed and built in France in 1769, but such vehicles were not called cars until the 1890s.

carafe [L18th] Adopted via French from Italian *caraffa*, carafe is probably based on Arabic *garafa* 'draw water'.

carat [LME] This measure of the purity of gold and a unit of weight for precious stones comes via French from Italian *carato*, from Arabi *kīrāṭ*, a unit of weight. The base is Greek *keration* used for both a **carob** seed and a unit of weight but literally 'little horn' describing the carob's elongated seedpod.

caravan [LME] The first use of caravan was for a group of people travelling together across a desert in Asia or North Africa. The word comes from French *caravane*, from Persian *kārwān*. The sense 'covered horse-drawn wagon' dates from the early 19th century; during this period it also described a third class 'covered carriage' on a railway. A **caravanserai** [L16th] is from Persian *kārwānsarāy*, literally a 'caravan palace': the word is either the same as the early sense of caravan or describes an inn with a central courtyard for travellers. **Van** [E19th] is a shortening of caravan, to which the word also sometimes refers. The earlier van [E17th], 'the foremost part of a group of people', found as part of the phrase **in the van of**, is also an abbreviated form, from **vanguard** [LME], whose first part was from Old French *avant* 'before' (*compare* VAMP). The workman's white van is such a familiar sight that **white van man** has recently entered the language to mean an aggressive male van driver, or more widely an ordinary working man with forthright views.

carbon, carbuncle *see* ANTHRACITE

carcinoma *see* CANCER

card [LME] A medieval word that comes via French *carte* from Latin *charta* 'papyrus leaf or paper', the source of **chart** [L16th], and **charter** [ME]. Its first recorded sense was 'playing card', source of many expressions we use today. To have a **card up your sleeve** is to have a plan or asset that you are keeping secret until you need it. If someone **holds all the cards** in a situation, they are in a very strong position, just like a card player who has a hand guaranteed to win. Someone who is secretive and cautious about their plans or activities might be said to be **keeping their cards close to their chest**. The image here is of a card player trying to prevent the other players from looking at their hand. If you **play your cards right** you make the best use of your assets and opportunities to ensure you get what you want, whereas to **lay your cards on the table** is to be completely open and honest in saying what your intentions are. Rather different from the above expressions is **on the cards** (in the US, **in the cards**), meaning 'possible or likely'. The cards being referred to here are ones used for fortune-telling.

In Britain a person unlucky enough to **get** or **be given their cards** is sacked from their job. The cards referred to are the National Insurance details and other documents that were formerly retained by the employer during a person's employment. A politician who is said to **play the race card** exploits the issue of race or racism for their own ends. The expression originates in a letter written by Lord Randolph Churchill (1849–95) in 1886 on the question of Irish Home Rule. Referring to the Orange Order of Protestant Loyalists, he said that 'the Orange card would be the one to play'.

Charles Dickens (1812–70) was fond of using card in the sense 'an odd or eccentric person', and his *Sketches by Boz* (1836) provides the first written use. It comes from **sure card**, meaning a person who was sure to succeed. **Discard** [L16th] was originally used in relation to rejecting a playing card.

cardiac *see* HEART

cardigan [M19th] This name is from the 7th Earl of Cardigan (1797–1868), leader of the Charge of the Light Brigade, whose troops are thought to have first worn this type of garment during the Crimean War.

cardinal [OE] The connection between a cardinal, 'a senior Roman Catholic priest', and cardinal, 'fundamental, most important', is a door hinge. The word derives from Latin *cardinalis*, from *cardo* 'hinge', and its senses share the idea of something being of pivotal

importance, on which everything else turns or depends.

career [M16th] The core idea behind the various meanings of career is that of progressing along a course of some kind. Based on Latin *carrus*, 'wheeled vehicle' (*see* CAR), career was first used in English to mean both 'a racecourse' and 'a short gallop at full speed, a charge'. From these developed the modern use, for the stages in a person's professional employment, the course of their working life. The verb use, 'to rush headlong, to hurtle', preserves the old sense.

cargo *see* CAR

Caribbean *see* CANNIBAL

carmine *see* VERMILLION

carnage, carnation *see* CARNIVAL

carnival [M16th] Originally a carnival was, in Roman Catholic countries, the period before Lent, a time of public merrymaking and festivities. It comes from medieval Latin *carnelevamen* 'Shrovetide'. The base elements of the Latin word are *caro, carn-* 'flesh' and *levare* 'to put away', before the meat-free fasting of Lent began. There is a popular belief that carnival is from *carne vale*, 'farewell, meat', but this is mistaken. Other flesh-related words that come from *caro* include **carnivorous** [L16th], **carnage** [E17th], **carnation** [L16th] (from the flower's 'fleshy' colour), **carrion** [ME], and **incarnation** [ME].

carob *see* CARAT

carp *see* CARPET

carpaccio *see* ITALIAN WORD PANEL

carpenter [ME] This comes via Old French from late Latin *carpentarius* (*artifex*) 'carriage (-maker)'. The base is late Latin *carpentum* 'wagon', of Gaulish origin.

carpet [ME] Originally tables or beds, not floors, were covered by a carpet, and it is the early 'tablecloth' meaning that is behind the

cardiac cardigan cardinal career cargo

expression **on the carpet**, 'being severely reprimanded by someone in authority'. The phrase originally had the meaning, 'under consideration or discussion', and referred to the covering of a council table, where official documents for discussion were placed. A matter up for discussion at a meeting was on the carpet, just as we might now say **on the table**. The modern sense of carpet is found when you **sweep something under the carpet** to hide or ignore a problem in the hope that it will be forgotten. The word carpet is from old Italian *carpita* 'woollen bedspread', which was based on Latin *carpere* 'to pluck, pull to pieces', the source of **carp** [ME], 'to criticise', and **excerpt** [M16th] 'pull bits out'. *See also* HARVEST

carriage *see* CAR

carrion *see* CARNIVAL

carry *see* CAR

cart [ME] Our word cart, deriving from Old Norse *kartr* and related to *CAR, was originally used to talk about a carriage of any kind, even a chariot, rather than the humble vehicle we are familiar with. If you **put the cart before the horse**, an expression first recorded in the early 16th century, you are doing things in the wrong order. A medieval version was **set the oxen before the yoke**.

carte blanche *see* FRENCH WORD PANEL

cartoon [L16th] Lovers of art will know that cartoons were not originally meant to be funny. They were originally full-size drawings made on paper as a design for a painting, fresco, or tapestry. The word seems to have become attached to cartoons in the modern sense in the 19th century, with the first record of its use coming from the magazine *Punch* in 1843. The word was applied to animated films in the early years of the 20th century. The word is from Italian *cartone*, literally 'big card', from Latin *carta* or *charta*, the source of *CARD. **Carton** [E19th] comes from the same source, but arrived in English via French, as does

cartridge [L16th] both typically made of light cardboard.

case [ME] Case 'an instance' is something that happens or befalls, coming via French from Latin *casus* 'a fall', also the source of **casual** [LME]. The case meaning 'container' is from Old French *casse*, the modern forms of which is *caisse* 'trunk, chest', based on Latin *capsa*, related to *capere* 'to hold' (*see* CAPABLE). Latin *capsa* is also the base of late Middle English **capsule**, a general term at first for 'a small container', and **cash** [L16th] originally meaning 'money-box'. The same base gave rise to late Middle English **casement**, which was first recorded as an architectural term for a hollow moulding.

cash *see* CASE

casino [M18th] Nowadays a casino is chiefly associated with gambling, but originally it was a public room used for dancing and music. The word is borrowed from the Italian for 'little house', which is ultimately from Latin *casa* 'cottage', the source of **chalet** [L18th].

casserole [E18th] This originally French word for a stew, or the pot in which it is cooked, is a diminutive of *casse* 'spoon-like container', from late Latin *cattia* 'ladle, pan' which came in turn from Greek *kuathion* 'little cup'.

cassock [M16th] This clerical garment has a disreputable history. It comes via French *casaque* 'long coat', from Italian *casacca* 'riding coat', probably based on Turkic *kazak* 'vagabond'. A cassock once referred to a long coat worn by some soldiers in the 16th and 17th centuries; the ecclesiastical use appears to have arisen in English in the 17th century.

castanet *see* CHESTNUT

caste [M16th] The general sense in early use was 'race, breed'. It is from Spanish and Portuguese *casta* 'lineage, race, breed', feminine of *casto* 'pure, unmixed', from Latin *castus* 'chaste', also the source of **castigate** [E17th], and **chasten** [M16th] 'make chaste', and **chaste** [ME] itself. The

carriage carrion carry cart carte blanche

common current use is to refer to the hereditary classes of Hindu society: Brahman (priest), Kshatriya (warrior), Vaisya (merchant or farmer), and Sudra (labourer).

castigate *see* CASTE

castle [OE] Castle goes back to Latin *castellum*, 'little fort' from *castrum* 'fort'. To build **castles in the air** is to have daydreams or unrealistic fantasies. It comes from a Latin phrase used by St Augustine, who became bishop of Hippo in North Africa in AD 396. Another version, originally a translation from medieval French, is to build **castles in Spain**. This country was probably chosen because it was a distant place where it would have been extremely unrealistic to build—most of it was under the rule of the Moors at the time the phrase was first used in French.

casual *see* CASE

cat [OE] The original Latin word for cat was *feles*, literally 'she who bears young' and also used of other animals such as polecats that were domesticated to keep down mice. This is the source of our **feline** [L17th]. In the early centuries AD *cattus* appears in Latin. It is generally thought to be Egyptian, as this is where cats were first domesticated, but a Slavic language is another possibility. Most modern European languages used a word derived from this. It is typical of the different roles played in English by words from Latin and Germanic sources that while feline is generally linked with positive words like 'grace', **catty** [L19th] is an insult. **Catgut** [L16th] is typically made from sheep not cats, and may come from a joke about the **caterwauling** [LME], from cat and a word related to 'wail', noise that can be produced from the strings. Cat features in many colourful English expressions. **A cat may look at a king**, meaning 'even a person of low status or importance has rights', is recorded from the mid 16th century. If you **let the cat out of the bag** you reveal a secret, especially carelessly or by

mistake. The French have a similar use of 'bag' in the phrase *vider le sac*, literally 'empty the bag', meaning 'tell the whole story'. **When the cat's away the mice will play** dates from the 15th century. To **put the cat among the pigeons** was first recorded in 1706, and appears then to have referred to a man causing a stir by surprising a group of women. **No room to swing a cat** probably refers not to the animal but to a **cat-o'-nine-tails**, a form of whip with nine knotted cords which was formerly used to flog wrongdoers, especially at sea. Something really good might be called **the cat's whiskers**, **the cat's pyjamas** or, in North America, **the cat's miaou**. Like the **bee's knees**, these expressions were first used in the era of the 'flappers', the 1920s. African-Americans started calling each other **cats** from the middle of the 19th century, a meaning that jazz musicians and fans took up. *See also* WHISKER.

cataclysm *see* CATARACT

catalogue [LME] Catalogue came via Old French and late Latin from Greek *katalogos*, from *katalegein* 'pick out or enrol'.

catamaran [E17th] This word describes a yacht or other boat with twin hulls in parallel; it is from Tamil *kattumaram*, which means literally 'tied wood'.

cataract [LME] Latin *cataracta* (from Greek *kataraktes*, 'rushing down') meant both 'waterfall or floodgate' and 'portcullis'. The first meaning led to the 'large waterfall' sense of the English word cataract, and the second is probably behind the medical sense describing the clouding of the lens of the eye. A person's vision is blocked by this condition as if a portcullis had been lowered over the eye. Other words in English containing *kata* 'down' include **cataclysm** [E17th] from *kluzein* 'to wash'; **catapult** [L16th] from *pallein* 'hurl'; and **catastrophe** [M16th] from *strophē* 'turning'.

catch *see* CAPABLE

Catch-22 In Joseph Heller's 1961 novel *Catch-22* an American air force pilot tries to

castigate castle casual cat cataclysm

avoid dangerous combat missions by feigning insanity. Unfortunately, expressing a desire to avoid combat duty was taken as obvious proof that he was sane, and so fit for duty. The phrase **Catch-22 situation** rapidly entered the language to describe a dilemma or difficulty from which there is no escape because it involves two mutually conflicting or dependent conditions.

category [LME] First used in philosophy, this comes via French or late Latin, from Greek *katēgoria* 'statement, accusation', from *katēgoros* 'accuser'.

caterpillar [LME] The **caterpillar** first appeared in English in the form *catyrpel*, probably an alteration of the Old French word *chatepelose*, literally 'hairy cat'. English used to have a word piller, meaning 'a plunderer or ravager' (related to **pillage**) and, given the damage that caterpillars do to plants, it is likely that this influenced how the word is spelt.

cathedral [ME] First used in the term **cathedral church**, a church containing the bishop's throne, cathedral comes from the Latin word for a seat or throne, *cathedra*, which is also the source of **chair** [ME]. The term **ex cathedra**, meaning 'with the full authority of office', is a reference to the authority of the pope; its literal meaning in Latin is 'from the chair'.

catholic [LME] This comes via Latin from Greek *katholikos* 'universal', with base elements *kata* 'in respect of ' and *holos* 'whole'. The general sense is 'all-embracing'.

catkin [L16th] This is from obsolete Dutch *katteken* 'kitten'.

cattle *see* CHATTEL

cauliflower [L16th] Cauliflower is a modified form of the Italian *cavoli fiori*, literally 'cabbage flowers'—*cavoli* comes from Latin *caulis* 'cabbage', the source also of **kale** [ME]. The original 16th-century English forms *colieflorie* and *cole-flory* had their first element influenced by the **cole** [OE] 'cabbage', and only later was the spelling changed to match the original Latin root.

causeway [LME] The first element of causeway is from *causey*, now an archaic or dialect form, from Anglo-Norman French *causee*, based on Latin *calx* 'lime, limestone'—material used for paving roads. The first recorded sense of *causey* was 'mound, embankment, dam'. A *causeyway* was a way across a mound or, a raised footpath by the side of a road which might be submerged in wet weather: this was then contracted to causeway.

caustic [LME] English caustic came via Latin from Greek *kaustikos*, from *kaiein* 'to burn', also the base of **cauterize** [LME].

cavalcade, cavalier, cavalry *see* CHIVALRY

cave [ME] Latin *cavus*, 'hollow', is the origin of a number of English words, including cave, **cavern** [LME], **cavity** [M16th], and **excavate** [L16th]. **Concave** [LME] is from *cavus* preceded by *con* 'with', while **convex** [L16th] is from the Latin for 'vaulted, arched'. In the days when more people knew Latin, there was a second English word spelled **cave**. This one, pronounced **kah**-vay, meant 'beware!', and was used from the mid 19th century by schoolchildren to warn their friends that a teacher was coming.

cay *see* QUAY

cease *see* CEDE

cede [E16th] *Cede* is from French *céder* or Latin *cedere* 'to yield, give way, go'. *Cedere* is a rich source of English words including **abscess** [M16th] 'going away' (of the infection when it bursts); **access** [Middle English] 'go to'; **ancestor** [ME] someone who went *ante* 'before'; **antecedent** [LME] from the same base as ancestor; **cease** [ME]; **concede** [LME] to give way completely; **decease** [ME] 'go away'; **exceed** [LME] to go beyond a boundary; **intercede** [L16th] go between; **predecessor** [LME] one who went away before; **proceed** [LME] to go forward;

category   caterpillar   cathedral   catholic

recede [LME] 'go back'; and **succeed** [LME] 'come close after'.

ceiling [ME] The reason ceiling has the -ing ending usually associated with action is that it was originally an action, from to *ceil* meaning 'line (the interior of a room) with plaster or panelling', perhaps from Latin *celare*, 'conceal'. The sense describing the upper interior surface of a room, dates from the mid 16th century.

celebrity [LME] A celebrity was originally a solemn ceremony, although the Latin source of celebrity and **celebrate**, from the same period and originally meaning to perform a public religious ceremony, is closer to our modern sense. It comes from Latin *celebritas*, from *celeber* 'frequented or honoured'.

cell [OE] Cell goes back to Latin *cella* 'storeroom, chamber', source also of **cellar** [ME]; in late Latin *cella* also denoted 'a monk's or hermit's cell'. *See also* SALT

cement [ME] This is from Old French *ciment* from Latin *caementum* 'quarry stone'. Cement was originally used for the material added to mortar to make something closer to **concrete**, a term only used for building material from the mid 19th century, but which was used in other senses from Late Middle English. It comes from Latin *concrescere* 'grow together'.

cemetery [LME] A cemetery is literally a place for sleeping. The word came from Greek *koimētērion*, 'dormitory', from *koiman* 'to put to sleep'. It was early Christian writers who first gave it the meaning of 'burial ground', applying it to the underground cemeteries or catacombs in Rome.

cenotaph [E17th] This comes via French and Latin from Greek *kenos* 'empty' and *taphos* 'tomb'.

censor [M16th] This was originally a term for two Roman magistrates whose job was to hold censuses and supervise public

morals. Their job came from *censere* 'assess'. Use to describe someone with the job of inspecting material before publication, dates from the mid 17th century. **Censure** [LME] and **census** [E17th] come from the same root.

cent, centigrade *see* HUNDRED

centre [LME] When you draw a circle with a pair of compasses, you use the point on one of the arms to prick a dot in the centre of the circle. The Greek word *kentron* meant 'sharp point', specifically the one on a pair of compasses, and for this reason the words descended from it, including the English centre, came to refer to the centre of a circle. What is now the American form **center** is in fact the older spelling, found in the works of Shakespeare. It was Dr Johnson's dictionary in 1755 that established centre as the preferred British spelling. **Concentrate** [M17th] literally 'centre together' reached English via Latin.

century [LME] In Latin *centuria* (from *centum* 'hundred') was used to refer to a group of 100, particularly a company in the ancient Roman army, made up of 100 men. Early usage of the English word carried the meaning 'a hundred', as in Shakespeare's 'a century of prayers' in *Cymbeline*. The '100 years' sense dates from the early 17th century, when it was used as a shortened form of the phrase 'a century of years'. A batsman who scores a century in cricket, a hundred runs, perpetuates the older sense. *See also* HUNDRED

cereal [E19th] This is from Latin *cerealis*, from *Ceres*, the name of the Roman goddess of agriculture.

cesspool [L17th] A cesspool, in early use, meant a trap under a drain to catch solids. It is perhaps an alteration, influenced by *pool*, of archaic *suspiral* 'vent, water pipe, settling tank', from Old French *souspirail* 'air hole' from Latin *sub-* 'from below' and *spirare* 'breathe'. Mid 19th-century **cesspit** was formed from cesspool. The old Irish expression **bad cess** meaning 'a curse on' is unconnected. It may be a shortening of assess (*see* SIZE). In the 15th century the native Irish had to supply their English rulers with goods at prices 'assessed' by the government. The shortening **cess** then became a word for 'tax', indicating how fair people thought the assessment was.

c'est la vie *see* FRENCH WORD PANEL

cha(r) *see* TEA

chair *see* CATHEDRAL

chakra *see* WHEEL

chalet *see* CASINO

chalice *see* POISON

chalk [OE] Old English *cealc*, the forerunner of chalk, also meant 'lime'. It came from Latin *calx* 'lime', which is also the source of **calcium** [19th]. When we say **by a long chalk**, meaning 'to a great degree, by far' (and **not by a long chalk**, 'not at all'), the '**long chalk**' refers to the length of a line of chalk marks or tallies drawn on a blackboard. This may originally have been in the context of a pub game, where points scored were marked up on the blackboard, or perhaps in the classroom, with a teacher chalking up pupils' marks for schoolwork. In either case, a long line of chalk marks against your name would mean you were a long way ahead of the others.

challenge [ME] Challenge was first recorded in the senses 'an accusation' and 'to accuse'. The Latin base is *calumnia* 'false accusation', which also gave **calumny** [M16th] 'a false statement damaging someone's reputation' in late Middle English.

chamber *see* CAMERA

chameleon [ME] A *LION and a *GIRAFFE feature in the history of the lizard's name. Chameleon is derived via Latin from Greek *khamaileon*, from *khamai* 'on the ground' and *leōn* 'lion'. So a chameleon was a 'ground lion'. It was often spelled *camelion*, which sometimes got mixed up with **camelopard**, an old word for a giraffe. So

for a time, in the 14th and 15th centuries, a *camelion* was also a name for the giraffe. From the 16th century people have been described as chameleons if they were fickle or continually changing their opinions.

champagne *see* CAMPAIGN

champion [ME] Title-deciding boxing matches are often contested between the challenger and the defending champion, the holder of the title. But, historically, both boxers would have been described as champions, as the word originally meant 'a fighting man'. It came from medieval Latin *campio* 'fighter or gladiator', from Latin *campus* 'a field, place of combat'. *See also* CAMPAIGN

chance [ME] The ultimate source of chance is Latin *cadere* 'to fall', the root of many other words including those listed at *ACCIDENT. In medieval times chance could mean 'an accident' as well as 'the way things happen, fortune'. There are a number of stories associated with the origin of the phrase **chance your arm**, meaning 'to take a risk'. One suggests that it was a slang expression used by tailors who, in rushing the job of sewing in a sleeve, risked the stitches coming loose. Or it may refer to the stripes on the sleeve of a military uniform that indicate a soldier's rank. Doing something that broke military regulations might put you at risk of losing one of your stripes. The most colourful explanation links the phrase with a feud between the Irish Ormond and Kildare families in 1492. According to the story the Earl of Ormond had taken refuge in St Patrick's cathedral in Dublin. The Earl of Kildare, wishing to end the feud and make peace, cut a hole in the cathedral door and put his arm through. The Earl of Ormond accepted his offer of reconciliation and shook his hand rather than cutting it off.

chandelier, chandler *see* CANDLE

change [ME] Change comes via Old French from Latin *cambire*, 'to exchange or barter', found also in **exchange** [LME]. The ultimate origin could be Celtic, which would

c'est la vie char charr chair chakra chalet

mean that the Romans picked up the word when they invaded the lands of the ancient Gauls and Britons. *See also* CHOP, RING

channel *see* CANNON

chant *see* ENCHANT

chaos [LME] A chaos from Greek *khaos* was originally 'a gaping void, chasm'. The word later came to refer to the formless matter out of which the universe was thought to have been formed, from which developed the current meaning, 'utter confusion and disorder'—first used by Shakespeare in *Troilus and Cressida. See also* GAS. In the 1980s scientists pondered the notion that a butterfly fluttering its wings in Rio de Janeiro could start a chain of events that would eventually change the weather in Chicago. They dubbed this **the butterfly effect**. It is a central idea of **chaos theory**, a branch of mathematics that deals with complex systems whose behaviour is highly sensitive to slight changes in conditions.

chap [L16th] A **chap** is now an ordinary man, but he was originally 'a buyer or customer'. The word was an abbreviation of **chapman** 'a pedlar', which came from Old English *ceap*, 'bargaining, trade', also the origin of *CHEAP and of English place names such as Chipping Norton. The current sense dates from early 18th century. *See also* CHOP

chapel [ME] The first place to be called a chapel was named after the holy relic preserved in it, the cape of St Martin. The Latin word *cappella*, meaning 'little cape', was applied to the building itself and eventually to any holy sanctuary. **Chaplain** [ME] is a related word, which referred initially to an attendant entrusted with guarding the cape. The Latin form remains unchanged in the musical term **a cappella**, which means 'sung without instrumental accompaniment' but is literally 'in chapel style'. *See also* CAP

chaperone *see* CAP

chapter [ME] Latin *capitulum* literally meant 'little head' from *caput*, but could also be used to mean, among other things, 'a

heading, a section of writing, a division of a book'. This is the origin of our word chapter, though the immediate source was Old French *chapitre*. If you want **chapter and verse** for a statement or piece of information, you want to be given an exact reference or authority for it. The phrase originally referred to the numbering of passages in the Bible. *See also* CAPITAL

character [ME] This goes back to Greek *kharaktēr* 'a stamping tool'. The first English sense was of a distinguishing mark made on something. By the early 16th century we find 'feature, or trait' from which the modern senses have evolved.

charge, chariot *see* CAR

chariot *see* CAR

charisma [M17th] The first recorded sense of *charisma* was 'a divinely conferred talent'. The word came via ecclesiastical Latin from Greek *kharisma*, from *kharis* 'favour, grace'. The **Charismatic** religious movement has, since the 1930s, gone back to the original sense of the word.

charity [OE] Charity begins at *carus*, the Latin word for 'dear'. This was the base of Latin *caritas*, 'dearness, love', which eventually gave us the English word. The early sense of charity, in the 12th century, was 'Christian love of your fellow men'. The modern sense developed from the fact that supporting the needy is one of the qualities of this. The saying **charity begins at home**, 'a person's first responsibility is for the needs of their own family and friends', dates back to the 14th century. A version in Beaumont and Fletcher's play *Wit without Money* (1625) goes 'Charity and beating begins at home'.

charlatan [E17th] This word first appeared in English, in the early 17th century, as a term for a fast-talking seller of quack remedies. It comes via French from Italian *ciarlatano*, from the verb *ciarlare* 'to babble'.

channel chant chaos chap chapel chaperone

charm [ME] In the Middle Ages a charm was an incantation or magic spell, and did not acquire its meaning of 'a quality of fascinating or being attractive to people' until the 17th century. The word comes from Latin *carmen* 'song or incantation'. *Compare* ENCHANT. In the late 1970s people started talking of politicians mounting a **charm offensive**, a campaign of flattery and friendliness designed to gain the support of others. This is a fine example of an oxymoron, a figure of speech in which apparently contradictory terms appear together.

chart, charter *see* CARD

charver *see* CHAV

charwoman [L16th] The first element of this word is from obsolete *char* or *chare* meaning 'a turn of work, an odd job, chore'. **Chore** [M18th] is a variant.

chase *see* CAPABLE

chasen *see* CASTE

chassis *see* SASH

chaste *see* CASTE

chat [ME] In medieval times chat was formed as a shorter version of **chatter**, which itself started life as an imitation of the sound made by people chatting away, rather as **jabber** [LME] and **twitter** [LME] imitated the sound they described. **The chattering classes** are liberal, well-educated people, often working in the media, who are fond of expressing their views on any and every subject. This name for them has been around since at least the early 1980s. The success of the website called **Twitter** has led to heated debate among users as to whether what they do should be called to twitter or to **tweet** [M19th]—yet another word imitating the sound of birds. *See also* JARGON

chattel [ME] A chattel, now often used in legal contexts as in **goods and chattels**, is 'a personal possession'. The source of the word

is Old French *chatel*, from medieval Latin *capitale*, from Latin *capitalis* 'of the head', from *caput* 'head' (*see* CAPITAL). From the same word comes **cattle** [ME]. At first it was an alternative form of chattel, but one which could also be used specifically for livestock. It started to be used specifically for cows and similar animals in the mid 16th century.

chauffeur [L19th] Early cars could be steam-driven rather than have petrol engines, which explains why this French word literally means 'stoker' from *chauffer* 'to heat'.

chauvinism [L19th] This term for 'exaggerated patriotism' or 'prejudiced support for one's own cause' comes from Nicolas Chauvin, a Napoleonic veteran noted for his extreme patriotism. He was popularized as a character by the Cogniard brothers in a play called *Cocarde Tricolore* (1831). After the fall of Napoleon, the term *chauvin* was used to ridicule any old soldier of the Empire who maintained admiration for the emperor and his acts.

chav [1990s] Baseball cap, fake designer sportswear, cheap jewellery—that is the uniform of the chav, a loutish, obnoxious youth who barged his way into the British consciousness in 2004. Popularized by websites and the tabloid press, the term caught on quickly, and soon women and older people too were being described as chavs. New words appear all the time, but chav caused great excitement to word scholars when it came on the scene. It seems to have been popular around Chatham in Kent during the late 1990s, and some people think that it is an abbreviation of the town's name, while others suggest it comes from the initial letters of 'Council House And Violent'. The most plausible suggestion is that it is from the Romany word *chavi* or *chavo*, 'boy, youth'. The related dialect word **chavvy** 'boy, child' was used in the 19th century and is still occasionally in use. The northeast variant of **chav**, **charver**, has been around since at least the 1960s, and **chav** can mean 'mate, pal' in Scots dialect. Chav was

charm chart charter charver charwoman

probably knocking around as an underground expression for a long time before it was taken up as a new way of insulting people. *See also* ROMANY WORD PANEL

cheap [OE] Nowadays something that is cheap is inexpensive or of low value. In Old English, though, *ceap* (derived from Latin *caupo* 'small trader, innkeeper') meant 'bargaining or trade'. *CHAP is based on the same word. The obsolete phrase **good cheap** meant 'a good bargain', and it is from this that the modern sense developed. In place names such as Cheapside and Eastcheap, cheap means 'market'. If you say that something is **cheap at the price**, you mean that it is well worth having regardless of the cost. A stronger alternative version of this is **cheap at twice the price**, and you will also hear the confusing inversion **cheap at half the price**.

cheat [LME] This started out as a shortening of **escheat**, a legal term for the reverting of property to the state when the owner dies without heirs. As an extension of this, the word came to mean 'to confiscate', and then 'to deprive someone of something unfairly'. Finally, the senses 'to practise deception' and 'to try to get an advantage by breaking the rules' came to the fore.

check [ME] Chess has given the word check its oldest meanings. It came into English via Old French *eschec* from Persian *šāh* 'king' (the origin of **shah**, as in the Shah of Iran), and was first used by chess players to announce that the opponent's king had been placed under attack. From there the meaning gradually broadened to 'to stop, restrain, or control' and 'to examine the accuracy of'. A squared pattern is described as **checked** or a **check** [LME] because of the appearance of a chessboard. **Checkmate** derives from Persian *šāh māt*, 'the king is dead'. **Chess** [ME] itself came into English during the 12th century from Old French *eschec*, or rather its plural form, *esches*, but probably goes back ultimately to the ancient Indian language Sanskrit. The game seems to have begun in India or China around the

6th century AD and to have been adopted in Persia, spreading to the West through the Arabs. The game was popular in medieval England. *See also* EXCHEQUER.

cheek [OE] The Old English word cheek, meaning both cheek and jaw, came to mean 'rude or disrespectful behaviour' in the mid 19th century. The sense probably comes from the idea of a person's cheeks moving as he rudely answers a superior back. **Cheeky** was first used around the same time. The affectionate reprimand **you cheeky monkey!** is particularly common in Lancashire, and is often used by the barmaid Betty Turpin in the ITV soap opera *Coronation Street*. A variation of the expression was popularized in the 1950s by the comedian Al Read, whose catchphrase was 'Right, monkey!' In **cheek by jowl**, meaning 'very close together', **jowl** [OE] simply means 'cheek'. In fact the original form of the phrase was **cheek by cheek**. To **turn the other cheek** is to make a deliberate decision to remain calm and not to retaliate when you have been attacked or insulted. The expression comes from the Gospel of Matthew: 'But I say to ye, That ye resist not evil; but whosoever shall smite thee on thy right cheek, turn to him the other.'

cheer [ME] In medieval English the word cheer meant 'face', coming ultimately from Greek *kara* 'head'. People came to use it to refer to the expression on someone's face, and hence to their mood or demeanour. This could be in either a positive or negative sense; you could talk, for example, about a person's 'sorrowful cheer' or 'heavy cheer'. '**What cheer?**' was once a common greeting meaning 'how are you?', and in the 19th century this eventually became worn down to **wotcha**. Over time cheer developed the specific meaning of 'a good mood' and then 'a shout of encouragement or joy'. A **Bronx cheer** is a rude noise made by blowing through closed lips with the tongue between them—what is also called a *RASPBERRY.

cheap   cheat   check   cheek   cheer

cheese *see* BIG

chemist [LME] The word **alchemy** [LME] was a medieval science that looked to transform matter, in particular to convert base metals into gold or find a universal 'elixir of life'. It was the medieval equivalent of chemistry, and was also the origin of the word. Alchemy came via Old French and medieval Latin from Arabic *al-kīmiyā*, which was from Greek *khēmia* 'the art of transforming metals'. *See also* ELIXIR

chenille [M18th] This term for a tufty velvety yarn is a use of a French word meaning 'hairy caterpillar', from Latin *canicula* 'small dog', the connection being the fur of all three.

cherry [ME] Cherry comes from Old French *cherise*, and at first *cheris(e)* was the English word for the fruit too. When people heard this word they seem to have thought that it must be a plural and so decided that the word for one of these fruit was cherry. *PEA is another example of the same process. The cherry is one of the few fruits native to Britain, and although delicious it has a short fruiting season. For these reasons it represents something pleasant or desirable in a number of common expressions.
To have **two bites** (or **a second bite**) **at the cherry** is to have more than one attempt or chance to do something. An extremely pleasant or enjoyable experience can be described as **a bowl of cherries**. And the **cherry on the cake** is an attractive feature that provides the finishing touch.

cherub [OE] Old English cherubin is ultimately (via Latin and Greek) from Hebrew *kerūb*, plural *kerūbīm*. A rabbinic folk etymology, which explains the Hebrew singular form as representing Aramaic *ke-rabyā* 'like a child', led to the representation of the cherub as a child.

chess *see* CHECK

chest [OE] The Greek word *kistē*, 'box or basket', is the source of chest. Not until the 16th century was the same word applied to the part of your body enclosed by the ribs and breastbone, acting as a protective 'box' for the heart, lungs, and other organs. **Cistern** [ME] is from the same root.

chestnut [E16th] Chestnuts have nothing to do with chests—the ultimate source is the Greek word *kastanea* 'chestnut' (ultimate source also of the Spanish **castanets** [E17th], presumably from the shape). A frequently repeated joke or story is known as **an old chestnut**. First recorded in the 1880s, the phrase probably comes from a play called *The Broken Sword*, written by William Dimond in 1816. In one scene a character called Zavior is in the throes of telling a story: 'When suddenly from the thick boughs of a cork tree—'. At this point he is interrupted by another character, Pablo, who says: 'A chestnut, Captain, a chestnut . . . Captain, this is the twenty-seventh time I have heard you relate this story, and you invariably said, a chestnut, till now.'

chic [M19th] Adopted from French, chic 'elegantly fashionable' is probably from German *Schick* 'skill'.

chicane [L17th] A chicane describes a sharp double bend forming an obstacle on a motor racing track; it is also an old word for **chicanery** [L16th] 'trickery'. The origin is the French noun *chicane*, and verb *chicaner* 'quibble', but earlier details are unknown.

chicken [OE] A word that probably has the same ancient root as *COCK. **Don't count your chickens before they're hatched** is recorded from the 16th century, and refers to one of Aesop's fables of 2,000 years earlier, in which a girl carrying a pail of milk to market dreams about buying chickens with the profit from the milk and becoming rich through selling eggs. In her daydream she sees herself as being so wealthy that she would simply toss her head at all her would-be lovers, at which point she tosses her head and spills the milk.

cheese   chemist   chenille   cherry   cherub

Chickens coming home to roost is a form of the proverb, dating from the 14th century, **curses, like chickens, come home to roost**.

chief *see* CAPITAL

chiffon [M18th] This word was originally used in the plural, for trimmings or ornaments on a woman's dress. It is from French, from *chiffe* 'rag'.

child [OE] In Anglo-Saxon times child frequently meant a newborn baby, a sense we retain in **childbirth** [M16th]. In the 16th century child was sometimes used to specify a female infant: 'A very pretty bairn. A boy or a child, I wonder?' (Shakespeare, *The Winter's Tale*). On a similar theme, the familiar saying **children should be seen and not heard** was applied originally not to children but to young women. It was described as early as 1400 as 'an old English saw' (or saying) in the form 'A maid should be seen, but not heard'. It was not until the 19th century that children became the subject.

chime *see* CYMBAL

chimney [ME] A chimney was at first 'a fireplace or furnace' and comes via Old French from late Latin *caminata*, perhaps from *camera caminata* 'room with a fireplace', via Latin *caminus* 'forge, furnace' from Greek *kaminos* 'oven'.

chin-chin *see* CHINESE WORD PANEL

chintz [E17th] Chintz was originally a painted or stained calico, imported from India. The source was the Hindi word *chīmṭ*, literally 'spattering, stain', which in English became *chint*. The plural of this unfamiliar word, being more frequently used, came over time to be mistaken for a singular and written *chints* and eventually chintz. The related word **chintzy** [M19th] means 'resembling or decorated with chintz' in British English, but in America means both 'cheap and of poor quality' and 'miserly, mean'.

chip [ME] The word chip was probably formed from an Old English word, *forchippian*, 'to cut off'. A person who is thought to resemble one of their parents in character or behaviour can be described as **a chip off the old block**. The phrase was originally found in the forms **chip *of* the same block** and **chip of the old block**, so that the person appeared made from the same material. To **have a chip on your shoulder** is to be aggressively sensitive about something, usually some long-standing grievance or cause of resentment. The expression is first recorded in American English. An explanation can be found in an early example from the *Long Island Telegraph* of 20 May 1830: 'When two churlish boys were determined to fight, a chip [of wood] would be placed on the shoulder of one, and the other demanded to knock it off at his peril.'

Another meaning of chip is 'a counter used in gambling games, representing money', and such gambling chips, especially as used in the game of poker, feature in a number of common phrases. If someone **has had their chips**, they are beaten or out of contention. The idea is of having run out of gambling counters or chips with which to place a stake. Similarly, **when the chips are down** you find yourself in a very serious and difficult situation. To **cash in your chips** is to die—you are no longer 'in the game'.

Deep-fried slices of potato have been known as **chips** since the time of Dickens. You might think of the phrase **cheap as chips** as being a recent invention, but it, too, goes back to at least the 1850s, when it was used in an advert in *The Times*.

chipolata [L19th] Chipolata sausages have nothing to do with chips—their name comes from Italian *cipollata*, meaning 'flavoured with onion' (the Italian for 'onion' is *cipolla*, which is related to English **chives** [LME]). And **chipmunk** [M19th] is also a completely different word, from the Native American language Ojibwa.

chisel *see* SCISSORS

chit *see* RAJ WORD PANEL

chief   chiffon   child   chime   chimney

All the tea in China

Chinese *civilization stretches back at least to the 3rd millennium* BC. *It is the source of many of the world's great inventions, including paper, the compass, gunpowder, and printing, not to mention china (porcelain) itself.*

BUT maybe the greatest contribution that the country and its language have made to the Western world is **tea**. The drink is first mentioned in English in 1655. The Chinese source *chá* also gives us the slang term **char**, as in 'a nice cup of char', used from the early years of the 20th century. The Chinese connection is remembered in the emphatic refusal **not for all the tea in China**, first found in US English in the early 20th century.

People drinking something stronger than tea might say **chin-chin**, or 'cheers!' This is a mangled pronunciation of *qing qing*, a Chinese greeting. Another 'doubled' word is **chop-chop**, or 'quickly'. *Chop* here is a pidgin Chinese rendition of Chinese *kuai* 'quick, nimble', and is also found in **chopstick**.

Our range of savoury relishes was extended when traders introduced us to **ketchup** at the end of the 17th century. The name may come from Chinese *k'ē chap* 'tomato juice'. Contact with imperial China in the early 19th century introduced Westerners to the Chinese custom of **kowtowing**—kneeling down and touching the forehead on the ground in worship or submission. The word means literally 'to knock the head'.

Ginseng is a plant whose root is credited with various health-giving and medicinal properties. Its Chinese name, *rénshén*, literally means 'man root', a reference to the root's forked shape, which supposedly resembles a person.

Gung-ho, meaning 'unthinkingly enthusiastic and eager, especially about fighting', dates from the Second World War. It is from Chinese *gōnghé* 'to work together', and was adopted as a slogan by the US Marines fighting in the Pacific under General Evans Carlson (1896–1947). He organized 'kung-hoi' meetings to discuss problems and explain orders to promote cooperation.

Increasing interest in our living spaces in the 1990s led to the popularity of **feng shui**, the ancient Chinese system of designing buildings and arranging objects in rooms to achieve a positive flow of energy and so bring happiness or good luck. It goes back a long way in English, and even had an entry in the *Encyclopaedia Britannica* of 1797. Not all our Chinese words are ancient, though. China's first manned space flight in 2003 gave us **taikonaut**, a Chinese astronaut—*taikong* means 'outer space'.

See also MANDARIN, TYPHOON, YEN

chiv *see* ROMANY WORD PANEL

chivalry [ME] The word chivalry springs from the fact that a knight rode a horse. Chivalry came into English from medieval Latin *caballerius*, which was based on Latin *caballus* 'horse'. **Cavalry** [M16th], **cavalier** [M16th], and **cavalcade** [L16th] come from the same Latin word. In its early use chivalry could describe knights, noblemen, and horsemen collectively, as in 'The eleven kings with their chivalry never turned back' wrote Thomas Malory (1405–1471) in *Le Morte D'Arthur* (1485). Later it came to refer to the qualities associated with an ideal knight, especially courage, honour, loyalty, and courtesy.

chives *see* CHIP

chivvy [L18th] This is probably from the ballad *Chevy Chase*, celebrating a skirmish (probably the battle of Otterburn in 1388) on the Scottish border. Chevy and chivy are early spellings. It was originally used as a word for a hunting cry; later to mean 'a pursuit', and so developed the sense 'to chase, worry' in the mid 19th century.

chocaholic *see* WORK

chock [ME] A chock, as in **'chocks away!'**, is a wedge or block placed against a wheel to prevent it from moving or to support it. It is probably from Old French *çouche* or *çoche*, meaning 'block or log'. **Chock-a-block** [M19th], 'crammed full', was originally a nautical expression which referred to a pair of pulley blocks with ropes threaded between to form a hoist or tackle—when they have been pulled so close together that the two blocks touch, further lifting is impossible. The expression was probably influenced by **chock-full**, a much older term meaning 'filled to overflowing'. Where this comes from is uncertain, though 'chock' here may have been a form of **choke** (ME from Old English *ceoce* 'jaw'), from the idea of being so full that you are almost choking.

chocolate [E17th] The first recorded use in English is as a drink made from chocolate; it was a fashionable drink in the 17th and 18th centuries. Samuel Pepys wrote in his diary in 1664: 'To a Coffee-house, to drink jocolatte, very good.' The word comes from French *chocolat* or Spanish *chocolate*, from Nahuatl (the language spoken by the Aztecs of Mexico) *chocolatl* 'food made from cacao seeds'. **Cacao** [M16th] and **cocoa** [E18th] are basically the same word, also from Nahuatl. Not from Mexico, though, is the expression **I should cocoa**. It is cockney rhyming slang for 'I should say so'.

choir [ME] The early spellings with a 'q' are from Old French *quer*, from Latin **chorus** (which entered English in the mid 16th century). The spelling change in the 17th century was due to association with the Latin. The spelling variant *quire* has never been altered in the English Prayer Book ('In Quires and Places where they sing, here followeth the Anthem').

choke *see* CHOCK

chokey [E17th] This slang term for 'prison' first appears in English in the original Hindi sense 'customs or toll house, police station'. The word is Anglo-Indian, from Hindi *caukī*, influenced by *choke*.

cholera, choleric, cholesterol *see* MELANCHOLY

chop [OE] In the sense 'to cut something into small pieces' chop is a variant of the closely related word **chap** [LME], 'to become cracked and sore'. Similarly, while a **choppy** sea nowadays is one with the surface broken up by many small waves, in the early 17th century the adjective meant 'full of cracks or clefts'. To **chop and change** is to keep changing your opinions or behaviour without warning and often for no good reason. Both chop and *CHANGE could once mean 'barter or exchange', and they were used in this phrase (which originally meant 'to buy and sell') from the 15th century onwards. As time went on, change came to be interpreted in its more usual sense, with chop reinforcing the idea of abruptness.

Australians and New Zealanders refer to something not very good as being **not**

chiv chivalry chives chivvy chocaholic chock

much chop. The chop here is a different word, which comes from Hindi *chāp* 'stamp, brand'. Europeans in the Far East used the Hindi word for documents such as passports which were given an official stamp, and it came to mean something that was genuine or had quality or class.

The word **chopstick** [L17th] is from a quite different word again, being based on the Chinese dialect term *kuaizi*, meaning 'nimble ones'. The *chop-* part (*kuai* in Chinese) means 'quick'—hence **chop-chop** [M19th], also originally based on a Chinese dialect expression. *See also* CHINESE WORD PANEL

chord [ME] The sense of a group of musical notes was originally spelt cord and was a shortening of **accord** [ME] in the sense 'bring into harmony', which came from Latin *accordere* literally 'to bring to heart'. The **accordion** [M19th] ultimately gets its name from the same source. The sort of chord found in mathematics is also a respelling of **cord**, but this time in the sense 'rope'. This was a Middle English word from Latin *chorda*, which came in turn from Greek *khorde* 'gut, string of a musical instrument'. The spellings of both chords was changed to be more like their classical sources.

chore *see* CHARWOMAN

chortle [1872] This was coined by Lewis Carroll (1832–98) in *Through the Looking Glass*; and is probably a blend of *chuckle* and *snort*.

chorus *see* CHOIR

chrome [E19th] This metal was given its name from Greek *khrōma* 'colour', because of the brilliant colours of chromium compounds.

chronic [LME] Words beginning **chron-** have something to do with time: the root being Greek *khronos* 'time'. A chronic illness is one that persists for a long time. In informal British English the word can also mean 'of very poor quality', as in 'the film was chronic',

a sense developing from the idea of unending tedium. *See also* ANACHRONISM, CRONY

chronicle, chronological, chronometer *see* ANACHRONISM

chubby [E17th] This originally meant 'short and thickset like a chub', a **chub** [LME] being a thick-bodied European river fish. The origin of its name is unknown.

chuck [L16th] This informal word meaning 'throw' is the same as the one meaning 'touch (someone) playfully under the chin', probably from Old French *chuquer*, 'to knock, bump' (of unknown ultimate origin). The chuck [L17th] of a drill is a variant of *CHOCK, with **chunk** [L17th] another variant. The phrase **the chuck** expressing rejection (**give somebody the chuck**) dates from the late 19th century, while the sense 'to vomit' is an Australianism from the mid 20th century.

chuffed [1950s] If you are really pleased or satisfied you are chuffed. This word dates from the 1950s and is from the English dialect word **chuff** [E17th] meaning 'plump or pleased'. To confuse matters, though, there is an entirely different dialect use of chuff [M19th] with the opposite meaning of 'surly or gruff'. So for a while chuffed was also being used to mean 'displeased or disgruntled': 'Don't let on they're after you, see, or she'll be dead chuffed, see? She don' like the law.' (Celia Dale, *Other People*, 1964). Chuff in the sense of the nether regions is another slang word from the mid 20th century of unknown origin.

chum [L17th] Before it came to mean 'a friend', chum was a slang word, used at Oxford University, for 'a room-mate'. It was probably a shortened form of **chamber-fellow**. *See also* CRONY

chunder *see* AUSTRALIAN WORD PANEL

chunk *see* CHUCK

chord chore chortle chorus chrome chronic

church [OE] The Old English word church, then spelled *circe* or *cirice*, is related to German *Kirche*, Dutch *kerk*, and Scots **kirk** [ME]. The source of all these words is medieval Greek *kurikon*, from Greek *kuriakon dōma*, 'Lord's house', based on *kurios* 'master or lord'.

churl, churlish *see* EARL

chute [E19th] The word chute 'sloping channel' was originally a North American usage; it is a French word originally meaning 'fall' (referring to water or rocks) from Latin *cadere* 'to fall'. The word in English has been influenced by shoot.

chutzpah *see* YIDDISH WORD PANEL

cider [ME] Cider goes back to Greek *sikera*, a word used by Christian writers to translate Hebrew *sēkār*, which meant 'strong drink'.

cigar [E18th] Cigar is from French *cigare*, or from Spanish *cigarro*, probably from Mayan *sik'ar* 'smoking'. Mid 19th-century **cigarette** 'little cigar' was also adopted from French. The abbreviation **ciggy** dates from the 1960s.

cinch [M19th] The first recorded use of cinch, 'something that is easy to achieve', was as a term for a girth of a saddle that was made from separate twisted strands of horsehair. It was used in Mexico and the western USA, and is a Spanish word. The link between the original meaning and the modern one is the idea of having a firm or secure hold on something.

cinema [E20th] A cinema shows moving pictures, and movement is the root idea of the word. The Greek verb *kinein* 'to move' (the source of **kinetic** [M19th] and other *kine-* words related to movement) is the base, and was used by the French brothers Auguste and Louis Jean Lumière to form the word *cinématographe* for their invention of an apparatus that showed moving pictures, which they patented in 1895. *Cinématographe* was anglicized to **cinematograph**, which in turn was abbreviated to **cinema**, first recorded in English in 1909.

circle [OE] The root of circle is Latin *circulus* 'small ring', from *circus* 'ring', the source of our word **circus** [LME]. A Roman circus was a rounded or oval arena lined with tiers of seats, where chariot races, gladiatorial combats, and other, often cruel, contests took place. Names like Piccadilly Circus were attached to open, more or less circular areas in towns where streets converged. Other words from the same root include **circuit** [LME] from Latin *circum ire* 'go around', and **circulate** [LME] 'move in a circular path'. **Come** or **turn full circle** is a reference to 'The Wheele is come full circle' in Shakespeare's *King Lear*. The wheel is the one thought of as being turned by the goddess Fortune and symbolizing change.

circuit, circulate *see* CIRCLE

circumference [LME] A circle's circumference is the boundary or line that encloses it. The term comes via Old French from Latin *circumferentia*. Formed from *circum*, 'around', and *ferre*, 'to carry'. English words beginning **circum-** all share some idea of 'going around' in their meaning. To **circumscribe** [LME] comes from Latin *circum* and *scribere* 'to write', **circumspect** [LME] literally means 'looking around', and **circumcise** [ME] 'to cut round'. If you **circumvent** a problem (from Latin *venire* 'to come'), you find a way round it, and if you **circumnavigate** [E17th] the world you sail round it. **Circumstances** [ME] come from Latin *cimcumstare*, 'stand around'.

circumflex *see* ACCENT

circus *see* CIRCLE

cistern *see* CHEST

cite *see* RECITE

city [ME] This is from Old French *cite*, from Latin *civitas*, from *civis* 'citizen'. From the same root come **civic** [M16th], **civility** [LME], **civilian** [LME], and **civilization** [E18th].

church churl churlish chute chutzpah

claim [Middle English] Latin *clamare* 'to call out' is the base of English claim. It also gives us **acclaim** [E17th] from *ad-* 'to' and *clamare* 'to shout', and **reclaim** [ME]. This was first used as a falconry term in the sense 'recall'. The sense 'make land suitable for cultivation' is recorded from the mid 18th century. **Clamour** [LME] comes from the same source.

clairvoyant [L17th] This was first recorded as meaning 'clear-sighted, perceptive', adopted from French *clair* 'clear' and *voyant* 'seeing' (from *voir* 'to see'). The sense of someone with the ability to perceive events in the future dates from the mid 19th century.

clam [E16th] It is not easy to prise apart a clam, and this tight grip lies behind the origin of the word. Clam originally meant 'a clamp', and probably had the same source as **clamp** [ME]. There is also an English dialect word clam, meaning 'to be sticky or to stick to something', which is related to **clay** [OE]. It is also where **clammy**—originally spelled *claymy*—comes from. *See also* HAPPY

clamour *see* CLAIM

clamp *see* CLAM

clan [LME] Clan is from Scottish Gaelic *clann* 'offspring, family', from Old Irish *cland*, derived from Latin *planta* 'sprout'.

clanger *see* DROP

clap *see* RAP

claptrap *see* POPPYCOCK

claret [LME] The Old French term *vin claret* 'clear wine' was originally applied to a light red or yellowish wine, as distinct from either a red or white wine. Claret was used in English with this meaning until around 1600, when people started using the word to talk about red wines generally. Nowadays the term refers particularly to the red wines imported from Bordeaux. In books or films about London gangsters you might come across claret used as a slang term for 'blood'.

This goes back at least as far as 1604, and was originally boxing slang.

clarinet [mid 18th century] This musical term is from French *clarinette*, a diminutive of *clarine* denoting a kind of bell; it is related to Middle English **clarion** originally 'a shrill narrow-tubed war trumpet', from medieval Latin *clario(n-)*, from Latin *clarus* 'clear'. From the same source come *CLARET, **clarity**, **clarify**, **clear**, and **declare**; all Middle English.

clay *see* CLAM

clean [OE] To **make a clean breast of it** is to confess all of your mistakes or wrongdoings. People used to think that the breast, or chest, was where a person's conscience was located.

In the proverb **cleanliness is next to godliness**, 'next' means 'immediately following'. The saying is quoted by John Wesley in one of his sermons, on the subject of dress: 'Slovenliness is no part of religion . . . Cleanliness is indeed next to godliness' (1791).

clear *see* CLARINET

cleave *see* CLOVE

clew *see* CLUE

climate [LME] This is from late Latin *clima*, *climat-*, from Greek *klima* 'slope, zone'. The term originally meant a zone of the earth between two lines of latitude, then any region of the earth, and later its atmospheric conditions.

climax [M16th] The word was first used in rhetoric for a number of propositions set forth in a series, increasing in force or effectiveness of expression. It comes from Greek *klimax* 'ladder, climax'. The sense 'culmination' arose in the late 18th century from popular misuse of the learned word.

clinic [M19th] Clinic is first recorded as the 'teaching of medicine at the bedside'. It is from French *clinique*, from Greek *klinikē (tekhnē)* 'bedside (art)', from *klinē* 'bed'.

claim clairvoyant clam clamour clamp clan

cloak [LME] The source of cloak was Old French *cloke*, a variant of *cloche* meaning 'bell' and, because of its shape, 'cloak'. The ultimate origin is medieval Latin *clocca* 'bell'. *See also* CLOCK. The expression **cloak-and-dagger** is used of plotting, intrigue, and espionage. As **cloak-and-sword**, a translation of the French phrase *de cape et d'épée*, it dates from the early 19th century. It originally referred to stories and plays featuring intrigue or melodramatic adventure, in which the main characters tended to wear a cloak and a dagger or a sword. The idea is, however, older: Chaucer wrote of **the smiler with the knife beneath his cloak**.

clobber [M20th] The clobber meaning 'to hit someone hard or defeat them completely' dates from the Second World War. Although the origin is not certain, it seems to have been RAF slang, and probably described striking a place hard in a bombing raid. The other sense of clobber, 'clothing or belongings', is a different word which dates from the late 19th century and is again of unknown origin.

clock [LME] Like *CLOAK, clock comes from medieval Latin *clocca* 'bell'. The English word originally meant 'bell', later taking on the sense 'the striking mechanism of a watch'. Gradually clock came to be applied not to the sound made by an instrument for telling the time but to the instrument itself. The verb sense 'to punch or hit in the face', first recorded in the 1920s, is originally Australian and comes from the slang use of clock to mean 'a person's face' (*see also* DIAL). The meaning 'to notice or watch', from the 1930s, refers to a person checking the time on a clock.

clockwise *see* WISE

clog [ME] The earliest meaning of clog was 'a block of wood', especially one fastened to the leg or neck of an animal to stop it moving too far. The term for a wooden-soled shoe is nearly as early and probably first referred to the thick wooden sole alone. The verb was first used to mean 'to hamper something', and from this developed the idea of hindering free passage through something by blocking it. Clogs were formerly worn by factory and manual workers in the north of England. **From clogs to clogs in three generations** is said to be a Lancashire proverb, meaning that it takes one generation to found a business, the next to build it, and the third to spend the profits, leaving the family penniless again.

clone [E20th] The word clone, from Greek *klōn* 'twig, cutting from a plant', is first recorded in 1903, when it referred to a group of plants produced by taking cuttings or grafts from an original. It has been used in the context of the genetic duplication of mammals since the early 1970s. Nowadays it is also used for someone who slavishly imitates someone else and for a computer that simulates another more expensive model. In gay culture a clone is a gay man who adopts an exaggeratedly macho appearance and style of dress.

closet [LME] Although closet is now the usual word in American English for a *CUPBOARD or wardrobe, it originally referred to a small private room, such as one for study or prayer. This idea of privacy led to the sense of hiding a fact or keeping something secret, which goes right back to the beginning of the 17th century. A person who is hiding the fact that they are gay has been described as **in the closet**, or as a closet homosexual, since the late 1960s. To **out** someone, meaning to reveal that they are gay, is a shortened way of saying 'to force them out of the closet'. Closet comes from **close** [ME], which both in the sense 'near' and 'shut' go back to Latin *claudere* 'to shut', also the source of **recluse** [ME], someone who shuts themselves away.

clot *see* CLOUD

cloud [OE] The Old English word cloud was first used to refer to a mass of rock or earth, and is probably related to **clot** [OE]. Only around the end of the 13th century did the meaning 'visible mass of condensed watery vapour' develop, presumably because people could see a resemblance in shape between a cloud and rocks.

cloak clobber clock clockwise clog clone

On cloud nine you are extremely happy. A possible source of the expression is the classification of clouds given in a meteorological guide published in 1896 called the *International Cloud Atlas*. According to this guide there are ten basic types of cloud, cumulonimbus being the one numbered nine. **Cumulonimbus** clouds are the ones that form a towering fluffy mass. They get their name from Latin *cumulus* 'a heap' found also in **accumulate** [LME]. 'Cloud nine' is said to have been popularized by the Johnny Dollar radio show in the USA during the 1950s. Johnny Dollar was a fictional insurance investigator who got into a lot of scrapes. Every time he was knocked unconscious he was taken to 'cloud nine', where he recovered. **Cloud cuckoo land** is a translation of Greek *Nephelokokkugia* (from *nephelē* 'cloud' and *kokkux* 'cuckoo'). This was the name the ancient Greek dramatist Aristophanes gave to the city built by the birds in his comedy *The Birds*. According to the proverb **every cloud has a silver lining**, even the gloomiest outlook contains some hopeful or consoling aspect. The saying is recorded from the 19th century, though John Milton expresses a similar sentiment in *Comus* in 1643: 'Was I deceiv'd or did a sable cloud / Turn forth her silver lining on the night?'

clove [ME] You might have two different types of clove in your kitchen cupboard, one in a jar on the spice rack and one in a garlic bulb. These are two different words. The spice clove comes from Old French *clou de girofle* (source of the name **gillyflower** for the similarly scented pink), meaning 'nail of the clove tree'. You can see why—cloves look like nails. The clove of garlic is an Old English word related to **cleave** [OE] and **cloven** [ME].

clown [M16th] The earliest recorded uses of clown means 'an unsophisticated country person'. Before long it was being applied to any rude or ill-mannered person, and by 1600 the word was also being used to refer to the character of a fool or jester in a stage play, from which the comic entertainer in a circus developed. For some reason

quite a few people seem to be afraid of clowns, and a word for the condition has been coined **coulrophobia**. The first element was borrowed from a Greek word for a stilt-walker, clowns not being known in the classical world.

club [ME] In the sense 'a heavy stick with a thick end' club comes from Old Norse *clubba*, and is related to **clump** [ME]. The use of the word to refer to a society or association of people who share a particular interest dates from the early 17th century. It appears to have derived gradually from the idea of a group of people forming into a mass like the thick end of a club.

clue [LME] Our word clue is a modern spelling of the old word **clew**, 'a ball of thread'. The idea here is of string or thread being used to guide a person out of a maze by tracing a path through it. The most famous example is that of the Greek hero Theseus, who killed the monstrous bull-headed Minotaur in its lair and then escaped from the Labyrinth, an underground maze of tunnels. This he was able to do because the princess Ariadne gave him a ball of twine, which he unravelled as he went in and followed back to find his way out again. From this a clue became anything that you can follow to get a solution.

clump *see* CLUB

coach [M16th] Coaches get the name from a small town in Hungary. The first vehicles to be called coaches were horse-drawn carriages, which in the 16th and 17th centuries were usually royal state vehicles. The word comes from French *coche*, from Hungarian *kocsi szekér*, which means 'wagon from Kocs', the town of Kocs being renowned for making carriages and wagons. When other, similar forms of transport such as railway carriages and single-decker buses were invented, in the 1830s and 1920s respectively, they were called coaches too. The use of the word to refer to a tutor (and later a trainer in sport) is related to the above meanings, based on the idea that a

clove   clown   club   clue   clump   coach

tutor 'carries' or 'drives' a student through an examination.

coal [OE] The Old English word *col* meant 'a glowing ember' rather than the substance that burns. The expression **haul over the coals** is a metaphorical extension of what was once an all-too-real form of torture. Coal from Newcastle upon Tyne in northeast England was abundant long before the Industrial Revolution, and to **carry** (or **take**) **coals to Newcastle** for something redundant has been an expression since the mid 17th century.

coalesce *see* ALIMONY

coast [ME] The Latin word *costa* meant 'rib or side', which is why coast meant 'rib' and 'the side of the body' from Anglo-Saxon days right up until the start of the 19th century. The sense is still found in French *côte de porc* (where the ˆ stands for a lost 's') for 'pork chop' referring to the rib bone, and in the word **cutlet** [E18th] 'a little *côte*'. The phrase **coast of the sea**—meaning 'side of the sea'—gave rise to the modern use, 'the part of the land adjoining the sea'. The verb originally meant 'to move along the edge of something' and 'to sail along the coast'. **The coast is clear** originally signalled that there were no enemies or coastguards guarding a sea coast who would prevent an attempt to land or embark by sailors or smugglers.

cob [LME] A small word with many distinct meanings, among them a loaf of bread, the central part of an ear of corn, a male swan, and a short-legged horse. What these senses all have in common is probably the underlying idea of being stout, rounded, or sturdy. The word, which may be related to Old English *copp* 'top or head', was originally used to refer to a strong man or leader. **Cobble** [LME], a rounded stone used for paving, derives from cob. **Cobbler** [ME], 'a person who mends shoes', is unconnected, and its origin is not known, although it is related to **cobble** meaning 'to repair shoes' and 'to assemble roughly'. **Cobblers**, 'rubbish', is rhyming slang from **cobbler's awls**, 'balls'.

cobalt [L17th] Cobalt is a hard silvery-white magnetic metal, often found in the ground alongside deposits of silver. The name comes from German *Kobalt*, a variation of the word *Kobold* meaning 'goblin or demon', and perhaps related to *GOBLIN. Medieval silver miners gave the metal this name because of the trouble it caused them. They believed that cobalt was harmful both to the silver ores with which it occurred and to their own health, though these effects were mainly due to the arsenic and sulphur with which it was frequently combined.

cobber *see* AUSTRALIAN WORD PANEL

cobweb [ME] An old word for a spider was a *coppe* or *cop*. This was a shortened form of the Old English *attercop*, for spider and literally meaning 'poison head', which turns up in a song sung by Bilbo Baggins in J.R.R. Tolkien's *The Hobbit* (1937). A spider's web came to be called a *coppeweb* or *copweb*, and this was later modified to **cobweb**.

coccyx [L16th] Your coccyx is the small triangular bone at the base of your spine. The name comes via Latin from Greek *kokkux* 'cuckoo', because the shape of this bone looks like a cuckoo's beak.

cock [OE] The ancient root of the word cock was probably suggested by the sound the bird makes. The same root is likely to have given us *CHICKEN as well. If you are **cock-a-hoop** you are extremely pleased, especially after some success or triumph. The expression dates from the 17th century and comes from an earlier phrase **set cock a hoop**. Cock here may be used in the sense of a tap for stopping the flow of liquid, so that the expression refers to turning on the tap of a beer barrel and allowing beer to flow freely before a drinking session. A **cock-and-bull story** is a ridiculous and implausible tale. The expression 'talk of a cock and a bull' is recorded from the early 17th century, and apparently refers to some rambling story or fable, a 'shaggy dog story', which is now lost. To **cock a snook**, first recorded in 1791, is to show open contempt or lack of respect for someone or something, originally by

coal coalesce coast cob cobalt cobber

touching your nose with your thumb and spreading out your fingers. Cock here means 'to stick out stiffly', but the origin of **snook** is not known. Because it is such an unfamiliar word, people have often taken to saying **snoot** (slang for 'nose') instead of snook. *See also* cox

cockney [LME] A cockney was originally a pampered or spoilt child. This use may derive from a similar word, *cokeney* 'a cock's egg', which, since cocks do not lay eggs, actually meant a poor specimen of a hen's egg, a small and misshapen one. The 'pampered child' meaning developed into an insulting term for someone who lives in the town, regarded as effeminate and weak, in contrast to hardier country dwellers. By the beginning of the 17th century the word was being applied to someone from the East End of London, traditionally someone born within the sound of Bow Bells (the bells of St Mary-le-Bow church in the City of London).

cockpit [L16th] At first a cockpit was a place for holding cock fights, so from the beginning the word had connotations of bloodshed and injury. This accounts for it being applied in the early 18th century to the area in the aft lower deck of a man-of-war where wounded sailors were treated during a battle. It then came to be used for the well from which you steer a sailing yacht. Finally, in the 20th century, **cockpit** acquired its modern meaning, the area or compartment that houses the controls of an aircraft or racing car.

cockroach [E17th] The early written form of cockroach was *cacaroch*, from the Spanish *cucaracha* 'cockroach'. People adapted the spelling to make it fit in better with the more familiar English words *cock and **roach** [ME], the freshwater fish, whose origin is unknown.

cocktail [E17th] The original use of cocktail was as a term to describe a creature with a tail like that of a cock, in particular a horse with a docked tail. Hunting horses and stagecoach horses generally had their tails shortened in this way, which led to the term being applied to a racehorse which was not a thoroughbred but 'of mixed blood', with a cock-tailed horse somewhere in its pedigree. It may be that the current sense of an alcoholic drink with a mixture of ingredients, which dates from the early 19th century, comes from this use, though the exact origin of the term is much debated.

cocoa *see* CHOCOLATE

coconut [E17th] Look at the base of a coconut and you will see three holes. These are the inspiration for its name. It was originally known as a **coco**, a Spanish and Portuguese word meaning 'a grinning face'.

code [ME] This was originally a term for a system of laws; the sense 'secret writing' developed in the early 19th century. It comes from Latin *codex*, which developed from a simple meaning of a 'a block of wood', to 'a block split into leaves or tablets' thus 'a book'. The related term **codicil** [LME] is from Latin *codicillus*, a diminutive of *codex*, and thus applies to a 'small' part of a legal document.

codger *see* CADGER

codicil *see* CODE

codswallop [M20th] Meaning 'nonsense or drivel', codswallop seems to be a fairly recent addition to English, with the earliest recorded use appearing in a 1959 script for the radio and TV comedy *Hancock's Half Hour*. It is sometimes said that the word comes from the name of Hiram Codd, who in the 1870s invented a bottle for fizzy drinks, although the evidence for this is sketchy. The **wallop** part may relate to the word's use as a 1930s slang term for beer or other alcoholic drink.

coffee *see* ARABIC WORD PANEL

coffin [ME] Coffin comes from the Old French word *cofin* meaning 'a little basket', and in medieval English could refer to a chest, casket, or even a pie. The sense 'a box in which a dead body is buried or cremated' dates from the early 16th century. A closely related word is **coffer** [ME]—both words

cockney   cockpit   cockroach   cocktail   cocoa

share the same source, Greek *kophinos* 'a basket'.

cogent *see* COGITATE

cogitate [L16th] This come from the Latin word *cogitare* 'to consider'. The first person singular of this is seen in Descartes's formula (1641) **cogito, ergo sum** 'I think therefore I am'. From the same verb comes **cogent** [M17th] 'logical and convincing'.

cognoscenti *see* QUAINT

cohort *see* COURTEOUS

coil *see* COLLECT

coincide [E18th] The early sense was 'occupy the same space': it comes from medieval Latin *coincidere*, from *co-* 'together with' and *incidere* 'fall upon or into'.

colchicum *see* PHEASANT

cold [OE] Cold goes back to an ancient root that was shared by Latin *gelu* 'frost', the root of **congeal** [LME], *JELLY, and *COOL. It appears in many common expressions, a number of which refer to parts of the body. If someone **gives you the cold shoulder** they are deliberately unfriendly. It is unlikely to be from 'a cold shoulder of mutton', for an unappetizing meal served to an unwelcome guest as is often claimed, but rather from a dismissive gesture of the body, involving a jerk or shrug of the shoulder. **Cold-hearted** first appeared in Shakespeare's play *Antony and Cleopatra*. The proverb **cold hands, warm heart** is much more recent: the earliest example is from the late 19th century.

The origin of **cold comfort**, meaning 'poor or inadequate consolation', is the idea that charity is often given in a cold or uncaring way. To **go cold turkey** is suddenly to give up taking a drug that you are addicted to, which can be an unpleasant process involving bouts of shivering and sweating that cause goose pimples reminiscent of the flesh of a dead plucked turkey. The expression dates from the 1920s. **The Cold War** was the state of political

hostility that existed between the Soviet countries and Western powers from 1945 to 1990 although the term has been recorded from the beginning of the Second World War.

cole *see* CAULIFLOWER

coleslaw *see* DUTCH WORD PANEL

collar *see* ACCOLADE

collect [LME] This comes from the Latin verb *colligere*, from *col-* 'together' and *legere* 'choose or collect'. The collect meaning 'prayer' [ME] is from Latin *collecta* 'a gathering together'—an obsolete use of collect was as a term for 'a gathering' for an act of worship. **Recollect** [E16th] is literally 'to collect again'. **Coil** [E16th] is less obviously from the Latin. Something coiled up is gathered in a specific way.

colossal [E18th] *Kolossos* was the Greek word for 'a gigantic statue', and was originally used to describe the statues of Egyptian temples. The most famous example was the huge bronze figure of Apollo that stood beside the harbour entrance at Rhodes, one of the Seven Wonders of the World. It was completed in 280 BC, but destroyed by an earthquake in 224 BC. This statue was known as the Colossus of Rhodes, **colossus** [LME] being the Latin, and subsequently English, version of the word. The idea that the statue stood astride the entrance to the harbour is widely held, but wrong. Nevertheless, it has given us the phrase **bestride like a colossus**, which is from Shakespeare's *Julius Caesar*: 'Why man, he doth bestride the narrow world / Like a Colossus.' The **Colosseum** has been the name since medieval times of the *Amphitheatrum Flavium*, a vast amphitheatre in Rome begun by the Emperor Vespasian around AD 75 and used for gladiatorial combats, fights between men and beasts, and mock battles.

colour [ME] In Old French it was spelled *colour*, in Latin *color*. The main English spelling has been colour since the medieval period, though **color**, now the usual spelling in American English, was sometimes used

cogent   cogitate   cognoscenti   cohort   coil

from the 15th century onwards. Since the late 16th century the distinguishing flag of a ship or regiment has been known as its colours, a meaning that lies behind a number of common English expressions. To **show your true colours** is to reveal your real character or intentions, especially when these are disreputable. A ship engaged in illegal trading or in time of war might fly a bogus flag to deceive the authorities or the enemy, a practice known as 'sailing under false colours'. If the ship subsequently revealed itself to the enemy by firing on them or fleeing, it was 'showing its true colours'. The phrase **nail your colours to the mast**, meaning 'to declare openly and firmly what you believe or support', is also naval: a ship in battle might nail its flag to the mast so that there was no possibility of it being lowered in defeat. And to **come through with flying colours** is to come successfully through a test, like a victorious warship returning to port with its flag unscathed.

comb *see* LIMB, UNKEMPT

combat *see* BATTLE

combine [LME] Combine is from late Latin *combinare* 'join two by two', from *com-* 'together' and Latin *bini* 'two (yoked) together'.

combustion [LME] This word is from late Latin *combustio(n-)*, from Latin *comburere* 'burn up'.

comestible *see* EAT

comet [OE] We get the word comet from Greek *komētēs* 'long-haired'. The ancient Greeks gazed into the night sky and observed a comet's long tail. To their eyes it resembled streaming hair, hence their name for what they called 'the long-haired star'.

commando [E19th] In early use commando was a word for an armed unit of Boer horsemen in South Africa. During the Second World War the name was adopted to describe troops specially trained to repel the threatened German invasion of England.

The word came into English from Portuguese, but is based on Latin *commandare* 'to command' from *com-* (giving emphasis) and *mandare* 'commit, command, entrust'. To **go commando** is to wear no underpants, said to be common among commandos. This curious phrase dates back to the 1980s and probably originated as American college slang, although it was popularized by its use in an episode of the 1990s TV comedy *Friends*. Also from South Africa and the same period is **commandeer** from Afrikaans. **Command** itself came into use in Middle English, taken from the Latin via French. From the same root come **remand** [LME] 'command back'; **commend** [ME], formed in the same way as command, but with the sense 'entrust' and **recommend** [LME]; and **demand** [ME] 'command formally'.

commemoration *see* MEMORY

commend *see* COMMANDO

commission [ME] Commission came into English via Old French from Latin *committere* 'entrust'. Late Middle English **commit** is from the same root. **Commissionaire** [M17th] came via French from medieval Latin *commissarius* 'person in charge', from *committere*. **Committee**, however, was formed in the late 15th century directly from commit and originally meant someone entrusting with something.

commode, commodity
see ACCOMMODATE

commonplace [M16th] This was originally written *common place*, a translation of Latin *locus communis*, rendering Greek *koinos topos* 'general theme', terms for a passage on which a speaker could base an argument. In the past people would keep **commonplace books** of such passages, and the quoting of these no doubt led to the modern sense of the word. **Topic** [LME] was originally a word for a set or book of general rules or ideas. It comes from Latin *topica*, from Greek *ta*

comb   combat   combine   combustion

topika, meaning literally 'matters concerning commonplaces' (the title of a treatise by Aristotle). Early use was as a term in logic and rhetoric describing a rule or argument as 'applicable in most but not all cases'. *See also* UTOPIA. **Common** itself [ME] comes via French from Latin *communis* 'common, general' also the source of **commune** [L17th], **communism** [M19th], **communication**, **communion**, and **community** [all LME].

commute [LME] In early use commute meant 'to interchange two things'. Its source is Latin *commutare*, from *com-* 'together' and *mutare* 'to change', the root of English words such as **moult** [LME], **mutant** [E19th], and **permutation** [LME]. The modern meaning, 'to travel between home and your place of work', comes from **commutation ticket**. This was the American term for a season ticket, where a number of daily fares were 'commuted' to, or changed into, a single payment. The Americans have been commuting since the 1860s, but the term did not make its way over to Britain until the 1930s.

companion [ME] A companion is literally 'a person who you eat bread with'. The word comes from Old French *compaignon*, from Latin *com-* 'together with' and *panis* 'bread'. Other English words that derive from *panis* include **pannier** [ME], **pastille** [M17th] a 'little loaf' of something, and **pantry** [ME]. **Company** [ME] and **accompany** [LME] come from the same root.

compare *see* PAIR

compassion, compatible *see* PASSION

compel *see* APPEAL

compensation *see* PENDANT

compete [E17th] This word is from Latin *competere* in its late sense 'strive or contend for (something)': the elements here are *com-* 'together' and *petere* 'aim at, seek'. As well as giving us **competition** [E17th] this is also the source of **competent** [LME]; while *petere* gives us: **impetus** [M17] and

impetuous [LME] 'seek towards, assail'; **petition** [ME] an act of seeking for something; **petulant** [L16th] originally immodest in what you seek; and **repeat** [LME] seek again.

compile [ME] This comes via Old French from Latin *compilare* 'plunder', 'plagiarize'.

complacent *see* PLEASE

complain *see* PLAINTIVE

complete [LME] Complete comes from Latin *complere* 'fill up, finish, fulfil'. This is also the source of **comply** [L16th] originally to fulfil an obligation; and of **compliment** [M17th] from Italian *complimento* 'fulfilment of the requirements of courtesy'; and its confusing partner **complement** [LME], something which contributes additional or contrasting features.

complexion [Middle English] This came via Old French from Latin *complectere* 'embrace, comprise'. The term originally referred to a person's physical constitution to temperament once believed to be determined by a combination of the four bodily *HUMOURS: blood, phlegm, yellow bile, and black bile. This gave rise, in the late 16th century, to the meaning 'natural colour and texture of a person's skin' as a visible sign of this temperament. **Complex** [M17th], something that comprises many things, is from the same source.

compliant *see* PLIGHT

compliment, comply *see* COMPLETE

compost [LME] Garden compost and fruit **compôte** do not seem to have much in common, but they both derive from French *compôte* 'stewed fruit'. This comes from Old French *composte*, from Latin *compositum* 'something put together'—source of **compose** [LME] and **decompose** [M18th], **composition** [LME], and **component** [M17th]. Compost has been used in the gardening sense since the late 16th century. The Latin word was formed from *com-* 'with' and the irregular verb *ponere* 'put, place'. From this we also get **impose** [LME] 'place

(up)on'; **oppose** [LME] 'place against';
*POSITIVE and **posture** [L16th]; **preposition**
[LME] something put in front, and **suppose**
[ME] literally something placed from below.

comprehend see PRISON

computer [E17th] The first computers
were not machines, but people. In the 17th
century a computer was a person who
make calculations, particularly someone
employed to do this in an observatory or in
surveying. The word was used in the late
19th century as a name for a mechanical
calculating machine, and the modern sense
dates from the 1940s. Its base is Latin
computare, 'to calculate'. *See also* COUNT

comrade [M16th] If a *COMPANION is,
literally, someone you share bread with,
then a comrade is someone you share a
room with. The origin of the word is Spanish
camarada 'a room-mate', from Latin *camera*
'a room'. Your comrade was originally
someone who shared the same room or tent
as you, often a fellow soldier. *See also*
CAMERA, CHUM

concave see CAVE

conceal see HELL

concede see CEDE

conceive see CAPABLE

concentrate see CENTRE

concern see CRIME

conch see CONKER

concise see DECIDE

concoct see COOK

concourse see CURSOR

concrete see CEMENT

concubine see CUBICLE

concur see CURSOR

condemn see DAMN

condescend see SCALE

condiment [LME] This word for a
substance that adds flavour to food,
is from Latin *condimentum* 'spice,
seasoning'.

condition see VERDICT

condom [E18th] This is often said to be
named after a physician who invented it,
but no such person has been traced, and its
origin is unknown.

conduct, conduit see DUCT

coney see RABBIT

confectionery see CONFETTI

confer see REFER

confetti [E19th] It was the custom during
Italian carnivals and public celebrations for
people to throw little sweets, known as
confetti. The Italian word comes from Latin
confectum 'something prepared'. As time
went on people threw small plaster balls
instead of sweets, which were meant to break
open in a cloud of white dust when they hit
someone. Charles Dickens describes the
custom in 1846: 'The spectators . . . would
empty down great bags of confetti, that
descended like a cloud, and . . . made them as
white as millers.' By the end of the 19th
century English had borrowed the Italian
word to refer to the coloured paper shapes
that wedding guests shower on the bride and
bridegroom after the marriage ceremony. A
related word is **confectionery** [L17th], both
words being traceable back to Latin *conficere*
'put together'.

confide, confident see FAITH

confiscate [M16th] The original
meaning of confiscate was 'to take
someone's property for the public treasury
as a punishment'. It comes from Latin
confiscare 'to store in a chest' or 'to take
something for the public treasury', based on
con- 'together' and *fiscus* 'chest or treasury',
also the root of **fiscal** [M16th].

comprehend computer comrade concave

conflagration *see* FLAGRANT

conflate [LME] The early meaning of this was 'fuse or melt down metal'; it is from Latin *conflare* 'kindle, fuse', from *con-* 'together' and *flare* 'to blow'.

conflict [LME] Conflict is from Latin *conflict-* 'struck together, fought', from the verb *confligere*, from *con-* 'together' and *fligere* 'to strike'.

conform *see* FORM

confound *see* CONFUSE

confront [M16th] If you confront someone you are literally face to face with them. It comes from Latin *confrontare*, formed from *con-* 'with' and *frons, front-* 'face'. Similarly **affront** [ME] comes from an Old French source meaning 'to strike someone on the forehead, insult them to their face' from Latin *ad frontem* 'to the face'.

confuse [ME] The early meanings of confuse were 'rout' and 'bring to ruin'. The word comes via French from Latin *confundere* 'mingle together, mix up'. **Confound** [ME] comes from the same word.

congeal *see* COLD

congregate [LME] The Latin word for a herd or flock was *grex*, giving *congregare*, meaning 'to collect into a herd or flock, to unite'. **Gregarious** [M17th], meaning 'fond of company', is also descended from *grex*, as are **aggregate** [LME] 'herd together'; **egregious** [M16th] 'standing out from the herd' and originally complimentary; and **segregation** [M16th] 'set apart from the herd'.

congress [LME] A congress once meant an encounter during battle: it is from Latin *congressus*, from *congredi* 'meet', literally 'walk together'. Use for any 'coming together' is reflected in obsolete or archaic uses such as social congress, sexual congress.

conjecture *see* JET

conjugal [E16th] Conjugal is based on the Latin word *jugum* 'yoke'. The word comes from Latin *conjugalis*, from *conjux* 'spouse'.

conjure [ME] The earliest meanings of conjure were 'to call on in the name of some divine or supernatural being' and 'to appeal solemnly to, entreat'—the *-jure* bit of the word is from Latin *jurare* 'to swear', which gave us words such as *JURY. A more familiar early meaning was 'to call on a supernatural being to appear by means of a magic ritual', from which the sense 'to make something appear as if by magic' developed. **A name to conjure with** comes from the idea of someone summoning the spirit of an influential or powerful person by saying their name out loud.

conker [M18th] Children originally played conkers not with horse chestnuts but with snail shells. The word conker is first recorded in the 1840s as a dialect word for a snail shell, and may have originally come from **conch** [ME], a kind of mollusc, which is probably also the origin of **conk** [E19th], meaning 'the nose'. On the other hand, conker could be related to **conquer** (ME, from Latin *conquirere* 'gain, win'), which was how conker was often spelled. Indeed, an alternative name for the game at one time was **conquerors**. Horse chestnuts seem to have replaced snail shells late in the 19th century.

connive [E17th] When someone connives at something wrong, they turn a blind eye to it. The word comes from French *conniver* or Latin *connivere* meaning 'to shut your eyes to something'. An early meaning of **connivance** [L16th] was 'winking'.

conquer *see* CONKER

conscience *see* SCIENCE

conscription *see* PRESS

consequence *see* SEQUEL

conserve [LME] This comes via French from Latin *conservare* 'to preserve', the elements of which are *con-* 'together' and

conflagration   conflate   conflict   conform

servare 'to keep'. **Conservatory** [M16th] was originally 'something that preserves', with the sense glass house dating from the mid 17th century. Other words from *servare* are **preserve** [LME] from *prae* 'in advance' and *servare*; **observe** [LME] with *ob* 'toward' with the sense 'pay attention to'; and **reserve** [ME] 'keep back'.

consider [LME] You used to consider with your eyes rather than your brain. Latin *considerare* meant 'to observe or examine something', but had an earlier meaning 'to observe the stars' and was based on *sidus* 'a star or constellation'. The earliest meaning of consider was 'to look at something very carefully', but this soon widened to the notion of thinking carefully about something.

consigliere *see* ITALIAN WORD PANEL

consist [LME] Fron Latin *consistere* 'stand firm or still, exist', *sistere* 'set, stand (still), stop', also the source of **assist** [LME] originally 'take your stand'; **desist** [LME] 'stand down, stop'; **exist** [E17th] 'come into being', literally 'stand out'; **insist** [L16th] 'stand upon [an argument]'; and **resist** [LME] 'stand back or against'.

consortium [E19th] A consortium is a partnership, from the Latin *consors* 'sharing, partner', from *con* 'with' and *sors, sort-* 'lot, destiny'. **Consort** [ME] is from the same word.

conspire *see* SPIRIT

constable [ME] The Latin phrase *comes stabuli* originally meant 'officer in charge of the stable'. One of the earliest surviving uses of the English word was as the title of the governor or warden of certain royal castles. It was used as a term for a police officer in the modern sense from the mid 19th century.

constellation *see* STAR

constipate *see* STIFF

constitution [ME] A constitution once referred to a law, as well as to a body of laws or customs. It comes from Latin *constituere* 'establish, appoint' from *con-* 'together' and *statuere* 'set up, place'. The latter is a rich source of English words including **destitute** [LME] literally 'placed away' so forsaken; **institute** [ME] something set up or established; **restitution** [ME] a re-establishing; **statue** [ME] something set up; and **substitute** [LME] someone set up instead of another. **Prostitute** [M16th] comes from Latin *prostituere* 'expose publicly, offer for sale', from *pro-* 'before' and *statuere* 'set up, place'.

consume *see* ASSUME

contact [E17th] Contact and **contagion** [LME] both go back to Latin *contingere* 'touched' formed from *con-* 'with' and *tangere* 'touch'. **Contaminate** [LME] is related.

contain *see* CONTENT

contaminate *see* CONTACT

contemporary *see* TEMPLE

contemptible [LME] In modern English contemptible is still widely used, whereas its root word, **contemn**, 'to treat or regard with contempt', is now rare and restricted to literary contexts. In 1914 the kaiser of Germany supposedly referred to the British army as **a contemptible little army**, in an order for his troops to 'walk all over General French's contemptible little army'. In fact the text, which became widely known and resented, appears to have been created by British propaganda. The veterans of the British Expeditionary Force of 1914 later became known as the Old Contemptibles.

contender *see* CONTENTION

content [LME] There are two words spelt content in English; one with the stress on the second syllable meaning 'happy' which comes from Latin *contentus* 'satisfied', the other with the stress on the first syllable meaning 'things included' from Latin *contenta* 'things contained'. Both Latin

consider　consigliere　consist　consortium

words go back to *continere* 'hold, contain' which also gives us **contain** [ME].

contention [LME] comes from Latin *contendere* 'strive with'. **Contender** [M16th] was originally a fighter rather than a competitor, a sense immortalized in **I could have been a contender**, spoken by Marlon Brando in the 1954 film *On the Waterfront*.

context *see* TEXT

continent [M16th] The geographical term continent is from the Latin phrase (*terra*) *continens* 'continuous land'. **Continue** [ME] comes from the same root.

contort *see* TORCH

contour [M17th] Contour comes via French, from Italian *contorno*: this is from *contornare* 'draw in outline', from *con-* 'together' and *tornare* 'to turn'.

contraband [L16th] This is from Spanish *contrabanda* 'smuggling', adopted from Italian *contrabando* 'unlawful dealing', from *contra-* 'against' and *bando* 'proclamation, *BAN'.

contract *see* TRAIN

contradiction *see* VERDICT

contrite [ME] The Latin word *contritus* meant 'ground down' and was based on *con-* 'together' and *terere* 'to rub or grind', also the source of *TRITE. The 'remorseful' meaning of contrite developed from the idea of a person's spirit being broken by a sense of sin.

control [LME] The early sense of this was 'check or verify accounts': usually by making reference to a duplicate register. It is from Anglo-Norman French *contreroller* 'keep a copy of a roll of accounts', from Latin *contrarotulus* 'copy of a roll'.

controversy [LME] This is from Latin *controversia*, from *controversus* 'turned against, disputed'.

conundrum [L16th] The origin of conundrum is itself a conundrum. In 1596 the English political writer Thomas Nashe used it as a term of abuse for a crank or pedant: 'So will I … drive him to confess himself a Conundrum, who now thinks he hath learning enough to prove the salvation of Lucifer.' The word later came to refer both to a whim and a pun. The current sense of 'a riddle or puzzle' dates from the late 17th century.

conurbation *see* URBANE

convalesce [LME] Convalesce is from Latin *convalescere*, from *con-* 'altogether' and *valescere* 'grow strong'.

convent [ME] Convent was originally spelled *covent*, a spelling that survives in the London place name **Covent Garden**. The word came into English via Old French from Latin *conventus* 'an assembly or company', based on *convenire* 'to come together'. **Convene** [LME], 'to call people together for a meeting', has the same origin; as does **convenient** [LME] 'assembling or agreeing'; **coven** [M17th] 'gathering of witches'; and **covenant** [ME] 'an agreement'.

conversation [ME] In Latin *conversare* meant 'to mix with people'. This is the source of conversation, which once meant 'living among' and 'familiarity or intimacy'. The poet John Milton used the word in this latter sense when he refers in 1645 to 'the good and peace of wedded conversation'. It could also at one time mean 'sexual intercourse', and **criminal conversation** was a legal term for adultery. The 'talking' sense dates from the late 16th century. *See also* CHAT

convert *see* VERSE

convex *see* CAVE

convict, convince *see* VICTORY

convoke *see* VOICE

convoluted, convolvulus *see* REVOLVE

cooee [L18th] While to **coo** [L17th] is an imitation of the soft murmur of a dove, cooee is a sound meant to carry over distance. It was adopted by early British settlers in Australia from the sound used by Aboriginals to signal to each other in the bush.

cook [OE] The Old English *coc*, the early form of **cook,** was always male. The word was applied either to the domestic officer in charge of the preparation of food in a large household or to a tradesman who prepared and sold food. Women who prepared dinner started being called cooks in the mid 16th century. The root of the word is Latin *coquus*, also the source of **concoct** [M16th] and *BISCUIT. Cook has been used to mean 'to tamper with' since the 1630s, giving us **cook the books**, meaning 'to alter records or accounts dishonestly'. The proverb **too many cooks spoil the broth** also dates back to the 16th century. It is not certain where the phrase **cook someone's goose** comes from. The reference could be to a goose being reared and fattened up for a forthcoming special occasion. Anyone who killed and cooked the goose before the proper time would have ruined the plans for the feast.

cookie *see* DUTCH WORD PANEL

cool [OE] As early as the 1880s, cool, an Old English word related to *COLD, was being used by black Americans to mean 'excellent, pleasing', and 'stylish'. It only became more widely known when people started associating it with jazz musicians with a restrained and relaxed style in the 1940s. It then declined in popularity for a decade or two before regaining its position as the top all-purpose affirmative. **Cool as a cucumber** is also older than might be expected, going back to the mid 18th century.

coop [ME] The Latin word *cupa* 'barrel' is the forerunner of **coop**, 'a cage or pen in which poultry are kept', and also gave us **cooper** [ME], meaning 'barrel-maker'. In medieval English a coop was a kind of basket that you placed over chickens that were sitting or being fattened.

coordinate [M17th] This was first recorded with the senses 'of the same rank' and 'place in the same rank'. It is formed from the prefix *co-* 'together' and the Latin base *ordo* 'order'. From this root come **inordinate** [LME] 'not ordered' and **subordinate** [LME] 'below in order'.

cop *see* COPPER

cope [ME] Nowadays to cope with something is to manage or deal with it effectively, but the word used to mean 'to meet in battle' or 'to come to blows'. Its source is the Latin word *colpus* 'a blow', which is also the root of **coup** [LME], 'a sudden seizure of power from a government' often used in its French form **coup d'état** [M17th]. **Coppice** [LME], woodland where the trees have regularly been cut back, and its shortening **copse** [L16th] also go back to *colpus*, from the idea that they have been cut back with blows.

copious [LME] Copious is from Latin *copia* 'plenty', also found in the symbol of fruitfulness the **cornucopia** [L16th] or '*HORN of plenty', and in **copy** [LME]. The radical change of meaning from the Latin came about because *copia* had a secondary meaning of 'permission, licence, opportunity'. Latin phrases such as *copiam describendi facere* 'permission to make a transcription' led to *copia* being used in medieval Latin to mean a copy.

copper [OE] The verb **cop** [E18th], meaning 'to catch', comes from a northern English dialect word *cap* meaning 'to capture or arrest'. This probably goes back to Latin *capere*, 'to take or seize'. So a **copper** was a catcher, which is why it became an informal word for a police officer in the 1840s. Apprehended villains have been saying '**it's a fair cop!**' since the 1880s. *See also* CAPABLE

Copper, the reddish-brown metal, comes from Latin *cyprium aes* 'Cyprus metal'. The island of Cyprus was the Romans' main source of copper.

cooee cook cookie cool coop coordinate cop

coppice, copse *see* COPE

copulate *see* COUPLE

copy *see* COPIOUS

coracle *see* CORGI

cord *see* CHORD

cordial [ME] The Latin word *cordis* meant 'to do with the heart', and this is the source and original meaning of cordial. It was not long before the adjective was being used to describe drinks as 'comforting' or 'stimulating the heart', and the core 'heart' meaning came to be applied to people too, in connection with actions or behaviour that seemed sincere and heartfelt—acting 'from the heart'. The root, Latin *cor* 'heart', is the source of many words, including *CHORD, **discord** [ME], and **courage** [ME]. *HEART itself came from the same ancient root.

cordon bleu *see* FRENCH WORD PANEL

corgi [1920s] Not many English words derive from Welsh, but **corgi** is one of them, literally 'a dwarf dog', from Welsh *cor* 'dwarf' and *ci* 'dog'. Others include **coracle** [M16th], **flummery** [E17th] originally in the food sense from Welsh *llymru*, *FLANNEL (probably), and *PENGUIN.

cork [ME] This is from Dutch and Low German *kork*, from Spanish *alcorque* 'cork-soled sandal'. The source elements are Arabic *al-* 'the' and (probably) Spanish Arabic *kork* based on Latin *quercus* 'oak, cork oak'.

cormorant [ME] Picture a glossy black cormorant, a large diving bird with a long neck, greedily gobbling down great quantities of fish, and you might agree that the description 'sea raven' seems rather fitting. This is indeed the meaning of the Latin *corvus marinus*, the source of the bird's name. Since the 16th century the word has also been used to describe an insatiably greedy person or thing.

corn [OE] Corn, meaning 'the seed of wheat and similar plants', is an Old English word whose root may date back as far as farming itself. The modern sense of **corny** is a development of an earlier sense, dating from the 1930s, that described something, especially music, of a simple and unsophisticated type that appealed to people living in the country. **Kernel** [OE] is based on corn and was originally a 'little corn or seed'. The other kind of corn [LME], the small area of thickened horn-like skin on your foot, comes from Latin *cornu* 'horn'. *Cornu*, which could also mean 'tip' or 'corner', is the source too of **corner** [ME]— you can think of a corner as the part of something that sticks out or forms the tip.

The trumpet-like **cornet** [LME] is now made from brass, but it was originally a wind instrument made out of a horn, and Latin *cornu* is again the source. The early 20th century **ice-cream cornet** gets its name because it resembles that of the instrument. One brand of ice cream is called a **Cornetto** ('little horn'), and this Italian word was also the name of an old musical instrument, a straight or curved wooden wind instrument with finger holes and a cup-shaped mouthpiece. *See also* HORN

cornea *see* HORN

corner, cornet *see* CORN

cornucopia *see* COPIOUS

coronary [M17th] In the 17th century **coronary** had the meanings 'like a crown' or 'suitable for making garlands', from Latin *corona*, 'a crown or wreath'. In medical contexts the term came to refer to blood vessels, nerves, or ligaments that encircle a part of the body like a crown, in particular the arteries surrounding the heart. A **coronary thrombosis**, frequently abbreviated just to coronary, is a blood clot forming a blockage in one of these arteries. Other crown-related words that descend from *corona* are **coronation** [LME], **coronet** [LME], and **coroner** [ME] (originally an official responsible for safeguarding the private property of the Crown), not to mention the word *CROWN itself.

coppice copse copulate copy coracle cord

corporation see MIDRIFF

corpse [ME] At one time corpses did not have to be dead. Until the early 18th century a corpse (from Latin *corpus* 'body') could be the living body of a person or animal, as in 'We often see...a fair and beautiful corpse but a foul and ugly mind' (Thomas Walkington, 1607). You would need to specify 'a dead corpse' or some similar expression if you were talking about a dead body. In time, you could simply say 'a corpse' and people would assume that you meant a dead person. The *p* used to be silent and the final *e* was rare before the 19th century. In fact, **corpse** and **corps** [L16th], 'a division of an army' are basically the same word. Latin *corpus* has given us several words, among them **corporation** [LME], **corpulent** [LME] or 'fat', **corset** [ME] a 'little body', and **incorporate** [LME]. A **corporal** [M16th] is in charge of a 'body' of troops.

correct [ME] If you correct something you put it straight, for it comes from the Latin *corrigere* 'make straight, amend'. Someone who is **incorrigible** [ME] cannot be straightened out or corrected.

corridor [L16th] Corridors are nothing to do with doors. They are 'running places'. The word comes from Italian *corridore*, from Latin *currere* 'to run'. It started out as a military term for a strip of land along the outer edge of a ditch, protected by a parapet. The modern sense of 'a long passage in a building' dates from the early 19th century. *See also* CURSOR. **Corridors of power** refers to the senior levels of government or the civil service, where all the important decision-making takes place behind the scenes. It was popularized by the title of C.P. Snow's novel *The Corridors of Power* (1964), though Snow did not coin the expression.

corroborate [M16th] If someone corroborates an account or story, the facts are strengthened. Corroborate was first recorded in the sense 'make physically stronger' from the Latin verb *corroborare* 'strengthen' from *robur* 'strength' source of **robust** [M16th].

corrode [LME] The second part of corrode is the same as the first part of *RODENT—a clue to the meaning of their Latin source *rodere*. It means 'to gnaw', so when something is corroded it is gradually worn away, as if by gnawing.

corrupt [ME] Corrupt comes from Latin *corrumpere* 'mar, bribe, destroy', from *cor-* 'altogether' and *rumpere* 'to break'. Also from *rumpere* are **disrupt** [LME] 'break apart'; **eruption** [LME] a breaking out; **interrupt** [LME] 'to break between'. *See* words at RUT

corset see CORPSE

cortex [LME] This is a Latin word meaning literally 'tree bark, husk'.

corvette see DUTCH WORD PANEL

cosmetic see COSMOS

cosmonaut see ASTERISK

cosmopolitan see POLICE

cosmos [ME] The fact that both cosmos and **cosmetic** [E17th] go back to the same word, Greek *kosmos* gives an interesting insight into the way the ancient Greeks thought. *Kosmos* had a central meaning 'order', but was also used to mean 'world' and the putting of oneself in order that involved 'adornment'.

cosset [M16th] In the 16th century a lamb brought up by hand as a pet was known as a cosset. The term was later used to refer to a spoiled child, and this is where the modern sense, 'to pamper someone', came from. The origin of the word is probably Old French *coscet* 'cottager'. *Compare* PET

cost [ME] This is from Old French *couster*, based on Latin *constare* 'stand firm, stand at a price'.

costume see CUSTOM

cot [OE] We have the British Empire to thank for the child's cot [M17th], which started life as an Anglo-Indian word for a light bedstead. The origin is the Hindi word

corporation   corpse   correct   corridor   cot

khāt 'bedstead or hammock'. A less familiar cot is an old word for a small, simple cottage, used nowadays as a term for a small shelter for livestock. Closely related to this word are **cottage** [LME], and **cote** [OE] as in **dovecote**, though that too once meant 'cottage'.

Cotswold *see* WILD

cotton *see* ARABIC WORD PANEL

couch potato [1970s] Someone who spends all day at home sitting in front of the television can be described as a couch potato. The phrase was coined in the US around 1976. It is actually a more ingenious expression than it might seem: a potato is a type of tuber (a vegetable that grows from a thick underground stem), and the slang term **boob tuber** was used at the time to refer to someone who was addicted to the **boob tube** or television. *See also* BOOB. **Couch** itself is Middle English and comes via Old French from Latin *collocare* 'lay in place'.

coulrophobia *see* CLOWN

coulter *see* CUTLASS

count [ME] The verb to count is from Latin *computare* 'to calculate', the root also of *COMPUTER, **account** [ME], and **recount** [LME] 'tell' (which can also be used for both 'narrate' and 'count'). **Counters** [ME] were originally used to help in counting; in the late 17th century the word came to be used for a surface across which goods were exchanged for money. The title of the count or foreign nobleman, corresponding to the English *EARL, is a completely different word, which was introduced by the Normans and comes from Latin *comes* 'companion, overseer, attendant'. **County** [ME] is from the same root, and seems originally to have referred to the lands or territory of a count, or to a meeting held to discuss the business of the county. *See also* CHICKEN, DUKE

counterpane [E17th] This is an alteration of *counterpoint*, from Old French *contrepointe*, based on medieval Latin *culcitra puncta* 'quilted mattress' (*puncta*, literally meaning 'pricked'). The change in the ending was due to association with the word *pane* in an obsolete sense 'cloth'.

country [ME] Country comes from medieval Latin *contrata terra*, meaning 'the land lying opposite, the landscape spread out in front of you'. This is based on Latin *contra* 'against or opposite' and *terra* 'land', the source of words at *TERRACE. **A country fit for heroes to live in** is a phrase associated with the British prime minister David Lloyd George (1863–1945). In a speech in 1918, he said 'What is our task? To make Britain a fit country for heroes to live in.' A person from a rural background who is unfamiliar with, and alarmed by, urban life can be called a **country mouse**. The allusion is to one of Aesop's fables, which contrasts the country mouse with the streetwise city-dwelling town mouse. In the fable each mouse visits the other, but is in the end convinced of the superiority of its own home.

coup *see* COPE

couple [ME] This comes via Old French from Latin *copulare* formed from *co-* 'together' and *apere* 'fasten'. The term **couplet** [L16th] used in poetry for a pair of successive (usually rhyming) lines, means literally 'little pair'. **Copulate** [LME] at first meant 'join' and is from the same source.

coupon [E19th] Our word coupon is borrowed from the French word meaning 'a piece cut off', from *couper* 'to cut'. In early use a coupon was a detachable portion of a stock certificate which you handed over in return for a payment of interest. It came to be applied to any ticket or voucher that entitles you to something or that you can exchange for goods or cash.

courage *see* CORDIAL

course *see* CURSOR

courteous [ME] Medieval courts were associated with good manners, hence the early meaning of courteous, 'having manners fit for a royal court'. It derived from

Cotswold cotton couch potato coulrophobia

Old French *corteis*, based on *cort* 'court'.
Courtesy [ME], 'the showing of politeness towards others', is from the same root, and got shortened to produce **curtsey** [E16th]. **Court** itself is from the same period and goes back to Latin *cohors* which had, as the English word has, the senses of both 'courtyard' and 'retinue', and is the source of the word **cohort** [LME] originally a tenth of a Roman legion.

cousin [ME] Our word cousin is from Old French *cosin*, which in turn comes from Latin *consobrinus* 'mother's sister's child'. By the time the word had entered English it could be used for the child of an aunt or uncle. It came to be used of any relative more distant than your brother or sister, and particularly in the past to a nephew or niece: 'How now brother, where is my cosen, your son?' (Shakespeare, *Much Ado About Nothing*).

cove *see* ROMANY WORD PANEL

coven, covenant *see* CONVENT

Coventry The phrase **send someone to Coventry**, for to refuse to speak to them, may be connected with the English Civil War (1642–49), although it is not recorded until the 1760s. The garrison of Parliamentarian soldiers stationed in Coventry was apparently deeply unpopular with the city's inhabitants, who refused to associate with them socially. Another theory is that this staunchly Parliamentarian city was where many Royalist prisoners were sent to be held in secure captivity.

cow [OE] The female animal is an Old English word. The verb cow, meaning 'to intimidate', is a different word, probably from Old Norse *kúga* 'to oppress'. *See also* BULL. The expression **till the cows come home**, 'for an indefinitely long time', dates from at least the 16th century. 'I warrant you lay a bed [in bed] till the cows came home', wrote Jonathan Swift in 1738.

cowabunga *see* JAPANESE WORD PANEL

coward [ME] The Latin word *cauda* 'tail' is the source of coward. This may be from

the idea of a frightened animal drawing its tail between its legs or 'turning tail' in flight. In heraldry **lion coward** is the term for a lion depicted with its tail drawn between its hind legs. Despite the similarity in spelling and meaning, the verb **cower** [ME] has a completely different origin, coming from German *küren* 'lie in wait'.

cox [M19th] The cox or **coxswain** [ME] is the person who steers a racing boat or similar craft. The *cox* part is from the old word **cock** [LME] 'small boat', which is not related to the bird but to Latin *caudex* or *codex* 'block of wood'. The second half of the word, **swain** [OE], now means 'a country youth or peasant' but was originally 'a young man attending a knight' and 'a male servant or attendant'. It is also the second half of **boatswain** [LME] (often abbreviated to **bo'sun**), a ship's officer in charge of equipment and the crew.

coy *see* REQUIEM

crabbed [ME] The **crab** [OE] is at the root of crabbed. Both original senses, the medieval 'perverse or wayward' and the later 'cantankerous and bad-tempered', come from aspects of a crab's behaviour, the way it walks sideways and its habit of snapping. **Crabby** is a later word, also derived from crab. The gambling game **craps** [E19th] may be from *crab* or **crab's eyes**, for the lowest throw (two ones) at dice, also known as **snake eyes**. *See also* CANCER, CRAYFISH

crack [OE] In Old English **crack** meant 'make a sudden sharp or explosive noise'. The drug known as crack, or crack cocaine, is a hard crystalline form of cocaine broken into small pieces and smoked. It gets its name from the 'cracking' noises the crystals make as they are heated. The 'crack' or lively socializing in a pub is an Irish use, first recorded in the 1920s and sometimes written **craic**, that comes from the Scottish sense 'chat, conversation'. You can talk about a time very early in the morning as the **crack of dawn**. The expression is first recorded in the late 19th century, in the form **crack of day**. The crack here is the crack of a whip, with an additional echo perhaps of break of day and daybreak, and the notion of the sky cracking or breaking open to reveal a sliver of light. The **crack of doom** is a peal of thunder which, according to the Book of Revelation, will announce the Day of Judgement. *See also* PAPER, POP

craft [OE] The Old English word craft meant 'strength or skill'. The sense 'a boat or ship', initially in the expression 'small craft', dates from the 17th century, and may originally have referred to vessels that only needed a small amount of skill to handle, in contrast to large ocean-going ships. People initially used **crafty** [OE] to mean 'skilful'; over time this developed the more negative sense of 'cunning or sly' that it has today.

craic *see* CRACK

crane [ME] The first meaning of crane, in the Middle Ages, was as the name for the long-legged wading bird that was then common in marshy places. The similarly long-legged lifting machine was also being called a crane as early as the 14th century. German, Dutch, and French also use their word for the bird for the machine.

cranium *see* MIGRAINE

crank [OE] The mechanical crank is found in Old English *cranc* recorded in *crancstæf*, a weaver's implement. The primary notion is 'something bent together' and it is related to *crincan* 'to bend', probably also the source of **cringe** [ME]. Crank [E17th] and **cranky** [L18th] meaning an eccentric or bad-tempered person are from a dialect word originally meaning 'weak, in poor health'.

crap [ME] Crap is related to Dutch *krappe*, from *krappen* 'pluck or cut off', and perhaps also to Old French *crappe* 'siftings', Anglo-Latin *crappa* 'chaff'. The original sense was 'chaff', later coming to mean 'residue from rendering fat' as well as 'dregs of beer'. Current senses meaning 'something of poor quality', 'rubbish', 'nonsense', 'excrement', date from the late 19th century and share the notion of 'rejected matter'. *See also* CRABBED

crass [LME] Crass, as in **crass stupidity**, was first recorded as meaning 'dense or coarse'. It comes from Latin *crassus* 'solid, thick'.

crater [E17th] The Greeks and Romans preferred to drink their wine mixed with water, and thought it very uncivilized to drink it neat. They would mix their wine in a large wide-mouthed bowl called in Greek a *kratēr* and in Latin a *crater*. English adopted this word as the term for the bowl-shaped hollow that forms the mouth of a volcano.

cravat [M17th] The term cravat comes from the French word *Cravate*, meaning 'Croat'. Croatian mercenaries in the French army during the 17th century wore a linen scarf round their necks, which subsequently became fashionable among the French population at large.

crayfish [ME] A crayfish is not a fish but a freshwater crustacean that looks like a small lobster. Its name came into medieval English from Old French *crevice*, and was probably related to *CRAB (although not to **crevice** [ME], which is from Old French *crever*, 'to burst or split'). The spelling was altered in the 16th century simply because people thought that it made more sense: it lives in water, so it must be a fish.

crayon [M17th] Crayon was adopted from French, from *craie* 'chalk', Latin *creta*, source also of the late 17th century word **cretaceous**, mainly used to describe the geological period when chalk was laid down.

crazy [L16th] The root here is the verb to **craze** [LME], which is now 'to drive mad, send crazy' or 'to develop a network of small cracks' but originally meant 'to break in pieces, shatter'. So a crazy person has had their sanity shattered. Crazy formerly meant 'broken, damaged' and 'frail, unwell, infirm'. *See also* DAFT

crease *see* CREST

creature [ME] The earliest recorded sense of creature in English is 'anything created', and the word is from Latin *creatura*

craft craic crane cranium crank crap crass

'a created being'. This is the meaning the poet William Cowper (1731–1800) had in mind when he wrote in 1783, 'The first boat or canoe that was ever formed…was a more perfect creature in its kind than a balloon at present.' **Create** [LME] originally meant 'to form out of nothing'. **Recreation** [LME] came via Old French from Latin _recreare_ 'create again, renew', which gives the word the notion of 'refreshment'.

credit [M16th] People first used the word credit (ultimately from Latin _credere_ 'to believe or trust') to mean 'belief' and 'trustworthiness'. The modern sense developed from the idea of, say, a shopkeeper's trust that a customer will pay for goods at a later time. _Credere_ also gave us **creed** [OE], **credence** [ME], **credential** [LME], **credible** [LME], and **incredulous** [L16th]. You can give **credit where credit is due** to show that you think someone deserves to be given praise. The earlier form of the saying was 'honour where honour is due', a phrase from the Bible, from the Epistle to the Romans: 'Render therefore to all their dues: tribute to whom tribute is due; custom to whom custom; fear to whom fear; honour to whom honour.'

creep _see_ CRIPPLE

crème de la crème _see_ FRENCH WORD PANEL

crescendo _see_ ITALIAN WORD PANEL

crescent [LME] The Romans referred to the thin curve of the waxing moon early in its cycle as _luna crescens_, 'growing moon'. _Crescens_ comes from Latin _crescere_ 'to grow', the source of many English words such as the late 19th century curved **croissant** (the French form of crescent), **accrue** [LME], **decrease** [LME], and **increase** [LME]. From being applied to the moon the word came to be applied to anything of that same shape. _See also_ CREW

crest [ME] Crest comes from Latin _crista_, meaning 'a tuft or plume'. **Crestfallen** [L16th], meaning 'dejected', is an extension of its original use to describe an animal or bird with a drooping crest. **Crease** [L16th] is

probably an alternative form of **crest**, the idea being that a fold in a length of cloth forms a ridge or crest.

cretaceous _see_ CRAYON

cretin [L18th] Cretin is now a term of abuse, but was originally a medical term for a person physically and mentally handicapped as a result of congenital thyroid deficiency. The word is from French _crétin_, from Swiss French _crestin_ 'Christian', used to mean 'human creature' but in this context with a compassionate sense of 'poor fellow'. Thyroid problems were once common in the Alps, where the soil lacks essential iodine.

crevice _see_ CRAYFISH

crew [LME] When crew came into English in the 15th century it initially referred to a band of soldiers acting as reinforcements. The origin of the word is Old French _creue_ 'an increase', ultimately derived from Latin _crescere_ 'to grow or increase' (_see_ CRESCENT). By the 16th century the word was being applied to any organized armed band or, more generally, a company of people. A **crew cut** is so called because this closely cropped hairstyle was first adopted by rowing crews at Harvard and Yale universities in the late 1930s. The **crew neck** came from the same source—rowers wore sweaters with close-fitting necks.

cricket [ME] This word is first recorded in an official document of 1598 in which a man of 59 swears that when he was a schoolboy he used to play cricket and other games on a particular bit of land in Guildford, Surrey. This would take the game back to the reign of Henry VIII. Cricket would have been very different then: the bats were more like hockey sticks, the wicket consisted of two stumps with one long bail and the ball was trundled along the ground rather than 'bowled' in the way that we understand. The word appears to be closely related to French _criquet_ 'a stick', although whether this originally referred to the wicket or the bat is not entirely clear. The idea of cricket being the epitome of honourable behaviour, as in

credit creep crème da la crème crescendo

'It's just not cricket!', dates from the mid 19th century. In 1867 *The Cricketer's Companion* told its readers: 'Do not ask the umpire unless you think the batsman is out; it is not cricket to keep asking the umpire questions.'

The other **cricket**, the grasshopper-like insect, is a completely different word. It comes from Old French *criquet* 'a cricket', based on *criquer* 'to crackle, click, or creak', probably suggesting the chirping sound the insect makes. *See also* OAF

crime [ME] The early meanings of crime were 'wickedness' and 'sin'. The word comes via Old French from Latin *crimen* 'judgement or offence', which was based on *cernere* 'to judge' also in **concern** [LME], **recriminate** [E17th], and **discern** [LME]. The expression **crime doesn't pay** was a slogan associated with the 1930s American radio crime series *The Shadow*, in which it was spoken by the Shadow at the end of each broadcast. It originated earlier, though, and was the title of a silent film in 1912.

crimson [LME] The colour crimson was originally a deep red dye used in colouring fine cloth and velvet and obtained from an insect called the **kermes** [L16th], whose body was dried and ground up to produce the dye. The name of the insect came ultimately from Arabic *qirmiz*. *See also* INGRAIN, PURPLE, VERMILION

cringe *see* CRANK

cripes [E20th] This old-fashioned exclamation, associated with Billy Bunter and the current mayor of London, Boris Johnson, is a euphemistic corruption of 'Christ'.

cripple [OE] This is a word of Germanic origin, related to **creep** [OE], perhaps meaning 'someone who can only creep'.

crisis [LME] At one time a crisis was specifically the turning point of a disease, a change that leads either to recovery or death. The source is Greek *krisis* 'a decision', from *krinein* 'to decide, judge' also the root of **critic** [E17th], **critical** [L16th], and **criterion** [E17th]. Its more general sense

'decisive point' dates from the early 17th century. **Crisis? What crisis?** is often attributed to the British Prime Minister James Callaghan, but it was in fact coined by a headline writer in the newspaper the *Sun*. Returning to London from a meeting in the Caribbean in January 1979 during the 'Winter of Discontent' when the country was plagued by strikes and economic problems, Callaghan was interviewed at London Airport. He gave the comment 'I don't think other people in the world would share the view there is mounting chaos.' The next day the *Sun*'s headline read: 'Crisis? What Crisis?'

crisp [OE] To the Anglo-Saxons curly or frizzy hair was crisp. The word comes from Latin *crispus* 'curled'. It started to be used to mean 'brittle' in the early 16th century, though it is not entirely clear why. **Potato crisps** first appeared under that name during the 1920s. The first edible crisps, though, were described in medieval cookery books and were crisp pastries made by dropping batter into boiling fat. Crisp was also an old term for the 'crackling' of roast pork, and this may be the sense behind the phrase **burned to a crisp**.

criterion, critic, critical *see* CRISIS

crochet *see* CROQUET

crockery [E18th] Crockery is from obsolete *crocker* 'potter', from **crock**, spelt in Old English *croc*, *crocca* 'earthenware pot'. The crock in the expression **old crock** is a different word, perhaps of Flemish origin. Originally a late Middle English Scots term for an old ewe, it came in the late 19th century to denote an old or broken-down horse. **Crone** [LME] has a related history coming from Middle Dutch *croonje*, 'old ewe, carcass' from Old Northern French *caroigne* meaning both 'carrion' and 'cantankerous woman'. *See also* CARNIVAL

crocodile [ME] The name of the crocodile comes from Greek *krokodilos* 'worm of the stones', from *krokē* 'pebble' and *drilos* 'worm'. This is a reference to the crocodile's habit of basking in the sun on the banks of a river. In medieval English the spellings *cocodrille* and *cokadrill* were common. If you accuse someone of shedding **crocodile tears**, you mean they are putting on a display of insincere sorrow. The expression dates from the mid 16th century and comes from the ancient belief that crocodiles wept while luring or devouring their prey. According to a 16th-century account of the sailor John Hawkins's voyages, the crocodile's nature 'is ever when he would have his prey, to cry and sob like a Christian body, to provoke them to come to him, and then he snatcheth at them'.

croissant *see* CRESCENT

crone *see* CROCK

crony [M17th] This derives from Greek *khronios* 'long-lasting', which was based on *khronos* 'time'. In the 17th century crony was Cambridge University slang for 'an old friend' or 'a contemporary'. *CHUM is the Oxford University equivalent. The first record of crony is from the diary of Samuel Pepys (1633–1703), a former Cambridge man, for 30 May 1665: 'Jack Cole, my old school-fellow…who was a great chrony of mine.' His spelling showed the word's direct relationship with the original Greek. The political sense of **cronyism**, 'the appointment of your friends and associates to positions of authority', originated in the US during the 19th century. *See also* CHRONIC

crook [ME] A crook was originally a hooked tool or weapon. The source is Old Norse *krokr* 'hook'. The word used to mean 'dishonest trick, guile' in medieval English, and although this sense had fallen from use by the 17th century it gave rise to villains being known as crooks in late 19th-century America. In Australia and New Zealand crook has meant 'bad, unpleasant', 'dishonest, unscrupulous', and 'ill, unwell' since the late 1890s. These uses might come from the old British thieves' slang sense 'stolen'.

croon [LME] Originally Scots and northern English, croon is from Middle Low German and Middle Dutch *krōnen* 'groan, lament'. The use of croon in standard English was probably popularized by poet Robert Burns (1759–96).

crop [OE] From around AD 700 to the late 18th century crop, related to **group** [L17th], had a sense 'flower head, ear of corn', which gave rise to the main modern meaning 'a cultivated plant grown on a large scale' and also to senses referring to the top of something, such as the verb uses 'to cut very short' or 'to bite off and eat the tops of plants'. The sense 'a very short hairstyle' goes back to the late 18th century but is particularly associated with the 1920s, when the **Eton crop**, reminiscent of the style then worn at the English public school Eton, was fashionable for young women.

To **come a cropper** is to suffer a defeat or disaster. The origin of the phrase may be the 19th-century hunting slang term 'cropper', meaning 'a heavy fall'. Cropper probably came from **neck and crop**, an expression meaning 'completely or thoroughly' and originally used in the context of a horse falling to the ground. Crop here referred either to the rider's whip (originally the top part of a whip) or the horse's hindquarters. This sense is found in Old French *croupe* 'rump', which appears as croup in Middle English, and is the source of the **crupper** [ME], the bit of harness that goes from the saddle under the horse's tail, and which lies behind the word **croupier** [E18th]. In early use, this was a term for a person standing behind a gambler to give advice, adopted from French, *cropier* 'pillion rider, rider on the croup'.

croquet [M19th] Different as they seem, croquet and **crochet** [M19th] are probably the same word. Croquet is thought to be a form of French *crochet* 'hook, shepherd's crook', which can mean 'hockey stick' in parts of France, and in English refers to a handicraft in which yarn is made up into fabric with a hooked needle. The lawn game in which you drive balls through hoops with a mallet seems to have been invented in France but introduced to Ireland, from where it spread to England in the 1850s and quickly became a popular sport among the

croissant   crone   crony   crook   croon   crop

aristocracy. The French word is also the source of the musical note called the **crotchet** [ME], from its shape, and also the old-fashioned term meaning a perverse belief, a hooked or twisted point of view, in use since Middle English, and giving us the term **crotchety** in the early 19th century.

cross [OE] The word cross was initially used in English to refer to a monument in the form of a cross. The source is Old Norse *kross*, which in turn goes back to *crux*, a Latin word that gave us *CRUCIAL, **crucible** [LME] originally a night light or the sort that might be hung in front of a **crucifix** [ME], and *EXCRUCIATING.

People **cross their fingers** to ward off bad luck. What they are doing is making a miniature 'sign of the cross', whether they know it or not. To **cross someone's palm with silver** is to pay them for a favour or service. It probably comes from the idea of tracing the shape of a cross on a fortune-teller's palm with a silver coin before you are told what the future has in store.

In 49 BC Julius Caesar, having defeated the Gauls, brought his army south to fight a civil war against Pompey and the Roman Senate. When he **crossed the Rubicon**, a small river marking the boundary between Italy and the Roman province of Gaul, he was committed to war, having broken the law forbidding him to take his troops out of his province. **Cross** meaning 'annoyed' dates back to the 17th century. It derives from the nautical idea of a wind blowing across the bow of your ship rather than from behind, which produced the senses 'contrary, opposing', and 'adverse, opposed', and then 'annoyed, bad-tempered'. **Crosspatch** [E18th] is based on the obsolete word **patch** meaning 'fool, clown', perhaps from Italian *pazzo* 'madman'.

crossword [E20th] A crossword was originally a **wordcross**. The puzzle is said to have been invented by the journalist Arthur Wynne, whose first crossword appeared in a Sunday newspaper, the *New York World*, on 21 December 1913. Some people are addicted to **cryptic** crosswords, whereas others find them totally obscure. Their meaning is literally 'hidden', which is the

translation of the Greek root *kruptos*, also the source of **crypt** [LME] and *GROTTO.

crotchet, crotchety *see* CROQUET

croup, croupier *see* CROP

crowd [OE] Old English *crūdan* meant 'to press, hasten'. In Middle English the senses 'move by pushing' and 'push one's way' arose, leading to the sense 'congregate', and hence (mid 16th century) to the noun.

crown [ME] A crown is now usually a grand jewelled affair, but the original idea was probably closer to a simple garland or headdress. The root was Latin *corona* 'wreath' (*see* CORONARY), which is from Greek *korōnē* 'something bent'—the Greek crown was a laurel branch or wreath of flowers bent around the head to honour a victor or official. *See also* TIARA

crucial [E18th] The Latin word *crux*, 'a cross', is the source for crucial. It was originally a technical term, especially in anatomy, meaning 'cross-shaped', and a close relative appears in the name of the knee's **cruciate ligament** [L19th]. The meaning 'decisive' or 'very important', as in 'at a crucial stage', can be traced back to the Latin phrase *instantia crucis* 'crucial instance', coined in the early 17th century by the English statesman and philosopher Francis Bacon (1561–1626). His metaphor was based on the idea of a signpost at a crossroad—a place where you have to choose which way to go next. *See also* CROSS, EXCRUCIATING

crucible, crucifix *see* CROSS

crud *see* CURD

crude [LME] This is from Latin *crudus* 'raw, rough'. **Cruel** [ME] comes from the same root.

cruise *see* EXCRUCIATING

cruiser *see* DUTCH WORD PANEL

crumb [OE] The word crumb did not always have a *b* at the end: this was added in

cross crossword crotchet crotchety croup

the 16th century, influenced partly by the related word **crumble** [LME] and partly by words like dumb and thumb, where the 'b' was silent. The dated exclamation **crumbs** is a euphemism for 'Christ' and dates from the late 19th century. **Crummy** [M19th], now meaning 'unpleasant' and 'in poor condition', was originally spelled **crumby** and meant 'crumbly' or 'covered in crumbs'.

crumple [ME] This is from obsolete *crump* 'make or become curved', from Old English *crump* 'bent, crooked'.

crupper *see* CROP

crusade *see* CROSS

crust *see* CUSTARD

crux *see* EXCRUCIATING

cry [ME] The word cry is first recorded with the meanings 'ask for earnestly', 'ask for loudly'. It comes via French from Latin *quiritare* 'raise a public outcry', literally 'call on the *Quirites* (Roman citizens) for help'. Early examples of cry centre around sound—sometimes in sorrow or distress. The association with tears is recorded from around the mid 16th century. **Decry** [E17th] originally had the sense 'decrease the value of coins by royal proclamation'.

crypt, cryptic *see* CROSSWORD, GROTESQUE

crystal [OE] Crystal started out as a term for ice or a mineral that looks like ice. It comes from Old French *cristal*, and ultimately from Greek *krustallos* meaning 'ice, crystal'. Its use as a term in chemistry dates from the early 17th century.

cubicle [LME] A cubicle is now any small partitioned-off area, but at first it was specifically a little place for lying down or a bedroom. The source is Latin *cubiculum*, from *cubare* 'to lie down', source also of **incumbent** [LME]. **Incubation** [E17th] is based on the same Latin word, as is **concubine** [ME], originally someone you go to bed with.

cuckoo [ME] The cuckoo is one of those birds whose name echoes the sound of its distinctive call—other examples are **curlew** [LME], **hoopoe** [M17th], **kittiwake** [M17th], and **peewit** [E16th]. You can describe an unwelcome intruder in a place or situation as a **cuckoo in the nest**. This comes from the cuckoo's habit of laying her eggs to be raised in another bird's nest. **Cuckold** [OE], referring to the husband of an unfaithful wife, also derives from *cucu*, and plays on the same cuckoo-in-the-nest idea, although it is not actually the husband who is being the 'cuckoo'. The reason that a silly or mad person is described as a cuckoo, or is said to have **gone cuckoo**, is probably that the bird's monotonously repeated call suggests simple-mindedness. **Kook**, 'an eccentric person', is short for **cuckoo**. It was first recorded in the 1920s but only really became common in the late 1950s.
See also CLOUD, COCCYX

cue *see* QUEUE

cuff [LME] Before it came to refer to the end of a sleeve, cuff meant 'a glove or mitten'. Its origin is unknown, and it does not appear to be connected to the verb sense 'to hit or punch', which is mid 16th century and also of unknown origin. The expression **off the cuff**, meaning 'without preparation', dates from the 1930s, and was first used in the USA. It comes from the idea of a person making a speech and relying on notes they have jotted down on their shirt cuffs rather than reading out a prepared script.

culinary *see* KILN

culprit [L17th] Formerly in England, when a prisoner in court pleaded not guilty the Clerk of the Crown said: 'Culprit, how will you be tried?' This expression, first recorded in 1678, may have started out as a mistake in reading the written abbreviation *cul. prist.*, which stood for Old French *Culpable: prest d'averrer notre bille*, '(You are) guilty: (We are) ready to prove our indictment.' *Cul prit* (later **culprit**) came to mean 'a guilty person'. Use may have been

crumple crupper crusade crust crux cry

influenced by **culpable** [ME] which comes from Latin *culpa* 'fault, blame'.

culture [ME] This goes back to Latin *colere* '**cultivate**', a word that appeared from the same source in the mid 17th century. In early examples, a culture was 'a cultivated piece of land'. In late Middle English the meaning was 'cultivation of the soil' and this developed during the early 16th century into 'cultivation of the mind or manners'. Reference to the arts and other examples of human achievement dates from the early 19th century.

cummerbund *see* RAJ WORD PANEL

cumulonimbus *see* CLOUD

cunning [ME] If you described someone as cunning in the Middle Ages you meant they were skilful or learned—there was no implication of slyness or deceit. The word probably comes from Old Norse *kunnandi* 'knowledge', from *kunna* 'to know', which is related to the verb **can** [OE]. Witches and wizards used to be known as 'cunning women' and 'cunning men', from an old sense of the word 'possessing magical knowledge or skill'.

cup [OE] An Old English word, from Latin *cuppa*. As early as 1640 cup could mean 'a sports trophy in the form of a cup', originally for horse-racing. To be **in your cups** is to be drunk. In the past you could also use the phrase to mean 'during a drinking bout'. It is unclear which meaning is intended in this passage in the biblical Apocrypha on the strength of wine: 'And when they are in their cups, they forget their love both to friends and brethren, and a little after draw out swords.'

cupboard [LME] In the late Middle Ages a cupboard, as its spelling might suggest, was a *BOARD, or table, on which you displayed cups, plates, and other pieces of crockery. We would now call this a sideboard. The modern meaning of cupboard emerged in the 16th century.

cupid, cupidity *see* EROTIC

cur [ME] A cur is now disparaging, whether used of dog or man. However, it was first used generally in the sense 'dog'. It probably comes from the phrase *cur-dog*, perhaps from Old Norse *kurr* 'grumbling', but used to mean 'house dog'.

curate [ME] The word curate, 'an assistant to a parish priest', comes from medieval Latin *curatus*, from Latin *cura* 'care' (because the parishioners are in his care), the source of a number of words including **cure** [ME], **curator** [LME], **accurate** [L16th] 'done with care', and **secure** [LME] 'free from care'. You can describe something that is partly good and partly bad as a **curate's egg**. This is one of those rare expressions whose origin can be precisely identified. A cartoon in an 1895 edition of the magazine *Punch* features a meek curate at the breakfast table with his bishop. The caption reads: 'BISHOP: "I'm afraid you've got a bad egg, Mr Jones." CURATE: "Oh no, my Lord, I assure you! Parts of it are excellent!" ' Only ten years later the phrase had become sufficiently familiar to appear in a publication called *Minister's Gazette of Fashion*: 'The past spring and summer season has seen much fluctuation. Like the curate's egg, it has been excellent in parts.'

curb [LME] A curb was a strap passing under the jaw of a horse and fastened to the bit, used for checking an unruly horse. This caused the horse to bend its neck, an action that produced the word. It derives from Old French *courber* 'to bend or bow', from Latin *curvare*, also the source of **curve** [LME]. The idea of 'holding back' led to the more general sense of a check or restraint. Curb is also the American spelling of what in British English is a **kerb** [M17th], a stone edging to a pavement or path. The original idea here was of a border or frame bending round something, for example, the top of a well or a trapdoor.

curd [LME] The original English word for curds was **crud**, which only acquired its sense 'filth, rubbish' in the USA in the 1940s. The swapping round of sounds in a word is called metathesis and is particularly common with 'r' and a vowel (*compare* BIRD). Since the late 16th century **curdle** has been used for the action of forming curds.

cure *see* CURATE

curfew [ME] Today a curfew is sometimes imposed during periods of emergency or conflict, as a way of keeping people off the streets, usually at night. In the Middle Ages, though, the curfew was the time by which people had to put out or cover the fire in their hearth—the objective was not to keep order but to stop houses burning down. Curfew is an Old French word, from *cuvrir* 'to cover' and *feu* 'fire'.

curious [ME] The word curious came into the language in the sense 'eager to know or learn something'. Its source is Latin *curiosus* 'careful', from *cura* 'care'. The word has had a variety of meanings over the centuries, including 'skilfully made', 'very accurate or precise', and 'having an exquisite taste'. The sense 'strange or unusual' appeared early on in the 18th century. Among booksellers curious used to be a euphemistic term for erotic or pornographic works.

The Curious Incident of the Dog in the Night-Time is the title of a best-selling 2003 novel by Mark Haddon but the words come originally from one of Sir Arthur Conan Doyle's Sherlock Holmes mysteries. In the story *Silver Blaze* (1884), Holmes draws Watson's attention to 'the curious incident of the dog in the night-time'. When Watson protests that 'the dog did nothing in the night-time', Holmes responds: 'That was the curious incident.' The point is that the dog did not raise the alarm because he already knew the person who had disturbed him. The saying **curiosity killed the cat** is first recorded around 1900. The older form is **care killed the cat**, which is first recorded in Ben Jonson's 1598 play *Every Man in His Humour*. **Curiouser and curiouser** is a quotation from Lewis Carroll's *Alice in Wonderland* (1865). ' "Curiouser and curiouser!" cried Alice (she was so much surprised that for a moment she quite forgot how to speak good English).'

curlew *see* CUCKOO

currant [ME] This comes from the phrase *raisons of Corauntz*, translating Anglo-Norman French *raisins de Corauntz* 'grapes of *Corinth*', which was their original source.

current *see* CURSOR

curry [L16th] The curry that you eat comes from *kari*, a word meaning 'sauce' in the South Indian and Sri Lankan language Tamil. Travellers were bringing back tales of this spicy new food as early as 1598, and in 1747 a book called *The Art of Cookery* told its readers how 'To make a Currey the Indian way'. *See also* VINDALOO

If you **curry favour** you try to win favour by flattering someone and behaving obsequiously. The expression dates from the early 16th century and has nothing at all to do with Indian cuisine. It comes from a different word, also spelled curry, meaning 'to groom a horse with a coarse brush or comb', which came into Middle English from Old French. Curry favour itself is an alteration of the medieval form *curry favel*. Favel or Fauvel was the name of a horse in a 14th-century French tale who became a symbol of cunning and deceit. So 'to groom Favel' came to mean to handle him in just as cunning a way, by flattering him or behaving in an ingratiating way. *See also* RAJ WORD PANEL

cursor [ME] Nowadays we call the movable indicator on our computer screen the cursor. In medieval English a cursor was a running messenger: it is a borrowing of the Latin word for 'a runner', and comes from *currere* 'to run'. From the late 16th century cursor became the term for a sliding part of a slide rule or other instrument, marked with a line for pinpointing the position on a scale that you want, the forerunner of the computing sense. *Currere* is the source of very many English words including **course** [ME] something you run along; **concourse** [LME] originally a crowd who had 'run together'; **current** [ME] originally meaning 'running, flowing'; **discursive** [L16th] running away from the point; **excursion** [L16th] running out to see things; **intercourse** [LME] originally an exchange running between people; and **precursor**

cure curfew curious curlew currant current

[LME] one who goes before; as well as supplying the *cur* part of **concur** [LME]; **incur** [LME]; **occur** [LME] (from *ob-* 'against'); and **recur** [ME].

curt [LME] 'In more temperate climes, hair is curt', writes Sir Thomas Herbert in his 1665 account of his travels in Africa and Asia, reflecting curt's original meaning, 'short or shortened'. The word comes from Latin *curtus* 'cut short, abridged', source also of **curtail** [LME]. By the 19th century you could use curt to describe people who were not only concise or brief in what they were saying, but rudely so.

curtsey *see* COURTEOUS

curve *see* CURB

cushion [ME] You can tell that the Romans knew a thing or two about reclining in comfort when you discover that they had separate words for a hip cushion (*coxinum*) and an elbow cushion (*cubital*). The former word, from Latin *coxa* 'hip or thigh', gave rise to Old French *cuissin*, from which we get cushion.

cushty *see* ROMANY WORD PANEL

cushy *see* RAJ WORD PANEL

cusp [L16th] When we say someone is **on the cusp of** something we mean that they are at a point of transition between two states. This probably comes from the astrological use of cusp as the term for the division between one astrological sign and another. The word comes from Latin *cuspis*, meaning 'a point', and can also be applied to the pointed end where two curves meet, such as the tip of a crescent moon.

custard [LME] A custard was originally a pie. Spelled *crustarde* or *custarde*, this was an open pie that contained meat or fruit in a spiced or sweetened sauce thickened with eggs. Over time the name gradually came to be applied to the sauce rather than the pie itself. The origin of the word was Old French *crouste* 'a crust' from Latin *crusta* 'rind, shell, crust', which is also where our word **crust** [ME] comes from.

custom [ME] Both custom and **costume** [E18th] come from the same root, Latin *consuetudo* 'custom, habit'—costume was originally the decor and clothing appropriate to a painting with a historical theme. A **customer** [LME] was a person who habitually bought from a particular tradesman, and **customs** [LME] were payments traditionally made to a lord or king.

cut [ME] There is evidence for the verb cut from the end of the 13th century. It may well have existed before that in Old English, but there are no written examples to prove it. You say something is **cut and dried** when it is completely settled or decided. There used to be a distinction between the cut and dried herbs sold in herbalists' shops and those that had been freshly gathered. The **cut of someone's jib** is their appearance or expression. A jib is a triangular sail set forward of the mast on a sailing ship or boat. Its proportions were variable and the characteristic shape of a particular jib helped to identify a ship. Hence the term came to be applied to the impression given by a person's appearance. Something **cuts the mustard** when it comes up to expectations or meets the required standard. In early 20th-century US slang mustard had the meaning 'the best of anything'. **Cut to the chase**, meaning 'come to the point', comes from film-making. The idea is of moving straight to the most exciting part.

cute [ME] This started out in the 18th century as a shortened form of **acute** (*see* ACCENT) and originally meant 'clever or shrewd'. The sense 'attractive or pretty' dates from late 19th-century America. **Cutesy**, meaning 'cute in a sickly or sentimental way', is also American, and was first recorded in 1914.

cuticle *see* HIDE

cutlass [L16th] The origin of cutlass for a sword with a slightly curved blade, is French *coutelas*, based on Latin *cultellus* 'small knife', source also of **cutlery** [ME] and **coulter** [OE], the cutting blade of a plough.

curt curtsey curve cushion cushty cushy

cutlet *see* COAST

cut-throat *see* DARE

cybernetics [1948] In 1948 the American mathematician Norbert Wiener wrote 'We have decided to call the entire field of control and communication theory, whether in the machine or in the animal, by the name Cybernetics.' He based the word on Greek *kybernetes* 'steersman'. He was not quite as original as we might think as the work *cybernétique* had been used for the art of governing exactly 110 years earlier in France. The word introduced cyber- as a combining form giving us a whole range of new words from the **cyberspace** [1982] used by computers to the more exotic **cyberpunk** genre of science fiction [1983], and **cybersex** [1991].

cycle, cyclone *see* WHEEL

cylinder [L16th] The shape and movement of a cylinder are captured in the word's origin. *Cylinder* comes via Latin from Greek *kulindros* 'roller'.

cymbal [OE] The shape of a cymbal is central to its name: it comes via Latin *cymbalum* from Greek *kumbalon*, from *kumbē* 'cup'. **Chime** [ME] was first recorded as meaning 'cymbal' as a noun, and 'ring out' as a verb. It is probably the Old English form, *cimbal* (which would have been pronounced with a 'ch' sound, the modern 's' sound coming from French) later interpreted as chime bell.

cynic [M16th] The original Cynics were members of a school of ancient Greek philosophers who displayed a contempt for wealth, luxury, and pleasure, believing that such things distracted a person from the quest for self-knowledge. The word comes from Greek *kunikos*. The Greek word probably derives from *Kunosarges*, the name of the school where one of their founders, Antisthenes, taught. This is more likely than the traditional story that the word comes from the Greek word for dog, *kuōn*, and so means 'doglike or churlish'. *See also* EPICURE, STOIC

Dd

dachshund *see* GERMAN WORD PANEL

daddy *see* POPE

daft [OE] In Old English a daft person was mild and gentle, qualities which tougher folk have often interpreted as signs of foolishness or mental incapacity. **Deft** [ME] was a related word, which first meant 'mild, meek' as well as 'skilful'. Daft came to refer to lack of intelligence during the Middle Ages, and from the 16th century it could also imply madness. It could also mean playfulness—the festivities of Christmas used to be referred to as **the daft days**. *See also* CRAZY, SILLY

dag *see* AUSTRALIAN WORD PANEL

daisy [OE] Daisies close at night and open again in the morning, revealing the yellow disc at their centre. This gives them their name, as daisy is a contraction of *day's eye*. Being dead and buried loses some of its solemnity and fear when you are **under the daisies** or are **pushing up daisies**. This light-hearted expression dates from the early 20th century, and the First World War poet Wilfred Owen (1893–1918) alludes to its use by soldiers in the trenches. **Fresh as a daisy** refers to the opening of the daisy in the morning, and to its welcome appearance in spring. It has been used by writers since at least the 14th century, when it appears in the works of the poet Geoffrey Chaucer (*c*.1343–1400).

dally *see* SHILLY-SHALLY

dame [ME] In its earliest use dame meant 'a female ruler'. It comes ultimately from Latin *domina* 'mistress', the root of which

also gave us *DANGER, **dominate** [E17th], **dominion** [ME], and *DUNGEON. Dame was used as a form of address to a woman of rank from the Middle Ages, and in the 17th century became a legal title—it is now the title given to a woman with the rank of Knight Commander or holder of the Grand Cross in the Orders of Chivalry. Alongside this elevated use ran a more popular strand, where a dame was the mistress of a house or school, or any elderly or mature woman. This gave us the **pantomime dame**, the comic middle-aged character usually played by a man, who makes her first appearance in print in the early 20th century. Dame is used in the USA for any girl or woman—as Oscar Hammerstein II told us in his 1949 song from the musical *South Pacific*, 'There is nothin' like a dame'. **Dam** [LME] in the sense 'mother (of an animal)' is also from dame (the sense 'a barrier' [ME] is Germanic). *See also* BABY, DAMSEL

damn [ME] The word damn goes back to Latin *damnare* 'to inflict loss on'. Originally to damn someone was to **condemn** them (a Middle English word from the same root), but associations with being condemned to hell have coloured much of the later history of the word. The desire to avoid profanity led to less offensive alternatives, such as **darn**, used since the 18th century. The older sense of 'to condemn' survives in the phrase to **damn with faint praise**, which was popularized by the 18th-century poet Alexander Pope in his 'An Epistle to Dr Arbuthnot'.

damp [ME] We do not think of something damp as being dangerous, but the word originally meant a noxious gas. This use survives in **firedamp** [L17th], a name for methane gas, especially when it forms an explosive mixture with air in coal mines. Damp did not come to refer to wetness until the 18th century. The **damp squib** which failed to go off has probably always marred firework displays—a squib is a small firework that burns with a hissing sound before exploding. From the middle of the 19th century the phrase began to be used of situations and events that were much less impressive than expected. Nowadays, the phrase is sometimes heard as 'damp squid',

dachshund daddy daft dag daisy dally

people substituting a more familiar and more familiarly damp word for the rarer squib. *See also* FIASCO, LEAD, LEMON. Both damp and **dank** [ME] are Germanic in origin, but were not originally connected.

damper [M18th] It stops the vibration of piano strings, absorbs shock in cars, and regulates the draught in chimneys, but originally a damper was a person or thing that dampened the spirits. This is what to **put a damper on** refers to. In Australia and New Zealand an unleavened loaf or cake of flour and water has been called a damper since the early 19th century.

damsel [ME] In romances any knight in shining armour worth his salt in a tale of chivalry scoured the country looking for a **damsel in distress** to rescue. Damsel is based on Latin *domina* 'mistress', which is also the source of *DAME and of modern French *mademoiselle*.

dance [ME] The word dance stepped into English from French in the Middle Ages. The **dance of death** was a medieval image in which Death led all types of people to the grave, emphasizing that everyone was equally faced with death. It was also known under its French name **danse macabre** (*see* MACABRE). The unlucky person who had to **dance attendance on someone** was kept waiting in an antechamber before being called in to speak to the elevated personage they had come to see. There they would no doubt fidget and kick their heels, as if dancing.

dandelion [LME] The toothed leaves of the dandelion explain the origin of its name. French *dent-de-lion* means 'lion's tooth'. The name came into English in the late Middle Ages. The usual term for the flower in French is now *pissenlit*, which has a parallel in English **pissabed** [M16th], another name for the dandelion. The plant was formerly well known for its diuretic properties.

dandruff [M16th] The first element is unknown; the second (-*ruff*) is perhaps related to Middle English *rove* 'scurfiness'.

dandy [L18th] Dandies emerged in the late 18th century. The word is perhaps a shortened form of **Jack-a-dandy**, a 17th-century term for a conceited fellow, where dandy is a pet form of the name Andrew. The original dandies, such as Beau Brummel, were not flamboyant, but understated and elegant. They reacted against the wigs and knee breeches of an older generation, and pioneered the forerunner of the business suit. Dandy quickly became a term of approval for anything of high quality, a use which continues in US expressions such as **fine and dandy**. *See also* DUDE

danger [ME] From the early Middle Ages into the 19th century danger meant 'jurisdiction, power', originally 'the power of a lord and master, power to harm'. This reflects its origin in Latin *dominus* 'lord', the root of which also gave us *DAME, **predominant** [M16th], and *DUNGEON. In the later Middle Ages danger developed its main modern sense.

dank *see* DAMP

danse macabre *see* DANCE, MACABRE

Darby and Joan [L18th] An anonymous poem of 1735 in *The Gentleman's Magazine* contained the lines: 'Old Darby, with Joan by his side, / You've often regarded with wonder: / He's dropsical, she is sore-eyed, / Yet they're never happy asunder.' People quickly began to use the names, whose exact origin is unknown, for any devoted old married couple.

dare [OE] This is a word with the deepest roots, related to forms in Greek and in Sanskrit, the ancient language of India. It originally meant 'to have the courage to do something'. By the late 16th century there also existed the sense 'to challenge or defy someone', which is the meaning behind **daredevil** [L18th], a contraction of 'someone ready to dare the devil'. This sort of formation is also seen in **cut-throat** [M16th] and **scarecrow** [M16th].

dark [OE] The origins of dark are mysterious, although it may be related to

damper damsel dance dandelion dandruff

German *tarnen* 'to conceal'. Ideas of secrecy and mystery are behind such phrases as to **keep someone in the dark** and **a dark secret**. Also mysterious is the **Dark Lady**, the anonymous woman to whom Shakespeare dedicated a number of his sonnets. Although there have been various suggestions as to who she was, the lady has never been certainly identified. A **dark night of the soul** is a period of great depression or soul-searching. The phrase was used by F. Scott Fitzgerald, author of *The Great Gatsby*, in 1936: 'In a real dark night of the soul it is always three o'clock in the morning.' It originated in the title of a poem by the Spanish mystic and poet St John of the Cross (1542–91), *Noche oscura*, 'Dark Night', which was rendered by a Victorian translator as 'Dark Night of the Soul'. One of the most famous opening lines in literature is 'It was a **dark and stormy night**', which begins *Paul Clifford* (1830) by the British novelist and politician Lord Edward Bulwer-Lytton. Today his name is a byword for bad writing, and there is an annual Bulwer-Lytton Fiction Contest for bad writing in the USA, but in his lifetime he was a successful writer who also became a reforming MP.

darling *see* DEAR

darn *see* DAMN

dashboard [M19th] This was originally a board or leather apron on the front of a vehicle to stop mud from being splashed by the horses' heels into the interior and of movable side pieces of a cart which served the same purpose. This was transferred to the control panel in motor vehicles at the beginning of the 20th century. To dash [ME] originally meant to strike against, so could apply to mud splashing. It developed the sense 'destroy, bring to nothing' in the 16th century, which is the source of to **dash someone's hopes**.

data [M17th] Originally recorded as a term in philosophy referring to 'things assumed to be facts', it is the Latin plural of **datum** 'a piece of information', literally 'something given'. Although plural, data is often treated in English English as a singular meaning 'information', although Americans and Australians use 'the data are...'. *See also* DICE. In the Middle Ages letters could be headed with the Latin formula *data* (*epistola*)...'(letter) given or delivered...' at a certain day or place. From this comes **date** [ME] in the time sense. The date you eat is also Middle English but comes from Greek *daktulos* 'finger', because of the finger-like shape of the plant's leaves.

daub [LME] This is from Old French *dauber* 'clothe in white', 'clothe', 'whitewash', 'plaster', from Latin *dealbare* 'whiten, whitewash' from *albus* 'white' (*see* ALBUM). All the English uses have developed from that of 'plaster'.

dauphin *see* DOLPHIN

dawn *see* DAY

day [OE] The ancient word day has a Germanic root which may have meant 'to burn', through association with the heat of summer. The **working day** came with increasing industrialization, in the early 19th century. This is the day you refer to if you **call it a day**, 'decide to stop doing something'. In the mid 19th century, when working people had fewer holidays, the expression was to **call it half a day**. If something unusual is **all in a day's work**, it is taken in your stride, as part of your normal routine. Jonathan Swift's *Polite Conversations*, which mocked the clichés of 18th-century society, suggest that the phrase was in circulation even then. **Daylight** dawned in the early Middle Ages (LME **dawn** itself is closely related to 'day'). It was always associated with seeing, and in the mid 18th century **daylights** appeared as a term for the eyes. This is not the meaning in to **beat the living daylights out of someone**, where 'daylights' are the vital organs, such as the heart, lungs, and liver (*see* LIGHT). The word 'living' is a later addition to the phrase, from the late 19th century. **Days of wine and roses** are times of pleasure, which will inevitably pass. The phrase comes from a line in a poem by the 19th-century poet Ernest Dowson: 'They are not long, the days of wine and roses'.

darling   darn   dashboard   data   daub

daze [ME] Daze was formed from **dazed**, from Old Norse *dasathr* 'weary'. In English the sense 'benumb with cold' may have been the earliest, and it is easy to see how this could develop into the senses confused or unable to operate normally. One development was dazed by excess light, which in the late 15th century developed its own form **dazzle**. In the USA in the late 19th century this developed in turn into **razzle-dazzle**, giving the new words **razzmattazz** [L19th] and **razzle** [E20th] from which very quickly developed the phrase **on the razzle.**

de rigueur *see* FRENCH WORD PANEL

dead [OE] Dead is related to Dutch *dood* and German *Tod* 'death', and to **death** itself. Their shared ancestor is the origin of *DIE. Often it is not enough to be dead: someone must be **as dead as a doornail** or as a *DODO. The comparison with the extinct dodo is understandable enough, but it is not clear why doornails are particularly associated with death. A doornail was one of the large iron studs that were once used on doors to give additional strength or simply for decoration. It may also have been the large stud struck by the knocker, which, subject to constant pounding, could be considered well and truly dead. The phrase goes back to the Middle Ages and was used by Shakespeare, in whose time a person could also be **as dead as a herring**. Death has prompted many reflections on the human condition. The Roman poet Claudian wrote *omnia mors aequat*, 'death levels all'—in English **death is the great leveller**. Shakespeare's *The Tempest* contains the line 'He that dies pays all debts', a thought that had become **death pays all debts** by the time of the novelist Sir Walter Scott. That **nothing is certain but death and taxes** has been a view since the early 18th century. The original **deadline** [M19th] was a line drawn around a military prison, beyond which any prisoner was liable to be shot. It is first mentioned in a document of the 1860s.

deaf [OE] The ancient ancestor of deaf also produced Greek *tuphlos* 'blind'. It probably referred to general dullness in perception, rather than dullness in any particular sense. Emphatic comparisons include **as deaf as an adder** and **as deaf as a post**. The traditional deafness of an adder is based on an image in the Psalms, 'the deaf adder that stoppeth her ear'. Actually, all snakes are deaf, not just the adder—they 'hear' by means of sensors that pick up vibrations in the ground such as footsteps.

deal *see* DOLE

dear [OE] Old English *dēore* is Germanic in origin and related to Dutch *dier* 'beloved', also to Dutch *duur* and German *teuer* 'expensive', showing that the word has long had the two senses it still has. **Darling** [OE] was a pet form of 'dear', while **dearth** [ME] started out as a time when things were expensive through scarcity.

death *see* DEAD

debacle *see* BACTERIUM

debate [ME] Debate is a word that has undergone a considerable shift in meaning. At its root is Latin *battere* 'to fight', and this was the original English meaning of debate. From that it acquired the sense 'quarrel' and 'dispute', which rapidly led to the more civilized idea of something deliberated and discussed. The phrase **debatable land** [ME] for borderland claimed by two nations, particularly the area fought over by England and Scotland, keeps the original sense.

debauch [L16th] This is from French *débaucher* meaning 'turn away from one's duty', 'entice away from the service of one's master'. The ultimate origin is debated, but one attractive suggestion is that it comes from *bauche* meaning 'place of work', giving an original sense 'draw away from the workshop'.

debt [ME] This comes via Old French from Latin *debitum* 'something owed', the past participle of *debere* 'owe'. **Debit** [LME] is from the same source.

decade [LME] One book by the Roman historian Livy, who lived at the time of Christ, was in ten parts, and the name for each division was translated into English as decade. The earliest uses of the word in English refer to the sections of a similar literary work. It did not come to refer to a period of ten years until the early 17th century. The root of decade, Greek *deka* 'ten', is also that of *DECIMATE and of the first element of units such as the **decilitre** and **decimetre** [L18th].

decant [17th] This is from medieval Latin *decanthare*, from the Latin prefix *de-* 'away from' and *canthus* 'edge, rim', a word used by the alchemists to denote the angular lip of a beaker. Greek *kanthos* 'corner of the eye' is the base.

decapitate *see* CAPITAL

decay *see* ACCIDENT

decease *see* CEDE

decide [LME] Decide was 'bring to a settlement' in early uses. It comes from Latin *decidere* 'determine', from *de-* meaning 'off' and *caedere* 'to cut'. *Caedere* is also found in **concise** [L16th] literally 'cut up'; **excise** [L16th] 'cut out'; **precise** [LME] 'cut in advance or short'; *SCISSORS, and **suicide** [M17th] 'cut or kill yourself'.

decilitre *see* DECADE

decimal *see* TEN

decimate [LME] When Roman legions mutinied, they would be decimated—one in every ten men would be selected by lot and executed. In its first recorded use in English, in the late 16th century, decimate refers to this practice, but by the mid 17th century people were using it of other acts of killing, destroying, or removing one in ten. They then lost sight of the military context, and soon any severe loss or destruction could be described as decimation. *See also* DECADE

decimetre *see* DECADE

deck [LME] Originally deck was a material such as canvas that was used as a covering, especially on a ship. By the end of the 15th century it was in use for the platform of

planks extending across a ship. A deck-chair was originally used for passengers who wanted to sit on a ship's deck. Because they were foldable, they could be put away if you needed to **clear the decks**. A **double-decker** [M19th] was originally a ship with two decks rather than a bus.

A pack of cards is usually called a deck in the USA, and the term was formerly also British—it is recorded in Shakespeare. The definition in Dr Johnson's *Dictionary of the English Language*, published in 1755, indicates the idea behind the term: 'A pack of cards piled regularly on each other', like the decks of a ship. In the USA a person who is **not playing with a full deck** is unintelligent. As a verb deck meant 'to decorate, adorn', as in 'Deck the halls with boughs of holly', from the early 16th century. In the 1940s a new meaning arose in the USA, 'to knock someone to the ground with a punch', probably from the naval expression **hit the deck**, which originally meant 'jump out of bed for a morning roll call'.

declare *see* CLARINET

decline *see* LEAN

decompose *see* COMPOST

decoy [M16th] A decoy was originally a pond with net-covered channels into which ducks and other wildfowl were enticed to be captured. The wildfowl were attracted by a **decoy duck**, a tame duck trained for the purpose or an imitation duck placed on the water. **Decoy** dates from the early 17th century and probably comes from Dutch *de kooi* 'the decoy', the second element of which goes back to Latin *cavea* *CAVE.

decrease *see* CRESCENT

decree [ME] Early decrees were edicts issued by an ecclesiastical council to settle a point of doctrine or discipline. The word is from Old French *decre*, from Latin *decretum* 'something decided', from *decernere* 'decide'. The *nisi* in the term **decree nisi** (late 19th century) is the Latin word for 'unless'; the phrase represents a court order stating when a marriage will end 'unless' a good reason to prevent divorce is produced.

decant decapitate decay decease decide

decrepit [LME] This word describing someone who is elderly and infirm owes its extended sense to the noise of creaking. The source is Latin *decrepitus*, from *crepare* 'to rattle, creak'.

decry *see* CRY

default *see* FALSE

deduce *see* DUCT

deep [OE] The word deep is related to **dip** [OE] and **dive** [OE], and in Old English could also mean **depth** [LME]. The phrase **in deep water**, 'in trouble or difficulty', has biblical origins. The writer of one of the Psalms begged, 'Let me be delivered from them that hate me, and out of the deep waters'. The deep waters of a swimming pool did not become familiar enough to provide linguistic inspiration until the 20th century. If you **go off the deep end** you have an emotional outburst, especially of anger, and to **jump** (or **be thrown**) **in at the deep end** is to face a difficult undertaking with little or no preparation or experience.

deer [OE] In Old English a deer was not just the animal we are familiar with now, it could be any four-footed creature. The meaning was narrowed down to its modern sense in the Middle Ages. The word goes back to Indo-European, to a root meaning 'breathing creature'.

defeat [LME] Early recorded senses were 'undo, destroy, annul'; it goes back to medieval Latin *disfacere* 'undo'.

defecate [LME] This originally meant 'clear of dregs, purify' from Latin *defaecare*, formed from *de-* (expressing removal) and *faex, faec-* 'dregs'. The current sense dates from the mid 19th century.

defect *see* EFFECT

defence, defend *see* FENCE

defer[1] *see* DIFFER

defer[2] *see* REFER

deficit *see* EFFECT

define *see* FINANCE

deflate *see* INFLATE

deflect *see* FLEX

deform *see* FORM

defrock *see* FROCK

deft *see* DAFT

defunct [M16th] 'Deceased' was the first recorded sense of this word which comes from Latin *defunctus* meaning 'dead'. The meaning, 'no longer in use or in fashion', dates from the mid 18th century.

degenerate *see* GENDER

degrade *see* GRADE

degree [ME] The source of degree is a French word based on Latin *de-* 'down' and *gradus* 'step' source of *GRADE. Early senses of the word include 'step, tier', 'rank' and 'relative state'. The use of degree for an academic qualification came from the medieval Mastership or Doctorate, which was attained in stages or degrees. The 'step' sense is found in the geometrical use [LME], measurement of heat [E18th], and in the expression **by degrees** or step by step.

deify *see* DIVINE

deign [ME] To deign is to do something that you consider beneath your dignity, and the word is bound up with 'dignity'. It goes back to Latin *dignare* 'to judge to be worthy', which was formed from *dignus* 'worthy', the source of **dignity** [ME], and **dignify** [LME], and the negative **disdain** [ME] 'consider unworthy'.

deject *see* JET

delete [LME] 'Destroy' was the early recorded sense of delete, from Latin *delere* 'blot out, efface'.

deliberate [LME] The sense of deliberate 'done intentionally' is older than the closely related, but slightly differently pronounced, deliberate 'to engage in careful

decrepit decry default deduce deep deer

consideration'. The first is medieval, the second from the mid 16th century. Both go back to a Latin word formed from *libra* 'scales', which captured the idea of weighing something up before coming to a conclusion. In the early 18th century the essayist Joseph Addison wrote that 'When love once pleads admission to our hearts...The woman that deliberates is lost'. This is the forerunner of the modern proverb **he who hesitates is lost**, which is not recorded until more than 150 years later.

delicious [ME] This comes from late Latin *deliciosus*, from Latin *deliciae* 'delight, pleasure'. **Luscious** [LME] may be an alteration of delicious.

delight [ME] For the first three centuries of its life delight was spelled *delit*, as was its French original. The *-gh-* spelling emerged in the 16th century, on the model of light and other native English words. Delight has no direct connection with *LIGHT, though, but goes back ultimately to Latin *delectare* 'to charm'. The English name of the sweet **Turkish delight** was originally **lumps of delight** (recorded from 1861). It was still a novelty when Charles Dickens wrote in his unfinished novel *The Mystery of Edwin Drood*: ' "I want to go to the Lumps-of-Delight shop." "To the —?" "A Turkish sweetmeat, sir." ' The first known written record of the name Turkish delight is from 1872.

delirium [M16th] This is a Latin word adopted into English, from the verb *delirare* 'deviate, be deranged'. The literal meaning is 'deviate from the furrow', from *de-* 'away' and *lira* 'a ridge between furrows'.

deliver [ME] Deliver goes back to Latin *liber* 'free', which is also the source of *LIBERTY. The word has been used for taking and handing over letters and goods since the late Middle Ages. The phrase to **deliver the goods**, 'to provide what is promised and expected', is from the USA, and the first known examples are from political debate in the 1870s. Highwaymen really did tell their victims to **stand and deliver**—the phrase is

mentioned in an early 18th-century account of the lives of highwaymen.

delta [M16th] The triangular area of sediment at the mouth of some rivers takes the name delta from its shape, which is like that of the triangular fourth letter of the Greek alphabet, called *delta*. The original delta was at the mouth of the River Nile, which was called **the Delta** from the mid 16th century. The shape of the Greek letter also gave its name to the **delta wing**, a triangular swept-back wing fitted on some jet aircraft, immediately after the Second World War.

delude [LME] This is from Latin *deludere* 'to mock', from *de-* (here with pejorative force) and *ludere* 'to play'.

deluge [LME] This is from an Old French variant of *diluve* 'flood', from Latin *diluvium*, from *diluere* 'wash away', also the source of **dilute** [M16th]. The English word **antediluvian** [M17th] meaning literally 'before the (biblical) Flood' is also based on Latin *diluvium*.

demagogue *see* DEMOCRACY

demand *see* COMMANDO

demented *see* MIND

demise *see* MESSAGE

democracy [L16th] The word democracy came directly from French in the mid 16th century, but goes back to Greek *dēmokratia*, from *dēmos* 'the people' and *kratia* 'power, rule'. *Demos* is also the source of **demagogue** [M17th] where it is combined with *agōgos* 'leading', and **epidemic** [E17th] which comes from *epidēmia* 'the prevalence of disease' which goes back to *epi* 'upon' and *dēmos* 'the people'.

demolish *see* MOLE

demon [ME] The Greek word *daimōn* is the root of demon. In ancient Greece a demon or daemon was a divine or supernatural being somewhere between gods and humans, or an attendant spirit or

delicious   delight   delirium   deliver   delta

inspiring force, a sense picked up by Philip Pullman in his *His Dark Materials* books. These demons were not evil; these did not appear until the writing of the Septuagint, a Greek version of the Hebrew Bible, in the 3rd and 2nd centuries BC. In Australia and New Zealand demon is a word for a police officer. This could be from **Van Dieman's Land**, an early name for Tasmania, or from **dee**, an old slang term for a detective, and *MAN. Either way, the criminals who first used it probably considered the usual sense of demon to be appropriate. *See also* DEVIL

demonstrate *see* MUSTER

demur [ME] Demur 'raise doubts or objections', was first recorded as meaning 'linger, delay'. The source of the verb is Old French *demourer*, based on Latin *de-* 'away, completely' and *morari* 'delay, stay'. **Demure** [LME] with which it is often confused, probably comes from the same French word, influenced by Old French *mur* 'grave' (from Latin *maturus* 'ripe or mature' source of **mature** [LME]). Early meanings of demure were 'sober, serious, reserved'. The sense 'reserved, shy' dates from the late 17th century.

dendrochronology *see* RHODODENDRON

denigrate [LME] To denigrate someone is to blacken their reputation. The original meaning of the word, in the late Middle Ages, was 'to make black or dark in colour'; the modern sense developed in the early 16th century. The root of the word is Latin *niger* 'black'.

denim *see* JEANS

denominate *see* NAME

denounce *see* ANNOUNCE

dent *see* INDENT

dental *see* INDENT, TOOTH

dentist *see* TOOTH

deny *see* NEGATIVE

depart *see* PART

depend *see* PENDANT

depict *see* PICTURE

depilatory *see* PILE

deplore [M16th] To deplore something was originally to weep over it, then regret deeply. The sense weakened over time until in the mid 19th century it was merely to disapprove strongly. The word comes from Latin *deplorare*, from *de-* 'away, thoroughly' and *plorare* 'bewail'.

deploy *see* DISPLAY

depot [L18th] Latin *depositum*, 'something put down', is the source of both depot and **deposit** [L16th], although depot entered English from French *dépôt*. The earliest meaning of depot was 'an act of depositing' rather than 'a place for storage', as it is now. The earliest depots were military establishments for stores, assembled recruits, and even prisoners of war.

deprave [LME] The first recorded sense of deprave was 'pervert the meaning or intention of something'; it comes from Latin *depravare*, from *de-* 'down, thoroughly' and *pravus* 'crooked, perverse'.

depreciate *see* PRICE

depredation *see* PRISON

depress *see* PRESS

deprive *see* PRIVATE

depth *see* DEEP

Derby [M19th] The 12th Earl of Derby founded the Epsom Derby, an annual race for three-year-old horses, in 1780. The simple form **Derby** as the name of the race is not recorded until the mid 19th century; 50 or so years later horse races in other countries, such as the Kentucky Derby in the USA, acquired the title. The significance of the event meant that in the early 20th century different sporting events

demonstrate   demur   dendrochronology

appropriated the name. Derby is also used in the USA for a bowler hat, and people attribute this to American demand for a hat of the type worn at the English Derby. The name first appeared in the late 19th century.

derelict [M17th] This is from Latin *derelictus*, the past participle of *derelinquere* 'abandon', from *de-* 'completely' and *relinquere* 'forsake', found also in **relinquish** [LME].

deride, derision *see* RIDICULE

derive *see* RIVAL

derrick [E17th] Derrick was first used to mean either the gallows or a hangman, and comes from the name of a London hangman who worked around 1600. This was then transferred to a tackle on a ship's mast, and from there extended to any hoisting device.

descend *see* SCALE

desert [ME] There are three words spelled desert, two of which are related. The word for 'a waterless, desolate area', and the (differently pronounced) word meaning 'to abandon' both ultimately go back to Latin *deserere* 'to leave, forsake'. The third desert usually appears in phrases such as to **get your just deserts**, 'to receive what you deserve'. It derives from Latin *deservire* 'to serve well', the source of **deserve** [ME]. The **dessert** [M16th] with a double 's' meaning 'a sweet course served at the end of a meal', is from French *desservir* 'to clear the table'.

design, designate *see* SEAL

desist *see* CONSIST

desk *see* DISC, DISH

desolate *see* SOLE

desperado [E17th] It looks like a Spanish word, but desperado is almost certainly one hundred per cent English—a pseudo-Spanish alteration of **desperate** [LME], probably created to sound more impressive and emphatic. Between the early 17th and

early 18th centuries a *desperate* was a desperate or reckless person, just like a desperado. An earlier meaning was 'a person in despair or in a desperate situation', which developed into 'a person made reckless by despair'. In both senses desperate is earlier than **desperado**, but the more exotic form ousted the original. The ultimate origin of desperate is Latin *desperare* 'to deprive of hope', the source of **despair** [ME].

despise [ME] Despise comes via Old French *despit* from Latin *despicere*, from *de-* 'down' and *specere* 'look at'. **Despicable** 'deserving to be despised' [M16th] comes from the same root, while **spite** [ME] is a shortening of the French.

despot [M16th] This comes, via French and medieval Latin, from Greek *despotēs* 'master, lord, absolute ruler' (in modern Greek used for a bishop). Originally, after the Turkish conquest of Constantinople, the term denoted a petty Christian ruler under the Turkish empire. The current sense dates from the late 18th century.

dessert *see* DESERT

destiny *see* LUCK

destitute *see* CONSTITUTION

destroy [ME] The word destroy comes via Old French *from* Latin *destruere*, from *de-* (expressing reversal) and *struere* 'build'.

desultory [L16th] Desultory 'lacking purpose or enthusiasm' also had the literal sense 'skipping about' in early use. The source is Latin *desultorius* 'superficial' (literally 'relating to a vaulter'), from *desultor* 'vaulter', from *desilire* 'to leap'.

detective [M19th] The development of an organized police force demanded a word such as detective, and it was duly formed in the 1840s from late Middle English **detect**. The first occurrences are in **detective police** and **detective policeman**; simple **detective** is a shortening of the latter. Charles Dickens was one of the earliest to draw attention to this innovation, reporting in his magazine

Household Words in 1850 that 'To each division of the Force is attached two officers, who are denominated "detectives".' *See also* SLEUTH

detergent [E17th] This was formed from the Latin verb *detergere*, from *de-* 'away from' and *tergere* 'to wipe'.

detest *see* TESTICLE

detonation [L17th] Detonation comes via French from Latin *detonare* 'thunder down'.

deuce [LME] The two different meanings of deuce both come from Latin *duus* 'two', by different routes. The earliest meaning, from the late 15th century, was 'a throw of two at dice'. The immediate source was the French word for 'two' (modern *deux*). In the mid 17th century this was reinforced by German *duus*, meaning 'bad luck or mischief' and by association 'the devil'. The connection arose because two is the worst or unluckiest throw you can have when playing with two dice. Expressions where deuce is interchangeable with devil (as in 'where the deuce …' or 'a deuce of a…') are now rather old-fashioned. In the late 16th century, **deuce** was a stage in the original form of tennis, now known as real tennis, which is played with a solid ball on an enclosed court. In real tennis deuce is five or more games all.

deviation *see* VIA

device [ME] The original sense of device was 'desire, intention', which is found now only in to **leave a person to their own devices**. It does occur in the title of the novel *Devices and Desires* by the crime writer P.D. James, taken from the *Book of Common Prayer*: 'We have erred, and strayed from thy ways like lost sheep. We have followed too much the devices and desires of our own hearts.' The source of device is a French form based on Latin *dividere* 'to divide'. Its sense developed from 'desire, intention' to 'a plan, scheme, trick' and then the usual modern meaning of 'a thing made or adapted for a particular purpose'.

devil [OE] The English word devil goes back to Greek *diabolos* 'accuser, slanderer', the source also of **diabolic** [LME], and similar words. In the Septuagint, a Greek version of the Hebrew Bible written in the 3rd and 2nd centuries BC, *diabolos* translated the Hebrew word for 'Satan'. The devil permeates popular wisdom. **The devil finds work for idle hands** appears first in English in the *Divine Songs* of the 18th-century hymn writer Isaac Watts, but goes back to the letters of St Jerome (*c*.342–420). **Why should the devil have all the best tunes?** is a question that has been attributed to the Victorian evangelist Rowland Hill, who encouraged the singing of hymns to popular melodies. The words **speak** or **talk of the devil** are often uttered when a person appears just after being mentioned. The expression dates back to the mid 17th century and comes from the superstition that if you speak the devil's name aloud he will suddenly appear.

The expression **the devil to pay**, 'serious trouble to be expected', is often said to have a nautical origin. The seam near a ship's keel was sometimes known as 'the devil', and because of its position was very difficult to 'pay', or seal with pitch or tar. There is not much evidence for this theory, though, and it is more probable that the phrase was a reference to a pact made with Satan, like that of Faust's, and to the inevitable payment to be made to him in the end. Shakespeare used the proverb **needs must when the Devil drives**, 'sometimes you have to do something that you would rather not', in *All's Well that Ends Well*, but he did not invent it: it is first found in a medieval work called *The Assembly of the Gods*. **Needs must** here means 'one needs must', or in today's language 'one must' or 'you must'. To **play devil's advocate** is 'to express an opinion that you do not really hold in order to encourage debate'. The devil's advocate was an official appointed by the Roman Catholic Church to challenge a proposal to make a dead person into a saint. His job was to present everything known about the proposed saint, including any negative aspects, in order to make sure the case was examined from all sides. The position was first established by Pope Sixtus V in 1587. It still exists, but the official is now known as the Promoter of the Faith. *See also* ANGEL, DEMON, DEUCE, EVERY, FALL

devious *see* VIA

devolve *see* REVOLVE

devotion, devout *see* VOTE

dexterous [E17th] The first meaning of dexterous was 'clever, mentally agile'. A little later it began to refer to physical coordination, and 'having skill with the hands' remains the primary modern sense. The word goes back to Latin *dexter* 'on the right', which is also the root of **dexterity** [E16th]: people have traditionally associated right-handedness with manual skill. *See also* AMBIDEXTROUS, SINISTER

diagnosis [L17th] This is a modern Latin formation from Greek, from *diagignōskin* 'distinguish, discern', from *dia* 'apart' and *gignōskein* 'recognize, know'.

diagonal *see* PENTAGON

diagram *see* GRAFT

dial [ME] The earliest senses of dial were 'a mariner's compass', 'sundial', and 'the face of a clock or watch'—all round objects marked out with gradations. The old slang meaning 'a person's face' would have been suggested by the fact that faces are roundish. The word's immediate source was medieval Latin *diale* 'clock dial', which came from Latin *dies* 'day', also the source of **diary** [L16th]. *See also* CLOCK

dialogue [ME] This comes via Old French and Latin from Greek *dialogos*, from *dialegesthai* 'converse with, speak alternately': the formative elements are *dia-* 'through, across' and *legein* 'speak'. The tendency in English is to confine the sense to a conversation between two people, perhaps by associating the prefix *dia-* with *di-*. *Dia-* is also found in **diameter** [LME] 'the measure across'; **diaphanous** [E17th] 'shows through'; **diaphragm** [LME] a barrier that is literally a 'fence through', and **diaspora** [L19th] a scattering across.

diameter *see* DIALOGUE

diamond [ME] The name of the gem derives from a medieval Latin alteration of Latin *adamans* *ADAMANT. Adamant was a legendary rock or mineral with many supposed properties. One of these was hardness, which was a reason why people sometimes identified it with diamond. **A diamond is forever** was used as an advertising slogan for De Beers Consolidated Mines from the late 1940s onwards, and in 1956 Ian Fleming used *Diamonds are Forever* as the title of his latest James Bond thriller, but the idea was first expressed by the American writer Anita Loos, in *Gentlemen Prefer Blondes* (1925). 'Diamonds are a Girl's Best Friend' was a song written by Leo Robin and Jule Styne for the 1949 stage musical of *Gentlemen Prefer Blondes*.

diaper [ME] In the USA babies wear diapers not nappies as in England. This is because the pads were originally made of diaper, a linen or cotton fabric woven in a repeating pattern of small diamonds. Napkins, towels, and cloths could also be diapers in Britain from the late 16th century, but napkin (*see* APRON) came to predominate in babywear. Before the 15th century diaper appears to have been a costly fabric of silk woven with gold thread. The original elements of the word are Greek *dia-* 'through, across' and *aspros* 'white', the overall sense being either 'white at intervals' or 'pure white'.

diaphanous, diaphragm
see DIALOGUE

diary *see* DIAL

diaspora *see* DIALOGUE

dice [ME] Originally—and still in the USA—a gambler would throw two **dice** but one **die**. This singular form is now rare in British English, surviving mainly in **the die is cast**, 'something has happened that cannot be undone' said by *CAESAR when he crossed the Rubicon (*see* CROSS). The word came from Latin *datum* 'something given, starting point', a form of *dare* 'to give'. This

devious devolve devotion devout dexterous

was interpreted as 'something given by chance or fortune' and applied to the dice determining the outcome of chance. Playing or gambling with dice is the idea behind **dicing with death**. Journalists began to use the expression in the early 20th century to convey the risks taken by racing drivers in the pursuit of success in their sport. It is probably the source of the adjective **dicey** meaning 'dangerous', first used by RAF pilots in the 1950s. *See also* BODICE

dick *see* ROMANY WORD PANEL

dicky [L18th] The informal British word dicky, meaning 'not strong, healthy, or functioning reliably', dates from the late 18th century, when it had the sense 'almost over'. The origin is not certain, but it may be from the given name Dick, in the old saying **as queer as Dick's hatband**. The pet form of Richard may also be behind **dicky bird**, a child's name for a bird. In **not a dicky bird**, 'nothing at all', it is rhyming slang for 'word'.

dictate *see* VERDICT

dictionary *see* LEXICON

diddle [E19th] In the farce *Raising the Wind* (1803) by the Irish dramatist James Kenney, the character Jeremy Diddler constantly borrows and fails to repay small sums of money. The informal term **diddle**, 'to swindle or cheat', appeared soon after the play's production, and is probably testimony to the impact the character made. The name Diddler may be based on an earlier word diddle (more often **daddle**) meaning 'to walk unsteadily'.

diddy [L18th] The informal word diddy meaning 'small' is probably a child's corruption of *little*.

die [ME] In surviving Old English texts the usual way of saying 'to stop living' is to *STARVE or to *swelt*, or by a phrase incorporating the word *DEAD. The form *swelt* survived in dialect, but has probably now died out. **Die** appeared in the early Middle Ages and came from an old Scandinavian word. To **die hard**, 'to

disappear or change very slowly', is now generally used of habits or customs, but its origins lie in public executions. It was originally used in the 1780s to describe criminals who died struggling to their last breath on the infamous Tyburn gallows in London. A few years later, during the Peninsular War (fought between France and Britain in Spain and Portugal from 1808 to 1814), Lieutenant-Colonel Sir William Inglis, commander of the 57th Regiment of Foot, lay severely wounded on the front line of the Battle of Albuera. He refused to be carried to safety, and urged his men to 'Die hard!' They followed his brave example, sustaining heavy loss of life, and all of the dead were found with their wounds on the front of their bodies. The battle was eventually won, and their heroism earned them the nickname 'the Die-hards'. In the early 20th century political circles took up the name to describe those who were determinedly opposed to reform, and the term **diehard** can still refer to someone who is stubbornly conservative or reactionary. *See also* DICE

diet [LME] In the context of food diet reaches back to Greek *diaita* 'way of life'. In the context of government and administration, for example, as the name of the legislative assembly in some European countries, diet comes from medieval Latin *dieta*, which meant both 'a day's work or pay' and 'councillors'. Martin Luther committed himself to the cause of Protestant reform at the **Diet of Worms**, a meeting of the imperial diet of the Holy Roman Emperor Charles V in 1521 in the German town of Worms on the Rhine.

differ *see* REFER

different [LME] The word different came ultimately from a form of Latin *differre*, which meant both '**defer**' and 'differ' in Latin, and is also the source of these two words in English. The modern proverb **different strokes for different folks** is of US origin. It came to prominence in newspaper reports of comments made by Muhammad

Ali about his knockout punches in fights with Sonny Liston, Floyd Patterson, and Karl Mildenberger during the 1960s. In the saying strokes means 'comforting gestures of approval or congratulation', but Ali was making a pun on the word's other meaning, 'blows'.

diffident *see* FAITH

diffract [E19th] If light is diffracted the waves it travels in are broken up in some way. The word is from Latin *diffringere* 'break into pieces'.

dig *see* DYKE

digger *see* AUSTRALIAN WORD PANEL

digit [LME] We all count on our fingers. This is how Latin *digitus*, 'finger, toe', came down to us as digit, 'numeral', in the late Middle Ages. **Digital** dates from the late 15th century, and the technical use of the word in communications arose in the mid 20th century.

dignify, dignity *see* DEIGN

dilemma [E16th] Recorded from the early 16th century, dilemma was originally a technical term of rhetoric and logic. It referred particularly to a form of argument involving a choice between equally unfavourable alternatives. The alternatives of a dilemma were traditionally called 'horns', translating the term used in Latin, the international language of European scholars in the 16th century. The expression **on the horns of a dilemma** captures this notion of double difficulty. The word came into English from Greek *dilēmma*, from *di-* 'twice' and *lēmma* 'premise, assertion'.

dilly-dally *see* SHILLY-SHALLY

dilute *see* DELUGE

diminish [LME] This is a medieval English blend of two obsolete words that share its meaning, 'to lessen': *diminue* and *minish*. Both ultimately go back to Latin *minutus* 'small', the source of *MINUTE in the same sense. In economics **the law of**

diminishing returns draws attention to the point at which profits are less than the amount of money invested. It originated in the first half of the 19th century with reference to profits from agriculture.

dine *see* DINNER

dingus [L19th] There are many words for something one cannot name or remember such as **thingamabob** [M18th] or more simply **thingy** [L18th]. Dingus is made on the same pattern, being a South African adoption from Afrikaans *ding* 'thing'.

dingy *see* GRUNGE

Dinkie *see* YUPPIE

dinkum [L19th] In the late 19th century **dinkum**, an English dialect word meaning 'hard work, honest toil', took up residence in Australasia. In **fair dinkum** it can describe an honest, straightforward person, a genuine article, or acceptable behaviour, and is particularly used to emphasize or seek confirmation of the genuineness or truth of something.

dinky [L18th] In Scottish and northern English dialect **dink** meant 'neatly dressed, spruce, trim'. Its origins are unknown, and it remained restricted to northern Britain. But from the late 18th century its derivative **dinky** spread: throughout Britain it means 'attractively small and neat', in the USA 'disappointingly small, insignificant'. In 1934 **Dinky toys** appeared, and these small but perfectly formed model cars are probably the first thing that come to many people's minds when they hear the word.

dinner [ME] Our words **dine** [ME] and dinner are both from the same root, Old French *desjeuner* 'to have breakfast', which survives in modern French as *déjeuner*, 'lunch', and *petit déjeuner*, 'breakfast'. The root was *jëun* 'fasting', which goes back to Latin *jejunus* 'fasting, barren' found also in **jejune** [E17th] which originally meant 'without food' and then 'not intellectually nourishing'. In Australia, New Zealand, and Canada to be **done like a dinner** is to be utterly

diffident diffract dig digger digit dignify

defeated or outwitted—the British equivalent is **done like a kipper**. The messy and unappetizing appearance of food set out for a dog is behind the expressions **a dog's dinner** (or **breakfast**), meaning 'a poor piece of work' a mess', and **dressed up like a dog's dinner**, 'wearing ridiculously smart or ostentatious clothes', which date from the 1930s.

dinosaur [M19th] The word dinosaur was coined in 1841, from Greek words meaning 'terrible lizard', the -*saurus*, also found in **saurian** [E19th] 'lizard-like'. People or things that have not adapted to changing times have been condemned as dinosaurs since the 1950s.

dint [OE] The phrase **by dint of** 'by means of' has violent origins. A dint was originally a stroke or blow with a weapon, and by dint of meant 'by force of', as in **by dint of sword**, an obsolete way of saying 'by force of arms'.

dip *see* DEEP

diploma [M17th] A diploma was originally a general word for a 'state paper'. It came via Latin from Greek *diplōma* 'folded paper', from *diploun* 'to fold', from *diplous* 'double'. **Diplomatic** [E18th] originally meant 'relating to original or official documents'.

direct *see* RECTANGLE

direction *see* ADDRESS

dirt [ME] The origin of dirt is old Scandinavian *drit* 'excrement'. In its earliest uses the English word retained both the meaning and the form, but gradually dirt superseded *drit*. Its history parallels that of *BIRD (earlier *brid*). By the time **dirty** appeared, in the later Middle Ages, dirt appears to have been the only form in use. The sense 'obscene, pornographic, smutty' dates from the 16th century, though most familiar phrases such as **dirty joke** and **dirty weekend** are first recorded in the 20th.

disabled *see* ABLE

disagree *see* AGREE

disappear [LME] The usual sense of disappear, 'to cease to be visible', appeared in the late Middle Ages. In the late 20th century English acquired a new construction, in which a person could be 'disappeared'—abducted or arrested for political reasons and secretly killed or detained without public knowledge. This came from Latin America, especially Argentina, and involves a translation of American Spanish *desaparecido*, applied to the many people who 'disappeared' under military rule in the 1970s.

disaster [L6th] In a disaster the stars are against you, for this is from Italian *disastro* 'ill-starred event', from *dis-* (expressing negation) and *astro* 'star' from Latin *astrum*. *See also* ASTERISK

disburse *see* PURSE

disc [M17th] The word disc goes back to Latin *discus*, which is the source of **discus** [M17th] and also of *DISH and Late Middle English **desk** (*discus* had come to be used for a stool or table in medieval Latin). Its earliest sense in English was the seemingly flat, round form that the sun, moon, and other celestial objects present to the eye. The anatomical disc, the sort that people 'slip', dates from the late 19th century, as does the type that turns on a record player. In the USA the usual spelling is **disk**, and this is now used everywhere with reference to computers, as in **floppy disk** and **disk drive**. *See also* JOCKEY

discard *see* CARD

discern *see* CRIME

discord *see* CORDIAL

discotheque [1950s] English writers commented on the French *discothèque* in the 1950s. Originally it was a record library (on the model of *bibliothèque* 'library'), then a club where recorded music was played for dancing. By the 1960s the English-speaking world had opened its own discotheques, and the USA very quickly shortened the word to **disco**. *See also* JUKEBOX

discretion [ME] In Latin *discretio* developed from 'separation' to 'fine judgement', an ability to separate ideas, the sense in which it entered English in the Middle Ages. The proverb **discretion is the better part of valour** was familiar in Shakespeare's time. The idea is even older, having a parallel in the works of the Greek dramatist Euripides in the 5th century BC.

discursive *see* CURSOR

discuss [LME] The basic sense of discuss is 'shaking and separating'. Latin *quatere* 'shake' is the base verb, combined with *dis-* 'apart' to form *discutere* meaning 'dash to pieces' and later 'investigate'.

disdain *see* DEIGN

disease [ME] At first disease was 'lack of ease, inconvenience, trouble', the meaning of the word in French, from which English adopted it in the early Middle Ages. The 'lack of ease' soon became associated with illness, and the original sense became obsolete.

disgruntled [M17th] Disgruntled people may go round muttering to themselves and complaining. Originally the word involved comparison with a pig making small or subdued **grunts** (an Old English word probably imitating the sound). The main element of disgruntled is **gruntle**, a dialect word used of pigs from the Middle Ages and of grumbling people from a little later. In the 17th century someone added *dis-* as an intensifier and created disgruntled. In the 20th century the comic novelist P.G. Wodehouse (1881–1975) removed the *dis-* again and introduced the humorous **gruntled**, 'pleased'. In *The Code of the Woosters*, published in 1938, he wrote: 'I could see that, if not actually disgruntled, he was far from being gruntled.'

disguise [ME] **Guise** came into English via French from a Germanic root with the

sense 'characteristic, manner, custom'. An early meaning of disguise was 'change one's usual style of dress', with no implication of concealing one's identity, but it soon developed a sense of concealment.

disgust *see* GUSTO

dish [OE] Dish is related to **desk**, which explains why corresponding forms in Dutch and German (*disch* and *Tisch*) mean 'table'. All derive from Latin *discus* (*see* DISC), which English took directly from Latin. Dishes remained containers until the 20th century, when technology gave us the dish-shaped aerial and the modern satellite dish. The sense 'a good-looking person' took off in the USA in the early 20th century, as did **dish the dirt**, 'to reveal scandal or gossip'.

dishevelled [LME] In the past, when no respectable man or woman would dream of going out without a hat, headscarf, or similar head covering, anyone seen bareheaded would be regarded as very scruffy and dishevelled. The word comes from Old French *chevel* 'hair', from Latin *capillus*, the source also of **capillary** [M17th]. The original sense was 'having the hair uncovered', then, referring to the hair itself, 'hanging loose', hence 'disordered, untidy'. *See* UNKEMPT

disk *see* DISC

dislocate *see* LOCAL

dismal [LME] This word originally referred to 24 days, two in each month, that medieval people believed to be unlucky. The name derives from Latin *dies mali* 'evil days', and first appeared in English in the early Middle Ages as **the dismal**. This was quickly spelled out more clearly as the **dismal days**. Soon dismal days could be any time of disaster, gloom, or depression, or the time of old age. In 1849 the Scottish historian and political philosopher Thomas Carlyle (1795–1881) nicknamed the difficult subject of economics (then known as 'political economy') the **dismal science**.

dismiss *see* MISSILE

discretion   discursive   discuss   disdain

disorient *see* ORIENT

disparage *see* PAIR

disparate *see* APPARATUS

dispel *see* APPEAL

disperse *see* ASPERSION

display [ME] The early meaning of this was 'unfurl (a banner or sail), unfold'. The word comes via Old French from Latin *displicare* 'scatter, disperse', which came to mean 'unfold' in medieval Latin and was also the source of **deploy** [L18th]. In English the notion of 'unfurling' led to 'causing to notice'. **Splay** [ME] was originally a shortening of display.

disport *see* SPORT

disrupt *see* CORRUPT

dissect *see* INSECT

disseminate *see* SOW

dissolute *see* SOLVE

dissonance *see* SOUND

distance [ME] The distant origin of distance lies in Latin *distare* 'to stand apart'. The apartness may be physical, as in the distance between two places, or intellectual. The earliest senses of distance in English are 'discord, debate', and 'a disagreement, a quarrel'. The expression to **go the distance**, 'to last for a long time', has its roots in the world of boxing, although it is also used in other sports. A boxer who 'goes the distance' manages to complete a fight without being knocked out. In baseball, the phrase is used to mean 'to pitch for the entire length of an inning', and in horse racing a horse that can 'go the distance' can run the full length of a race without tiring.

distend [LME] This comes from Latin *distendere*, from *dis-* 'apart' and *tendere* 'to stretch'.

distil *see* STILL

distort *see* TORCH

distress *see* DISTRICT

district [E17th] A district was originally the territory under the jurisdiction of a feudal lord. The word is from French, from medieval Latin *districtus* which meant 'the constraining and restraining of offenders' indicating the right to administer justice in a given area. It goes back to Latin *distringere* 'hinder, detain', found also in **distress** [ME], and its shortened form **stress** [ME].

disturb *see* TROUBLE

ditch *see* DYKE

ditto [E17th] A Tuscan dialect form of Italian *detto* 'said', from Latin *dictus*, is the root of ditto. In the 17th century it meant in Italian '(in) the aforesaid month'. English merchants began to use it in accounts and lists, where the word is usually represented by double apostrophes (**ditto marks**) under the word or figure to be repeated: the symbol would be read out as 'ditto'. In the later 18th century clothiers and tailors used it as shorthand for 'the same material', and a **suit of dittos** was a suit of the same material and colour throughout.

divan [L16th] The divan travelled across Europe from the court of the Ottoman Empire in the East. The Ottoman divan was its privy council, presided over by the sultan or his highest official, the grand vizier. Travellers first referred to it in English in the late 16th century. Turkish *dīvān* came from a Persian word with a range of meanings: 'brochure', 'anthology', 'register', 'court', and 'bench'. The last gave rise to the usual sense of divan in English, a piece of furniture. Originally, a divan was a low bench or raised part of a floor forming a seat against the wall of a room, a style which was common in Middle Eastern countries. European imitations of this led to the sense 'a low flat sofa or bed' in the late 19th century, while **ottoman** [L18th] was used for a similar object; an upholstered box that doubled as a seat.

dive *see* DEEP

disorient   disparage   disparate   dispel

divide [ME] English adopted divide from Latin *dividere* 'to force apart, remove' in the Middle Ages. The maxim **divide and rule**, recommending that a ruler or government set factions against each other so that they will not unite against the powers that be, is also of Latin origin: *divide et impera*. People often attribute it to the Renaissance Italian statesman and political philosopher Machiavelli (*see* MACHIAVELLIAN), but in fact he denounced the principle. **Dividend** [LME] comes from the same Latin root, and originally meant 'something to be divided', while **individual** [LME] comes from the Latin for 'not divisible'. *See also* WIDOW

divine [LME] Divine 'godlike' came via Old French from Latin *divinus*, from *divus* 'godlike' (related to *deus* 'god', source of Middle English **deify**). The gradual weakening of the word to a general term of praise, which started in the late 15th century, can be compared with 'heavenly'. The phrase **the divine right of kings** stating that legitimate kings derive their power from God alone, came into specific use in the 17th century under the Stuart kings.

divorce [LME] In early times divorce covered many ways of ending a marriage: one spouse could simply leave or send the other away; the marriage could be annulled, declared invalid from the beginning (as in the divorce of Henry VIII from Catherine of Aragon); or the couple could formally enter into a legal separation. The word itself is recorded from the late Middle Ages and came from Latin *divortium*, based on *divertere* 'to turn in separate ways'. A divorced person has been a divorcee since the early 19th century. The term came from French, and at first usually appeared in its French forms, *divorcée* for a woman and *divorcé* for a man.

divulge *see* VULGAR

dizzy [OE] In Old English dizzy meant 'foolish'. The medieval sense 'having a whirling feeling in the head' led to 'scatterbrained' and in late 19th-century USA to the **dizzy** *BLONDE. In the 20th century the US novelist Dashiell Hammett

defined the stereotype when he wrote of 'A dizzy blonde that likes men and fun and hasn't got much sense'. The blonde who had been dizzy from the 1870s became *DUMB in the 1930s.

do *see* DOOM

docile *see* PHYSICIAN

dock [OE] In a criminal courtroom dock is the official term for the enclosure where a defendant stands or sits. It was not always so orderly: originally a dock was crammed full of the thieves and petty criminals whose trial was scheduled for the day. The word may well be identical with Flemish *dok* 'chicken coop, rabbit hutch', and first appears in the late 16th century. The Late Middle English dock meaning 'area of water for the loading, unloading, or repair of ships' has a parallel in Dutch *dok* and early German forms, but its earlier history is lost. The plant dock, effective against nettle stings, is the oldest of the group, being recorded in Old English.

doctor, doctrine, document *see* PHYSICIAN

dodo [E17th] The dodo was a large, heavily built flightless bird found on Mauritius in the Indian Ocean until it was hunted to extinction, because, apparently, of its lack of fear of human beings. When sailors and colonists came to the island in the 16th and 17th centuries they discovered that it was very easy to catch and kill, a characteristic which gave it its name: dodo comes from Portuguese *duodo*, meaning 'simpleton'. By the end of the 17th century the dodo had died out. Its fate prompted the expression **as dead as a dodo**, 'completely dead or extinct'. *See also* DEAD

doff [LME] To doff, 'to remove an item of clothing, especially a hat', is a contraction of **do off**. It has an exact parallel in **don**, 'to put on', which was originally **do on**. Both forms date from the late Middle Ages.

dog [OE] The word dog appears only once in surviving Old English literature, and until the Middle Ages hound was the ordinary

divide   divine   divorce   divulge   dizzy   do

word for a dog. The low status of dogs is shown by phrases like **a dog's life**, **not have a dog's chance**, and **to treat someone like a dog**. For something to **go to the dogs** is certainly undesirable, but even such luckless animals might sometimes get hold of a tasty treat or a warm bed, for **every dog has its day**. Dogs can be savage, and **dog eat dog** signifies a situation of fierce competition. This rather chillingly makes reference to, and reverses, the proverb **dog does not eat dog**, which dates back to the mid 16th century in English and has a precursor in Latin *canis caninam non est*, 'a dog does not eat dog's flesh'. **Every dog is allowed one bite** is based on the rule, probably dating from the 17th century, by which an animal's owner was not liable for harm done by it unless he knew of its vicious tendencies. A **dog in the manger**, 'a person inclined to prevent others having or using things that they do not want or need themselves', derives from a fable in which a dog lies in a manger to prevent the ox and horse from eating hay. People have invoked the idea since the 16th century. A change in the status of dogs is found in the idea of the dog being **man's best friend,** which seems to be a Victorian one, a change emphasized by **love me, love my dog**. *See also* BOLLOCK, CANARY, DINNER, HAIR, HAVOC

dogma [M16th] Dogma comes via late Latin from Greek *dogma* 'opinion', from *dokein* 'seem good, think'.

doily [L17th] This ornamental mat made either of lace or of paper with a lace pattern, is from *Doiley* or *Doyley*, the name of a 17th-century London draper. It was originally a term for a woollen material used for summer wear, said to have been introduced by this draper. The current sense was originally part of the phrase **doily napkin** and dates from the early 18th century.

dolce vita, dolce far niente *see* ITALIAN WORD PANEL

doldrums [L18th] To most people **the doldrums** refers to a state or period of stagnation or depression, but to sailors it is an equatorial region of the Atlantic Ocean

with calms, sudden storms, and light unpredictable winds. For sailing ships, being becalmed in the doldrums was a serious occupational hazard. The earliest form of the word, in the late 18th century, was singular *doldrum*, and it meant 'a dull, sluggish, or stupid person'. It may come from **dull**, which originally meant 'stupid' [OE].

dole [OE] A dole was originally a division or share, which in the Middle Ages developed the sense of 'gift', particularly food, both senses surviving in modern English when we speak of doling out food to people. The dole, for unemployment benefits appears in the early 20th century. To **deal** [OE] is closely related, but the sense of deal for a type of wood is Middle English from Middle Low German or Dutch *dele* 'plank'.

doll [M16th] Doll started life as a pet form of the name Dorothy, and a doll was originally a man's 'pet' or lover. The sense 'small model of a human figure' dates from the late 17th century—before this time people used **poppet** or **puppet** (*see* PUP) to refer to the child's toy. The sense 'attractive girl' is US slang from the 1840s. *See also* BABE, DAME. **Dolly** was being used as a pet form of doll by the late 18th century and **dolly tub** meaning 'washtub for clothes' [L19th] is based on a dialect use of dolly as a term for various things thought to resemble a doll in some way. Here the dolly was a short wooden pole for stirring the washing.

dollar *see* US WORD PANEL

dolphin [LME] The name for this small whale goes back through French and Latin to Greek *delphin*. The form *delphin* existed in English from the early Middle Ages, but dolphin, from its French equivalent, appeared in the later Middle Ages and finally ousted the earlier word during the 17th century. In another guise the French word entered English as **dauphin**, the eldest son of the king of France. This is from the family name of the lords of the Dauphiné, an area of southeast France. In 1349 the future Charles V acquired the lands and title

dogma   doily   dolce vita   dolce far niente

of the Dauphiné, and when he became king he ceded both to his eldest son, establishing the pattern of passing them to the crown prince.

domain [LME] A domain was formerly 'heritable or landed property'. The word is from French *domaine* which goes back ultimately to Latin *dominus* 'lord'. The computing use dates from the 1980s. *See also* DAME

dome [E16th] Latin *domus* 'house' entered English directly as dome in the 16th century in the sense 'a stately building'; it also passed through Italian *duomo* and French *dôme* to enter English for a second time as dome 'a rounded vault' in the mid 17th century. *Domus* is also found in **domestic** [LME] 'relating to the house' and in **domicile** [LME] 'home'.

Domesday book *see* DOOM

domestic, domicile *see* DOME

dominate, dominion *see* DAME

don *see* DOFF, ITALIAN WORD PANEL

donjon *see* DUNGEON

donkey [L18th] Before the late 18th century a donkey was an *ASS. At first the word donkey was used only in slang and dialect, and its origin is lost. Early references indicate that it rhymed with *MONKEY, and this has prompted some to suggest that it comes from the colour **dun** [OE] or from the man's name Duncan. The expression **for donkey's years**, 'for a very long time', is a pun referring to the length of a donkey's ears and playing on an old pronunciation of *ears* which was the same as that of *years*. The British expression **yonks**, with the same meaning, may derive from it. *See also* EASEL

doodle [E17th] If you are a doodler, you may not be pleased to know that the original meaning of doodle was 'a fool, a simpleton'. The word came from German *dudeltopf* or *dudeldopp* in the early 17th century. The modern senses, 'to scribble absent-mindedly' and 'a rough drawing', date from

the 1930s. The Second World War **doodlebug**, or German V-1 flying bomb, may have got its name from the 1930s slang sense 'a small car or railway locomotive', or from the English dialect use 'cockchafer'. A cockchafer is a large beetle which flies around slowly at dusk, making a deep hum.

doolally [E20th] This British term for 'temporarily insane' originated in India in the military sanatorium at Deolali, which also doubled as a transit camp where soldiers would await their boat home at the end of their duty tour. As boats only left between November and March, some soldiers were there for many months, during which boredom set in and behaviour began to deteriorate. Men could go doolally, the Englishman's pronunciation of 'Deolali'.

doom [OE] The ancient root of doom meant 'to put in place' and is also the root of **do** [OE]. By the time that written English records began the emphasis had narrowed to putting law and order in place: the Old English senses of doom include 'a law, statute', 'a judicial decision', and 'the right to judge'. In the context of the end of the world, the word 'judgement' was not used until the 16th century—before that the usual term for Judgement Day was **doomsday** (source of the name the **Domesday Book** for the survey of the land ordered by William the Conqueror in 1085 for tax purposes, because it was the final authority on such things). In the Middle Ages this was also shortened to doom, a use that survives only in **the crack of doom**. '**We're doomed!**' was the catchphrase of the gloomy Scottish undertaker Frazer, played by John Laurie, in the BBC TV comedy *Dad's Army* (1968–77). The 1947 musical *Finian's Rainbow* popularized **gloom and doom**, which became a catchphrase when it was made into a film in 1968. The idea seemed appropriate to a world threatened by nuclear war.

doornail *see* DEAD

dose [LME] The Greek physician Galen, who lived between 129 and 99 BC, used *dosis*, the Greek word for 'a gift', for 'a

domain   dome   Domesday book   domestic

portion of medicine'. In **like a dose of salts**, 'very quickly and efficiently', the salts referred to are **Epsom salts** or magnesium sulphate. They have had a variety of medicinal uses since the 18th century, most notably as a very effective and fast-acting laxative. The name Epsom salts comes from the town of Epsom in Surrey, where the crystals were first found.

dossier [L19th] The word dossier is from a French word for a bundle of papers with a label on the back, from *dos* 'back', based on Latin *dorsum*. **Endorse** [LME] goes back to the same idea and root. A document on Iraq and the evidence for weapons of mass destruction was distributed to journalists by the British government in 2003. When it was found to contain multiple inaccuracies the press rapidly named it the **dodgy dossier**.

dot [OE] The word dot appears only once in Old English manuscripts, meaning 'the head of a boil'. It then disappears until the late 16th century, when it re-emerges in the sense 'a small lump or clot'. The sense 'small mark or spot' dates from the mid-17th century. In **on the dot**, 'exactly on time', the dot is one appearing on a clock face to mark the hour. Writers and printers sometimes use a dot in place of a number or letter that they do not know or do not want to specify, and this may be the origin of **the year dot**, 'a very long time ago'—the dot could also be a zero.

double *see* TWO

double entendre *see* FRENCH WORD PANEL

doubt [ME] In English doubt goes back to Latin *dubitare* 'to hesitate, waver', from *dubium* 'doubt' (from which **dubious** [M16th] also derives). The immediate sources were French forms in which the -*b*- had been lost, and people never pronounced the *b*- in doubt—it was a learned spelling to show that the writer knew the original Latin word. The first **doubting Thomas** to refuse to believe something without proof was the apostle Thomas. In the biblical account Thomas

refused to believe that Christ was risen again until he could see and touch the wounds inflicted during the Crucifixion.

dough *see* BREAD, DUFF, LADY

dour [LME] This word meaning 'relentlessly severe' was originally Scots. It is probably from Scottish Gaelic *dúr* 'dull, obstinate, stupid', perhaps from Latin *durus* 'hard'.

dove [ME] The dove gets its name from Old Norse *dufa*. In politics a dove, a person who advocates peaceful or conciliatory policies, contrasts with a *HAWK, a more warlike hardliner. The terms emerged in the early 1960s at the time of the Cuban missile crisis, when the Soviet Union threatened to install missiles in Cuba within striking distance of the USA. More generally, the dove has long been a symbol of peace and calm, in reference to the dove sent out by Noah after the Flood (*see* OLIVE), and is also a symbol of the Holy Spirit in Christian iconography.

dowfart *see* DUFF

down [OE] Downs are gently rolling hills. The word down may be of Celtic origin and related to early Irish *dún* and obsolete Welsh *din* 'fort', which go back to an ancient root shared by *TOWN. The everyday down, 'towards a lower place', is also Old English. It is a shortening of **a-down**, itself a reduction of **off down** 'off the hill'. The phrase **down and out**, 'completely without resources, defeated in life', probably comes from boxing. It referred to a boxer who was knocked out by a blow. Since the late 19th century a **down-and-out** has been a person without money, a job, or a place to live. The fluffy down that forms the first covering of a young bird is unrelated. It came in the Middle Ages from an old Scandinavian word.

drab *see* TRAPPINGS

draconian [L19th] Draco was a Greek lawmaker of the 7th century BC. His drafting of Athenian law was notorious for its severity. Since the late 19th century

draconian has described excessively severe laws and punishments, although **draconic** was used in the same way from the early 18th century.

drag [ME] The word **drag** comes from the same Old Norse root as **draw** [OE], **draught** [ME], the type of cart known as a **dray** [LME], and possibly **drudge** [ME]. The sense 'a boring or tiresome person or thing' developed in the early 19th century from the idea of an attachment that drags and hinders progress. The cumbersomeness of contemporary women's dress may also be behind the use of drag for 'women's clothing worn by a man', which is recorded from the 1870s. A street has been a **drag** since the middle of the 19th century. A description of London life in 1851 records a woman 'whose husband has got a month for "griddling in the main drag" (singing in the high street)'. The term later became better known in the USA, especially in **the main drag**.

dragon [ME] Dragon goes back to Greek *drakōn* 'serpent', and this was one of the first senses in English in the Middle Ages. In early texts it can be difficult to distinguish the genuine large snake or python (at that time known only from report) from the mythical fire-breathing monster. The dragon is a popular Chinese symbol, and this is behind the expression to **chase the dragon**, 'to smoke heroin'. A 1961 *Narcotic Officer's Handbook* explains: 'In "chasing the dragon" the heroin and any diluting drug are placed on a folded piece of tinfoil. This is heated with a taper and the resulting fumes inhaled through a small tube of bamboo or rolled paper. The fumes move up and down the tinfoil with the movements of the molten powder, resembling the undulating tail of the mythical Chinese dragon.'

drama [E16th] This came via late Latin from Greek *drama*, from *dran* 'do, act' source also of **drastic** [L17th]. The Latin **dramatis personae** has been used since the mid 18th century for a list of the characters in a play.

draper, drapery *see* TRAPPINGS

drastic *see* DRAMA

drat [E19th] This is a shortening of the phrase 'od rat', a euphemism for **God rot**.

draught, draw *see* DRAG

drawers *see* TROUSERS

dray *see* DRAG

dread [OE] The original word for 'to fear greatly, regard with awe' was **adread**, shortened to **dread** in the Middle Ages. Among Rastafarians, members of the Jamaican cult that believes Emperor Haile Selassie of Ethiopia was the Messiah, dread is dread of the Lord, and more generally a deep-rooted sense of alienation from contemporary society. Rastafarians wear **dreadlocks**, a hairstyle in which the hair is washed but not combed, and twisted while wet into tight braids. Dreadlocks are sometimes simply dreads. These uses were originally Jamaican, but came to wider attention in 1974 in 'Natty Dread', a song performed by Bob Marley and the Wailers. *See also* NATTY. The most familiar **dreadnought** is a type of large, fast battleship equipped with large-calibre guns, the first of which, HMS *Dreadnought*, was launched in 1906. But before that, in the early 19th century, a dreadnought was a very warm coat worn in cold weather, or a fearless person.

dream [ME] Although it corresponds to Dutch *droom* and German *Traum* and thus comes from a Germanic root, dream is not recorded in Old English. In the main modern sense dream did not appear until the Middle Ages, although an earlier dream meaning 'joy' and 'music' did occur in Old English and may be related. Dreams are often pleasant, sometimes unrealistically so, and numerous popular phrases refer to this. To go **like a dream** is recorded from the early 20th century; **in your dreams** is from the 1980s. The **city of dreaming spires** is Oxford. The name comes from a line in the poem 'Thyrsis' (1866) by Matthew Arnold.

dreary [OE] In Saxon times dreary was 'gory, bloody'. It came from a word meaning

drag dragon drama draper drapery drastic

'gore' which was related to Old English *drēosan* 'to drop, fall', the source of dreary **drizzle** [M16th]. The modern sense 'depressingly dull and bleak' did not develop until the mid 17th century.

dreck *see* YIDDISH WORD PANEL

drench *see* DRINK

dribble, driblet *see* DRIP

drink [OE] Old English *drinc* 'drink' had a close relative *drenc* which is the source of **drench** [OE].The colloquial phrase **the drink** referring to the sea, dates from the mid 19th century, but **drink like a fish** goes back to at least the early 17th when John Fletcher and James Shirley wrote a play called *The Night-Walker* which contains the line 'Give me the bottle, I can drink like a Fish now, like an Elephant'. **Drunk** comes from the past tense of drink. We now use the American **drunk as a skunk**, but Chaucer describes someone as drunk as a mouse; and drunk as a rat or even a wheelbarrow have been used in the past. **Drunkards** have been with us since at least the 13th century.

drip [OE] Drip is Old English but the slang use of the word to refer to a 'feeble or dull person', dates only from the middle of the 20th century. Drip had a variant drib, source of **dribble** [M16th]. The original sense was 'shoot an arrow short or wide of its target', also a sense of *drib*, which survives in the expression **dribs and drabs** [E19th]. A **driblet** meaning 'a small drop or stream of liquid' dates from the late 16th century when it meant a 'small sum of money'. *DROP is related, and so is **droop** [ME].

drizzle *see* DREARY

droll [E17th] Droll 'curious and unusual in a way that provokes dry amusement', is from French *drôle*, perhaps from Middle Dutch *drolle* 'imp, goblin'.

droop *see* DRIP

drop [OE] In the course of its history people have dropped all sorts of things: bombs, names, aitches, goals, LSD, hints, stitches, and more. Since the 1940s they have been dropping clangers, although the slightly less obtrusive brick has also been let slip since the 1920s. To **drop a clanger** is 'to make an embarrassing mistake or tactless remark'. Clangers only turn up in this phrase, but presumably they are things that make a very loud noise on hitting the ground and so draw immediate attention to the person responsible for dropping them.

drown [ME] Although it makes its first appearance in the Middle Ages, drown probably existed in Old English. It was originally a northern English form, and is related to the old Scandinavian word *drukkna* 'to be drowned', which comes from the same root as *DRINK, in which people sometimes **drown their sorrows**. The idea that **a drowning man will clutch at a straw** has been expressed since the 16th century. Before the 20th century the proverb involved 'catching' at straws: clutch adds a vivid sense of desperation. '**Not waving but drowning**' is the title of a 1957 poem by the English poet and novelist Stevie Smith (1902–71): 'I was much too far out all my life / And not waving but drowning.' Smith also popularized the phrase 'A good time was had by all', which was the title of a collection of poems in 1937.

drudge *see* DRAG

drum [ME] Recorded from the late Middle Ages, drum is probably from Dutch or German *tromme*, which imitates the sound of a drumbeat. The English word may be an alteration of **drumslade**, from German *trommelslag* 'drumbeat'. In Australia and New Zealand drum is a term for 'a piece of reliable inside information'. The meaning dates from the early 20th century, and perhaps derives from the use of the musical instrument to give signals. The idea behind **drumming up** support is that of a person going around beating a drum to attract attention. We talk of someone being **drummed out** of a place or institution with reference to the military drumbeat that accompanied the ceremony of dismissing a soldier from a regiment. And a lesson is **drummed into** someone in the regular, repetitive way that a drum is beaten.

dreck drench dribble driblet drink drip

drunk, drunkard see DRINK

dub [OE] It has been possible to dub someone a knight since the Norman Conquest: the king conferred the rank by ceremonially touching the person being honoured on the shoulder with a sword. The word dub came from a shortened form of Old French *adober* meaning 'to equip with armour' or 'to repair'. The sense of giving an unofficial title, name, or nickname to someone developed from this ritual conferring of a knighthood.

Since the 1920s to dub a film has been to provide it with an alternative soundtrack, now usually in another language. Dub is also a kind of reggae music in which some vocals and instruments are removed and the bass guitar accentuated. In these uses dub is a shortening of **double** (see TWO).

dubious see DOUBT

duck [OE] The name of the waterfowl, and duck meaning 'to lower the head and body quickly' go back to the same ancient root. The earliest sense of the latter was 'to suddenly go underwater and emerge, to dive', which connects directly with the behaviour of ducks—a duck is a bird that 'ducks' underwater. Stock exchange traders in the mid 18th century originally used the expression **lame duck** to describe a person or company unable to pay their debts. The idea behind it may be that a lame duck could easily fall victim to a hunter or predator: in the case of a debtor, he would be at the mercy of his creditors. Since the 19th century lame duck has also described a politician or government in their final period of office, after their successor has been elected. In cricket a duck is a batsman's score of nought. This is short for **duck's egg**, used for the figure 0 because of its similar outline. To **break your duck** is to score the first run of your innings. *See also* GOOSE, LOVE

duct [M17th] Duct comes from Latin *ductus* meaning both 'leading' and 'aqueduct' formed from *ducere* 'to lead'. The verb has produced numerous words in English including **abduct** [E17th] to lead away; **conduct** [ME] lead with; **conduit** [ME]; **deduce** [LME] draw a conclusion from something; DUKE; **educate** [LME] 'lead out'; **induce** [LME] lead in; **introduce** [LME] bring into (a group etc); **produce** [LME] 'lead forward'; **reduce** [LME] bring back; **seduce** [LME] lead away (originally from duty, with the sexual sense developing in the M16th); **subdue** [LME] 'draw from below'.

dude [L19th] This slang term is probably from German dialect *Dude* 'fool'. It appeared in New York at the beginning of 1883 for a man who was the equivalent of the English *DANDY, fastidious in his dress. At the same time the word was applied to a non-westerner or city-dweller spending his holidays on a ranch in the western USA, a 'dude ranch'. In the 20th century it came to mean simply 'a man, a guy'. *See also* CAT

duff [L18th] People have obviously long found the sound of duff expressive, and it has a wide variety of uses. One of them begins with **duffer** 'a useless person or thing'. This is recorded from the mid 19th century and may be an alteration of **dowfart**, an old Scottish term meaning 'a stupid person', from **dowf** 'spiritless'. Golfers shortened **duffer** to **duff** in the early 19th century and used it to mean 'to mishit a shot or ball', which spread into the wider community as 'to make a mess of something, bungle'. This duff may be the source of duff 'of poor quality, worthless', or may link to another set of words, also going back to a duffer. In this sense duffer appeared in the mid 18th century as thieves' slang for a person who sells worthless articles and passes them off as valuable. The origin is unknown, but it seems to have travelled to Australia and reappeared in the mid 19th century as 'a cattle rustler'. The phrase **up the duff** 'pregnant' may be related: it shares the Australian connections, as it is first recorded in Australia in the mid 20th century. The violent duff, as in to **duff someone up**, is recorded from the 1960s and may also be connected, though this is less likely. Everything about duff is hedged about with uncertainty, and the only duff whose history is known for certain is that of **plum**

drunk drunkard dub dubious duck

duff, a northern English dialect form of **dough**.

duke [OE] The word duke is recorded in Old English, but it goes back to Latin *dux* 'leader', which is related to *ducere* 'to lead' (*see* DUCT). The earliest meaning of duke was 'the ruler of a duchy'—it referred to sovereign princes in continental Europe, and did not describe a member of the British nobility until the end of the 14th century. *See also* COUNT, EARL, PRINCE

dulcet [LME] Dulcet as in **dulcet tones** was spelt *doucet* earlier, from an Old French diminutive of *doux*, from Latin *dulcis* 'sweet'. The Latin form influenced the modern spelling.

dull *see* DOLDRUMS

dumb [OE] In Old English dumb signified 'unable to speak', and could apply to both humans and animals (**dumb beasts**). The sense 'stupid, unintelligent' dates from the Middle Ages. These days the 'stupid' sense has come to dominate the word to such an extent that it has overshadowed the original meaning, so using it in that sense can cause offence. **Speech-impaired** or a similar alternative is safer. The original meaning does, however, lie behind the **dumb-bell** [E18th], which originally referred to an apparatus similar to that used to ring a church bell but without the bell making it therefore noiseless or 'dumb'. It is also behind **dummy** [L16th]. The original sense was 'a person who cannot speak', then [M18th] 'an imaginary fourth player in whist'. This gave rise to 'a substitute for the real thing' (e.g. a rubber teat, a blank round of ammunition), and 'a model of a human being' (mid 19th century).

A person considered stupid began to be called a **dumbo** in the USA in the 1950s, probably inspired by the 1941 Disney cartoon film *Dumbo*, which featured a flying elephant. The elephant's name was probably based on *JUMBO. Worry about things being **dumbed down**, or having their intellectual content reduced so as to be accessible to a larger number of people,

seems very recent, but the phrase goes back to 1933. *See also* BLONDE, DIZZY, LIMB

dumpy [M18th] Dumpy 'short and stout' is from **dumpling** [E17th] which is apparently from the rare adjective **dump** 'of the consistency of dough'.

dun *see* DONKEY

dunce [E16th] In the Middle Ages the Scottish 13th-century theologian and scholar John Duns Scotus was a profoundly influential figure. His works were university textbooks, and his followers so numerous that they had a name, Scotists. But from the 16th century the Scotists' views became old-fashioned and they were attacked and ridiculed, especially for making unnecessarily fine distinctions. The Scotists acquired a new name: Dunsmen or Dunses. A Duns was a 'hair-splitter', 'a dull pedant', and 'a person who is slow at learning'. The last is the sense of dunce which survives to this day.

dungeon [ME] The word dungeon had two main senses when it was first used in the 14th century: 'the great tower or keep of a castle' and 'an underground prison cell'. The first is now usually spelled **donjon** and regarded as a separate word. The core meaning was 'lord's tower', and the word goes back to Latin *dominus* 'lord, master', through which it is related to *DAME and *DANGER.

dunk [E20th] This colloquial word is from Pennsylvanian German *dunke* 'dip', from German *tunken* 'to dip or plunge'.

dunny *see* AUSTRALIAN WORD PANEL

duo *see* TWO

dupe [L17th] 'A victim of deception', dupe is from dialect French *dupe* 'hoopoe' (*see* CUCKOO), from the bird's supposedly stupid appearance.

duplicate *see* TWO

durable [ME] This came via Old French from Latin *durabilis*, from *durare* 'to last,

duke dulcet dull dumb dumpy dun dunce

harden'. **Obdurate** [LME] comes from the same root.

dust [OE] Our word dust is related to Dutch *duist* 'chaff, meal dust, bran', and the ancient meaning appears to have been 'material that rises in a cloud of smoke'. Various biblical uses of dust have settled in the language. To **shake the dust off your feet** derives from the Gospel of Matthew: 'And whosoever shall not receive you, nor hear your words, when ye depart out of that house or city, shake off the dust of your feet.' The phrase **dust and ashes**, used to convey a great sense of disappointment or disillusion, is found in the books of Genesis and Job. It refers back to the legend of the Sodom apple or Dead Sea fruit, whose attractive appearance tempted people but which tasted only of dust and ashes when eaten. A **dusty answer** is a curt and unhelpful reply. The expression comes from the 1862 poem 'Modern Love' by George Meredith: 'Ah, what a dusty answer gets the soul / When hot for certainties in this our life!'

Dutch [LME] From the Middle Ages up to the 17th century Dutch was not restricted to the people and language of the Netherlands, but referred to much of north and central Europe, taking in the peoples of modern Germany and the Low Countries. In 1579 the seven provinces that form the basis of the republic of the Netherlands gained independence and united, adopting the kind of German spoken in Holland as their national language. This change in the political landscape led to the more specific uses of Dutch in modern English. During the 17th century there was great rivalry between the English and the Dutch. The English attributed various undesirable characteristics to their neighbours, including **Dutch courage**, 'strength or confidence gained from drinking alcohol', which managed to imply that the Dutch were both cowards and drunkards. Their language was insulted in **double Dutch**, 'gibberish'. In some phrases the Dutch appear to have been singled out simply because they are foreign, as in **I'm a Dutchman**, used to express disbelief. In the American expression **Dutch uncle**, 'a kindly but authoritative figure', the choice serves to emphasize that the person referred to is not a blood relation. The original wording was 'I will talk to him like a Dutch uncle', meaning 'I will give him a lecture'. Another expression that was originally American is **go Dutch**, 'to share the cost of something equally', first recorded in 1914—the implication, more obvious in **Dutch treat**, was presumably that the Dutch were mean.

Going Dutch

*Is your boss a bit gruff? Maybe he is given to snooping—you probably wish he would go for a cruise on his yacht, maybe to the Netherlands, where all of these words come from. The English and **Dutch** languages are closely related, and despite three 17th-century naval conflicts Britain and the Netherlands have long been connected.*

THE 'boss' of all our Dutch words is **boss**, which is from *baas* 'master'. It started life in the USA at the beginning of the 19th century, and when it arrived in Britain was restricted to workmen's slang. If the boss is addicted to **snooping** he is now spying, but originally he would be stealing tasty items of food and eating them on the sly—the meaning of the

dupe   duplicate   durable   dust   Dutch

Dutch source *snoepen*, and the first English use in the 1840s.

*BOOZE is a Dutch word, and so are two of our most popular alcoholic drinks. The full name for **brandy** was originally **brandy wine**, a term that entered English in the early 17th century from Dutch *brandewijn*, literally 'burnt wine'. 'Burning' referred to the heating of low-strength alcohol over a fire so that the alcohol was given off as a vapour that condensed as brandy. **Gin** is flavoured with juniper berries, and was traditionally made in the Netherlands. In the early 18th century the word was spelled **genever** or **geneva**, which came via Dutch from Old French *genevre* 'juniper'. To avoid confusion with Geneva in Switzerland the drink was sometimes called Hollands geneva or just Hollands.

Many words to do with the sea and sailing came the short distance across the North Sea to Britain, most of them in the 17th century. The source of **cruise** was probably Dutch *kruisen* 'to cross', which is related to *CROSS itself. The names of the **corvette**, the **sloop**, the **smack,** and the **yacht** are all Dutch: the last of these is from *jaghte* 'light sailing vessel', which was derived from *jaghtschip* 'fast pirate ship'.

Words for items of food that have entered the English language from Dutch include **coleslaw**, literally 'cabbage salad', **cookie**, and **gherkin**. In Dutch a cookie was a *koekje*, or 'little cake', which was its meaning when it appeared in Scotland in the 1750s.

In English **frolic** first meant 'playful, happy' when it entered the language in the early 16th century from Dutch *vrolijk*. A less cheerful word is **gruff**, originally meaning 'coarse'. Like **cookie** it started life in Scotland rather than England, in the late 15th century. In Dutch a **bumpkin** is either 'a little tree' or 'a little barrel'—either way, it probably referred to the ungainly figure of a short, stout countryman.

See also CABOODLE, EASEL, GROOVE, TREK, WAGON

dye [OE] Both main uses of **dye**, 'a substance used to add or change colour' and 'to add a colour to', are recorded in Old English. Soon afterwards they both disappeared, the first until the late 16th century, the second until the late Middle Ages. The world in the meantime was not colourless, so the absence of dye from written records is a puzzle. The basis of **dyed in the wool**, 'unchanging in a belief or opinion', is the fact that yarn dyed in its raw state, before it is woven into a piece of fabric, has a much more even and permanent colour. The practice goes back many centuries, and the sense of 'unchanging' is also very old. Nowadays people often use the expression to refer to someone's political or sporting affiliation.

dyke [ME] There are two almost contradictory aspects to dyke: it means both 'something dug out' and 'something built up'. The first group of senses began in the medieval period and derives from the old Scandinavian word *dík* or *diki*, which corresponds to native English **ditch** [OE] and is related to **dig** [ME]. At much the same time related German and Dutch forms gave us the second group, initially in the sense 'a city wall, a fortification'. A possible linking idea appears in the sense 'dam'—a dam entails both the building up of an

Dutch uncle   Dutch treat   dye   dyke

obstruction and the creation of a pool. The Dutch build dykes to prevent flooding from the sea. This is the context of the phrase to **put your finger in a dyke**, 'to attempt to stem the advance of something undesirable'. It comes from a popular story of a heroic little Dutch boy who saved his community from flooding, by placing his finger in a hole in a dyke, thereby preventing it getting bigger and averting the disastrous consequences.

The word dyke is also a derogatory term for a lesbian, especially a masculine-looking one. Originally found in the fuller form **bulldyke**, it has been in use since at least the 1920s, but no one is sure of its origin.

dynasty [LME] Dynasty comes via late Latin from Greek *dunasteia* 'lordship, power'.

dysentery [LME] This comes via Latin from Greek *dusenteria*, from *dusenteros* 'afflicted in the bowels', from *dus-* 'bad' and *entera* 'bowels', found in medical terms such as **enteritis** [E20th].

dyspepsia [E18th] This came via Latin from Greek *duspepsia*, from *duspeptos* 'difficult to digest'.

dystopia *see* UTOPIA

dynasty   dysentery   dyspepsia   dystopia

each *see* EVERY

eagle [ME] Eagle comes from Old French *aigle* which came in turn from Latin *aquila* 'eagle' also the source of **aquiline** [M17th]— an aquiline nose is hooked like an eagle's beak. Renowned for its keen sight and soaring flight, the eagle is considered the king of birds. The **bald eagle** is the emblem of the USA, and *Eagle* was the name of the lunar module during the first moon landing, on 20 July 1969. The phrase **the eagle has landed** was said by astronaut Neil Armstrong on that day: 'Houston, Tranquillity Base here. The Eagle has landed.' It was later used by Jack Higgins as the title of his 1975 thriller about an attempt to assassinate Winston Churchill. *See also* BIRD

ear [OE] Unsurprisingly, since their meanings are so dissimilar, the ear that allows you to hear and the one that bears seeds are different words. The first is an Old English word that goes right back to an ancient root that was shared by Latin *auris*, from which we get **aural** [M19th]. The second seems to come ultimately from the same root as Latin *acer* meaning pointed or sharp. To **earmark** [L16th] something is to set it aside for a particular purpose. Originally, though, it referred to the practice of marking the ear of an animal as a sign of ownership.

You might say that **your ears are burning** if you are subconsciously aware of being talked about or criticized. This phrase has been around in English since at least the early 1600s, but the idea is an ancient one, which the 1st-century AD Roman scholar Pliny mentioned in his *Natural History*. In 1738 Jonathan Swift wrote, 'Miss, didn't your Left Ear burn last Night? . . . Because . . . you were extolled to the Skies.'

earl [OE] In Saxon days an earl was a man of noble rank, as opposed to a **churl** (source of **churlish**), or ordinary peasant, or a **thane**, who was a man granted land by the king. At the time of King Canute's rule in the early 11th century, the governor of a large division of England such as Wessex was called an earl. As the court started to be influenced by the Normans, the word was applied to any nobleman who held the continental title of *COUNT. *See also* DUKE

early [OE] The word early, like **late**, is from Old English, and is found in many idioms and proverbs. **The early bird gets the worm** is first recorded in 1636, and **early to bed, early to rise, makes a man healthy, wealthy, and wise** goes as far back as 1496. **Early doors**, meaning early on in a game or contest, has become a cliché of sports reporting, but originally referred to admission to a music hall some time before the start of the performance, which was more expensive but gave you a wider choice of seating. The first record of its use is from 1883. The practice died out in the 1950s but the phrase was resurrected in footballing circles in the 1970s in its current sense, with the legendary English football manager Brian Clough (1935–2004) providing the first recorded example.

earth [OE] It is impossible to tell which meaning of earth came first in English: the senses 'the ground', 'our planet', and 'soil' are all found in Old English. Related words in other languages are German *Erde* and Dutch *aarde*, as in **aardvark** (*see* SOUTH AFRICAN WORD PANEL). Earth meaning 'the underground lair of a badger or fox' dates from the late Middle Ages. 'The earth' has been used in idioms like **pay the earth**, **cost the earth** and **expect the earth** since the 1920s. Many of the earliest examples are by the comic novelist P.G. Wodehouse (1881–1975)—he probably did not invent them, but spotted new slang expressions of the day. We think of **earthling** as being a term from science fiction, but it actually goes back at least as far as 1593: 'We (of all

each   eagle   ear   earl   early   earth

earthlings) are God's utmost subjects' (Thomas Nashe, *Christ's Tears*).

earwig [OE] Earwigs have nothing to do with wigs. The *-wig* bit is related to wiggle, which makes a lot more sense. It was once thought that the insect crawled into people's ears, and the same idea is found in other languages: in French an earwig is a *perce-oreilles*, literally 'ear-piercer', and in German it is *Ohrwurm*, or 'ear worm'. The Germans also used *Ohrwurm* as a term for those irritating snatches of music that go round and round in your head, and **ear worm** has been used in this sense in English since the 1980s. These tunes are also called **sticky tunes** in English, or a **cognitive itch**, while the Brazilians call them *chiclete de ouvido* or **ear chewing gum.**

ease *see* EASY

easel [L16th] An easel is literally a donkey, coming into English in the 1630s from Dutch *ezel*. The use is similar to that of *HORSE in **clothes horse**, where the load-bearing object is likened to a beast of burden.

east [OE] All of the words for compass points are Old English. East is from an ancient root shared by the Latin word for dawn, *aurora* (as in the **aurora borealis** [E19th], or northern lights). It is also related to **Easter**, another Old English word, which is probably connected with *Ēastre*, the name of a Germanic goddess associated with spring and the dawn. The title of the James Dean film *East of Eden* (1955) is taken from the Book of Genesis: 'And Cain went out from the presence of the Lord, and dwelt in the land of Nod, on the east of Eden.'

easy [ME] Both easy and **ease** [ME] go back via Old French *aisier* to Latin *adjacens* 'lying close by', source also of **adjacent** [LME]. **Easy-peasy** 'childishly easy' is only recorded from the 1970s. The 'peasy' is simply a rhyme and the childish word intensifies the sense.

eat [OE] For such a fundamental concept, it is unsurprising that eat is an

Old English word, with an ancient root shared by Latin *edere* 'to eat'. This is the source not only of **edible** [L16th], but also **comestible** [LME] 'something edible', **edacious** [E19th], a rare word for 'greedy', and **obese** [M17th] from *obedere* 'eat completely'. There are also many phrases associated with eating. **Eat, drink, and be merry, for tomorrow we die** is a combination of two Biblical sayings, 'A man hath no better thing under the sun, than to eat and to drink, and to be merry' (Ecclesiastes) and 'Let us eat and drink; for tomorrow we shall die' (Isaiah). **You are what you eat** is a proverb that first appeared in English in the 1920s. It is a translation of the German phrase *Der Mensch ist, was er isst*, 'Man is what he eats', which was said by the philosopher Ludwig Feuerbach (1804–72). If you **eat your heart out** you suffer from excessive longing or grief. As **eat your own heart** the phrase was first used in Edmund Spenser's *The Faerie Queene* (1596): 'He could not rest; but did his stout heart eat.' *See also* FRET

eaves [OE] In Old English eaves, then spelled *efes*, was a singular word, but the *-s* at the end made people think it was a plural, which is how we treat it today. If you **eavesdrop** you secretly listen to a conversation. The word was formed in the early 17th century from the old word **eavesdropper** [LME], 'a person who listens from under the eaves'. Eavesdropper came from the noun **eavesdrip** or **eavesdrop**, 'the ground on to which water drips from the eaves'. This was a concept in an ancient law which banned building closer than two feet from the boundary of your land, in case you damaged your neighbour's land by 'eavesdrop'.

ebullient *see* BULLETIN

eccentric [LME] Eccentric started life in the astronomical sense, meaning 'a circle or orbit not having the earth precisely in its centre', before taking on its main modern meaning of 'unconventional and slightly strange' as it were 'off centre' in the mid

17th century. It comes from Greek *ekkentros*, from *ek* 'out of' and *kentron* 'centre'.

echelon [L18th] Echelon came into English in the military sense describing a formation of troops. The arrangement of troops in echelon is described in its source, for it comes from French *échelon*, from *échelle* 'ladder', from Latin *scala* (*see* SCALE). The notion of 'steps of a ladder' is reflected in modern figurative use in the context of company hierarchy or strata of society.

echo [ME] In Greek mythology Echo was the name of an oread or mountain nymph whom the goddess Hera deprived of speech to stop her chattering. The unfortunate creature was left able only to repeat what others had said. She fell in love with the handsome *NARCISSUS, and when he rejected her she wasted away with grief until there was nothing left of her but her voice. In another, nastier version of the story she was loved by the god Pan but turned him down; in revenge he drove a group of shepherds mad and made them tear her to pieces. The fragments were hidden in the earth, including her voice, which could still imitate other sounds. The name of the nymph was probably a personification of the Greek word *ēkhō*, which was related to *ēkhē* 'a sound'.

éclair *see* FRENCH WORD PANEL

eclipse [ME] Eclipse comes via Old French and Latin from Greek *ekleipsis* which was formed from *ekleipein* 'fail to appear, forsake its accustomed place'.

ecology [L19th] The word ecology is thought to have been invented in 1869 by the German biologist Ernst Haeckel. Originally spelled **oecology**, it is based on the Greek word *oikos* 'house'—in this case the natural environment is seen as the home of all the plants and animals that live within it.

economy [LME] Like *ECOLOGY, economy and **economical** come from Greek *oikos* 'house', and in the 15th century they were spelled **oikonomy** and **oikonomical**. Economy was then 'the art or science of managing a household' and 'the way in which household finances are managed'. The sense expanded in the 17th century to cover the management of a country's finances. Being **economical with the truth** is a euphemism for lying or deliberately withholding information. Mark Twain commented in *Following the Equator* (1897), 'Truth is the most valuable thing we have. Let us economize it.' The phrase itself did not gain widespread popularity until its use in 1986 during a government attempt to prevent the publication of *Spycatcher*, a book by a former MI5 officer, Peter Wright. Giving evidence at the trial, the head of the British Civil Service reportedly said of a letter: 'It contains a misleading impression, not a lie. It was economical with the truth.'

ecstasy [LME] The base of the word ecstasy is Greek *ekstasis*, which meant 'standing outside yourself'. Ecstasy first referred to a state of frenzy or distraction, of literally being 'beside yourself' with fear, passion, or other strong emotion. This meaning is now encountered only rarely, but was famously used by Wilfred Owen in his war poem 'Dulce et Decorum Est' (written in 1917): 'Gas! Gas! Quick, boys!— An ecstasy of fumbling, Fitting the clumsy helmets just in time.' The word came during the 16th and 17th centuries to mean a condition of emotional or religious frenzy or heightened emotion: if you were **in ecstasy** you were transported by any emotion, not just happiness or pleasure. The illegal drug Ecstasy is first referred to in 1985, in the *Los Angeles Times*. It gained its 'street' name because of its euphoric effects—the chemical name is methylenedioxymethamphetamine, or MDMA.

edacious, edible *see* EAT

edify [ME] In the Middle Ages to edify was to construct a building. This reflected the word's origin, Latin *aedificare*, from *aedis* 'house, dwelling' and *facere* 'to make'. It quickly took on the extended sense of

echelon echo éclair eclipse ecology economy

'building up' someone in moral or intellectual terms. *Aedis* also gave us **edifice** [LME], a formal word for a building.

educate *see* DUCT

eerie [ME] The word eerie 'strange and frightening' was originally northern English and Scots in the sense 'fearful'. The focus then moved from feelings of fear to the cause of the fear. It probably comes from Old English *earg* 'cowardly'.

effect [LME] Effect 'result, consequence' from Latin *effectus*, from *efficere* 'accomplish, work out', formed from *ex-* 'out, thoroughly' and *facere* 'do'. Its negative is **defect** [LME], while **deficit** [L18th] is from Latin *deficit* 'it is lacking', from the verb *deficere*. The Latin word was used formerly in inventories to record what was missing. **Feckless** [L16th] 'lacking in efficiency or vitality' is based on Scots and northern English dialect *feck*, a shortening of *effeck*, a variant of effect.

effete [E17th] Today effete is usually used of a young man who is affected and rather effeminate, but the word originally referred to animals and meant 'no longer fertile, too old to bear young'. It comes from Latin *effetus*, from *ex-*, meaning 'out', and *fetus* 'breeding, childbirth, offspring'—the same word as English **foetus** [LME] (US **fetus**). The meaning developed into 'having exhausted strength or vigour' and in the late 18th century on to 'feeble, over-refined'.

effluent *see* AFFLUENT

egalitarian *see* EQUAL

egg [ME] In the Middle Ages the Old Norse word **egg** started to take over from the earlier ey or eye (plural eyren). The two terms were used side by side for some time, and in 1490 the printer William Caxton wrote about how difficult it was to decide which word to use. *See also* COCKNEY. If you **have egg on your face** you look foolish or ridiculous. The first recorded example is from 1950s America. It probably comes from the idea of a messy eater having traces of food around their mouth, but it could

also refer to a bad actor being pelted with eggs. Calling someone a **good egg** or **a bad egg**—something famous for its unpleasant smell—is now associated with the 1920s and writers such as P.G. Wodehouse, but the expressions are older than that. A disliked or unpleasant person was first called a bad egg in the 1850s; the first person to reverse the words and come up with good egg seems to have been Rudyard Kipling, in 1903. *See also* CURATE. The advertising slogan **Go to work on an egg**, used in Britain by the Egg Marketing Board during the 1960s, is often credited to the novelist Fay Weldon, who used to work as an advertising copywriter. She now says that it was written by another member of her team. The proverb **don't teach your grandmother to suck eggs** has been in use since the early 18th century to caution someone against giving unwanted advice, in particular trying to tell a more experienced or knowledgeable person how to do something that they already know. Why should your grandmother be sucking eggs in the first place is not certain, but presumably the suggestion is that she has no teeth. An intellectual or highbrow person is sometimes called an **egghead** because of the association of an egg-like bald head with age and wisdom. This particular use dates from the early years of the 20th century. **Eggplant** [M18th], an alternative for aubergine, was first used to describe a variety with white egg-shaped fruit. Egg as in to **egg someone on** is a different word. It comes from Old Norse *eggja* 'to incite'.

ego [E19th] This is the Latin word for 'I'. It came into English later than **egotism** [E18th] or **egoism** [L18th]. **I** [OE] goes back to the same Indo-European root.

egregious *see* CONGREGATE

ejaculate, eject *see* JET

elaborate *see* LABOUR

elapse *see* LAPSE

elastic [M17th] First recorded in the 1650s, elastic was originally used to describe the way that gas is able to expand to fill whatever space is available. In those days

educate   eerie   effect   effete   effluent

some people thought that gas particles acted like a coiled spring, an idea that led elastic to take on its modern sense. The word comes from Greek *elastikos*, from *elaunein* 'to drive'.

elbow *see* BOW

elect *see* ELEGANT

electricity [E17th] The word **electric** seems to have come before electricity, having been first used by the scientist William Gilbert in a Latin treatise called *De Magnete* (1600). Gilbert, the man who discovered how to make magnets and coined the term **magnetic pole**, spelled it as *electricus*. Electricity is first recorded in 1646, in the writings of the physician Sir Thomas Browne. Both were based on the Latin word *electrum* 'amber', the connection being that rubbing amber produces an electric charge which will attract light objects.

elegant [LME] These days, someone elegant will generally be well dressed, but the basic idea behind the word is of being discerning and making careful choices. It comes from Old French *élégant* or Latin *elegans*, from *eligere* 'to choose or select', which was the origin of **elect** [LME], **eligible** [LME], and **elite** [L18th].

element [ME] Latin *elementum* 'principle, rudiment' is the source of element. In medieval times people thought that everything was made up from four elements: earth, air, fire, and water. They also believed that each kind of living creature had a natural affinity with one of these elements: most commonly these were air and water, although the salamander, for example, was supposed to live in fire. From this idea came that of a person's natural or preferred environment, and of **being in your element** if you are doing something that you love. **The element** was sometimes used specifically to mean 'the sky', and **the elements** became a term for strong winds, heavy rain, and other kinds of bad weather. **Elementary** is particularly associated with Sherlock Holmes saying 'Elementary, my

dear Watson', although the phrase is not actually found in any of Sir Arthur Conan Doyle's books. Holmes did certainly say 'My dear Watson', and he said 'Exactly, my dear Watson'; but the famous phrase does not appear until 1915, in *P. Smith, Journalist* by P.G. Wodehouse.

elephant [LME] Perhaps surprisingly, elephant did not come to us from an African or Indian language, but via Latin from Greek. The Greek word *elephas* meant both 'ivory' and 'elephant'. It is found in the work of the poet Homer, who probably lived in the 8th century BC, and may have been taken up by the Greeks from an ancient language of the Middle East. Elephant appeared in English in the 14th century, but before that people called them *oliphants* or *elps*. The related word *olfend* was used to mean 'a camel'—in those days northern Europeans had only vague notions of exotic animals. *See also* CAMEL, CHAMELEON, GIRAFFE, ROOM, WHITE

elevate [LME] The word elevate is from Latin *elevare* 'to raise', based on *levis* 'light', found also in **alleviate** [LME] 'lighten', **levity** [M16th], **relieve** [ME], and the **leaven** [ME] used in bread-making to lighten the loaf.

elevator *see* ESCALATE

eleven *see* ELF

elf [OE] An Old English word related to German *Alp* 'nightmare'. Elves were formerly thought of as more frightening than they are now: dwarfish beings that produced diseases, caused nightmares, and stole children, substituting changelings in their place. Later they became more like fairies, dainty and unpredictable, and in the works of J.R.R. Tolkien (1892–1973) they are noble and beautiful. Originally an elf was specifically a male being, the female being an **elven**: Tolkien revived **elven** and used it to mean 'relating to elves'. **Elfin**, meaning 'relating to elves' and also used to describe a small, delicate person with a mischievous charm, was first used by Edmund Spenser in *The Faerie Queene* (1590–96). *See also* OAF

eligible *see* ELEGANT

elbow   elect   electricity   elegant   element

eliminate [M16th] 'Drive out, expel' was the early sense of eliminate from Latin *eliminare* 'turn or thrust out of doors', based on *limen*, 'threshold'. The sense 'kill, murder' dates from the early 18th century.

elite *see* ELEGANT

elixir [LME] The root of both elixir and **Xerox** is Greek *xēros* 'dry'. Elixir came into English via Arabic *al-'iksīr*, from Greek *xīrion* 'powder for drying wounds'. It was first used in alchemy, as the name of a sought-after preparation that was supposed to change ordinary metals into gold, and one that could prolong life indefinitely (the **elixir of life**). Xerox, a name for a copying process that uses dry powder, dates from the early 1950s. *See also* CHEMIST

ell *see* BOW

elocution, eloquent *see* VENTRILOQUIST

emancipate [E17th] The word emancipate is from Latin *emancipare* 'transfer as property', from *e-* (a variant of *ex-*) 'out' and *mancipium* 'slave'. In Roman law it was the setting free of a child or wife from the power of the *pater familias*, the head of the household, a sense found in the 20th century in the campaigns for the emancipation of women. **Enfranchise** [LME] has a similar history coming from French *enfranchir* from *franc* 'free', also the source of **frank** [ME]. In early medieval France only the conquering Franks (who also gave their name to the country) were fully free. **Franchise** [ME], originally legal immunity, comes from the same source.

embargo [E17th] A Spanish word, from *embargar* 'to arrest'. When it was first used in English, embargo referred to an order prohibiting ships from entering or leaving a country's ports, usually just before a war. These days it is an official ban on trade with a particular country.

embark *see* BARK

embarrass [E17th] Although it came into English from French, embarrass was probably based on Portuguese *baraço* 'halter'. The first English sense was 'to encumber or impede': the notion of difficulty or problems led to the use of **embarrassed** to mean 'in difficulties through lack of money', as in **financially embarrassed.** The familiar modern meaning was not recorded until the early 19th century.

embassy [L16th] Originally this had the spelling variant *ambassy*, showing its relationship to Late Middle English **ambassador** (which is also found spelt *embassador*), and as well as being an official residence, it denoted the position of ambassador or the sending out of ambassadors. The source is Old French *ambasse*, based on Latin *ambactus* 'servant'.

embrace *see* BRACELET

embrocation [LME] This comes via medieval Latin from Greek *embrokhē* 'lotion'.

embryo [LME] This comes via late Latin from Greek *embruon* 'foetus', from *em-* 'into' and *bruein* 'swell, grow'.

emend *see* MEND

emerald [ME] The word emerald can be traced back to Greek *smaragdos*, and ultimately to an ancient Hebrew verb meaning 'flash or sparkle'. In early English examples the word's meaning is vague, and does not necessarily refer to a green stone. Ireland has been called **the Emerald Isle**, on account of its lush greenery, since as long ago as 1795. *See also* DIAMOND

emerge *see* MERGE

emigrant *see* MIGRATE

eminent [LME] Eminent 'outstanding' and **eminence** [ME] go back to Latin *eminere* 'jut, project'. The French expression *éminence grise*, literally 'grey eminence' for someone who has power without an official position, has been used in English since the 1930s. The term was originally used in French of His Eminence the

Cardinal Richelieu's grey-cloaked private secretary, Père Joseph (1577–1638). The Latin *eminere* is also found in **pre-eminent** [LME] and **prominent** [LME].

emission [LME] An emission is literally something sent out, coming from Latin *emittere* 'to send out'. An **emissary** [E17th] is a person sent out, and comes from Latin *emissarius* 'scout, spy', from *emittere*. Emit [E17th] is from the same source.

emmet *see* ANT

emollient *see* MOLLUSC

emolument [LME] Emolument comes from Latin *emolumentum* which was probably, in its original use, a payment made to a miller for grinding corn. Latin *emolere* meant 'to grind up' (the prefix *e-* here adding the notion of 'thoroughly'). Compare the less pretentious word 'salary' which started out as a 'payment for *SALT*.

emotion [M16th] The modern meaning of emotion is surprisingly recent and very different from its original sense. In the 16th century the word first meant 'a public disturbance or commotion', as in 'There were…great stirs and emotions in Lombardy' (1579). The root is Latin *movere*, 'to move', and the second sense was 'a movement or migration'. The main current meaning of 'a strong feeling such as joy or anger' was not used in writing until the early 1800s. The **emoticon**, a blend of emotion and *ICON* dates from the 1990s.

empathy *see* PATHETIC

emperor [ME] The root of emperor is the Latin word *imperare* 'to command', which is also the ultimate source of **empire** [ME], **imperative** [M16th], **imperial** [LME], and **imperious** [L16th]. Latin *imperator* meant 'military commander', which was given as a title to Julius Caesar and to Augustus, the first Roman emperor, and was adopted by subsequent rulers of the empire. In English, emperor first referred to these Roman rulers, and then to the head of the Holy Roman Empire. *See also* EVIL

emporium [L16th] An emporium is unconnected with *EMPEROR, but comes via Latin from Greek *emporion*, from *emporos* 'merchant', based on the word for 'journey'.

empty [OE] In Anglo-Saxon times empty meant 'at leisure', unoccupied, and also 'unmarried' as well as 'not filled'. It came from Old English *æmetta* 'leisure'. The proverb **empty vessels make most noise**, meaning that foolish people are always the most talkative, dates back to the work of the 15th-century poet John Lydgate.

emulsion [E17th] Nowadays we tend to think of it mainly as a household paint for walls and ceilings, whose name comes from the scientific sense of 'a fine dispersion of minute droplets of one liquid in another', but emulsion was originally a milky liquid made by crushing almonds in water. Its root is the Latin word *mulgere* 'to milk'.

enchant [LME] Enchant is from French *enchanter*, from Latin *incantare*, which was based on *cantare* 'to sing'. These Latin words gave us **chant** [LME], **canticle** [ME] a 'little song', and **incantation** [LME]. The original meanings of enchant were 'to put under a spell' and 'to delude'. **Enchanter's nightshade** [L16th] was believed by early botanists to be the herb used in potions by the enchantress Circe of Greek mythology, who charmed Odysseus' companions and turned them into pigs. *See* CHARM, INCENTIVE

encyclopedia [M16th] An encyclopedia is literally a 'circle of learning'. In ancient Greece a child was expected to receive a good all-round education, an *enkuklios paideia* in Greek. The word came to be spelled *enkuklopaideia* and made its way into English in the 1530s. Its first English meaning was 'general course of instruction', the meaning 'large work of reference' not appearing until 1644. The Latin-style spelling **encyclopaedia** is still sometimes used, partly because some encyclopedias, notably the *Encyclopaedia Britannica* (first published in 1768), use it in their title.

end [OE] To **make ends meet** or **make both ends meet**, 'earn enough money to live on', was formerly also **make the two ends of**

the year meet. It probably refers to the idea of making your annual income stretch from the beginning to the end of the year. The phrase goes back to at least 1661. If you are **at the end of your tether** you have no patience or energy left to cope with something. People in North America tend to say that they are **at the end of their rope**. The image behind both expressions is that of a grazing animal tethered on a rope so that it can move where it likes, but only within a certain range. When it reaches the end of its tether—when the rope is taut—it can go no further. **At the end of the day** has become one of those clichés that enrages teachers and linguistic purists. It is now continually parroted by sports players and commentators, but does not seem to have been used before the 1970s.

endorse *see* DOSSIER

enema [LME] This comes via late Latin from Greek, from *enienai* 'send or put in', from *en-* 'in' and *hienai* 'send'.

enemy [ME] An enemy is not your friend. So far, so obvious, but this is, in fact, the derivation of the word. It came into the language at the end of the 13th century from Old French *enemi*, from Latin *inimicus*, which was based on *in-* meaning 'not' and *amicus* 'friend'. *Inimicus* is the source of **inimical** [L17th] or 'hostile', and *amicus* of **amicable** [M16th] or 'friendly'.

energy *see* WORK

enfant terrible *see* FRENCH WORD PANEL

enfranchise *see* EMANCIPATE

engage [LME] **Gage** is an old word that means 'a valued object deposited as a guarantee of good faith' and, as a verb, 'to give as a pledge'. An Old French word related to **wage** [ME] and wedding (*see* MARRY), it is the root of engage. Engage originally meant 'give as a pledge' and 'pawn or mortgage', later coming to express the ideas 'to pledge or guarantee' and 'to enter into a contract'. People have been getting **engaged to be married** since the beginning of the 18th century: the first recorded example is by

Henry Fielding (1707–54), author of *Joseph Andrews* and *Tom Jones*.

engender *see* GENDER

engine [ME] Engine is from Old French *engin*, from Latin *ingenium* 'talent, device', the source also of **ingenious** [LME]. Like many English words that now start with *en-*, it could also be spelled *in-*. Its original senses were 'ingenuity, cunning', and 'natural talent, wit, genius', which survives in Scots as **ingine**. From there it became 'the product of ingenuity, a plot, or snare', and also 'a tool or weapon', specifically a large mechanical weapon, such as a battering ram or heavy catapult, constructed by **engineers** [ME]. By the first half of the 17th century something like our idea of an engine had arisen, a fairly complex device with moving parts that worked together.

English [OE] England and the English get their names from the Angles, an ancient Germanic people who came to England in the 5th century AD and founded kingdoms in the Midlands, Northumbria, and East Anglia. Their name came to refer to all of the early Germanic settlers of Britain—the Angles, Saxons, and Jutes—and their language, which we now call Old English. The first written example of English (spelled *Engliscne*) comes from the *The Treaty of Alfred and Guthrum*, an agreement between King Alfred the Great and Guthrum, the Viking ruler of East Anglia. Its exact date is uncertain, but it was probably written around 880. For an account of how the Angles got their name *see* ANGLE, and *see also* BRITISH. The proverb **An Englishman's home is his castle** has been around in various forms since at least 1581. Dickens uses it in *The Pickwick Papers* (1837): 'Some people maintains that an Englishman's house is his castle. That's gammon [nonsense].'

engross [LME] Both engross and **gross** [ME] come ultimately from the Latin word *grossus* 'large'. Engross comes from the Latin phrase *in grosso* 'wholesale' and originally meant 'to buy up the whole of a commodity in order to sell it at a monopoly price'. It

end   endorse   enema   enemy   energy

is also linked to Middle English **grocer**—originally a person who sold things 'in the gross' or in large quantities. *See also* RETAIL

enhance *see* ALTITUDE

enigma [M16th] An enigma is now a person or thing that is mysterious or difficult to understand, but it was originally a riddle, or an obscure speech. The word came from Latin, based on Greek *ainissesthai*, 'to speak allusively'. *See also* RIDDLE. One of the codes broken by the codebreakers at Bletchley during the Second World War was known as *Enigma*.

enjoy *see* JOY

enormous [M16th] Enormous is from Latin *enormis*, from *e-* 'out of' and *norma* 'pattern, standard' (the root of **norm** [E19th], and **normal** [M17th]). In early use it meant 'abnormal, unusual, extraordinary' and also 'abnormally bad, monstrous, shocking' as well as 'huge'. This bad sense is still found in **enormity** [LME], which strictly means 'a grave crime or sin' or 'the extreme seriousness of something bad', although today people increasingly use it to mean simply 'great size or scale'.

enquire *see* QUESTION

enrage *see* RAGE

enrol *see* ROLL

ensign *see* SEAL

enteritis *see* DYSENTERY

entertain [LME] This is based on Latin *inter* 'among' and *tenere* 'to hold'. It originally meant 'maintain, continue'; in the late 15th century it developed into 'maintain in a certain condition, treat in a certain way'. The meaning 'show hospitality' developed from this in the same period. The noun **entertainment** dates from the early 16th century; its use for a public performance intended to amuse is early 18th century.

enthusiasm [E17th] The origin of enthusiasm is Greek *enthous* 'possessed by a god, inspired', from *theos* 'god', which is the root of many words including **atheist** [M16th], **pantheon** [OE], and *THEOLOGY. Until relatively recently enthusiasm, **enthusiast**, and **enthusiastic** had stronger and less favourable meanings than they do today. Enthusiasm was originally, in the early 17th century, religious mania or divine inspiration, often involving 'speaking in tongues' and wild, uncontrollable behaviour. An enthusiast was a religious fanatic or fundamentalist, or a hypocrite pretending to be one. Over the next hundred years or so the force of enthusiasm and its related words weakened so that they arrived at something like our modern meanings.

entice [ME] Early senses of entice included 'incite' and 'provoke (to anger)'. It is from Old French *enticier* which probably had a root meaning 'set on fire', and was an alteration of Latin *titio* 'firebrand'.

entrails [ME] The root meaning of entrails is 'insides'. It is from Old French *entrailles*, from medieval Latin *intralia*, an alteration of Latin *interanea* 'internal things', based on *inter* 'among'.

entrepreneur *see* FRENCH WORD PANEL

enumerate *see* NUMBER

enunciate *see* ANNOUNCE

envelope [LME] An envelope was originally any kind of wrapper or covering, not just something to put a letter in. It is from the same word as envelop, 'to wrap up or surround', from Old French *envoluper* the *en-* meaning 'in', but the origin of the rest is lost. To **push the envelope** is to go up to, or beyond, the limits of what is possible, an idea that comes from aeronautics. Since the Second World War the envelope or flight envelope has been the set of combinations of speed, altitude, and range within which a particular kind of aircraft can fly safely. If a test pilot is pushing the envelope he is flying the plane at the very limits of its performance. The phrase came into wider circulation after 1979 following its use in

The Right Stuff, a book by American author Tom Wolfe about the early days of the American space programme, later made into an Oscar-winning film.

envoy *see* VIA

envy [ME] One of the traditional seven deadly sins, envy is said to lead to damnation in Christian theology. Early senses included 'hostility, enmity'. It comes from Latin *invidere* 'regard maliciously, grudge', formed from *in-* 'into' and *videre* 'to see', also found in **invidious** [E17th].

ephemera [L16th] An ephemera or ephemeron was originally a fever lasting only one day, an insect with a very short lifespan, or a plant thought to last a day. Some ancient writers thought there were two plants of this name, one that sprang up and died in a day, the other that carried a poison causing death within a day. The word was then applied to a person or thing of short-lived interest. It appeared in its current plural sense in the 1930s, to describe items like tickets, posters, and greetings cards that were of no enduring value except to collectors. Ephemera and its contemporary **ephemeral** 'lasting for a very short time', are from Greek *ephēmeros* 'lasting only a day', from *hēmera* 'day'.

epicentre [L19th] This is from Greek *epikentros* 'situated on a centre', from *epi-* 'upon' and *kentron* 'centre'. It originally meant the point immediately above an earthquake, but has been used as an emphatic form of 'centre' since at least 1970.

epicure [LME] In ancient times an Epicure was a follower of the Athenian philosopher Epicurus (341–270 BC). The Epicures or **Epicureans** were 'hedonists' who believed that pleasure was the highest good, although the pleasure they had in mind was restrained. They valued mental pleasure more highly than physical, and thought that the ultimate pleasure was freedom from anxiety and mental pain, especially from needless fear of death and the gods. In their view the gods existed but did not concern themselves with humans.

Because they talked of 'pleasure' (*hēdonē* in Greek, as in **hedonist** [M19th]) as the most desirable objective, people later thought of them as dedicated to having a good time all of the time. Nowadays, the word is restricted in meaning to someone with a particular interest in good food. *See also* CYNIC, STOIC

epidemic *see* DEMOCRACY

epilogue [LME] An epilogue, a comment or conclusion at the end of a book or play comes via Latin from Greek *epilogos*, from *epi* 'in addition' and *logos* 'speech'.

epiphany [ME] Epiphany is the festival commemorating the manifestation of Christ to the Gentiles as represented by the Magi or the three wise men who brought gifts to the infant Jesus. It is from Greek *epiphainein* 'reveal'. An alternative Greek name for the festival is *Theophania* 'divine revelation', which lies behind the personal name Tiffany, originally given to girls born at the festival.

episode[1] [L17th] An episode was originally a section between two choric songs in Greek tragedy. The word is from Greek *epeisodios* 'coming in besides'. The use of the word for an instalment in a radio and, eventually, television drama is early 20th century.

episode[2] *see* PERIOD

epitaph [LME] Old French *epitaphe* came via Latin from Greek *epitaphion* 'funeral oration', from *ephitaphios* 'over or at a tomb', from *epi* 'upon' and *taphos* 'tomb'.

Epsom salts *see* DOSE

equal [LME] A word that came from Latin *aequus*, which is also at the root of **adequate** [E17th], **equable** [M17th], **equanimity** [E17th], **equate** [ME], **equity** [ME], **equivalent** [LME] 'of equal worth', **equator** [LME] the circle where day and night are equal, **iniquity** [ME], and, via French, **egalitarian** [L19th]. George Orwell's political satire *Animal Farm* (1945) is the

envoy envy ephemera epicentre epicure

source of the quotation 'All animals are equal but some animals are **more equal than others**.' Another historic use of equal is from the American Declaration of Independence (1776): 'We hold these Truths to be self-evident, that all men are created equal, that they are endowed, by their creator, with certain unalienable rights, that among these are life, liberty, and the pursuit of happiness.' *See also* FIRST

equestrian [M17th] Both equestrian and **equine** [L18th] 'like a horse' are from Latin *equus* 'horse', a word that goes right back to the earliest times—unsurprisingly, as horses would have been so important to ancient peoples. Its root was also the source of the Greek equivalent to *equus*, *hippos*, which is where we get **hippopotamus** or 'river horse'.

equinox *see* NIGHT

equip [E16th] Equip is from French *équiper* 'equip', probably from Old Norse *skipa* 'to man (a ship)', from *skip* 'ship'.

equity, equivalent *see* EQUAL

equivocate *see* VOICE

eradicate *see* ROOT

ergonomic *see* WORK

ermine [ME] This is from Old French *hermine*, probably from medieval Latin (*mus*) *Armenius* 'Armenian (mouse)'. White ermine fur is the winter coat of the common weasel, and it needs dependable snowfall, such as is found in Armenia, for the coat to turn white.

erode *see* RODENT

erotic [M17th] French, the language of love, gave us erotic, although the ultimate source was Greek *erōs* 'love', and the name of the Greek god of love, the son of Aphrodite and the equivalent of the Roman Cupid who gets his name for the Latin for 'desire', the source of **cupidity** [LME]. He is usually pictured as a naked boy with wings, carrying a bow and arrow to wound his

victims with the pains of love. **Erogenous** [L19th] comes from the same source.

err [ME] Like **error** [ME] and **erratic** [LME], err comes to us from Latin *errare*, which meant 'to stray, wander' but could also mean 'to make a mistake'. The idea of straying or going off the correct course is still found in erratic, and also in the old term **knight errant** [ME], so called because they wandered far and wide in search of adventure. **Arrant** is a Middle English variant of errant, and **aberrant** [M16th] is literally a 'wandering away' from the right path. The proverb **to err is human, to forgive, divine** is so old that it is found in Latin (*humanum est errare*, 'it is human to err'), and also in the 14th-century work of Geoffrey Chaucer: 'The proverb says that to sin is human, but to carry on sinning is the devil's work.' The precise wording that we are familiar with comes from *An Essay on Criticism* (1711) by the poet Alexander Pope.

ersatz *see* GERMAN WORD PANEL

eruption *see* CORRUPT

escalate [E20th] To escalate was originally 'to travel on an escalator'. The word came from **escalator** and was coined in the early 1920s, when escalators were still new and exciting. It is now so familiar that it is quite a surprise to realize that we have only been using it to mean 'increase rapidly' and 'become more intense or serious' since the 1950s. Escalator itself started life in 1900, as a trade name in America. It was derived from the early 19th-century word **escalade**, which meant 'to scale a fortified wall by ladder', and was suggested by **elevator**, the US word for 'lift', which had been around since the 1880s.

escape [ME] This is from Old French *eschaper*, based on medieval Latin *ex-* 'out' and *cappa* 'cloak', with the idea of leaving your pursuer just clutching your cloak. **Escapade** [M17th] comes from the same source and originally had the same meaning. *See also* SCAPEGOAT

escheat *see* CHEAT

equestrian　　equinox　　equip　　equity　　err

Eskimo [L16th] The traditional word for the indigenous people inhabiting northern Canada, Alaska, Greenland, and eastern Siberia is Eskimo. The word is from Native American language Algonquian, and may have originally meant 'people speaking a different language'. It was formerly thought that the original meaning was 'person who eats raw meat' and because this was seen as insulting, the word is now avoided by many. The peoples inhabiting the regions from the Canadian Arctic to western Greenland prefer to call themselves **Inuit**, first recorded in English in the mid 18th century and the plural of *inuk* 'person'. There are comparatively few words in English from the Inuit language. **Kayak**, which came into English in the 18th century, is one of them, and **igloo** [M19th] from *iglu* 'house', is the most notable other.

espresso *see* ITALIAN WORD PANEL

esquire [LME] An esquire was originally a young man of gentle birth, who attended a knight. Esquire comes from an Old French word which means 'shield bearer' and comes from Latin *scutum* 'shield'. **Squire** is really the same word. Esquire later came to refer to a man belonging to the higher order of English gentry, below a knight, and from there became a polite title added to the name of a man, at first only one regarded as a 'gentleman'.

essay [LME] Essay is a variant of **assay** [ME] 'try, test', going back to Latin *exigere* 'ascertain, weigh'. In writing contexts, it referred initially to 'a first draft' but came to mean 'a composition'. This use seems to have been taken from the French philosopher and essayist Montaigne (1533–92) whose *Essais* were first published in 1580.

essence [LME] Essence comes via Old French from Latin *essentia*, from *esse* 'to be'. An early meaning was 'being, existence'. In alchemy it was used in the phrase **fifth essence** or *QUINTESSENCE. Alchemists believed this substance to be latent in all bodies and thus to be extractable by distillation: this probably led to essence's

use for 'an extract obtained from a plant with therapeutic qualities', reinforced by the sense 'indispensable quality or constituent'.

estate [ME] Estate and its shortening **state** [ME] are the same word, both going back to Latin *status* [L18th] 'state, condition'. The sense of estate for 'property' comes from a late Middle English development via the idea of 'state of prosperity'. *See also* PRESS

estimate [LME] This is from Latin *aestimare* 'determine, appraise', also the source of Middle English **esteem** for how people value or regard you.

estuary [M16th] This was originally a tidal inlet of any size. The source is Latin *aestuarium* 'tidal part of a shore' from *aestus* 'tide'. The term **Estuary English** was coined by David Rosewarne in 1984 for an accent which developed along the Thames Estuary from London English and which has rapidly become the dominant urban accent in southern England.

etch [M17th] This is from Dutch *etsen*, from German *ätzen*, from a base meaning 'cause to eat'. This type of engraving is done by 'eating away' the surface of metals, glass, and stone, by the application of acid.

ether [LME] This comes via Latin from Greek *aithēr* 'upper air', from the base of *aithein* 'burn, shine'. Originally it meant a substance believed to occupy space beyond the sphere of the moon. It was then used, from the mid 17th century, as a name for the rarefied substance formerly believed to permeate all space,, a sense behind **ethereal** [E16th]. The use of a volatile liquid as an anaesthetic is found from the mid 18th century. **Ethernet**, a blend of *ether* and *network* dates from the 1970s.

ethic [LME] At first this term referred to ethics or moral philosophy. It comes via Old French from Latin *ethice*, from Greek *(hē) ēthikē (tekhnē)* '(the science of) morals'. The base is Greek *ēthos* 'nature, disposition', source of **ethos** [M19th].

Eskimo espresso esquire essay essence

ethnic [LME] This, like gentile (*see* GENTLE), was first used for a person not belonging to the Christian or Jewish faith. It comes via ecclesiastical Latin from Greek *ethnikos* 'heathen', from *ethnos* 'nation'. Current senses date from the mid 19th century. The phrase **ethnic minority** arose in the 1940s; references to **ethnic cleansing** are found in texts from the 1990s.

ethos *see* ETHIC

etiquette [M18th] A French word which means literally 'label or ticket' and also 'list of ceremonial observances at a royal court'. Its Old French root is the source of our word *TICKET. It is not completely clear why the word moved from meaning 'ticket or label' to 'code of correct behaviour', but people probably started thinking of an *étiquette* as a list of correct forms of behaviour.

etui *see* TWEEZERS

eucalyptus, eulogy *see* EUPHEMISM

eunuch [OE] This word came via Latin from Greek *eunoukhos*, literally 'bedroom guard', from *eunē* 'bed' and a second element related to *ekhein* 'to hold'.

euphemism [L16th] This word is from Greek *eu* 'well' and *phēmē* 'speaking' from *phēnai* 'to speak', which is also where **prophet** [ME] came from. Several other English words start with *eu* meaning 'well'. The **eucalyptus** tree [E19th] is literally 'well covered': it is so called because the unopened flower is protected by a sort of cap. If you give a **eulogy** [LME] you praise, or speak well of, someone: the *-logy* part, found in a great many English words, comes from Greek *logos* 'speech, word, reason'. If something is **euphonious** [L18th] it is pleasing to the ear – *phōnē* 'sound' is the Greek root (the mid 19th-century **euphonium**, which not everyone finds pleasing, comes from the same word). Finally, **euthanasia** [E17th] is literally 'an easy death': *thanatos* is 'death' in Greek. The *euro-* in **Europe** and related words is unconnected. Europe is from *Europa*, the name of a princess of Tyre, in modern-day Lebanon, who was admired by the god Zeus.

He turned himself into a bull and swam across the sea to Crete with the princess on his back. Once in Crete Europa bore Zeus three sons, and eventually gave her name to the continent of Europe.

eureka [E17th] In the 3rd century BC the Greek mathematician and inventor Archimedes of Syracuse in Sicily, was asked by the king Hiero to test his new crown to find out whether it was really solid gold as the maker claimed, or was an alloy made up to be the same weight. The story goes that the solution eluded Archimedes until he overfilled his bath, which overflowed as he got in. Suddenly the solution to the problem hit him. He realized that he could test whether or not the crown was pure gold by putting it in water and seeing whether it made the water overflow as much as a similar volume of genuine gold did. He is said then to have run through the streets shouting 'Eureka!', or rather *heurēka*, which means 'I have found it' in Greek. The name **Archimedes' principle** is given to the law stating that a body immersed in a liquid is subject to an upward force equal to the weight of liquid it displaces.

Europe, euthanasia *see* EUPHEMISM

evangelism, evangelist *see* GOSPEL

evaporate *see* VAPOUR

even [OE] In the sense 'flat and smooth', even is an Old English word. Even as in **evening** [OE] is from a different Old English word, one related to German *Abend* 'afternoon'. **An even break**, meaning 'a fair chance', was popularized by the American comedian W.C. Fields (1886–1946) in his catchphrase, 'Never give a sucker an even break', which itself went on to become the title of one of his best-known films. There does not seem to have been a real Stephen behind the phrase **even Stephen** or **even Stephens**, meaning 'completely even or equal'. It probably comes from *Journal to Stella* by Jonathan Swift: 'Now we are even, quoth Stephen' (1711). If a ship is **on an even keel** it is not tilting to the

ethnic ethos etiquette etui eucalyptus

side. The keel is the supporting structure along the base of a ship; even here it is in the old sense 'in a level position, horizontal'.

every [OE] An Old English word that is related to **ever** and **each**. Every occurs in two well-known proverbs. **Every little helps** has a rather rude origin. It appears to be from a 1590 work by the French writer Meurier, which translates as 'Every little helps, said the ant, pissing into the sea.' In the first English example, ten years later, the ant is replaced by a wren. **Every man for himself and the devil take the hindmost** alludes to a chase by the Devil, in which the slowest will be caught.

evict *see* VICTORY

evidence [ME] This came via Old French from Latin *evidentia*, from *evident-* meaning 'obvious to the eye or mind', from *e-* (a variant of *ex-*) 'out' and *videre* 'to see'. This also gives us **evident** [LME].

evil [OE] Like *GOOD and *BAD, evil goes back to the earliest times, and many have reflected on its nature over the centuries. 'The evil that men do lives after them', wrote Shakespeare in *Julius Caesar*. The proverb **See no evil, hear no evil, speak no evil** is often represented by the image of 'three wise monkeys', who are pictured covering their eyes, ears, and mouth with their hands. The carving of the original monkeys is found on a shrine at Nikko in Japan. The idea of **a necessary evil** goes back to Greek. The first necessary evil was marriage, and the first example in English, from 1547, refers to a woman. In his State of the Union address of February 2002, US President George W. Bush said of Iraq, Iran, and North Korea that they constituted 'an **axis of evil**, arming to threaten the peace of this world'. The phrase is now used to encapsulate the Bush administration's stance in foreign relations, much as **the evil empire** (inspired by the *Star Wars* films) summed up Ronald Reagan's view of the Soviet Union.

evoke *see* VOICE

evolve [E17th] The word evolve was first used in the general sense 'make more complex, develop'. It comes from Latin *evolvere*, from *e-* (a variant of *ex-*) 'out of' and *volvere* 'to roll', also the source of **evolution,** from the same period. Early senses related to physical movement, first recorded as a tactical 'wheeling' manoeuvre in the realignment of troops or ships. Current senses stem from a notion of 'opening out' and 'unfolding', giving rise to a general sense of 'development'.

exaggerate [M16th] To exaggerate was originally 'to pile up, accumulate', and later 'to make much of, emphasize'. It comes from Latin *exaggerare* 'to heap up', from *agger* 'heap'. Mark Twain is usually credited with saying, in response to an incorrect story that he had died, 'Reports of my death have been greatly exaggerated'. In fact, he said 'The report of my death was an exaggeration'—in the *New York Journal*, on 2 June 1897.

exalt *see* ALTITUDE

example [LME] Example goes back to Latin *exemplum* 'sample, imitation', from *eximere* 'take out'. **Sample** [ME] comes from the same root via French.

exasperate [M16th] Exasperate is from Latin *exasperare* 'irritate to anger', based on *asper* 'rough'.

excavate *see* CAVE

exceed *see* CEDE

except *see* CAPABLE

excerpt *see* CARPET

exchange *see* CHANGE

exchequer [ME] In around 1300 an exchequer was 'a chessboard'. The word came into English from Old French *eschequier*, which was based on medieval Latin *scaccus* 'check'—the origin of our word *CHECK. It took on its current, very different sense from the department of state that dealt with the revenues of the Norman kings

every evict evidence evil evoke evolve

of England. In those days they kept the accounts by placing counters on a chequered tablecloth, which was called the Exchequer.

excise *see* DECIDE

exclude [LME] Exclude is from Latin *excludere* 'shut out', from *ex-* 'out' and *claudere* 'to shut'. The same root gives us, via French, a **sluice** gate used to shut off water flow, while **seclude** [LME] comes from *claudere* combined with *se-* 'apart'.

excruciating [L16th] The source of excruciate is Latin *excruciare* 'to torment or torture', which was based on *crux*. This meant 'a cross', of the kind used to crucify someone, and is the root not only of *CROSS but also of *CRUCIAL, and **crux** [M17th]. In English to **excruciate** someone was originally to torture them.

excursion *see* CURSOR

excuse [ME] This comes via Old French from Latin *excusare* 'to free from blame', from *ex-* 'out' and *causa* 'accusation, cause'.

execrate *see* PRIEST

exhale *see* INHALATION

exhaust [M16th] First used in the general sense 'draw off or out', exhaust is from Latin *exhaurire* 'drain out'.

exhilarate [M16th] This is from Latin *exhilarare* 'make cheerful', based on *hilaris* 'cheerful' source of **hilarity** [LME].

exist *see* CONSIST

exit [M16th] Exit was used during the time of Shakespeare as a stage direction meaning 'he or she goes out', which is the word's literal meaning in Latin. (The plural equivalent, 'they go out', is **exeunt**.) One of the best-known uses of the word is in a speech from Shakespeare's *As You Like It*: 'All the world's a stage, / And all the men and women merely players: / They have their exits and their entrances; /And one man in his time plays many parts, / His acts being

seven ages.' Shakespeare is also responsible for what must be the must famous of all stage directions, from *The Winter's Tale*: '**Exit, pursued by a bear**'. People started using exit to mean 'a way out' at the end of the 17th century. The sounds of the Latin were softened in French to become the source of **issue** [ME].

exodus *see* PERIOD

exonerate [LME] Exonerate 'absolve from blame' is from Latin *exonerare* 'free from a burden', from *ex-* 'from' and *onus, oner-* 'a burden', source of **onerous** [LME] 'burdensome'.

exorcize [LME] This word comes from Greek *exorkizein* 'exorcise', from *ex-* 'out' and *horkos* 'oath'. The word originally meant 'conjure up or command (an evil spirit)'; the specific sense of driving out an evil spirit dates from the mid 16th century.

exotic [L16th] English exotic is from Greek *exōtikos* 'foreign', from *exō* 'outside'. The notion of 'foreign origin' gave the word a dimension of glamour, hence phrases such as **exotic dancer**, first introduced in the USA, for a stripper.

expand *see* PACE

expect [M16th] First meaning 'to wait for', expect entered English from Latin *exspectare* 'to look out for', from *spectare* 'to look'. *Spectare* is also the source of spectacle and many other English words (*see* SPECIES). '**England expects** that every man will do his duty' was the British admiral Lord Nelson's memorable last signal to his fleet before the Battle of Trafalgar, on 21 October1805. *See* BLIND and KISS for more about Nelson.

expel *see* APPEAL

expense [LME] Expense goes back to Latin *expendere* 'pay out', and shares a root with Old English **spend**.

experiment [ME] This goes back to Latin *experimentum*, from *experiri* 'to try'. **Experience** [LME] and **expert** [ME],

excise exclude excruciating excursion excuse

someone who has tried and found out about something, go back to the same verb.

expire *see* SPIRIT

explain [LME] The words explain and **explanation** both date from late Middle English and their source is Latin *explanare*, based on *planus* 'plain'. Early senses included 'smooth out' and 'spread out flat'. In the early 16th century it came to mean 'give details of (a matter)', and later 'make intelligible by clarification'.

expletive [LME] This word is from late Latin *expletivus*, from *explere* 'fill out', from *ex-* 'out' and *plere* 'to fill'. The general sense 'word used merely to fill out a sentence' [E17th] was applied specifically to an oath or swear word in the early 19th century. The phrase **expletive deleted** gained a high profile in the 1970s in the submission of recorded conversations involving President Nixon to the Committee on the Judiciary of the House of Representatives (30 April 1974).

explode [M16th] In Roman days bad performers were exploded, for explode comes from Latin *explodere* 'to drive off with hissing or clapping, to boo off the stage', from *ex-* 'out' and *plaudere* 'to clap' (*see* PLAUDIT). Early meanings of explode were 'to reject scornfully', and 'to show to be false' (still used in phrases like **explode a theory**). The modern sense appeared in the late 18th century via the sense 'to force out violently and noisily'. **Implode** was formed on the pattern of explode in the late 19th century using *in-* 'within'.

explore [M16th] This comes via French from Latin *explorare* 'search out', from *ex-* 'out' and *plorare* 'utter a cry'.

export *see* TRANSPORT

express [LME] In the sense 'to convey in words or by behaviour', express originally meant 'to press out, obtain by squeezing', and its root is Latin *pressare* 'to press'. Express meaning 'intended for a particular purpose' is from another Latin word meaning 'to press', *primere*, and is the source of **express train** and other uses that involve high speed. As early as 1845 an express train went 'expressly' or specifically to one particular place, not stopping at intermediate stations. This would have been a relatively fast train, and led to the word being interpreted as meaning 'fast, rapid'.

extempore [M16th] This word is from Latin *ex tempore* 'on the spur of the moment' (literally 'out of the time').

extenuate *see* THIN

exterior *see* EXTREME

exterminate [LME] This is from Latin 'drive out, banish', from *ex-* 'out' and *terminus* 'boundary'. This was the sense used when the word entered English. The sense 'destroy' [M16th] comes from the Latin of the Vulgate Bible.

extinct [LME] The early recorded sense of this was 'no longer alight'. This is from Latin *exstinguere* 'to **extinguish**' [M16th]. Extinct is used in connection with species of animals that have died out, from the late 17th century.

extort *see* TORCH

extra *see* EXTRAORDINARY

extract *see* TRAIN

extracurricular *see* EXTRAORDINARY

extradition [M19th] This is an adoption from French, from the prefix *ex-* meaning 'out, from' and *tradition* meaning 'delivery'. In an extradition procedure, a person is taken out of a foreign country and delivered to the home country.

extraordinary [LME] This looks as though it is from **extra** and **ordinary**, but is actually comes from Latin *extra ordinem*, meaning 'outside the normal course of events'. In English **extra** means 'beyond, outside' in many words such as **extramarital** [E19th] 'outside marriage', **extracurricular** [E20th] 'outside the curriculum', and **extraterrestrial** [M19th].

expire explain expletive explode explore

When it means 'additional' or 'especially', as in **extra-special**, it is really a shortened version of extraordinary, which in the 17th and 18th centuries often meant 'additional, extra', as in an extract from the diary of the traveller Celia Fiennes, written in 1710: 'You pay a penny extraordinary for being brought from Tunbridge town.'

extravagant [LME] Extravagant came to us from medieval Latin *extravagari*, from *extra-* 'outside' and *vagari* 'to wander' (the source of **vagabond** and **vagrant**, *see* VAGUE). It first meant 'unusual, unsuitable', and 'diverging greatly', then 'excessive or elaborate', not coming to mean 'spending or costing a great deal' until the early 18th century. An **extravaganza** [M18th] is an elaborate and spectacular entertainment or production. It is basically the same word as mid 17th-century **extravagance**, but came into English from Italian *estravaganza* in the 1750s, when it meant 'extravagance in language or behaviour'.

extreme [LME] This comes via Old French from Latin *extremus*, literally 'outermost', the superlative of *exterus* 'outer' source of **exterior** [E16th].

extrude [M16th] This is from Latin *extrudere*, from *ex-* 'out' and *trudere* 'to thrust'.

exuberant [LME] 'Overflowing, abounding' were the early senses recorded for exuberant from French *exubérant*, from the Latin verb *exuberare* 'be abundantly fruitful'. The base is Latin *uber* 'fertile'. The usual sense now is 'overflowing with delight', first recorded in the early 16th century.

exude [L16th] The word exude 'discharge' is from Latin *exsudare*, from *ex-* 'out' and *sudare* 'to sweat'.

exult *see* SALIENT

eye [OE] An Old English word that has given rise to a huge number of phrases in English. **The eyes are the window of the soul** is a proverb that goes back at least to 1545, when it is found in the form 'The

eyes...are the windows of the mind, for both joy and anger...are seen through them'. The same idea was expressed by the Roman orator Cicero in the 1st century BC: 'The face is a picture of the mind as the eyes are its interpreter.' **An eye for an eye and a tooth for a tooth** refers to the law set out in the Old Testament book of Exodus: 'Thou shalt give life for life, eye for eye, tooth for tooth, hand for hand, foot for foot, wound for wound.' **The eye of a needle** is a tiny opening through which it would seem impossible to pass. The reference is to the Gospel of Matthew, where Jesus said, 'It is easier for a camel to go through the eye of a needle, than for a rich man to enter into the kingdom of God.'

A person who has **an eye for the main chance** is on the lookout for an opportunity to profit. The origins of this expression lie in the gambling game of hazard, in which the person about to throw the dice calls out a number between five and nine. This number is called the **main** or the **main chance**, and if someone rolls it they have won. If you would **give your eye teeth for** something you would do anything in order to have it. The eye teeth are the two pointed teeth in the upper jaw, so called because they are more or less immediately below the eyes, and are essential for tearing off chunks of food. They are more usually called **canine** teeth from the Latin for dog, referring to this animal's prominent examples. To **give someone the hairy eyeball** is to stare at them coldly or contemptuously. The image behind this American expression is of someone glaring with their eyes narrowed and partly closed: the hairy eyeball is the effect of seeing the eyeball through the eylashes. **Keep your eyes peeled** comes from the idea of 'peeling' the covering from your eyes to see as clearly as possible. It goes back to the 1850s in the USA, but now is particularly associated with *Police 5*, a long-running British TV show that appealed to the public for information to solve crimes. The catchphrase of the presenter, Shaw Taylor, at the end of each programme was 'Keep 'em peeled!'

eyelid *see* LID

extravagant extreme extrude exuberant

Ff

fabric [LME] Fabric comes from Latin *fabrica* 'something skilfully produced'. A fabric was originally 'a building', and then 'a machine or appliance' and 'something made', which led to the main current meaning 'cloth, textile'. The related verb **fabricate** [LME] originally just meant 'to manufacture, construct', but towards the end of the 18th century it began to be used in the sense 'make up facts that are not true'. *See also* FORGE

fabulous [LME] The Latin word *fabula* 'story', ultimately from *fari*, meaning 'to speak', is the source of both fabulous and **fable** [ME], and perhaps of **fib** [M16th], which may be a shortening of the obsolete *fible-fable* 'nonsense'. A fable is a short story which conveys a moral, and is particularly associated with the legendary 6th-century BC Greek storyteller Aesop, whose fables have given the language many expressions (*see*, for example, at CHICKEN). In early use fabulous meant 'known through fable' or 'not based on fact'. The idea of 'astonishing' led to it being understood as both 'beyond belief' and 'wonderful, marvellous'. As the 60s started to swing, fabulous was shortened to **fab**, and the Beatles were nicknamed **the Fab Four**, while in the 1990s TV comedy *Absolutely Fabulous* (sometimes shortened to *Ab Fab*), 'Fabulous, sweetie!' was the standard encouragement. *See also* FATE

façade [M17th] This is an adoption of French *façade*, from *face* 'face'. Primarily used of buildings, it started to be used in a figurative way for the face you put on to meet people, from around the middle of the 19th century.

face [ME] The word face, from Latin *facies* 'form, appearance, face', is used in many expressions. To **fly in the face of**, meaning 'to do the opposite of', is recorded from the 16th century. It is taken literally from the notion of a dog attacking someone by springing directly at them. To **lose face**, meaning to be humiliated, is a direct translation of a Chinese phrase. The 16th-century dramatist Christopher Marlowe coined the phrase **the face that launched a thousand ships** to describe the great beauty of Helen, whose abduction by Paris caused the Trojan War. **Facet** [E17th] is literally a 'little face' from French *facette*.

facetious [L16th] This comes via French from Latin *facetia* 'jest', from *facetus* 'witty'.

facility [E16th] Latin *facilis* 'easy' is the base of facility. Originally meaning ease in doing something, facility developed into something that makes it easier to do something in the early 19th century, *Facilis* also give us **facile** [LME], **facilitate** [E17th], and **faculty** [LME].

facsimile [L16th] This was originally written *fac simile*, meaning the making of an exact copy, usually a copy of a piece of writing. It is modern Latin, from Latin *fac* 'make' and *simile* 'like'. The abbreviation **fax** dates from the 1940s.

fact *see* FACTORY

factory [L16th] The first factories were far from any urban area, in India and southeast Asia. A factory in the late 16th century was a trading company's foreign base or station. The first use of the word in something like the modern sense came in the early 17th century, but until the Victorian era a building where goods were produced was more usually called a **manufactory**. The root of **factory** is Latin *facere* 'to make or do', the source of a great many English words such as **fact**, **factor**, **feat**, and **feature** (all LME). The sense 'a place where things are made' probably came from Latin *factorium* 'oil press'.

faculty *see* FACILITY

fabric fabulous façade face facetious

fad *see* FIDDLE

fade [ME] The early sense of fade was 'grow weak, waste away'. The word comes from Old French *fade* 'dull, insipid', probably a blend of Latin *fatuus* 'silly, insipid' (source of E17th **fatuous**), and *vapidus* 'vapid' (*see* VAPOUR). The sense 'lose freshness' (faded colours) developed in English alongside the meaning 'lose strength'.

fae *see* FAIRY

faff [L18th] Originally a dialect word for 'blow in puffs or small gusts', faff was describing the wind, imitating the sound. The current sense may have been influenced by dialect **faffle** initially meaning 'stammer, stutter', later 'flap in the wind', which came to mean 'fuss or dither' at about the same time as faff in the late 19th century.

faggot [ME] Faggot was first recorded in the sense 'bundle of sticks for fuel'. It comes via Old French *fade* from Italian *fagotto*, which was based on Greek *phakelos* 'bundle'. Towards the end of the 16th century, the word came to be used as an abusive term for a woman; later, in the early 20th century, this was applied as offensive slang in US English to a male homosexual. The abbreviation **fag** dates from the 1920s. Faggot also came to be used for any general bundle or collection of things by the end of the 15th century, and this is the source of faggot for the traditional English dish known as a faggot [M19th], which is made up from miscellaneous bits of chopped pork and offal bundled together.

fail *see* FALSE

faint [ME] The word faint is related to **feign**, both coming from French *faindre* and initially used in the original French sense of 'feigned, simulated', from Latin *fingere* 'to form, contrive' also the source of **fiction** [LME] and **figment** [LME]. Another early meaning was 'cowardly', a sense now preserved only in the proverb **faint heart never won fair lady**. The sense 'hardly perceptible' dates from the mid 17th century. **Feint** [L17th] originally used in fencing for a deceptive blow is from the same source, while the mid 19th-century use of feint for lightly lined paper is simply a respelling of faint.

fair [OE] The word fair is recorded from Old English in the sense 'pleasing, attractive'. In early uses its opposite is often given as *FOUL, as in the phrase **by fair means or foul**. This opposition remains in the phrases **fair play** and **foul play**, both of which first appeared in the late 16th century. The sense *BLONDE developed in the mid 16th century from the sense attractive. Fair applied to handwriting to mean 'neat, legible' dates from the late 17th century. From this we get **fair copy**, the final corrected copy of a document. People have been saying **all's fair in love and war** to justify what they are doing since the early 17th century. **The fair** (or **fairer**) **sex**, a term for women, is recorded from the 17th century.

The kind of fair with stalls and amusements is a completely different word. It comes via Old French from Latin *feria* 'holy day', as fairs were often held on religious holidays. *See also* COPPER, DINKUM

fairy [ME] Although we now think of fairies as small, delicate creatures they come from a powerful source—Latin *fata* 'the Fates' (*see* FATE). The old spelling *faerie* is first recorded in *The Faerie Queene*, the title of a poem by Edmund Spenser celebrating Queen Elizabeth I (the figure of the 'Faerie Queene' herself was taken to stand for Elizabeth). Faerie was originally the collective form of the word, with **fae** or nowadays **fay** as the singular.

faith [ME] Both faith and **fidelity** [LME] come from the Latin word *fides*. **Fido**, a traditional name for a dog, is also related—it represents the Latin for 'I trust'. Other words from the same source include **confident** [L16th], **confide** [LME], and **diffident** [LME] which originally meant 'lacking in trust'. **Fiancée**, the French for 'promised', which goes back to *fides* is related. *See also* INFIDEL

fall [OE] Even in Old English the difference between fall and **befall** was that the first was used literally while the second was used figuratively in the sense such as 'happened'. When we say of a disappointed person that **his face fell**, we are using an expression which was originally a translation from Hebrew: 'And Cain was very wroth [angry], and his countenance fell.' If we say of someone who has given up an attempt that they have **fallen by the wayside**, we are echoing the parable of the sower, told by Jesus to his disciples in St Matthew's Gospel. The person who has stopped trying to achieve something is compared with seed which 'fell by the wayside' and was eaten by birds, and therefore produced no crop. The same story gives us an expression for a suggestion which is badly received or ignored: it is said to **fall on stony ground**. This refers to the seed in the parable which 'fell on stony places' and withered. In Christian, Jewish, and Muslim tradition a **fallen angel** is an angel who rebelled against God and was cast out of heaven. The *DEVIL was the head of the fallen angels. These are largely negative senses, but a more positive expression is found in **fall on your feet**, used to indicate that you emerge unhurt from a difficult or damaging situation. The reference is to cats, which always seem to land elegantly after a fall or jump. SEE ALSO FELL, US WORD PANEL

false [OE] Along with **default** [ME], **fail** [ME], and **fault** [ME], false comes from Latin *fallere* 'to deceive'. A **false dawn** is a light which in Eastern countries is briefly seen about an hour before sunrise. The expression, the translation of an Arabic phrase, is often used to describe a promising situation which has, or is likely to, come to nothing.

fame [ME] In early use fame could mean not only 'celebrity' but 'reputation', a sense that survives in the old term for a brothel, a **house of ill fame**. The word comes from Latin *fama* 'report, fame'. The desire to win fame has often been seen as a positive force to stir somebody up to action: in the 17th century John Milton wrote 'Fame is the spur that the clear spirit doth raise . . . To scorn delights, and live laborious days.' The writer Howard Spring borrowed *Fame is the Spur* as the title of a novel that was made into a film in 1947. **Famous** [LME] is from the same root. To be **famous for fifteen minutes** comes from the prediction by the American artist Andy Warhol in 1968 that 'In the future everybody will be world-famous for fifteen minutes.' A few years later **famous for being famous** is recorded to describe someone whose only real distinction is their celebrity status.

family [LME] A person's family was originally the servants of their household. It then came to be 'all the people who live in one house, including parents, children, and servants', before it settled on its modern meaning. The word is from Latin *famulus* 'household servant', as is **familiar** [ME]. The former British Prime Minister Harold Macmillan made a speech in 1985 where he opposed the government's policy of privatizing state assets and supposedly accused them of **selling the family silver**. What he actually said was: 'First of all the Georgian silver goes, and then all that nice furniture that used to be in the saloon. Then the Canalettos go.' Family is also used, chiefly in the US, as a slang term for the members of a local unit of the Mafia; a use popularized in the 1972 film *The Godfather* by Francis Ford Coppola. The phrase **in the family way** meaning 'pregnant' from the late 18th century, was in use earlier meaning 'in a domestic way, in a domestic setting'.

famous *see* FAME

fan [OE] The spelling fan can represent two quite different words. The first, meaning 'a device to create a current of air', goes back to the Old English noun *fann*, a word of Latin origin. It was a device for blowing air through harvested grain to winnow it, removing the husks or chaff from the seed. The second fan, meaning 'enthusiast, supporter', is short for **fanatic** [M16th]. Its earliest uses are recorded from the end of the 17th century, but it became particularly established in American English during the 19th century. In Latin *fanaticus* meant 'inspired by a god' and came from *fanum* meaning 'a temple'. In its first English appearances fanatic was used as an adjective to describe the kind of frenzied speech or behaviour typical of someone possessed by a god or demon. As a noun it originally meant 'a mad person' and then 'a religious maniac'. **Fanzine** was coined in the 1940s in the US for a magazine produced by amateur enthusiasts of science fiction, though fanzines are now often about music, film, or sport. The word is a blend of **fan** and **magazine**.

fancy *see* FANTASTIC

fang [OE] Fang first meant booty or spoils. It comes from Old Norse *fang* 'to capture, grasp'. A sense 'trap, snare' is recorded from the mid 16th century; both this and the original sense survive in Scots. The current sense 'large, sharp tooth' (also mid 16th) reflects the same notion of 'something that catches and holds'.

fantastic [LME] A word originally meaning 'existing only in the imagination, unreal' that comes from Greek *phantastikos* 'vision'. **Fantasy** [LME] is of similar origin, as is **fancy** [LME], a contracted version of fantasy. The modern use of fantastic to mean 'wonderful, excellent' dates from the 1930s. The playful phrase **trip the light fantastic**, meaning 'to dance', goes back to John Milton's 1645 poem *L'Allegro*: 'Come, and trip it as you go / On the light fantastic toe.' **Pant** [ME] 'to breath spasmodically' goes back to the root verb of fantastic, *phainon* 'to show', via Old French *pantaisier* 'be agitated, gasp'; as do **phantom** [ME] from *phantasma* 'mere appearance' and **phenomenon** [L16th] which meant 'things appearing to view' in the original Greek.

fanzine *see* FAN

farce [E16th] In 1796 the cookery writer Hannah Glasse wrote, 'Make a farce with the livers minced small.' Farce was an adoption of a French word meaning 'stuffing', its first sense in English. It took on its modern English meaning when applied to comic interludes which were 'stuffed' into the texts of religious plays. From this the term was

used for a complete comic play, these days one that involves a lot of slapstick. *See also* INTERLUDE

fare, farewell *see* FORD

farm *see* FIRM

fart *see* FEISTY

fascinate [L16th] 'Bewitch, put under a spell' was the first sense recorded for fascinate which comes from Latin *fascinare* 'bewitch'.

fascism [E20th] The term fascism was first used of the right-wing nationalist regime of Mussolini in Italy (1922–43), the *Partito Nazionale Fascista* ('National Fascist Party'), and later applied to the regimes of Franco in Spain and of the Nazis in Germany. It comes from Latin *fascis* 'bundle'. In ancient Rome the *fasces* were the bundle of rods, with an axe through them, carried in front of a magistrate as a symbol of his power to punish people.

fashion [ME] If you were out of fashion in the early 1500s you were not outmoded, you were 'out of shape'. Fashion originally meant 'make, shape, or appearance' as well as 'a particular style', and it was not until the mid 16th century that it developed the sense of 'a popular style of clothes or way of behaving'. **In fashion** and **out of fashion** were both used by Shakespeare to mean 'in vogue' and 'out of vogue'. In *Julius Caesar*, when the defeated Brutus plans to kill himself, he says, 'Slaying is the word. It is a deed in fashion.'

fast [OE] The two meanings of fast, 'at high speed' and 'abstain from food', are different words, both Old English. The first originally meant 'firmly fixed in place', a meaning surviving in such uses as 'colour-fast' and 'make a rope fast', and in its close relative **fasten** [OE]. **Fast and loose** was an old fairground gambling game in which the player put a finger into one of the two figure-of-eight loops of a twisted belt or rope so that it caught in a loop when the belt or rope was pulled away. If it was not held, or 'fast', the punter lost the money. The

fancy   fang   fantastic   fanzine   farce   fare

person organizing the game could easily make sure the loops always came free by twisting them in a particular way, which is where we get the expression **play fast and loose**, 'behave irresponsibly or immorally'. **Fast food** has been eaten since the beginning of the 1950s in the USA. The first McDonald's restaurant opened there in 1940, but it was in 1948 that it was reorganized to offer a simple menu of speedily served burgers, fries, and drinks which has spread worldwide. The first UK restaurant was opened in 1974. *See also* US WORD PANEL

fastidious [LME] This comes from Latin *fastidiosus*, from *fastidium* 'loathing'. The word originally meant 'disagreeable, distasteful', later 'disgusted'. Current senses ('attentive to accuracy', 'concerned about personal cleanliness') date from the 17th century.

fat [OE] People have been described as fat since Anglo-Saxon times. The English writer George Orwell said in 1939, 'I'm fat, but I'm thin inside. Has it ever struck you that there's a thin man inside every fat man, just as they say there's a statue inside every block of stone?' Cyril Connolly echoed this in 1944 when he said that 'Imprisoned in every fat man a thin one is wildly signalling to be let out.' For some women **fat is a feminist issue**—the title of a 1978 book by Susie Orbach. The Bible gives us **live on the fat of the land** as a way of saying that we have the best of everything. It comes from the Book of Genesis, in Pharaoh's promise to Joseph and his family, 'Ye shall eat the fat of the land'. Fat here represents an old sense of the noun meaning 'the richest or choicest part of something', which now survives only in this phrase. **The fat is in the fire** is recorded from the mid 16th century, when it referred to the complete failure of a plan. People spending time chatting in a leisurely way can be said to be **chewing the fat**. The origin of the expression is not entirely clear—it may have first been used in the Indian Army—but the most likely explanation is that it derives from the similarity between the movements of the jaw in chewing

through fat or gristle and those involved in talking animatedly. *See also* OPERA, PRODIGAL

fate [LME] This comes from Latin *fatum* 'what has been said', from *fari* 'to speak', source also of *FABULOUS. The main sense of *fatum* was 'the judgement or sentence of the gods', but it came to mean a person's 'lot', or what would happen to them. **The Fates** were the three goddesses of Greek and Roman mythology who presided over the birth and life of humans. Each person was thought of as a spindle, around which the three Fates (Clotho, the spinner, Lachesis, who measured the thread, and Atropos, who cut it off) would spin the thread of human destiny.

father [OE] The Old English word **father** is related to Dutch *vader* and German *Vater*. The proverb **like father, like son** means that a son's character and behaviour can be expected to resemble that of his father. In this exact form it is recorded from the early 17th century, but the idea with slightly different wording goes back to the Middle Ages. **Father Christmas** is of obscure origin. His conventionalized image is comparatively recent: in late medieval Europe he became identified with St Nicholas (Santa Claus); in England Father Christmas was a personification of Christmas, a genial red-robed old man who appeared in many 16th-century masques and in mummers' plays. There was a great revival of the celebration of Christmas in the 19th century and Father Christmas acquired (from St Nicholas) the association of present-bringing.

fatigue [M17th] The early use of the word was to mean 'a task or duty causing weariness'; this is seen in the military use of the plural **fatigues**, duties sometimes allocated as a punishment. It comes via French from Latin *fatigare* 'tire out'. The opposite is found in **indefatigable** [E17th].

fatuous *see* FADE

fatwa *see* ARABIC WORD PANEL

faucet *see* US WORD PANEL

fastidious fat fate father fatigue fatuous

fault *see* FALSE

faun [LME] In Roman mythology a faun was a lustful rural deity represented as a man with goat's horns, ears, legs, and tail. The word comes from the name of Faunus, a god of flocks and herds, who was associated with wooded places. He had a sister, Fauna, whose name in turn gives us **fauna**, which since the late 18th century has been used to mean 'the animals of a particular region or period'. **Flora** [L18th], 'the plants of a particular region or period' comes from the name of Flora, an ancient Italian goddess of fertility and flowers, source also of **floral** [M18th], **floret** [L17th], **florid** [M17th], and **florist** [E17th]. *See also* FLOWER.

The identically sounded **fawn** [LME] meaning 'a young deer' comes from Old French *faon* and is based on Latin *fetus* 'offspring'. The word did not mean 'a light brown colour' until much later, in the late 19th century. The verb fawn is earlier, and is a quite different word. In Old English *fagnian* meant 'make or be glad', often used of a dog showing delight by wagging its tail, grovelling, or whining. Fawn was then used to convey the idea of a person giving a servile display of exaggerated flattery or affection, particularly in order to gain favour.

Faustian *see* SELL

favela *see* SHANTY

favour [ME] The early sense was 'liking, preference'. It comes via Old French from Latin *favor*, from *favere* 'show kindness to'. In the late 16th century, a favour was something given as a sign of preference, a gift as a token of affection. An example of this is the favour worn conspicuously by medieval knights. Sometimes a ribbon or cockade worn at a ceremony such as at a wedding or coronation was known as a favour too. The **feather in your cap** would originally have been a favour.

fawn *see* FAUN

fax *see* FACSIMILE

fay *see* FAERY

faze [M19th] This informal word meaning 'disturb, disconcert' was originally US, a variant of dialect *feeze* 'drive or frighten off', from Old English *fēsian*.

feast [ME] People have been celebrating special occasions with a feast since the Middle Ages, and appropriately the word goes back to Latin *festus* meaning 'joyous'. **Festival** [ME] derives from the closely related Latin word *festivus*. A **festoon** [M17th] comes from the same root, being at first a festival ornament. In the Christian Church the date of some festivals like Easter, known as **movable feasts**, varies from year to year. A **skeleton at the feast** is someone or something who casts gloom on what should be a happy occasion. This goes back to a story told in the 5th century BC by the Greek historian Herodotus. In ancient Egypt a painted carving of a body in a coffin was carried round the room at parties, and shown to guests with the warning that this was how they would be one day.

feat *see* FACTORY

feather *see* FAVOUR, WING

feature *see* FACTORY

febrifuge *see* FEVER

feckless *see* EFFECT

fee [ME] A word bound up with the medieval feudal system, in which the nobles held Crown land in exchange for military service while the peasants were obliged to work their lord's land and give him a share of the produce. A fee was originally a **fief** [E17th] or feudal estate, from which it developed through the meanings 'the right to an office or pension', 'a tribute to a superior', and 'a benefit or reward' to the modern sense. The word comes from Old French *feu* or *fief*, and is related to **feudal** [E17th].

feeble [ME] This word is from Old French *fieble*, which was earlier spelt *fleible*, from

fault faun Faustian favela favour fawn fax

Latin *flebilis* 'lamentable' from *flere* 'to weep'.

feign, feint *see* FAINT

feisty [L19th] A small farting dog is the surprising idea behind the word feisty, meaning 'spirited and exuberant'. It comes from the earlier and now obsolete word *feist* or *fist* meaning 'small dog', from *fisting cur* or *fisting hound*. This was a derogatory term for a lapdog, deriving from the old verb *fist*, meaning 'to break wind'. *Fist* may also be the source of **fizzle**, which in the 16th century meant 'to break wind quietly'. **Fart** itself goes back to Old English times and was formerly a more respectable word than it is now—Geoffrey Chaucer used it in *The Canterbury Tales*.

feline *see* CAT

fell [OE] The verb fell meaning 'to cut down' is recorded from Old English, and is related to *FALL. Fell as a noun meaning 'hill' is a different word, not found until the Middle Ages. It comes from the Old Norse word for a hill, *fjall*. Fell as an adjective meaning 'wicked' comes from an Old French word meaning 'wicked' or 'a wicked person', the same root as **felon** [ME]and **felony** [ME]. Today it is probably most familiar in the phrase **at one fell swoop**. This originally referred to the sudden descent of a bird of prey in deadly pursuit of its quarry, but came to be used to mean 'at a single blow' or 'all at one go'. In Shakespeare's *Macbeth*, when Macduff hears that his wife and children have been killed at Macbeth's orders, he cries out, 'What! All my pretty chickens and their dam / At one fell swoop?' *See also* BLIND

female [ME] The spelling of female changed in the Middle Ages to match **male**, which is a quite different word. Female came via Old French *femelle* from Latin *femella*, which was a diminutive form of *femina* 'woman' source also of **feminine** [LME], whereas **male** [LME] is based on Latin *masculus*, from *mas* 'a male person'. *See also* CHAUVINISM, MACHO. The saying **the female of the species is more deadly than the male** comes originally from the 1911 poem 'The Female of the Species' by Rudyard Kipling. Whether the animal in question is a cobra, a she-bear, or a woman, the warning of where the greatest danger lies is the same, 'For the female of the species is more deadly than the male'.

femme fatale *see* FRENCH WORD PANEL

fence [ME] The words fence and **fend** [ME] were originally shortenings of **defence** and **defend** (both Middle English), which came from Latin *defendere* 'ward off, guard'. Use of fence for 'railing' developed early. Association with the art of fencing arose in the late 16th century.

feng shui *see* CHINESE WORD PANEL

ferment [LME] This comes via Old French from Latin *fermentum* 'yeast', from *fervere* 'to boil'.

ferret [LME] Latin *fur* 'thief' is the root of ferret, which entered English from Old French *fuiret*. Ferrets are known for stealing birds' eggs, and this was probably why they got their name.

ferry *see* FORD

fertile *see* REFER

festival, festoon *see* FEAST

fetish [E17th] Before its modern sense of 'an obsession' or 'an unusual form of sexual desire', a fetish was an object worshipped in West Africa for its supposed magical powers, or used as an amulet or charm. Early European visitors used the Portuguese word *feitiço* 'charm, sorcery' for it.

fetus *see* EFFETE

feudal *see* FEE

fever [OE] Fever has been with us since Anglo-Saxon times, when we borrowed the word from Latin *febris*. A fever makes you hot and bothered, and the word may ultimately go back to a root meaning 'to be restless'. In herbal medicine the plant

feverfew [OE] was traditionally seen as a cure for fever. In Latin the name was *febrifugia*, from *febris* 'fever' and *fugare* 'drive away', from which we get the medical term **febrifuge** [L17th] for a drug that reduces fever. Closely related to *fugare* is *fugere* 'to flee' found in **fugitive** [LME], **refuge** [LME], and **refugee** [L17th].

few [OE] The ancient root of few is shared by Latin *paucus* 'small', which gives us the English word **paucity** [LME]. The name **the Few** for the RAF pilots who took part in the Battle of Britain in 1940 comes from a speech by Winston Churchill in August of that year: 'Never in the field of human conflict was so much owed by so many to so few.'

fiancée *see* FAITH

fiasco [M19th] A fiasco is a ridiculous or humiliating failure. The word was borrowed from Italian in the 19th century. In that language it meant originally 'a bottle', but the phrase *far fiasco*, literally 'make a bottle', was used in the theatre to mean 'fail in a performance'. In medieval English a **flask** [ME] was a cask or skin for holding liquor. The word came from medieval Latin *flasca* (along with LME **flagon**) but the 17th-century sense 'glass container' was influenced by Italian *fiasco*.

fib *see* FABULOUS

fiction *see* FAINT

fiddle [OE] In Old English fiddle was the usual word for a stringed instrument like a violin, based on Latin *vitulari* 'to celebrate, be joyful', which may come from *Vitula*, the name of a Roman goddess of joy and victory. In the sense 'to swindle' fiddle was first used in the 1630s. The connection with the instrument probably came from the idea that the 'fiddler' or player could make people 'dance to his tune'. Expressions like **fiddle-de-dee** and **fiddle-faddle**, meaning 'nonsense', come from the idea of violin-playing being a trivial or pointless exercise, and in turn **fiddle-faddle** is the origin of **fad**.

When we criticize someone for concerning themselves with trivial affairs while ignoring serious matters, we may say that they are **fiddling while Rome burns**. This looks back to a story about the Roman emperor Nero. According to one historian, when Rome suffered from a disastrous fire Nero reacted by singing a song about the fall of Troy and accompanying himself on some instrument—not a fiddle, which had not been invented then. To **play second fiddle** is to take a less important role. The idea here is that you are there to support the person taking the leading part.

fidelity *see* FAITH

fidget [L17th] The word fidget is from obsolete *fidge* 'to twitch'; it may be related to Old Norse *fikja* 'move briskly, be restless, or eager'.

Fido *see* FAITH

fief *see* FEE

figment *see* FAINT

figure [ME] The word figure, which comes ultimately from Latin *figura* 'shape, figure, form' came into English with the same wide range of meanings it has today, from 'distinctive shape of a person', 'representation of something', to 'numerical symbol'.

file [OE] Of the three different words that take the form file in English, the oldest is the word for the smoothing tool, which is Old English. The other two, the folder and the queue, both go back to Latin *filum* 'thread' found also in **filament** [L16th], **filigree** [L17th] which was originally spelt *filigrane* and formed from *filum* and *granum* 'seed', and **fillet** [ME] originally a ribbon tied round the head and subsequently used for any long, thin strip. The folder sense, from Late Middle English, comes about because it was originally used of paperwork kept in order by being threaded on string. The line of people, which is late 16th century, comes via French, from the idea of people strung out.

filial *see* AFFILIATE

filibuster [L18th] A filibuster was an 18th-century pirate of the Caribbean. The word links a number of languages, reaching back through Spanish and French to *vrijbuiter*, from *vrij* 'free', and *buit* 'booty', a Dutch word from which we also get **freebooter**. In the 19th century the Spanish *filibustero* was used for American adventurers who stirred up revolution in Central and South America, and filibuster came to be used in the USA to describe behaviour in congressional debates intended to sabotage proceedings. From this we get the current sense, 'a very long speech made in Parliament to prevent the passing of a new law', which links the long-ago pirates with politicians of today.

filigree, fillet *see* FILE

fillip [LME] Back in the Middle Ages fillip meant simply 'a flick of the finger', and probably came into use because the sound was felt to represent the movement. **Flip** [M16th] is probably a shortening, expanded in turn in the early 17th century to form **flippant**.

finance [LME] The word finance is from Old French, from *finer* 'make an end; settle a debt', from *fin* 'end'. The original sense was 'payment of a debt, compensation, or ransom', which later developed into 'taxation, revenue'. Current senses date from the 18th century. **Fine** [ME] in the sense money you pay, comes from the same source and was originally a sum paid to settle a lawsuit, while the other sense of fine, 'high quality' leading to 'thin', also Middle English, goes back to the earlier sense 'thoroughly finished', and lies behind **refine** [L16th], **define** [LME], **finery** [L17th], and **finesse** [LME]. **Finish** [ME] itself goes back to the same root.

finger [OE] Finger is Germanic in origin and the source of many expressions including: **point the finger** (of scorn) **at** [E19th], the emphatic **lay a finger on somebody** [M19th], **fingers crossed** [1920s], and **pull one's finger(s) out** [1940s].

finish *see* FINANCE

fire [OE] In ancient and medieval thought fire was seen, along with water, air, and earth, as one of the four elements. The word goes back to an ancient root that also gave us the Greek word for fire, *pur*, the source of **pyre** [M17th] and **pyromaniac** [M19th]. The phrase **fire and brimstone** is a traditional description of the torments of hell. In the biblical book of Revelation there is a reference to 'a lake of fire burning with brimstone'. **Brimstone** [OE] is an old word for sulphur, and literally means 'burning stone'. A fire-and-brimstone sermon is one that gives vivid warning of the dangers of going to hell if you misbehave. To **set the world on fire** is to do something remarkable. An earlier British version was to **set the Thames on fire**, and a Scottish one is **set the heather on fire**. Whichever version is used, it tends to be with a negative implication. In Anthony Trollope's novel *The Eustace Diamonds* (1873) Lady Glencora is clear about the limitations of 'poor Lord Fawn' who 'will never set the Thames on fire'.

firedamp *see* DAMP

firm [ME] Firm meaning 'not yielding to pressure' comes from Latin *firmus*, also the root of **farm** [ME], which originally meant a tax or rent. Firm meaning 'a company or business' has the same root, but the immediate origin is different. The Latin word had also given rise to Italian *firma* 'confirmed by signature', and in the late 16th century this was adopted into English to mean 'an autograph or signature'. Over time it came to mean the name under which business was transacted by an organization, as in 'trading under the firm of "Grant & Co."'. Finally, in the late 18th century, firm became the term for a company.

first [OE] The Old English word first goes back to an ancient root which is shared by Latin *primus* (as in *PRIME), and Greek *prōtos* (as in **protein** [M19th] and **prototype** [M16th]). The expression **first come, first served** goes back to the Middle Ages and is found in the poetry of Geoffrey Chaucer. It was originally used in the context of milling, when a mill would serve the whole community. The first person to bring their corn to the mill would be the first person to have it ground. The **first among equals** is the member of a group that has the highest status. It is a translation of the Latin phrase *primus inter pares*, which was used as a title by Roman emperors. Many will know it today as the title of a Jeffrey Archer novel published in 1984. In Scotland to **first-foot** [E19th] is to be the first person to cross the threshold of a house in the New Year. Traditionally, it is thought lucky for that person to be a dark-haired man.

fiscal *see* CONFISCATE

fish [OE] A fish was originally any animal living exclusively in water, as distinct from the 'birds of the air', and the 'beasts of the field'. In Christian art a fish is a symbol of Christ, and is often found in paintings in the underground catacombs of ancient Rome— for this reason modern Christians sometimes have a stylized fish on their car's number plate. The connection may go back to the first letters of the Greek words for 'Jesus Christ, Son of God, Saviour', which were read as *ikhthus*, Greek for 'fish', found in words such as **ichthyologist** [E18th] for someone who studies fish, and the fish-like dinosaur the **ichthyosaur** [M19th]. We have been eating **fish fingers** for more than 50 years. Their inventor Clarence Birdseye, founder of the Birds Eye food company, launched them in 1955. The idea of being a **fish out of water**, or a person in a completely unsuitable environment, is very old, going back to the days of Geoffrey Chaucer, who wrote that 'A monk when he is reckless [meaning 'neglectful of his duty'] is like a fish that is waterless'. *See also* RED, WIFE

fissure [LME] This comes from Latin *fissura*, from *findere* 'to split' also the base of **fission** [E17th] 'splitting'.

fizzle *see* FEISTY

flab [1950s] Flab was formed in the 1950s from the late 17th-century **flabby**, itself a

form of **flappy** [L16th] from Middle English **flap**, which probably, along with its further variant **flop** [E17th], imitates the sound of something flapping. The slang use **be in a flap about** something dates from the early 20th century. **Flabbergast**, first mentioned in 1772 as a new piece of fashionable slang and probably an arbitrary invention, may have been modelled on flabby. **Flaccid** [E17th] comes from *flaccus*, the Latin for 'flabby'.

flag [LME] The flag that means 'a stone slab' is recorded from medieval English, and may be one of the words given to us by the Vikings, making it a relative of **flaw** [ME] originally a snowflake, then a fragment, becoming a defect in the 15th century. The flag which is used as the emblem of a country has been with us since the mid 16th century, and is a different word. It is likely to represent the sound of something flapping in the wind, although it may also be connected with an obsolete word *flag* meaning 'hanging down'. When we want to make clear our support for something we might say that we **show the flag**. Originally this was used of a naval vessel making an official visit to a foreign port. Flag meaning 'become tired' is probably related to the 'emblem' flag. It first meant 'flap about loosely, hang down'. In June 1940, after Dunkirk and before the Battle of Britain, Winston Churchill rallied the House of Commons with the words: 'We shall not flag or fail . . . We shall fight on the beaches, we shall fight on the landing grounds, we shall fight in the fields, and in the streets, we shall fight in the hills; we shall never surrender.'

flagon *see* FIASCO

flagrant [LME] Early senses of flagrant with meanings such as 'glorious' and 'blazing' were positive. The word comes from the Latin word *flagrare* 'to blaze', as in **conflagration** [LME], and is recorded from the late 15th century. **Flamboyant** [M19th] and **flame** [ME] itself go back to the same root. The Latin original is also found in the phrase *in flagrante (delicto)* literally 'in blazing crime', and usually used to mean that someone has been caught in bed with someone else's partner.

flair [L19th] This word for 'instinctive aptitude' comes from French, from *flairer* 'to smell', based on Latin *fragrare* 'smell sweet', source also of **fragrant** [LME] and **fragrance** [M17th]. The notion is one of having the ability to detect the 'scent, essence' of something and the know-how to react accordingly.

flak *see* GERMAN WORD PANEL

flamboyant, flame *see* FLAGRANT

flamingo [M16th] This tall wading bird may be connected with **flamenco** [L19th], the style of Spanish Gypsy music and dance. In Spanish *flamenco* means both 'flamingo' and 'flamenco', and also 'like a Gypsy', 'strong and healthy-looking', and 'Flemish'. How 'Flemish' is related to the other meanings is not clear: it may be from the pink cheeks of north Europeans, or because of an apparent reputation that the people of Flanders had in the Middle Ages for flamboyant clothing. The name of the bird was probably influenced by Latin *flamma* 'flame', on account of its bright pink colour. *See also* SPANISH WORD PANEL

flannel [ME] Ever since the Middle Ages we have worn flannel, which probably comes from Welsh, from the word *gwlân* 'wool'. In 1920s the sense of 'bland, vague talk used to avoid a difficult subject' developed from the central idea of a soft, warm fabric—it seems to have started as military slang. *See also* CORGI, OAF

flap, flappy *see* FLAB

flash [ME] We think of flash in terms of fire and light, but in the Middle Ages it originally meant 'splash water about', and like **plash** [E16th] and **splash** [M18th] probably came from the sound of the word. The association with fire may have developed from the resemblance of the word to flame (*see* FLAGRANT). The idea of 'ostentatious stylishness or display of wealth' goes back to the 17th century. When calling a sudden, brief success **a flash in the**

pan we are referring to early firearms. Sometimes the gunpowder would burn fiercely but ineffectually in the 'pan', the part that held the priming charge, without igniting the main charge. The result was a flash and some smoke, but the gun did not fire—what Shakespeare in *Macbeth* called 'sound and fury signifying nothing'.

flask *see* FIASCO

flat [ME] Flat in the sense 'smooth and even' is from Old Norse *flatr*. **Flatline** came into use in the 1980s for 'to die', from the continuous straight line displayed on a heart monitor when a heart stops beating. Flat meaning 'apartment is from the early 19th century and related to the first flat. It originally meant a storey of a building and is an alteration of the obsolete Germanic word *flet* 'floor, dwelling'.

flatulent [L16th] This word came via French from modern Latin *flatulentus*, from Latin *flatus* 'blowing'.

flaunt *see* FLOUT

flavour [LME] Originally flavour was associated with smell rather than taste, and meant 'fragrance'. Linked in English with **savour** [ME] which comes from Latin *sapere* 'to taste', it comes from an Old French word which might be a combination of Latin *flatus* 'blowing' and *foetor* 'unpleasant smell'. The current meaning of 'a distinctive taste' dates from the 17th century. In the 1930s American ice-cream parlours ran campaigns to promote a particular **flavour of the month**, giving us the phrase we use today to mean 'something that is currently very popular.'

flaw *see* FLAG

flea [OE] The first use of flea is recorded as early as the 8th century. Fleas are jumping insects, and since the late 19th century we have used **fit as a flea** to describe an active, healthy person. People have been sent away with **a flea in their ear** since the 15th century, and the idea dates back earlier in France. The telling-off or rejection is so 'sharp' that it is likened to the pain of a flea

flair   flak   flamboyant   flame   flamingo

bite. **Flea markets** [E20th] and **fleapits** [M20th], or scruffy cinemas, get their names from the idea that they are places which harbour fleas.

flesh [OE] The most tangible part of the human body is flesh, and since the Middle Ages people have described their children, brothers, sisters, and other family members as **their own flesh and blood**. In the Book of Genesis God takes out one of Adam's ribs when he was sleeping, and made it into a woman, Eve. Adam said, 'This is now bone of my bones, and **flesh of my flesh**: she shall be called Woman, because she was taken out of Man.' To **go the way of all flesh** is to die. It is from a 17th-century English translation of the Bible, which in most bibles is rendered as 'Go the way of all the earth'. **Fleshpots** [E16th], 'places providing luxurious living', also come from the Bible, in which they are literally pots in which meat is boiled. In the book of Exodus, when the Israelites are making their laborious way through the desert after their escape from Egypt, they lament, 'Would to God that we had died by the hand of the Lord in the land of Egypt, when we sat by the flesh pots, and when we did eat bread to the full.'

flex [E16th] This comes from the Latin *flectere* 'to bend'. The electrical flex [E20th] is a shortening of flexible cord or cable, **flexible** being late Middle English and from the same source, as is **deflect** [M16th] 'bend away'. An **inflection** [LME] was originally an act of bending inwards, gaining its grammatical sense in the mid 17th century. **Flexitime** has been being worked, by those lucky enough to get it, since the 1970s.

flip, flippant *see* FILLIP

flirt [M16th] Like words such as **biff** [M19th], **bounce** [E16th], flick [*see* FILLIP], and **spurt** [L16th], and many others often sharing the same sounds, flirt apparently arose because it somehow 'sounded right' to convey the idea it represented. In the case of flirt the elements *fl-* and *-irt* probably suggest sudden movement—the original verb senses were 'to give someone a sharp blow', 'to move or propel suddenly', and 'to

sneer at'. As a noun it first meant 'joke, gibe', and 'flighty girl', with a notion originally of cheekiness rather than of playfully amorous behaviour.

flittermouse *see* BAT

flog [L17th] Originally a slang word, which might be from Latin *flagellare* 'to whip', or could just have been formed in imitation of the noise of a whip being wielded. Flog meaning 'to sell' started life as military slang, probably during the First World War. *See also* HORSE

floozy [E20th] These days floozy (or floozie) has a dated feel, and is only really used in jokey contexts. It is not that old a word, though, and does not seem to have been used before the 20th century. It might come from the English dialect word *floosy*, meaning 'fluffy, soft', or from **flossy** [M19th], which is literally 'like silk, silky' but can mean 'saucy, cheeky', or 'showy, flashy' in the USA.

flop *see* FLAB

flora, floral, floret, florid, florist *see* FAUN

flossy *see* FLOOZY

flotsam [E17th] This legal term for wreckage found floating on the sea or washed up on the beach, comes ultimately from French, from the verb *floter* 'to float'. **Flotsam and jetsam** is useless or discarded objects. Jetsam came originally from **jettison** [LME], a term for the deliberate throwing of goods overboard to lighten a ship in distress, which came ultimately from the Latin verb *jactare* 'to throw'. In the 16th century it was shortened to give us first the spelling *jetson* and then our modern word **jetsam**. There are strict legal distinctions made between what you can do with flotsam and with jetsam.

flour *see* FLOWER

flout [M16th] Flout, which appeared in the 16th century and means 'to openly disregard a rule or convention', may come

flesh flex flip flippant flirt flittermouse

from a Dutch word *fluiten* meaning 'whistle, play the flute, hiss derisively'. There is a German dialect expression *pfeifen auf*, literally 'pipe at', which is used in a similar way. Flout is often confused with **flaunt** [M16th], 'to display something ostentatiously', but there is no connection— the origin of flaunt is unknown.

flower [ME] Despite the big difference in meaning, flower and **flour** are the same word. In Middle English **flower** was spelt 'flour', but by the 17th century this spelling was limited to the specialized sense of 'ground grain'. Flour developed from the meaning 'flower' or 'best part of something'. It was then used for 'the finest quality of ground wheat', and from this developed the sense we have today. The word comes through French from a Latin root which also gives us flora and flourish (*see* FAUN).

flu *see* INFLUENZA

fluent, fluid, flume *see* AFFLUENT

flummery *see* CORGI

flush [ME] Flush as in **flushed cheeks, flush the lavatory** was first recorded in the sense 'move rapidly, spring up', especially in the context of a bird'. It is symbolic, *fl-* frequently beginning words connected with sudden movement; perhaps, in this case, influenced by **flash** and **blush**. The sense 'level with' [M16th] is probably the same word, probably from the image of a river running full and level with its banks. The term for a hand of cards all of the same suit is perhaps from French *flux* (formerly *flus*), from Latin *fluxus* 'a flow', and dates from the early 16th century. This specialized use may be compared with English *run* also used in cards contexts.

fluster [E17th] The early sense was 'make slightly drunk'. It is perhaps of Scandinavian origin and related to Icelandic *flaustra* 'hurry, bustle'.

flux *see* AFFLUENT

fly [OE] In Old English a fly was any winged insect. In the 17th century the clergyman Edward Topsell wrote of 'the black flies called beetles'. A **fly in the ointment** is a minor irritation that spoils the success or enjoyment of something. The phrase goes back to a verse in the biblical book of Ecclesiastes, 'Dead flies cause the ointment of the apothecary to send forth a stinking savour.' To **fly a kite** has had various incarnations in slang. It now means 'to try something out to test public opinion', but in the 19th century it was to raise money on credit. In the USA telling someone to **go fly a kite** is to tell them to go away. The **flies** on trousers or in a theatre come from the idea that they are only partly attached to their base, as if they could fly off.

fob [L16th] To **fob someone off** meant 'to cheat, deceive' in medieval days. Although the origin is uncertain, it may be related to German *foppen* 'deceive, cheat, banter', or to **fop** [LME] originally used to mean a fool. In the mid 17th century a fob was a small pocket in the waistband of a pair of breeches, for carrying a watch or other valuables. The use of the word to mean a chain attached to a watch developed from this. Again the origin is uncertain, but there may be a link with the earlier English verb, or there could be a connection with the idea of 'deceive', because the pocket was 'secret'.

focus [M17th] In Latin *focus* meant 'hearth, fireplace', and the optical sense of 'the burning point of a lens', the point at which rays meet after reflection or refraction, may have developed from this. It was first used in 1604 in Latin in this sense by the German astronomer Johannes Kepler (1571–1630). By the beginning of the 18th century the word had appeared in the writings of such eminent figures as the philosopher Thomas Hobbes (1588–1679), the scientist Robert Boyle (1627–91), and the mathematician and physicist Isaac Newton (1643–1727). The **focus groups** of modern marketing are much more recent, dating from the early 1960s. Latin *focus* became **foyer** in French, in the sense 'hearth'. It came to be used in French for the 'green-room' in a theatre, and then for the area that the public could gather in during intervals, a

flower flu fluent fluid flume flummery

sense first found in English in 1859. *See also* FUEL

fodder *see* FOOD

foetus *see* EFFETE

fog [LME] In medieval English fog was a name for a type of coarse grass. Its origin is uncertain, but it may be related to Norwegian *fogg*. It gave rise to the adjective **foggy**, 'covered with fog grass', which also had the meaning 'thick, murky, boggy'. The weather term **fog** was probably formed from foggy.

fogey [L18th] This word for an old-fashioned or narrow-minded person is first found in the late 18th century, in Scots use. It is related to an earlier slang term *fogram*, and may be connected with *foggy* in the senses 'flabby, bloated' or 'moss-grown'. In the 1980s **young fogeys** appeared—young people noticeable for their conservative tastes and ideas. The phrase is first recorded as far back as 1909, but became popular with the publication of *The Young Fogey Handbook* in 1985.

fond [LME] The root of both fond and fun is the medieval word *fon*, which meant 'a fool'. Fond originally meant 'foolish, silly', or 'mad', and did not acquire the modern sense 'affectionate' until the end of the 16th century—Shakespeare appears to have been the first to use 'fond of', in *A Midsummer Night's Dream*. Someone you are fond of came to be called a *fondling* in the mid 17th century. The word may have fallen out of use, but lives on in to **fondle**, formed from fondling in the late 17th century.

fondue *see* FOUND

font *see* FOUNTAIN

food [OE] Recorded since the beginning of the 11th century, food is related to **fodder** [OE] and **foster** [OE], originally found in the sense 'feed, nourish'. It can refer to mental as well as physical nourishment—the expression **food for thought** to indicate something that deserves serious consideration has been in use since the early 19th century. **Cannon fodder** for soldiers regarded as expendable dates from the First World War.

foodaholic *see* WORK

fool [ME] The root of fool is Latin *follis*, which originally meant 'bellows, windbag', and came to mean 'an empty-headed person', in the same way that **windbag** (LME, but E19th in this sense) does in English. The use of fool to mean a jester or clown also goes back to the Middle Ages. People in the 16th century seem to have been particularly aware of the ways in which someone may come to grief through lack of wisdom, especially in their dealings with others. **A fool and his money are soon parted**, **a fool at forty is a fool indeed**, and **there's no fool like an old fool** all come from this period. Two centuries later foolish behaviour was still a matter for concern—in 1711 the poet Alexander Pope published the line which has become proverbial, '**Fools rush in** where angels fear to tread.' Eager prospectors have been mistaking worthless minerals such as iron pyrites, or **fool's gold**, for gold since the late 19th century. The term **foolscap** for a paper size dates from the late 17th century, and is said to be named after a former watermark representing a fool's cap. Sadly, a traditional story that after the Civil War Parliament gave orders that a fool's cap should replace the royal arms in the watermark of the paper used for the Journals of the House of Commons apparently has no basis in fact.

foot [OE] An Old English word that appears as far back as the epic poem *Beowulf*, probably written in the 700s, foot comes from an ancient root which also gives us Greek *pous*, the root of words as varied as *ANTIPODES, *OCTOPUS, and **podium** [M18th], and Latin *pes* 'foot' (*see* PAWN). The measure equal to 12 inches was originally based on the length of a man's foot.

When we use **feet of clay** to suggest that a respected person has a fundamental flaw, we are reaching back to a story from biblical times. In the book of Daniel, Nebuchadnezzar, the king of Babylon, dreamed about a magnificent idol which had feet 'part of iron and part of clay', and which was broken into pieces. The prophet Daniel interpreted this to mean that the kingdom would eventually fall. To **have one foot in the grave** is to be near death. Although the idea dates back to the 17th century, it is now particularly associated with the 1990s British TV comedy *One Foot in the Grave*, starring Richard Wilson as the unlucky but defiant Victor Meldrew, who had been forced into early retirement. *See also* FIRST

football [LME] Football is truly the world sport, but it means different things in different places. In Britain it is Association football or *SOCCER, or to some people *RUGBY is football. In the USA it is American football, and in Australia Australian Rules. In most forms of football, the ball is handled as well as kicked, and this seems to have been the case when similar games were played in ancient Greece, Rome, and China. In medieval Europe it was a rowdy game with vague rules and large numbers of participants, and often banned by rulers. The first written evidence of the term football comes in 1424, when James I of Scotland decreed that 'na man play at the fut ball under the payne of 4d' (meaning that there was a fine of fourpence for anyone playing football). In Britain a **political football** is a controversial or much-debated issue—one that is 'kicked around' in discussion—whereas in the USA a football is a briefcase containing the codes the President would use to launch a nuclear attack, carried by an aide and kept available at all times. The comparison was made because in American football, players hold on to the ball tightly, letting go only to pass to a colleague.

footle [L19th] This word for engaging in fruitless activity is perhaps from dialect *footer* 'to idle, potter about', from 16th-century *foutre* 'worthless thing': this comes from Old French, with a literal meaning 'have sexual intercourse with', but with a long history of much milder associations than the English equivalent.

footpad *see* PAD

fop *see* FOB

force *see* FORGE

ford [OE] This is a Germanic word, closely related to **ferry** [ME] which comes from Old Norse, and to **fare** [OE]. This originally meant both to journey, travel—as in **farewell** [LME] 'go well, safe journey'—and the journey itself. From this developed the sense payment for a journey in late Middle English.

foreign, forensic *see* FOREST

forest [ME] You would not necessarily link forest and **foreign**, but they have the same Latin root. Forest came via French from the Latin phrase *forestis silva*, literally 'wood outside', from *foris* 'out of doors, outside' and *silva* 'a wood'. The first word moved into English and became our 'forest'. In early use forest had a special legal sense. It was an area, usually belonging to the king, that was intended for hunting, a mixture of woodland, heath, scrub, and farmland not as thickly wooded as forests today. It had its own **forest laws**, and officers appointed to enforce them. The New Forest in Hampshire was reserved as Crown property by William the Conqueror in 1079 as a royal hunting area, and still has its own rules and officers, or **verderers** [M16th], a word that comes from Latin *viridis*, 'green'—compare the expression **greenwood** [ME]. **Forfeit** [ME] which originally meant 'a crime or offence', with the meaning of a fine or penalty developing from this, is also from *foris*, as are **forum**, literally 'what is out of doors' in Latin, but used to mean 'market place' and then 'meeting place'. **Forensic** [M17th] comes from Latin *forensis* 'in open court, public', from *forum*. Because we so often hear the expression forensic science in the context of solving a mystery, it is sometimes forgotten that the term means the application of medical knowledge to support the law.

forfeit *see* FOREST

football footle footpad fop force ford

forge [ME] In early use, to forge meant not only to work metal but also had the general sense 'make, construct'. The word comes from Latin *fabricare* 'to fabricate', from *fabrica* 'manufactured object, workshop' source of *FABRIC. The sense 'make a fraudulent imitation' arose early in the word's history. Forge as in **forge ahead** is a different word. It was first used of ships and may be a variant of **force** [ME] which comes from Latin *fortis* 'strong', source also of **fort** [LME].

fork [OE] Rather than things to eat your dinner with, forks were originally agricultural implements. The fork used for holding food dates from medieval times, when Anglo-Saxon table manners were presumably affected by Norman ways. The word is from Latin *furca* 'pitchfork, forked stick'. A snake's divided tongue is often described as forked, and snakes have been symbols of deceit since the serpent that tempted Adam and Eve in the Garden of Eden. So to speak **with forked tongue** is to speak untruthfully. People have been **forking out**, or reluctantly paying money, since the 1830s or earlier. The phrase comes from the earlier literal meaning, 'to divide or move with a fork'. An earlier use in connection with money is found in **Morton's Fork** although this is really an example of fork used for a dilemma in which either choice brings discredit. John Morton (*c.*1420–1500) was the Archbishop of Canterbury and minister of Henry VII who tried to levy forced loans by arguing that the rich could afford to pay, and so could those who lived frugally since they must have amassed savings.

forlorn [OE] In Old English forlorn meant 'morally corrupted', but the core idea was 'lost', from the verb *forlese* 'to lose'. In the 16th century the current sense of 'pitifully sad' developed. A **forlorn hope** is a persistent or desperate hope that is unlikely to be fulfilled. The phrase came into the language as a mistranslation of Dutch *verloren hoop* 'lost troop'. It originally referred to a band of soldiers picked to begin an attack, many of whom would not survive. The current sense, based on a

misunderstanding of 'forlorn', is recorded from the mid 17th century.

form [ME] Form goes back to Latin *forma* 'a mould or form', and is an element in many English words such as **conform** [ME] make like something else; **deform** [LME] 'mis-shape'; and **reform** [ME] 'put back into shape'. **Formal** [LME] originally meant 'relating to form', and developed the sense 'prim, stiff' in the early 16th century. **Format** [M19th] came via French and German from Latin *formatus (liber)* 'shaped (book)'. **Formula** [E17th] was in Latin a 'little form' and was at first a fixed form of words used in ceremonies. Use in chemistry is from the mid 19th century.

fornication [ME] Latin *fornix*, the source of this word, originally meant a vault or arch. In Rome prostitutes would ply their trade under certain arches such as those around the Colosseum (*see* COLOSSAL). From this *fornix* acquired the sense 'brothel' and then passed into Late Latin as a term for extra-marital sex.

forsake *see* SAKE

forsooth *see* SOOTHE

fort *see* FORGE

fortissimo *see* ITALIAN WORD PANEL

fortnight *see* NIGHT

fortune [ME] The Roman goddess Fortuna, who personified luck or chance, gave us the English word fortune and **fortuitous** [M17th]. The saying **fortune favours the brave**, is found in English from the late 14th century, but the same idea can be traced back to classical times. The Roman poet Virgil included the line '*audentes fortuna iuvat*' or 'fortune favours the brave' in his epic poem the *Aeneid*. *See also* HOSTAGE

forum *see* FOREST

fossil [M16th] Fossils are the petrified remains of ancient or prehistoric creatures that are dug up, and fossil comes from Latin

forge fork forlorn form fornication forsake

fodere 'to dig'. It was originally used for a fossilized fish which was found in the earth. In those days before the theory of evolution people believed that it had lived underground too. The use of the word for a person or organization seen as outdated or resistant to change is found from the mid 19th century.

foster *see* FOOD

foul [OE] The Old English word foul comes from an ancient root shared by Latin *pus* (adopted into late Middle English) Latin *putere* 'to stink' (source of LME **putrid**), and the original sense was 'stinking or disgusting'. **Foul play** indicating unfair conduct or treachery is recorded from the late 16th century, and sports players have been able to complain of 'a foul' since the 1750s. *See also* FAIR

found [ME] The word found 'establish' goes back to Latin *fundare* 'to lay a base for', from *fundus* 'bottom, base', source also of **foundation** [LME], **founder** [ME] 'sink', and **fund** [M17th] from a secondary sense of *fundus* 'landed property'; and **profound** [ME] 'deep'. Found 'melt and mould' is from French *fondre* (source of the melted cheese **fondue** [L19th]), from Latin *fundere* 'melt, pour' (found also in **fuse** [L16th]), and dates from the early 16th century.

fountain [ME] A fountain was originally used to mean a natural spring of water rather than an artificial one, and comes from Latin *fontana* 'spring'. Fount '**source**' (the French for 'spring', in English from the Late Middle Ages) was formed in English in the late 16th century. The baptismal **font** [OE] comes from the same root, although the printing font [L16th], made from melted and cast metal, comes from *fondre* (*see* FOUND).

fourth estate *see* PRESS

fowl *see* BIRD

fox [OE] An Old English word that is related to German *Fuchs*. As well as featuring in folklore (*see* GRAPES) it is also a traditional quarry of hunters. Oscar Wilde

described 'The English country gentleman galloping after a fox—the unspeakable in full pursuit of the uneatable'. Today the fox is as much an urban animal as a rural one, and its meaning has also shifted significantly. The US sense 'an attractive woman' is first recorded in the early 1960s, but the related adjective **foxy** was used before the First World War. This is an unusual development, in that fox is strictly masculine, the female being a **vixen** [LME]. The two words are not as far apart as they might at first seem. Vixen was originally *fixen*, but in the past, as today, in the West Country an 'f' was often pronounced as a 'v', given *vox* and *vixen* and for some reason the West Country form stuck for the female. In the late 16th century vixen came to be a term for a bad-tempered woman (otherwise a *SHREW) so was not available for the new, sexual, sense. **Foxed** to describe a book with brownish spots on it dates from the mid 19th century and comes from the colour of the spots matching the reddish-brown of the animal.

foyer *see* FOCUS

fraction [LME] Medieval mathematicians called numbers that were not whole numbers fractions. The name came from Latin *frangere* 'to break', also the root of **fracture**, **fragile**, and **fragment** (all LME), and ultimately of **frail** [ME]. People who struggled to learn about fractions may not be surprised to learn that the word is also linked to **fractious** [E18th], or 'bad-tempered'.

fragrance, fragrant *see* FLAIR

frail *see* FRACTION

France, franchise, frank *see* EMANCIPATE

frantic *see* FRENETIC

fraternal, fraternity *see* FRIAR

fraught [LME] Something fraught is now usually filled with danger or anxiety, but at first the word simply meant 'laden' or

foster foul found fountain fourth estate

'equipped'. It comes from medieval Dutch *vracht* 'ship's cargo', source also of **freight** [LME].

fray [LME] The spelling fray represents two distinct words. The verb meaning 'to unravel' comes from Latin *fricare* 'to rub', found also in **friction** [M16th]. A person eager to fight might 'plunge into the fray'. This comes from the same root as the old legal term *AFFRAY, Old French *afrayer* 'to disturb, startle'. Someone **frazzled** [E19th] with exhaustion might not be surprised to hear that the word is probably linked with fray meaning 'to unravel'.

frazzled *see* FRAY

free [OE] The adjective free appears in the writings of King Alfred (reigned 871–99) and comes from an ancient root meaning 'to love', from which we also get *FRIEND. **Freedom** is also Old English. The French philosopher Jean-Jacques Rousseau (1712–78) wrote, 'Man was born free, and everywhere he is in chains', while in the 1960s TV series *The Prisoner* Patrick McGoohan cried 'I am not a number, I am a free man!' We now use **freelance** [E19th] as a term for a self-employed person working for a number of different companies, but in the early 19th century it was written as two words, and used to describe a medieval knight who offered his services as a mercenary. **Freemasons** [LME] were originally skilled workers in stone who travelled to find employment and had a system of secret signs and passwords that gained them access to work on important building projects. In the 17th century they began to admit honorary members, and membership of their societies or 'lodges' became a fashionable status symbol.

freebooter *see* FILIBUSTER

freeze *see* FROST

freight *see* FRAUGHT

French [OE] French and France come from the Franks who invaded the area in the 6th century (*see* EMANCIPATE). For centuries the French and English were enemies, which has influenced the way French is used in English. Unceremonious guests have taken **French leave** since the 18th century. The expression is said to come from the French custom of leaving a dinner or ball without saying goodbye to their host or hostess. It is first recorded just after the Seven Years War (1756–63), when France and Britain were struggling for supremacy overseas. It is perhaps not entirely surprising to find that the French themselves take a different view: the equivalent French expression is *filer à l'Anglaise* 'to escape in the style of the English'. The British also regard the French as rather naughty, as the terms **French kiss**, **French knickers**, and **French letter** (for a condom) indicate. This idea is far from new, as the following phrase from *Tom Jones* (1749) by Henry Fielding indicates: 'I would wish to draw a Curtain over…certain *French* novels.'

frenetic [LME] This comes via French and Latin from Greek *phrenitikos*, from *phrenitis* 'delirium', and was initially used to mean 'insane'. Originally **frantic** [LME] was merely an alternative form of the word. **Frenzy** [ME] is from the same root.

frequent [LME] 'Profuse, ample' was the meaning of frequent in early examples. It comes from Latin *frequens*, 'crowded, frequent'.

fresco *see* ITALIAN WORD PANEL

fresh [OE] In Anglo-Saxon times, when meat was salted to last through the winter, fresh meant 'not salt'. The sense of 'newly made, not faded, or worn' developed in the Middle Ages. Fresh meaning 'cheeky' or 'impudent' appeared in the 19th century, and may have been influenced by German *frech* 'saucy'. A desire for new areas of activity may be expressed as wanting **fresh fields and pastures new**. The phrase is a misquotation from a poem by the 17th-century poet John Milton, 'Tomorrow to fresh woods, and pastures new'.

fray frazzled free freebooter freeze freight

Ooh-la-la!

*When they invaded Britain in 1066 the Normans brought over their language, and for the next 300 years the kings and nobility of England spoke French. More recently **French** has given us many expressions that can imply sophistication or a certain naughtiness.*

THE English view of the French as immoral or sexy goes back a long way (*see* FRENCH). Since the 1860s we have called something mildly indecent **risqué**, literally 'risked', whereas a word or phrase open to two interpretations, one of which is less innocent than the other, is a **double entendre** or 'double understanding'. A seductive woman who is likely to cause distress to any man who becomes involved with her is a **femme fatale**, or 'fatal woman'.

By the Victorian era the British upper classes had adopted French cooking, and French cooks were **de rigueur** (literally 'in strictness') or obligatory, with the result that French became the language of good eating. Someone who wants to produce food to the standard of **haute cuisine** or 'high cookery' might follow a **cordon bleu** course. The name refers back to the 'blue ribbon' which since the 1820s has marked a first-class cook but before the French Revolution indicated the highest order of chivalry. Ordering **à la carte** is choosing dishes as separate items rather than as a set meal, literally 'according to the menu card'. You may prefer the **prix fixe**, a set meal of several courses served at a 'fixed price', or make do with an **hors d'oeuvre**, a small savoury dish which is literally 'outside the work'. Or you could simply eat an **éclair**, which in French is not only a cream cake but also 'a flash of lightning', 'a flash or glint', or 'a moment'—*un repas éclair* is a quick meal. The cake's name could have been suggested by the fact that its light texture makes it very quick to eat—the word is defined by the *Chambers Dictionary* as 'a cake, long in shape but short in duration'.

The traditional English prejudice against the French, who were not only their nearest rivals but were Catholics to boot, moderated after the fall of Napoleon in 1815, and people took up several French expressions. The best example of a particular type might be described as the **crème de la crème** or 'cream of the cream'. Someone who likes to leave things to follow their own course without interfering follows a policy of **laissez-faire**, from the French for 'allow to do'. If things do not turn out as you hope, you might console yourself with shrugging your shoulders and saying **c'est la vie**, the equivalent of 'that's life', or **plus ça change**—short for **plus ça change, plus c'est la même chose**, 'the more it changes, the more it stays the same', an 1849 quotation by the French novelist and journalist Alphonse Karr (1808–90).

If you give someone complete freedom to act as they wish, you give them **carte blanche**. The literal meaning 'blank paper' carried the idea of a blank sheet on which to write anything desired, originally the terms of a peace treaty. You would probably not give the opportunity to your **bête noir**—an expression, literally 'black beast', for someone you greatly dislike. Originally an **enfant terrible** was, as the name suggests, a 'terrible child' who embarrassed its parents with untimely remarks, but it is now a person who behaves in an unconventional or controversial way.

That mainstay of corny sitcoms, the **au pair** is a young foreign girl who helps with housework or childcare in exchange for food and accommodation. She has been around since 1960 or so, but in the 19th century an *au pair* arrangement was one in which each party paid the other in kind, by performing services. The phrase means 'on equal terms'. **Entrepreneur** has been used in English since the 1820s. It first meant 'a director of a musical institution' and 'a person who organizes entertainments', but later in the 19th century broadened to refer to somebody who runs a business and takes the risks it entails. The US president George W. Bush is said to have proclaimed, 'The problem with the French is that they don't have a word for entrepreneur'—a good story but one with no evidence to back it up.

fret [OE] If we tell an anxious person not to fret, we are telling them not to worry, but in Old English the word meant 'devour, consume'. It is from the same root as *EAT. The fret in **fretsaw** [M19th], and **fretwork** [E17th] is a different word, from Old French *freté* 'trelliswork', while the fret on a guitar neck is yet another word, of unknown origin.

friar [ME] This is from Old French *frere*, from Latin *frater* 'brother', source also of such words as **fraternal** [LME] and **fraternity** [LME].

friction *see* FRAY

Friday *see* TUESDAY

fridge *see* FRIGID

friend [OE] In the Old English poem *Beowulf*, the king's great hall is described as being filled with friends. This is the first recorded use of the word, which is from an ancient root meaning 'to love' that is shared by *FREE. The proverb **a friend in need is a friend indeed** can be traced back in English to the 11th century. More recent is **your flexible friend**, that faithful plastic

companion on many a shopping trip. The slogan was used for the credit card Access from 1981.

frigid [LME] This comes from Latin adjective *frigidus* 'cold', from the noun *frigus* 'cold'. The word is also behind **refrigerate** [LME]. The **refrigerator** for preserving food appears in the mid 19th century, and was shortened to **fridge** in the 1920s.

fritter *see* FRY

frock [LME] This comes from Old French *froc*, of Germanic origin. The original sense 'priest's or monk's gown' is preserved in **defrock** [L16th].

frog [OE] In the Middle Ages to call someone a frog was a general term of abuse. In the 17th century it was used particularly for a Dutchman, but by the late 18th century it was being applied to the French: this was probably partly due to alliteration, and partly to the reputation of the French for eating frogs' legs. Someone who is finding it hard to speak because they are hoarse may be described as having **a frog in the throat**. The expression dates from the late 19th

fret friar friction Friday fridge friend

century, but 'frog' here goes back to an earlier meaning of a soreness or swelling in the mouth or throat. Frog for a decorative fastening does not seem to be the same word and its origin is unknown.

frolic *see* DUTCH WORD PANEL

frost [OE] This is one of our earliest English words, recorded from the 8th century and related to **freeze** [OE]. Not until the 19th century do we start to hear of **Jack Frost**. The *Sporting Magazine* of 1826 recorded ruefully of the effects of frozen ground, 'Jack Frost, however, put a veto on our morning's sport.' *See also* ICE

frugal *see* FRUIT

fruit [ME] Fruit comes from Latin *fructus* 'enjoyment of produce, harvest' from *frui* 'to enjoy'. The Latin for fruit also had the sense 'profit, value' which is why it is also the source of **frugal** [M16th] 'economical, thrifty'. In America fruit is a term for a gay man. It could come from the US slang sense 'a dupe, an easy victim', with the idea of a fruit that is easily 'picked', or with the derogatory implication of homosexuals being 'soft' like fruit. **Fruitcake** (M20th in this case) meaning 'a mad person' is a play on **nutty** in **as nutty as a fruitcake**, also mid 20th century. **Fruity** in the sense 'sexually suggestive' draws on the idea of being 'ripe and juicy' and dates from the early 20th century. *See also* NUT. **Forbidden fruit** looks back to the biblical account of the fruit of the tree of knowledge of good and evil, which was forbidden to Adam in the Garden of Eden, and which he was disastrously tempted to eat. *See also* APPLE

frump [M16th] This is probably a contraction of late Middle English *frumple* 'wrinkle', from Middle Dutch *verrompelen*. The word originally referred to a mocking speech or action; later as *frumps* it meant 'the sulks'; this led to the word's use for a bad-tempered, and eventually a dowdy woman [E19th].

fry [ME] The word meaning 'to cook in hot fat or oil' comes from the Latin verb *frigere*, which meant both 'to roast' and 'fry'. Fry as a term for 'young fish' is a quite different word, which comes from Old Norse. If you move from a bad situation to one that is worse you have moved **out of the frying pan into the fire**, an expression used by the scholar and statesman Sir Thomas More in the mid 16th century. **Fritters** [LME] are fried food and get their name from Late Latin *frictura* 'a frying'. To fritter time or money [E18th] is a different word. It is based on an old verb *fitter* meaning 'to break into fragments, shred', and may be related to German *Fetzen* 'rag, scrap'.

fuchsia *see* PINK

fudge [E17th] Today we think of fudge as primarily a sweet, and maybe also as a word thrown around as an insult by politicians who are always accusing each other of 'fudging' facts or figures. But the first use of the word was in the sense 'to turn out as expected', and also 'to merge together'. It then came to mean 'to fit together in a clumsy or underhand manner', or 'to manipulate facts and figures'. People started exclaiming 'fudge!' to express scorn or annoyance in the 18th century. The word probably came from the old term **fadge**, which meant 'to fit'. People have been enjoying the sweet since the 1890s or so, originally in America. The meaning was probably suggested by the old sense 'to merge together', because of the way in which you mix up the sugar, butter, and milk or cream to make the fudge.

fuel [ME] Fuel comes ultimately from Latin *focus* 'hearth' (*see* FOCUS), so there has been a shift in meaning from where the fire was laid to what was being burned. **Fuel poverty** has recently been prominent but is found from the 1970s for the inability to afford adequate domestic heating, lighting, and power. *See also* FOSSIL

fugitive *see* FEVER

fumigate [M16th] We would fumigate a room today if we wanted to disinfect it, but the earliest use was 'to perfume', of which it is also the root, from the same period, from the pleasant smell of incense. It comes

frolic frost frugal fruit frump fry fuchsia

ultimately from Latin *fumus* 'smoke', which also gives us **fume** [LME]. *See also* FUNK

fun [L17th] The earliest sense of this surprisingly recent word is 'trick' or 'hoax'. It seems to come ultimately from a dialect pronunciation of Middle English *fon* 'a fool' (*see* FOND). Our current sense dates only from the 18th century, and in 1755 Dr Johnson described it disapprovingly as 'a low cant [slang] word'. He would probably have sympathized with the view given in the humorist A.P. Herbert's *Uncommon Law* (1935): 'People must not have fun. We are not here for fun. There is no reference to fun in any Act of Parliament.' Things can be **funny** [M18th] in several different ways. The expressions **funny ha-ha** and **funny peculiar**, encapsulating the distinctions in meaning between what is amusing and what is strange, were coined by the writer Ian Hay in his novel *The Housemaster* (1936). **Funny money** dates from the 1930s when it was used in the US for forged money.

fund *see* FOUND

fungus [LME] This is the use of a Latin word in English; it is perhaps from Greek *spongos*. The word has sometimes been used to mean 'a beard' since the early 20th century which is probably a shortening of the term **face fungus**.

funk [E17th] People started using **funk** and **funky** in musical contexts during the 1950s: before that, **funky** was a black English expression that meant 'worthless, bad', which reversed its meaning in the same way as *BAD and *WICKED to mean 'excellent'. In the early 17th century, though, funk meant 'a musty smell'. It may come from French dialect *funkier* 'blow smoke on', which was based on Latin *fumus* 'smoke' (the root of *FUMIGATE). Funk

meaning 'a state of panic or anxiety' was Oxford University slang in the mid 18th century, in the phrase **in a blue funk**. It could refer to the slang sense of funk as 'tobacco smoke', or it could be from an old Flemish word *fonck*, 'disturbance, agitation'.

furl *see* ALLY

furlong [OE] Old English *furlang* is from *furh* 'furrow' and *lang* 'long', and meant the standard length of a furrow in a common field, which was regarded as a nominal square of ten acres. It was also used as the equivalent of the Roman measurement the *stadium*, one eighth of a Roman mile, which gave rise to the current sense. *Stadium* came from Greek *stadion* 'race track' and **stadium** came to be used in this sense in the early 17th century, with **sports stadium** appearing in the mid 19th century.

furnish, furniture *see* VENEER

fuse *see* FOUND

fusilli *see* ITALIAN WORD PANEL

fuss *see* FUZZ

futon *see* JAPANESE WORD PANEL

fuzz [L16th] If you are 'caught by the fuzz' you are arrested by the police. This fuzz is a different word from the one that means 'a frizzy mass', and may be a form of **fuss**, from the idea of the police 'making a fuss'. It has been used since the 1920s and originated in the USA. The other fuzz entered English in the late 17th century, probably from Dutch or German, although **fuzzy** is recorded earlier, in around 1600, when it meant 'spongy'. **Fuzzy logic** is a form of logic in which a statement can be partially true or false rather than having to be absolutely one or the other.

fun fund fungus funk furl furlong furnish

Gg

'a blunder', in which sense it came into English in the early 20th century.

gaga [E20th] Gaga 'slightly mad' is from French, 'senile, a senile person'. It is a based on *gâteux*, a variant of the hospital slang word *gâteur* 'bed-wetter'.

gage *see* ENGAGE

gaggle [ME] Gaggle as in **gaggle of geese**, originally imitated the noise that a goose makes. Many word were invented in the 15th century for groups of people or animals; unlike most of the others, gaggle was actually adopted in use.

gain [LME] This comes from the French *gaignier* 'gain' and was at first used to mean 'booty'. The origin is Germanic. The phrase **gain ground** was originally military, used when land was taken from an enemy. **No gain without pain** dates from the 1990s. *See also* UNCOUTH

gala *see* GALLANT

galaxy [LME] If you look into the sky on a dark moonless night you can see a band of pale light crossing the sky, made up of vast numbers of faint stars that appear to be packed closely together. This is the **Milky Way,** a direct translation of what the Romans called *via lactea*. The Greeks were also reminded of milk and named it *galaxias kuklos* 'the milky vault', from *gala* 'milk', the origin of our word galaxy. It was adopted into medieval English and at first referred specifically to the Milky Way, though later it applied to any system of millions of stars. In current sporting usage, especially in football, **galactico** is a term for one of a team's superstar players. A Spanish word, it is chiefly associated with the club Real Madrid, whose high-profile signings Luis Figo, Zinedine Zidane, Ronaldo Lima, and David Beckham were collectively dubbed *Los Galácticos*, literally 'the galactics', because they were 'bigger than stars'.

gall *see* YELLOW

gallant [ME] Gallant at one time could describe an attractive or fine-looking

---

gab, gabby *see* GOBSMACKED

gad [LME] Gad as in **gad about** was probably formed from obsolete *gadling* which first meant 'companion' but later had the meaning 'wanderer, vagabond'. The origin is Germanic. Another view is that it is from obsolete *gad* meaning 'rush about like an animal stung by gad-flies', which is a possibility, but some of the evidence does not support this theory.

gadget [L19th] Sailors were the first people to talk about gadgets. The word started out in nautical slang as a general term for any small device or mechanism or part of a ship. This is the earliest recorded use, dated 1886: 'Then the names of all the other things on board a ship! I don't know half of them yet; even the sailors forget at times, and if the exact name of anything they want happens to slip from their memory, they call it a chicken-fixing, or a gadjet, or a gill-guy, or a timmey-noggy, or a wim-wom.' The word is probably from French *gâchette* 'a lock mechanism' or *gagée* 'tool'. *See also* WIDGET

gaff [ME] One type of gaff is a stick with a metal hook used for landing large fish: it comes from Provençal *gaf* 'a hook'. In British slang a gaff can also be someone's home, a use dating from the 1930s and probably derived from an old term for a fair or music hall. The gaff 'in blow the gaff', though, may be linked to an early 19th-century sense, 'noise or pretence'. Letting out a secret indiscreetly could also be regarded as a **gaffe** [E20th], an embarrassing blunder or *faux pas*, which brings us back to metal hooks. In French *gaffe* means 'a boat hook' and, informally,

gab gabby gad gadget gaff gaga gage

woman. Here is the poet John Lyly writing in 1579: 'This gallant girl, more fair than fortunate, and yet more fortunate than faithful'. It was also once used to mean 'excellent, splendid, or noble', as in 'A more gallant and beautiful armada never before quitted the shores of Spain' (William H. Prescott, 1838). Gallant came into English in the Middle Ages in the sense 'finely dressed', from Old French *galant* 'celebrating', from *gale* 'pleasure or rejoicing', also the source of **gala** [E17th]. The modern sense 'politely attentive to women' was adopted from French into English in the 17th century. **Gallivant** [E19th], meaning 'to go from place to place in pursuit of pleasure', may be a playful alteration of gallant.

gallery [LME] Galilee, the northern region of ancient Palestine where Jesus lived, may be the ultimate source of gallery, which entered English from Italian *galleria* 'gallery', or 'church porch'. Its medieval Latin source was perhaps an alteration of *Galilea* 'Galilee', which was used as the name for a porch or chapel at the church entrance. The idea behind this was probably that the porch was at the end of the church furthest away from the altar, just as Galilee, an outlying portion of the Holy Land, was far from Jerusalem. From the mid 17th century the highest seating in a theatre was called the gallery, and this was where the cheapest seats—and the least refined members of the audience—were found. Hence, to **play to the gallery**, an expression dating from the late 19th century, is to act in a showy or exaggerated way to appeal to popular taste.

gallivant *see* GALLANT

gallon [ME] This unit of volume for liquids is from Anglo-Norman French *galon*, from medieval Latin *galletum* 'pail, liquid measure'. The origin may be Celtic.

gallop *see* WALLOP

galore [E17th] When the Scottish writer Sir Walter Scott wrote in his journal in 1826, 'Sent off proofs and copy galore before breakfast', he was using a word that originated in Ireland. Galore 'in abundance'

comes from Irish *go leor*, which means 'to sufficiency, enough'.

galosh [ME] A galosh was originally a type of clog. It comes via Old French from late Latin *gallicula*, a diminutive of Latin *gallica* (*solea*) 'Gallic (shoe)'. The current use of the word for a waterproof overshoe dates from the mid 19th century.

galumph [1872] Now meaning 'move in a clumsy and ponderous way', galumph started out in the sense 'prance in triumph'. It was coined by Lewis Carroll in *Through the Looking Glass* and may be a blend of **gallop** and **triumph**.

galvanize [E19th] Galvanize was first used to mean 'to stimulate a muscle or nerve by electricity'. It was based on the name of the Italian scientist Luigi Galvani (1737–98), who discovered that frogs' legs twitched violently when he ran electricity through them. Galvani believed that such convulsions were caused by 'animal electricity' found in the body, an idea that inspired Mary Shelley to write *Frankenstein* in 1818. To galvanize iron or steel is to coat it with a layer of zinc to stop it from rusting, originally done by means of an electrical current.

game [OE] The original meaning of game, dating back to Old English, was 'amusement, fun, or pleasure'. Shakespeare uses it in this sense in *Love's Labour's Lost*: 'We have had pastimes here and pleasant game'. Other early meanings included 'a jest or joke', and 'a laughing stock'. The sense of an 'animal hunted' [LME] developed from the earlier sense of 'pleasure of the hunt'. The adjective sense 'full of fight, spirited' (now used also to mean 'ready and willing'), comes from a use of the noun as a term for a fighting cock. Australians say that a brave person is **as game as Ned Kelly**, referring to the 19th-century outlaw and folk hero who led a band of horse and cattle thieves and bank raiders. To be **on the game** is to be involved in prostitution. Although the expression dates from the late 19th century, the use of game to mean 'sexual activity' is much older, as in Shakespeare's reference to

gallery gallivant gallon gallop galore galosh

'daughters of the game' in *Troilus and Cressida*. At one time, being on the game was also thieves' slang for thieving or housebreaking. Rather different from **playing the game**, behaving in a fair or honourable way or abiding by the rules. The expression is recorded from the late 19th century and memorably used in Henry Newbolt's poem 'Vitai Lampada' (1897), celebrating public school values: 'And it's not for the sake of a ribboned coat, / Or the selfish hope of a season's fame, / But his Captain's hand on his shoulder smote – / 'Play up! play up! And play the game!'

People say **game** in situations, especially in sport, when one side has suddenly got themselves back into a contest and anyone can still win. The expression comes from darts, where it signals the start of play. Game meaning 'injured, lame' [L18th] as in **game leg** was apparently originally north Midland dialect (as *gam*) but its origin is unknown. A variant dialect form of game is **gammy** which in the mid 19th century meant 'bad, false'.

gamut [OE] To **run the gamut** is to experience or display the complete range of something. In medieval music gamut was originally the name of the lowest note in the scale, but the term also came to be applied to the full range of notes which a voice or instrument can produce. In time it started to be used outside musical contexts. According to the acerbic American critic and humorist Dorothy Parker, the film actress Katharine Hepburn 'ran the whole gamut of emotions from A to B'. This word is from medieval Latin *gamma ut*, and applied to bass G an octave and a half below middle C. The Greek letter Γ (gamma) was used for bass G, with *ut* indicating that it was the first note in the lowest of the hexachords or six-note scales. Notes in each hexachord were named using syllables of a Latin hymn for St John the Baptist's Day in which each line began on the next note of the scale: *Ut* queant laxis *re*sonare fibris *Mi*ra gestorum *fa*muli tuorum, *Sol*ve polluti *la*bii reatum, Sancte Iohannes. A seventh note, *si*, was added later, from the initial letters of *Sancte Iohannes* 'St John'. The scheme was adapted in the 19th century for the Tonic Sol-fa.

gang [OE] A gang is literally a group of people who 'go about' together. The word comes from Old Norse *gangr* or *ganga*, 'gait, course, or going', and is related to Scots *gang* 'to go'. In early use gang meant 'a journey', and later developed the senses 'way or passage', and 'a set of things which go together'. In the early 17th century it started to be applied to people too, specifically a ship's crew or a group of workmen, and soon any band of people going about together, especially when involved in some disreputable or criminal activity, could be described disapprovingly as a gang. Both **gangway** [OE] and **gangplank** [M19th] are based on the original 'going' sense of the word. **Gangster**, dating from the late 19th century, was altered in US Black English in the 1980s to **gangsta**, and applied both to a member of a gang and to a type of rap music.

gannet [OE] Old English *ganot* is Germanic in origin and related to Dutch *gent* 'gander'. The word is used sometimes to describe a greedy person—first used of a greedy sailor in 1920s slang.

gaol *see* JAIL

garage [E20th] This is an adoption of a French word, from *garer* 'to shelter'.

garbage [LME] A word probably borrowed from Old French that originally meant 'offal or giblets'. These days its main modern use of 'rubbish, refuse' is commoner in American than in British English, but this sense goes back to the 16th century. In computing the saying **garbage in, garbage out** (often abbreviated as **GIGO**) is used to state the fact that incorrect or poor-quality input is bound to produce faulty output.

garden [ME] Garden comes from Old French *jardin* and has an ancient root that is also the ancestor of *YARD. You can say **everything in the garden is lovely** (or **rosy**) when all is well. This early 20th-century catchphrase originated in a song made popular by the English music hall star Marie Lloyd (1870–1922). If someone makes you believe something that is not true by giving

gamut gang gannet gaol garage garbage

you misleading clues or signals, they can be said to be **leading you up the garden path**. The phrase was first used in the early 20th century in the form **lead you up the garden**, suggesting that the original idea was of someone enticing a person they wanted to seduce or flirt with into a garden, away from the safety of the house.

garderobe *see* GUARD

gargantuan [L16th] Gargantua is the name of a large-mouthed giant with a huge and insatiable appetite from the book of the same name, published in 1534, by the French satirical writer Rabelais. In one episode Gargantua accidentally swallows six pilgrims while eating a salad. Gargantuan, meaning 'enormous or gigantic', comes from the name of Rabelais' colossal guzzler.

gargle [E16th] The words gargle and **gargoyle** [ME] are closely related, linked by the idea of throats. Gargle comes from French *gargouiller* 'to gurgle or bubble', from *gargouille* 'throat'. A gargoyle, a grotesque figure of a human or animal carved on a building, especially one that acts as a waterspout, with water passing through its throat and mouth came from the same source.

garment *see* GARNISH

garner *see* GRAIN

garnish [ME] Nowadays you might garnish a plate of food with a sprig of parsley which seems a far cry from what the word meant in the Middle Ages, 'to equip or arm yourself'. Over time the sequence of meanings evolved like this: 'to equip or arm yourself', 'to fit out with something', 'to decorate or embellish', and finally 'to decorate a dish of food for the table'. The source is Old French *garnir* (also the root of **garment** [ME]), which meant both 'to fortify or defend', and 'to provide, equip, or prepare'.

garret [ME] 'Watchtower' was the first meaning recorded for garret. It comes from Old French *garite*, which (like ME **garrison**) is from *garir* 'to defend, provide'. The word's

use for a room on the top floor of a house arose early in its history, in the late 15th century.

gas [M17th] Gas is an invented word, coined in the 17th century by the Belgian chemist and physician Joannes Baptista van Helmont (1577–1644), who was the first scientist to realize that there are gases other than air, and who discovered carbon dioxide. Van Helmont based the word on Greek *khaos*, *CHAOS. It did not really catch on until the 19th century, with earlier scientists like Robert Boyle preferring to think of gases as different types of *AIR. Gas for lighting or heating purposes dates from the late 18th century. The first experiments using coal-gas for lighting are said to have been made by the rector of Crofton, Dr Clayton, in about 1688; gas-lighting in its practical application was due to William Murdock (1754–1839).

gasket [E17th] A gasket was at first a cord securing a furled sail to the yard of a sailing ship. It may come from French *garcette* 'thin rope'. The term for a flat ring used as a seal in an internal combustion engine dates from the early 20th century.

gather *see* GOOD

gauntlet [LME] To **throw down the gauntlet** and **run the gauntlet** use two different gauntlets. If someone **throws down** (or **takes up**) **the gauntlet**, they issue (or accept) a challenge. In medieval times a gauntlet (from Old French) was a glove worn as part of a medieval suit of armour. The custom was for a knight to challenge another to a fight or duel by throwing his gauntlet to the ground. The other knight would pick it up to show that he accepted the challenge. To **run the gauntlet** has nothing to do with gloves, but refers to a former military form of punishment recorded from the mid 17th century. A soldier found guilty of an offence, particularly stealing from his fellows, was stripped to the waist and forced to run between two lines of men armed with sticks, who beat him as he went past. **Gauntlet** here is a version of an earlier word **gantlope**,

garderobe gargantuan gargle garment

from Swedish *gatlopp*, from *gata* 'lane' and *lopp* 'course'. **Run the gantlope** was first recorded in English in 1646, but **gantlope** was soon replaced by **gauntlet**, a more familiar word.

gay [ME] In its original sense of 'light-hearted and carefree, exuberantly cheerful', gay goes back to the 14th century and derives from Old French *gai*. By the 17th century the meaning had extended to 'addicted to social pleasures', often with an implication of loose morality, as in, for example, the expression **gay dog** (a man fond of revelry), or these lines from William Cowper's poem 'To a Young Lady' (1782): 'Silent and chaste she steal along / Far from the world's gay busy throng'. In slang use the word could describe a prostitute. The use of gay to mean 'homosexual', now the main meaning, is unambiguously found in examples from the 1930s, though there is evidence that it may have been used in this sense earlier.

gazette [E17th] The word gazette came via French from Italian *gazzetta*, a shortening of the Venetian dialect *gazeta de la novità* 'a halfpennyworth of news'—the news-sheet sold for a *gazeta*, a Venetian coin of very little value. The verb phrase to be **gazetted** [L17th] meant 'be the subject of an announcement in a gazette', and 'be named in a gazette as being appointed to a military command'. **Gazetteer** is also early 17th century when it meant 'journalist': The current use of the word for a geographical index comes from a late 17th-century gazetteer called *The Gazetteer's: or, Newsman's Interpreter: Being a Geographical Index*.

gazump [1920s] These days we associate gazumping with the buying and selling of houses, a use that dates from the 1970s. It now means 'to raise the price of a house after accepting an offer from a prospective buyer', but in the early 20th century it simply meant 'to swindle', deriving from Yiddish *gezumph* 'to overcharge'. In the late 1980s the opposite term **gazunder** (a combination of **gazump** and **under**) was coined to describe the practice of lowering the amount of an offer that the seller has already accepted while threatening to withdraw if the new offer is not accepted.

geek [L19th] This is originally US slang from the related English dialect word *geck* 'fool', from a Germanic source. It is related to Dutch *gek* 'mad, silly'. In Webster's *New International Dictionary of the English Language* of 1954, the definition read: *Geek*, a carnival 'wild man' whose act usually includes biting off the head of a live chicken or snake'.

geezer [late 19th century] An informal word for a 'man', geezer represents a dialect pronunciation of the earlier form *guiser* (related to *DISGUISE) meaning 'mummer, someone who dresses up'. In recent use it sometimes has a connotation of shady dealing.

geisha *see* JAPANESE WORD PANEL

gender [LME] The words gender and **engender** [ME] go back via Old French to Latin **genus** 'birth, family, nation', a word that was reborrowed in the early 17th century for scientific classification, although it had been in use 50 years earlier in logic. In modern French the 'd' was lost to produce **genre**, a word reborrowed in the early 19th century. **Generation** [ME], **generate** [E16th], **engender** [ME], **generosity** [LME], **genial** [M16th], and **degenerate** [LME] are all from the same source.

gene [E20th] The word gene is from German *Gen*, from *Pangen* (from Greek *pan-* 'all' and *genos* 'race, kind, offspring'), a supposed ultimate unit of heredity. **Genetic** [M19th] started out meaning 'arising from a common origin': this is from **genesis** [OE] 'creation', on the pattern of pairs such as *antithesis* and *antithetic*.

generate, generation, generosity *see* GENDER

genesis, genetic *see* GENE

genial, genre *see* GENDER

gentle [ME] The root word shared by **genteel** [L16th], **gentile** [LME] 'not Jewish', and gentle is Latin *gentilis* 'of a family or nation, of the same clan', which came from *gens* 'family, race'. Genteel and gentle originally had similar meanings. Genteel first meant 'stylish, fashionable', and 'well bred'—the ironic or derogatory implications that it now tends to have date from the 19th century. The original sense of gentle was 'nobly born', from which came 'courteous, chivalrous', the idea behind **gentleman** [ME]. *See also* BLONDE. **Jaunty** [M17th] is an anglicization of the French for gentle, *gentil* and was first used to mean 'gentile'.

genuine [L16th] 'I rather choose to keep to the Language of the Sea, which is more genuine, and natural for a mariner.' So wrote Woodes Rogers, the English privateer, in 1712. Genuine is used here in its original sense, 'natural or proper'. The source of the word is Latin *genuinus*, from *genu* 'knee', with reference to the Roman custom of a father formally acknowledging that a newborn child was his by placing the baby on his knee.

genus *see* GENDER

geriatric [1920s] This word is made up of Greek *gēras* 'old age' and *iatros* 'doctor'.

germ [LME] This came via Old French from Latin *germen* 'seed, sprout'. At first it meant a portion of an organism capable of developing into a new one or part of one. The sense 'micro-organism' dates from the late 19th century when it was first used vaguely to mean the 'seed' of a disease. **Germinate** [L16th] is from the same root.

Überbabes and spritzers

War inevitably influenced Germany's 20th-century contributions to our language, but **German** *has given us many other terms, including some that handily fill in where there is no English equivalent.*

TAKE dogs, for example. The **poodle** is now considered to be a cute, pampered little breed of dog, but it was bred as a hunting dog to retrieve waterfowl shot by its master, and its name is from German *Pudelhund* 'puddle dog'. The **dachshund** is often called a 'sausage dog' because of its long body, but it is literally a 'badger dog'—the breed was used to dig badgers out of their setts.

Since the 1920s we have criticized objects regarded as garish or sentimental as **kitsch**. At times this may be seen as a type of intellectual snobbery—in May 1961 *The Times* made a reference to 'highbrows...who consider that the quality of the pure entertainment as such is generally *kitsch* or trash'. We might feel that this sort of thing was **ersatz**, or 'artificial', and add that it should be **verboten**, or 'forbidden'.

But there is no avoiding the language of war. **Flak** or 'anti-aircraft fire', borrowed directly from German in the 1930s, is an abbreviation of *Fliegerabwehrkanone*, literally 'aviator-defence-gun'. By the 1960s it was sufficiently established in English for the extended sense 'strong criticism' to develop.

gentle   genuine   genus   geriatric   germ

In September 1940 **blitz** appeared in *Daily Express* reports of the heavy air raids made by the **Luftwaffe** (the German air force, a combination of 'air' and 'weapon') on London. **Blitz** is a shortening of **blitzkrieg**, which had been used the previous year to describe the German invasion of Poland. In German *Blitzkrieg* means 'lightning war'. The metaphorical use 'a sudden concerted effort to deal with something' came up in the *Guardian* in 1960: 'The women did only the bare essentials of housework during the week, with a "blitz" at weekends.'

A **spritzer** is a mixture of wine and soda water named after the German word for 'a splash'. In the 1980s this drink was certainly in tune with the **zeitgeist**, or 'spirit of the time'. Since the 1990s we have used the German word for 'over', *über*, to form words expressing the idea of the ultimate form of something—supermodels are sometimes referred to as **überbabes**.

German was the language used by the Austrian psychoanalyst Sigmund Freud (1856–1939) and his Swiss collaborator Carl Jung (1875–1961), and has given us several words for feelings. **Angst**, vague worry about the human condition or the world in general, entered English in the 1940s. **Weltanschauung**, from *Welt* 'world' and *Anschauung* 'perception', means 'individual philosophy, world view'. Until the 1890s English had no word for the regrettably familiar feeling of pleasure derived from another person's misfortune, and so imported one from Germany—**schadenfreude** combines 'harm' and 'joy'.

See also DUDE, HAMSTER, HEROIN, LAGER, QUEER, TRADE

gerrymander [E19th] Half-man, half-lizard—that is a **gerrymander**. In political contexts gerrymandering is manipulating the boundaries of electoral districts to give an advantage to a particular party or class. The term was coined when Elbridge Gerry, governor of Massachusetts in 1812, created a new voting district that appeared to favour his party. Because the shape of this new district vaguely resembled the outline of a salamander, a map, embellished with claws, wings, and fangs, was published in the Boston *Weekly Messenger*, with the title *The Gerry-Mander*.

gesture *see* JEST

ghastly *see* AGHAST

gherkin *see* DUTCH WORD PANEL

ghetto [OE] Italian *getto* 'a foundry' is probably the source of this word for a part of a city, especially a slum area, occupied by a minority group. The first ghetto was established in 1516 on the site of a foundry in Venice. Alternatively, it may come from Italian *borghetto*, meaning 'a little borough'. In Italy the word referred to the quarter of a city to which Jews were restricted, a use that became more widespread elsewhere, as in the Warsaw ghetto.

ghost [OE] In Old English ghost meant 'a person's spirit or soul'. This sense is preserved in to **give up the ghost**, which originally meant 'to die', the original idea being of soul as the source of life, although it now often refers to equipment that has broken down beyond repair. **The ghost in the machine** refers to the mind viewed as distinct from the body. It was coined by the British philosopher Gilbert Ryle (1900–76) in *The Concept of the Mind* (1949), and was also the title of a book in 1967 by polymath Arthur Koestler (1905–83). *See also* AGHAST

gerrymander   gesture   ghastly   gherkin

ghoul [L18th] Ghoul is from Arabic *gūl*, a desert demon believed to rob graves and devour corpses.

gift [ME] A word related to **give** [OE] and deriving from Old Norse *gipt*. **Don't look a gift horse in the mouth** is a proverb that goes back to the 16th century (in the form **do not look a given horse in the mouth**), but it can be found even earlier in a 5th-century Latin version in the writings of St Jerome. A common way of estimating a horse's age is to look at the state of its teeth, so if you were buying a horse you might want to have a good look into its mouth first. If someone gave you a horse as a present, it might seem ungrateful to start checking how old it was.

GIGO *see* GARBAGE

gigolo [1920s] The original sense was 'dancing partner': it comes from French, formed as the masculine of *gigole* 'dance hall woman', from colloquial *gigue* 'leg'.

gillyflower *see* CLOVE

gilt *see* BLUE, GINGER

gin *see* DUTCH WORD PANEL

ginger [OE] The word ginger can be traced back to a word in Sanskrit (the ancient language of India), which became *zingiberis* in Greek and eventually made its way into English around AD 1000. There is no connection between this and the adverb **gingerly** [E16th]. In early usage this was used to describe the way a person danced or walked, and meant 'with small elegant steps' or 'daintily'. Later it developed a more negative meaning, 'mincingly'. The modern meaning, 'carefully or cautiously', dates from the 17th century. Gingerly may come from Old French *gensor* 'delicate', and ultimately from Latin *genitus* 'born' or 'well born' (*see* GENDER). A **ginger group**, a group within a political party or movement that presses for stronger action on an issue, comes from an old practice by unscrupulous horse dealers of putting a piece of ginger up the bottom of a worn-out horse in order to make it seem more lively

and frisky. This led to the metaphorical use of **ginger up** to mean 'to make more lively', and ginger group developed from this. In the past gingerbread was traditionally decorated with gold leaf. This is why **take the gilt off the gingerbread** means 'to make something no longer appealing or to spoil the illusion'. **Gilt** [ME] is the old past participle of **gild** (from the same root as gold); these days we use **gilded**.

ginseng *see* CHINESE WORD PANEL

gippy *see* GYP

giraffe [L16th] The giraffe was known in Europe in the medieval period, but people then called it the **camelopard** (*see* CAMEL). The modern name is from Arabic *zarāfa*.

girl [ME] The origin of girl is not known for certain. It could once refer to a child or young person of either sex—not until the 16th century was a female child specified. The variant **gal** started to appear in the late 18th century. The phrase **the girl next door**, describing an ordinary and likeable young woman, was popularized by a film of that name in 1953. A **girl Friday** is a female assistant or secretary—it derives from the name of Man Friday in Daniel Defoe's *Robinson Crusoe* (1719), who helped the shipwrecked Crusoe, and was given publicity by the 1940 film *His Girl Friday*, although it had been in use since the 1920s.

gizzard [LME] The early spelling was *giser* which is from Old French, based on Latin *gigeria* 'cooked entrails of fowl'. The final *-d* was added in the 16th century.

give *see* GIFT

glad [OE] The meaning of glad has weakened over time—it originally meant 'bright, shining' (it shares a common root with German *glatt* 'smooth' and Latin *glaber* 'smooth, hairless'), then had the sense 'delighted and rejoicing', but nowadays just means 'pleased'. If you are in your **glad rags**, you are dressed in your smartest clothes. The expression was first used in American English at the end of the 19th century, about the same time that **glad eye**, 'a look

ghoul gift GIGO gigolo gillyflower gilt gin

intending to attract the opposite sex', first appeared in British English. *See also* HAPPY

glamour [E18th] Although the two words are rarely associated with each other, glamour and **grammar** are related. Glamour was originally a Scots word meaning 'enchantment or magic' or 'a magic spell or charm'—if someone **cast the glamour over** you, they enchanted or bewitched you—and was an altered form of grammar. Greek *gramma* 'a letter of the alphabet, something written down' was the source of grammar, which in medieval times had the sense 'scholarship or learning'. Learning and the study of books was popularly associated with astrology and occult practices, hence the connection with magic. 'Magical beauty' became associated with glamour in the mid 19th century, and from the 1930s the word was particularly used of attractive women. In the early 1970s a new kind of glamour was displayed largely by men—**glam rock**, in which acts wore exaggeratedly flamboyant clothes and glittery make-up. *See also* PRESTIGE

glare *see* GLASS

glass [OE] The substance glass goes back to ancient Mesopotamia or Phoenicia (modern Lebanon and Syria). **Glasses** 'spectacles' dates from the mid 18th century, although before that people would use a single glass or 'an eye glass'. 'Men seldom make passes / At girls who wear glasses' is by the American wit Dorothy Parker (1893–1967). The proverb **people who live in glass houses shouldn't throw stones**, dates from the 17th century. People started complaining of the existence of a **glass ceiling**, meaning an unofficial barrier to advancement at work, especially for a woman, in the early 1980s. **Glaze** [LME], to equip with glass, comes from glass and was first used of eyes, in Shakespeare's *Richard II*: 'For Sorrowes eyes glazed with blinding tears, Divides one thing entire to many objects.' **Glare** [ME] first found in the sense 'dazzling shine' may be related.

glib [L16th] There are a number of other words, such as greasy, oily, and slimy, that link the idea of smoothness and slipperiness with insincere speech or behaviour. To give a glib answer is to speak fluently but insincerely and shallowly; one of its first meanings, in the late 16th century, was 'smooth or unimpeded'. It is ultimately of Germanic origin and related to Dutch *glibberig* 'slippery', and German *glibberig* 'slimy'.

glister *see* GLITTER

glitch [1960s] Although nowadays a glitch can be any kind of hitch or snag, the word was originally used by US electronic engineers in the 1960s to mean 'a sudden surge of electrical current'. Astronauts began using the word to talk about any sudden malfunction of equipment. It may derive from Yiddish *glitsh* 'a slippery place'.

glitter [LME] Things have glittered since the 14th century, and the word comes from Old Norse *glitra*. **All that glitters is not gold** dates back at least to the early 13th century: Shakespeare uses it, in the form **all that glisters is not gold**, in *The Merchant of Venice*. **Glister** is probably from the Middle Dutch variant of the word. **Glitzy**, 'showily attractive', first appeared in the USA in the 1960s. It was based on glitter, and probably influenced by **ritzy** and perhaps also by German *glitzerig* 'glittering'. Ritzy comes from the luxurious Ritz hotels, and is first recorded used by P.G. Wodehouse in 1920.

glove [OE] Old English *glōf* is Germanic in origin. From the Middle Ages gloves carried strong social symbolism. Gloves could be used to challenge someone to combat (*see* GAUNTLET) or to confer office. Fine-quality gloves were a sign of status and often given as presents. To **fit like a glove** and **hand in glove** both date from the late 18th century although the latter was in existence earlier as **hand and glove**. The expression **to take the gloves off** meaning 'to use no mercy' dates from the 1920s, although 'to handle without gloves'—the opposite of **with kid gloves** (the softest kind)—dates from the early 19th century. The maxim to rule with an **iron fist** or **hand in a velvet glove** has been ascribed to several rulers including Napoleon.

glamour glare glass glib glister glitch

glucose *see* LIQUORICE

glue [ME] Both glue and **gluten** [L16th] go back to *gluten* the Latin for 'glue', also found in **agglutinate** [M16th].

gnome [M17th] You would not really confuse a gnome with a *PYGMY, but the terms are closely related. It was probably the Swiss physician Paracelsus (*c.*1493–1541) who coined gnome as a synonym of *Pygmaeus*, the name given to a member of a mythical race of very small people believed to live in parts of Ethiopia and India. The **gnomes of Zurich** are Swiss financiers or bankers, thought of as having a sinister influence over international monetary funds. Former British Prime Minister Harold Wilson popularized the phrase in 1956: 'All these financiers, all the little gnomes in Zurich and other financial centres about whom we keep on hearing'. **Gnomic** [E19th] meaning 'clever but hard to understand', as in 'gnomic utterances', is a different word. It comes from Greek *gnōmē* 'thought, judgement', which was related to *gignōskein* 'to *KNOW'. *See also* NAFF

gnu *see* SOUTH AFRICAN WORD PANEL

go [OE] Words do not get much shorter, more common or more important than go. **Go-cart** was first recorded in the late 17th century when it denoted a baby walker: the first element is from the obsolete sense 'walk'. The variant **go-kart** for a small racing car arose in the 1950s with kart as a deliberate alteration of cart. **What goes around comes around** is a modern proverb first used in the USA, although the idea was expressed in different ways much earlier. Also from the USA is **when the going gets tough, the tough get going**, a favourite family saying of President John F. Kennedy's father Joseph, although it is not certain if he actually coined it. It was later used as a slogan for the 1985 film *The Jewel of the Nile* with a hit theme song sung by Billy Ocean. Another film-related expression is **go ahead, make my day**, originally uttered by Clint Eastwood's character Harry Callaghan in *Sudden Impact* (1983), as he aimed his .44 Magnum gun at a gunman, daring him to

shoot. The phrase was appropriated by Ronald Reagan in 1985, when the president was threatening to veto legislation raising taxes. *See also* PEAR-SHAPED

goanna *see* MONITOR

goblin [ME] This is from Old French *gobelin* from *Gobelinus*, the name of a mischievous spirit said to haunt the region of Évreux in northern France in the 12th century. The term may be related to German *Kobold*, the name of a German spirit that haunted houses or lived underground in caves and mines, although another possible source is Greek *kobalos* 'goblin'. *See also* COBALT, GREMLIN, HOBBY

gobsmacked [1980s] The word gobsmacked presumably refers either to the shock of being hit in the mouth or to the action of clapping your hand to your mouth in astonishment. **Gob**, an informal word for 'mouth' [M16th], may come from Scottish Gaelic *gob* 'beak or mouth'. **Gab**, as in the **gift of the gab** and the adjective **gabby**, both early 18th century, are variants of gob. There is another **gob** [LME], 'a lump of something', that came into English from Old French *gobe* 'mouthful or lump' which may also be Celtic: **gobble** [E17th] is probably based on this gob.

God [OE] The Old English word God is related to similar words in German and in Scandinavian languages, but not to the Latin and Greek words, which were *deus* (*see* DIVINE) and *theos* (as in **theology** [LME]). The top gallery in a theatre is known as **the gods**—the original term in the 1750s was **the regions of the gods**, because the seats were high up and therefore close to the heavens. **Godfather** and **godmother** has been used since around AD 1000. **Godfather** meaning 'a leader of the American Mafia' has been a familiar term since Mario Puzo's novel *The Godfather* (1969) filmed in 1972, but was first recorded in the early 1960s. The origins of the British national anthem **God save the Queen** (or **King**) are not known for sure, but the song was definitely sung in London theatres in 1745, when the country was threatened by the Jacobite uprising led by the Young Pretender, Bonnie Prince Charlie, and the words and tune probably date from the previous century. 'God save the king' was a password in the navy as early as 1545—'long to reign over us' was the correct response. The exclamations **gosh** [M18th] and **golly** [M18th] were originally ways to avoid taking God's name in vain. *See also* LAP

golden [ME] Our word **gold** is Old English, from an ancient root meaning 'yellow'. Golden is medieval, and replaced the earlier word *gilden*. People first used **golden age** in the mid 16th century to refer to an idyllic period in the past. It translates the Greek and Roman poets' name for the first period of history, when the human race was believed to live in an ideal state. In business a **golden handshake**, from the late 1950s, is money paid by an employer to a retiring or redundant employee, usually a senior one. This has led to a number of similar terms, including **golden hello** (a substantial payment offered to induce a senior executive to leave one company and join another) and **golden handcuffs** (a series of payments made over a period to encourage someone to stay with a company).

golf [LME] The first recorded mention of golf is in 1457, in a Scottish edict that banned certain games (including football) because King James II thought they distracted people from archery practice. It seems to have been a Scottish game originally, although the word may be related to Dutch *kolf* 'a club or bat'. It is now popular around the world, but according to the American writer Mark Twain, golf is 'A good walk spoiled'. *See also* BIRD

golly *see* GOD

goo [E20th] This word for 'a sticky substance' was originally US and is perhaps from **burgoo** [M18th], originally a nautical slang term for porridge, but now a thick soup or stew particularly associated with Kentucky. It is based on Persian *bulġūr* 'bruised grain', a word found in **bulgar wheat** [M20th].

good [OE] The ancient root of good probably meant 'to bring together, unite' which was also the source of **gather** [OE]. In 1957 British Prime Minister Harold Macmillan said, 'Let us be frank about it: most of our people have never had it so good'. '**You Never Had It So Good**' was the US Democratic Party slogan during the 1952 election campaign. Also in 1952, Kentucky Fried Chicken opened its first outlet, and for many years its slogan has been 'It's finger-lickin' good'. **Good Friday**, the Friday before Easter Day, on which Christ was crucified, uses good in the old sense 'observed as holy'. Our word **goodbye** [L16th] is actually a shortened form of the phrase **God be with you**. In time good replaced God, in line with phrases such as **good morning** and **goodnight**. Sweets and cakes have been **goodies** since the mid 18th century, and the childish exclamation **goody** is first recorded not much later. **Goody goody gumdrops** was the catchphrase of Humphrey Lestocq, the host of the British children's TV show *Whirligig* in the 1950s.

googly [E20th] One way to bowl a maiden over in cricket is to deliver a googly, a deceptive ball which bounces in the opposite direction from the expected one. The word is first recorded in 1903, but beyond that nothing is known about its origin. The Australian term for a googly, **bosie**, comes from the name of the English cricketer Bernard Bosanquet (1877–1936).

goolies [1930s] In Britain goolies are testicles, but in Australia they are stones. The two are probably different words: the first was probably picked up by British soldiers in India from Hindi *golī* 'ball, pill, bullet'; whereas the second may be from the Aboriginal word *goolie*, 'a stone'.

goon [M19th] To most people a goon is associated with the creators of the radio comedy series *The Goon Show* in 1951. The original sense of the word was 'a stupid or hapless person'—it came from the name of the US cartoon character Alice the Goon, created by the cartoonist E.C. Segar (1894–1938) and appearing in the *Popeye* strips that also introduced Eugene the Jeep

golden golf golly goo good googly goolies

(*see* JEEP). Segar probably took the name from the dialect term **gooney** 'a simpleton', recorded from the 1580s. In the USA a goon also became a thug hired to terrorize people, and in the Second World War the term was given by British and US prisoners of war to their German guards.

goose [OE] Geese have long been a mainstay of the farmyard, and are found in several idioms. If someone **kills the goose that lays the golden eggs** they destroy a reliable and valuable source of income. In one of Aesop's fables a man finds that one of his geese lays eggs of pure gold, which make him rich. But he grows dissatisfied with just one egg a day, and kills the goose in the mistaken belief that it will be filled with golden eggs. There is no gold inside it and no longer any more golden eggs. The US film producer Sam Goldwyn, famous for idiosyncratic expressions like 'include me out', is supposed to have said: 'That's the way with these directors, they're always biting the hand that lays the golden egg.' In America a **goose egg** is a score of zero in baseball and other sports. This derives from the egg shape of 0, in just the same way as does the cricketing term *DUCK (originally 'a duck's egg'). We associate the military marching step known as the **goose-step** with the Nazis, but the term was recorded much earlier than the 1930s, at the beginning of the 19th century. Goose-stepping soldiers advance by swinging each leg stiffly forwards without bending it at the knee, in a way reminiscent of geese. To goose someone [L19th] is to poke their bottom as a joke. This meaning probably comes from the way that geese can be aggressive and ready to peck at people unexpectedly. A **gooseberry** [M16th] may be a modified version of German *Krausebeere* or the French dialect *gozelle*, or it may simply have been created by combining the existing words **goose** and **berry**. The 'unwanted third party' sense, as in 'playing gooseberry', dates from the 19th century. *See also* GOSSAMER, SAUCE

gopher [L18th] This animal may get its name from Canadian French *gaufre*

'honeycomb': the gopher 'honeycombs' the ground with its burrows.

Gorblimey *see* BLIMEY

gorge [ME] The Old French word *gorge* meant 'throat' and was adopted into English with the same meaning, hence to gorge yourself is to shovel food down your throat. It came to mean 'the contents of the stomach', and when we talk about **someone's gorge rising** in disgust it is in this sense. A gorge is also a narrow valley between hills, a sense that emerged in the middle of the 18th century from the idea of this geographical feature being narrow like a throat.

gorgio *see* ROMANY WORD PANEL

gorilla [M19th] In the 5th or 6th centuries BC the Carthaginian explorer Hanno wrote an account of his voyage along the northwest coast of Africa. In the Greek translation of Hanno's account there appears a supposedly African word *gorillai*, the name of a wild or hairy people. This was adopted in 1847 by the US missionary Thomas Savage as the name of the large ape. *See also* GUERRILLA

gormless [M18th] The original spelling was *gaumless* formed from dialect *gaum* 'understanding', from Old Norse *gaumr* 'care, heed'.

gosh *see* GOD

gospel [OE] The Good News Bible is an English translation of the Bible, published in 1976, whose name refers to the root meaning of gospel itself. The word is not related to *GOD, but was formed from Old English *gōd* 'good' and *spel* 'news, a story', and was a translation of Greek *euangelion* 'good news', the source of our words **evangelism** [E17th] and **evangelist** [ME]. The rock musical *Godspell*, based on the Gospel of St Matthew and first produced in 1971, took its title from the original spelling of the word.

gossamer [ME] Gossamer literally means 'goose summer', another name for St Martin's

goose gopher Gorblimey gorge gorgio gorilla

Summer, in early November, when geese were eaten. This is also the time of the year when you are likely to see cobwebs spun by small spiders, floating in the air or spread over a grassy surface, and so these cobwebs came to be called gossamer.

gossip [OE] In Old English *godsibb* or gossip was the word for a godparent. It literally meant 'a person related to one in God' and came from *god* 'God' and *sibb* 'a relative', the latter word found in **sibling** [OE]. Gossip came to be applied to a close friend, especially a female friend invited to be present at a birth. From this developed the idea of a person who enjoys indulging in idle talk, and by the 19th century idle talk or tittle-tattle itself.

gothic *see* VANDAL

Götterdämmerung *see* TWILIGHT

gout [Middle English] This comes from Old French *goute*, from medieval Latin *gutta* whose literal meaning is 'a drop', a sense still found in phrases such as **gouts of blood**. The disease gout got its name because it was believed to be caused by the dropping of diseased matter from the blood into the joints. *See also* GUTTER

govern [ME] Govern is from Old French *governer* (and of Middle English **government**), from Latin *gubernare* 'to steer, rule' which came in turn from Greek *kubernan* 'to steer'. **Governess** [ME] was originally *governeress* meaning 'a female ruler'.

gown [ME] Old French *goune* is the source of gown, from late Latin *gunna* 'fur garment'.

grade [E16th] A grade is literally a step from Latin *gradus* 'step', and was originally used in English as a unit of measurement, a use largely replaced by *DEGREE, from the same source. The word is also found in **graduate** [LME] 'take a degree', **gradient** [M19th], **gradual** [LME] 'done by degrees', and **degrade** [LME]. The expression to **make the grade** is an American expression from the early 20th century.

graffiti [M19th] Although we think of graffiti as being scribbled, painted, or sprayed on a wall, it was originally scratched on. The word first appeared in English in the mid 19th century and was applied to ancient wall drawings or inscriptions found in ruins in Rome or Pompeii. This was an adoption of an Italian word in the plural form (the singular being *graffito*), from *graffio* 'a scratch'.

graft [LME] A graft is a shoot from one plant fixed into a slit made in another to form a new growth. Originally spelled *graff*, it derives from Greek *graphion* 'stylus, pointed writing implement', from *graphein* 'to write', source of the **graphite** [L18th] in your pencil, **graphic** art [M17th], and **diagram** [E17th]. The tapered tip of the shoot was thought to resemble a stylus. The other graft [M19th], 'hard work', may be related to the phrase **spade's graft** 'the amount of earth that one stroke of a spade will move', based on Old Norse *groftr* 'digging'.

grain [ME] The first meaning of grain, which is from Latin *granum* 'seed', also found in **granary** [L16th], **granule** [M17th], and **granite** [M17th] with its grain-like markings, was, a single seed of a plant. From this developed the idea not only of a seed-like particle such as a grain of sand, salt, or gold but also of an arrangement of fibres that resembles small seeds or grains side by side, such as the 'grain' of a piece of wood. If something **goes against the grain** it is contrary to your natural inclination. This, dating from the mid 17th century, comes from carpentry. While **grange** is used today for a country house it was originally a barn for grain and comes from medieval Latin *granica (villa)* 'grain house', based on *granum*. **Garner** [ME] was originally also a word for a granary, and comes via French from the same source.

grammar *see* GLAMOUR

gramophone *see* PHONETIC

granary, grange, granite, granule *see* GRAIN

gossip   gothic   Götterdämmerung   gout

grape [ME] A grape was originally not an individual berry but the whole bunch. It can be traced back to Old French *grap* 'hook', specifically a vine hook used for harvesting grapes. **Grapple** [ME], first used to refer to a grappling hook, has a similar origin, and a **grapefruit** [E19th] is so called because it grows in clusters, like grapes. To **hear something on the grapevine** is to get information by rumour or by unofficial communication. The expression comes from the American Civil War, when news was said to be passed 'by grapevine telegraph'. **Bush telegraph** [L19th], originally an Australian term, is based on a similar idea. The phrase **sour grapes** describes an attitude of pretending to despise something because you cannot have it yourself. The source is Aesop's fable of the fox and the grapes. In the story a fox tries to reach a bunch of juicy grapes hanging from a vine high above his head. After several attempts he gives up and stalks off, muttering that they were probably sour anyway.

graphic, graphite *see* GRAFT

grapple *see* GRAPE

grass [OE] The Old English word grass is descended from the same root word as both *GREEN and **grow** [OE]. According to the well-known saying, **the grass is always greener on the other side of the fence**, a sentiment echoed in the works of the Roman poet Ovid: 'The harvest is always more fruitful in another man's fields.' A woman whose husband is often away for long periods can be referred to as a **grass widow**. In the early 16th century, though, this was a term for an unmarried woman with a child, probably from the idea of the couple having lain on the grass together instead of in bed. People have been smoking grass, or cannabis, since the 1940s, originally in the USA. The word has meant 'an informer', or 'to inform' since the decade before that. In this sense it is probably short for **grasshopper**, rhyming slang for **shopper**, a person who 'shops' someone. Graze [ME] is from Old English *grasian* 'eat grass'. *See also* NARK

grate [ME] Grate 'to shred' is from Old French *grater* 'grate, scratch', of Germanic origin; it is related to German *kratzen* 'to scratch'. People have being saying that something **grates upon** them since the early 17th century. The grate in a fire was originally a general word for 'a grating': it comes from Old French, based on Latin *cratis* 'hurdle', also found in **griddle** [ME], **grill** [M17th], **grille** [M17th], and **grid** [M19th].

grave *see* ACCENT, GROOVE

gravity *see* GURU

gravy [ME] In medieval cookbooks gravy describes a spicy sauce, usually consisting of broth, milk of almonds, spices, and wine or ale. Only in the late 16th century did it start to refer to a sauce made out of meat juices. The most likely explanation for the word's origin is that someone misread Old French *grané* as *gravé*, which is quite possible given the similarity between 'u' and 'n' and that *u* was used to represent *v* in medieval manuscripts. *Grané* probably derived from *grain* 'spice', from Latin *granum* '*GRAIN'. Gravy has also meant 'money that is easily acquired' since the start of the 20th century, and to **board the gravy train** is to obtain access to an easy source of financial gain. Here 'gravy train' is perhaps a play on 'gravy boat', a long, narrow jug used for serving gravy.

graze *see* GRASS

grease [ME] The ultimate source of grease is Latin *crassus* 'thick or fat', and in medieval English the word meant 'the fat part of the body of an animal' and 'fatness'. To **grease someone's palm**, a phrase that dates from the early 16th century, is to bribe them. The metaphor comes from the idea of applying grease to a machine to make it run smoothly. The idea behind **like greased lightning**, 'very quickly', is that lightning, the fastest thing imaginable, would presumably be even faster if greased. *See also* GLIB

Greek [OE] The word Greek comes from Latin *Graeci*, which was the name the

grape graphic graphite grapple grass

Romans gave to the people who called themselves the Hellenes. If you cannot understand something at all, you can say **it's all Greek to me**—the use of Greek to mean 'unintelligible language or gibberish' dates from around 1600. In Shakespeare's *Julius Caesar* the conspirator Casca, noting that Cicero gave a speech in Greek, adds 'for mine own part, it was Greek to me'. Greek also has a negative connotation in the proverb **beware** (or **fear**) **the Greeks bearing gifts**. This is a reference to the Trojan War. In Virgil's *Aeneid* the Trojan priest Laocoon says, 'I fear the Greeks even when they bring gifts', warning his fellow Trojans not to take into their city the gigantic wooden horse that the Greeks have left behind on their apparent departure.

green [OE] The defining characteristic of green is that it is the colour of living plants and the word shares an earlier ancestor with *GRASS. The colour has also long been associated with a sickly complexion, and phrases such as **green and wan** and **green and pale** were once common. To be **green around the gills** is to look or feel ill or nauseous—a person's gills are the fleshy parts between the jaw and the ears, by analogy with the gills of a fish. An inexperienced person has been called green since the Middle Ages, in reference to the colour of unripe corn, and naïve or gullible people have been green since the beginning of the 17th century (*see also* SALAD). Traditionally green has also been the colour of jealousy and envy. In *Othello* Shakespeare gave us a memorable term for jealousy, **the green-eyed monster**: 'O! Beware my lord of jealousy / It is the green-eyed monster which doth mock / The meat it feeds on.' A person with **green fingers** (or, in the USA, a **green thumb**) is good at growing plants. The phrase originated as the title of a 1934 book of garden verse by the British comic writer Reginald Arkell. The association of the colour with the environmentalist lobby dates from the early 1970s in West Germany. British Conservative MP Norman Lamont is widely credited with introducing the phrase **the green shoots of recovery**, in relation to the performance of the economy after a recession, but what he said at the Tory Party conference of 1991 was 'The green shoots of economic spring are appearing once again'. *See also* YELLOW

greenwood *see* FOREST

gregarious *see* CONGREGATE

greige *see* BEIGE

gremlin [1940s] It was pilots who first talked about gremlins, mischievous sprites responsible for any unexplained mechanical problems suffered by their planes. The earliest mention of them comes from the USA in the 1920s, but they are particularly associated with the Second World War. The word may be a combination of *GOBLIN and *Fremlins*, a type of beer—so these were the sort of creatures you see when you have had one too many.

grenade [M16th] The Old French word *grenate*, the root of grenade, is a shortened form of *pome grenate* '*POMEGRANATE', literally 'many-seeded apple'. The connection is the supposed resemblance between the shape of the bomb and that of the fruit. Early on in its history grenade could also refer to the fruit. Continuing the fruity theme, a hand grenade has, since the First World War, been informally known as a *PINEAPPLE.

grey [OE] An Old English word that since the Middle Ages has been used to describe the weather when the sky is overcast. The extension of this to mean 'dismal or sad' dates from the early 18th century. The following 1969 quotation from *The Times* appears to be one of the earliest instances of the word carrying connotations of 'faceless or anonymous': 'The identity of these grey men of politics should be revealed.' A **grey area** is an ill-defined situation which does not readily fit into an existing category. It is so called because it is 'not black or white', and cannot be simply analyzed or put into a single category. The expression was first used in the late 1940s in reference to countries that had Communist sympathies but were not completely pro- or anti-Communist. The name of the **greyhound** has nothing to do with the colour grey. It

green greenwood gregarious greige gremlin

comes from Old English *grighund*, which meant 'bitch hound'. In the late 19th century an **ocean greyhound** was a steamship specially built for great speed.

grid, griddle *see* GRATE

grill, grille *see* GRID

grim [OE] The meaning of grim has weakened over the centuries from its first appearance in Old English as 'fierce or cruel'. To **hang** (or **cling**) **on like grim death** dates from the mid 19th century, but the use of grim for the forbidding appearance of the figure of Death is recorded much earlier. The **Grim Reaper** [M19th] is a representation of Death in the form of a cloaked skeleton wielding a long scythe.

grin [OE] When grin entered English in the 11th century it meant 'to bare the teeth in pain or anger', far from the happy expression the word suggests nowadays. This former sense is preserved in the expression **grin and bear it**, 'to suffer pain or misfortune stoically'. An earlier version of the phrase is **grin and abide**. Not until the late 15th century did grin begin to be used for various sorts of smile, developing from a forced, unnatural one, through a rather vacant, silly one, to the cheerful and broad smile we associate with the word today. **Groan** [OE] is related.

grindstone [ME] A grindstone is a thick revolving disc of stone on which knives and tools are sharpened. If someone got control over you and treated you harshly, making you work hard and continuously they are **keeping your nose to the grindstone**. A word related to **grind** [OE] is **grist** [OE], 'corn that is to be ground'. You can describe something which can be turned to good use, such as experience or knowledge, as being **grist to the mill**. The phrase comes from the 17th-century proverb **all is grist that comes to the mill**.

grizzly [E19th] A grizzly is a large North American bear which has brown fur with white-tipped hairs. Fearsome though the bear's appearance is, its name has nothing to do with the word **grisly**. In fact grizzly is a variant of **grizzled** [LME], 'streaked with grey hair'. This comes from Old French *gris* 'grey', whereas grisly is from Old English *grislic*, meaning 'terrifying'. **Grizzle** [M18th] meaning 'to cry or whine' is a different word again. It started life in the dialect of Devon and Cornwall, and originally meant 'to grin or laugh', so has taken the opposite route to *GRIN.

groan *see* GRIN

grocer *see* ENGROSS

grog [M18th] This word for alcoholic drink is said to be from *Old Grog*, the reputed nickname (given to him because of his grogram cloak) of Admiral Vernon (1684–1757): in 1740 he first ordered diluted rum to be served out to sailors instead of the traditional neat rum. **Grogram** [M16th] was a heavy fabric which got its name from French *gros grain* 'course grain', also found in the name of the lighter silk fabric **grosgrain** [M19th].

groove [ME] In early use a groove was a mine, shaft, or pit. The word comes from Dutch *groeve* 'furrow or pit', and is related to **grave** [OE]. From the 17th century it was used to refer to a channel or furrow cut in something and, in the 20th century, a spiral track cut into a record into which the stylus fits. The latter sense lies behind the phrase **in the groove**, 'performing consistently well or confidently', which was first used of jazz musicians and dates back to the 1930s. This is also where we get the adjective **groovy** from, first recorded meaning 'excellent' in the 1930s, specifically in the context of playing jazz well. Groovy was a teenage slang term by the 1940s and became prominent in the 1960s. It was revived by Mike Myers in the *Austin Powers* film spoofs.

grosgrain *see* GROG

gross *see* ENGROSS

grotesque [M16th] We think of something grotesque as being ugly or distorted, either in a comic or a repulsive way, but when the word first appeared in

grid griddle grill grille grim grin

English in the 16th century it simply described the style of painting found in a grotto, specifically the murals discovered in ancient Roman ruins. These decorative wall paintings involved interweaving human and animal forms with flowers and foliage. Grotesque comes from Italian *grottesca*, which was used in the phrases *opera grottesca* 'work resembling that found in a grotto', and *pittura grottesca* 'painting resembling one found in a grotto'. **Grotty**, meaning 'unpleasant or unwell', source of **grot** 'dirt', comes from grotesque. It was introduced to the public in 1964 in the Beatles' film *A Hard Day's Night*. **Grotto** itself ultimately comes from Greek *kruptos* 'hidden', which is also the source of **crypt** (*see* CROSSWORD).

grouch [L19th] The words grouch and **grudge** [LME] are variants of obsolete *grutch*, from Old French *grouchier* 'to grumble, murmur', of unknown origin. Early 19th-century **grouse** may be related.

group *see* CROP

grouse SEE GROUCH

grow *see* GRASS

grub, grubby *see* GRUNGE

grudge *see* GROUCH

gruesome [L16th] Although gruesome first appeared in English in the late 16th century, based on Scots *grue* 'to feel horror, shudder', it was rare before the late 18th century. It was popularized in the novels of Sir Walter Scott: 'He's as grave and grewsome an auld Dutchman as e'er I saw' (*Old Mortality*, 1816). *Grewsome* was the more common spelling until around 1850.

gruff *see* DUTCH WORD PANEL

grunge [1960s] Before it became associated with rock music, grunge was generally used to mean 'grime or dirt'. It was formed from **grungy**, a word that was coined in the 1960s, probably by blending

grubby (from the state you get in when you **grub** [ME] or dig) and **dingy** (a M18th word of unknown origin, but perhaps related to dung). In the 1990s **grunge** became the term for a style of rock music in which the guitar is played raucously and the lyrics delivered in a lazy vocal style. Among well-known practitioners of grunge were Seattle-based groups such as Nirvana and Pearl Jam.

grunt *see* DISGRUNTLED

guarantee [L17th] A guarantee and a **warranty** [ME] are basically the same thing and go back to a common source. **Warrant** [ME] and warranty are earlier, coming from Norman French, showing the typically Norman 'w' variant of French *garantie*. Guarantee seems to have come from the Spanish equivalent and to have been influenced by the French form.

guard [LME] An Old Germanic element meaning 'to watch, guard' lies behind both guard and **ward**. Ward came into English from Old English *weard* 'watchman, guard'. The sense 'child protected by a guardian' is late Middle English, and the sense of a hospital ward, where you are watched over by nurses or wardens, is mid 18th. Meanwhile, Germanic-speaking Franks had taken over areas of Europe that were mainly Romance speaking, and introduced the word into Romance. The *w* became a *g(u)* and the word became *g(u)arde* in Old French from which the *g-* forms were introduced into English. The *g-* and *w-* forms (found as alternatives in other words in modern French and English, as in the name William or Guillaume) are also found in **warden** [ME] and **guardian** [LME]. **Wardrobe** [LME], a place where you look after clothes, has an alternative **garderobe** [ME]. These were once interchangeable. However, garderobe is now mainly restricted to a term for a medieval lavatory. Wardrobe could have this sense in the past, for both words developed the sense of a small room where you could be private, and from there somewhere you could do something in private (*compare* **privy** under PRIVATE).

grouch   group   grouse   grow   grub   gruff

guerrilla [E19th] A Spanish word that means literally 'little war'. When it was first used in reports of the Peninsular War, fought between the French and the British in Spain and Portugal from 1808 to 1814, it meant 'irregular war carried on by small bodies of men' as well as 'a member of an independent group of fighters'.

guinea pig [M17th] The guinea pig comes from South America—not Guinea in Africa, or New Guinea in the South Pacific. Guinea pigs are chubby and can squeal like pigs, but why guinea was chosen nobody is really sure. The word could have been confused with Guyana, which *is* in South America, or was possibly used as an example of a far-off, exotic country that no one knew much about. Guinea pigs have been bred by humans for some 3 000 years, and are no longer found in the wild. Their use in animal testing led to the word's acquiring the sense 'a person or thing used as a subject for experiment' in the 1920s.

guise *see* DISGUISE

gulf [LME] The Greek word *kolpos* had a number of meanings relating to a curved shape, including 'bosom', 'the trough between waves', 'the fold of a piece of clothing', and 'gulf or bay'. This is where our word gulf came from, via Italian and Old French. We can talk about a gulf between two groups, meaning a great division or difference between them. This was probably influenced by a passage in the Gospel of Luke: 'Between you and us there is a great gulf set'.

gullible [E19th] A gullible person was originally someone who could be 'gulled', or deceived. **Gull** in this sense is now rare, but was a very common word from the 16th to the 19th centuries, and was used by Shakespeare. It may have come from gull, an old dialect term for an unfledged bird, which had nothing to do with gull as in **seagull**: this was a medieval word that probably came from a Celtic language such as Welsh or Cornish.

gum [ME] In the sense 'a sticky secretion produced by some trees and shrubs', gum can be traced all the way back to an ancient Egyptian word *kemai*. Among its more recent meanings it has been applied to a type of sweet pastille (as in 'fruit gum') since the early 19th century, and to **chewing gum** from the mid 19th century in the US. The other type of **gum**, inside your mouth, comes from an Old English word meaning 'the inside of the mouth or throat'. **Gumshoe** is an American term for a detective. Dating from the early 20th century, it relates to rubber-soled shoes, called gumshoes or sneakers, suitable for doing something stealthily.

gun [ME] The first device to be called a gun in English may have been a kind of catapult used in medieval warfare to hurl rocks or arrows at the enemy. It is possible that the term may have derived from a pet form of the Scandinavian name Gunnhildr (from *gunnr* and *hildr*, both meaning 'war'). Giving female personal names to weapons has been a common practice over the centuries. Examples include Mons Meg, a 15th-century cannon in Edinburgh Castle; Brown Bess, the nickname for a musket used by the British army in the 18th century; and Big Bertha, a large German gun used in the First World War.

If someone refuses to compromise or change, we can say that they are **sticking to their guns**. This comes from the battlefield, where sticking to your guns meant remaining at your post despite being under constant bombardment. To **be gunning for** someone is to be looking for a chance to attack them. In the 17th century, though, to go gunning was to go hunting. **Gunboat diplomacy** is foreign policy supported by the use or threat of military force. It is first mentioned in the 1920s, in reference to US policy in China.

gung-ho *see* CHINESE WORD PANEL

gunk [1930s] This was originally a US usage and came from the proprietary name of a detergent.

guru [E17th] This is from Hindi and Punjabi, from Sanskrit *guru* 'weighty, grave, dignified' (comparable with Latin *gravis*

guerrilla   guinea pig   guise   gulf   gullible

'heavy' source of **gravity** [LME]): this led to 'elder, teacher'.

gusto [E17th] If you do something with gusto, you do it with real relish or enjoyment. The word is borrowed from Italian, and came from Latin *gustus* 'taste', source also of **disgust** [L16th]. One of its early meanings was 'a particular liking for something', as in this line from William Wycherley's play *Love in a Wood* (1672): 'Why should you force wine upon us? We are not all of your gusto.' This sense eventually dropped out of use, with the 'keen enjoyment' sense becoming common from the beginning of the 19th century.

gut [OE] Gut is probably related to Old English *gēotan* 'to pour'. Guts was used commonly for 'stomach, bowels'; it became more informal and also came to mean 'force of character, courage' from the late 19th century. The notion of 'basic' as in **gut reaction** arose in the 1960s.

gutter [ME] 'We are all in the gutter, but some of us are looking at the stars,' wrote Oscar Wilde in *Lady Windermere's Fan* (1892). A gutter was originally a watercourse, either a natural or an artificial one, and the word comes via Old French *gotiere* from Latin *gutta* 'a drop'. In the 16th century this became 'a furrow or track made by running water', from which developed the main modern meaning. **The gutter** became the habitat of very poor people in the mid 19th century, and newspapers that pursue sensational stories about the private lives of public figures have been known as **the gutter press** since the end of that century. *See also* GOUT

guy [L16th] Expressions such as **fall guy**, **wise guy** and **tough guy** are all American in origin, and it used only to be Americans who called men (and now women) guys at all. This use of the word dates from the late 19th century, as a development of an earlier sense applied to a person of grotesque appearance. Before it came to be applied to people, though, the word was used—as it still is today—to describe an effigy of Guy Fawkes, one of the Gunpowder Plot conspirators and Catholic extremists who intended to blow up James I and his parliament in 1605. People traditionally burn a Guy on a *BONFIRE each year on 5 November, the anniversary of the plot. To guy someone is now to make fun of them, but it was previously to carry an effigy of them around the streets. It came from the practice of **guying**, or carrying a Guy around on 5 November. The **guy rope** on a tent is unconnected, and probably comes from a German word.

gymkhana *see* RAJ WORD PANEL

gymnasium [L16th] Ancient Greek men exercised naked. This fact is preserved in the origin of the word gymnasium, which came into English from Latin but is ultimately from Greek *gumnazein* 'to exercise or train naked', *gumnos* being the Greek word for 'naked'. The shortened form **gym** first appeared in the late 19th century.

gyp [L19th] If something **gives you gyp**, it causes you pain or discomfort. No one knows for certain where **gyp** comes from, but one theory holds that it is a dialect alteration of **gee-up**, an instruction to a horse to urge it to move faster. This is certainly plausible, as an earlier meaning of the expression was 'to scold or punish someone severely'. **Gippy** as in **gippy tummy** is from a different source. A gippy tummy was originally painful diarrhoea experienced by British troops in the Second World War in Egypt and is a corruption of the country's name (*see also* GYPSY).

Gypsy [M16th] When Gypsies first appeared in Britain in the 16th century no one was quite sure where they had come from. Their dark skin and hair led people to believe that they were from Egypt, and they were called *Gipcyans*, short for Egyptians. In fact Gypsies probably originated in the Indian subcontinent, and their language, Romany, is related to Hindi. *See also* BOHEMIAN, ROMANY WORD PANEL

gusto   gut   gutter   guy   gymkhana

gyrate [E19th] The Greek word *guros* meaning 'a ring' is the base of English *gyrate*. This passed into Latin as *gyrare* 'to revolve'. Different as it may seem, to **veer** [L16th] is thought to be from the same source. It comes directly from French *virer* which is thought to be an alteration of *gyrare*. The original use in English was nautical in reference to the wind, meaning 'change gradually'; it came to mean 'change course' from the early 17th century.

gymnasium   gyp   Gypsy   gyrate

Hh

hack [OE] The word hack meaning 'to cut with rough or heavy blows' goes back to ancient times. Modern computer enthusiasts have used it in the sense 'to gain unauthorised access to computer systems and data' since the 1980s, although **hacker** appeared earlier, in the 1970s. The sense 'to cope' as in **I can't hack it** dates from the 1950s. It has no relation to hack 'a writer or journalist producing dull, uninteresting work'. This word originally referred to a horse for everyday riding, especially one hired out and consequently often tired and overworked. It is a shortening of **hackney**, probably taken from Hackney in East London, where horses were once pastured. This gave us the **hackney carriage** [L18th], originally a horse-drawn vehicle plying for hire and still the official term for a taxi. The idea of tiredness and overwork continues in **hackneyed**, 'overused, unoriginal, and trite'. *See also* JADE, NAG

hackle [LME] Hackles are the long feathers on the neck of a fighting cock or the hairs on the top of a dog's neck, which stand up when the animal is aggressive or excited. So if you **make someone's hackles rise** you make them angry or indignant. In the Middle Ages a hackle or **heckle** was also an instrument with parallel steel pins used to prepare flax for spinning by splitting the fibres and pulling them straight. This vigorous action was transferred to giving speakers an equally hard time or **heckling** them in the early 19th century. The word goes back to an ancient root related to *HOOK. *See also* TEASE

hag [ME] This word used disparagingly (old hag) is literally 'an evil spirit in female form, a witch': it derives perhaps from Old English *hægtesse*, *hegtes*, related to Dutch *heks* and German *Hexe* 'witch', source of **hex** [E19th].

haggard [M16th] A word from falconry, where it is a technical term for an adult hawk caught for training. Unlike hawks bred or raised in captivity, haggards are wild and untamed. Wild-looking people, or their wild-looking eyes, began to be described as haggard in the 17th century, and from there the word developed the sense 'looking exhausted or unwell'. The word may be related to *HEDGE. *See also* HAWK

haggis *see* SCOTTISH WORD PANEL

haggle *see* HASSLE

hail *see* WASSAIL

hair [OE] In English the state of people's hair is used to reflect how they feel and behave—since the 1990s if you have a **bad hair day** you have a day when everything seems to go wrong. If you **don't turn a hair** you are unflustered. It was first used in the early 19th century of horses who did not show any signs of sweating, which would curl and roughen their coat. If you **let your hair down** you become uninhibited. This idea started in the mid 19th century as to **let down the back hair**, with the notion of relaxing and becoming less formal. The expression **the hair of the dog**, for a hangover cure, is a shortening of **a hair of the dog that bit you**. It comes from an old belief that someone bitten by a rabid dog could be cured of rabies by taking a potion containing some of the dog's hair. **Harsh** [ME] comes from the related Middle Low German *harsch* 'rough', the literal meaning of which was 'hairy', from *haer* 'hair'.

halcyon [LME] The halcyon was a bird that in medieval times was thought to breed in a nest floating on the sea, and to charm the wind and waves so that the sea was calm. It was identified as a kingfisher, most of which actually nest in riverbanks, and the word comes from the Greek term for a kingfisher, *alkuōn*. The **halcyon days** were originally 14 days of calm weather which were supposed to occur when the halcyon was breeding. Today the phrase refers to a period of time in the past that was idyllically happy and peaceful, as in 'those halcyon days when students received full government grants'.

hale *see* WASSAIL

half [OE] The ancient root of half meant 'side', and this was the first meaning in English—a half of something was one of its two sides. The phrase **at half cock**, 'when only partly ready', comes from early firearms, and describes a flintlock pistol misfiring. The cock was the lever which was raised into position ready to be released when the trigger was pulled. A pistol at half cock had the lever raised halfway and held by the catch, which in theory ensured that it could not be fired even if the trigger was pulled. Inevitably the occasional pistol would be faulty and go off early, at half cock. *See also* HANG. The **halfpenny** was the smallest unit of the old British currency from 1961 until decimalization. A **halfpennyworth**, also spelled **ha'p'orth** to represent a common pronunciation, was a small amount, and so the proverb **don't spoil the ship for a ha'p'orth of tar** recorded from 1623, reflects on the miserliness that can spoil something of much greater value. The saying is not nautical, but referred to the use of tar to keep flies off sores on sheep: *ship* was a dialect pronunciation of sheep.

hallmark [E18th] Articles made of gold, silver, or platinum have been taken to Goldsmiths' Hall in London to be tested since the Middle Ages, and then stamped with a mark to guarantee purity. This was the original hallmark. Goldsmiths' Hall is the home of the Worshipful Company of Goldsmiths, one of the traditional Livery Companies of the City of London.

hallo *see* HELLO

hallucination [E17th] The word hallucination is from Latin *hallucinari* 'go astray in thought', from Greek *alussein* 'be uneasy or distraught'.

halo [M16th] This was originally a circle of light such as that around the sun; it came via medieval Latin from Greek *halōs* which referred to the 'disc of the sun or moon'. From around the middle of the 17th century, the word came to be applied to the circle of light depicted around Christ's head or those of the saints. Its use for an effect in photography is found from the 1940s.

haloo *see* HELLO

ham [OE] It is unlikely that ham actors get their name from salted meat. The word meaning 'an excessively theatrical actor' arose in the USA in the late 19th century and may be based on *AMATEUR, although **hamfatter** was also used at this time to mean 'an inexpert performer'—the 'ham' connection could be from the idea of being 'ham-fisted'. The radio ham or amateur radio enthusiast appeared in the early 20th century. The word ham goes back to an ancient root meaning 'to be crooked'. The earliest sense was 'the back of the knee', but in the 15th century people began to apply it to the back of the thigh, or the thigh and buttocks, and from there to the thigh and hock of an animal used as food. **Hamster** [E17th] is unconnected. It is a German word—odd, as the hamster is found from central Europe through Asia to China, but not in Germany. Odder still is the fact that the German word's origin means 'corn weevil', a kind of beetle.

hamburger *see* US WORD PANEL

hammer [OE] Old English *hamor* has a Germanic origin, related to German *Hammer*, and Old Norse *hamarr* 'rock, crag'. The original sense was probably 'stone tool or weapon'. The expression **hammer and tongs** [E18th] meaning 'with energy and speed' comes from the blacksmith showering blows on the iron taken by the help of tongs from the fire.

hammock [M16th] This was *hamaka* in the extinct Caribbean language Taino. It became *hamaca* in Spanish, which was used at first in English. The last syllable was altered in the 16th century to conform to English words ending in *–ock*.

hale   half   hallmark   hallo   hallucination

hand [OE] Since the Middle Ages hand has had the secondary meaning 'a person', as in **farmhand** or **deckhand**. **All hands** is the entire crew of a ship—the orders **all hands on deck** and **all hands to the pump** call upon all members of the crew, and now of any team, to assist. The phrase **hand over fist** also came from sailing. Originally it was **hand over hand**, describing the action of a sailor climbing a rope or hauling it in. By the 1820s the idea of speed had been extended to other contexts such as the rapid progress of a ship in pursuit of another, and soon after it was being used much more generally of any action done quickly. Nowadays, it is almost always making money that is done hand over fist. Horse racing gave us **hands down**. A jockey who won hands down was so certain of winning that he could lower his hands, relax his grip on the reins, and stop urging on his horse. A **handle** [OE] gets its name because it is held in the hand. *See also* HANDSOME

handbag [M19th] The Conservative MP Julian Critchley introduced handbag to mean 'to attack or crush verbally'. In 1982 he said of Margaret Thatcher, then British prime minister, that 'she can't look at a British institution without hitting it with her handbag'. The article in *The Economist* that reported his comment went on to say that 'Treasury figures published last week show how good she has proved at handbagging the Civil Service'. Football managers or commentators sometimes describe a minor fight or scuffle between players as being **handbags**, or **handbags at three** (or **ten**) **paces** as if describing duelling. The expression seems to have originated in the mid to late 1980s.

handicap [M17th] This word derives from a old pastime that involved one person claiming an article belonging to another and offering something in exchange. The participants then appointed an umpire to adjudicate the difference in value, and then all three deposited forfeit money in a cap, the two opponents showing their agreement or disagreement with the valuation by putting in their hands and then bringing them out either full or empty. This sport was called **hand in cap**, later reduced to handicap. The word is first recorded in the mid 17th century, but the practice appears in the 14th-century poem *Piers Plowman*, and is known elsewhere in continental Europe from an early date. The **handicap race** (originally **handicap match**), in which an umpire determines what weight each horse carries in order to equalize their chances, dates from the mid 18th century.

handkerchief *see* KERCHIEF

handle *see* HAND

handsome [ME] The original sense, showing that the root word is *HAND, was 'easy to handle or use'. In the mid 16th century this developed to 'suitable' and 'apt, clever'. The current senses 'good-looking' and 'striking, of fine quality' followed soon after. In the proverb **handsome is as handsome does** the original reference was to chivalrous or genteel behaviour.

hang [OE] To hang someone as a punishment was originally to crucify them. Later it came to involve using a rope, now the only sense in which the past form **hanged** is used. But in early times it was the only possibility: **hung** did not appear until the 16th century. The phrase to **hang fire** originates with the complex firing mechanism of the old flintlock pistol. A small quantity of gunpowder would be loaded into a metal hollow above the trigger, and when the trigger was released a spark from a flint would ignite the gunpowder, which in turn would ignite the main charge, causing it to explode and propel the shot out of the barrel. Sometimes the powder in the pan would fail to explode immediately, perhaps because it was damp, and merely smoulder, causing a delay in the firearm going off. When this happened it was said to hang fire. *See also* HALF. The **hinge** [ME] on which you hang a door is closely related to hang.

hanky-panky [M19th] People have been talking in disapproving terms of hanky-panky since the 1830s. Then it tended to mean 'trickery' or 'dishonest behaviour',

hand handbag handicap handkerchief

whereas since the 1930s it has mainly referred to sexual indiscretions. The word is possibly an alteration of **hocus-pocus**, which was said by conjurors as they performed their tricks, rather like 'abracadabra!'. This appeared in the early 17th century based on a pseudo-Latin phrase *hax pax max Deus adimax* used by conjurors as a magic formula. **Hoax** [L18th] may be a shortening of hocus-pocus.

haphazard [late 16th century] This is composed of Middle English hap (*see* HAPPY) 'luck, fortune' (from Old Norse *happ*) and **hazard**, which was initially a gambling game played with two dice in which the chances are complicated by arbitrary rules. It reached English in the Middle Ages through Arabic, Spanish, and French, but goes right back to Persian or Turkish *zar* 'dice'. In the 16th century hazard came to mean 'a chance' and 'a risk of loss or harm'.

hapless *see* HAPPY

happy [ME] Before the 14th century you could be *GLAD but not happy. The word is from **hap** 'fortune, chance', which entered English a century or more earlier and which is no longer used in everyday English, except in **hapless** [LME] meaning 'unfortunate', its development **happen** [LME] and *PERHAPS. To be happy was at first to be favoured by fortune—but came to refer to feelings of pleasure in the early 16th century. **Happy as a sandboy** is said because sandboys (who would have been grown men as well as boys) were 'happy' or 'jolly' because they were habitually drunk. A dictionary of slang terms published in 1823 explains that **jolly as a sandboy** referred to 'a merry fellow who has tasted a drop'. This is reflected in a pub in Charles Dickens's *The Old Curiosity Shop*, published in 1840: 'The Jolly Sandboys was a small road-side inn . . . with a sign, representing three Sandboys increasing their jollity.' Sandboys sold sand for use in building, for household chores such as cleaning pots and pans, and to spread on floors to soak up spillages, especially in pubs. In Australia you can also be **as happy as Larry**, which may be connected with the renowned 19th-century

boxer Larry Foley, or owe something to **larry** [L19th], a dialect word meaning 'a state of excitement' that appears in the novels of Thomas Hardy. A North American equivalent is **as happy as a clam** or **as happy as a clam at high water**: when the tide is high, the clams are covered by seawater and are able to feed to their hearts' content.

hara-kiri *see* JAPANESE WORD PANEL

harass [E17th] This came from French in the early 17th century and is probably from *harer* 'to set a dog on'. The notion of intimidation arose during the 19th century, with **sexual harassment** acquiring particular prominence in the 1970s. The sound and sense of harass may be similar to those of **harry**, but the two are unrelated: **harry** [OE] goes back to an ancient root meaning 'army, host', which also gave us the bird called a **harrier** [M16th], but not the dogs [LME], which got their name from the hares they were bred to hunt.

harbour [OE] Old English *herebeorg* was 'a shelter, refuge'. It came to be used as a shelter for ships in late Middle English. In Old English **haven** was the word used for harbour. The sense 'cherish privately' arose early and was used of any feelings; it gradually became associated principally with grievance and resentment. A **harbinger** [ME] was originally someone who went ahead to find lodgings for an army.

harem [M17th] This is from Arabic *harīm* which is literally 'prohibited, prohibited place', thus 'sanctuary, women's quarters' and, by extension, 'women'.

harlequin [16th] Harlequin is the name of a mute character, masked and dressed in a diamond-patterned costume, who played a leading role in the **harlequinade** [L18th], a section of a traditional pantomime. As pantomime developed from being a prologue into a dramatized story, it included a transformation scene in which Harlequin and his mistress Columbine performed a dance. Harlequin comes from French, from the earlier *Herlequin* (or *Hellequin*), the leader of a legendary troop of demon horsemen. It may ultimately be related to Old English *Herla cyning* 'King Herla', a mythical figure found in early British legend. *See* PANTOMIME

harlot [ME] In the 13th century a harlot was a term of abuse for a male beggar or villain. It then came to refer to a jester or comedian and to a male servant before it started to mean 'a promiscuous woman' in the mid 15th century. It was much used in early English versions of the Bible as a less offensive word than 'whore'.

harmony [LME] Harmony comes from Latin *harmonia* 'joining, concord', from Greek *harmos* 'joint'.

harpsichord *see* PIANO

harrier, harry *see* HARASS

harsh *see* HAIR

harvest [OE] The meaning of harvest in Old English was 'autumn'. Since early autumn was the season for the cutting and gathering in of ripened crops, this passed during the Middle Ages into 'the process of gathering in crops' and 'the season's yield or crop'. The word harvest itself has ancient roots: it is related to Latin *carpere* 'to pluck' (*see* CARPET) and Greek *karpos* 'fruit'. *See also* AUTUMN

hash [L16th] A hash is a dish of cooked meat cut into small pieces and then reheated in gravy. Its 16th-century origin is a French word meaning 'an axe', from which *HATCHET and the use of **hatch** meaning 'to mark a surface with close parallel lines to represent shading' also derive. The **hash sign** (the sign #) only dates from the 1980s and is probably also from this use of hatch. In the 18th century hash developed the sense of 'a jumble of mismatched parts', which forms the basis of the modern expression to **make a hash of**. *See also* HOTCHPOTCH

hassle [late 19th century] This was originally a dialect word in the sense 'hack or saw at'. The origin is unknown but it may

be a blend of **haggle** (LME from an Old Norse word for 'hack, mangle') and **tussle** (LME, probably the same word as **tousle**, of Germanic origin).

hatchet [ME] English took over French *hachette* in the Middle Ages. It derives from *hache* 'an axe'—*see* HASH. To **bury the hatchet**, 'end a quarrel or conflict', refers to a Native American custom which involved burying a hatchet or tomahawk to mark the conclusion of a peace treaty between warring groups. The custom is described as early as 1680; the current sense of the phrase emerged around 70 years later. In 1974 the then British Prime Minister Harold Wilson observed wryly of his Cabinet: 'I've buried all the hatchets. But I know where I've buried them and I can dig them up if necessary.' Since the 1940s a **hatchet man** has been somebody employed to carry out controversial or disagreeable tasks, such as dismissing people from their jobs or writing journalistic pieces to destroy a person's reputation. The original hatchet man, in the USA during the late 19th century, was a hired Chinese assassin who carried a hatchet with the handle cut off.

haughty *see* ALTITUDE

haute cuisine *see* FRENCH WORD PANEL

haven *see* HARBOUR

haversack [M18th] This comes via French from obsolete German *Habersack* which described a bag used by soldiers to carry oats as horse feed. The word came from dialect *Haber* 'oats' and *Sack* 'sack, bag'.

havoc [LME] A victorious army commander would once have given his soldiers a signal to start plundering: he would **cry havoc**. The sense of plunder gradually passed into destructive devastation, and the army itself would **make havoc**. Outside the battlefield other people and other circumstances eventually began to **work havoc** or, from the 20th century, to **create** or **wreak havoc** and to **play havoc with something**. The word havoc itself is a medieval alteration of

harlot harmony harpsichord harrier harry

French *havot* of unknown origin. The word was memorably used by Shakespeare in *Julius Caesar*: 'Cry, "Havoc!", and let slip the dogs of war.' *See also* MAYHEM

hawk [OE] In politics a hawk, a person who advocates hard-line or warlike policies, contrasts with a *DOVE, a peacemaker. The terms emerged in the early 1960s at the time of the Cuban missile crisis, when the Soviet Union threatened to install missiles in Cuba within striking distance of the USA. To hawk meaning 'to carry about and offer goods for sale' was formed in the late 15th century, probably by removing the ending from **hawker**, 'a person who travels around selling goods'. The latter word is not recorded until the early 16th century, when hawkers came to legal notice as something of a nuisance to be suppressed, but was most likely in use long before it was written down. It is related to **huckster** [ME], from a root meaning 'to haggle, bargain'. *See also* HAGGARD

hay [OE] An ancient word that goes back to around AD 800 in Old English. The phrase to **make hay**, 'to make good use of an opportunity while it lasts', is a shortening of the proverbial recommendation **make hay while the sun shines**, which has been in use since the 16th century. Since the late 19th century North American farmers have employed **haywire** to bind bales of hay and corn. Others found other uses for it, so that haywire came to describe anything patched together or poorly equipped. By the 1920s to **go haywire** meant 'to go wrong', and in the 1930s it was extended to cover people who were mentally disturbed or out of control.

hazard *see* HAPHAZARD

head [OE] English head—in Old English *hēafod* – has parallels in numerous related languages, including Dutch *hoofd* and German *Haupt*. The earlier, more logical, version of **head over heels**, 'turning over completely in forward motion', was **heels over head**. The modern form dates from the late 18th century. It often describes an extreme condition, as in **head over heels in love** or **head over heels in debt**. A variant is

head over ears, which is an alteration of earlier, and much more logical, **over head and ears**. The expression to **give someone their head** comes from horse riding. Giving a horse its head meant allowing it to gallop freely rather than checking its pace by using the reins. The same image and meaning is to be found in the phrase to **give someone free rein,** which these days people sometimes write as **free reign**, as if the idea was allowing someone to rule freely.

health *see* WELL

hearse [ME] In English a hearse has always been a part of a funeral, but its origin is agricultural. The word derives from Old French *herce*, which meant 'a harrow' and goes back to Latin *hirpex*, a name for a kind of large rake. This came from Oscan, an extinct language of southern Italy known only from early inscriptions, where *hirpus* meant 'wolf': people were making a comparison between a wolf's teeth and the teeth of a rake. The earliest uses of hearse in medieval English were for a triangular frame, shaped like an ancient harrow, used for carrying candles at certain church services, and a canopy placed over the coffin of a distinguished person while it was in church. The modern meaning, 'a vehicle for conveying the coffin at a funeral', appeared in the mid 17th century.

heart [OE] The Greek word *kardia*, from which English took **cardiac** [LME], is directly related to heart. The shared root existed before their ancestor developed into different language families in Europe, Asia, and northern India. Since Anglo-Saxon times people have regarded the heart as the centre of emotions and feelings. If you **wear your heart on your sleeve**, you make your feelings clear for all to see. In a television interview in 1987 the former British Prime Minister Margaret Thatcher advised against it, saying: 'To wear your heart on your sleeve isn't a very good plan; you should wear it inside, where it functions best.' The phrase has its origins in chivalry. In the Middle Ages, when jousting was a popular form of entertainment, a knight would tie a favour to his sleeve—a ribbon, glove, or other small

hawk hay hazard head health hearse

item belonging to the lady given as a sign of her love or support.

heat [OE] The words heat and *HOT go back to the same Germanic ancestor. **If you can't stand the heat, get out of the kitchen** is associated with the Democratic statesman Harry S. Truman, who was president of the USA between 1945 and 1953. When he announced his retirement in 1952 he did express the sentiment, in the form **if you don't like the heat...** but attributed it to one of his military advisers, Major General Harry Vaughan.

heath, heathen *see* PAGAN

heave *see* HEFTY

heaven [OE] The ultimate origin of heaven is unknown, although parallel forms exist in related languages. Heaven has always referred to the sky and to the abode of God, regarded as beyond the sky. In Christian theology there is only one heaven, but some Jewish and Muslim people considered there to be seven, of which the seventh was the highest. There souls enjoyed a state of eternal bliss, and so **in seventh heaven** came to mean 'very happy, ecstatic'. *See also* MOVE, PARADISE

heavy *see* HEFTY

heck *see* HELL

heckle *see* HACKLE

hectare *see* HUNDRED

hectic [LME] This came via late Latin from Greek *hektikos* 'habitual'. The original sense was 'symptomatic of one's physical condition' associated specifically with the symptoms of tuberculosis (known as hectic fever); this led in the early 20th century to the sense 'characterized by feverish activity'.

hedge [OE] Hedges mark boundaries, but are also a means of protection or defence. The idea of protecting yourself is strong in to **hedge your bets**. In strict betting terms this means putting money on more than

one horse in a race, but you can also hedge other financial liabilities, including speculative investments. Originally people would **hedge in** a bet. This is related to an earlier application of hedge in, in which debts were incorporated into a larger debt for which better security was available. Much more recently, in the 1960s, **hedge fund** became the term for an offshore investment fund that engages in speculation using credit or borrowed capital.

hedonist *see* EPICURE

heel *see* HELL

hefty [M19th] This was originally a US dialect word formed from late Middle English **heft** 'the weight of someone', which came from Old English **heave**, also the source of Old English **heavy**. **Heave-ho** [LME] was originally a nautical expression, used when hauling a rope.

helicopter [L19th] The first helicopter did not appear until the 1920s, but the word had already been invented by then, first of all in French—the science fiction writer Jules Verne wrote of a helicopter in *The Clipper of the Clouds* (1886). The French word was based on Greek *helix* 'spiral' and *pteron* 'wing', which gave us the name of the flying reptile the **pterodactyl** [E19th].

heliophobia, heliotrope *see* PHOBIA

hell [OE] Hell descends from an ancient Indo-European root with the sense 'to cover, hide' which also gave rise to Latin *celare* (root of **conceal** [ME] and *OCCULT) and to English **hole** (*see* HOLD), **helmet** [LME], and **heel** 'to set a plant in the ground and cover its roots'. This was originally unconnected with the Old English word for the part of the foot, but rather came from *helian* 'cover'.

The infernal regions are regarded as a place of torment or punishment, and many curses and exclamations, such as **a hell of a—** or **one hell of a—**, depend on this. These expressions used to be shocking, and until the early 20th century were usually printed as h—l or h—. Alterations such as **heck** [L19th] served the same softening purpose in speech as well as in writing. The saying **hell hath no fury like a woman scorned** is a near quotation from a 1697 play by William Congreve: 'Heaven has no rage like love to hatred turned, Nor Hell a fury like a woman scorned.' The dramatist Colley Cibber had used very similar words just a year earlier, and the idea was commonplace in the Renaissance. It can be traced back to the Greek dramatist Euripides of the 5th century BC. Strictly the 'fury' is one of the Furies of Greek mythology, frightening goddesses who avenged wrong and punished crime, but most people now use and interpret it in the sense 'wild or violent anger'. The proverb **the road to hell is paved with good intentions** dates from the late 16th century, but earlier forms existed which omitted the first three words. Grumpy and misanthropic people everywhere will agree with the French philosopher Jean-Paul Sartre who wrote in 1944: **'Hell is other people.'**

hello [L19th] This, like **hallo** [M16th] a form found well into the 20th century and still common in the policeman's ''Allo, 'Allo, 'Allo', is a variant of the earlier word **hollo** [E16th] and **halloo** [M16th]. They all come from cries used to urge on hunting dogs, and keep in touch will others in the field. **Holler** [L17th] is yet another form, now mainly found in the USA. *Compare* COOEE.

helmet *see* HELL

help [OE] Old English help lies behind **helpmate**. This is found in the late 17th century as *helpmeet* which comes from Genesis 2:18 where Eve is described as 'an help meet for' Adam. 'Meet' means suitable, but as the word became more obscure in the early 18th century it was changed to mate.

helter-skelter *see* PELL MELL

hemp *see* CANVAS

hen [OE] Ultimately the word hen is related to Latin *canere* 'to sing'. Apart from singing hens, what could be rarer than hen's teeth? Hens do not have teeth, so to describe something as **as rare as hen's teeth** is tantamount to saying that it is non-existent.

The phrase was originally used in the USA during the mid 19th century. The **henpecked** husband has long been a staple of comedies and seaside postcards, and the word goes back to *The Genuine Remains* (1680) by Samuel Butler. The expression comes from the way that hens will sometimes peck at the feathers of other birds.

henchman [ME] The original sense of this was probably 'a groom'. It is from Old English *hengest* 'stallion', and *MAN. The first part also features in the names of the semi-mythological leaders Hengist and Horsa (meaning 'horse'), who supposedly came to Britain at the invitation of the British King Vortigern in 449 to assist in defeating the Picts. From the Middle Ages a henchman was a squire or page of honour to a person of great rank; in Scotland he was the principal attendant of a Highland chief. The word was taken up by Sir Walter Scott, whose novels were hugely popular throughout the 19th century, and Scott gave henchman to the wider world. The current sense, 'a criminal's follower', began in the mid 19th century in the USA.

heptagon, heptathlete *see* SEVEN

herb [ME] Herb came via Old French from Latin *herba* 'grass, green crops, herb'. Although herb has always been spelled with an *h*, pronunciation without it was usual until the 19th century and is still standard in the US.

heroin [L19th] The similarity in spelling between heroin and **hero** [ME] is not accidental. The name of the drug is a German word formed in the late 1890s from Latin *heros* 'hero', in reference to its effects, for the feelings of euphoria it can produce meant that in early tests users reported that they felt 'heroic'. Hero itself in an early Greek word.

hesitate [E17th] This comes from Latin *haesitare* 'to stick fast, leave undecided', from *haerere* 'to stick, stay'.

hex *see* HAG

hello helmet help helter-skelter hemp hen

hexagon *see* SIX

heyday [E16th] From the early 16th century people shouted **hey-day!** to express joy, surprise, or some other intense emotion. It may have come from Low German *heida!* or *heidi!*, 'hurrah!'. By the end of the same century **heyday** meant 'a state of high spirits or passion'. Perhaps through a false association with *DAY, it began to refer to the period of a person's or thing's greatest success or activity in the mid 18th century.

hey presto *see* PRESTIGE

hide [OE] The hide meaning 'the skin of an animal' goes back far in prehistory to a root that also developed into Latin *cutis* 'skin' (the source of **cuticle** [LME]). A person who is **hidebound** [M16th] is unable or unwilling to change because of tradition or convention. The word originally referred to physical condition, first of cattle who were so badly fed or so sick that their skin clung close to their back and ribs, and then of emaciated people. The hide meaning 'to put or keep out of sight' is also Old English but unrelated. *See also* BUSHEL. Someone who is **on a hiding to nothing** is unlikely to succeed, or at least unlikely to gain much advantage if they do. The term apparently arose in the world of horse racing, when a trainer, owner, or jockey was expected to win easily and so could gain no credit from success but would be disgraced by failure. The word is the same as that in a **good hiding**, and means 'a beating'—the idea is one of beating the hide or skin off someone. *See also* HUNDRED

higgledy-piggledy [L16th] This is a rhyming jingle probably used with reference to the herding together of pigs in a disorderly and confused way.

high [OE] High is one of those small words that plays a part in a large number of expressions. In the calendar of the Christian Church there used to be two sorts of special day: a **high day** and a holiday. **Holiday** [OE] was originally **holy day** and was a day set apart for religious observance. A high day was a much more important religious festival commemorating a particular sacred person or event. These together give us **high days and holidays**. Being high on drugs is associated with the 1960s, but the expression goes back at least to the 1930s. Alcohol can also be classed as a drug, and you can read of a man being 'high with wine' as early as 1627.

The first records of **high, wide, and handsome**, 'expansive and impressive', are from US newspapers in the 1880s. In 1932 a book on *Yankee Slang* comments that it is a common shout at rodeos: 'Ride him, Cowboy, high, wide, and handsome.' The expression to **be for the high jump** might conjure up athletics, but behind it lies a much grimmer scene. It dates from the early 20th century, when it was a slang term used by soldiers to mean 'to be put on trial before your commanding officer'. The image is actually of a person being executed by hanging, with the jump being the effect of the gallows trapdoor being suddenly opened beneath their feet. See also HOG

hilarity *see* EXHILARATE

himbo *see* BIMBO

Hindi, Hindu *see* INDIAN

hinge *see* HANG

hinny *see* MULE

hippopotamus *see* EQUESTRIAN

history [LME] History goes back to a very ancient root that is also the source of Latin *videre* 'to see' (*see* VIEW) and of the Old English word *wit* 'to have knowledge'. More immediately it came from Greek *historia* 'finding out, narrative, history'. In its earliest use in English a history was not necessarily assumed to be true: it could be any narrative or story, an idea echoed by the American motor manufacturer Henry Ford (1863–1947) when he said '**History is more or less bunk**.' To **make history**, 'to do something that influences the course of history', dates from the mid 19th century. A less positive view of history appears in the phrase to **be history**, 'to be dead or no

hexagon heyday hey presto hide hidebound

longer relevant to the present', which is recorded from the 1930s.

hit [OE] The earliest sense of hit, in the Old English period, was 'to come upon, meet with, find'. Popular successes, first of all plays, and then songs, have been called hits since the beginning of the 19th century. In the 1990s the phrase to **hit the ground running** became something of a cliché. It seems to refer to soldiers disembarking rapidly from a helicopter, though no one has been able to trace it back to any particular conflict. Marksmanship and shooting are behind a number of phrases, including to **hit the mark**, 'to be successful in an attempt or accurate in a guess' and **hit-and-miss** 'done or occurring at random', which is more understandable in its earlier form **hit-or-miss** [E17th].

hitch [ME] The earliest sense of hitch was 'to move or lift up with a jerk'. The meaning 'to fasten or tether' dates from the early 17th century, and is the one that features in such expressions as to **get hitched** for get married and to **hitch your wagon to a star**. The US philosopher and poet Ralph Waldo Emerson introduced this second phrase in 1870 in the sense 'to have high aspirations'. A hitch meaning 'an obstacle' is probably from the word's use to mean 'a knot in a rope'.

hive [Old English] This Germanic word is probably related to Old Norse *húfr* 'hull of a ship' and Latin *cupa* 'tub, cask'. Early hives were conical and made of straw.

hoard *see* HORDE

hoax *see* HANKY-PANKY

hob *see* HUB

hobby [LME] In medieval times men and boys given the name Robin were sometimes known as Hobin or Hobby, in much the same way that today they might be called Bob or Bobby. This became a pet term for a pony, just as Dobbin—also from Robin—was used for a carthorse. This gave us the **hobby horse** [M16th], a figure of a horse made of wickerwork and worn over the head in a Morris dance or pantomime. Later it

became a stick with a horse's head, for a child to ride when playing. The connection with pleasure or play led to the use of hobby horse for what we now call a hobby. Since the early 19th century hobby has taken over this sense and **hobby horse** now usually means 'a preoccupation or favourite topic'. The *hob* in **hobgoblin** [M16th] is also from a pet form of Robin or Robert.

hobnob [E19th] In the 18th century drinkers would toast each other alternately with the words 'hob or nob' or 'hob and nob', probably meaning 'give or take' or 'have or have not'. Toasting each other in this way was 'to drink hob or nob', or, from the early 19th century, simply to hobnob. The image of convivial companionship led to the sense 'to be on familiar terms, to talk informally', which during the 20th century acquired negative associations of mixing socially with those felt to be of higher social status. It was the convivial connotations that probably persuaded McVitie's to come up with the name HobNobs for their new biscuit in 1985.

hocus-pocus *see* HANKY-PANKY

hodgepodge *see* HOTCHPOTCH

hog [OE] This may be one of the small number of English words that comes from the language of the Celts, who lived in Britain before the Romans and Saxons. It is probably related to Welsh *hwch* and Cornish *hoch* 'pig, sow'. A number of explanations have been offered for the expression to **go the whole hog**, which was first used in the USA in the early 19th century. The earliest examples are in political contexts, so its origins may lie in the large political rallies which were then common. At these rallies various ploys were used to woo potential voters, notably the provision of vast quantities of free food: a whole pig —or hog, in American English—might be roasted. Another idea is that the phrase comes from a fable about Muslims in *The Love of the World: Hypocrisy Detected*, published in 1779 and composed by William Cowper (an English poet and hardly an expert on Islam). According to this fable certain Muslims,

hit   hitch   hive   hoard   hoax   hob   hobby

forbidden to eat pork by their religion but strongly tempted to have just a little, suggested that Muhammad had meant to ban only one particular part of the pig. But they could not agree which part that was, and between them they ate the whole animal, each one telling himself that his own portion did not contain the part that was forbidden. To **live high on the hog** is to have a luxurious lifestyle. The phrase probably comes from the idea of eating the best bits of a pig, which were higher up on the animal, as opposed to the offal and trotters. The verb use, 'to take all of something in a greedy way', comes from the proverbial greed of the pig. It was first used in the USA, in the 1880s.

hoi polloi [M17th] In Greek *hoi polloi* means 'the many'. It has been used since the middle of the 17th century as a snooty way of referring to ordinary people, 'the masses'. Strictly, as *hoi* means 'the' you should avoid saying 'the hoi polloi', but writers as well known as Dryden and Byron have said 'the hoi polloi'.

hold [OE] The ancient root of hold probably meant 'to watch over'. Hold, 'a large compartment in the lower part of a ship or aircraft' has a different origin, is late 16th century and derives from **hole** [OE] and is related to **hollow** [OE], and possibly **hull** [ME]. The phrase **no holds barred**, 'with no rules or restrictions', comes from the sport of wrestling. Certain holds, such as gripping round the throat, are banned as too dangerous. Sometimes, though, no-holds-barred contests would be set up where participants could do almost anything they liked.

holiday *see* HIGH

holler *see* HELLO

hollow *see* HOLD

holocaust [ME] A holocaust was originally a sacrificial offering burned completely on an altar, from Greek *holokauston*, from *holos* 'whole' and *kaustos* 'burned'. From the 18th century it could also mean 'a great slaughter or massacre', and

this is the sense most widely known today. **The Holocaust** was the mass murder of more than 6 million Jews and other persecuted groups under the German Nazi regime between 1941 and 1945. The term was introduced by historians during the 1950s, but as early as 1942 newspapers were referring to the killing of Jews by the Germans as 'a holocaust'. The Hebrew equivalent is *sō'āh* or **Shoah**, literally 'catastrophe', which is sometimes used in English.

holy [OE] Holy is related to Dutch and German *heilig*, and derives from the same root as **whole**. The **holy of holies** originally referred to the inner chamber of the sanctuary of the Jewish temple in Jerusalem, which was separated by a veil from the outer chamber and entered only by the High Priest on the Day of Atonement. The attitude of self-conscious virtue or piety that is **holier than thou** also has a biblical source, in Isaiah, which deplores 'a rebellious people...Which say, Stand by thyself, come not near to me; for I am holier than thou'. *See also* HIGH

home [OE] Home is an ancient word related to a Sanskrit term meaning 'safe dwelling'. The Greek poet Hesiod, who lived around 700 BC, expressed the same sentiment as **there's no place like home**, although its best-known expression is in the sentimental song 'Home Sweet Home' by John Howard Payne, first sung in the opera *Clari, the Maid of Milan* in 1823: 'Mid pleasures and palaces though we may roam, / Be it ever so humble, there's no place like home.' The saying **home is where the heart is** dates from the late 19th century. **A woman's place is in the home** dates from the 19th century.

homestead *see* STEAD

honcho *see* JAPANESE WORD PANEL

honest, honesty *see* HONOUR

honeymoon [OE] In the 16th century the first month of a couple's marriage was their honeymoon whether or not they went away on holiday—very few then did. The

hoi polloi   hold   holiday   holler   hollow

original reference was not to a 'moon' or month at all, but to 'sweet' affection changing like the moon.

honour [ME] Latin *honor* is the source of honour and of **honest** and **honesty** (both Middle English). The idea that **there is honour among thieves** was expressed even in the early 17th century. The English philosopher Jeremy Bentham was the first to put it in print in its modern form when he wrote in 1802: 'A sort of honour may be found (according to a proverbial saying) even among thieves.' The plant honesty is named from its diaphanous seed pods, translucency symbolizing lack of deceit.

hoodwink *see* WINK

hoof [OE] If a government makes policy **on the hoof**, it does so without proper thought and preparation. The original reference was to livestock that was alive and not yet slaughtered; the earliest example in print dates from 1818. The human foot is also treated like a cow's or horse's in the phrase to **hoof it** 'to walk as opposed to ride', which dates from as far back as the mid 17th century. To **hoof** meaning 'to dance', and **hoofer** 'a dancer' both arose in US slang in the 1920s.

hook [OE] Hooks have many uses: for catching hold of things, for hanging things on, for controlling sheep, for carrying bait, and others. The angler's hook features in **hook, line and sinker**, used to emphasize that someone has been completely deceived or tricked. The items all form part of fishing tackle, where a sinker is a weight used to sink the fishing line in the water. The image behind the expression is of a hungry fish deceived by the bait into gulping everything down. The expression **off the hook**, 'no longer in trouble or difficulty', is almost the opposite: the idea here is of a fish managing to wriggle off the hook that lodged in its mouth when it took the bait.

The type of hook referred to in **by hook or by crook**, 'by any possible means', is not certain. The expression goes back to the 14th century and probably comes from farming, with the crook being a shepherd's

hooked staff and the hook a 'billhook', a heavy curved pruning knife. How these implements might have been used together comes from the writer and political reformer William Cobbett, who in 1822 described an ancient English forest law. According to this, people living near woodland were allowed to gather dead tree branches for fuel, using the hook to cut them off or the crook to pull them down. To **play hookey**, or play truant, is a 19th-century US expression. It probably comes from **hook off** or **hook it**, meaning 'to go away'.

hooligan [L19th] The Hooligans were a fictional rowdy Irish family in a music hall song of the 1890s, and a comic Irish character called Hooligan appeared in a series of adventures in the magazine *Funny Folks*. One or other may have given their name to the hooligan, a phenomenon who made his debut in newspaper reports of cases in police courts in 1898. The **football hooligan** is first mentioned in the mid 1960s. *See also* THUG, VANDAL

hoopoe *see* CUCKOO

Hooray Henry *see* SLOANE

hope [OE] The word hope is an ancient Germanic term. That **hope springs eternal** is thanks to the poet Alexander Pope, who wrote in his *Essay on Man* in 1732: 'Hope springs eternal in the human breast. Man never is, but always to be blessed.' *See also* PANDORA'S BOX

horde [OE] A horde was originally a tribe or troop of nomads, such as the Tartars led by Genghis Khan, who migrated from place to place in search of new pasture or plunder. The word comes from Polish *horda*, which is itself from Turkish *ordu* 'royal camp', from which the language name **Urdu** [L18th] also derives. The word is often confused with **hoard** [OE] a Germanic word for 'a secret stock or store'.

horizon [LME] The word horizon came via late Latin *horizon* from Greek *horizōn* (*kuklos*) 'limiting (circle)'.

honour hoodwink hoof hook hooligan hoopoe

Horlicks *see* BOLLOCKS

horn [OE] The word horn is related to *CORN 'a painful area of thickened skin', and **cornea** [LME] through its ancestor Latin *cornu* 'horn'. In to **draw** (or **pull**) **in your horns**, 'to become less assertive or ambitious', the image is of a snail drawing in its eyestalks and retreating into its shell when disturbed. *See* DILEMMA

hornbeam *see* BEAM

horology, horoscope *see* YEAR

horror [ME] The Latin word *horror* was formed from *horrere*, meaning 'to stand on end' (referring to hair), and 'to tremble, shudder'. This is the source of our word **horror** and of related words such as **horrible** [ME], and **horrify** [L18th]. *See also* ABHOR, CAPRICE

hors d'oeuvre *see* FRENCH WORD PANEL

horse [OE] An ancient word that has relatives in most northern European languages. The root may also be the source of Latin *currere* 'to run' (*see* CURSOR). Horse racing has given numerous expressions to the language. The saying **horses for courses** is from the idea that each racehorse is suited to one particular racecourse and will do better on that than on any other. A.E.T. Watson's *The Turf* in 1891 was the first to record this observation, which he describes as 'a familiar phrase on the turf'. The underlying idea of **straight from the horse's mouth** is that the best way to get racing tips is to ask a horse directly. One of the first examples comes from a 1913 edition of the *Syracuse Herald*: 'Lionel hesitated, then went on quickly. "I got a tip yesterday, and if it wasn't straight from the horse's mouth it was jolly well the next thing to it."' People often say something like, 'Oh, **wild horses wouldn't . . .**', meaning that nothing could persuade them to do that particular thing, not realizing the horrific reference—it comes from the old custom of executing criminals by tying each of the four limbs to four horses and then urging the horses on, tearing the person into four

pieces. To **flog a dead horse** is to waste energy on a lost cause or a situation that cannot be altered. **Dead horse** used to be workmen's slang for work that was charged for before it was done: to **work** or **work for a dead horse** was to do work that you had already been paid for.

An early form of the proverb **you can lead a horse to water but you can't make him drink** was 'They can but bringe horse to the water brinke, But horse may choose whether that horse will drinke' (1602). The **horse chestnut** was formerly said to be a remedy for chest diseases in horses, and its name is a translation of Latin *Castanea equina*. In **horsefly** [LME], **horseradish** [L16th], and similar terms **horse** implies 'large of its kind'. See also DARK, EASEL, EQUESTRIAN, GIFT

hospital [ME] Latin *hospis* meant both 'host' and 'guest'. This has given us **host** [ME] itself (in the meaning 'a person who entertains other people as guests'), **hostel** [ME], and *HOTEL, as well as **hospice** [E19th], hospital, **hospitality** [LME], and **hostile** [L16th]. Although the immediate source of **guest** [OE] is Old Norse *gestr*, the history of the word can be traced back to an ancient root shared by Latin *hostis*.

hostage [ME] The word hostage has no connection with host (*see* HOSPITAL) in any of its uses—it goes back to Latin *ob* 'towards, against' and *sedere* 'to sit', used to mean 'the state of being a hostage'. Originally an ally or enemy would hand over a hostage as security for the fulfilment of an undertaking. Now hostages are 'taken' as well as 'held', and are very seldom handed over voluntarily. In a **hostage to fortune**, the word fortune means 'fate', with the idea being that future events are no longer under a person's control but in the hands of fate. In a rather jaundiced reflection on marriage the English philosopher Francis Bacon wrote in 1625: 'He that hath wife and children, hath given hostages to fortune; for they are impediments to great enterprises, either of virtue, or of mischief.'

hostel *see* HOTEL

hostile *see* HOSPITAL

hot [OE] Hot shares an ancestor with
*HEAT. It has been used to describe sexual
arousal since the Middle Ages, but a
dictionary of US slang published in 1947 is
the first to record **the hots** for desire, which
may have originated in **hot pants**, first
recorded in the 1920s and revived in Britain
in the early 1970s to describe the women's
fashion for skimpy shorts. People have used
hot air for empty talk that is intended to
impress since the late 19th century. *See also*
BLOW

hotchpotch [LME] In the late Middle
Ages English acquired the word hotchpot
for 'a confused mixture'. It came from
French *hochepot*, which was formed from
hocher 'to shake' and *pot* 'pot'. **Hotchpot** is
still used in English law in the context of
joining together all of a dead person's
property so that it can be divided equally. In
its everyday sense, though, people quickly
changed it to hotchpotch, so that the
elements rhymed for emphasis. The same
rhyming impulses then changed it to
hodgepodge, now mainly used in North
America.

hotel [M18th] English adopted the French
word *hôtel* in the mid 17th century. For the
first century of its life people used it only in
French phrases and to refer to the large
town mansions of French aristocrats, but
since the mid 18th century the modern
sense, 'a place providing accommodation
and meals for paying guests', has prevailed.
The French word was originally spelled
hostel, and this older form came into
English in the Middle Ages, in the general
sense 'a place to stay'. It was also used for an
inn or what we would now call a hotel. The
word **hostel** has since become restricted to
places for specific groups of people such as
students and migrant workers. The word
goes back to Latin *hospis* (*see* HOSPITAL).

hound *see* DOG

hour [ME] Hours came into English from
French, and goes back to Greek *hōra*
'season, hour'. *YEAR is a distant relation.
The Old English equivalent was *TIDE. **The**

eleventh hour, meaning 'the latest possible
moment', comes from the parable of the
labourers in the Gospel of Matthew, in
which someone pays people he hired at the
beginning of the day the same daily rate as
those he hired at the last or eleventh hour.
The phrase **their finest hour** was part of
Winston Churchill's speech in the House of
Commons on 18 June 1940, before the Battle
of Britain began: 'Let us therefore brace
ourselves to our duty, and so bear ourselves
that, if the British Empire and its
Commonwealth lasts for a thousand years,
men will still say, "This was their finest
hour."'

house [OE] The word house is related to
Dutch *huis* and German *Haus*, and their
ancient ancestor may have been a root
meaning 'to hide' found also in **huddle**
[L16th]. The **House of Commons** was first
called by that name in the early 17th
century, quickly followed by the **Houses of
Parliament**, and the **House of Lords**. The
house music heard in clubs from 1986
onwards was probably named after the
Warehouse, a club in Chicago where the
music was first popular. *See also* HUSSY

how *see* NATIVE AMERICAN WORD PANEL

hub [E16th] Although hub is recorded
from the early 16th century, it did not
appear in any dictionary until the 19th. It
seems to have been an English dialect term
that first meant '**hob**' (a variant spelling
recorded from the late 16th century), which
before the days of modern cookers was a
surface behind or beside a fireplace used for
heating pans, originally made of piled up
clay. The sense 'the central part of a wheel'
dates from the mid 17th century and was
probably suggested by the shape of the
original 'hub'.

huckster *see* HAWK

huddle *see* HOUSE

hue and cry [LME] In early times any
person witnessing or surprising a criminal
committing a crime could **raise a hue and
cry**, calling for others to join in their pursuit
and capture. In law the cry had to be raised

hostile hot hotchpotch hotel hound hour

by the inhabitants of the district in which the crime was committed, or otherwise the pursuers were liable for any damages suffered by the victim. The origin of the expression is in legal French *hu e cri* 'outcry and cry'. The first element has no connection with hue 'colour', which is a native English word related to Swedish *hy* 'skin, complexion', and originally meant 'form, appearance', only developing the colour sense in the mid 19th century.

hulk [OE] A hulk was originally a large cargo or transport ship. The word is probably of Mediterranean origin and related to Greek *holkas* 'cargo ship'. In the late 17th century it came to apply to an old ship stripped of fittings and permanently moored, especially one used for storage or as a prison. Large, clumsy people began to be described as hulks in the late Middle Ages.

hull *see* HOLD

human [LME] In the beginning human and **humane** were the same word. The forms were used interchangeably until the 18th century, when human took over the scientific and general senses relating to people and **humane** became restricted to the meanings 'showing compassion', and 'without inflicting pain'. Both derive from Latin *humanus*, from *homo* 'man, human being'.

humble [ME] A word that goes back to Latin *humilis* 'low, lowly, base', also found in **humility** [ME], which was formed from *humus* 'earth'. English adopted it from French in the Middle Ages. Before the mid 19th century there was no humility involved in eating **humble pie**. Humble pie was more correctly **umble pie**, made from the 'umbles' or innards of a deer of other animal. People considered offal to be inferior food, so began to pun on the similar-sounding **humble**. The first recorded example of to **eat humble pie**, 'to make a humble apology and accept humiliation', is from a collection of the dialect of East Anglia, published in 1830.

humour [ME] In the Middle Ages scientists and doctors believed that there were four main fluids in the body and that the relative proportions of these determined an individual's temperament. Blood gave a cheerful or *SANGUINE disposition; phlegm made somebody stolidly calm or *PHLEGMATIC; choler or yellow bile gave a peevish and irascible, or choleric character; and *MELANCHOLY or black bile caused depression. These substances were the four humours, or **cardinal humours**. From this notion **humour** acquired the sense 'mental disposition', then 'state of mind, mood' and 'whim, fancy' (hence to **humour someone**, 'to indulge a person's whim'). The association with amusement arose in the late 17th century. The origin of **humour** directly refers to fluids—it derives from Latin *humor* 'moisture', from *humere* 'to be moist', source also of **humid** [LME].

hump [E18th] If something annoying makes you **get the hump** the word is being used in something like its original sense. Hump arrived in English in the mid 17th century and is probably related to German *humpe* 'hump', and to Dutch *homp* 'lump, hunk of bread'. Its earliest use was to mean 'a complaint', especially in the rhyming phrase **humps and grumps**, the ancestor of **get the hump**. With reference to a personal deformity it dates from the early 18th century.

hundred [OE] Old English had two words for this number. One was *hund*, which came from an ancient root shared by Latin *centum*—as in **cent** (L18 for the money), **centigrade** [E19th], *CENTURY, and many other *cent-* words—and Greek *hekaton* (the source of **hectare** [E19th]). The other was hundred, which was formed from the same element plus another meaning 'number'. Hundred was also then used to refer to a division of a county or shire that had its own court. This unit may originally have been equivalent to a hundred hides of land—a **hide** is an ancient measure typically equal to between 60 and 100 acres, which varied from area to area because it was a measure of the area of land which would feed a family and its dependants.

hulk hull human humble humour hump

hunky dory [M19th] If everything is hunky dory it is going well, with no problems. It is American, and comes from the old slang word **hunky**, meaning 'all right, safe and sound', from Dutch *honk* 'home, base': the reason for the *dory* is unknown. Hunky here has nothing to do with hunky meaning 'strong and fit'—this is from **hunk** [E19th], 'chunk or lump', which is probably also Dutch or perhaps German in origin.

hurly-burly *see* TOPSY-TURVY

hurricane [M16th] When Christopher Columbus arrived in the Caribbean in 1492 he encountered the Arawak. These peaceful people did not long survive the coming of the Spanish, and are thought to have died out as a result of the diseases carried by the Europeans and attacks by their aggressive neighbours, the Carib. One part of their culture lives on in the term hurricane for a violent storm, specifically a tropical cyclone in the Caribbean. The word came into English via Spanish *huracán* from the name of the Arawak god of the storm, Hurakan. *See also* TYPHOON, TORNADO

husband [OE] In Old English a *WIFE was simply 'a woman', and a husband was 'a male head of a household' or 'a manager or steward', a sense preserved in expressions such as **to husband your resources**. The word is from Old Norse *húsbondí* 'master of a house'. Not until the 13th century or so did a husband become the married partner of a woman. Around then the word also took on the meaning 'a farmer or cultivator' and also the verb use 'to cultivate', both of which are no longer used but are preserved in **husbandry** [ME], 'the cultivation and care of crops and farm animals'.

husky [M16th] Husky for a hoarse-sounding person (one with a husky voice) and the term husky for an Arctic dog are unconnected. The first comes from **husk** [ME] meaning 'the dry outer covering of a fruit or seed', a medieval word from Dutch *hūskjin* 'little house'—the husk was pictured as the 'house' of the seed it contained. The name of the powerful dog used for pulling sledges probably comes from a Native American language, and came from Newfoundland dialect *Huskemaw* a form of *ESKIMO, first used in English in around 1830. Our use is from the shortening of **husky dog** or 'Eskimo dog'.

hussy [LME] 'You brazen hussy!' is now the sort of thing someone might call a female friend as a joke, but until the mid 20th century hussy was a serious term for an immoral woman. The original hussy was far more respectable, though—she was a housewife. Hussy developed in the mid 16th century from **housewife** [ME], which was the word's first meaning. Some hundred years later it became a rude or playful way of addressing a woman, and also a derogatory term implying a lack of morals.

hydraulic, hydrotherapy *see* WATER

hygiene [L16th] The word hygiene goes back to Greek *hugieinē* (*tekhnē*) meaning '(art) of health', from *hugiēs* 'healthy'.

hyphen [E17th] This word came into English via late Latin from Greek *huphen* 'together'.

hypnotic [E17th] This goes back to Greek *hupnōtikos* 'narcotic, causing sleep', from *hupnoun* 'put to sleep'.

hysteria [E19th] In ancient times doctors (all male) regarded hysteria as a disease of women cause by a disturbance of the womb. In the early 19th-century English pathologists (also male) formed the English name from Greek *hustera* 'uterus, womb'. Earlier terms for the condition had been **hysteric** [M17th] or **hysterical passion**, reflecting the same view, and **the vapours** [M17th].

Ii

I *see* EGO

ice [OE] The primary purpose of **breaking the ice** was to allow the passage of boats through frozen water, but by the end of the 16th century people were using the phrase to mean 'to begin an undertaking'. The modern sense, 'to do or say something to relieve tension or get conversation going', began in the 17th century. Ice has represented a person's cold nature or unfriendly manner since at least the time of Shakespeare. In the early 19th century the poet Lord Byron wrote in his *Don Juan*: 'And your cold people are beyond all price, When once you've broken their confounded ice.' **Ice cream** has been around longer than you might think. The term first appeared in the mid 18th century, but the earlier equivalent **iced cream** is known from the late 17th. In 1848 the novelist William Makepeace Thackeray could use the shortened form **ice** in *Vanity Fair*: 'He went out and ate ices at a pastry-cook's shop.' Since the early 18th century both **icing** and ice have been names for sugar paste for cakes. The American equivalent is **frosting** [1756]. The idea behind both is that the white sugar looks like ice. The phrase **the icing on the cake**, 'an attractive but inessential addition or enhancement', has been recorded since the 1920s

iceberg [L18th] The earliest meaning of iceberg in English was for a glacier which is seen from the sea as a hill. The term came in the late 18th century from Dutch *ijsberg*, from *ijs* 'ice' and *berg* 'hill'. The expression **the tip of the iceberg**, 'the small visible part of a larger problem that remains hidden', is surprisingly recent, being recorded only from the 1950s.

ichthyologist, ichthyosaur *see* FISH

icicle [ME] Before a hanging, tapering piece of ice was an icicle it was an **ickle**. In the early Middle Ages people put **ice** and **ickle** together to form a compound; writers spelled the term as two words into the 17th century, but then speakers lost sight of its origins and icicle emerged as the standard term.

icon [M16th] Greek *eikōn*, the source of icon, meant 'likeness, image'. The earliest use in English was for a simile, a figure of speech in which two things are compared, as in 'as white as snow'. Later it meant 'a portrait, a picture', and especially an illustration in a natural history book. The 'portrait' sense partly continues in the modern use for 'a devotional painting of a holy figure'. The use to mean a celebrated figure such as a sporting or pop star dates from the early 1950s. Icons in computing, those symbols or graphic representations on VDU screens, appeared with the release of the Apple Macintosh computer in 1984. At various times in the history of the Christian Church, reformers, among them English Puritans in the 16th and 17th centuries, have condemned and destroyed religious images. Such a zealot is an **iconoclast** [M17th], a breaker of images—the -*clast* bit is from Greek *klan*, 'to break'. An iconoclast is now also a person who attacks a cherished belief or respected institution.

idiom [L16th] This goes back to Greek *idiōma* 'private or peculiar phraseology', from *idiousthai* 'make one's own' from Greek *idios* 'own, private'. **Idiosyncrasy** [E17th] is from *idios* combined with *sun* 'with' and *krasis* 'mixture', and originally meant 'physical constitution peculiar to an individual'.

idiot [ME] This comes via Latin *idiota* 'ignorant person', from Greek *idiōtēs* 'private person, layman, ignorant person' based on *idios* 'own, private', and reflecting the attitude in the ancient world to those who did not take an active part in public life.

idle [OE] Old English *īdel* included the sense 'empty, useless': it was often found in the combination *idle yelp* 'boasting'. However, the sense 'lazy' or 'with nothing to do' was inherent in the original meanings of the word.

idol [ME] Both **idyll** [L16th] and idol go back to Greek *eidos* 'form, shape, picture'. Its earliest uses in English were for false gods, images that people revered as objects of worship, and that Jewish and Christian tradition condemned. Outside religion, any object of excessive devotion has been called an idol since the mid 16th century, mainly in a condemnatory way. No one wanted to be a **pop idol** until the end of the 20th century, but in the 21st century it is such a common ambition that the reality TV contest *Pop Idol* has been an outstanding success. It is the 'picture' element that is prominent in idyll—a picture in words. When English adopted the word it meant 'description of a picturesque scene or incident', which is the sense in the title of Alfred Lord Tennyson's series of poems based on Arthurian legend, *The Idylls of the King*. Tennyson's popularization of the term in the mid 19th century led to the word **idyllic** and the development of the usual modern sense, 'an extremely happy, peaceful, or picturesque period or situation'.

igloo *see* ESKIMO

ignition [E17th] Ignition initially meant heating something to the point of combustion or chemical change. The Latin *ignire* 'set on fire', from *ignis* 'fire' is also found in **igneous** rock [M17th] for solidified magma.

ignorance [ME] Ignorance is from Latin *ignorare* 'not to know', the source of **ignore** [LME], and **ignoramus** [L16th]. The poet Thomas Gray first expressed the thought that **ignorance is bliss** in 1742: 'Thought would destroy their paradise. / No more; where ignorance is bliss, / 'Tis folly to be wise.' In 1615 King James I attended a production of a farcical play by George Ruggle, a fellow of Clare College, Cambridge. Its title was *Ignoramus*, the name of a character in the play, and it satirized lawyers and their ignorance. The use of ignoramus for 'an ignorant person' appeared almost immediately afterwards. In Latin *ignoramus* means 'we do not know', which in legal Latin became 'we take no notice (of it)'. The original use of ignoramus in English was as the judgement that grand juries formerly made on indictments brought before them that they considered to be backed by too little evidence: they would 'find an ignoramus'.

ill [ME] Ill is from Old Norse *illr* 'evil', and the commonest modern sense, 'suffering from an illness or feeling unwell', developed in the later medieval period. Before then a person would be *SICK, as they still are in the USA. The idea of harm and evil is prominent in many English proverbs, such as **it's an ill wind that blows nobody any good**. This refers to the days of sailing ships. The wind might be blowing in the wrong direction for you, but it was sure to be blowing the right way for someone, somewhere—it would be a very bad or 'ill' wind that was of no help to anyone.

illusion [ME] The first sense recorded for illusion was 'deception, attempt to fool'. It came via Old French from Latin *illudere* 'to mock, ridicule, make sport of', from *in-* 'against' and *ludere* 'play'. The prime modern sense of 'a false idea or belief' dates from the late 18th century.

image [ME] The word image goes back to Latin *imago* 'imitation, likeness, idea', also behind **imitation** [LME]. **Imagine** [ME] is closely related, coming from a combination of Latin *imaginare* 'form an image of, represent' and *imaginari* 'picture to oneself '.

imam *see* ARABIC WORD PANEL

imbecile [M16th] Originally a person described as imbecile was physically weak. The root meaning may be 'without a supporting staff', from Latin *baculum* 'stick, staff' (*see* BACTERIUM). The current sense dates from the early 19th century.

imbibe *see* BEER

idle idol igloo ignition ignorance ill illusion

imitation *see* IMAGE

immaculate [LME] For centuries Christian theologians had argued over whether God had preserved the Virgin Mary from the taint of original sin from the moment she was conceived. In 1854 the Vatican declared in favour of **the Immaculate Conception** and it became a dogma of the Roman Catholic Church. The term involves the earliest, sense of **immaculate**, 'free from moral stain', from Latin *in-* 'not' and *macula* 'spot'. The physical sense, 'spotlessly clean or neat', dates only from the early 19th century. Similarly, **impeccable** [M16th] originally meant 'incapable of sin', and is still used in this sense in theology, where it has an opposite, **peccable** [E17th] 'liable to sin'.

immigrate *see* MIGRATE

immune [LME] Latin *immunis* 'exempt from public service' (literally 'not ready for service') is the source of immune and **immunity**. The early sense of immune was 'free from (a liability)' and this general meaning was common from the 15th to 17th centuries. The sense 'able to resist infection' dates from the late 19th century.

imp [E17th] Plants were the original imps. The word goes back to Greek *phuein* 'to plant'. The Old English sense 'a young shoot of a plant' became 'a descendant, especially of a noble family' in the late Middle Ages, and from there developed into 'a child of the devil'. Mischievous children began to be called imps in the mid 17th century. The Hillman company gave the name Imp to its new small car in 1963—it never matched the success of its rival, the Mini.

impact *see* IMPINGE

impale *see* PALE

impart, impartial *see* PART

impeccable *see* IMMACULATE

impel *see* APPEAL

imperative, imperial, imperious *see* EMPEROR

impersonate *see* PERSON

impetuous *see* COMPEL

impetus *see* COMPETE

impinge [M16th] The word impinge is from Latin *impingere* 'drive something in or at', from *in-* 'into' and *pangere* 'fix, drive'. The word originally meant 'thrust at forcibly'. **Impact** [E17th] comes from the past form of the same source.

implacable *see* PLEASE

implode *see* EXPLODE

implore [E16th] The word implore comes from Latin *implorare* 'invoke with tears'.

import *see* TRANSPORT

important [LME] This comes from Latin *importare* 'be of consequence'.

importune [M16th] Portunus, the name of the god who protected harbours (from *portus* 'harbour'), lies behind this word. A lack of the safety and calm associated with his protection is found in this word and in **inopportune** 'troublesome, bringing problems'.

impose *see* COMPOST

improvement [LME] The early spelling was *emprowement* used to mean 'profitable management, profit'. It derives from Anglo-Norman French, based on Old French *prou* 'profit', ultimately from Latin *prodest* 'is of advantage'.

impudent [LME] In the Middle Ages people who were impudent were lacking in shame or modesty rather than presumptuous or cheeky, for it comes from the Latin *pudere* 'to be ashamed'. The modern sense developed in the mid 16th century.

impulsive *see* APPEAL

imitation immaculate immigrate immune

in *see* INN, INNINGS, UTTER

inadvertent *see* ADVERTISEMENT

inane [M16th] This is from Latin *inanis* 'empty, vain'. The sense 'silly, senseless' dates from the beginning of the 19th century.

inaugural [L17th] This is the adoption of a French word coming from Latin *inaugurare* 'take omens from the flight of birds'. *See* AUSPICIOUS

incandescent [L18th] This comes via French, from Latin *incandescere* 'glow', based on *candidus* 'white' (*see* CANDIDATE). The prefix *in-* here intensifies the meaning. The **incense** [ME] that you burn comes from the related *candere* 'to glow', while the word meaning 'to inflame with anger' comes from the related *incendere* 'set fire to' also found in **incendiary** [LME].

incantation *see* ENCHANT, INCENTIVE

incapacity *see* CAPABLE

incarcerate [M16th] Latin *carcer* 'prison' is the base of this word from medieval Latin *incarcerare* 'imprison'.

incarnation *see* CARNIVAL

incendiary, incense *see* INCANDESCENT

incentive [LME] Modern management gurus may not realize it, but when they advocate incentives they are invoking magic. The word is closely related to **incantation** [LME], 'words said as a magic spell or charm'. The root of both is Latin *incantare* 'to chant, charm', from *cantare* 'to sing', the source also of **chant** [LME]. In the general sense 'a thing that motivates or encourages someone to do something', incentive entered English in the Middle Ages, but it took until the 1940s for incentives to be offered to workers. The first **incentive payments** were proposed in early 1940 as a way to encourage US farmers to plant new crops. *See also* ENCHANT

inch [OE] The inch and the *OUNCE have the same ultimate origin, both going back to Latin *uncia* 'twelfth part'. The observation **give someone an inch and they will take a mile** dates from the mid 16th century. Originally people often took an **ell** rather than a mile (an ell is an old measure equal to just over a metre, used especially for cloth). The inch in the name of some Scottish islands, such as Inchcolm, is a completely different word, deriving from Scottish Gaelic *innis* 'island, land by a river'.

incident *see* ACCIDENT

incision [LME] Latin *incidere* 'cut into' is the source of several words: incision; **incisive** [LME] first used in the sense 'cutting, penetrating'; **incise** [M16th]; and **incisor** [L17th] from a medieval Latin word meaning literally 'cutter'.

incline *see* LEAN

incognito [M17th] The word incognito, 'having your true identity concealed', came from Italian in the mid 17th century. The Latin root is *cognoscere* 'to know' (*see also* QUAINT). At first incognito could mean simply 'unknown', without any implication of disguise or concealment, and was used mainly of royals or dignitaries who did not want to be recognized. In the 20th century the theatre critic Kenneth Tynan (1927–80) wrote, 'The disguise . . . renders him as effectively incognito as a walrus in a ballet-skirt'.

incorporate *see* CORPSE

incorrigible *see* CORRECT

increase *see* CRESCENT

incredulous *see* CREDIT

incubation, incumbent *see* CUBICLE

incur *see* CURSOR

indefatigable *see* FATIGUE

indent [LME] Although their meanings have in common an idea of a gap or notch, there are two completely unrelated words indent in English. One, meaning 'to make a dent or impression in', is formed directly from **dent** [ME] 'a hollow made by a blow or pressure', which is a variant form of *DINT. The other goes back to Latin *dens* 'tooth', the source of **dental** [L16th] and related words. Its first meaning was 'to give a zigzag outline to', like a set of sharp teeth. The legal term **indenture** [LME], 'a legal document, contract, or agreement', is related. Before the days of easy duplication, lawyers would write out the same contract twice on a single piece of parchment or paper. They would then separate the two sections with a serrated or wavy edge and give one to each party. If ever there was a dispute, the fact that the two edges fitted together was proof that they were the same agreement.

index [LME] In Latin *index* meant 'forefinger, informer, sign', Its second part is related to *dicare* 'to make known', also the source of **indicate** [E17th] and related words. The earliest uses in English refer to the finger that we would now usually call the **index finger**. Because this finger is used for pointing, index came to mean 'a pointer', either a physical one or some piece of knowledge that points to a fact or conclusion. And because a list of topics in a book points to their location in the text, publishers and scholars gave such a list the name index in the late 16th century.

Indian [M16th] Christopher Columbus set sail from Europe in 1492 with the main object of reaching Asia and proving that the world was round. When his ships reached the New World—in fact some Caribbean islands—he believed that he had reached India, and so it seemed natural to give the name Indian to the indigenous inhabitants of the Americas. The name of the West Indies arose from the same mistake. People felt the need to make clearer this double use of Indian, for the peoples of the Indian subcontinent and of the Americas. At first the latter were often called Red Indians, but this is now considered offensive. **American Indian** was another solution, but many now prefer to avoid the term Indian altogether, and use **Native American**. **Indian summer**, a period of unusually dry, warm weather in late autumn, refers to North America rather than Asia. The phenomenon is first mentioned towards the end of the 18th century in the USA, and was not adopted in Britain until the late Victorian period. India itself is named after the mighty River Indus, which flows from Tibet through Kashmir and Pakistan into the Arabian Sea, and the word is related to **Hindi** [E19th] and **Hindu** [M17th]. India gives its name to **indigo** [M16th], originally meaning 'Indian dye'.

indicate *see* INDEX

indigo *see* INDIAN

individual *see* DIVIDE

indolent [M17th] It now means 'lazy', but indolent was originally a medical term, referring to an ulcer or tumour that caused no pain to the patient. This reflects its root, Latin *in-* 'not' and *dolere* 'to suffer or give pain'.

indomitable [M17th] 'Untameable' was the early sense, from late Latin *indomitabilis* 'not able to be tamed'.

induce *see* DUCT

industry [LME] The first sense recorded for industry was 'hard work'. It comes from Latin *industria* 'diligence'. The meaning 'trade, manufacture' is found from the mid 16th century.

inept *see* APT

inert, inertia *see* ART

infant [LME] This is from Latin *in-* 'not' and *fari* 'to speak'. According to law, an infant is a person who has not reached the age of legal majority, so is unable to speak for themselves in law. The Italian equivalent *infante* meant 'youth' and also 'foot soldier', from which arose *infanteria*, a body of foot soldiers. English adopted this as **infantry** in the late 16th century.

infect [LME] The words infect and **infection** [LME] are both from Latin *inficere* 'to taint, dip in', from *in-* 'into' and *facere* 'put, do'.

infer [LME] The early sense recorded for infer is 'bring about, inflict' from Latin *inferre* 'bring in, bring about', which in medieval Latin came to mean 'deduce'. The base elements are *in-* 'into' and *ferre* 'bring'. Infer expresses the idea that something in the speaker's words enables the listener to 'deduce' what is meant; **imply** [LME] from Latin *implicare* 'fold in', expresses the notion that something in the speaker's words 'suggests' a certain meaning.

inferno [M19th] In the early 14th century the Italian poet Dante Alighieri wrote *The Divine Comedy*, describing his journey through hell and purgatory and finally to paradise. The description of hell in particular, the 'Inferno', had a lasting impact on the European imagination. The word came to mean 'hell' and then 'any fire raging out of control'. Italian *inferno* comes from Latin *infernus* 'below, subterranean', which is also the source of **infernal** [LME], and is related to **inferior** [LME].

infest [LME] This has the sense 'torment, harass' in early examples. It goes back to Latin *infestare* 'assail', from *infestus* 'hostile'. The current sense 'trouble in large numbers' dates from the mid 16th century.

infidel [LME] An infidel is a person who is 'not faithful'. The word goes back to Latin *infidelis* (the source, too, of **infidelity** [LME]), from *fides* *FAITH, and originally referred to a person of a religion other than your own. To a Christian an infidel was usually a Muslim, who would consider a Christian an infidel in return, and to a Jew an infidel would be a Gentile.

inflate [LME] The Latin verb *flare* 'to blow' is the base of inflate, which literally means 'blow into'. **Deflate** [M19th] is its opposite.

inflection *see* FLEX

inflict *see* AFFLICT

influenza [M18th] Italy saw an outbreak of a severe respiratory ailment in 1743. The English minister to Tuscany, Sir Horace Mann, wrote of Rome that 'Everybody is ill of the *Influenza*, and many die'. The epidemic spread throughout Europe, and in English influenza became the general term for this type of contagious viral infection. The English shortened influenza to the more familiar **flu** in the mid 19th century. Italian *influenza* means '**influence**' and derives from Latin *fluere* 'to flow'. The Italian word also had the sense 'an outbreak of an epidemic', and so 'an epidemic'. *Compare* MALARIA

ingenious *see* ENGINE

ingrain [LME] This was originally written as *engrain* in the sense 'dye with cochineal or in fast colours' from the old use of *GRAIN meaning 'kermes, cochineal' (*see also* CRIMSON). In the late Middle Ages truly fast colours were rare.

ingredients *see* PROGRESS

inhalation [E17th] The Latin *halare* 'to breathe' lies behind both to **inhale** [E18th] and the much earlier **exhale** [LME].

inimical *see* ENEMY

iniquity *see* EQUAL

initial [E16th] Initial comes from Latin *initium* 'beginning', from *inire* 'go in (to)'.

inject *see* JET

injury *see* JUDGE

ink [ME] Roman emperors used a purple fluid for writing their signatures, which was called in Latin *encaustum*, from Greek *enkaiein* 'to burn in'. Ink formed from this, reached English through French in the Middle Ages. The black liquid ejected by a cuttlefish to confuse predators has been called ink since the late 16th century.

inn [OE] An inn was originally any dwelling place or lodging. The word is related to **in**— an inn is a place you live or stay *in*. Medieval

infer   inferno   infest   infidel   inflate

translators used it for Latin *hospitium*, meaning 'a residence for students'. This survives in the **Inns of Court** in London, the buildings of the four legal societies with the exclusive right of admitting people to the English bar. The usual modern sense of 'a public house' dates from the late Middle Ages—an inn specialized in providing accommodation and refreshment for travellers, as opposed to a tavern [ME, from Latin *taberna*], which was just for drinking. **Inmate** [L16th] was probably originally an 'inn mate' and was initially a person who shared a house, specifically a lodger or subtenant. In the 16th and 17th centuries there were strict by-laws about harbouring poor people as inmates: this was a practice that caused the number of local paupers to increase.

innards [early 19th century] This represents a dialect pronunciation of *inwards*, used as a noun. The more respectable **intestine** [L16th] means much the same, coming from the Latin for 'internal'.

innate *see* NATION

inner *see* UTTER

innings [OE] In cricket a team or batsman has an innings or turn at batting, but in baseball a batter has an **inning**. The word inning itself goes back to Old English, when it meant 'putting or getting in', and derives from **in**. Cricket has given many expressions to English, among them to **have had a good innings**, 'to have had a long and fulfilling life or career'. The first example of this extended meaning is in Charles Dickens's *The Pickwick Papers*, published in 1836.

innocent [ME] Literally meaning 'not harming', innocent goes back to Latin *in-* 'not' and *nocere* 'to hurt, injure', which also lies behind **nuisance** [LME], **noxious** [LME] 'harmful', its opposite **innocuous** [L16th], and **obnoxious** [L16th].

innovate *see* NEW

innuendo [M16th] Early legal documents would introduce an explanation of a word

with innuendo, meaning 'that is to say, to wit', as in 'he (*innuendo* the plaintiff) is a thief' from a mid 17th-century glossary. Innuendo comes from a Latin word meaning 'by nodding at, by pointing to', from *in* 'towards' and *nuere* 'to nod'. In the late 17th century it became possible to have an innuendo, 'an explanation', and also the modern sense, 'an oblique remark or hint'.

inoculate [LME] Originally inoculation was a task of gardeners rather than of doctors and nurses. To inoculate something was to graft a bud or shoot into a plant of a different type. This corresponds to its Latin source *inoculare* 'to graft', from *in-* 'into' and *oculus* 'eye, bud' (as in **binocular** [E18th] and **ocular** [L16th]). The horticultural sense dates from the late Middle Ages. As a medical procedure people could inoculate a person from the early 18th century—its first uses referred to the treatment of smallpox. *See also* VACCINE

inopportune *see* IMPORTUNE

inordinate *see* COORDINATE

inquest [ME] English words that come from Latin *inquirere* 'to ask for information' often have spellings with either *en-* or *in-*, with *en-* representing the older form acquired through French and *in-* a return to the Latin root. This is the case, for instance, with **enquire** [ME] or **inquire** [LME], **enquiry** [LME] or **inquiry** [M16th], and used to apply to **inquest**, although the spelling **enquest** has not been used since the 18th century. In Britain an inquest is now usually an inquiry by a coroner's court into the cause of a death; formerly it could be any official inquiry into a matter of public interest.

Another word from Latin *inquirere* is **inquisition** [LME]. In the mid 13th century Pope Gregory IX established a tribunal for the suppression of heresy. This was the first Inquisition, which was active chiefly in northern Italy and southern France, and became notorious for the use of torture. In 1478 **the Spanish Inquisition** began to target converts from Judaism and Islam, later extending its reach to Protestants. It

innards innate inner innings innocent

operated with great severity and was not suppressed until the early 19th century. Mention the word to many people, and they will immediately cry, 'No one expects the Spanish Inquisition!' The classic Monty Python sketch featured Michael Palin as Cardinal Ximinez, who appears suddenly with two junior cardinals when anyone innocently says, 'I didn't expect a kind of Spanish Inquisition'.

insane *see* SANE

inscribe *see* SCRIPTURE

inscrutable [LME] Inscrutable is from ecclesiastical Latin *inscrutabilis*, from *in-* 'not' and *scrutari* 'to search' also found in **scrutiny** [LME].

insect [E17th] Insects have bodies that are divided into segments, and segments are the basic idea behind the word. Insect was formed in the 17th century from Latin *animal insectum* 'segmented animal', and originally referred to any small cold-blooded creature with a segmented body, for example, a spider, not just what we would call insects. The root word is *secare* 'to cut', which gave us **dissect** [L16th], **section** [LME], and **segment** [L16th].

insecure *see* SURE

insignia *see* SEAL

insinuate [E16th] This word was first used in legal contexts in the sense 'enter (a document) on the official register'. Latin *insinuare* 'introduce tortuously' is the source, from *in-* 'in' and *sinuare* 'to curve', from *sinus* 'a bend' found in the **sine** of mathematics, **sinuous,** and the **sinus** (all late 16th century). Nearly all the English senses were already in Latin.

insipid [E17th] The word insipid goes back to late Latin *insipidus*, from *in-* 'not' and *sapidus,* from *sapere* 'to taste'.

insist *see* CONSIST

insolent [LME] Early uses included the sense 'extravagant, going beyond

acceptable limits'. Insolent comes from Latin *insolent-* meaning 'immoderate, unaccustomed, arrogant' formed from *solere* 'be accustomed'.

insomnia *see* SOMNOLENT

inspire *see* SPIRIT

instead *see* STEAD

instinct [LME] The word instinct is from Latin *instinctus* 'impulse', from the verb *instinguere*: the base is Latin *stinguere* 'to prick' which gives a core notion of 'urge'.

institute *see* CONSTITUTION

insular [M16th] The earliest use of insular, in the mid 16th century, was as a noun meaning 'an islander'. Islanders were popularly regarded as narrow-minded and ignorant of people and cultures outside their own experience, and the adjective insular later developed this meaning. The word itself goes back to Latin *insula* 'island', the source also of **isle** (*see* ISLAND), and of **insulate** [M16th], and **insulin** [E20th]. The hormone insulin, produced by the pancreas, gets its name from the islets of Langerhans, the group of pancreatic cells that secrete it. Paul Langerhans was the 19th-century German anatomist who first described them.

insult [M16th] An insult was originally an attack or assault, especially a military one. Sir Walter Scott (1771–1832) in his poem *Marmion* wrote: 'Many a rude tower and rampart there / Repelled the insult of the air.' The word goes back to Latin *insultare* 'to jump or leap upon'. The phrase to **add insult to injury** comes from the 1748 play *The Foundling* by Edmund Moore.

insurrection *see* SURGE

intellect [LME] The words intellect, **intelligence,** and **intelligible**, all from the same period, go back to Latin *intellegere* literally 'to choose between' but used for 'to understand'.

intend [ME] The early spelling was *entend* which meant 'direct the attention to', from Old French *entendre* from Latin *intendere* 'intend, extend, direct', literally 'stretch towards'. **Intense** [LME] comes from a past form of the Latin, and **superintendent** [M16th] is from Latin *superintendere* 'to oversee'.

intercede *see* CEDE

intercept *see* CAPABLE

intercourse *see* CURSOR

interim [M16th] The Reformation produced upheaval in 16th-century Europe, and nowhere more so than in Germany. The Holy Roman Emperor Charles V attempted to settle the differences between the German Protestants and the Roman Catholic Church, making three provisional arrangements pending a settlement by a general council. This was called **the Interim**, and was reported in English in a diplomatic letter of July 1548. In Latin *interim* meant 'meanwhile'. Very quickly people were using interim for other provisional arrangements, and then for 'an intervening time, the meantime'.

interloper [L16th] An interloper was originally an unauthorized trader trespassing on the rights of a trade monopoly. The word was coined in the late 16th century, and is truly a hybrid. The first element derives from Latin *inter* 'between, among', while the second is extracted from **landloper**, an old word for a vagabond or tramp taken from Dutch.

interlude [ME] Performances of medieval miracle plays could last all day, so to provide variety and relieve tension, performers would introduce short and often humorous dramatic pieces between the acts, which were the original interludes. The word derives from Latin *inter* 'between, among' and *ludus* 'a play'. By the 17th century people were using interlude for the interval of time between the acts of a play, and by the 18th for any intervening time, space, or event.

intermediate *see* MEDIOCRE

interrupt *see* CORRUPT

intersperse *see* ASPERSION

interval [ME] The word interval is from Old French *entrevalle*, based on Latin *intervallum* 'space between ramparts, interval', from *inter-* 'between' and *vallum* 'rampart'.

intestate *see* TESTICLE

intestine *see* INNARDS

intoxicate *see* TOXIC

intrepid *see* TREMENDOUS

intrigue [E17th] There is an intriguing link between **intrigue** and **intricate** [LME]. Both ultimately derive from Latin *intricare* 'to entangle, perplex'. Intricate came directly from the Latin word in the late Middle Ages, whereas intrigue lived an independent life, developing into Italian *intrigare*, which passed through French into English in the 17th century. The original English meaning was 'to trick, perplex'. The modern sense 'to arouse curiosity or interest' dates only from the late 19th century and shows the influence of a later development in French.

introduce *see* DUCT

Inuit *see* ESKIMO

inundate *see* WATER

invade [LME] The early sense was 'attack or assault (a person)'. The source is Latin *invadere*, from *in-* 'into' and *vadere* 'go'.

invention [ME] 'Finding out, discover' rather than creating is the base sense of invention, which comes from Latin *invenire* 'discover, come upon' from *in-* 'into, upon', and *venire* 'come'. **Inventory** [LME] 'a list of what is found' is from the same source.

invest [M16th] The root of invest is Latin *vestis* 'clothes', also the source of **vest** [LME], and which shares an Indo-European root with **wear** [OE]. Latin *investire* meant 'to put clothes on someone', and was the sense of invest when it entered English in the mid 16th century. Someone being formally installed in a job or office would once have been ceremonially dressed in special clothing, and this is behind the sense 'to formally confer a rank or office on someone'. The main modern use of the word is financial—putting money into a commercial venture with the expectation of profit. This came into English under the influence of a related Italian word in the early 17th century, apparently through a comparison between putting money into various enterprises and dressing it in a variety of clothing.

investigation *see* VESTIGE

inveterate *see* VETERAN

invidious *see* ENVY

invigilate *see* VIGIL

invigorate *see* VIGOUR

invoke *see* VOICE

involve *see* REVOLVE

invulnerable *see* VULNERABLE

iris [LME] In classical mythology Iris was the goddess of the rainbow and a messenger of the gods. People saw the rainbow as a bridge or road let down from heaven for her to carry her messages along. The Latin and Greek word *iris*, taken from her name and meaning 'rainbow', is also in **iridescent** and the name of the chemical element **iridium**, which forms compounds of various colours. The name iris for the membrane behind the cornea of the eye appears to derive from the variety of its colours. As a name for a flowering plant, iris dates from the late Middle Ages.

irk [ME] Work irks many people, and may be related to irk, which possibly derives from Old Norse *yrkja* 'to work, take effect upon'. Its earliest sense in English was 'to be annoyed or disgusted'.

iron [OE] The English word iron probably came from Celtic and was related to Latin *aes* 'bronze' and English **ore** [OE]. There are many different tools and implements described as **irons** because they are or were originally made of iron, such as branding irons and fire irons. The expression to **have many irons in the fire**, 'to have a range of options', comes from the way such tools are made. Blacksmiths have to heat the iron objects in a fire until they reach the critical temperature at which they can be shaped. If they have several items in the forge at the same time they can remove one and hammer it until it has cooled, then return it to the fire to heat up again and work on another. Another phrase from the work of a blacksmith is to **strike while the iron is hot**, 'to make use of an opportunity immediately'.

In a speech made in March 1946, Winston Churchill observed that 'an iron curtain has descended across the Continent [of Europe]'. People often cite this as the origin of **the Iron Curtain**, the notional barrier separating the former Soviet bloc and the West before the decline of communism after 1989, but the phrase had been used in reference to the Soviet Union in the 1920s, and had the more general meaning of 'an impenetrable barrier' as far back as the early 19th century. Its origins actually lie in the theatre. Today's theatres employ a flame-resistant fire curtain, which in the late 18th century would have been of metal, a genuine iron curtain. In 1948 the term **Bamboo Curtain** arose to refer to the then-impenetrable barrier between China and non-Communist countries. Margaret Thatcher, then soon to become British prime minister, was given the nickname **the Iron Lady** in January 1976 by the Soviet newspaper *Red Star*. The paper accused her of trying to revive the Cold War. **Irony** [E16th] has no connection with iron. It came from Greek *eirōneia* 'pretended ignorance'. *See also* VELVET

Islam *see* ARABIC WORD PANEL

island [OE] In spite of their similarity of form and meaning, island and isle [ME] are completely unrelated. The first is a native English word, with parallels in early forms of other north European languages, whereas the second came through French from Latin in medieval times. The first part of Old English *īegland* is *īeg* 'island', from a root meaning 'watery'. People wrongly associated it with isle, and in the 16th century changed the spelling accordingly. In fact there was no 's' in isle in the Middle Ages either: it was spelled *ile*, as it was in French at the time of its adoption.

In the 15th century both French and English people connected the word—this time correctly—with Latin *insula*, and added the 's'. *See also* INSULAR, PENINSULA. The English poet and preacher John Donne (1572–1631) memorably expressed the view that the lives and fates of humans are interconnected in *Devotions upon Emergent Occasions* (1624): 'No man is an island, entire of itself; every man is a piece of the Continent, a part of the main;...any man's death diminishes me, because I am involved in mankind; And therefore never send to know for whom the bell tolls; it tolls for thee.' **Isolated** [M18th] is related to isle, coming from Latin *insulatus* 'made into an island'.

issue *see* EXIT

Make mine a cappuccino

The **Italian** *loves of food, music, and the good life have injected bright colours into English usage. At the other extreme, the Italian language of crime, captured on film and TV, has infiltrated talk of murkier areas of life.*

I F you want pasta cooked so that it is still firm when you bite into it, you should ask for it to be **al dente**, literally 'to the tooth'. Varieties of pasta include **fusilli** or 'little spirals' and **penne** or 'quills'—most were unknown in English until the 20th century, but **vermicelli** or 'little worms' and *MACARONI date back to the 17th century. A determined meat-eater might ask for **carpaccio**. This name for thin slices of raw meat comes from the surname of the medieval Italian painter Vittore Carpaccio (*c*.1460–1525/ 1526), because of his characteristic use of red pigments, resembling raw meat.

Baroness Frances Bunsen (1791–1876) was a diplomat's wife who travelled widely. A letter about one of her trips has given us the first mention of the **pizza**, in 1825: 'They gave us ham, and cheese, and *frittata* [a kind of omelette], and *pizza*.' The Italian word simply means 'pie'.

Some kinds of Italian food suggest their appeal rather than their look or shape, such as the veal dish **saltimbocca**, whose name means literally 'leap into the mouth'. The dessert **tiramisu** was unknown to English until the 1980s, since when the combination of coffee-and-brandy-soaked sponge

invulnerable   iris   irk   iron   Islam   island

and mascarpone cheese has become irresistible. The name comes from *tira mi sù* 'pick me up'.

After the meal you might have the strong black **espresso**, whose name comes from *caffè espresso* 'pressed-out coffee', or the milder **latte**, from *caffè latte* 'milk coffee'. A **macchiato**, espresso with a dash of frothy steamed milk, is short for *caffè macchiato*, literally 'stained or marked coffee'. In Italian **cappuccino** means 'Capuchin monk', probably because the drink's colour resembles a Capuchin's brown habit. The Capuchins are a branch of the Franciscan order that takes their name from the sharp-pointed hood worn by the monks—*cappuccio* in Italian, which is from the same root as **cape**. It is now found on every high street, but cappuccino has been known in English only since the 1940s.

A life of heedless pleasure and luxury is a **dolce vita**, or 'sweet life', a phrase brought into English by the 1960 film *La Dolce Vita*, directed by Federico Fellini. A lazy person who likes the idea of pleasant idleness is attracted to **dolce far niente**, literally 'sweet doing nothing'.

The term **fresco** for a painting done rapidly on wet plaster on a wall or ceiling means 'cool, fresh' in Italian. The same word is part of **al fresco**, meaning 'in the open air'—in English this phrase tends to refer to eating outdoors, as in this example from *GQ* magazine: 'Open 7 days a week...with *al fresco* dining in fine weather'. The phrase dates back to the 1750s in English and was used by Jane Austen.

Sheet music was first printed during the Renaissance by Italians, which is why Italian is the language of musical terms, a number of which have moved into the wider language. We might talk of excitement reaching a **crescendo**, a word originally used to indicate gradually increasing loudness in a piece of music. Someone might be speaking **fortissimo**, 'very loudly', or **sotto voce**, 'in a quiet voice'—literally 'under the voice'. Italian has also given us the names for different ranges of singing voice, including **alto** 'high', **soprano**, from *sopra* 'above', and **baritone**, which is ultimately from Greek *barus* 'heavy' and *tonos* 'tone'. Many of the great opera singers have been Italian, and *OPERA itself is the Italian word for 'work'.

Films like *The Godfather* (1972) and *Goodfellas* (1990), and the more recent television series *The Sopranos*, have familiarized us with some of the enigmatic vocabulary associated with the *MAFIA. Members practise **omertà**, or a code of silence, which is a dialect form of **umità** 'humility'. Within the group the adviser to the leader, who resolves internal disputes, is known as the **consigliere**, literally 'member of a council'. Presumably it is only after his arts have failed that someone may reach for his **lupara**, or sawn-off shotgun, a slang term that comes from *lupa* 'she-wolf'. A high-ranking member of the Mafia is a **don**, a word also used for a British university teacher, which comes from Latin *dominus* 'master'.

See also CONFETTI, FIASCO, GHETTO, GRAFFITI, INFERNO, INFLUENZA, MALARIA, PANTALOONS, PASTE, TENOR

item [LME] Originally item was used to introduce each new article or particular in a list or document. In Shakespeare's *Twelfth Night* Olivia mocks attempts to shower her with exaggerated praise: '[My beauty] shall be inventoried and every particle and utensil labelled to my will, as, *item*, two lips, indifferent red; *item*, two grey eyes, with lids to them; *item*, one neck, one chin, and so forth.' This use for 'likewise, also' reflects its source, Latin *item* 'just so, similarly, moreover'. From there item started to refer to a statement or maxim of the type often introduced by the word 'item', then to an individual article or unit. A couple have been **an item** since around 1970, at first in the USA.

ivory [ME] The Latin word *ebur*, from which ivory derives, is related to ancient Egyptian *āb* or *ābu* 'elephant'. Before poachers reduced elephant numbers, ivory was an important item of commerce, used for many functional items as well as for ornaments. The 'white' piano keys were made of ivory, and to **tickle** or **tinkle the ivories** is a familiar expression for 'to play the piano'. An **ivory tower** is a state of privileged seclusion or separation from the facts and practicalities of the real world. The phrase is an early 20th-century translation of French *tour d'ivoire*, used in 1837 by the critic and writer Charles Augustin Sainte-Beuve.

Isolated issue item ivories ivory ivory tower

jabber *see* CHAT

jack [LME] In the Middle Ages Jack, a pet form of John, was used to refer to any ordinary man, much as Tom, Dick, and Harry is today. By the 16th century it also meant a young man, and from this we get an alternative name for the **knave** (from the Old English for 'boy') in cards. In the 18th century a jack was a labourer, which gives us the second part of words like **lumberjack** [M19th] and **steeplejack** [L19th]. A jack was also an unskilled worker as contrasted with the master of a trade who had completed an apprenticeship, from which we get the saying **jack of all trades and master of none**. On the other hand, the apprentice could assert his equality with the words **Jack is as good as his master**. *See also* JOCKEY

A jack can also be a thing of smaller than normal size. Examples include the jack in bowls—a smaller bowl placed as a mark for the players to aim at—and jack as in **Union Jack** [L17th], which is strictly speaking a small version of the national flag flown on board ship. **Jack-o-lantern** as a name for a pumpkin lantern made at Halloween looks back to an earlier use of the phrase. In the 17th century it was a name for a **will-o'-the-wisp** [E17th], a light seen hovering at night over marshy ground, from another common first name—exchanging the idea of Jack with a lantern for Will with a 'wisp', or handful of lighted hay. **I'm all right, Jack** is an early 20th-century catchphrase used to express selfish complacency, which became the title of a film starring Peter Sellers in 1959. The **Jack Russell terrier** is named after a 19th-century English clergyman, known as 'the Sporting Parson', who was famed in hunting circles for breeding these terriers. Today a **jackpot** [L19th] is a large cash prize in a game or lottery. The term was originally used in a form of poker, where the pool or pot accumulated until a player could open the bidding with two jacks or better.

jacket [LME] Jacket is from Old French *jaquet*, a diminutive of *jaque*, a word for a kind of tunic. The origin of the French word is uncertain, but it may have been identical with the common given name *Jacques* (a form of James—*compare* JACK) and be associated with a garment worn by the common people. An alternative theory takes *jaques de mailles*, a tunic of chain mail, as the original form and links it via Spanish *jaco* to Arabic *sakk* 'breastplate'.

jade [LME] Since the Middle Ages a worn-out horse has been described as a jade, although the origin of the word is unknown. When a tired person describes themselves as **jaded** [L16th], they are looking back to this use, rather than to the sense of jade as 'a headstrong or disreputable woman', which developed in the mid 16th century. *See also* HACK, NAG. Jade as a name for a hard bluish-green precious stone is a different word. It comes from Spanish *piedra de ijada*, literally 'stone of the side or flank', from the belief that it was a cure for colic. This word dates from the late 16th century.

jag, jagged *see* JOG

jail [ME] The words jail and **cage** [ME] both go back to Latin *cavea* 'hollow, cave, cell', from *cavus* 'hollow' the source of *CAVE. In Late Latin the *-ea* at the end of *cavea* softened to a 'ya' or 'ja' sound, which explains the sound changes between the source and the forms we use. Jail arrived in medieval English in two forms, from Old French *jaiole* and Anglo-Norman *gaole*, which survives in the old-fashioned British spelling **gaol**.

jam [E18th] The British have been eating a preserve called **jam** since the 18th century. The best jam is packed with fruit, and its name probably comes from the verb jam meaning 'cram' or 'squeeze'. The saying **jam tomorrow and jam yesterday, but never jam today** comes from Lewis Carroll's *Through the Looking-Glass* (1872), where the White

jabber   jack   jacket   jade   jag   jagged

Queen explains to Alice that, 'The rule is, jam tomorrow and jam yesterday—but never jam today.' In Britain if you are **jammy** you are lucky, but in Australia you are rather posh or affected. In Victorian slang the word first simply meant 'excellent'. **Traffic jams** are an everyday reality, but the first jams were on rivers, not roads. From the beginning of the 19th century loggers talked of jams of logs being floated downriver—the original **logjam**. By the 1850s references to 'carriage jams' can be found. *See also* MONEY

jamb [ME] Jamb as a term for a post of a doorway or window is from Old French *jambe* 'leg, vertical support', based on Greek *kampē* 'joint'.

janitor [M16th] A caretaker or doorkeeper in North America is referred to as a janitor, a word that was borrowed into English from Latin *junua* 'door'. This comes from Janus, the name of an ancient Italian god regarded as the doorkeeper of heaven, and the guardian of doors and gates. He was traditionally represented with two faces, so that he could look both backwards and forwards. **January** comes from a Latin word meaning 'month of Janus', and marks the entrance to the year.

jar [LME] The jar that is a shock is late Middle English and is probably meant to be imitative. It was first used in the sense 'disagreement, dispute'. The jar you put things in dates from the late 16th century and comes via French from Arabic *jarra* 'earthen water vessel'. It has been used to mean a drink of beer since the 1920s.

jargon [LME] Modern life is full of jargon, language used by a particular group that is difficult for other people to understand. It comes from Old French *jargoun* 'the warbling of birds', and in medieval English meant 'twittering, chattering' and also 'gibberish'. Our current sense had developed by the 17th century. *See also* CHAT

jaundice *see* YELLOW

jaunty *see* GENTLE

jaywalk [E20th] The 'jay' in the word is the same as the bird, which has been used colloquially to mean 'silly person'.

jazz [E20th] We have been enjoying jazz since the early years of the 20th century, but no one is completely sure about the word's origin, although an enormous number of suggestions have been made, including an African origin. It seems that the original

How do you sudoku?

*From the ancient culture of the samurai to modern electronic gadgets, cutting-edge business terms, and foods such as sushi, **Japanese** has provided English with some distinctive Far Eastern touches.*

THE **samurai** were a powerful military class in feudal Japan, from the 7th to the 19th century, who carried the **katana**, a long, single-edged sword. Samurai warriors expert in **ninjutsu**, or stealthy spying, were known as **ninja**, from *nin* 'stealth, invisibility' and *sha* 'person, agent'. The term became well known from the **Teenage Mutant Ninja Turtles**, four cartoon turtles who first appeared in a US comic book in 1984. They were skilled ninja warriors, with a battle cry of 'Cowabunga!' (originally surfers'

jamb janitor jar jargon jaundice jaunty

slang), who battled criminals and alien invaders from their home in the sewers of Manhattan.

According to the **bushido**, or code of honour, a disgraced samurai was expected to commit suicide by the gruesome method of **hara-kiri** or **seppuku**. As the literal meaning of *hara-kiri* ('belly-cutting') implies, the samurai had to disembowel himself with a single stroke of a knife or short sword across the belly. As soon as he had made the cut his head was severed by a friend or 'second' to spare him further suffering.

Japanese martial arts, or forms of unarmed combat, were first known in Europe in the late 19th century. The name **aikido** is literally 'spirit way', **karate** means 'empty hand', **judo** is 'gentle way', and **ju-jitsu**, from which judo evolved, means 'gentle skill'.

By no means all Japanese terms used in English are aggressive. A **geisha**, or 'performing arts person', is a hostess trained to entertain men with conversation or dance and song—the geisha has been known in English since the end of the 19th century, as has the unsprung mattress the **futon**. **Bonsai**, the practice of cultivating artificially dwarfed potted plants or small trees, is literally 'tray planting', and came into English in the early 20th century, while **origami**, the art of folding paper, is a still more recent import, recorded only from the 1950s.

As the Second World War turned against them, Japanese pilots in the Pacific became suicide bombers, loading their aircraft with explosives, and deliberately crashing on to enemy targets. These were known as **kamikaze** attacks. The word *kamikaze* means literally 'divine wind', and referred originally to a supposedly divine wind which blew up in 1281 and destroyed the navy of the invading Mongols. Today the term is used of any reckless or apparently self-destructive behaviour, as in 'A wonderfully exhilarating night of gung-ho attacking and kamikaze defending' (*Guardian*, 2006).

After the war America occupied Japan, and many of its servicemen were stationed there. They brought back the word **honcho**, 'the person in charge', from Japanese *honchō* 'group leader'. It first appeared in print in 1947.

It was only at the end of the 1970s that British people first became aware of the often excruciating possibilities of **karaoke**. Both the word and the entertainment were borrowed from Japanese, where its literal meaning is 'empty orchestra'.

In the 1990s **manga** cartoons and **anime** cartoon films became popular in the West. Anime was taken by the Japanese from French and just means 'animated', whereas **manga** is from *man* 'indiscriminate', and *ga* 'picture'.

A **tamagotchi** is an egg-shaped electronic toy featuring a pet whose animated image is displayed on a screen, and whose needs are met by pushing buttons. The name is made up of the two words *tamago* 'egg' and *votchi* 'to watch'. It was chosen in 1996 by Japanese schoolgirls from a shortlist prepared by market researchers for the manufacturers.

The beginning of the 21st century saw many people become obsessed with Japanese number puzzles, in particular **sudoku**, which involves filling in a nine-by-nine grid of squares with the numbers 1 to 9. Its name is based on *su* 'number' and *doku* 'single', and is a shortening of its original Japanese name *Sūji wa dokushin ni kagiru*, which can be translated as 'only single numbers allowed' or 'numbers can only occur once'.

Since the 1980s an increasing number of Japanese business terms have become known in the West. In the **kanban** or **just-in-time system** the supply of components in a factory is regulated by the use of a card or sheet sent along the production line and to suppliers, ensuring that parts arrive exactly when they are required. **Kaizen** is a business philosophy of continuous improvement in working practices and personal efficiency. All this striving for improvement can be a strain for the **salarymen** and **office ladies**, as male and female workers are known—the term **karoshi**, 'death caused by overwork', was coined in the late 1980s.

See also MARCH, TSUNAMI, TYCOON

meaning may have been something like 'liveliness, energy, spirit'—in 1912 a baseball player said of his new way of pitching: 'I call it the Jazz ball because it wobbles and you simply can't do anything with it.' The first known musical use came in 1915 in Chicago. Jazz was also used with sexual connotations, and its source could be the slang word **jism** (M19th of unknown origin) 'semen'. **And all that jazz**, meaning 'and all that stuff, etcetera', has been around since the 1950s, but is currently particularly known as a song from the 1975 musical *Chicago*.

jealous [ME] This comes via Old French *gelos* and medieval Latin *zelosus* from Greek *zelos*, also the source of **zeal** [LME].

jeans [LME] Jeans go back to the late 15th century, when the name *jean fustian* was used for a kind of heavy cotton cloth. It meant literally 'fustian (a type of cloth) from Genoa', a city in Italy. Jeans as we know them today date from the 1860s, when Levi Strauss (1829–1902), founder of the **Levi's** company, started to make durable denim work trousers which became popular with cowboys in the Wild West. **Denim** [L17th]

was originally **serge denim**, from French *serge de Nîmes* 'serge of Nîmes', a city in the south of France. Serge is a woollen cloth, but modern denim is made of cotton.

Jeep [Second World War] The name of the Second World War Jeep originally came, in American English, from the initials 'GP', standing for 'general purpose'. It was probably also influenced by the name of 'Eugene the Jeep', a resourceful creature with superhuman powers that first appeared in the *Popeye* comic strip in 1936. *See also* GOON

jejune *see* DINNER

jelly [LME] In the Middle Ages jelly was a savoury dish of meat or fish set in a mould of aspic. The first references to fruit-flavoured jellies are not found until the late 18th century. The word comes ultimately from the Latin word *gelare* 'to freeze'. *See also* COLD

jeopardy [ME] The early spelling of jeopardy was *iuparti*. The word comes from Old French *ieu* (modern *jeu*) *parti* 'an evenly divided game', and was originally used in chess and similar games to mean a problem

jealous jeans Jeep jejune jelly jeopardy

or position in which the chances of winning or losing were evenly balanced. This led to the modern sense 'a dangerous situation' and the legal use 'danger arising from being on trial for a criminal offence'.

jerk [M16th] The word jerk was first recorded meaning 'a stroke with a whip'; it is probably imitative of the action. The slang use meaning 'fool, stupid person' is originally a US usage dating from the 1930s.

jerry-built [M19th] Poorly built houses have been described as jerry-built since the mid 19th century. The term is nothing to do with **Jerry**, a derogatory name for a German, probably based on the word 'German', that came out of the First World War. One suggestion is that jerry-built comes from the name of a firm of builders in Liverpool, or it may allude to the walls of Jericho, which in the biblical story fell down at the sound of Joshua's trumpet. The **jerrycan** [Second World War] *does* come from Jerry—it was originally used by Germans, but was adopted by the Allies in the Second World War.

jest [LME] In the Middle Ages a jest was not a joke but a notable exploit. It was spelled *gest*, and came from the Latin word *gesta* 'actions, exploits'. It has the same root as **gesture** [LME]. Jest came to be used for a narrative of someone's deeds, and from that became a word for 'an idle story' and then 'a joke'.

jet [L16th] The name jet for a hard black semi-precious mineral comes ultimately from the Greek word *gagatēs* 'from Gagai', a town in Asia Minor. When we refer to a jet of water or gas, or a jet aircraft, we are using a quite different word. It comes from a late 16th-century verb meaning 'to jut out', from French *jeter* 'to throw', which goes back to the Latin *jacere* 'to throw'. **Jut** [M16th] is a variant of jet in this sense. *Jacere* is found in a large number of English words including **abject** [LME] literally 'thrown away'; **conjecture** [LME] 'throw together'; **deject** [LME] 'thrown down'; **ejaculate** [L16th] from *jaculum* 'dart, something thrown'; **eject** [LME] 'throw out'; **inject** [L16th]

'throw in'; **jetty** [LME] something thrown out into the water; **project** [LME] 'throw forth'; **subject** [ME] 'thrown under'; **trajectory** [L17th] 'something thrown across'. Especially if you use budget airlines, air travel today is far from glamorous, but in the 1950s the idea of flying abroad by jet aircraft was new and sophisticated. At the start of that decade people who flew for pleasure came to be known as the **jet set**.

jetsam, jettison *see* FLOTSAM

jetty *see* JET

jewel [ME] Originally jewel meant a decorative piece worn for personal adornment, but later it came to specify an ornament containing a precious stone, or the stone itself. The origin suggests that adornment was linked with entertainment, as the word comes from French *jeu* 'game, play', and perhaps ultimately from Latin *jocus* 'jest'. *See also* JOKE, JUGGLE. **The jewel in the crown** is the most valuable or successful part of something. It was popularized as the title of a 1966 novel by Paul Scott, and of a 1980s BBC TV series that was based on this and other novels by Scott. The phrase was used in the early 1900s as a name for the colonies of the British Empire.

jiggery-pokery [L19th] This late 19th-century expression means 'deceitful or dishonest behaviour'. It is probably a variant of Scots *joukery-pawkery*, from *jouk* 'to skulk'.

jihad *see* ARABIC WORD PANEL

jingo [L17th] Originally a word said by conjurors when performing a magic trick, rather like *ABRACADABRA, jingo became used more widely in the expression 'by jingo!' to show how much in earnest a person was. In 1878 the British Prime Minister Benjamin Disraeli (1804–81) was determined to send a fleet into Turkish waters to resist Russia. Popular support for his policy included a music-hall song with the chorus: 'We don't want to fight, yet by Jingo! If we do, We've got the ships, we've got the men, and got the money too.' **Jingoism** as a word for an aggressive patriotism

jerk   jerry-built   jest   jet   jetsam   jettison

associated with vociferous support for a policy favouring war appeared in the language in the same year.

jink [L17th] This was originally Scots in the phrase **high jinks** referring to antics at drinking parties. These usually consisted of throwing dice to decide who should perform a silly task to amuse the others in the company, or who should drink a large draught of alcohol; a forfeit was involved. The word is probably symbolic of nimble motion. Current senses associated with a sudden change in direction date from the 18th century.

jism *see* JAZZ

jive [1920s] This was originally used in the US usage for meaningless or misleading speech. Its origin is unknown, but may be African. It came to be used for a type of fast jazz and for the slang of African American jazz musicians, with the meaning 'a dance performed to jazz' found in the 1940s.

jockey [L16th] A pet form of the man's name Jock, a northern form of *JACK, jockey was originally used, rather like Jack, for any ordinary man, boy, or underling. From this came a specialized sense of a servant as a mounted courier, which in the 17th century gave rise to today's meaning. In American slang a jockey was a specific kind of worker—so a **beer jockey** was a barmaid, a **garage jockey** a garage attendant, and a **typewriter jockey** a typist. From there it was natural to call someone who played records a **disc jockey**, in the 1940s.

jocund *see* JOKE

jodhpurs *see* RAJ WORD PANEL

jog [E16th] One of the most visible changes in society since the 1960s has been the number of joggers pounding round the streets. Few joggers will be aware that the original meaning of jog was 'to stab'. The word is related to **jag**, as in **jagged** [LME], and in Scotland and northern England to jag is still 'to prick'. The 'stab' sense was medieval; after that jog meant 'to shake or push' or 'to give a gentle nudge', and also 'to

walk or ride in a heavy or jolting way, trudge'.

join [ME] Join comes via Old French *joindre*, from Latin *jungere* 'to join' also found in **joint** [ME], used in butchery contexts from the late 16th century; **juncture** [LME] originally meaning 'joining'; and **junction** [E18th] which also started out in the sense 'joining'. Its use in transport is found from the late 18th century.

joke [L17th] Joke seems to have been a slang word at first, but it may well come from Latin *jocus* 'jest, wordplay', found also in **jocund** [LME], and **juggle** [LME]. *See also* JEWEL

jolly *see* YULE

Jones [E20th] *Keeping up with the Joneses* was the title of a comic strip by 'Pop' which first appeared in the New York *Globe* in 1913. 'Jones', which comes from the common given name John (*see* JACK), was used simply because it is one of the commonest British and American family names. Since the 1960s Jones has been used as a term for a drug habit or the cravings of an addict, although it took only a decade for the term to enter general slang for a craving, so you can now be **jonesing** for a coffee or even something in the shops. Its origin is not known, although there has been no shortage of theories, from Jones being the name (or pseudonym) of a dealer to linking it with Great Jones Alley in New York, said to be a hang-out of junkies.

jostle [LME] The early spelling was *justle*, from *just*, an earlier form of **joust** (*see* ADJUST). The original sense was 'have sexual intercourse with'; current senses date from the mid 16th century.

jot [LME] Greek *iōta* (ι), the smallest letter of the Greek alphabet, gave us jot as a word for a very small amount—'i' and 'j' being interchangeable forms in medieval writing. To stress that someone cannot have any part of something, we might use the phrase **not one jot** or **not one iota**, which reflects the warning given by Jesus in St Matthew's

Gospel that 'Till heaven and earth pass, one jot or **tittle** shall in no wise pass from the law' (a *tittle* here is a small stroke or accent). To jot something down appeared in the early 18th century and seems to have developed from the idea of a short sharp action as in writing a jot.

journal [LME] In the Middle Ages a journal was a book listing the times of daily prayers. It comes ultimately from the late Latin word *diurnalis* 'belonging to a day'. The use of the word to mean a personal diary, which in theory you filled in every day, comes in at the beginning of the 17th century. Journal meaning 'a daily newspaper' is first recorded from the early 18th century, but must be earlier as **journalist,** in the modern sense, dates from the late 17th century. The earliest senses of **journey** in Middle English were 'a day, a day's travel, a day's work'. Like journal, the word comes ultimately from the Latin *dies* 'day'. Today we use **journeyman** [LME] as a term for a worker or sports player who is reliable but not outstanding. This goes back to the Middle Ages when it was the name for someone who had served his apprenticeship but was not yet a master of his craft. He still worked for someone else, and got his name from the fact that he was paid by the day.

joust *see* ADJUST

jovial [L16th] When we describe a cheerful person as jovial, we are looking back to the Latin word *jovialis* 'of Jupiter'. This refers to the supposed influence of the planet Jupiter on those born under it. Jove is a poetical equivalent of Jupiter, the name of the most important god of the ancient Romans. *See also* SATURNINE

jowl *see* CHEEK

joy [ME] Joy is from Old French *joie*, based on Latin *gaudium*, from *gaudere* 'rejoice'. In **rejoice** [ME] the *re-* makes the sense more intense; **enjoy** [LME] comes from the Old French *enjoier* 'give joy to'.

jubilee [LME] Jubilee comes from a shortening of Latin *jubilaeus annus*, meaning 'year of jubilee', an expression based on *yōbēl* the Hebrew name for a special year, celebrated in Jewish history every 50 years, when slaves were freed and the fields were not cultivated. The original sense of the Hebrew word was 'ram's-horn trumpet', with which the jubilee year was proclaimed. So in its strictest sense a jubilee is a 50th anniversary, although we celebrate **silver jubilees** (25 years) or **diamond jubilees** (60 years), with the original jubilee described as a **golden jubilee**. The Latin form of the Hebrew word, with a 'u' rather than an 'o' as the second letter, shows that the word was associated in people's minds with the Latin *jubilare* 'shout for joy' which is the source of English words such as **jubilant** [M17th], and **jubilation** [LME].

judge [ME] The word judge, recorded in English since the Middle Ages, looks back to a Latin word based on *jus* 'law' (the source also of **just** [LME], **justice** [OE], **injury** [LME]), and *dicere* 'to say'. Judges are often thought of as solemn and impressive figures, and the expression **sober as a judge** goes back to the 17th century, with sober originally meaning 'serious, grave' rather than 'not drunk'.

judo *see* JAPANESE WORD PANEL

juggernaut [M19th] If you are stuck behind an articulated lorry, or juggernaut, on the motorway, a beach resort on the Bay of Bengal is probably not what springs to mind. But Juggernaut (in Sanskrit *Jagannātha*, 'Lord of the World') is the name given to the form of the Hindu god Krishna worshipped in Puri, eastern India, where at a festival each year his huge image is dragged through the streets in a heavy chariot. The use of the word for a large, heavy vehicle came into English, along with many other Hindi words, in the mid 19th century.

ju-jitsu *see* JAPANESE WORD PANEL

jukebox [1930s] In the USA a **juke** was a nightclub or bar that provided food, drinks, and music for dancing. The word was based on a term from the Creole language of the

journal joust jovial jowl joy jubilee judge

Gullah, an African-American people living on the coast of South Carolina and nearby islands. In their language *juke* meant 'disorderly'.

July *see* OCTOPUS

jumbo [E19th] In the early 19th century jumbo was applied to a large and clumsy person. The word became well known when it was used as a name for an elephant at London Zoo. He was sold to the Barnum and Bailey circus in 1882, despite massive public protest. Since 1964 it has referred to a large jet airliner, in particular the Boeing 747.

jump [E16th] Like **bump** [M16th] and **thump** [M16th], jump was probably formed because it 'sounded right', and seemed to express the sound of feet hitting the ground. It was first used around 1500. To **jump the gun**, or act too soon, comes from the idea of an athlete starting a race a split-second before they hear the starting gun. A **jumpsuit** was a term first used in the USA in the 1940s for the outfit worn by parachutists when making their jumps. **Jumper** [M19th] is unrelated. In the 19th century it was a loose outer jacket worn by sailors and is now a woollen jersey in UK English, but a style of dress in the USA. It may come from Scots *jupe*, 'a loose jacket or tunic', which in turn came through French from Arabic *jubba*.

juncture, junction *see* JOIN

jungle [L18th] This Hindi word has a root in the Sanskrit for 'rough and arid', and in Indian use jungle first meant simply 'rough, uncultivated ground, wasteland' rather than 'land overgrown with dense forest and tangled vegetation'. **The law of the jungle** is from *The Jungle Book* (1894) by Rudyard Kipling. In Kipling's book, the law of the jungle is not necessarily selfish: 'Now this is the Law of the Jungle—as old and as true as the sky...the strength of the Pack is the Wolf, and the strength of the Wolf is the Pack.' Since the 1920s a **concrete jungle** has been an unattractive urban area perceived as a harsh, unpleasant environment, where the 'law of the jungle' prevails. *Blackboard Jungle* was the title of the 1954 novel by Evan

Hunter about an undisciplined school, filmed the following year.

junior [ME] This word was first used as an adjective following a family name. It is a use of a Latin word, the comparative ('younger') of *juvenis* 'young'.

junk [LME] In the Middle Ages junk was a name for old or inferior rope. By the mid 19th century the current sense of 'old and discarded articles, rubbish' had developed. From there came the slang sense 'heroin or other narcotic drugs' in the 1920s, the source of **junkie** [1920s] 'a drug addict'. **Junk food** has been making us obese since the early 1970s. The junk which is a flat-bottomed sailing boat used in China and the East Indies is a quite different word. Dating from the mid 16th century, it comes through French or Portuguese from the Malay word *jong*.

junket [LME] Today a junket is a dish of sweetened curds. Originally, though, it was a rush basket, and the word goes back to Latin *juncus* 'a rush'. In early translations of the Bible it was the word used for the little boat of bulrushes in which the infant Moses was placed by his mother. It came to mean 'cream cheese' or 'dish of sweetened curds', because they were at one time drained in a rush basket. Junkets might be served at a feast, and by the 16th century the sense 'a feast, a party' arose, from which came, in the early 19th century, 'a pleasure trip'. The meaning 'a trip or excursion made by government officials and paid for by public funds' developed more recently.

jury [LME] This comes from the Latin word *jurare* 'to swear'. Early juries had to swear that they would give true answers to questions asked of them which related to their personal knowledge of an event they had witnessed or experienced. If you did not do this you committed **perjury** [LME] from the Latin for 'false oath'.

just, justice *see* JUDGE

jut *see* JET

juvenile *see* YOUNG

July jumbo jump juncture junction jungle

Kabbalah *see* CABAL

Kaiser *see* CAESAR

kaizen *see* JAPANESE WORD PANEL

kale *see* CAULIFLOWER

kaleidoscope [E19th] Sir David Brewster, the 19th-century inventor of the kaleidoscope, also coined the name for his invention. It is made up of elements from the Greek words *kalos* 'beautiful', *eidos* 'form', and *skopein* 'to look at', also the root of **scope** [M16th].

kamikaze *see* JAPANESE WORD PANEL

kanban *see* JAPANESE WORD PANEL

kangaroo *see* AUSTRALIAN WORD PANEL

kaput [L19th] This word meaning 'no longer working' comes from German *kaputt*, from French (*être*) *capot* '(be) without tricks in the card game of piquet'.

karaoke *see* JAPANESE WORD PANEL

karate *see* JAPANESE WORD PANEL

karoshi *see* JAPANESE WORD PANEL

katana *see* JAPANESE WORD PANEL

kayak *see* ESKIMO

kedgeree *see* RAJ WORD PANEL

keepsake *see* SAKE

kempt *see* UNKEMPT

ken *see* KNOW

kennel *see* CANARY

keratin *see* RHINOCEROS

kerb *see* CURB

kerchief [ME] The early spelling was *kerchef*, from Old French *cuevrechief*, from *couvrir* 'to cover' and *chief* 'head'. It was formerly used to describe a woman's head-dress, a type of cloth covering over the hair.

The word was used meaning 'cloth' as the second element of **handkerchief** from the mid 16th century.

kermes *see* CRIMSON

kernel *see* CORN

ketchup *see* CHINESE WORD PANEL

kettle [OE] Originally a kettle was any container used to heat water over a fire. There may be a clue as to how **a pretty kettle of fish**, where the pretty is ironical, developed in a travel book of the 1790s. This describes 'a kettle of fish' as a term used in Berwick-upon-Tweed for a high-society picnic where freshly caught salmon were cooked in kettles on the banks of the River Tweed. Kettle goes back to Latin *catinus* 'a deep container for cooking or serving food'. The first example of **the pot calling the kettle black**, meaning that a person's criticisms of another could equally well apply to themselves, dates from 1693.

key *see* QUAY

khaki *see* PERSIAN WORD PANEL

kibbutznik *see* YIDDISH WORD PANEL

kick [LME] Although it is such a common word, nobody seems to know the origin of kick. If you **kick against the pricks** the image is that of an ox fruitlessly kicking out at a whip or spur: the more it kicks, the more the driver goads it. The expression comes from the Bible story of Saul of Tarsus. He was an opponent of the followers of Jesus, and was going to Damascus to arrest any Christians in the city. On his journey he had a vision and heard the question, 'Saul, Saul, why persecutest thou me?' When he asked who the speaker was he was told, 'I am Jesus who thou persecutest: it is hard for thee to kick against the pricks.' After seeing the vision Saul became a Christian convert, under the new name Paul. If you **kick over the traces** the 'traces' in this expression are the two side straps which attach a draught horse to the vehicle it is pulling. If the animal is uncooperative or skittish and kicks out over these straps, the driver has difficulty in trying to regain control. To **kick the bucket** meaning 'to die' has been in use since the late 18th century, although its exact origins are not clear. One gruesome suggestion is that a person who wanted to commit suicide by hanging themselves might stand on a bucket while putting the noose round their neck and then kick the bucket away. Another idea looks back to an old sense of 'bucket' meaning 'a beam used for hanging something on'. This meaning was also found in Norfolk dialect, in which it referred specifically to a beam from which a pig about to be slaughtered was suspended by its heels.

kid [ME] Young goats are traditionally a source of soft pliable leather for fine gloves. In the 19th century this gave us the expression **handle with kid gloves** to mean 'to deal very tactfully and gently with'. Our familiar use of kid for a young person developed in the 19th century, but probably looks back to late 17th-century slang use to mean a baby or young child. The verb **kidnap**—its second syllable is a slang word, *nap*, meaning 'to take or seize'—originally referred to the 17th-century practice of stealing children to provide servants or labourers for the new American plantations.

kill [ME] Like *KICK, kill is of unknown origin, although it may be related to **quell** which meant 'kill' in Old English. To **be in at the kill** is to be present at or benefit from the successful conclusion of an enterprise. The image comes from the idea of the climax of a hunt. In 1814 the future William IV, contemplating the defeat of Napoleon, wrote triumphantly, 'The game is up with Bonaparte, and I shall be in at the kill.' Medicine in the 18th century was a risky

business, hence **kill or cure**. Achieving two goals at once is always an attractive thought. Since the 17th century one way of expressing the idea has been to refer to the hope of bird scarers in fields that they can **kill two birds with one stone**. To **kill someone with kindness** dates back to the mid 16th century, and appeared in the title of a play of the early 17th century, Thomas Heywood's *A Woman Killed with Kindness*. The film *The Killing Fields*, released in 1984, dealt with the horrific events in Cambodia during the Khmer Rouge dictatorship of 1975–9, when thousands of people were executed in **killing fields** and many more died of starvation. The term is first recorded in the early years of the 20th century and is a variation of **killing ground**, a place where seals were slaughtered.

kiln [OE] The words kiln and **culinary** [M17th] come from the Latin word *culina* 'kitchen, cooking stove'.

kilt *see* SCOTTISH WORD PANEL

kilter [E17th] The word kilter, meaning 'good condition or order', emerges in English dialect use in the 17th century, and is recorded in areas from Northumberland to Cornwall. It survives in mainstream language only in the phrase **out of kilter**, meaning 'out of balance'.

kind [OE] In Old English the original senses of kind were 'nature, the natural order', and 'innate character', which led to our use of the word for 'a class or type of similar people or things'. Kind is also related to **kin** [OE] and through it to *KING. In medieval times it was used as an adjective to mean 'well born', and the association of good breeding with good manners in turn gave us the familiar meaning of 'considerate and generous'.

kinetic *see* CINEMA

king [OE] The first kings in England were the chiefs of various tribes or 'kins' of Angles and Saxons who invaded the country and established their own small states (*see* KIND). To say that something expensive costs **a king's ransom** is to look back to feudal

kid kill kiln kilt kilter kind kinetic king

times, although the expression itself is not recorded before the 16th century. In the Middle Ages prisoners of war could be freed on payment of a ransom which varied according to the rank of the prisoner. A king would require a vast sum of money to be paid to secure his release.

kink [L17th] Originally a nautical term referring to a twist in a rope, kink is from Middle Low German *kinke*, probably from Dutch *kinken* 'to kink'. The adjective **kinky**, based on kink arose in the mid 19th century meaning 'having twists'; the sense 'perverted' dates from the 1950s.

kiosk *see* PERSIAN WORD PANEL

kirk *see* CHURCH

kiss [OE] An action or event causing certain failure for an enterprise may be described as **the kiss of death**. Although the phrase is relatively recent it is thought to refer to a story in the Bible. In the biblical account of the arrest of Jesus in the Garden of Gethsemane, Judas Iscariot identified Jesus to the soldiers who would arrest him by greeting him with a kiss. The expression is often used of apparently beneficial or well-meaning actions that somehow tempt fate, and have the opposite result to that intended. A much earlier traditional expression for an act of betrayal, a **Judas kiss**, refers to the same story. The last words of Lord Nelson, fatally wounded at the Battle of Trafalgar in 1805, are usually quoted as **'Kiss me, Hardy'**, spoken to Thomas Hardy, the captain of Nelson's ship, *HMS Victory*. According to eyewitness accounts he did say this, but it was not his final speech. His real last words were either 'Drink, drink. Fan, fan. Rub, rub', asking the doctor to give him a drink, fan him, and rub him to relieve his pain, or 'Thank God, I have done my duty'.

kit [ME] If you were told in the Middle Ages to **get your kit off** it would be a wooden tub you removed, not your clothes. Kit comes from Dutch *kitte*, meaning 'wooden vessel', later applied to other containers. Its use for a soldier's equipment, dating from the late

18th century, probably comes from the idea of a set of such articles packed in one container. *See also* CABOODLE

kitchen [OE] An Old English word based on Latin *coquere* 'to cook'. **Everything but the kitchen sink**, meaning 'everything imaginable', seems to have started life in the Second World War. A 1948 dictionary of forces' slang says that it was used in the context of a heavy bombardment: 'They chucked everything they'd got at us except, or including, the kitchen sink.' **Kitchen-sink drama** refers in particular to post-war British drama which used working-class domestic settings rather than the drawing rooms of conventional middle-class theatre.

kite [OE] In Old English this word was used for the bird of prey, remarkable for its ability to hang effortlessly in the air as it searches for food. The bird's name was transferred to the toy that floats in the air in the same way in the mid 17th century.

kitsch *see* GERMAN WORD PANEL

kittiwake *see* CUCKOO

kitty [E18th] The pet name for a cat is a shortening of the earlier word **kitten** [LME]. Both ultimately go back to *chitoun*, an Old French pet form of *chat* 'cat'. When a successful person is said to **scoop the kitty** their success has nothing to do with cats, but looks back to the use of kitty in northern English as a word for a prison. By the end of the 19th century it was being used generally in gambling as a name for the pool of money that is staked—to be scooped up by the luckiest player.

kiwi *see* AUSTRALIAN WORD PANEL

klutz *see* YIDDISH WORD PANEL

knapsack [E17th] This goes back to Dutch *knapzack*, probably from German *knappen* 'to bite (food)' and *zak* 'sack'. It was first used by soldiers for carrying necessities such as food supplies.

knave *see* JACK

kink kiosk kirk kiss kit kitchen kite

knee *see* KNUCKLE

knickers [L19th] A writer for the magazine *Queen* offered some good advice on warm underwear in 1882: 'I recommend...flannel knickers in preference to flannel petticoat.' At that time knickers, then with long legs, were becoming part of every woman's wardrobe and part of the vocabulary. The word, originally meaning 'short trousers', comes from an abbreviation of **knickerbockers** [M19th]. The use of **knickerbockers** for loose-fitting breeches arose from the knee breeches worn by Dutch men in Cruikshank's illustrations to Washington Irving's *History of New York* (1809), which was supposedly by 'Dietrich Knickerbocker'. By the 1970s somebody who was becoming upset and angry might be warned against **getting their knickers in a twist**.

knight [OE] To Anglo-Saxons knight meant 'boy, youth, or servant', but in medieval times this developed into a name for a man of honourable military rank. Knights in traditional stories are rescuers of people in danger or distress, giving us a **knight in shining armour**. A **white knight** is, in Stock Exchange language, a person or company that makes an acceptable counter-offer for a company facing a hostile takeover bid from a **black knight**. A 17th-century highwayman might be called ironically a **knight of the road**. The phrase has survived into the modern language as a jokey term for someone like a sales representative or a lorry driver who habitually travels the roads. *See also* DAMSEL, ERR, PAGE, ESQUIRE

knit *see* KNOT

knock [OE] The origin of this word is probably an attempt to imitate the sound. When you decide to finish an idea or plan you may say that you are going to **knock it on the head**, a phrase well established in English by the late 16th century. To **knock spots off** someone is to outdo them easily. The expression probably comes from the world of competitive shooting. Contestants keen to show off their skilled marksmanship would be required to shoot out the pips or spots on a playing card. The winner would be the person who shot out the most pips—and who might then be described as having 'knocked spots off' their rivals. The sense 'speak disparagingly about' is recorded from the late 19th century in US usage.

knot [OE] The words knot and **knit**, both Old English, are closely related. Something travelling fast might be described as going **at a rate of knots**. A knot here is a measure of speed, equivalent to one nautical mile an hour. In the days of sailing ships a line with knots tied at fixed intervals and a float at the end was run out into the sea over a certain time to gauge the ship's speed. If the line unwound very rapidly, with each knot appearing in quick succession, then the ship was going 'at a rate of knots'. *See also* NATTY

know [OE] The ancient root of know is shared by *CAN and **ken**, 'to know' in Scots (all Old English), and also by Latin *noscere*, and Greek *gignōskein* 'to know', source of words such as *AGNOSTIC. To **know in the biblical sense**, meaning 'to have sex with', comes from biblical uses such as the verse in the book of Genesis: 'And Adam knew Eve his wife; and she conceived, and bare Cain.' To **know the ropes** is to be thoroughly acquainted with the way in which something is done. The phrase comes from the days of sailing ships, when skill in handling ropes was essential for any sailor—an alternative is **know their onions**. The ancients valued self-knowledge as the way to wisdom—inscribed on the Greek temple of Apollo at Delphi were the words **know thyself**. The line '**It's life, Jim, but not as we know it**' is the mainstay of anyone trying to do an impression of Dr Spock from the TV series *Star Trek*, but he never said it in the programme. He did say that there was 'no life as we know it', but the quoted phrase is from the 1987 song 'Star Trekkin'' by the Firm. *See also* GNOME

knuckle [ME] In medieval times a knuckle was the rounded shape made by a joint like the elbow or knee when bent, but over the years it became limited to the joints of the fingers. The word may ultimately be related to **knee** [OE]. Someone prepared to **knuckle down** to something is ready to concentrate on a task, but the phrase originally comes from a game. People playing marbles in the 18th century set their knuckles down on the ground before shooting or casting the 'taw', a large marble. Something which threatens to go beyond the limits of decency can be described as being **near the knuckle**. This was originally used more generally to mean 'close to the permitted limits of behaviour'.

kook *see* CUCKOO

kop [M19th] The Taylor Report after the Hillsborough disaster of 1989, in which 96 Liverpool fans were killed in a crush at the ground of Sheffield Wednesday FC, recommended that major soccer grounds in England should become all-seated, and spelled the end for the traditional terrace or kop. The original and best-known kop was the one at Anfield, home of Liverpool FC, which was known in full as Spion Kop. The name came from the site of a battle in 1900 during the Boer War, in which troops from Lancashire, including many from Liverpool, led the assault. In Afrikaans *kop* means 'hill', and so was an appropriate name for a high bank of terracing.

kosher [M19th] Only food that is kosher may be eaten by Orthodox Jews. Animals must be slaughtered and prepared in the prescribed way, meat and milk must not be cooked or consumed together, and certain creatures, notably pigs and shellfish, are forbidden altogether. The word is from Hebrew *kāsēr* 'right, proper', and was first used in English in the mid 19th century—the slang sense, 'genuine and legitimate', is almost as old, going back to the 1880s.

kowtow *see* CHINESE WORD PANEL

kvetch *see* YIDDISH WORD PANEL

kylie *see* AUSTRALIAN WORD PANEL

kook   kop   kosher   kowtow   kvetch   kylie

Ll

laager *see* SOUTH AFRICAN WORD PANEL

labour [ME] Labour came into English through French from Latin *labor* 'toil, distress, trouble', also found in **laboratory** [E17th] a place of work, and **elaborate** [L16th] 'produced by much labour'. In the late 18th century the Scottish economist Adam Smith used the word technically for work directed towards providing the needs of a community, and paved the way for the use of labour in political contexts. The British **Labour Party** was formed in 1906 to represent ordinary working people. A task requiring enormous strength or effort is a **labour of Hercules** or a **Herculean labour**. In Greek mythology Hercules had superhuman strength and performed twelve tasks or 'labours' imposed on him as a penance for killing his children in a fit of madness. After his death he was ranked among the gods.

labyrinth [LME] The word was first used to refer to the mythological maze constructed by the Greek craftsman Daedalus for King Minos of Crete to house the Minotaur, a creature half-man half-bull. It comes from Greek *laburinthos*. By the early 17th century it was being used both for mazes in landscaped gardens and for something intricately complicated.

lace [ME] This comes from Latin *laqueus* 'noose' which was also found as an early sense in English and is still the basic sense of the Spanish-American equivalent, **lasso** [M18th]. The fine openwork fabric of looping threads was known as lace from the middle of the 16th century. The verb lace, to mean 'fortify' and 'flavour' as in to lace a drink, is from the late 17th century. **Lacerate** [LME] is unrelated, coming from Latin *lacerare* 'to mangle, tear'.

lackadaisical [M18th] 'Feebly sentimental' was among the early meanings of lackadaisical which comes from the archaic interjection **lackaday** (earlier alack-a-day), and its extended form **lackadaisy**.

laconic [M16th] The Spartans or Laconians of ancient Greece were known for their austere lifestyle and pithy speech. When Philip of Macedon threatened to invade Laconia in the 4th century BC, he wrote to its governing magistrates to try to frighten them into submission, saying that if he entered Laconia he would raze it to the ground. They are reported to have sent a one-word reply—'If'. Since the 16th century laconic has meant 'using very few words'. *See also* SPARTAN

lacrosse *see* NATIVE AMERICAN WORD PANEL

lactic *see* LETTUCE

lad [ME] Like *BOY, the word lad appeared from nowhere in the early Middle Ages. By the mid 16th century it was being used for 'a boisterously spirited young man', and **laddism** was first mentioned in the 1840s. It was in the early 1990s, though, that laddism and **new lads** became a social phenomenon, driven by the rise of the rock group Oasis and the launch of the **lad's mag** *Loaded* in 1994. A young woman who is **a bit of a lad** has been a **ladette** since around 1995.

lady [OE] The root meaning of lady was 'kneader of bread'. Old English *hlafdige*, from which the modern word developed, comes from an early form of *LOAF and a word meaning 'knead' from which **dough** also derives. The corresponding male form is *LORD, in Old English *hlafweard* 'keeper of bread'. In spite of the humble associations of baking, a lady in Anglo-Saxon times was a powerful woman who ruled over a household and made its staple food. These days a certain type of lady meets during the day in expensive restaurants—they are the **ladies who lunch**. The source of this expression is the title of a 1970 song by Stephen Sondheim from the musical

Company, which pokes fun at members of the affluent charity fund-raising set.

lager [M19th] The fuller name for lager, no longer much used, is **lager beer**. It comes from German *Lagerbier* 'beer brewed for keeping', from *Lager* 'storehouse', which shares its root with an animal's **lair** [OE], and also with **lie** [OE]. Since the 1980s we have had the **lager lout**, the young man who drinks too much and then behaves in an unpleasant or violent way. *See also* BEER

lagoon *see* LAKE

lair *see* LAGER

lairy [M19th] For a century or more lairy has been Australian and New Zealand slang for 'ostentatious, flashy'. British English has adopted this use, to join an earlier, originally Cockney sense 'cunning or conceited', as well as the meaning 'aggressive, rowdy'. The word is a form of **leery** [L17th], which means 'cautious or wary' and is related to **leer** [M16th] 'to look at in a lecherous way', from Old English *hleor* '*CHEEK'.

laissez-faire *see* FRENCH WORD PANEL

lake [OE] A lake was once a pond or pool: it is from Old French *lac*, from Latin *lacus* 'basin, pool, lake'. A small *lacus* was a *lacuna*, which became *laguna* in Spanish and Italian, and became **lagoon** [E17th] in English.

lam *see* LAMBASTE

lama [M17th] This honorific title applied to a spiritual leader in Tibetan Buddhism is from Tibetan *bla-ma* (the initial *b* remaining silent); the literal meaning is 'superior one'.

lambaste [M17th] The early sense recorded for lambaste was 'beat, thrash': it comes from late 16th-century **lam** meaning 'beat soundly' and mid 16th-century **baste** meaning 'thrash', both probably of Scandinavian origin. The sense 'criticize harshly' dates from the late 19th century. The US expression **on the lam** 'in flight' developed from lam in the late 19th century.

lampoon [M17th] The source of English lampoon meaning 'publicly criticize by using ridicule or irony' is French *lampon*. This is said to be from the refrain of popular French drinking songs in the 1600s *lampons* 'let us drink!', from *lamper* 'gulp down'.

land [OE] Celtic words such as Irish *lann* 'enclosure' and Welsh *llan* 'enclosure, church' are related to land, as well as the closer Dutch *land* and German *Land*. **In the land of the living** is now a jokey way of saying that someone is alive or awake. The expression is biblical, occurring for example in the Book of Job: 'Man knoweth not the price thereof; neither is it found in the land of the living.' **The land of Nod** is also biblical, first used for the state of sleep by Jonathan Swift, who based it on the place name **Nod** in Genesis: 'And Cain went out from the presence of the Lord, and dwelt in the land of Nod, on the east of Eden'. **Landscape** [L16th] was first used as a term for a picture of natural scenery: it comes from Middle Dutch *lantscap*, from *land* 'land' and *-scap* (the equivalent of the English suffix *-ship*).

landlubber *see* LOAF

language [ME] The word language is from Old French *langage*, based on Latin *lingua* 'tongue', which is also found in **linguist** [L16th], and goes back to an Indo-European root shared with **lick** [OE]. The expression to **lick someone into shape** comes from the old tradition that bear cubs were born a formless mass, and had literally to be licked into shape by their mothers. **Lingo** [M17th] is probably from the Portuguese form of *lingua*.

languish [ME] Early senses included 'become faint, feeble, or ill'; in the early 18th century it came to mean 'assume a languid or sentimentally tender expression' and was aptly applied to Sheridan's character Lydia Languish in *The Rivals* performed for the first time in 1775. The word goes back to Latin *laxus* 'loose, lax' found also in **lax** [LME], **relax** [LME] where the *re-* intensifies the sense; **relay** [LME], **release** [ME], and

lager   lagoon   lair   lairy   laissez-faire   lake

laxative [LME] something that loosens the bowels. *See* SLAKE

lanolin *see* WOOL

lap [OE] Originally a lap was a fold or flap of a garment, which gave rise to **lapel** in the 17th century. By the Middle Ages it was also the front of a skirt when held up to catch or carry something, and from there the area between the waist and the knees as a place where a child can be nursed or an object held. Since the 1980s erotic dancers or striptease artists have also performed a **lap dance** while sitting on the laps of—or at least dancing close to—paying customers. **In the lap of the gods** can be traced back to several passages in the works of the Greek epic poet Homer, thought to have been written during the 8th century BC. The idea is that the course of events is determined by the gods, and so is completely outside human control. The phrase probably comes from the image of someone trying to placate or influence a person in authority by placing gifts in their lap as they sit ready to pass judgement. The lap of a race comes from extending the sense of a fold to that of a coil or something going round, but to lap in the sense a cat laps milk is unconnected and comes from a Germanic source.

lapse [LME] Lapse is from Latin *lapsus*, from *labi* 'to glide, slip, or fall' reinforced by Latin *lapsare* 'to slip or stumble'. **Elapse** [L16th] comes from the same root.

larboard *see* PORT

larder [ME] In the past, and in many peasant societies, the pig has been a vital source of food for the winter: it can be salted and preserved, and traditionally you can eat every part of it except its squeak. This is reflected in the word **larder**, which in origin is a place for storing bacon. It comes from the French word meaning 'bacon' that also gave us **lard** [ME], and the **lardon** [LME], a cube or chunk of bacon.

large [ME] Large is found in early examples with the meaning 'liberal in giving, lavish, ample in quantity'. It came via Old French from Latin *largus* 'copious': also

behind **largesse** [ME] 'liberality, munificence'.

lark [E19th] Old English *laferce* developed into Scottish and northern English **laverock**, and in the Middle Ages was contracted to **lark**, which become the standard name for this songbird. References to the early-morning singing of the lark date back to the 16th century. People often refer to an early riser as a lark, while a late-to-bed counterpart is an *OWL. The phrase **up with the lark**, 'up very early in the morning', also plays on the word 'up', since the lark sings on the wing while flying high above its nest. In to **lark about** or **around**, and in the sense 'something done for fun', lark may be a shortening of **skylark**, which was formerly used in the same way, or it may be from dialect *lake* 'to play', from a Scandinavian word.

larrikin *see* AUSTRALIAN WORD PANEL

larry *see* HAPPY

larva [M17th] 'A disembodied spirit or ghost' was the first use of this Latin word which means literally 'ghost, mask'. The common modern use as a term for the active immature form of an insect is due to the Swedish botanist Linnaeus (1707–78).

laser *see* RADAR

lass [ME] The word lass is based on the Old Norse feminine adjective *laskura* 'unmarried'.

lasso *see* LACE

late *see* EARLY

latent [LME] The word latent comes from Latin *latere* 'be hidden'.

lateral [LME] This word meaning 'at or to the side' is from Latin *lateralis*, 'side, broad' also found in **latitude** [LME].

lath *see* LATTICE

lather [OE] Old English *læthor* was 'washing soda' or its froth. Of Germanic origin, *lather* is related to the Old Norse noun *lauthr*, from an Indo-

What the Romans did for us

*As well as education, wine, roads, under-floor heating, and the fresh water system, the Romans gave us words and phrases. Far from being a dead language, **Latin** is alive and well, and may be found in a sentence near you.*

ENGLISH is full of words of Latin origin that came into the language by way of the French-speaking Norman invaders of 1066. But we also use many phrases that came into English later, typically in the 17th and 18th centuries, and remain in their original Latin form.

In Latin **index** referred to the 'forefinger' or 'index finger', with which you point. From this we got our term for a list of topics in a book which 'point' to the right page. When we decide to leave by a door marked **exit**, we may not know that in Latin this meant 'he or she goes out'. The phrase **in flagrante delicto**, literally 'in blazing crime', means in English 'in the very act of wrongdoing', and particularly refers to sexual misconduct. If someone is caught *in flagrante delicto* they are generally found in bed with someone else's partner.

If we want to say that someone really knows about something we might say that they are **bona fide**, Latin words meaning 'with good faith'. A remark that has no logical connection with a previous statement is a **non sequitur**—literally, 'it does not follow'. A particular stipulation or condition is a **caveat**, a word which means literally 'let a person beware'. If a person is preparing to buy something, you might say **caveat emptor**, 'let the buyer beware', to remind them that it is the buyer alone who is responsible for checking the quality of the goods before the purchase is made.

Someone who dislikes sailing might be very glad to find themselves back on **terra firma** or 'firm land'. If they had heard too much of the delights of the sea, they might say that they had been lectured about it **ad nauseam**, or 'to sickness'. They might be wary of decisions taken on an **ad hoc** basis, Latin for 'to this', used in English to mean 'created or done for a particular purpose'. Sometimes you have no chance to influence what happens, as things may be done in your absence, or **in absentia**.

In 1992, following the marital troubles of her children and a disastrous fire at Windsor Castle, the Queen said in a speech that it had turned out to be an **annus horribilis**. This term for a year of disaster or misfortune is an alteration of an established Latin phrase **annus mirabilis** 'wonderful year'.

Changes are often received with apprehension, especially by people who would prefer to preserve the existing state of affairs or **status quo**—literally 'the state in which'. The band Status Quo had their first hit, 'Pictures of Matchstick Men', in 1968 and are still going strong. Another band with a Latin name are Procol Harum, who released the enigmatic 'A Whiter Shade of Pale' in 1967. The band's name is a misspelled version of a Latin phrase meaning 'far from these things' – it should really be *procul his*.

The legal world is full of Latin. If someone is not of sound mind they are said to be **non compos mentis**, literally 'not having control of the mind'. Journalists may sometimes feel frustrated at not being able to report freely on a case because it is **sub judice** 'under a judge'—under judicial consideration and so prohibited from public discussion.

Latin supplies a number of well-known mottoes. **E pluribus unum**, or 'one out of many', is the motto of the United States. In 1913 King George V approved **per ardua ad astra**, 'through struggle to the stars', as the motto of the Royal Air Force.

Some Latin phrases lie behind our most familiar abbreviations. If we want to emphasize the importance of something, we may say or write **NB**—short for *nota bene*, or 'note well'. **QED**, pointing out that a fact or situation demonstrates the truth of what you are saying, stands for *quod erat demonstrandum*, 'which was to be demonstrated'. A long list of items may finish with **etc.**, standing for *et cetera* 'and the rest'. Advancing age may be referred to jokingly as **Anno Domini**, Latin for 'in the year of the Lord', which also gives us the abbreviation AD. The passage of time inevitably leads to **RIP**, short for *requiescat in pace*, 'rest in peace', although the same cannot be said to apply to Latin itself.

European root shared by Greek *loutron* 'bath'. The sense 'agitation' as in **get into a lather** dates from the early 19th century.

latitude *see* LATERAL

latrine [ME] Although this was found in Middle English, it was rare before the mid 19th century. It came via French from Latin *latrina* 'privy', a shortening of *lavatrina*, from *lavare* 'to wash'.

latte *see* ITALIAN WORD PANEL

lattice [Middle English] A lattice is a structure made of laths and comes from Old French *lattis*, from *latte* '**lath**' [OE], of Germanic origin. The ordered criss-cross pattern associated with the word has led to its application in many contexts, particularly in science.

launder [ME] In the sense 'to wash clothes or linen', launder was originally a contracted form of *lavender*, a medieval word meaning 'a person who washes

clothes'. It goes back to Latin *lavare* to wash, the source of **lava** [M18th] originally an Italian word for 'steam' narrowed down to mean a stream of lava; **lavatory** [LME]; and **lavish** [LME] where the sense of 'profusion' comes from the French for a deluge of rain; and **lotion** [LME] which in the past could also be used for the action of washing as well as for a liquid rubbed on. **Lavender** [LME] probably does not come directly from *lavare*, but its form was altered to look as if it did, because lavender was used to scent washing. The Watergate scandal in the USA in the early 1970s, in which an attempt to bug the national headquarters of the Democratic Party led to the resignation of President Richard Nixon, gave the world **money laundering**. Before bathrooms and running water, people washed from a basin or bowl. This is what a lavatory originally was—vessel for washing. In the mid 17th century the word came to refer to a room with washing facilities, from which developed the modern sense of a *TOILET.

lava, lavatory, lavish *see* LAUNDER

latitude latrine latte lattice launder lava

law [OE] The words **legacy** [LME], **legal** [LME], **legitimate** [LME], and **loyal** [E16th] all descend from Latin *lex* 'law', the source also of law. The phrase **law and order** is found from the late 16th century. It was Charles Dickens who first said **the law is an ass**, or rather his character Mr Bumble did in *Oliver Twist*: '"If the law supposes that," said Mr Bumble... "the law is a ass... a idiot."' *See also* JUNGLE

lawn [M16th] This is an alteration of dialect *laund* 'glade, pasture', from Old French *launde* 'wooded district, heath', of Celtic origin. The current use for short mown grass dates from the mid 18th century. The lawn [ME] that is a fine fabric is probably from *Laon*, the name of a city in France important for linen manufacture.

lax, laxative *see* LANGUISH

lead [OE] Two entirely different strands come together in the spelling lead, with different pronunciations. The lead that rhymes with 'bead' shares an ancient root with *LOAD; the **lead** that rhymes with 'bed' and means 'a metal' is related to Dutch *lood* 'lead' and German *Lot* 'plumb line, solder'. The image in to **lead someone by the nose**, 'to control someone totally', is of an animal being led by a ring in its nose. Boxing gave us to **lead with your chin** 'to behave or talk incautiously'. It refers to a boxer's stance that leaves his chin unprotected. *See also* BALLOON

league *see* ALLY

lean [OE] The two words spelled lean are of different origins. Both are Old English, but the one meaning 'be in a sloping position' shares a root of Latin *clinare*, as in **incline** [ME]; **decline** [LME]; and **recline** [LME]. We sometimes talk of **lean years** or **a lean period**. This expression comes from the story of Joseph in the Bible. He successfully interprets Pharaoh's disturbing dream, in which seven plump, healthy cattle come out of the river and begin to feed. Seven lean, malnourished animals then leave the river and proceed to eat the plump cattle. According to Joseph's interpretation, there will be seven years of plenty in Egypt

followed by seven lean years. Pharaoh, impressed by Joseph, appoints him vice-regent to prepare the country for the ordeal of the seven lean years. A person who is **lean and hungry** is active and alert-looking. The phrase comes from Shakespeare's *Julius Caesar*—'Yond' Cassius has a lean and hungry look.'

leave *see* LIFE

leaven *see* ELEVATE

leech *see* PHYSICIAN

leer, leery *see* LAIRY

left [OE] The original core sense of left in Old English is 'weak'—the majority of people are right-handed, and the left-hand side was regarded as the weaker side of the body. The political application of left originated in the French National Assembly of 1789, in which the nobles as a body took the position of honour on the president's right, and the Third Estate—the French bourgeoisie and working class—sat on his left. *See also* AMBIDEXTROUS, SINISTER. In baseball **left field** is the part of the outfield that is to the left from the perspective of the batter. In US English something that is **left-field** or **out of left field** is surprising or unconventional, or possibly ignorant or mistaken. The connection with baseball probably came from the fact that in many early ball parks the left field was larger than the right, making it more difficult to retrieve balls hit there and sometimes leading to delay and general confusion.

leg [ME] Leg took over from the earlier word *SHANK. It is from Old Norse *legg*. The use of leg for a short section (**leg of a journey**) found from the 1920s, has developed from the nautical application of the term in the early 17th century when it described a short rope branching out into two or more parts.

legacy, legal *see* LAW

legend [ME] A legend was first 'the story of a saint's life', coming from Old French *legende*, from medieval Latin *legere* 'to read',

law   lawn   lax   laxative   lead   league   lean

also found in **legible** [LME]. The sense 'a traditional story popularly regarded as historical' dates from the early 17th century when the word is also first found meaning 'motto, inscription'.

legitimate *see* LAW

leisure [ME] Leisure is from Old French *leisir*, based on Latin *licere* 'be allowed'. The phrase **a lady of leisure** defining a woman who has lots of free time, dates only from the 1940s.

lemon [ME] The root of lemon and also **lime** [M17th] is an Arabic word, *lim*, that was a collective term for citrus fruit. On fruit machines the lemon is the least valuable symbol, and this may be behind **the answer is a lemon** 'the response or outcome is unsatisfactory'. Especially in the USA, a lemon may be a substandard or defective car, of the type all too often bought from shady used-car dealers.

lengthwise *see* WISE

lens [L17th] Lens means 'lentil' (ME, from the same word) in Latin. The word was used for a lens because it is the same shape.

Lent *see* SPRING

Leo *see* LION

leopard [ME] Two Greek words combine in the root of **leopard**: *leōn*, the source of *LION, and *pardos*, the source of **pard**, an old word for a leopard (*see further at* PANTHER). The saying **the leopard does not change his spots** is inspired by the Book of Jeremiah in the Bible: 'Can the Ethiopian change his skin, or the leopard his spots?' *See also* CAMEL, GIRAFFE

leotard *see* TUTU

leprechaun [E17th] The name of the small, mischievous sprite of Irish folklore is based on old Irish words meaning 'small body'. The spelling of Irish has always been a mystery to the uninitiated: when the **leprechaun** first appeared in English literature in the 17th century, it was named

lubrican; the modern form dates from the 19th century.

lesbian [L19th] Sappho was a Greek lyric poet of the early 7th century BC who lived on the Greek island of Lesbos (often now found in the Greek spelling Lesvos). Despite the fact that we know very little of her life, and that there is an unsupported tradition that she killed herself for love of a young man, the fragments of her poems also express her affection and admiration for women, and so people came to associate her with female homosexuality. In the late 19th century she inspired two descriptive terms, **lesbian**, from her island home of Lesbos, and **sapphic**.

lethal [L16th] When the souls of the dead in Greek mythology drank the water of Lethe, a river in Hades, the underworld, they forgot their life on earth, and so the word *Lēthē* meant 'forgetfulness'. Many ancient Romans were familiar with this, and along the line they altered their Latin word *letum* 'death' to *lethum*, to be closer to the Greek. The altered Latin form is the source of English lethal 'deadly'. **Lethargy** [LME] comes from a related Greek word.

letter [ME] English adopted letter from Old French in the 13th century. Its ultimate source is Latin *lit(t)era*, from which **literal** [LME], **literature** [LME], and **alliteration** [E17th] also derive—the Latin word meant 'written communication or message' as well as 'letter of the alphabet', and both senses came over into English. The phrase **to the letter** 'to the last detail' has a parallel in French *au pied de la lettre*, which people of a literary bent have also used in English. *See also* ALPHABET

lettuce [ME] Lettuce came into English from Old French *letues* or *laitues*, from Latin *lactuca*, whose root was *lac* 'milk'—the connection was the milky juice that lettuce produces. Latin *lac* also gave us **lactic** [L18th], 'relating to milk'.

leukaemia *see* LIGHT

level [ME] The ultimate root of level is Latin *libra* 'scales, balance', also the source of the sign of the zodiac **Libra** [LME]. It has many senses in English, the earliest being 'an instrument used to determine if a surface is horizontal', as in **spirit level** [M18th]. Since the 1980s the image of **a level playing field** has been a cliché of business and politics. In games, an uneven playing surface will favour the home side, who will be more familiar with its hazards. *See also* DELIBERATE

leviathan [LME] In the Bible Leviathan is a sea monster, sometimes identified with a whale, sometimes with a crocodile, sometimes with the Devil. In 1651 Thomas Hobbes published a treatise of political philosophy called *The Leviathan*, in which the monster in question is sovereign power. Modern uses of **leviathan** for 'an autocratic monarch or state' derive from this. Hobbes himself considered that an absolute monarch was essential to maintain an ordered state in a world in which 'the life of man is solitary, poor, nasty, brutish, and short'. Leviathan has been used for something huge since the early 17th century.

Levis *see* JEANS

levity *see* ELEVATE

lewd [OE] Old English *lǽwede* is of unknown origin. The original sense was 'belonging to the laity' as opposed to the church; in Middle English the sense became 'belonging to the common people, vulgar', and later 'worthless, vile, evil' which led to the current sense 'sexually crude and offensive'.

lexicon [E17th] While a **dictionary** [E16th] goes back to the Latin *dicere* 'to speak', lexicon comes from Greek *lexikon (biblion)* '(book) of words', from *lexis* 'word', from *legein* 'speak'.

liable *see* RELY

liaison [M17th] Originally a cookery term, liaison is from French *lier* 'to bind'. The more general use of the word to mean 'intimate connection' or more specifically 'sexual relationship' dates from the early

19th century. The verb **liaise**, 'communicate and cooperate', was used from the 1920s as military slang formed from liaison.

libel [ME] When first used a libel was 'a document, a written statement': it came via Old French from Latin *libellus*, a diminutive of *liber* 'book', source of **library** [LME]. Now used as a legal term referring to a published false statement damaging to someone's reputation, it dates from the early 17th century. Libel contrasts with slander (*see* SCANDAL) which is spoken.

liberty [LME] The root of liberty is Latin *liber* 'free', the source also of **liberal** [ME], **libertine** [LME], and **livery** [ME], and *DELIVER. During the French Revolution the rallying cry was '**liberty, equality, fraternity**'. Supporters of change wore the **cap of liberty**, a red conical cap of a type that had originally been given to Roman slaves when they were freed.

libido *see* LOVE

Libra *see* LEVEL

library *see* LIBEL

licence [LME] Latin *licere* 'be lawful or permitted' is the base of licence, which came into English via Old French from Latin *licentia* 'freedom, licentiousness' which in medieval Latin came to mean 'authority, permission'. The phrase **poetic licence,** meaning deviation from a recognized rule for artistic effect, is found from the early 16th century. The verb **license** [LME] gained its *-se* spelling from the pattern of noun/verb pairs such as 'practice' and 'practise'. *See also* SHAKE

lick *see* LANGUAGE

lid [OE] Old English *hlid* has a Germanic origin, with a base meaning 'cover', still found in **eyelid** [ME].

lidar *see* RADAR

lido [L17th] This word for a public open-air swimming pool or bathing beach comes from Italian *Lido*, the name of a famous

leviathan Levis levity lewd lexicon liable

Venetian bathing beach. This comes from Italian *lido* 'shore', from Latin *litus*, also found in words like **littoral** [M17th].

lie *see* LAGER

life [OE] The English word life is related to German *Leib* 'body', and also to **leave** [OE], and *LIVE. The expression **as large as life** goes back to the days when portrait painting was common. Professional artists were expensive, and a good way of showing off your wealth was to have a portrait painted that was life-size. Early versions of the expression, dating from the mid 17th century, are **greater** or **bigger than the life**, with the modern form first recorded in the early 19th century. When someone lives **the life of Riley** they are enjoying a luxurious and carefree existence. *Reilly* or *Riley* is a common Irish surname, and the phrase may come from a popular song of the early 20th century called 'My Name is Kelly'. This included the lines: 'Faith and my name is Kelly Michael Kelly, / But I'm living the life of Reilly just the same.' It is probable that the songwriter, H. Pease, was using an already existing catchphrase, but the song would have made it more widely known.

lift *see* LOFT

ligament, ligature *see* RELY

light [OE] The two words spelled light have different sources. The light referring to the rays that stimulate sight shares an ancestor with Greek *leukos* 'white' (found in **leukaemia** [M19th] a disease that affects the white blood cells), and Latin *lux* (source of **lucid** [L16th]). The light referring to weight comes from the same ancient root as **lung** [OE]—the lightness of the lungs distinguishes them from other internal organs. This sense of light survives in **lights** [ME], the lungs of sheep, pigs or bullocks, used as food, especially for pets. If someone does something that creates a tense or exciting situation, people might say that they **light the blue touch-paper**. A touch-paper is a type of fuse that will burn slowly when touched by a spark. It is now only used with fireworks, but in the past would also

have been a means for igniting gunpowder. The word **lighten** [ME] 'shed light on' is the source of **lightning** [ME].

limb [OE] There was no 'b' in limb until the 16th century: the earlier form was *lim*. Old English *thuma* similarly became **thumb** in the 13th century. Words such as Old English **comb** and **dumb** that had always ended in -b may have influenced the new spelling. The limb in **out on a limb** is the branch of a tree, a sense of the same word. The image conjured up is of someone clinging precariously to the end of a projecting branch, with nothing or no one to assist them in their difficult situation.

limbo [LME] In some versions of Christian theology limbo is the abode, on the border of hell, of the souls of unbaptized infants and of just people who died before Christ's coming. The word represents a form of Latin *limbus* 'edge, hem, border'. From the late 16th century it developed uses such as 'an uncertain period of awaiting a decision' and 'a state of neglect or oblivion'. There is no linguistic connection with the West Indian dance the limbo recorded from the 1950s, which is an alteration of **limber** [M16th] 'lithe, supple'.

lime *see* LEMON

limelight [E19th] Before electricity or gas lighting, theatres lit up important actors and scenes using limelight. This was an intense white light produced by heating up a piece of lime in a flame of combined oxygen and hydrogen, a process invented around 1825 by Captain T. Drummond of the Royal Engineers. From the end of the 19th century, as modern lighting ended the need for real limelight, the word came to be more common in the sense 'the focus of public attention'.

limerick [L19th] The city of Limerick, on the River Shannon in the west of the Irish province of Munster, gets its name for the Irish for 'bare patch of ground'. In a country famous for its *CRACK, or enjoyable sociability, tradition has it that in the past it was the custom for people to improvize a piece of nonsense verse. The audience would then follow every performance with a chorus containing the words 'Will you come up to Limerick?' Through this the town gave its name to the humorous five-line poem made particularly popular by Edward Lear in *A Book of Nonsense* (1845).

limey *see* AUSTRALIAN WORD PANEL

limousine [E20th] In French a limousine was a cloak with a cape, of a type worn in Limousin, a region of central France. People saw a resemblance between this distinctive garment and early forms of motor car in which the driver's seat was outside in a separate compartment covered with a canopy. The name, first recorded shortly after 1900, passed to large, luxurious cars driven by a chauffeur separated from the passengers by a partition. The word was abbreviated to **limo** in the 1960s, while in the 1980s the **stretch limo** made its appearance.

limp [LME] Limp meaning 'walk unevenly or with difficulty' was originally used with the sense 'fall short of': it is related to obsolete *limphalt* 'lame', and is probably of Germanic origin. Use of the word in nautical, aviation, and other transport contexts such as **limp into port, limped over the airfield** is found from the 1920s. Limp in the sense 'lacking firmness' dates from the early 18th century. It may be related to the other limp, but its origin is uncertain.

linctus [L17th] This word for a cough mixture is an adoption of a Latin word which comes from *lingere* 'to lick'. It is literally a mixture meant to be lapped up by the tongue.

lingerie [M19th] The original lingerie had far more practical associations than the word has today, for it comes from the French *linge* 'linen' from Latin *linum* 'flax, linen'. This also lies behind Old English **linen**, which was probably borrowed by Germanic people before the Anglo-Saxon invasion, and is also the source of **line** [LME] in the sense 'cover the inside of' from

the use of linen as a liner. Flax could also be made into rope or string, and this is probably the source of the other **line** [OE], for a straight mark or row.

lingo, linguist *see* LANGUAGE

links [OE] This word used commonly in golf contexts was first found as *hlinc* meaning 'rising ground'; it is perhaps related to *LEAN. Links in Scottish use describes gently undulating sandy ground near the sea-shore covered with turf or coarse grass, which gave us the golfing sense. It is unconnected to the singular **link** [LME] which was originally a loop, and comes from Old Norse *hlekkr*.

lion [ME] The lions known in parts of Europe and around the Mediterranean in early times were not African but Asiatic lions, rare animals in the 21st century. The name lion came into English from French, and ultimately from Greek *leōn*. The Anglo-Saxons had used the Latin form **Leo**, which was overtaken by lion for the animal, but which is still the name of a constellation and sign of the zodiac.

In ancient Rome lions and other wild beasts provided entertainment in the amphitheatres. Christians and other dissidents were left at their mercy in the arena, a practice behind our phrase to **throw someone to the lions**. After the terrible slaughter of British soldiers during the First World War, the phrase **lions led by donkeys** became popular as a way of encapsulating the idea that the men had been brave, but had been let down by their senior officers. It is not clear who first came up with the description, but the French troops defeated by the Prussians in 1871 were described as 'lions led by packasses'. From medieval times until the opening of London Zoo in the 19th century, the Tower of London contained a menagerie of unusual animals, among which were lions. Not surprisingly, they were a great attraction for visitors to the city, and the phrase to **see the lions** sprang up with the meaning 'to see the sights or attractions of a place'. From there a lion became a celebrity or noted person, a sense which gave us **lionize**, 'to treat as a celebrity', in the 1830s. *See also* BEARD

lip [OE] Old English *lippa* is from an Indo-European root shared by Latin *labia* 'lips'. The word is used in several phrases expressing an attitude or reaction: **bite one's lip** [ME], **keep a stiff upper lip** [E19th], which despite its association with a certain type of Englishman actually comes from the USA, and **smack one's lips** [E19th].

liquorice [ME] Contrary to appearances, liquorice has no connection with **liquor** [ME] which comes directly from Latin. The word goes back to a Greek compound formed from *glukus* 'sweet' (source of **glucose** [M19th]), and *rhiza* 'root' (as in **rhizome** [M19th]). Liquorice is made by evaporating the juice of the root of certain members of the pea family. **Liquorice allsorts** were introduced in 1899. The story behind their invention is that a salesman from the company, Bassett's, was visiting a client and showing him samples of the various liquorice sweets that the company made. The client was unimpressed by any of them until the salesman gathered up his samples to leave and in doing so dropped them all, creating a mix of sweets that the client liked.

list [L16th] In the sense 'a number of connected items or names', list came from French in the late 16th century. The origin of the French word appears to be the root of another list that already existed in English, with the meaning 'a border, edge, or strip'— presumably from the strip of paper on which a list would have been written. Its main use now is for the selvedge or sewn edge of a piece of fabric. The origins of to **enter the lists** 'to issue or accept a challenge' have nothing to do with signing up, but go back to the days of knights and jousting tournaments. These lists were the enclosed area where jousts took place or rather the barriers surrounding this area— but the meaning was extended to refer to the yard itself. If you chose to enter the lists you were formally agreeing to take part in combat. There was another list, now obsolete, meaning 'desire, wish' which still

survives in **listless** [ME] literally 'without desire'.

literal, literature *see* LETTER

litter [ME] The earliest, medieval meaning of litter was 'a bed', which was also that of its source, Latin *lectus*. Its journey to the modern sense 'rubbish lying in a public place' took until the mid 18th century. The link is bedding made of straw or rushes, once used by poorer people, who put it down on the floor and then discarded it when soiled. A litter of animals such as kittens probably gets its name from the mother's giving birth in a sheltered sleeping place.

little [OE] Like *SMALL, this is recorded from the earliest times. The proverb **a little learning is a dangerous thing** quotes a line from Alexander Pope's *Essay on Man* (1711); nowadays people often substitute 'knowledge' for 'learning'.

littoral *see* LIDO

live [OE] In the sense 'to be alive', live goes back to the same root as *LIFE. The other live, with a different pronunciation, is a mid16th-century shortening of **alive** [OE]. The proverb **live and let live** is identified as Dutch in the earliest known reference, from 1622. *Live and Let Die*, the 1954 James Bond book, filmed in 1973, subverted it. The rhyme 'He who fights and runs away / Lives to fight another day' gives us the phrase **live to fight another day**. The idea is found in the works of the Greek comic playwright Menander, who lived from around 342 to 292 BC.

livery *see* LIBERTY

livid [LME] First recorded meaning 'of a bluish leaden colour', livid comes from Latin *lividus*, from *livere* 'be bluish'. It was often used to describe the skin of someone cold or very ill. The sense 'furiously angry' dates from the early 20th century.

load [OE] The ancient root of load is related to that of the metal *LEAD. The word **lode** meaning 'a vein of ore' and found also in **lodestone** [E16th] was originally just a different spelling of load. In earlier use load and lode were used interchangeably for both sets of meanings. The expression **loads of** 'lots, heaps' goes back as far as Shakespeare's *Troilus and Cressida*, where the original spelling was 'loades a'. In the 20th century **loadsa** started appearing in print as one word, and in the late 1980s the comedian Harry Enfield created the character Loadsamoney, a flash Tory who boasted about the money he had made and threw wads of cash around. Loadsamoney was seen as epitomizing the 'get-rich-quick' ethos of the Thatcher years.

loaf [OE] Originally loaf meant 'bread' as well as 'a shaped quantity of bread'. In the British expression **use your loaf**, 'use your common sense', loaf probably comes from the rhyming slang phrase **loaf of bread** meaning 'head'. It is first recorded in a 1920s dictionary of army and navy slang as '*Loaf*, head, e.g., Duck your loaf, i.e., keep your head below the parapet'. To loaf [M19th] or spend time in an aimless, idle way is not connected with bread, but comes from **loafer**, which itself is probably based on German *Landläufer* 'a tramp', related to the word **landlubber** [E18th]. *See also* BREAD, LADY, LORD

lobby [M16th] Both lobby and **lodge** [ME] go back to medieval Latin *lobia* 'covered walk, portico'. The earliest uses of the word refer to monastic cloisters, but after Henry VIII dissolved the monasteries it moved into the world of the rich subjects who turned them into houses. A lobby became an antechamber or entrance hall, and is now often the foyer (*see* FOCUS) of a hotel. The British Houses of Parliament, and other parliaments, have a central lobby where MPs can meet constituents and members of pressure groups, and two division lobbies where MPs assemble to vote. To lobby meaning 'to try to influence a legislator' originated from this arrangement in the USA. **Logistics** [L19th], originally the supplying of troops, developed in French from lodge.

lobscouse *see* SCOUSE

lobster [OE] Lobsters and **locusts** [ME] are linguistically the same. Latin *locusta*, from which both derive, had both meanings. A look at close-up pictures of the two clearly shows the similarity. Lobster was used as a contemptuous name for British soldiers from the mid 17th century. Originally applied to a regiment of Roundhead cuirassiers who wore complete suits of armour; later the term was associated with the red military coats once worn by British soldiers. In US slang, lobster was used to describe 'a slow-witted or gullible person' from the late 19th century.

local [LME] Local is from Latin *locus* 'place'. At first used to mean 'concerned with place or position', it was applied more specifically to a small area with respect to its inhabitants from the late 17th century. **Locals** described the inhabitants themselves from the mid 19th century. The same root is found in **allocation** [LME] from *allocare* 'allot', **dislocate** [L16th] 'displace', **locate** [E16th], **locomotive** [E17th], something that could move its place, and **locale** [L18th]. This is from French *local*, the same as the English word, but with an 'e' added to show the change in pronunciation (*compare* MORAL and morale).

lock [OE] They seem like very different words, but the lock that is a fastening mechanism and the lock of hair may be related. Both are Old English, and possibly derive from a root that meant 'to bend'. All the elements in **lock, stock, and barrel** are parts of an old-fashioned firearm, although only the stock and barrel are found in modern guns. The lock was the mechanism for exploding the charge, the stock is the part to which the firing mechanism and barrel are attached, and the barrel is the cylindrical tube out of which the shot or bullet is fired. The expression first appears in the early 19th century in the alternative version **stock, lock, and barrel**, used by the novelist Sir Walter Scott.

locomotive *see* LOCAL

locust *see* LOBSTER

lode, lodestone *see* LOAD

loaf   lobby   lobscouse   lobster   local   lock

lodge *see* LOBBY

loft [OE] In Old English *loft* meant 'air, sky' as well as what was up in the air, an upper room. It comes from Old Norse, and shares a Germanic root with **lift** [OE]. **Sky** [ME] was also a borrowing from Scandinavian and originally meant 'cloud'. The word was applied to a shade of blue in the mid 17th century; the phrase **out of a clear blue sky**, for something as unexpected as rain or thunder out of such a sky, made its appearance towards the end of the 19th century; **the sky's the limit** dates from the 1920s. When Anglo-Saxons wanted to talk about the sky they could also use the word *wolcen*, welkin in modern English, but now only used in the expression to **make the welkin ring**.

log [ME] The word log is first recorded in the Middle Ages in the sense 'a bulky mass of wood'. The ship's log or official record of events during the voyage got its name from a device used to find out the rate of a ship's motion, a thin quarter-circle of wood loaded so as to float upright in the water and fastened to a line wound on a reel (*see* KNOT). The captain would record the information obtained from this in a journal, or log. *See also* JAM, SLEEP

loggerheads [L16th] The origins of **at loggerheads** are obscure. The earliest meanings of loggerhead, dating from the late 16th century, were 'a disproportionately large head' and 'a stupid person' (similar to mid 16th-century **blockhead**). Around half a century later the word was applied to various animals with very large heads, notably the **loggerhead turtle**. Finally, in the 1680s, it described a long-handled iron instrument with a bulbous end, used for heating liquids. The last sense is probably the source for the modern expression, as it arose at the same time and the implement may also have been used as a weapon.

logic [LME] Logic came via Old French from late Latin, and from Greek *logikē (tekhnē)* '(art) of reason'; the base is Greek *logos* 'word, reason', found also in **prologue** [ME] 'words said before'. **Logo**, a 1930s

shortening of **logogram**, 'a sign representing a word or phrase, shorthand', or of the printing term **logotype**, 'a single piece of type that prints a word, phrase, or symbol' (both E19th) also goes back to *logos*.

logistics *see* LOBBY

logjam *see* JAM

Lolita [M20th] In Vladimir Nabokov's novel *Lolita* (1958), Humbert Humbert, a man in his late 30s, becomes sexually obsessed with Dolores Haze, a 12-year-old girl whom he dubs Lolita, a pet form of Dolores. The book's disturbing subject matter created a scandal when it was published in the USA, but it gave the world two words for 'a sexually precocious young girl', **Lolita** itself and **nymphet**.

lollipop [L18th] Late 18th-century children enjoyed a particular kind of sweet that dissolved easily in the mouth. Its dialect name was a **lollipop**, which may come from another dialect word, **lolly** meaning 'tongue', though there is no written record of this until a century later. Lollipops are now flat, rounded boiled sweets on a stick. The shortened form **lolly** appeared in the mid 19th century, and is still a general word for a sweet in Australia and New Zealand.

long [OE] The long referring to length and the long meaning 'to desire' are unrelated, though both have ancient Germanic roots. The phrase **long in the tooth** was first used to describe horses, and comes from the way you can estimate a horse's age by looking at its teeth: if the gums have receded and the teeth consequently look very long, you know the animal is rather old. *See also* GIFT. The background to **long time no see**, would nowadays probably be seen as politically incorrect. It was originally an American expression and arose in the early 20th century as a supposedly humorous imitation of the broken English spoken by a Native American. This dubious past is long forgotten and the phrase is now freely used on both sides of the Atlantic. *See also* ARM

loo [1940s] The upper-class author Nancy Mitford first put **loo**, meaning 'lavatory', into print in her 1940 novel *Pigeon Pie*. People have put forward different theories about its origin, but none is conclusive. Perhaps the most plausible suggests the source as **Waterloo**, a trade name for iron cisterns in the early 20th century. A popular but unlikely one, not least because of their relative dates, refers it to **gardyloo**, a cry used in 18th-century Edinburgh to warn passers-by that someone was about to throw slops out of a window into the street. It is based on pseudo-French *gar de l'eau* 'mind the water' (real French would be *gare l'eau*). Another French phrase is behind a third suggestion, that British servicemen in France during the First World War picked up *lieux d'aisances* 'places of ease', used for 'a lavatory'.

loon [late 19th century] This word for 'a silly person' comes from the North American loon [M17th], a large water bird also known as a diver. It gets its name from its distinctive cry. The sense silly is from the bird's actions when escaping from danger; perhaps influenced by **loony**, a mid 19th-century abbreviation of **lunatic** [ME] from Latin *luna* 'moon'. In the past people thought that the phases of the moon could affect people.

loose [ME] The medieval word loose is related to Old English **lose** and **loss,** and also to the ending -less, signifying 'without'. The sense 'immoral, promiscuous' dates from around 1470 from the original sense 'free from bonds'. The term **a loose cannon** sounds as if it should be centuries old, perhaps from the days of warships in Napoleonic battles. In fact, the first recorded uses are from the late 19th century, and the phrase only really gained currency in the 1970s. That said, it does come from the idea that a cannon which has broken loose from its mounting would be a particularly dangerous hazard on any ship, but especially a wooden one. *See also* FAST

loot [E19th] Like *THUG, the word loot has its origins in the experience of the British in India. Soldiers picked it up for 'valuables plundered from an enemy' from their Hindi-speaking counterparts—it goes back to a word meaning 'to rob' in Sanskrit, the ancient language of northern India. The slang sense 'money' developed in the 1940s.

loquacious *see* VENTRILOQUIST

lord [OE] The root meaning of lord was 'keeper of bread'. Old English from *hlafweard*, it comes from early forms of *LOAF and *WARD. The corresponding female form is *LADY, in Old English *hlafdige* 'kneader of bread'. The Devil has many names, among them **Lord of the Flies**, the literal meaning of the Hebrew form **Beelzebub**. In 1954 William Golding published *Lord of the Flies* in which a group of schoolboys marooned on an uninhabited island revert to savagery and ritualistic behaviour.

lose, loss *see* LOOSE

lotion *see* LAUNDER

lousy [ME] Lousy is based on **louse**, an Old English word of Germanic origin. It meant both 'full of lice', and 'dirty, contemptible' from early times. The sense 'swarming, full, abundantly supplied' as in **lousy with tourists**, **lousy with money** arose in US English in the mid 19th century.

louvre [ME] The first sense recorded was to describe a domed structure on a roof with side openings for ventilation: *louvre* comes from Old French *lover, lovier* 'skylight', probably of Germanic origin and related to lodge (*see* LOBBY).

love [OE] As you might expect, love is almost as old as time. The word's ancient root is also the source of Latin *lubido* 'desire' (which gave us **libido** [E20th]). **Love is blind** goes back to classical times, but first appeared in English in Geoffrey Chaucer's *Canterbury Tales* in the 14th century. Lewis Carroll appears to have been the first to use **love makes the world go round**, in *Alice's Adventures in Wonderland* in 1865—he may have based it on a French folk song with the lines *c'est l'amour, l'amour, l'amour, Qui fait la monde à la ronde*, 'it is love, love, love that makes the world go round'. In 1967 the Beatles sang 'All You Need is Love', and a slogan associated with the weepie film *Love Story* (1970) was 'Love means never having to say you're sorry'. **The love that dare not speak its name** is homosexuality. The description is by the poet Lord Alfred Douglas, whose association with Oscar Wilde led to Wilde being imprisoned in Reading gaol for homosexual activity.

The use of love in tennis and squash for a score of zero apparently derives from the phrase to **play for love**, that is for the love of the game, not for money. A popular explanation connects it with French *l'oeuf* 'egg', from the resemblance in shape between an egg and a zero (*see also* DUCK).

One caricature of actors is that they all gushingly call each other 'love'. In the late 20th century an actor, or anyone actively involved in entertainment, came to be a **luvvy**, a respelling of **lovey**, an affectionate term of address used since the mid 18th century.

lox *see* YIDDISH WORD PANEL

loyal *see* LAW

lozenge [ME] Lozenge, which primarily conveys a diamond shape, is from Old French *losenge*, probably derived from Spanish *losa*, or Portuguese *lousa* 'slab', and late Latin *lausiae (lapides)* meaning '(stone) slabs'. The word's use to mean 'tablet' arose in the early 16th century from their original diamond shape. *Compare* **tablet** *at* TABLE

lucid *see* LIGHT

Lucifer [OE] This is a Latin word originally, meaning 'light-bringing, morning star', from *luc-* 'light' and *-fer* 'bearing'. It was sometimes used in poetry to refer to the planet Venus appearing in the sky before sunrise. It was also used for the rebel archangel (Satan) by association with the biblical quotation 'How art thou fallen from heaven, O Lucifer, son of the morning' (Isaiah 14:12).

luck [LME] The native English word for that which determines events was weird, which only came to mean strange or supernatural in the early 19th century. **Destiny** [ME] came later via French from Latin *destinare* 'make firm, establish', *FATE from Italian, and luck from German. The idea of **lucky at cards, unlucky in love** is already a commonplace in Jonathan Swift's *Polite Conversation* in 1738: 'Well, Miss, you'll have a sad husband, you have such good luck at cards.'

ludicrous [E17th] The early sense of ludicrous was 'sportive, intended as a jest': it is based on Latin *ludicrus*, probably from *ludicrum* 'stage play'.

luff *see* ALOOF

luggage [L16th] Luggage is basically something you **lug** about, from a late Middle English word, which is probably Scandinavian. The connection to lug for 'ear' is uncertain.

lumber [LME] The earliest lumber in English meant 'to move in a slow, heavy, awkward way'. Its origin is not known, but its form may have been intended to suggest clumsiness or heaviness, rather like **lump** [ME]. This may have been the origin of lumber in the sense 'disused furniture and articles that take up space', but people also associated the term with the old word lumber meaning 'a pawnbroker's shop', which was an alteration of **Lombard** or 'person from Lombardy'. The mainly North American sense 'timber sawn into rough planks' appears to be a development of the 'disused furniture' meaning, as is the verb to **be lumbered** or burdened with something unwanted. The slang phrase **in lumber**, 'in trouble', originally meant 'in pawn, pawned'.

lumberjack *see* JACK

luminous [LME] Luminous is from Old French *lumineux* or Latin *luminosus*, from *lumen, lumin-* 'light'.

lump *see* LUMBER

lunatic *see* LOON

lunch [E19th] Until the 19th century a light midday meal was a **luncheon** [L16th],

lox   loyal   lozenge   lucid   Lucifer   luck

and when the shortened form **lunch** appeared in the 1820s people regarded it as either lower-class or a fashionable affectation. Luncheon was probably derived from Spanish *lonja* 'slice'. *See also* LADY, SUPPER. The modern proverb **there's no such thing as a free lunch**, was first used in the 1960s among US economists. It was probably suggested by the practice, dating from the mid 19th century, of some bars providing free lunch if you bought a drink.

lung *see* LIGHT

lupara *see* ITALIAN WORD PANEL

lupine *see* WOLF

lurch [M16th] The lurch in **leave someone in the lurch**, 'to leave an associate without support when they need it', derives from French *lourche*, the name of a 16th-century game resembling backgammon. As well as a game, lurch then was a score or state of play in which one player was enormously ahead of the other. The unsteady, uncontrolled lurch is a different word from the late 17th century—it was originally a sailors' term, which described the sudden leaning of a ship to one side.

lurid [M17th] The early sense of lurid was 'pale and dismal in colour'. It comes from Latin *luridus*, related to *luror* 'a wan or yellow colour'.

luscious *see* DELICIOUS

luvvy *see* LOVE

luxury [ME] From the Middle Ages to the early 19th century luxury was 'lust, lasciviousness'—the Latin source *luxuria* also implied indulgence as a vice— although the modern English sense 'great comfort or elegance' has also appeared in the mid 17th century.

lycanthropy *see* WOLF

lynch [M19th] During the War of American Independence (1775–83) a Captain William Lynch of Pittsville, Virginia, headed a self-constituted court with no legal authority which persecuted 'Tories', or people who supported the British side. People called this illegal punishment **Lynch's law** or **lynch law**. The penalties handed out were beatings or tarring and feathering, but by the mid 19th century to lynch a supposed offender was generally to hang him.

lynx *see* OUNCE

lung   lupara   lupine   lurch   lurid   luscious

Mm

Tudor and Elizabethan politics. It advised rulers that the acquisition and effective use of power may necessitate unethical methods that are undesirable in themselves. People simplified and exaggerated his ideas, and his name became a byword for unscrupulous, deceitful, and cunning methods.

machine *see* MECHANICAL

ma *see* MUM

mac *see* MACKINTOSH, MAIDEN

macabre [L19th] One of the medieval miracle plays presented the slaughter of the Maccabees, family members and supporters of Judus Maccabaeus, who led a religious revolt in Judaea in 165 BC. This gruesome event probably gave rise to macabre, 'disturbing, horrifying', originally in the phrase **dance of macabre**, a term for the dance of death (*see* DEATH). The name Maccabaeus may come from a Hebrew word meaning 'hammer'.

macaroni [E16th] When 'Yankee Doodle went to town a-riding on a pony' and 'stuck a feather in his hat and called it macaroni', he was not confusing his headgear with pasta. He was presenting himself as a dandy — completely unconvincingly, reflecting the English view of Americans, then still under British colonial rule, as lacking sophistication. In 18th-century Britain the macaronis were young men who had travelled abroad and exaggeratedly imitated continental fashions. The pasta dish pre-dated this trend. Its name also survives in **macaroon** [L16th], which came through French, changing its recipe on the way. Italian *macaroni* goes back to Greek *makaria* 'food made from barley'. *See also* PASTE, ITALIAN AND US WORD PANELS

macchiato *see* ITALIAN WORD PANEL

Machiavellian [M16th] Niccolò Machiavelli was an Italian statesman and scholar who lived from 1469 to 1527. His best-known work is *The Prince*, translated into English in 1532 and highly influential in

macho [1920s] When Mexicans described a man as *macho*, it was usually to compliment him on his vigour and virility. But when English-speaking Americans adopted the word from Mexican Spanish in the 1920s it acquired overtones of 'masculine in an overly assertive or aggressive way'. The Spanish word *macho* derives from Latin *masculus* 'male', the source of **masculine** [ME]. **Machismo**, also from Mexican Spanish and based on *macho*, dates from the 1940s.

mackintosh [M19th] This word for a waterproof garment was named after Charles Macintosh (1766–1843), the Scottish inventor who patented the waterproof cloth of the original mackintosh, made of two layers of cloth bonded together by India rubber dissolved in naphtha. The abbreviation **mac** is found from the early 20th century. The Apple Macintosh computer has nothing to do with waterproofs, but was named after a popular North American apple, the McIntosh, with a slight change of spelling for legal reasons.

mad [OE] In English mad has always meant 'insane'. In extreme cases a person can be **as mad as a hatter** or **as mad as a March hare**. The comparison with hatters has a sound scientific basis: in the past some hatters really did become mentally ill. Felt hats were made from fur, and one of the processes in their manufacture involved brushing a solution of mercurous nitrate on to the fur to make the fibres mat together. As a result of inhaling the mercury fumes some hat-makers suffered from mercury poisoning, which can produce symptoms such as confused speech, hallucinations, and loss of memory. The phrase was around

ma   mac   macabre   macaroni   macchiato

in the 1830s, but from 1865 it was popularized by the Mad Hatter, one of the characters in Lewis Carroll's *Alice's Adventures in Wonderland*. As mad as a March hare arose from the excitable behaviour of hares at the beginning of the breeding season.

'**Mad, bad, and dangerous to know**' was how Lady Caroline Lamb described the poet Lord Byron after their first meeting at a ball in 1812. Byron was a dashing figure whose name gave rise to the adjective **Byronic** for a man who is alluringly dark, mysterious, and moody. '**Mad Dogs and Englishmen** / Go out in the midday sun' is the beginning of a 1931 song by the English dramatist, actor, and composer Noël Coward. The word **madding** is a rather poetic way of saying 'acting madly'. It is most familiar through the phrase **far from the madding crowd**, 'private or secluded'. Many will associate it with the title of one of Thomas Hardy's classic novels, but Hardy took the title from a line in Thomas Gray's poem 'Elegy Written in a Country Church-Yard', published in 1751: 'Far from the madding crowd's ignoble strife'. **Mad scientists** have been with us since the 1940s, but **mad cow disease** for bovine spongiform encephalopathy only since the 1980s.

madonna [L16th] In Italian *madonna* means 'my lady'—the second element goes back to Latin *domina* 'mistress', the root of which also gave us *DAME, *DANGER, *DOMINION, and *DUNGEON. At first in English it was used as a title or mock title for an Italian woman, but in the 17th century **the Madonna** began to refer to the Virgin Mary.

madrigal *see* MOTHER

Mae West *see* SEE

mafia [M19th] The first printed reference to the **Mafia** dates from 1866. The secret criminal society started in Sicily where *mafia* meant 'bragging'. Other communities harboured similar organizations: a **Chinese mafia** is reported in California in 1891 and a **Russian mafia** in 1903, and by the 1940s any group regarded as exerting a secret and sinister influence could be given the name. *See also* GOD

magazine [L16th] The first magazines were storehouses, often for ammunition and provisions for war. The word comes from Italian *magazzino* and goes back to Arabic. From the mid 17th century books providing information useful to particular groups of people often had magazine in their title. The use for a periodical publication providing a range of stories and articles developed from this: the first was *The Gentleman's Magazine; or, Monthly Intelligencer*, launched in 1731. Military uses of the word developed at the same time. A container for holding a supply of cartridges to be fed automatically into the breech of a gun came to be called a magazine in the 1860s.

magenta [M19th] This colour owes its name to Magenta in northern Italy, the site of a battle in 1859 fought shortly before the dye was discovered.

maggot [LME] Around 2003 a photograph circulated on the internet purporting to show a man with **maggots in the brain**. The maggots were just an urban myth—one story said that the condition resulted from eating the Japanese raw-fish dish sashimi; another that it resulted from swimming in water where parasitic fish could enter the urinary tract (the *candiru*, a small catfish of the Amazon basin, does occasionally do this). The scare was new, but not the idea. When the Gothic novelist Charlotte Dacre published *Zofloya, or the Moor* in 1806, with its plot of murder and a Satanic lover, a reviewer pronounced that she must be 'afflicted with the dismal malady of maggots in the brain'. Maggot is probably an alteration of the earlier word **maddock**, meaning 'maggot' or 'earthworm', influenced by *Maggot* or *Magot*, pet forms of the names Margery or Margaret. *Compare* PIE

magic [LME] The Magi were the 'wise men' from the East who visited the infant Jesus soon after his birth. They were said to have been kings, called Caspar, Melchior, and Balthasar, who brought gifts of gold, frankincense, and myrrh. The singular form is **magus**, and it was originally a term for a member of a priestly caste of ancient Persia regarded as having unusual powers, and the word, filtered through Greek and Latin, is the origin of our magic and **magician** [LME]. Magic has been used for something remarkable, as in the expression a **magic touch**, since the mid 19th century and as an exclamation of approval meaning 'excellent' since the 1950s.

magistrate [LME] Magistrate is from Latin *magistratus* 'administrator', from *magister* 'master'. This also gives us **master** [OE], its weakened form **mister** [M16th], and *MISS.

magnet [LME] The term magnet was originally used for a natural magnet or lodestone (*see* LOAD). It comes via Latin for the Greek term for a lodestone, *magnes lithos*. See also ELECTRICITY

magnify [LME] Early uses have strong biblical associations and included 'show honour to (God)' (Luke 1:46: 'My soul doth magnify the Lord': part of the *Magnificat*, a canticle used in Christian liturgy) and 'make greater in size or importance' (Job 20:6: 'Though he be magnified up to the heavens'). 'Make larger by means of a lens' is a sense dating from the mid 17th century. It goes back to Latin *magnus* 'great' as does **magnificent** [LME] originally 'serving to magnify'.

maiden [OE] The ancient root of maiden is also that of Scottish and Irish Gaelic *mac* 'son', the element in surnames beginning **Mac-** or **Mc-**, and seems to have referred to a young person of either sex. In the Middle Ages maiden was shortened to **maid**, and the two continued alongside each other, both meaning 'a young female' and 'a virgin of any age', and also 'a female servant', for which maid is now the usual term. This ambiguity led to words and phrases such as *GIRL or young lady replacing maiden and maid in the 'young female' sense. Cricketers trying to bowl a **maiden over** are hoping to ensure that no runs are scored from the six balls they are bowling. The idea, dating from the 1850s, is that the over is 'virgin' or 'unproductive'.

mail [ME] Modern English has two different words spelled mail. The mail that refers to the postal system came immediately from French, but is related to Dutch *maal* meaning 'wallet, bag'. This is also the oldest sense in English, and **mails** in the USA and Scotland is still a term for baggage. The use of a postal service arose in the mid 17th century from the bag in which letters were carried. From there it developed to the contents of the bag. 'An item delivered' is the origin of newspaper titles such as the *Daily Mail*. At the same time mail also came to apply to a person or vehicle delivering letters and packages, and then to the postal system itself. British usage favours *POST for both the system and the material delivered, while mail is dominant in North America and Australia. For electronic messages, though, mail and **email** are universal—the ordinary post is **snail mail**.

In **coat of mail** the word came from Latin *macula* 'stain, blemish, mesh of a net', seen also in *IMMACULATE. Originally it referred to the individual metal rings or plates that make up the armour, so a knight would have worn a **coat of mails**. See also BLACKMAIL

maim *see* MAYHEM

mainline *see* TRAIN

majesty *see* MAJOR

major [ME] Latin *major* means 'greater' from *magnus* 'great' (*see* MAGNIFY), a sense still found in old-fashioned schools where 'Smith major' might be used to label the older of two brothers. The military rank is found from the late 16th century, while the sense 'serious, excessive' as in **a major foul-up** dates only from the 1950s. The **mayor** [ME] of a place, the title **majesty** [ME], and the **majority** [M16th] all get their names from the same source.

make *see* MATCH

malady *see* MALARIA

magistrate magnet magnify maiden mail

malaise *see* MALICE

malapropism [M19th] 'As headstrong as an allegory on the banks of the Nile' are some of the words of Mrs Malaprop, a character in *The Rivals*, a comedy by Richard Sheridan produced in 1775. Her most notable characteristic is an aptitude to misapply long words. The play was a great success, and the character clearly memorable, giving English the malapropism. Sheridan had based her name on the earlier term **malapropos** [M17th] from French *mal à propos* 'inappropriate'. *See also* SPOONERISM

malaria [M18th] Before people understood that malaria was transmitted by mosquitoes, they attributed the disease to an unwholesome condition of the atmosphere in marshy districts. It was particularly prevalent in Italy, and especially near Rome. In a letter of 1740 the writer and statesman Horace Walpole wrote of 'A horrid thing called the mal'aria, that comes to Rome every summer and kills one'. Italian *mal'aria* is a contraction of *mala aria* 'bad air'. **Malady** [ME] comes from a similar source, being from Lain *male* 'ill' and *habitus* 'having (as a condition)'.

male *see* FEMALE

malice [ME] Malice goes back to Latin *malus* 'bad', the source also of **malign** [ME], **malaise** [M18th], and the first part of **malevolent** [E16th], the second half being from Latin *velle* 'to wish'. Since the 15th century malice has been a legal term, found especially in **malice aforethought**, the intention to kill or harm which distinguishes murder from manslaughter.

mall [M17th] The game **pall-mall** was popular in the 17th century. Players used a mallet to drive a boxwood ball through an iron ring suspended at the end of a long alley, itself also called a pall-mall. The game got its name, via French, from the Italian for 'ball' and 'mallet'. Pall Mall, a street in central London known for its large number of private clubs and formerly a fashionable place to promenade, was originally a pall-mall for the game. From the 18th century other sheltered places for walking came to be called malls—the first reference to a mall for shopping dates from 1950 in the USA. **Malleable** [LME] got its name from the same source as mall, for it originally meant 'able to be hammered' and goes back, like **mallet** [LME] and **maul** [ME], to Latin *malleus* 'hammer'.

malus *see* BONUS

mama *see* BABY, MUM

mammal [E19th] This is an anglicized form of modern Latin *mammalia*, from *mamma* 'breast', the ability to produce milk being one of the distinguishing features of mammals.

mammoth [E18th] In Siberia people used to dig up fossil remains and frozen carcasses of a large elephant-like hairy mammal with long curved tusks. They called this in Russian the *mamont*, which probably came from a Siberian word meaning 'earth horn'. In the early 18th century English acquired this as **mammoth**. The word began to refer to anything of a huge size in the early 19th century. *See also* COLOSSAL

man [OE] The English word man goes back to an age-old root that also gave *manu*, 'humankind', in Sanskrit, the ancient language of India. From Anglo-Saxon times, man meant both 'a person of either sex' and 'an adult male', as well as the human race in general. Shakespeare's *Hamlet* provided the phrase **man and boy**, when the gravedigger says, 'I have been sexton here, man and boy, for thirty years.' The original **man for all seasons** was Sir Thomas More, the scholar and statesman who wrote *Utopia* and was beheaded for opposing Henry VIII's marriage to Anne Boleyn. It came into prominence in 1960 as the title of a play about More by Robert Bolt. A clergyman is a **man of the cloth**. The writer Jonathan Swift first used 'the cloth' to refer to the clergy in 1710. A clergyman's 'cloth' had meant his profession since the mid 17th century, and before that other occupations which stipulated a special dress code or uniform, notably the law and the military, had also been referred to as a person's 'cloth'.

malaise malapropism malaria male malice

Man for humans in general survives in expressions such as **the man in the street**. The judge Lord Bowen, who died in 1894, used **the man on the Clapham omnibus** (Clapham is a district of south London) to refer to any ordinary reasonable person, such as a juror is expected to be. '**Man cannot live by bread alone**' is found in two passages of the Bible, one from the Old Testament in Deuteronomy, and the other from the New Testament in the Gospel of Matthew. The proverb **man proposes, God disposes** goes back to the 15th century, but also reflects a 14th-century French saying. The ancient Greek philosopher Plato provided a precedent for **man is the measure of all things**, recorded in English from the mid 16th century.

As a way of addressing someone, man goes right back to the Anglo-Saxons and was common in the 18th and 19th centuries, although the old uses tended to sound impatient or encouraging—'Pick up your feet, man!' The modern use of man, often expressing surprise, admiration, or delight, came from the speech of black Americans. *See also* MOUSE

manacle, manicure *see* MANAGE

manage [M16th] Managers now manage businesses, but the first things to be managed were horses. The earliest sense of manage in English was 'to handle or train a horse', or put it through the exercises of the **manège** [M17th]. This French word, used in English to mean 'an area in which horses and riders are trained' and 'horsemanship', is at root the same word as manage—both go back through Italian to Latin *manus* 'hand', the source also of **manacles** [ME] which restrain your hands; **manicure** [L19th] care of your hands; **manipulate** [E19th] to handle something; *MANNER; *MANOEUVRE; **manual** [LME] either done with your hands or a handbook; and **manuscript** [L16th] something written by hand.

mañana *see* SPANISH WORD PANEL

mandarin [L16th] Few words can claim such different meanings as a language, a fruit, and a civil servant; but mandarin can. A mandarin was an official in a senior grade

of the former imperial Chinese civil service. The word is not Chinese, though, but came into English from Portuguese in the late 16th century, and goes back to a term meaning 'counsellor, minister' in Sanskrit. The use of mandarin for a leading civil servant in Britain, as in 'Whitehall mandarins', comes from this and dates from the early 19th century. In 1703 Francisco Varo published his *Arte de la Lengua Mandarina*, the first grammar of any spoken form of Chinese, which described the Chinese used by officials and educated people in general. In 1728 Mandarin first appeared in English for the language, and it is now the name for the standard, official form of Chinese. Mandarin was first applied to a citrus fruit in Swedish. The reason for the name is not certain—it might refer to the colour of Chinese officials' silk robes, or to the high quality of the delicious little oranges, playing on the old term China *ORANGE. A translation of a Swedish travelogue introduced the mandarin orange to English in 1771.

manège *see* MANAGE

manga *see* JAPANESE WORD PANEL

manger [ME] In Christianity the manger is a symbol for the birth of Jesus, as told in the Gospel of Luke: 'And she brought forth her firstborn son, and wrapped him in swaddling clothes, and laid him in a manger; because there was no room for them in the inn.' This word for an animal's feeding trough goes back through Old French *manger* 'to eat' (seen also in **mangetout peas** [E19th] and BLANCMANGE) to Latin *manducare* 'to chew'. The name of the skin disease **mange** [LME] has a very similar origin. The parasites that cause it give rise to intense itching, and another meaning of *manger* was 'to itch from bites'. **Mangy** had become an insult by the mid 16th century. See also DOG.

manifest [LME] Manifest and the originally Italian **manifesto** [M17th] both come from Latin *manifestare* 'to make public'.

manikin [M16th] This is from Dutch *manneken* 'little man'. The same word, through French gives us **mannequin** for a model [E20th].

manipulate *see* MANAGE

manky [1950s] This word meaning 'inferior, worthless, off-colour' is probably from obsolete *mank* 'mutilated, defective', from Old French *manque* 'lack', from Latin *mancus* 'maimed'.

mannequin *see* MANIKIN

manner [ME] Latin *manus* 'hand' is ultimately the source of manner, as it is of *MANAGE and many other words, via the idea of 'way of handling'. The first sense in English was 'sort, kind', followed by 'usual practice or behaviour', then 'customary rules of behaviour in society', and (in the plural) 'polite or well-bred social behaviour'—the kind of **manners** that parents try to teach their children. The phrase **as if to the manner born**, 'naturally at ease in a particular job or situation', derives from a passage in Shakespeare's *Hamlet*. Since at least the mid 19th century this has also appeared as 'to the manor born', a confusion picked up in the title of the British television series *To the Manor Born*, first shown in 1979. *See also* MANSION

manoeuvre [M18th] Soldiers, sailors, and farmers come together in the words manoeuvre and **manure** [LME], which share the Latin origin *manu operari* 'to work with the hand', from *manus* 'hand' (*see* MANAGE, MANNER). The earliest sense of manoeuvre, which came from French in the mid 18th century, was 'a planned movement of military or naval forces'. Old French gave us **manure** in the late Middle Ages. Then it had the senses 'to cultivate land' and 'to administer or manage land or property'— the use for dung used on the land dates from the mid 16th century.

mansion [LME] The rich person's mansion and the minister's **manse** have the same origin. They both derive from Latin *mansio* 'place where someone stays', from *manere* 'to stay' (the source of **remain** [LME] and **manor** [ME]). A mansion was originally the home of a medieval lord of the manor, but the word later extended to any large, impressive house. 'The principal house of an estate' was also the original sense of manse; it became increasingly restricted to an ecclesiastical residence, and is now a house occupied by a Church of Scotland or other Nonconformist minister. A **son** or **daughter of the manse** (like Prime Minister Gordon Brown) is a child of a Church of Scotland minister. *See also* PALACE

manual *see* MANAGE

manufactory *see* FACTORY

manure *see* MANOEUVRE

manuscript *see* MANAGE

marathon [L19th] In 490 BC the Athenians won a victory over an invading Persian army at Marathon on the coast of Attica in eastern Greece. The Greek historian Herodotus described how the herald Pheidippides ran the 150 miles from Athens to Sparta to get help before the battle. According to a later tradition a messenger ran from Marathon to Athens, a distance of 22 miles, with news of the victory, but fell dead on arrival. The first modern Olympic games in 1896 instituted the marathon as a long-distance race— fortunately for competitors, based on the shorter version of the story.

marble [ME] Marble goes back to Greek *marmaros* 'shining stone', a limestone used for building and sculpture. The small balls of the children's game have been called marbles since the late 17th century, though they are now mostly made of glass. In the game players take turns at shooting their own marble at marbles inside a ring, trying to knock other's marbles out of the ring to win them. Some players lose some or all of their marbles—the idea behind **marbles** as a term for someone's mental faculties.

marcel *see* PERMANENT

march [LME] There are three English words march, if you include **March**. The march with the sense 'to walk in a military manner' came from French *marcher* 'to walk' in the late Middle Ages. If you **march to a different tune** you consciously adopt a different approach or attitude to the majority of people. The variant **march to a different drummer** was inspired by an observation from the 19th-century US essayist and poet Henry David Thoreau: 'If a man does not keep pace with his companions, perhaps it is because he hears a different drummer.'

Another march means 'the border or frontier of a country', now found mainly in the geographical term **the Marches**, used for the area of land on the border of England and Wales, such as the counties of Shropshire and Monmouthshire. It too came from French, but is probably related to mark, from the idea of a boundary marker.

The month is named after Mars, the Roman god of war, and was originally the first month of the Roman calendar. Weather lore from the early 17th century tells us that **March comes in like a lion, and goes out like a lamb**—traditionally the weather is wild at the beginning of March, but fair and settled by the end. The name of the god Mars is also the source of **martial** [LME], 'relating to fighting or war', which entered English in the late Middle Ages. The **martial arts**, sports such as judo, karate, and kendo, originated in Japan, China, and Korea and first came to European attention in the late 19th century, though the general term martial arts is not recorded until 1920. *See also* MAD

Mardi Gras *see* SHRIFT

mare [OE] Old English *mearh* 'horse', *mere* 'mare' are from a Germanic base with related words in Celtic languages meaning 'stallion'. The sense 'male horse' died out at the end of the Middle English period. The same root lies behind **marshal** [ME], originally someone in charge of horses.

Margaret *see* MAGGOT, PEARL, PIE

margarine [L19th] This comes from French, based on Greek *margaron* 'pearl', by association with the pearly appearance of its early ingredients. The abbreviation **marge** has been in use since the 1920s. *See* PEARL

marguerite *see* PEARL

marine [ME] The root of marine is Latin *mare* 'sea', the source also of **mariner** [ME], **maritime** [M16th], and **mermaid** [ME]. **Marinate** [M17th] and **marinade** [L17th] are closely related, having originally been used of pickles and coming from a word for 'salt water, brine'. Marines were originally any men serving on board a ship, but later the meaning was restricted to troops who were trained to serve on land or sea, now particularly the Royal Marines or, in the USA, the Marine Corps. These facts shed little light on the likely source of the expression **tell that to the marines**, used to express disbelief. It may have begun with a remark made by King Charles II (1630–85). He advised that implausible tales should be checked out with sailors, who, being familiar with distant lands, might be the people best qualified to judge whether they were true or not. Another idea picks up a clue left in the longer version **tell that to the horse marines**. The horse marines were an imaginary troop of cavalry soldiers serving on board a ship, used as an image of total ineptitude or of people completely out of their natural element. The idea is that such people are so clueless that they will believe anything they are told.

marital *see* MARRY

market *see* MERCURY

marmalade [LME] Oranges were not the original fruit in marmalade. Early marmalade was a solid quince jelly that was cut into squares for eating; in 1524 King Henry VIII was given 'a box of marmalade'. The word is recorded in English in the late 15th century, and comes from Portuguese *marmelada* 'quince jam'. The story that marmalade was originally made for Mary Queen of Scots when she was ill and comes from *marie malade* 'ill Mary' has no foundation. The Scots are, however,

Mardi Gras   mare   Margaret   margarine

generally credited with inventing the kind of marmalade we are familiar with, and the first marmalade factory was built in Dundee in 1797, by the Keiller family.

maroon [L16th] The Maroons were descendants of runaway slaves who lived in the mountains and forests of Suriname and the West Indies. Their name came from French *marron* 'feral', from Spanish *cimarrón* 'wild'. In the early 18th century to maroon someone became to put them down on a desolate island or coast and to leave them there, especially as a punishment. None of this has anything to do with the colour maroon, which derives from French *marron* 'chestnut'. The earliest examples of maroon in English, from the late 16th century, refer to this lustrous reddish-brown nut, with the colour dating from the late 18th century. The noise of a chestnut bursting in a fire accounts for maroon as the name of a firework that makes a loud bang, often with a bright flash of light, used as a signal or warning.

marry [ME] Both marry and **marriage** [ME] come from Old French *marier* 'to marry', which goes back to Latin *maritus* 'a husband', source also of **marital** [E16th]. Traditional advice on marriage includes **marry in haste and repent at leisure**, from the late 16th century, and **never marry for money, but marry where money is**, first formulated in Alfred Lord Tennyson's poem 'Northern Farmer, New Style' (1870). A **marriage of convenience** is one concluded to achieve a practical purpose. The essayist Joseph Addison used the expression in the early 18th century, translating French *mariage de convenance*. Whatever the married state, we have been assured since the mid 16th century that **marriages are made in heaven**, and since the mid 17th that **marriage is a lottery**. It is typical of the way we use words from different sources in English that we speak of a marriage, from French, in the abstract, but when we talk of the actual, concrete celebrations we usually use **wedding**, which has been in use since Anglo-Saxon times going back to a Germanic root meaning 'to pledge'.

marshal *see* MARE

martial *see* MARCH

marvel *see* MIRACLE

marzipan [M16th] The sugary paste used on cakes has taken an exotic journey starting at the port of Martaban on the coast of southeast Burma (Myanmar), once famous for the glazed jars it exported, containing preserves and sweets. In the course of a long trek through Persian and Arabic into European languages, the name Martaban transmuted into Italian *marzapane*, with a shift of meaning from the container to its contents. From the 16th to the 19th centuries the usual form in English was **marchpane**. It was not until the 19th century, when English reborrowed the Italian word, that marzipan became established.

mascara [L19th] Acting and clowning are indirectly linked in mascara, from Italian *maschera*, which goes back to an Arabic word meaning 'buffoon'. Most of the earliest English uses refer to theatrical make-up, though the first known, from 1886, suggests a more discreet use by gentlemen: 'For darkening the eyebrows and moustaches without greasing them and making them prominent'. Through Italian *maschera* mascara is also linked to **mask** [M16th] and **masquerade** [L16th].

mascot [L19th] The French operetta *La Mascotte* by Edmond Audran had its première on 29 December 1880. The next year the word made its first appearance in English. French *mascotte* derives from *masco* 'witch' in the dialect of southern France. At first mascot meant simply 'a person or thing supposed to bring good luck' and did not have to be carried or displayed, as now.

masculine *see* MACHO

mash [OE] Brewing provides the earliest context of mash. The mash is a mixture of ground malt and hot water which is left to stand to form the infusion called 'wort'. The first example of mash meaning 'mashed

maroon   marry   marshal   martial   marvel

potatoes' is from 1904, by the British MP and novelist A.E.W. Mason: 'I...go into a public-house...and have a sausage and mash and a pot of beer.' The word may ultimately be related to **mix**. This is from Latin *mixtus* which became *mixte* in Old French. This was heard by English speakers as 'mixed' and a new verb, to mix, was formed. As an abbreviation for 'mobile army surgical hospital' **MASH** goes back to 1950. The term was made famous in the 1970 film *M*A*S*H*, set in a field hospital during the Korean War. The film gave rise to a long-running TV series (1972–83).

mask *see* MASCARA

masochism [L19th] Sexual pleasure derived from pain features in several stories by the 19th-century Austrian writer Leopold von Sacher-Masoch. The German term *Masochismus* was used in 1890, and by 1892 English had adopted it as masochism. *See also* SADISM

masquerade *see* MASCARA

mass [OE] There is no relation at all between late Middle English mass 'a large body with no definite shape' and Old English Mass 'the celebration of the Christian Eucharist'. The first goes back to Greek *maza* 'barley cake'. The other derives ultimately from Latin *mittere* 'to dismiss, send', and so is connected with *MESSAGE, **missive** [LME], and **amass** [LME], as well as with words such as *PERMIT. The use for the religious service may come from its last words in Latin, *Ite, missa est* 'Go, it is the dismissal'. Ordinary people have been called **the masses** since at least 1837, and they have been supplied with goods by **mass production** since 1893.

massacre [L16th] This is from French, from Old French *macecre* 'slaughterhouse, butcher's shop'.

master *see* MAGISTRATE

matador *see* SPANISH WORD PANEL

match [OE] Match in the sense 'be the same as' comes from an Old English word

meaning 'mate, companion' which probably goes back to the same root as Old English **make**. Use of the word to mean 'contest, competitive trial' dates from the early 16th century. The match associated with fire was first used to mean 'candle wick'. It is from Old French *meche*, perhaps from Latin *myxa* meaning 'spout of a lamp, lamp wick'. The wooden match we are familiar with today dates from the early 19th century.

mate *see* MEAT

maternal, matriarch, matrimony, matrix, matter *see* MOTHER

mattress [ME] The word *mattress* came via Old French and Italian from Arabic *matrah* 'carpet or cushion', from *taraha* 'to throw'.

mature *see* DEMUR

matzos *see* YIDDISH WORD PANEL

maul *see* MALL

mausoleum [LME] This word came via Latin from Greek *Mausōleion*, from *Mausōlos*, the name of a king of Caria in the 4th century BC. It was originally applied to his tomb in Halicarnassus.

maven *see* YIDDISH WORD PANEL

maverick [M19th] In the middle of the 19th century Samuel Augustus Maverick owned such a large herd of cattle in Texas that he left the calves unbranded. People in the USA noted this unusual practice and began to use maverick for any unbranded calf or yearling. From the 1880s the word came to signify 'individualistic, unorthodox, or independent-minded'.

May [OE] Maia was one of the seven daughters of the Titan *ATLAS in Greek mythology. In Roman mythology she came to be identified with Maia Majesta, a goddess of fertility and of the spring, who is said to have given her name to the month of May. Since the late Middle Ages may has also been a name for hawthorn blossom or

mask masochism masquerade mass

the hawthorn, which in Britain typically flowers in May. Many people believe that the proverb warning us not to leave off old or warm clothes until the end of May, **ne'er cast a clout till May be out**, refers to hawthorn blossom, but the first recorded example makes it clear that the word applies to the month. **May Day** has been known since the 13th century as a time for springtime festivities and the election of a pretty girl as **May queen** or **Queen of the May** to preside over them. In some countries it is now a holiday in honour of working people. The international radio distress signal **Mayday** is a representation of French *m'aider*, short for *venez m'aider* 'come and help me'.

mayhem [E16th] Between the 15th and 19th centuries mayhem was a crime which involved maiming a person so that they could no longer defend themselves. In origin the word is a form of **maim** [ME], which came through French but whose ultimate origin is unknown. The modern sense 'violent or extreme disorder' originated in the USA in the 19th century.

mayonnaise [E19th] Most books say that mayonnaise comes via French *mahonnais* from Port Mahon, the capital of Minorca, which was taken by the French in 1756. The first reference to mayonnaise anywhere is not found until 1804, though, when the success was hardly fresh in the French mind, and the spelling was with -*y*- rather than -*h*- from the beginning. The chef M.A. Carême (1784–1833), explained the word as from French *manier* 'to handle' referring to the method of preparation. It could also be a corruption of French *bayonnaise*, meaning 'from the town of Bayonne'.

mayor *see* MAJOR

maze [ME] This is probably a shortening of Old English **amaze**. Maze was first used for delirium, but had come to be used for a labyrinth by late Middle English.

McCoy [M19th] The source of **the real McCoy** is far from clear. The trouble is that

McCoy is a relatively common surname and so there are numerous candidates for the post of the original McCoy. The earliest example of the phrase, dating from 1856, is Scottish, uses the form **McKay**, and describes a brand of whisky: 'a drappie [drop] o' the real McKay'. The distillers G. Mackay and Co. apparently adopted 'the Real Mackay' as an advertising slogan in 1870, and this was the form familiar to novelist Robert Louis Stevenson, who used it to mean 'the genuine article' in a letter in 1883. It seems clear that the expression was well established as **the real McKay** by the end of the 19th century, but in the early part of the next century most examples have the **McCoy** spelling and are American. Possibly the most likely reason for this spelling change is one Norman Selby, also known as Charles 'Kid' McCoy. He was an American boxer who became welterweight champion in 1896 after knocking out Tommy Ryan, his sparring partner, to whom he had previously pretended to be ill and unfit. Apparently he often used this trick of feigning illness, only to appear fighting fit on the day itself, prompting commentators to wonder whether this was **the real McCoy**.

meal [OE] Meal meaning 'the edible part of any grain or pulse' goes back to an ancient root shared with Latin *molere* 'to grind', which shares a root with *MILL. The meal at which food is eaten has a root meaning 'to measure'. In Old English meal also meant 'a measure', a use which survives in **piecemeal** [ME] 'a bit at a time'. The expression to **make a meal of** dates from the early 17th century in the sense 'to take advantage of', but the notion 'to make something unduly laborious' goes back only to the 1960s. The idea behind **mealy-mouthed**, 'afraid to speak frankly or straightforwardly', is of a person having their mouth full of meal and so being afraid to open it fully. It is first recorded in the 1570s, and probably comes from an old German proverb.

mean [OE] The word mean means many things in English. The ancient root of Old English mean 'to intend to convey' is related to *MIND. The original meaning of mean 'not

mayhem   mayonnaise   mayor   maze   McCoy

generous, small-minded' [ME] was 'common to two or more people', reflecting its ancient root, shared with Latin *communis* 'common' (*see* COMMONPLACE). Modern uses developed from 'low on the social scale' through 'inferior', while a complete reversal comes in the informal sense 'excellent', dating from the early 20th century. Use as a term of approval has a precursor in expressions involving a negative, **no mean . . .** : in the Bible St Paul declared 'I am . . . a Jew of Tarsus . . . a citizen of no mean city.' The mathematical use of mean, 'an average' [ME], goes back to Latin *medianus* 'middle', source also of **median** [LME]. This is the mean behind means 'a method', as in a **means to an end**, a thing that is not valued or important in itself but is useful in achieving an aim.

meander [L16th] The River Menderes in southwest Turkey rises in the Anatolian plateau and winds some 384 km (240 miles) to the Aegean Sea. It features in Homer's *Iliad* and was known in ancient times as the Maeander, and its winding course gave its name to meander.

measles [ME] The spelling in Middle English was *maseles*, probably from Middle Dutch *masel* 'pustule'. The spelling change was from association with Middle English *mesel* 'leprous, leprosy'. **Measly** dates from the late 16th century when it described a pig or pork infected with measles; the current sense 'contemptibly small, mean' dates from the mid 19th century.

measure *see* MOON

meat [OE] Meat is related to **mete** [OE], an old word meaning 'to measure', and **mate** [LME] through the idea of a mate being someone you share food with. It goes back to an ancient root shared with **meditate** [L16th]. The earliest sense of meat was simply 'food'. This survives in the proverb **one man's meat is another man's poison**, which is recorded in English from the late 16th century but has a parallel in the work of the Roman poet and philosopher Lucretius of the 1st century BC. Other early meanings

include 'an item of food', now found only in **sweetmeat** [LME]. *See also* FLESH

mechanical [LME] Both mechanical and **machine** [M16th] go back to Greek *mēkhanikē* 'machine'. Originally mechanical and **mechanic** [LME] were more or less interchangeable, but nowadays the first primarily means 'operated by or relating to a machine' or 'done without thought, automatic', and the second refers to a skilled worker. An old meaning of both is 'a manual labourer or artisan', as in 'A crew of patches, rude mechanicals, / That work for bread, upon Athenian stalls' from Shakespeare's *A Midsummer Night's Dream* (rude here meaning 'unsophisticated').

medal [L16th] Medal goes back to medieval Latin *medalia* 'half a *denarius*', there being little difference in appearance between a coin and a medal. **Medallion** dates from the mid 17th century and originally meant 'a larger medal'.

meddle *see* MEDLEY

median *see* MEAN

medieval [E19th] This is based on modern Latin *medium aevum* 'middle age'.

mediocre [L16th] Mediocre is from Latin *mediocris* used to mean 'of middle height or degree', but literally 'somewhat rugged or mountainous', from *medius* 'middle' and *ocris* 'rugged mountain'. *Medius* also gives us **medium** [L16th] and **intermediate** [LME], while **meridian** [LME] goes back to Latin *meridianum* 'noon' from *medius dies* 'middle of the day'.

meditate *see* MEAT

Mediterranean *see* OCEAN

medium *see* MEDIOCRE

medley [ME] A medley was originally a fight, and is the same word as **melee** [M16th], 'a confused fight or scuffle'. The source is French, and goes back to Latin *misculare* 'to mix', the source of mix (*see* MASH) and related to **meddle** [ME]. The

meander   measles   measure   mechanical

mixing and mingling of combatants in hand-to-hand fighting led to medley having a variety of uses that involve a mixture of parts. It was applied to a collection of songs or tunes performed as a continuous piece in the 17th century, and the swimming event with each part involving a different stroke appeared in the 1920s.

meerkat *see* SOUTH AFRICAN WORD PANEL

meet *see* MOOT

megastar *see* STAR

megrim *see* MIGRAINE

melancholy [ME] According to the medieval theory of the four humours (*see* HUMOUR), melancholy or black bile caused depression. The word goes back to Greek *melankholia*, from *melas* 'black' (source of mid 19th-century **melanin** and **melanoma**) and *kholē* 'bile' (source of **cholera** [LME], **choleric** [ME], and **cholesterol** [L19th]). Today it tends to refer to a pensive or moody sadness rather than deep depression.

Melba [E20th] We have all seen entertainers retire and make a comeback, or do numerous farewell performances. In Australia and New Zealand they would be said to **do a Melba**. At the beginning of the 20th century Dame Nellie Melba (1861–1931) was one of the most famous opera singers in the world, and she continued to perform long after her official retirement. Melba was not her real name— she was born Helen Porter Mitchell near Melbourne in Australia, and took her stage name from that city. Outside her native country many associate her name with various dishes created in her honour by the French chef Georges-Auguste Escoffier (1846–1935). He is said to have devised the dish of ice cream and peaches with raspberry sauce that he called **peach Melba** in London around 1892, though the first known record is from 1909; in 1897, when Dame Nellie was ill and took to a plain diet, he apparently recommended very thin crisp toast, promptly dubbed **Melba toast** or **toast Melba**.

melee *see* MEDLEY

mellifluous [LME] Latin *mel* 'honey' and the verb *fluere* 'to flow' are the base elements of mellifluous. **Mellow** [LME] may look as if it should be related, but it is not. It first meant 'ripe, soft, sweet and juicy' and may be a development of Old English *melu* '*MEAL'.

melody [ME] This goes back to Greek *melos* 'song'. **Melodrama** [E19th] was adopted from French and is a blend of *melos* 'music' and French *drame* 'drama'.

melt *see* MOLLUSC

memory [ME] English adopted the Latin word *memoria* twice, first directly from Latin in the Middle Ages as memory, then in the 15th century through French as **memoir**. The earliest sense of memoir was 'a memorandum'; people's memoirs, either recording historical events or recounting their own lives, appeared in the 17th century. Latin *memoria* is formed from *memor* 'mindful', from which **memorable** [LME]; **remember** [ME]; **remind** [M17th]; **reminisce** [E19th]; and **commemoration** [LME] also come. A 1903 song introduced the world to **memory lane**, while another song took the same title in 1924. In both lyrics people 'wandered', whereas nowadays we **take a trip down memory lane** when we indulge in pleasant or sentimental memories. In medieval times and later, merchants, lawyers, and diplomats would write **memorandum that** … at the head of a note of something to be remembered or a record of what had been done. In Latin *memorandum* means 'it is to be remembered', and is a form of *memorare*, 'to bring to mind'. **Memento** [LME] is also pure Latin. It was at first a prayer of commemoration and is an order to 'remember!'.

memsahib *see* RAJ WORD PANEL

menace [ME] The root of menace is Latin *minae* 'threats'. The original English sense, which survives mainly in legal contexts, was also 'a threat'—the Larceny Act of 1861 made it a criminal offence to **demand**

meerkat   meet   megastar   megrim   Melba

money with menaces, and the phrase has been used in subsequent Acts dealing with similar offences. In the sense 'a person or thing that threatens danger or catastrophe', menace is recorded from the mid 19th century, but has since progressively weakened to mean 'an inconvenience, an annoyance, a nuisance'. There are two cartoon characters called **Dennis the Menace:** the British Dennis is in a strip cartoon and made his first appearance in issue 452 of the comic the *Beano* on 17 March 1951. The American Dennis is a character in a single-cell cartoon and appeared just five days earlier in sixteen American newspapers.

mend [ME] Even though it is found slightly earlier, mend is thought to be a shortening of **amend**, which along with **emend** are recorded within a few years of each other. They all go back to Latin *emendare* 'to free from faults, correct'.

menopause *see* MONTH

mensch *see* YIDDISH WORD PANEL

menstruate *see* MONTH

mental *see* MIND

menthol *see* MINT

mention *see* MIND

menu [M19th] When people first used menu in English they treated it as a foreign word, printing it in italic type, and perhaps pronouncing it in a 'French' way. The word means 'detailed list' in French, and is a use of *menu* 'small, detailed' from Latin *minutus* 'small', the source of *MINUTE, *MINCE, **minutiae** [M18th] 'small, precise or trivial details', the delicate dance the **minuet** [L17th], and *DIMINISH. Applied to a list of dishes available in a restaurant, it dates from the mid 19th century; by the 20th it was fully anglicized, and by the 1960s could also mean 'a list of facilities or commands displayed on a computer screen'.

mercury [OE] Mercury was the Roman god of eloquence, skill, trading, and thieving, and was the messenger of the gods. His name came from Latin *merx* 'merchandise', the source also of **market** [OE], **merchant** [ME], and **mercenary** [LME]. In later Latin *mercurius* was also the name of a silvery-white metal, liquid at room temperature. The use probably arose from the fluidity of the metal being likened to the rapid motion associated with the god. In English the metallic element was first called mercury in the Middle Ages—its earlier name was **quicksilver** (*see* QUICK).

mercy [ME] In the Latin of the early Christian Church, *merces*, which had meant simply 'reward' in classical times, came to be used for 'heavenly reward' and also 'pity, favour'. These are the senses in which mercy first appears in the Middle Ages. The phrase **to be thankful for small mercies** is first recorded in Sir Walter Scott's novel *The Heart of Midlothian*, published in 1818.

merge [M17th] Latin *mergere* 'to dip, plunge' is the source of merge and **emerge** [L16th]. Merge was initially used to mean 'immerse' oneself in a particular way of life, with the modern sense appearing in the 19th century via business use.

meridian *see* MEDIOCRE

mermaid *see* MARINE

mess [ME] Current senses of mess, 'a dirty or untidy state', and 'a confused situation full of problems', date only from the 19th century. Back in the Middle Ages a mess was 'a portion of food', and especially 'a portion of liquid or pulpy food'. This is the meaning in the phrase to **sell for a mess of pottage** (pottage is soup or stew), which refers to the biblical story, told in Genesis, in which Esau sells his birthright to his brother Jacob. At medieval banquets diners were divided into small groups, usually of four people, who sat together and were served from the same dishes. Such a group was also a mess, and is still so on board ship and in military canteens. From this developed the sense 'a place providing meals and recreational facilities for members of the armed forces', as in **the officers' mess**.

message [ME] The root of message is a form of Latin *mittere* 'to send' that is the source of *MASS and *MISSILE as well as of **messenger** [ME] and **demise** [LME]. The phrase to **shoot** (or **kill**) **the messenger**, 'to treat the bearer of bad news as if they were personally to blame for it', is recorded only from the 1960s, but breaking bad news has always been a thankless task. The idea occurs at least twice in Shakespeare—in *Coriolanus* there is reference to beating the messenger—and the ancient Greek dramatist Sophocles expressed it as 'No one loves the messenger who brings bad news.'

metabolism *see* MIDWIFE

metal [ME] The words metal and **mettle** [E17th] were once the same. Both could refer to a physical material and to a quality. In the 17th century the quality came to be particularly 'vigour, spiritedness', originally of horses but later also referring to people. By the mid 18th century the form mettle was being restricted to this, and metal to the material. Their ultimate origin is Greek *metallon* 'mine, quarry, metal'.

metamorphosis [LME] Metamorphosis came into English via Latin from Greek *metamorphoun* 'transform, change shape'. It was introduced from the *Metamorphoses*, a large collection of verse stories by Ovid (43 BC–AD 17 or 18), about transformations of gods and mortals into the shapes of objects, plants, or animals. In the 1980s **morph**, derived from metamorphosis, came to be used in computer animation for the merging of one image into another, although the idea was already familiar to young television viewers in the UK from the character of Morph, a stop-motion plasticine character created by Aardman Animations from 1977, who would mutate in the same way.

metaphorical, metaphysics *see* MIDWIFE

mete *see* MEAT

meteor [M16th] In early use the term was used for any atmospheric phenomenon: it comes via modern Latin from Greek *meteōron* 'of the atmosphere', from *meteōros* 'lofty'. The same source gave us **meteorology** [E17th].

method [LME] Originally a method referred to a medical treatment for a disease, coming via Latin from Greek *methodos* 'pursuit of knowledge', based on *hodos* 'way'. **Methodist,** the 18th-century evangelistic movement founded by Charles and John Wesley and George Whitefield is probably from the notion of following a specified 'method' of Bible study.

meticulous [M16th] At first meticulous meant 'fearful, timid' for it came from Latin *metus* 'fear'. It came to mean 'over-careful about detail', then lost its negative associations, giving the current sense 'showing great attention to detail' by the early 19th century.

metropolis *see* POLICE

mettle *see* METAL

microbe [L19th] Microbe is from French based on the Greek elements *mikros* 'small' and *bios* 'life'. The word was coined by C. Sédillot in March 1878.

midget [E19th] This is first used of anything that is very small, and only for an unusually small person from the mid 19th century. It is a development of Old English **midge**, the small biting fly.

midriff [OE] The second part of **midriff** is Old English *hrif* 'belly', which goes back to the same root as Latin *corpus* 'body', the source of many English words including **corporation** [LME], one of whose meanings is 'a protruding abdomen'.

midwife [ME] The original sense of midwife seems to have been 'a woman who is with the mother'. *Mid-* here is not connected to middle, but is an old word meaning 'with' that is related to Greek *meta* 'with', which appears in English words beginning **meta-**, such as **metabolism**

message metabolism metal metamorphosis

[L19th], **metaphorical** [M16th], and **metaphysics** [M16th]. 'A woman' (rather than 'a married woman') is the oldest sense of *WIFE, still used in Scotland.

migraine [LME] People unfortunate enough to suffer from migraine know that this sort of throbbing headache usually affects one side of the head—reflected in the origin of the word. It is a highly shortened form of Greek *hemi-* 'half' and *kranion* 'skull', the source of English **cranium** [M16th]. Until the 20th century the form **megrim**, also used for a fit of being difficult, was more common than **migraine**.

migrate [E17th] The word migrate was initially a general word for 'move from one place to another'. It comes from Latin *migrare* 'to move, shift'. People could **immigrate** from the early 17th century, but **emigrants** only appeared in the mid 18th century.

mild *see* MOLLUSC

mile [OE] Where Roman legions marched they left roads, bridges, and other works of civil engineering. One thousand paces (or two thousand steps) marched by disciplined troops became a fixed and useful unit of measurement of distance—in Latin this was *mille passus* or *mille passuum* 'one thousand paces', later shortened to simple *mille*. The word entered most of the languages of Europe. When you urge someone to **go the extra mile**, 'to make a special effort to achieve something', you are echoing the Bible. In the Sermon on the Mount, in the Gospel of Matthew, Jesus says, 'And whosoever shall compel thee to go a mile, go with him twain' (two). *See also* INCH, MISS, MILLION

militant [LME] The root of militant, Latin *miles* 'soldier', is shared by **military** [LME], **militate** [L16th] originally 'serve as a soldier', and **militia** [L16th]. For most of its history the main sense of militant has been 'engaged in warfare', but from the late 19th century militant has particularly meant 'aggressively active in pursuing a political or social cause'. In Britain the **Militant**

tendency was a Trotskyite political organization which published a weekly newspaper, *Militant*, between 1964 and 1997.

milk [OE] The ancient root of milk may have meant 'to rub', and so would refer to hand-milking animals by pulling on their teats. It is connected with the Latin word *mulgere* 'to milk', the source also of *EMULSION. The phrase **the milk of human kindness** comes from Shakespeare's *Macbeth*. Lady Macbeth expresses her suspicion that her husband might not use violence to seize the Scottish throne: 'Yet I do fear thy nature; it is too full o' the milk of human kindness / To catch the nearest way.' In the Book of Exodus in the Bible the Promised Land of Israel is described as 'a land flowing with **milk and honey**' giving us a term for prosperity and abundance.

Milky Way *see* GALAXY

mill [OE] Early mills ground corn into flour using water or wind power. The root of mill is Latin *molere* 'to grind', also the source of *MEAL 'the edible part of any grain or pulse', and **molar** [ME] the grinding tooth. Since the early 19th century people have been able to **put someone through the mill**, or cause them to have a difficult experience. A **millstone** [OE] is a large circular stone used to grind corn. The origins of **a millstone around your neck**, 'a heavy burden of responsibility', lie in a far more unpleasant practice. It is thought to come from an ancient method of execution which involved throwing a person into deep water with a heavy stone attached to their neck.

millennium *see* MILLION

milliner [LME] In the 16th century the city of Milan in northern Italy was famous for making small articles of women's dress and other fancy goods. Those who sold them were the original milliners (or 'milaners'). In time the word became restricted to 'a person who makes or sells women's hats'.

million [LME] In Latin *mille* means 'a thousand'—as in *MILE and **millennium**

migraine   migrate   mild   mile   militant

[M17th]. In million, the thousand got multiplied by itself. This seems to have happened in Italian, where the word *millione* (now *milione*) was formed. In 1956 Frank Sinatra and Celeste Holm enjoyed great success with the duet 'Who wants to be a **millionaire?**' from Cole Porter's *High Society*. The answer in the song is 'I don't', but the television company ITV found that they were in a small minority when they introduced the quiz show *Who Wants To Be A Millionaire?* in September 1998. Thousands have applied to be contestants and millions have been won; the show has given several catchphrases to the language, including '**phone a friend**' and '**is that your final answer?**' The top prize in the British show is a million pounds, but the first millionaires had a thousand French francs. The poet Lord Byron wrote in a letter in 1816: 'He is still worth at least 50-000 pds— being what is called here a "Millionaire" that is in Francs and such Lilliputian coinage, introducing the word to English.'

mime, mimic *see* PANTOMIME

minaret [L17th] This word for a slender tower (for example, part of a mosque) comes via Turkish from Arabic *manār(a)* 'lighthouse, minaret', based on *nār* 'fire or light'.

mince [LME] The words mince, *MINUTE 'small', *MENU, and *DIMINISH all derive ultimately from Latin *minutus* 'small'. Mince in the sense 'expressing yourself candidly', now found mainly in **not mince your words**, goes back to Shakespeare: in *Henry V* King Henry says to the French princess he is courting, 'I know no ways to mince it in love, but directly to say, I love you.' This use produced 'to say in an affectedly refined way' and then 'to walk in an effeminately dainty way', as early as the 1560s. In the sense 'ground meat' mince was earlier **mincemeat** [M17th] and even earlier **minced meat**. The mincemeat put in pies at Christmas originally contained meat as well as fruit. To **make mincemeat of**, to defeat easily in a fight or contest, dates from the late 17th century.

mind [OE] English mind shares its ancient root with Latin *mens* 'mind', from which **demented** [M17th], **mental** [LME], and **mention** derive. The mind can do many wonderful things, including 'boggling'. The phrase **the mind boggles**, meaning that someone becomes astonished or overwhelmed at the thought of something, is first recorded in the 1890s. **Boggle** itself is probably a dialect word related to **bogle** 'a phantom or goblin' and **bogey** 'an evil or mischievous spirit'. Someone may have warned you to **mind your Ps and Qs**, 'be careful to behave well and avoid giving offence'. The expression has been known since the 1770s, but its exact origins are uncertain. One obvious suggestion is that it comes from a child's early days of learning to read and write, when they might find it difficult to distinguish between the two tailed letters *p* and *q*. Another idea suggests that printers had to be very careful to avoid confusing the two letters when setting metal type. **Mind how you go!**, meaning 'be careful, look after yourself', has been common in Britain since the 1940s. It was popularized by the long-running BBC TV series *Dixon of Dock Green* (1955–76), in which it was a catchphrase of the avuncular PC George Dixon, along with **evening all**.

miniature [E18th] When monks and scribes decorated the initial letters of chapters in illuminated manuscripts, they often painted small images. It was not the smallness that miniature originally referred to, though, but the colour of the paint used for the capital letters. Latin *minium* was a word for the red pigment *VERMILION. It is the source of Italian *miniatura*, which originally referred to the illuminating of manuscript letters but came to be used for small portraits, and gave us miniature in the late 16th century. **Mini** is an abbreviation of miniature that became popular in the early 20th century. The Mini car, originally known as the Mini Minor, was launched by the British Motor Corporation in 1959, and became an iconic vehicle of the swinging 60s that was immortalized in the film *The Italian Job* (1969). The other mini of the 60s was the **miniskirt**, which symbolized the decade's sexual permissiveness. The French fashion designer André Courrèges is credited with its invention, although it was popularized by Mary Quant. The word is first recorded in 1965, the year when the fashion was first seen.

minstrel [ME] Originally a minstrel would be employed to provide a variety of entertainment. Minstrels sang, played music, told stories, juggled—whatever their employer demanded. A minstrel could be closer to a jester or buffoon than the singer of heroic and lyrical poetry that later writers romantically portrayed. Sir Walter Scott's poem *The Lay of the Last Minstrel*, published in 1805, was instrumental in developing this view. It is a romance based on an old Border ballad, put into the mouth of an ancient minstrel, the last of his race. The Irish poet Thomas Moore, who died in 1852, also played his part: in the song 'The Minstrel Boy' he wrote of 'the warrior bard' with 'his wild harp slung behind him'. The original meaning of minstrel was simply 'a servant'. It goes back to Latin *minister* 'servant', the source also of **minister** [ME].

mint [OE] Latin *moneta* is the source of both mint and of *MONEY. The phrase **in mint condition**, 'new or as new', refers to a newly minted coin, and people have **made a mint**, or a great deal of money, since the late 16th century. The mint [OE] that refers to the plant used as a flavouring is an entirely different word, which goes back to Greek *minthē* which also lies behind **menthol** [M19th].

minuet *see* MENU

minute [LME] English words spelled minute have two different pronunciations and entered English by different routes, but share an origin in Latin *minutus* 'small', the source also of *MINCE, *MENU, and many other words. The closest to the original Latin sense is minute 'small'. The minute referring to a period of 60 seconds comes through medieval Latin *pars minuta prima* 'first minute part'. The use of minute in the minutes of a meeting goes back to the times before printing, when a scribe would make a rough version of a record or memorandum

in 'small writing' (Latin *scriptura minuta*) before the fair copy was made in the more formal style of writing called 'book hand'. *See also* HOUR, SECOND

miracle [ME] In Latin a *miraculum* was 'an object of wonder' and was formed from *mirus* 'wonderful'. These also lie behind **admiration** [LME] and **marvel** [ME].

miscellany [L16th] This goes back to the Latin *miscellus* mixed from *miscere* 'mix' (*see* MASH). This also lies behind **promiscuous** [E17th]. Its early sense was 'consisting of elements mixed together', giving rise to 'indiscriminate', and 'undiscriminating', from which the notion of 'casual' arose.

mischief [LME] In early examples, mischief denoted 'misfortune' or 'distress'. It came from Old French *meschever* 'come to an unfortunate end', based on *chef* 'head'.

misery [LME] Misery comes via French from Latin *miser* 'wretched', which also gives us **miser** [LME].

mishmash *see* PELL MELL

misnomer *see* NAME

miss [OE] To miss, meaning 'to fail to hit', goes back to Old English. On the surface of it the proverb **a miss is as good as a mile** is puzzling. The original longer form, from the early 17th century, is clearer: **an inch in a miss is as good as an ell** (an ell is an old measure of distance, *see* BOW). As a title for a young girl or an unmarried woman miss is a shortening of **mistress** [ME], which itself is from the same Old French root as master (*see* MAGISTRATE).

missile [E17th] The root of missile is a form of Latin *mittere* 'to send', found also in words such as **dismiss** [LME] and *MESSAGE. The earliest missiles were gifts, such as sweets, thrown to crowds by Roman emperors. From there the word came to mean, in the 1650s, an object which is forcibly propelled at a target—the modern sense of a rocket or similar weapon is first found in 1945. **Mission** [M16th] is also from Latin *mittere*. *Mission: Impossible* was an

minstrel   mint   minuet   minute   miracle

American TV series that was first shown between 1966 and 1973, and in 1996 used as the basis of a film of the same name.

missive *see* MASS

mister *see* MAGISTRATE

mistress *see* MISS

mite [OE] Old English *mīte* describing a tiny arachnid related to the ticks is a word of Germanic origin. Late Middle English mite now used in phrases such as **poor little mite** is probably from the same Germanic word but it described, during this period, a small Flemish copper coin (from Middle Dutch *mīte*). The 'small size' is reflected in the phrase **the widow's mite**, which refers to Mark 12:42 'And there came a certain poor widow, and she threw in two mites, which make a farthing': although some sneered at her poor contribution it had virtue because she had given all she had.

mitten [ME] Mittens often used to be made of fur, and the name may derive from French *mite*, a pet name for a cat which probably imitated its mewing. This implies that the fur in question was cat's fur—the medieval world could not afford to be sentimental about its animals. The word mitten was shortened to **mitt** in the mid 18th century, in the sense 'fingerless glove'. From the late 19th century **mitt** was also used for 'a person's hand', as in to **get your mitts up**. *See also* GAUNTLET, GLOVE

mix *see* MASH

mobile [LME] In the 21st century the first thing that comes to mind when you hear the word mobile is probably a portable phone. At least that is the case in Britain—in the USA and elsewhere people are more likely to say **cellphone**. The term **mobile phone** was first recorded in the USA in 1945, but it was not until the 1980s that the mobile or cellphone became more widely available, and even then it was out of reach of the ordinary person. A 1984 source refers to one 'available now with a suggested price of $1,995'. The word mobile itself dates in English to the late 15th century and goes back to Latin *movere* 'to move', the source of *MOVE. It started to be used of people's ability to move between social levels at the beginning of the 20th century, and a person can now be **upwardly mobile** or **downwardly mobile**. In Latin *mobile vulgus* meant 'the common people, the fickle crowd'. English adopted the phrase in the late 16th century, and two centuries later shortened it to mobile and then even further to simple **mob**. This became a term for a gang of criminals in the early 19th century, and in 20th-century America **the Mob** became an alternative name for the Mafia.

moccasin *see* NATIVE AMERICAN WORD PANEL

mocker The phrase to **put the mockers on**, 'to put an end to, thwart', is originally Australian. It dates from the early 20th century and may come from Yiddish *make* 'sore, plague', or be the same word as mocker [LME] meaning 'someone who mocks'. Another Antipodean mocker, meaning 'clothes, dress', was brought back from Egypt by New Zealand troops after the First World War. It is based on Egyptian Arabic *makwagi* 'presser of clothes'-in Egypt and other Middle Eastern countries there are clothes-pressing establishments with changing rooms where people can shed the outfits they are wearing and have them pressed. Mock [LME] meaning 'to make fun of' is a quite different word, from Old French *mocquer* 'to ridicule'.

model *see* MOULD

modem [M20th] The term modem is a blend of *modulator* and *demodulator*.

modern [LME] Modern is from late Latin *modernus*, from Latin *modo* 'just now'.

mods *see* ROCK

module *see* MOULD

moggie [L17th] This informal word for a cat is a variant of Maggie, a pet form of the name Margaret.

missive mister mistress mite mitten mix

mogul [L16th] If you are a skier you are probably familiar with the mogul, the hump or bump that disrupts your progress. This has nothing to do with the movie mogul. The skier's mogul comes from Austrian German *Mugel* 'hillock'. The media mogul is a use of **Mogul**, a member of the Muslim dynasty of Mongolian origin, which ruled much of India from the 16th to the 19th centuries. This historical term is now more usually spelled **Mughal**. It is originally from Persian *mugul* 'Mongol'.

mohair see ARABIC WORD PANEL

molar see MILL

mole [OE] English has several unrelated words spelled mole. The oldest refers to a small blemish on the skin; in Old English this meant 'a discoloured spot on cloth'. Next to appear was the mole that now means 'a structure serving as a pier, breakwater, or causeway', which goes back to Latin *moles* 'mass' (the earliest sense in English) which also lies behind **demolish** [M16th]. The mole that is a burrowing animal stayed underground until the later Middle Ages, and went under other names before then—in Old English it was a want, and then also a **mouldwarp**. The novels of John le Carré popularized the term mole for a spy who gradually achieves an important position within the security defences of a country: it first appeared in *Tinker, Tailor, Soldier, Spy* in 1974. The world of espionage seems to have adopted the use from le Carré, rather than vice versa. *See also* MOUNTAIN

mollify see MOLLUSC

mollusc [L18th] Most molluscs have hard shells, but they need these because they are so soft underneath, which gives them their name, from Latin *mollis* 'soft'. This also lies behind **mollify** [LME] originally to make soft, **emollient** [M17th], and share an Indo-European root with Germanic **melt** [OE] and **mild** [OE].

moment [LME] The Latin word *momentum* is the source of our words moment and **momentum** [OE]. Its root is

movere, 'to move'. At the end of a bullfight the matador faces the bull and prepares to make the final sword thrust. In Spanish this is *la hora de la verdad*, translated into English as **the moment of truth**. The first recorded use was by the writer Ernest Hemingway in his 1932 book *Death in the Afternoon*.

monarch [LME] The word monarch comes via late Latin from Greek *monarkhēs*, from *monos* 'alone' and *arkhein* 'to rule'. *Monos* also lies behind **monastery** [LME] which comes from *monazein* 'to live alone', while **monk** [OE] comes from *monakos* 'solitary'.

money [ME] In ancient Rome money was coined in a temple to the goddess Juno, where she was identified with a pre-Roman goddess called Moneta and known as Juno Moneta. Latin *moneta* has come down to English as money, and also as *MINT. **Money is the root of all evil** comes from the biblical Book of Timothy, where it is stated more carefully that 'the love of money is the root of all evil'. People down the ages have agreed that **money can't buy happiness**, though this exact form appeared only in the 19th century. In 1964 the Beatles sang that 'Money can't buy me love'. In Britain money gained with little effort is **money for jam** or **money for old rope** (*see* ROPE). These expressions, dating back to the early 20th century, probably originated in military slang. In 1919 *The Athenaeum* stated that money for jam came from the 'great use of jam in the Army'. *See also* COLOUR, LOAD, MUCK

monitor [E16th] Today's familiar uses of monitor, for a computer or TV screen or for checking the progress or quality of something, date only from the mid 20th century. A much earlier sense was 'a reminder or warning', reflecting its origin in Latin *monere* 'to warn', the source also of **admonish** [ME], **monster** [LME], and **monument** [ME]. A **monitor lizard** is a large tropical lizard, in Australia also called a **goanna** (a L19th corruption of iguana), whose name derives from the way its reactions can warn people of the presence

mogul mohair molar mole mollify mollusc

of a venomous creature. In schools from the 16th century a monitor was a pupil with responsibility for supervising and disciplining other pupils, who in the past might have done some teaching.

monk *see* MONARCH

monkey [M16th] The origin of monkey seems to go back to a name given to the monkey character in medieval beast epics, which may ultimately be Arabic. Historically, *APE was used as the general term for all apes and monkeys, and appears much earlier in English. People often associate monkeys with mischief and mimicry. British **monkey tricks** 'mischievous behaviour' are **monkeyshines** [M19th] in the USA. The use of **monkey business** for 'mischievous behaviour' seems to have come from India. If you **don't give a monkey's** you do not care at all. This phrase, recorded from the late 19th century, is a shortening of something ruder, such as **don't give a monkey's ass** or **f—**. The slang sense of a monkey, for £500 (or, in Australia, $500), is much older than you might expect, going back to the 1830s, and **a pony**, or £25, is from the late 18th century. *See also* BRASS, CHEEK

monocle [M19th] This goes back to Latin *monoculus* 'one-eyed' in contrast with binoculars (recorded from E18th, but only from 1871 in the normal modern sense) which are used with both eyes. The element *mono* 'one', which was borrowed by Latin from Greek, is found in many words including **monochrome** [M17th] combined with Greek *chroma* 'colour'; **monogamy** [E17th] with *gamos* 'marriage; **monologue** [M17th] with *logos* 'word, speech'; and **monopoly** [M16th] from *polein* 'sell'.

monolithic *see* XYLOPHONE

monologue, monopoly *see* MONOCLE

monoxylic *see* XYLOPHONE

monster *see* MONITOR

month [OE] A month corresponds to the period of time of the moon's revolution, and the words month and *MOON are related. Their ancient ancestor is also the source of Greek *mēn* 'month', from which English took **menstruate** [LME], **menopause** [L19th], and similar words. Shops and entertainments now open on Sundays, but in the past this was not necessarily so. Where Christianity was the dominant religion, restrictions on pleasure and activity meant that Sundays were quiet, private days. This may be behind the expression **a month of Sundays**, 'a very long, seemingly endless period of time'. The expression is known from 1836 in *The Clockmaker* by Thomas Chandler Haliburton: 'Mr. Slick . . . told him all the little girls there would fall in love with him, for they didn't see such a beautiful face once in a month of Sundays.'

monument *see* MONITOR

moody [OE] In Anglo-Saxon times if you were moody you were brave, passionate, or strong-willed. The word came from *mod* source of **mood**, which had a range of meanings including 'mind', 'thought,' and 'fierceness'. From this moody developed to mean 'angry' and by the 13th century had developed the modern sense.

moon [OE] The words moon, *MONTH, and **measure** [ME] all go back to the same ancient root. Since the earliest times people have looked at the full moon and seen a face or figure there, which has been identified as **the man in the moon** since the Middle Ages. The patterns on the moon's disc were formerly also seen as a man leaning on a fork and carrying a bundle of sticks or as a man with his dog and a thorn bush, while other cultures have seen a rabbit, hare, frog, or other animal. The expression **over the moon**, 'extremely happy', though it goes back to the early 18th century, is now particularly associated with post-match remarks from victorious footballers and football managers (along with its opposite, **sick as a parrot**). The origins of it lie in a nursery rhyme beginning 'Hey diddle diddle, The cat and the fiddle, The cow jumped over the moon'. The distance and unattainability of the moon is behind such

monk monkey monocle monolithic month

phrases as to **cry for the moon** 'to ask for what is impossible or unattainable' and to **promise someone the moon**. For a dog to **bark at the moon** is a singularly pointless act, and people have used it to express futility since the mid 17th century. *See also* BLUE

moose *see* NATIVE AMERICAN WORD PANEL

moot [OE] Groups of law students are sometimes given the exercise of discussing an imaginary doubtful law case for practice. This is an old training method, which died out in the 19th century but has since been reintroduced into university law courses. A discussion of this kind is a moot, and in the USA a **moot court** is a mock court at which law students argue imaginary cases. These legal assemblies are behind a **moot point**, one which is subject to debate or is no longer of any practical purpose. Originally moot was used more widely, of any meeting or assembly. The word derives from the same root as **meet** [OE].

moped [1950s] This is made up of syllables from the Swedish phrase (*trampcykel med*) *mo*(*tor och*) *ped*(*aler*) 'pedal cycle with motor and pedals'.

moral [LMEn] Moral is from Latin *moralis*, from *mos*, 'custom', (plural) *mores* 'morals', also behind **morose** [M16th]. As a noun the word was first used to translate *Moralia*, the Latin title of St Gregory the Great's exposition of the Book of Job. It was subsequently applied to the works of various classical writers. In the mid 18th century the identical French word was adopted into English and an 'e' added to the English spelling to indicate the French stress on the second syllable, to produce **morale**.

moratorium [L19th] This is a use in English of a modern Latin word meaning 'a delaying'.

morbid [M17th] Morbid is from Latin *morbus* 'disease'. It was first used to mean 'indicative of disease' and did not come to be used for 'gloomy, unhealthy' until the late 18th century.

morgue *see* MORTUARY

morning [ME] In Old English the word for the beginning of the day was *morgen*, which survives in the literary words **morn** and **morrow**. In the Middle Ages **morn** was extended to morning on the model of **evening** (*see* EVEN). Excessive drinking has resulted in **the morning after** (more fully **the morning after the night before**) since the late 19th century.

moron [E20th] Early use was as a medical term for an adult with a mental age of about 8–12. It comes from Greek *mōron*, the neuter of *mōros* 'foolish'.

morose *see* MORAL

morph *see* METAMORPHOSIS

morrow *see* MORNING

morsel [ME] This is an English use of Old French *morsel* 'a little bite', from Latin *mordere* 'to bite'.

mortal *see* MURDER

mortar [OE] A Latin *mortarium* was the sort of mortar you use with a pestle to grind things. The gun got its name in the mid 16th century because its dumpy shape reminded people of a mortar. The mortar you use for bonding bricks is recorded from the mid-13th century and probably got its name from the same mortar, because the ingredients are ground up. *See also* PISTON

mortuary [LME] In the Middle Ages a mortuary was a gift claimed by a parish priest from a deceased person's estate. The word derives from Latin *mortuus* 'dead', the source also of **mortgage** [LME], literally a 'dead pledge' because the debt dies when the pledge is redeemed; and **mortify** [LME] 'deaden', and related to *MURDER. The current sense, 'a room or building in which dead bodies are kept', dates from the mid 19th century. In Paris the bodies of people found dead formerly were taken to a building at the eastern end of the Île de la Cité, where they were kept until identified. It was called the Morgue (from a French word

moose   moot   moped   moral   moratorium

for haughtiness or sad expression). By the 1830s **morgue** was being used in English for other mortuaries; the parallel use of French *morgue* is not recorded until the 1940s and was borrowed back from English.

moth [OE] In Anglo-Saxon times a moth was any parasitic pest such as a maggot or worm, especially the larva of the clothes moth. The name eventually extended to the adult clothes moth, and then to other similar insects. People have been able to use a **mothball** to protect stored clothes since the 1890s; shortly after that **in mothballs** came to mean 'unused but kept in good condition for future use'. *Compare* BUTTERFLY

mother [OE] English mother, Dutch *moeder*, and German *Mutter* share their ancient ancestor with Latin *mater* (source of **madrigal** [L16th], **maternal** [LME], **matriarch** [L16th], **matrimony** [LME], **matrix** [LME], and **matter** [ME] the last two containing the idea of something from which something is made or born). The root probably came from the use of the sound *ma* made by babies, identified by mothers as a reference to themselves. The British expression **some mothers do 'ave 'em**, commenting on a person's clumsy or foolish behaviour, was apparently originally a Lancashire saying. The comic Jimmy Clitheroe popularized it, as 'don't some mothers 'ave 'em, in his BBC radio programme *The Clitheroe Kid*, which ran from 1958 to 1972. The phrase gained further currency as the title of a 1970s BBC television comedy series *Some Mothers Do 'Ave 'Em*, in which Michael Crawford starred as the clumsy, accident-prone Frank Spencer. The former Iraqi dictator Saddam Hussein is remembered as having promised **the mother of all battles** on the eve of the first Gulf War. On 7 January 1991 *The Times* reported that he had no intention of relinquishing Kuwait and was ready for the 'mother of all wars'. The proverb **necessity is the mother of invention** is first recorded in 1658, in *Northern Memoirs* by R. Franck: 'Art imitates Nature, and Necessity is the Mother of Invention.' The idea can be traced back further to classical times, to the Roman satirist Persius, who stated that 'The belly is the teacher of art and giver of wit'.

motley [LME] The word motley originally described a fabric woven from different-coloured threads, and was later extended to refer to the multicoloured costume traditionally worn by a court jester. To **wear motley** is to play the fool, and a **motley fool** is a professional jester. **On with the motley** is a quote from the English translation of Leoncavello's 1892 opera *Pagliacci*, about the real-life troubles of a group of comic actors, while **motley crew** was in use of a mixed bunch of sailors by the mid 18th century. **Mottle** was formed in the late 18th century from motley.

motor [LME] In early use a motor was a person who imparted motion. It derives from a Latin word meaning 'mover', based on *movere* 'to move'. The current sense of the noun dates from the mid 19th century.

mottle *see* MOTLEY

mould [ME] The root of mould 'a hollow container used to give shape to hot material when it cools' is Latin *modulus*, source of **model** [L16th] and **module** [L16th]. The mould that is a furry growth of fungi is unconnected, and came from a Scandinavian word into late Middle English. The origins of the expression to **break the mould**, 'to change to a markedly different way of doing things', comes from the manufacture of objects cast in moulds. Destroying a mould afterwards ensured that no further copies could be made. The phrase dates from the 1560s and probably comes from a translation of the Italian epic poem *Orlando Furioso*, written by Ludovico Ariosto in 1532: 'Nature made him and then broke the mould.' Mould in the sense 'earth' as in **leaf mould** is a Germanic word found in Old English (*see* MOLE).

moult *see* COMMUTE

mountain [ME] The Latin word *mons* 'mountain' was extended in French to create the ancestor of mountain. It is also the source of **mount** [OE], **paramount** [M16th] 'highest', and **amount** [ME]. The story

moth   mother   motley   motor   mottle   mould

behind the proverb **if the mountain won't come to Muhammad, Muhammad must go to the mountain**, was told in 1625 by the philosopher Francis Bacon. Muhammad was once challenged to prove his credentials as a prophet by summoning Mount Safa to come to him. Inevitably, the mountain did not move in response to his summons, but Muhammad had a ready answer for this. He observed that if the mountain had moved it would have crushed him and all his followers to death. Therefore it was only right that now he should go to the mountain and give thanks to God for his mercy in sparing them all from this disaster. The phrase to **move mountains** means both 'to achieve apparently impossible results' and 'to make every effort'. In the first sense it goes back to Paul's First Epistle to the Corinthians: 'And though I have the gift of prophecy, and understand all mysteries, and all knowledge; and though I have all faith, so that I could remove mountains, and have not charity, I am nothing.' The contrast of size between mountains and molehills has been exploited since the late 16th century hence **make a mountain out of a molehill**.

mountebank *see* BANK

mouse [OE] English mouse, Dutch *muis*, and German *Maus* share their ancient ancestor with Latin and Greek *mus*. The essential meaning of the word, that of a small rodent, has remained unchanged. *See also* MUSCLE. The shared initial *m* sound, as well as differences of size and character, has prompted contrasts with *MAN. A person might mock another's timidity by asking, 'Are you a **man or a mouse**?' Robert Burns's poem *To a Mouse* reminded people in 1786, as it does today, that 'The best laid schemes o' Mice an' Men, Gang aft agley' ('often go awry'). John Steinbeck's *Of Mice and Men*, published in 1937, told the story of two farm labourers, one of huge strength but low intelligence, the other who both exploited and protected the first. The computer mouse appeared in the 1960s and was so called from its small size and cord suggesting the tail. A person who spent most of their time sitting using a computer

or surfing the internet got the name **mouse potato** in the 1990s, in imitation of **couch potato** (*see* COUCH). People began setting **mousetraps** in the 15th century: before that the usual word was **mousefall**, still used in Scots dialect. The phrase **a better mousetrap**, 'an improved version of a well-known article', comes from an observation attributed to the US philosopher and poet Ralph Waldo Emerson in 1889, though it is also claimed by Elbert Hubbard: 'If a man write a better book, preach a better sermon, or make a better mousetrap than his neighbour, tho' he build his house in the woods, the world will make a beaten path to his door.' Agatha Christie took *The Mousetrap* as the title for her most successful play, a murder mystery premiered in London in 1952, and still going strong as the longest continuously running play of all time. She took the title from Hamlet's mockingly named play by the same title with which he traps his uncle.

move [ME] Latin *movere* 'to move' is the source of *MOBILE and *MOMENT as well as of move. People have **moved with the times** since 1875, and were prepared to **move heaven and earth** to get what they wanted in the 1790s. In 1873 the English poet Arthur O'Shaughnessy wrote of creative artists, 'Yet we are the movers and shakers / Of the world for ever, it seems.' In the 1950s **mover and shaker** was borrowed for 'a powerful person who initiates events and influences people'. *See also* MOUNTAIN

movies *see* US WORD PANEL

muck [ME] English muck is from an early Scandinavian word that goes back to a ancient root meaning 'slippery, slimy' from which **mucus** [M17th] also descends. The verb first meant 'to clean muck from' and 'to spread manure', from which we get **muck up** or make a mess of and **muck around**, 'to behave in a silly or aimless way'. Down-to-earth northerners might often comment that **where there's muck there's brass**. This form of the proverb, using brass in the sense 'money', is recorded in print only from the 1960s, but an earlier version was **where there's muck there's money**. The

mountebank   mouse   move   movies   muck

Australians introduced **Lady Muck** and **Lord Muck** at the beginning of the 20th century as names for a socially pretentious woman or man. The first **muckraking** was done by poor people, who would collect manure from the filthy streets of the city in the hope of selling it or finding something valuable. Since the start of the 20th century it has been used for searching out and publicizing scandal about people. **Mucker** or 'friend' was originally military slang, first recorded in the 1940s. It probably comes from the idea of a friend being a person who 'mucks in' or shares tasks cheerfully.

mud [LME] German probably gave mud to English, in the Middle Ages. The expression **someone's name is mud**, 'someone is in disgrace or unpopular', draws on an 18th- and 19th-century slang use of mud meaning 'a stupid or foolish person'. **As clear as mud** is found from the early 19th century; **drag through the mud** arose in the mid 19th century, and **mud sticks** is recorded from the late 19th century. **Here's mud in your eye,** said before drinking, dates from the 1920s. **Muddle** [LME] originally meant 'wallow in mud'.

mug [E16th] A mug was first of all a measure of salt, then a large earthenware vessel or bowl. In the 18th century drinking mugs commonly represented a grotesque human face. This may be the origin of mug in the sense 'a face', which in turn probably gave rise to mug as an insult for a stupid or gullible person, from their blank or unintelligent expression. In 19th-century slang mug was particularly a term for someone who has been duped by a card sharp or confidence trickster—this is behind **a mug's game**. People were robbed and attacked in public places before the 1860s, but before then the words mug and **mugger** would not have been used. They go back to the 'face' sense: to mug was originally a boxing term meaning 'to punch an opponent in the face' or 'a blow to the face'.

Mughal *see* MOGUL

mujahideen *see* ARABIC WORD PANEL

mule [OE] A mule results from crossing a donkey and a horse, strictly a male donkey and a female horse (the technical name for the offspring of a female donkey and a stallion is **hinny** [L17th] from Latin *hinnus*). Mules have traditionally been used as beasts of burden, and are also traditionally regarded as stubborn. Someone stubborn, stupid, or physically tough has been called a mule since the 15th century. As a name for a courier for illicit drugs, mule dates from the 1920s in US slang. The name of the animal goes back to Latin *mulus*. It has no connection with mule in the sense 'a slipper or light shoe without a back'. This comes from a term for the reddish shoes worn by magistrates in ancient Rome, Latin *mulleus calceus*.

mum [LME] Like **ma** [E19th] and **mama** [M16th], mum [L16th] and **mummy** [M18th] go back eventually to the first semi-articulate sounds made by children, which tend to be 'ma, ma'. *MOTHER itself probably has the same origin. The expressions **mum's the word** and to **keep mum** are perhaps most associated with life during the Second World War, conjuring up warnings about careless talk costing lives—for example, 'Be like dad. Keep mum.' Both phrases are much older, being recorded as far back as the early 16th century. The word mum itself was used on its own in medieval times to mean 'hush!' or 'shh!', and probably originated as a representation of the sound you make when you close your lips firmly together and try to speak. It also gave us **mumble** [ME]. Ancient Egyptian mummies are named after the substance in which the dead person's body was embalmed. Mummy in this sense goes back to Arabic *mūmiyā* 'bitumen' for 'the body of an embalmed person or animal' mummy is recorded in English from the early 17th century.

munitions *see* AMMUNITION

murder [OE] The ancient root of murder is shared by Latin *mors* 'death', from which **mortal** [LME] also derives, as do words at *MORTUARY. In his *Canterbury Tales* Geoffrey Chaucer wrote 'Murder will out'. The idea is older, but his concise way of expressing it ensured that it became proverbial. From the 18th century *BLUE was thought of as the colour of plagues and of harmful things in general, and someone being attacked would **cry** or **scream blue murder** to emphasize their plight. The phrase now refers to making a noisy protest.

muscle [LME] The ancient Romans saw a resemblance between a flexing muscle in the upper arm and the movements of a *MOUSE. Latin *musculus*, from *mus* 'mouse', meant 'little mouse' and also 'muscle'. It entered English through French in the 14th century. The edible mollusc the **mussel** [OE] is the same word, and the accepted spellings of both words remained variable into the 19th century.

muse [ME] People who muse look thoughtful and reflective, and the word probably originally referred to facial expression, as it is related to **muzzle** [LME] (*see also* AMUSE). It has no connection with the Muses of classical mythology, the nine goddesses regarded as inspiring learning and the arts. The Greek word for a Muse, *mousa*, is also the source of **music** [ME] and **museum** [E17th]. An institute called **the Museum** was established at Alexandria in about 280 BC by Ptolemy I of Egypt, and became the most renowned of the museums in the ancient world. The word **museum** means 'seat of the Muses, place dedicated to the Muses'. Old astronomers imagined the universe to consist of transparent hollow globes that revolved round the earth carrying the heavenly bodies and making a harmonious sound known as the **music of the spheres**. Many other things have been regarded as making music, such as birds, running brooks, and packs of hounds—since the 1930s a man and woman making love have been said to **make beautiful music together**.

mush [L17th] Mush in the sense of something soft is a variant of *MASH, and was first recorded meaning 'maize porridge'. The cry of mush to dogs pulling a sledge is probably a variant of French *marchez!* 'go!'

or *marchons!* 'let's go!'. *See also* ROMANY WORD PANEL

music *see* MUSE

musket [L16th] The name of the old type of long-barrelled gun comes from Italian, and is probably a use of *moschetto* 'sparrowhawk'. It was not uncommon for ballistic weapons to take their names from birds of prey, and arrows and crossbows had previously been called sparrowhawks. The soldier armed with a musket was immortalized in *The Three Musketeers* by the 19th-century French novelist Alexandre Dumas, though film versions of the story are more memorable for their sword fights. In the 17th and 18th centuries the **musketeers** formed part of the household troops of the French king.

Muslim *see* ARABIC WORD PANEL

muslin [E17th] Muslin means 'cloth made in Mosul' in Iraq. The place was called *Mussolo* in Italian and the cloth was called *mussolina*. This was adopted into French as *mousseline* (also used for a light sauce since the early 20th century) which in turn gave the English form.

mussel *see* MUSCLE

muster [LME] The word muster has a military swagger to it, conjuring up a picture of troops gathering for inspection or in preparation for battle. In Australia and New Zealand, though, the things most often mustered are cattle, sheep, and other livestock that are scattered and need to be rounded up. The phrase to **pass muster**, 'to be accepted as adequate or satisfactory', was originally to **pass the musters** and referred to soldiers undergoing inspection without getting into trouble with senior officers. The word itself goes back to Latin *monstrare* 'to show', the source also of **demonstrate** [M16th] and **remonstrate** [L16th].

mutant *see* COMMUTE

mutton [ME] A word that came from French but which is probably Celtic in

muscle muse mush music musket Muslim

origin and related to Scottish Gaelic *mult* and Welsh *mollt*. Mutton is technically the meat of sheep more than a year old The insult **mutton dressed as lamb** describes an older person dressed in a style suitable for somebody much younger. There is a long tradition of using mutton of women in a derogatory way. It was used as a slang term for prostitutes from the early 16th century, and the phrase to **hawk your mutton** meant 'to flaunt your sexual attractiveness' or, of a prostitute, 'to solicit for clients'. **Muttonhead** was used as a term for a stupid person of either sex from the beginning of the 19th century, and this is probably the source of **mutt** [L19th] for both a stupid person and a dog. *See also* BEEF

muzzle *see* MUSE

myriad [M16th] This was originally a Greek term for 'ten thousand'.

mystery [ME] Mystery goes back to Greek *mustērion*, which is related to **mystic** [ME] and **mystify** [E19th]. In ancient Greece mysteries were secret religious ceremonies witnessed only by the initiated, who were sworn never to disclose their nature. In Christianity the word means either a truth long kept secret but now revealed through Christ, or something of symbolic significance. The first English uses of mystery were in religious contexts, but it soon spread into wider use for something inexplicable or beyond human comprehension, and then for simply a puzzle or conundrum. In the heyday of British coach parties the **mystery tour** to an unspecified destination was popular. The Beatles went one stop further with their *Magical Mystery Tour*, an album and TV film of 1967.

N n

nabob *see* RAJ WORD PANEL

nachos [M20th] A Mexican chef called Ignacio 'Nacho' Anaya is thought to have invented nachos, a snack consisting of small pieces of tortilla topped with melted cheese and spices, in the 1940s. An alternative origin could be the Spanish word *nacho*, which means 'flat-nosed'.

nadir *see* ZENITH

naff [M20th] The first recorded example of naff, meaning 'lacking taste or style', is from the script of the BBC radio programme *Round the Horne* by Barry Took and Marty Feldman (1966): 'I couldn't be doing with a garden like this. I mean all them horrible little naff gnomes.' One of the most popular theories about its origin is the suggestion that the word was formed from the initial letters of *N*ormal *As F*— or *N*ot *A*vailable *F*or *F*—ing, but more likely is the idea that it is from Polari (a form of theatrical slang incorporating Italian words, rhyming slang, and Romany, used especially by gay people), and that it comes ultimately from Italian *gnaffa* 'despicable person'. **Naff off**, meaning 'go away!', is probably a different word, which may be a variant of **eff**, as in 'eff off!' Its first recorded use is from Keith Waterhouse's novel *Billy Liar* (1959): 'Naff off, Stamp, for Christ sake!' It was often used in the script of the BBC comedy series *Porridge* as an acceptable substitute for the bad language characteristically used in prison, and in 1982 Princess Anne was famously supposed to have told reporters to 'Naff off!' when they photographed her after she had fallen from her horse.

nag [ME] In the sense 'to find fault persistently', nag was originally a northern English expression meaning 'to gnaw or nibble' that probably came from Scandinavia or Germany. The first written evidence is from the early 18th century, but may well be earlier, as dialect expressions are often used for a long time before they appear in print. Nag meaning 'an old or worn-out horse' is a different word. It may be from early Dutch, or it could be related to **neigh** [OE]. *See also* HACK, JADE

nail [OE] When the word nail emerged in the Old English period it already had its main modern meanings of 'small metal spike' and 'fingernail'. To **nail a lie** is to expose a falsehood, an idiom known from the early nineteenth century. The reference is most likely to shopkeepers nailing forged coins to their shop counter to expose them and put them out of circulation. If money is paid **on the nail** it is paid without delay, immediately. The phrase may come from the *Satires* of the Roman poet Horace, who used *ad ungulum*, 'on the nail', to mean 'to perfection' or 'to the utmost'. This referred either to Roman sculptors making the finishing touches to their work with a fingernail, or to carpenters using a fingernail to test the accuracy of a joint. An American equivalent was **on the barrelhead**, an upturned barrel being a simple shop counter.

naïve *see* NATION

naked [OE] The Old English word naked comes from the same ultimate root as **nude** [LME], Latin *nudus*. The sense of 'blatant, clear, unashamed', as in **naked ambition**, dates from the 13th century. **The naked truth**, meaning 'the plain truth, without concealment or embellishment', dates back to the 14th century. It may originally have developed as a translation of the Latin phrase *nudaque veritas* in the *Odes* of the Roman writer Horace, or have come from fables personifying Truth as a naked woman, in contrast to Falsehood, who is elaborately dressed. **Stark naked** is an alteration of **start naked**, which probably meant 'naked even to the tail', as a start was an animal's tail—as in the red-rumped bird the **redstart** [L16th]. First recorded as early as 1530, stark naked developed into **starkers** in the 1920s. The change was made the easier because stark, which had meant 'hard, stiff' in Old English had come to mean 'absolutely, utterly' in late Middle English, as in **stark staring mad**. Words related to stark include the **starch** [OE] used for stiffening clothes and probably the **stork** [OE] from the bird's stiff posture.

namby-pamby [M18th] This began as a play on the name of the English writer Ambrose Philips, who died in 1749. His poems were ridiculed as insipid and over-sentimental by writers including the poet and essayist Alexander Pope.

name [OE] The Latin word *nomen* is the source of name and of related words in English, such as **denominate** [M16th], **misnomer** [LME], **nominate** [LME], and **noun** [LME]. **What's in a name?** alludes to Shakespeare's *Romeo and Juliet*. Juliet is saying the fact that Romeo belongs to the rival Montague family is irrelevant: 'What's in a name? That which we call a rose / By any other name would smell as sweet.' **No names, no pack drill** means that punishment for a misdeed cannot be meted out if everyone involved keeps silent about what has happened. Pack drill is a form of military punishment in which an offender has to perform parade-ground exercises carrying a heavy pack. It dates back to the First World War and soon spread from army circles, especially as a joking aside advising someone to be careful how much they say about a particular person or matter.

namesake *see* SAKE

nanny [E18th] Both for a person taking care of young children and in **nanny-goat**, this is a pet form of the name Ann. The **nanny state** is found from the 1960s. **Nan** (1940s) is an abbreviation of nanny and a child's pronunciation of **gran**.

nano- Placing **nano-** before a word indicates that the thing referred to is submicroscopically small; technically, it refers to a factor of a thousandth of a million (10^{-9}). A **nanosecond** is one thousand

millionth of a second, while **nanotechnology** deals with the manipulation of individual atoms and molecules. **Nano-** comes from the Greek word *nanos*, meaning 'dwarf'. It was adopted in English as early as 1947, although *nano-* words only entered most people's consciousness in the 1990s, when technology using very small components had been developed. By 2005 the concept was familiar enough for the Apple computer company to call its new slim-line iPod music player the iPod Nano.

napkin, nappy *see* APRON

narcissus [OE] The flower narcissus, a kind of daffodil, takes its name from a handsome youth in Greek mythology. Narcissus fell so deeply in love with his own reflection in a pool that he pined away and died, but the narcissus flower sprang up at the spot. **Narcissism**, 'excessive admiration of your own physical appearance', comes from the infatuation of Narcissus with his own beauty, and seems to have been invented by the poet Samuel Taylor Coleridge in 1822. As a technical term in psychology it is particularly associated with the theories of the psychotherapist Sigmund Freud. The source of narcissus is not known, and it is probable that the Greeks borrowed it from an earlier language, but in the past it was associated with Greek *narkoun* 'to make numb' source of **narcotic** [LME]. *See also* ECHO

nark [M19th] The original meaning of nark was 'an annoying or troublesome person', a sense which survives in Australia and New Zealand, and in the verb nark, 'to annoy'. The word is from Romany *nok* or *nak*, 'nose'. *SNOUT and **snitch** (L17th, of unknown origin) are other words that mean both 'nose' and 'informer', and the word **nosy** itself implies an inappropriate interest in other people's business.

nasal *see* NOSE

nasty [LME] The origins of nasty, which was first recorded in the Middle Ages, are uncertain, although it is probably related to

Dutch and Swedish words with similar meaning. It originally meant 'filthy, offensively dirty', but its force has been gradually toned down, although in America it remains a more strongly negative term than it is in Britain. The phrase **something nasty in the woodshed** comes from the comic novel *Cold Comfort Farm* (1932) by Stella Gibbons: Aunt Ada Doom's peculiarities are explained by the fact that when she was small she had seen something nasty in the woodshed, but we are never told what. **Nasty piece of work** or **nasty bit of work**, 'an unpleasant person', is a slang term first found in a 1923 book by the author 'Bartimeus' (the pseudonym for Lewis Anselm da Costa Ricci). 'Bartimeus' wrote books on a nautical theme, such as *Naval Occasions* and *Seaways*, and it is possible that the expression originated as naval slang. In informal English nasty can also be a noun, meaning 'a nasty person' or 'an unpleasant or harmful thing'. Today it is most often found in connection with gratuitously violent or pornographic films or **video nasties**, a use first recorded in the early 1980s.

nation [ME] This word came via Old French from Latin *natio*, from *nasci*, meaning 'to be born'. The link between 'country' and 'birth' was the idea of a people sharing a common ancestry or culture. The Latin verb *nasci* is the source of many familiar English words connected with birth, among them **innate** [LME] inborn or natural; **native** [LME]; **nativity** [ME] birth; **nature** [ME]; **naïve** [M17th]; and *RENAISSANCE (literally 'rebirth'). Also related is the name of the former province of **Natal** in South Africa, which was first sighted by the explorer Vasco da Gama on Christmas Day 1497. He called it **Terra Natalis** or 'land of the day of birth', in recognition of Christ's birth. A similar idea lies behind **Noel** [LME], 'Christmas', which is a French word that comes ultimately from Latin *natalis*. **England is a nation of shopkeepers** is supposed to have been Napoleon's scornful dismissal of the enemy across the Channel. Napoleon was not the first to use the phrase, though; the economist Adam Smith and possibly also the American revolutionary Samuel Adams referred to 'a nation of shopkeepers' in 1776.

Time for a powwow

*The clichéd 'cowboys and Indians' world of the Western has had a big influence on our use of American Indian or **Native American** words. But the contributions to English of the native cultures of the continent are often wider and older than that.*

THE team game **lacrosse** is played chiefly in girls' schools in Britain, but to North Americans it is a man's sport. French missionaries in the 17th century saw Native Americans playing the game, and gave it its name, from French *jeu de la crosse*, 'game of the hooked stick'.

In Westerns Indians always greet people with **how!** This is nothing to do with the English word **how**—it seems to be based on an expression used by north-eastern American peoples, possibly *háo* or *hou* in the Sioux or Omaha languages. A **powwow** is now a conference or discussion, but was originally a ceremony involving feasting and dancing. The word, first used during the 1620s, is from *powah* or *powwaw*, meaning 'priest or healer' in the Narragansett language of New England.

narcissus nark nasal nasty nation

Although **scalp** is a Scandinavian word, it is strongly associated with the American Indian practice of cutting or tearing the scalp from an enemy's head as a battle trophy. This was first recorded in the 17th century, and since around 1750 **scalp** has also meant 'a trophy or symbol of victory', as in 'Home games against France and Wales will give them a chance to take a scalp' (*Scottish Rugby*, 1991).

Wigwam, a word which means 'their house' in Ojibwa (a language of central Canada), was first used in English in the 1620s. A wigwam is a dome-shaped hut or tent, whereas a **tepee**, from Sioux *tīpī* 'dwelling', is conical. A **totem** is an object or animal believed to have spiritual significance, and Indians of the northwest USA and Canada hang or carve totems on a **totem pole**. **Totem** is from Ojibwa *nindoodem* 'my totem', and was first recorded in the mid 18th century.

The names of many US and Canadian animals and plants are Native American—**moose** and **skunk** are from Abnaki (a language of Maine and Quebec) *mos* and *segankw*, **raccoon**, and **terrapin** are from Algonquian *aroughcun* and *turepé*. A **moccasin** is a dangerous kind of viper, and also a soft-soled leather shoe based on a Native American style of footwear. The word comes from the Powhatan language of Virginia.

See also HATCHET, INDIAN, LONG, POSSUM, WAR, WEST

natty [L18th] The informal word natty, 'smart or stylish', probably comes from *NEAT. It was first recorded in 1785, in *The Classical Dictionary of the Vulgar Tongue* by Francis Grose, which was a collection of slang terms that Dr Johnson had deliberately left out of his dictionary of 1755. **Natty lads** in those days were young thieves or pickpockets. A quotation from the poet Shelley (1812) shows the modern meaning: 'As natty a beau, As Bond Street ever saw.' Among Rastafarians natty is used to describe hair that is uncombed or matted, as in dreadlocks; in this context it is a form of **knotty**. A **natty dread** is a Rastafarian. *See also* DREAD

nature *see* NATION

naughty [LME] Today naughty generally refers to children or animals that misbehave in a fairly harmless way, but until quite recently it was a stronger word meaning 'wicked' or 'morally bad', as in 'An Oxe of mine being a naughty beast, through ye default of mine owne fence hath goared a Cow of your Worships' (1592) or ''Tis a villanous Error of some naughty Men' (1699). Naughty comes from the Old English word **naught**, 'nothing', and originally meant 'possessing nothing, poor, needy'. The sense 'mildly rude or indecent', found in expressions such as 'naughty bits', dates from the mid 16th century.

nausea [LME] Nausea originally meant 'seasickness' and is based on the Greek word *naus*, 'ship' also the source of the English word **nautical** [M16th]. **Noise** [ME] also comes from nausea—as it developed through Latin and early French, nausea took on a series of meanings that went from 'seasickness' to 'upset, malaise', and 'disturbance, uproar', and so to 'noise', which was the word's spelling and meaning when it first appeared in medieval English.

navvy [E19th] A navvy is a labourer employed in building a road or railway. The word is a 19th-century shortening of

navigator [L16th], which in the 18th century was a labourer employed in the rapidly expanding enterprise of canal construction (in parts of England a canal is known as a **navigation**). Navigate comes from the Latin word for ship, *navis*, which gave rise to **navy** [LME], and also, because of its shape, to the **nave** [L17th] or long central part of a church. The ultimate root of *navis* is the Greek word for ship, *naus* (*see* NAUSEA).

neat [LME] Neat came into English via French *net*, from Latin *nitere*, meaning 'to shine'. It was first used in a sense quite similar to its main modern meaning, but with a greater emphasis on the handsome appearance of the thing described, as in this quotation from the 16th century, 'O thou Jerusalem full faire...much like a Citie neat'. The sense 'undiluted', as in 'neat whisky', derives from the old use 'free from impurities, clean', first found in the late 15th century. The slang sense 'excellent' was American, from the beginning of the 19th century.

nebbish *see* YIDDISH WORD PANEL

neck [OE] In Old English the word neck (then spelled *hnecca*) was quite rare, and actually referred to the back of the neck. Our idea of 'neck' was expressed by the words *halse* and *swire*, which today survive only as Scottish and northern English dialect terms. A number of common phrases involve necks. **Neck and neck**, meaning 'level in a race or contest' dates back to 1672: it refers to two horses struggling to establish the lead in a race. Horses have been winning races **by a neck** since at least 1791. **The same neck of the woods**, 'the same small area or community', derives from neck used in the sense 'narrow strip of woodland', which is recorded from the mid 17th century, originally in the USA. People have used **necking** to mean 'kissing and cuddling' since the early 19th century, presumably from the idea of clasping someone affectionately around the neck. *See also* SAVE

nectar [M16th] In Greek and Roman mythology nectar was the drink of the gods. Today you might sometimes hear a delicious drink being described as nectar, and in America it is the usual term for a thick fruit drink. The word took on its usual modern meaning 'a sugary fluid secreted in flowers' in the early 17th century. **Nectarine** [E17th], now the name of a smooth-skinned kind of peach, was originally an adjective meaning 'like nectar'.

needle [Old English] Old English *nædl*, of Germanic origin, is related to Dutch *naald*, and German *Nadel*, from an Indo-European root shared by Latin *nere* 'to spin' and Greek *nēma* 'thread'. The colloquial use of the verb in the sense 'irritate, annoy' dates from the late 19th century.

neep *see* PARSNIP

negative [LME] Negative comes from Latin *negare* 'to **deny**', a Middle English word from the same source. The photographic negative dates from the mid 19th century.

negotiate [E17th] The words negotiate and **negotiations** [LME] came into English from the Latin verb *negotiari*, which was made up of the two parts *neg-*, meaning 'not', and *otium*, 'leisure', the same image as *BUSINESS. *Otium* is also the root of the English word **otiose** [L18th], 'serving no practical purpose, pointless'.

neigh *see* NAG

neighbour *see* BOOR

nelly [M20th] The expression **not on your nelly** was originally used in the form **not on your Nelly Duff**. In the 19th century **Nelly Duff** was rhyming slang for 'puff' (meaning 'breath of life'), and so the phrase is roughly equivalent to **not on your life**. Nobody now knows who Nelly was, if indeed she was ever a real person.

nemesis [L16th] This word for someone's or something's downfall is Greek; the literal meaning is 'retribution', from *nemein* 'give what is due'.

neon [L19th] This gas, used in fluorescent lamps and illuminated advertising signs,

neat nebbish neck nectar needle neep

was named in 1898 by its discoverers, the scientists Sir William Ramsay and M.W. Travers. Neon is simply the Greek word for 'new thing'. The same Greek word is the source of the many English words that start with *neo-* and refer to a new or revived form of something, such as **neoclassical** [L19th], **neocolonialism** [M20th], and **neo-Nazi**, a word that appeared in 1944 before the Nazis had even been ousted from power.

nephew [ME] A nephew could originally also be a grandson—the word nephew comes via Old French *neveu*, from Latin *nepos* 'nephew, grandson'. **Nepotism** [M17th], or favouritism towards friends or relations, also comes from *nepos*. The reference is to privileged treatment formerly given to the 'nephews' of popes, who were in many cases their illegitimate sons. **Niece** [ME] comes from Latin *neptis* the feminine form of *nepos*.

nerd [M20th] Originally an American term, nerd in the sense of 'boring, unfashionable person' was first recorded in 1951. The word itself appeared the previous year in *If I Ran the Zoo* by Dr Seuss, who seems to have invented it: 'I'll sail to Ka-Tro / And Bring Back an It-Kutch, a Preep and a Proo / A Nerkle, a Nerd, and a Seersucker, too!' Some think that this is the origin of nerd, but Dr Seuss used the word in nonsense verse as the name of a kind of animal, and there is no connection with the obsessive computer fan we are familiar with. Another theory links the word with the name of Mortimer Snerd, a dummy used by the American ventriloquist Edgar Bergen in the 1930s.

ness see NOSE

nest [OE] A nest was originally a 'sitting-down place'. The Old English word comes from the same ancient roots as **nether** [OE] and **sit** [OE]. The related word **nestle** [OE] first meant 'build a nest', and did not take on its modern meaning until the 16th century. **Niche** [E17th], 'a shallow recess' or 'a comfortable or suitable position', is another related word.

neuralgia see NOSTALGIA

Never-Never Land [L19th] Although **Never-Never Land** is now usually associated with J.M. Barrie's *Peter Pan* (1904), the name was used at the end of the previous century to refer to the remote outback, in particular to the unpopulated northern part of the Northern Territory and Queensland in Australia, from which a person might never return. Barrie's imaginary country was first called **Neverland** or **Never Land**, but in *When Wendy Grew Up* (1908) the longer name was introduced. **The never-never** is an informal term for hire purchase or, today, for buying by credit card. It originated in the 1890s, also in Australia.

new [OE] New comes from the same root as Latin *novus*, the source of the English words **innovate** [M16th], *NOVEL, **novice** [ME], and **renovate** [E16th]. The noun **news** [LME] is simply the plural of new. It came into use as a translation of Old French *noveles* or medieval Latin *nova*, meaning 'new things'. The proverb **no news is good news**, although modern-sounding, can be traced back at least as far as the time of King James I, who wrote in 1616 that 'No newis is bettir then evill newis'. It may be based on the Italian phrase *Nulla nuova, buona nova* ('No news, good news'). **Newfangled** [ME] is from new and a second element related to an Old English word meaning 'to take'.

newt [LME] Like *NICKNAME, the name of the newt is an example of the phenomenon known as 'wrong division' or 'metanalysis', whereby people came to attach the last letter of one word to the beginning of the next. Originally the animal was **an ewt**. **Ewt** was an Old English term for a newt, as was **eft**. *See also* ADDER, APRON

nice [ME] In medieval English nice meant 'foolish, silly, ignorant', from its Latin source *nescius* 'ignorant'. It developed a range of largely negative senses, from 'dissolute', 'ostentatious, showy', 'unmanly, cowardly', and 'delicate, fragile' to 'strange, rare', and 'coy, reserved'. In *Love's Labour Lost* Shakespeare talks of 'nice wenches', meaning 'disreputable women'. The word

nephew   nerd   ness   nest   neuralgia

was first used in the more positive sense 'fine or subtle' (as in **a nice distinction**) in the 16th century, and the current main meanings, 'pleasant' and 'kind', seem to have been in common use from the mid 18th century. This example from a letter written in 1769 sounds very contemporary: 'I intend to dine with Mrs. Borgrave, and in the evening to take a nice walk.' The development of the word's senses from negative to positive is similar to that of *PRETTY. **Nice guys finish last** is credited to Leo Durocher, manager of the Brooklyn Dodgers baseball team from 1951 to 1954. In his 1975 autobiography *Nice Guys Finish Last* he is quoted as saying of a rival team: 'Take a look at them. All nice guys. They'll finish last. Nice guys. Finish last.'

niche *see* NEST

nick [LME] Nick has a great many meanings that are apparently unrelated. The first, most basic meaning is 'make a nick or notch in', from which developed various senses to do with striking something or hitting a target. The meaning 'to apprehend, take into custody', as in 'You're nicked!', is first found in the play *The Prophetesse* (1640) by John Fletcher and Philip Massinger: 'We must be sometimes witty, to nick a knave.' The sense 'to steal' is more recent, dating from the 1820s.

The noun nick first meant 'notch, cut, or groove'; the sense 'condition' ('you've kept the car in good nick') seems to come from Worcestershire and Gloucestershire dialect, and was first recorded at the end of the 19th century. **In the nick of time** developed from an old meaning 'the precise or critical time or moment', and was in the mid 16th century simply **in the nick** or **the very nick**. The slang sense 'prison' or 'police station' was originally Australian, with the first written evidence in the *Sydney Slang Dictionary* of 1882. **Old Nick**, a name for the devil, is probably a shortening of the man's name Nicholas. One theory as to why this familiar name was adopted links it with the Italian politician and philosopher Niccolò Machiavelli (*see* MACHIAVELLIAN), although he is reputed to have been unscrupulous and scheming rather than downright evil.

Another is that it is short for Iniquity (*see* EQUAL), which was the name for the character symbolizing Vice in old morality plays—Old Iniquity is found as a name for the devil in the 19th century. Other names for the devil in parts of Britain are Old Harry, Old Horny, Old Ned, and Old Scratch, so maybe there is no particular reason why Nick should have been chosen.

nickname [LME] In the Middle Ages a nickname was **an eke-name**, or 'an additional name'—**eke** meant 'additional'. People misinterpreted an eke-name as **a neke name** or, later, a nickname. *See also* NEWT

niece *see* NEPHEW

night [OE] Although an Old English word, night comes ultimately from the same root as Latin *nox*, the source of **equinox** [LME] and **nocturnal** [LME]. **Fortnight** [OE] is an Old English contraction of 'fourteen nights', and reflects an ancient Germanic custom of reckoning time by nights rather than days. The original **night of the long knives** was the legendary massacre of the Britons by the Saxon leader Hengist in 472. According to the 12th-century Welsh chronicler Geoffrey of Monmouth, the Saxons attended a meeting armed with long knives, and when a prearranged signal was given each Saxon drew his weapon and killed the Briton seated next to him. The phrase is now more commonly associated with the brutal suppression of the Brownshirts (a Nazi militia replaced by the SS) on Hitler's orders in 1934. It is also used of any decisive or ruthless sacking, in particular the occasion in 1962 when British Prime Minister Harold Macmillan dismissed a third of his cabinet at the same time. **Nightmares** are nothing to do with horses. In the Middle Ages a nightmare [ME] was thought of as an evil female spirit or monster that lay on sleeping people and suffocated them: the -*mare* part comes from Old English and meant 'suffocating evil spirit'.

-nik *see* YIDDISH WORD PANEL

nil *see* ANNIHILATE

niche nick nickname niece night -nik nil

nimby [1980s] Nimby, short for Not In My Back Yard, refers to a person who objects to the siting of something unpleasant in their own neighbourhood while not objecting to similar developments elsewhere. Although first recorded in 1980, in the USA, it is associated by most people with the British politician Nicholas Ridley, who in 1988 attacked country dwellers as selfish for opposing development, calling their attitude 'pure Nimbyism'. It was later discovered that he himself was opposing the building of new houses near his own country home.

nincompoop [L17th] The word nincompoop perhaps came from Nicodemus, the name of a Jewish Pharisee in the New Testament who became something of a byword for slow-wittedness. Nicodemus secretly visited Jesus one night to hear about his teachings. Jesus explained, 'Except a man be born again, he cannot see the Kingdom of God', which puzzled the Pharisee, who took Jesus literally and said 'How can a man be born when he is old?'. The -poop part of the word may have come from the old verb **poop**, which meant 'to deceive or cheat'. In a similar vein **ninny** [L16th] may be a pet form of the name Innocent.

nine [OE] All of our main number words go back to the most ancient times. Nine is Old English but can be traced back to a root that was shared by Latin *novem* and Greek *ennea*. The phrase **dressed up to the nines** dates from the early 18th century. At first it meant 'to perfection, to the greatest degree', but by the mid 19th century was particularly associated with smart dress, as in 'When she's dressed up to the nines for some grand party' (Thomas Hardy, 1896). One theory is that it comes from the name of the 99th Wiltshire Regiment, known as **the Nines**, which was famous for its smart appearance. But their reputation seems to have dated from the 1850s, which means that it is unlikely to account for this much earlier phrase. *See also* TALK

ninja, ninjutsu *see* JAPANESE WORD PANEL

ninny *see* NINCOMPOOP

nit [OE] A nit is the tiny egg of a human head louse, and was in use for something small or insignificant by Shakespeare's day. However, **nitwit** is not recorded until the 1920s and **nit-picking** or pedantic fault-finding did not come into the language until the 1950s. The idea here is of painstakingly searching through someone's hair for nits. In Australia children shout 'nit!' to warn their friends when a teacher is approaching. The person who is keeping watch is said to **keep nit**. Nit is this context is probably an alteration of **nix** [L18th], which comes from German *nichts*, 'not'.

nocturnal *see* NIGHT

nod [LME] The word nod came into English from German. The proverb **a nod's as good as a wink to a blind horse**, now usually 'a nod's as good as a wink', is first recorded in a letter written in 1793. The use of **a nod and a wink** to mean 'a hint or suggestion' is first found in 1710, several decades earlier than the proverb: it seems that the 'blind horse' was tacked on to the original phrase for fun.

noel *see* NATION

noise *see* NAUSEA

nominate *see* NAME

nomophobia *see* PHOBIA

nonchalant [M18th] This is an English use of a French word meaning literally 'not being concerned', from the verb *nonchaloir*; the *chaloir* element is from Latin *calere* 'be warm, be roused with zeal'.

nonpariel *see* PAIR

noon [OE] Noon originally meant 'the ninth hour from sunrise', approximately 3pm. It came from the Latin phrase *nona hora* 'ninth hour'. The time change appears to have occurred in the Middle Ages: examples of **noon** meaning 'midday' are found from around 1225, and by the 14th century it seems to be the usual sense. The

nimby nincompoop nine ninja ninjutsu

Church service of **nones** gives a clue as to why its meaning shifted. Nones—from the same root as **noon**—are prayers generally said at 3pm, but among Benedictine monks in Italy the service was held closer to midday.

norm, normal see ENORMOUS

Norman [ME] The Normans who invaded England in 1066 were not simply Frenchmen. They were a people of mixed Germanic and Scandinavian origin who settled in Normandy from about AD 910 under their chief Rollo, and became dominant in western Europe and the Mediterranean. Their name is a form of **Northman**, which was first used in Old English in reference to Scandinavians, especially Norwegians (the related form **Norseman** [E19th] comes from the Dutch word for 'north'). The form Norman was in use by the 13th century, by which time it referred specifically to the people from Normandy.

nose [OE] The Latin root of nose is *nasus*, which is the source of our word **nasal** [ME], and is also related to **ness** [OE], meaning a headland or promontory. A **nostril** [OE] is literally a 'nose hole'. In Old English the word was spelled *nosterl* or *nosthyrl*, and came from *nosu* 'nose' and *thyrl* 'hole'. **Nozzle** was originally an early 17th slang form of 'nose'. To **cut off your nose to spite your face** was proverbial in both medieval Latin and French, and has been found in English since the mid 16th century. Since the 1780s a nose has been a spy or police informer. The idea of such a person being a 'nose', or 'sticking their nose in', is also found in words such as *NARK and *SNOUT, and in **nosy**. The first **nosy parker** appeared in a postcard caption from 1907, 'The Adventures of Nosey Parker', which referred to a peeping Tom in Hyde Park. Nosy itself goes back to 1620, in the sense 'having a big nose', and to at least the 1820s in the sense 'inquisitive'. The common surname Parker was originally a name for the caretaker of a park or large enclosure of land.

nosh see YIDDISH WORD PANEL

nostalgia [L18th] As the saying goes, 'Nostalgia isn't what it used to be'. In English nostalgia first meant 'acute homesickness', coined in the 18th century from the Greek words *nostos*, 'return home', and *algos*, 'pain', as a translation of the German word *Heimweh* or 'homesickness'. The familiar modern meaning, 'longing for the past', had become established by the early 20th century. There are a number of medical terms also derived from *algos*, all relating to physical pain, such as **neuralgia** [E19th] 'pain in a nerve', and **analgesia** [E18th] 'relief of pain'.

nostril see NOSE

nosy see NARK, NOSE

notorious [LME] When it appeared in the late 15th century notorious first meant just 'commonly or generally known, famous', as, for example, in the 1588 quotation 'Manie of you … are men verie notorious for their learning and preaching'. However, the negative meaning had already emerged by the time the *Book of Common Prayer* was published in 1549: 'Suche persones as were notorious synners.' The word comes from Latin *notus* 'known', which is also the root of the English words **note** [ME], **notice** [LME], **notify** [LME], and **notion** [LME].

noun see NAME

novel [LME] As an adjective novel first meant 'recent'. It entered English in the 15th century via Old French from the Latin *novellus*, which came from *novus*, 'new'. Novel meaning 'a book' is at root the same word, deriving from Italian *novella* (*storia*) 'new (story)', also from *novellus*. People first started speaking of a literary novel when referring to *The Decameron* by Boccaccio, which we would nowadays call a collection of short stories. Novel in the modern sense first started being used in the 1630s. At first it was contrasted with *ROMANCE, novels being shorter and having more connection to real life.

novice see NEW

norm normal Norman nose nosh nostalgia

noxious *see* INNOCENT

nozzle *see* NOSE

nubile [M17th] Today a nubile girl is young and sexy, but originally she was simply old enough to marry, with no implication of attractiveness. The word comes from Latin *nubilis*, from the verb *nubere*, 'to put on a veil, get married'. In English nubile at first had the same meaning as in Latin, but this use is now only found in anthropology and other technical contexts. *Nubere* is also the source of the English word **nuptial** [LME], 'to do with weddings', and ultimately derives from the Latin word for a cloud (the link is the obscuring veil), *nubes*, which is the root also of **nuance** [L18th].

nucleus [M17th] The nucleus of something is literally its 'little nut'. In Latin *nucleus* meant 'kernel, inner part', and was a diminutive of *nux* 'nut'. Nucleus originally referred to the bright core at the centre of a comet's head, and then to the central part of the earth. Today its main technical meaning is 'the positively charged central core of an atom'. This was identified by Sir Ernest Rutherford (1871–1937), regarded as the founder of nuclear physics, in 1911.

nude *see* NAKED

nuisance *see* INNOCENT

null *see* ANNUL

numb [LME] Old English used to have a verb *nim* meaning 'take'. It was one of those verb, like *sing*, that show the past form by changing the vowel. In this case the past was *nome* 'taken'. This then evolved into numb for sensation that had been taken away.

number [ME] The source of number, and of **enumerate** [E17th] and **numerous** [ME], is the Latin word *numerus*. The first written use of **your number is up** was by the English essayist Charles Lamb in a letter written in 1806, in which the reference is to someone drawing a winning ticket in the 'lottery of despair'. Other suggestions have been made as to the phrase's origins. One links it to various passages in the Bible that refer to the 'number of your days', meaning the length of your life. Another proposes that the number in question is a soldier's army number, associated with identifying casualties on the battlefield and the fatalistic expectation of a bullet with 'your name and number' on it.

nuncio *see* ANNOUNCE

nuncle *see* UNCLE

nuptial *see* NUBILE

nut [OE] The Old English word nut is related to the Latin *nux*, also meaning 'nut', and to *NUCLEUS. The informal meanings 'crazy or eccentric person' and 'person who is excessively interested in a particular thing', both date from the early 20th century. They probably come from the informal sense 'a person's head'. This latter sense is the one behind phrases such as **do your nut**, or get very cross, and is the root of **nutty** meaning 'mad or crazy'. It is also the source of the verb 'to nut', or butt with the head, which is first found in the 1930s. *See also* FRUIT. A **nutshell** has been used since the late 16th century to symbolize compactness or shortness. Shakespeare's Hamlet says, 'I could be bounded in a nutshell, and count myself a king of infinite space, were it not that I have bad dreams.' The idea is thought to have come from the supposed existence of a copy of Homer's epic poem, the *Iliad*, which was small enough to fit into an actual nutshell, mentioned by the Roman scholar Pliny (AD 23–79) in his *Natural History*.

nutty *see* FRUIT, NUT

nymphet *see* LOLITA

Oo

oaf [E17th] The word **oaf** goes back to Old Norse *alfr* 'an *ELF'. It originally meant 'an elf's child, a changeling', and from this came to be used for 'an idiot child', and then 'fool' or 'halfwit'. Finally, in the early 20th century, it acquired the general sense of 'large clumsy man', a sense used by Rudyard Kipling in *The Islanders* (1903) when he referred to cricketers and footballers as 'flannelled fools at the wicket' and 'muddied oafs at the goals'.

oak [OE] The name of the oak is related to Latin *aesculus*, a word for a species of oak sacred to the Roman god Jupiter. Oak was traditionally used in shipbuilding, which gave the 18th-century actor David Garrick the line for a song about the British navy, '**Heart of oak** are our ships'. **The Oaks** is the name of an annual flat horse race for three-year-old fillies run on Epsom Downs, over the same course as the Derby. It was first run in 1779 and was named after a nearby estate, presumably distinguished for its oak trees. *See also* ACORN

oasis [E17th] In the classical world Oasis was the name of a particular fertile spot in the Libyan desert. It came ultimately from an ancient Egyptian word for 'dwelling place'. By the early 19th century the word was being used for a place of calm in the midst of trouble or bustle. In Sir Arthur Conan Doyle's *The Sign of Four* (1890), a character describes his richly furnished house as being 'an oasis of art in the howling desert of South London'.

oat [OE] Oats are used as feed for horses, making them friskier and more energetic, and if you show signs of being lively and buoyant you may be said to be **feeling your oats** [M19th]. To be **off your oats** [L19th], on the other hand, means that you have no appetite for food. **Wild oats** are weeds found in cornfields which resemble cultivated oats. They have no value as a crop, so you would be wasting your time sowing them instead of good grain. Since the 16th century **sowing your wild oats** has been a term for behaving wildly or promiscuously when young, while to **get your oats** [1920s] is to have sex.

obdurate *see* DURABLE

obese *see* EAT

obey [ME] Latin *oboedire* 'pay attention to' is based on *audire* 'to hear' (*see* AUDIENCE). In the traditional Church of England wedding vows the husband promised 'to love and cherish' his wife 'till death us do part', while the wife promised to '**love, cherish, and obey**' her husband. **She who must be obeyed**, was the title of the beautiful sorceress Ayesha in the adventure story *She* (1887) by Sir H. Rider Haggard, although many now know it better from Sir John Mortimer's television series and books about Rumpole of the Bailey, where Rumpole uses it to refer to his wife.

object [LME] Object as a noun meaning 'a thing you can see and touch' and as a verb meaning 'to say that you disagree with something' are related, both going back to the same Latin word, *obicere*. This meant 'to throw at something else'. The earliest meaning in English was 'put something in the way of something else', and from this we get the idea of 'oppose'. An obstacle placed in the path is something that can be seen, and this gives us the noun sense.

oblige *see* ALLY

obnoxious *see* INNOCENT

obscene [L16th] The word obscene comes from Latin *obscaenus* 'ill-omened or abominable', a sense it could have into the 19th century. However, its primary sense in English has always been 'offensive, indecent.'

oaf oak oasis oat obdurate obese obey

observe *see* CONSERVE

obsess [LME] The word obsess had the early sense 'haunt, possess', referring to an evil spirit. It comes from Latin *obsidere* 'besiege'.

obvious *see* VIA

occasion *see* ACCIDENT

occident *see* ORIENT

occur *see* CURSOR

ocean [ME] The first mention of ocean in English looks back to the classical world. The ancient Greeks believed the world was surrounded by a great river, which they called *okeanos*. Ocean originally described the body of water ('the Great Outer Sea' as contrasted with the Mediterranean and other inland seas) regarded as enclosing the earth's single land mass, that of Europe and Asia, which at the time was the only land known. The **Mediterranean** is the sea 'in the middle of the earth' or 'enclosed by land', from Latin *medius* 'middle' and *terra* 'land'. *See also* ATLAS, PEACE

octopus [M18th] This is from Greek *oktōpous*, from *oktō* meaning eight and *pous* 'foot'. The prefix gives us words like **octagon** [L16th] an eight-sided figure and **octogenarian** [E19th], someone aged between 80 and 89. In the modern world **October** [OE] is the tenth month, but the word comes from Latin *octo* because it was the eighth month in the Roman calendar. It became the tenth month after the addition of **July** (named after Julius Caesar), and **August** (named after the Emperor Augustus) in the 1st century BC.

ocular *see* INOCULATION

odd [ME] The first meaning of odd, an Old Norse word, was 'having one left when divided by two', as in 'odd numbers'. This led to 'single, solitary', and then 'strange, unusual'. In the betting sense **odds** have been around since the end of the 16th century. If you **lay odds** or **give odds** you are offering a bet with odds favourable to

the other person betting. The opposite is to **take odds**, where you offer a bet with odds unfavourable to the other person betting. A person who talks loudly and opinionatedly is sometimes said to be **shouting the odds**—the idea here is of someone calling out the odds on a racecourse, encouraging punters to bet. When we say of something that **it makes no odds** we mean that it will not alter things in any way. This is not the gambling sense of odds, but an old use of the word with the sense 'difference in advantage or effect'.

odour [ME] Today an odour (from Latin *odor*) tends to be an unpleasant smell, but in medieval times it was a sweet smell or perfume. This gives us the expression **odour of sanctity** for a state of holiness—a sweet scent was supposedly given off by the bodies of saints when they were at or near death. To be **in good odour** (*or* **in bad odour**) with someone is to be in (or out of) favour with them, a use that has been around since the end of the 17th century.

office [ME] In the Middle Ages office meant a duty that went with someone's position or employment. It goes back ultimately to Latin *officium* 'performance of a task', which in turn comes from the combined elements of *opus* 'work' (source of English **opus** in the early 19th century and of **operation** [LME]) and *facere* 'to do'. The sense of 'a place for business' is recorded from the later Middle Ages. Someone **officious** [LME] was originally obliging or efficient in carrying out their office. The word developed its modern negative sense at the end of the 16th century.

ogre *see* ORC

oil [ME] The English word oil goes back to Latin *oleum*, which referred especially to *OLIVE oil. If someone sits up writing or reading until very late they are **burning the midnight oil**, an expression looking back to

when the main source of artificial
light would be an oil lamp. Oil paints are
traditionally used for portraits, and since
the early 20th century the unkind verdict
that someone is **no oil painting** has been a
way of saying that they are not attractive.
Water and oil cannot be mixed. People who
are incompatible may be described as being
like **oil and water** together. In classical
times, there was a belief among seamen—
recorded by the Roman statesman and
scholar Pliny the Elder (AD 23–79)—that
pouring oil into a stormy sea could calm the
waves. This is probably what lies behind the
proverbial expression **pour oil on troubled
waters**, meaning to try to settle a
disagreement by soothing those involved.

ointment *see* UNCTION

OK [M19th] The word OK came from the
USA, and is probably an abbreviation of *orl
korrect*, a jokey spelling of 'all correct', that
was used as a slogan during the presidential
re-election campaign of Martin Van Buren
(1782–1862) in 1840. It was reinforced by the
initials of his nickname Old Kinderhook,
derived from his birthplace.

old [OE] This word shares an ancient root
with Latin *alere* 'to nourish', which links it
with *ALIMONY. **The old boy network**
providing mutual assistance (and often
career advancement) among people from
the same social and educational
background goes back to the 1950s.
Members of such a group might well refer to
ideas of group loyalty and tradition in terms
of **the old school tie**—values seen as
associated with wearing the tie of a
particular public school. The first writers to
use this phrase were those astute social
commentators Rudyard Kipling and George
Orwell in the 1930s. **An old wives' tale** is a
widely held traditional belief now thought
to be unscientific or incorrect. This phrase,
with its earlier variant **an old wives' fable**,
has been part of the language since the 16th
century. It is first found in William Tyndale's
translation of the Bible, where the faithful
are instructed to 'cast away' such stories.
Some behaviour becomes inappropriate as
you get older, and there is a risk for some of

being considered a **dirty old man**. First
recorded in the 1930s, the phrase was
Harold Steptoe's familiar rebuke to his
father in the TV comedy *Steptoe and Son*
(1962–74).

olive [ME] The word olive comes from
Greek *elaion* 'oil'. To **hold out an olive
branch** is to make an offer of peace and
reconciliation. Olive branches as emblems
of peace and goodwill feature in both
classical mythology and biblical tradition.
In ancient Greece olive crowns were
presented to winners in the Olympic Games
and to worthy civic dignitaries, and brides
would wear olive garlands. In the story of
Noah and the Ark in the Bible, a dove
returns to Noah with an olive leaf (often
described as a branch) to indicate that God
is no longer angry and that the waters of the
flood have begun to recede. *See also* DOVE

ombudsman [1950s] There are not
many words in English that come directly
from Swedish, but this is one of them. In the
1950s we adopted the Swedish word for
'legal representative' as a term for an official
appointed to investigate individual
complaints against companies or the
government, though the British
Parliamentary Commissioner for
Administration, as the office is formally
known, dates from 1967.

omen *see* ABOMINABLE

omerta *see* ITALIAN WORD PANEL

ominous *see* ABOMINABLE

omnibus [E19th] The 1820s saw the
introduction in Paris of a horse-drawn
vehicle that carried passengers along a fixed
route for a fare. This was called a *voiture
omnibus*, a 'vehicle for everybody'. When it
came to London the vehicle was called
simply an omnibus. Though 'omnibus' was
taken from French, its origin is a Latin form
meaning 'for all', based on *omnis* 'all', and by
the 1930s people had shortened this rather
pompous, learned word to **bus**. In the 1830s
an omnibus came to be a volume
containing several works previously
published separately. *Omnis* also gives us

ointment OK old olive ombudsman omen

words such as **omnivorous** [E17th] literally 'all-eating', and **omniscient** [E17th] 'knowing everything', and **omnipotent** [ME] 'all powerful'.

one [OE] Like the other main number words, one goes back to Old English. It shares an ancient root with Latin *unus*, and so is linked with such words as **unique** [E17th], **unity** [ME], and **unison** [LME]. The **one that got away** is a term for something desirable that has eluded capture. The phrase comes from the angler's traditional way of trying to impress by boasting 'You should have seen the one that got away'. A **one-horse town** is a small town with hardly any facilities, particularly in the USA. Such towns are associated with the Wild West, and the term is first recorded in a US magazine of 1855. The previous year, though, there is a record of a specific place of that name: 'The principal mining localities are...Whiskey Creek, One Horse Town, One Mule Town, Clear Creek [etc.].' Also American is the **one-trick pony**, a person with only one talent or area of expertise. This goes back to the days of travelling circuses in the early 20th century. It would be a poor circus whose pony had only one trick. **Once and future** refers to someone or something that is eternal, enduring, or constant. It probably comes from T.H. White's *The Once and Future King* (1958), a series of novels about King Arthur. In White's story the enchanter Merlyn says to Arthur: 'Do you know what is going to be written on your tombstone? *Hic jacet Arthurus Rex quondam Rexque futurus.* Do you remember your Latin? It means, the once and future king.' A bad experience can make you wary of the same thing happening again, a feeling which might be summed up concisely with the words **once bitten, twice shy**. The expression has been around since the late 19th century, although in the USA you might say instead **once burned, twice shy**.

onerous *see* EXONERATE

onion [LME] Onions have been part of the vegetable garden since medieval times, and the name comes ultimately from Latin

where it was the word for a large pearl, but used in non-standard speech for an onion. To **know your onions** is to be very knowledgeable about something. The phrase was first used in the USA in the 1920s, when there were a number of similar phrases that involved knowing a lot about foodstuffs, and onions may simply have been chosen as a widely used vegetable. Another idea is that onions is short for 'onion rings', rhyming slang for 'things', but this does not fit with an American origin. The same is true of another theory, that there is a link with the lexicographer C.T. Onions, one of the first editors of the *Oxford English Dictionary*. Despite his eminence as a scholar it seems unlikely that his name would have been widely known on both sides of the Atlantic.

opera [M17th] An adoption from Italian which goes back to Latin *opus*, meaning literally 'labour, work' (*see* OFFICE). In mid 1970s America the saying **the opera isn't over till the fat lady sings** became a way of warning that something had not been finally settled, and that an outcome could still change. The reference is probably to the final solo of an operatic heroine, often played by a large woman.

operation *see* OFFICE

opium [LME] The name of this drug comes ultimately from the Greek word *opion* 'poppy juice'. The **opium of the people** is something regarded as giving people a false sense of security and contentment. The phrase originated as a direct translation of the German *Opium des Volks*, as used by the founder of modern Communism, Karl Marx, in 1843–44.

opossum *see* POSSUM

opportune [LME] Since medieval times we have used opportune of something that has happened at a good or convenient time. Originally, though, the word was associated with a much more specific meaning. It comes from Latin *opportunus*, from *ob-* 'in the direction of' and *portus* 'harbour', referring to the favourable wind which

one onerous onion opera operation opium

brought ships into the harbour.
Opportunity [LME] comes from the same root. The phrase **opportunity knocks** is used to mean that a chance of success might happen, often with the implication that every person has a chance to succeed. It was the title of a hugely popular TV talent show broadcast from the late 1950s to 1978, with a revival in the late 1980s.

oppose *see* COMPOST

optic, optician *see* AUTOPSY

optimism [M18th] Philosophers in the 18th century coined optimism for the theory that this is the best of all possible worlds. The word goes back to Latin *optimum* 'best thing'. By the early 19th century it had gained wider currency, and was being used to mean a general tendency to hope for the best. The opposite, **pessimism** (from Latin *pessimus* 'worst'), was also coined in the 18th century, when it meant 'the worst possible state or condition'.

option [M16th] This goes back to Latin *optare* 'choose'. **Keep your options open** is only recorded from the 1960s. You choose a specific child to **adopt** [LME] and this comes from the related word *adopatare* 'choose for yourself'.

opus *see* OFFICE

orange [LME] The name of the orange, first recorded in English in medieval times, goes back through Arabic to Persian, although the native home of the fruit may have been southeast Asia. The Arabs brought what we now call the **Seville orange**, or **bitter orange**, to Sicily in the Middle Ages, and from Sicily it was introduced to the rest of Europe. In the 16th century the Portuguese brought the sweet orange from China, and gave us the fruit which we now know simply as the orange, at first distinguished as a **China orange**. The children's game of **oranges and lemons** is recorded from the early 19th century but is probably a lot older. The song lists the bells of a number of London churches, beginning with St Clement's, and the final line runs

'Here comes a chopper to chop off your head.' This has led to the theory that the song looks back to the days of public executions, when the condemned person was taken in procession to execution while the church bells were tolled. There may also be an association with the marriages of King Henry VIII, and the beheading of two of his wives. The **Orangemen** of Northern Ireland are members or supporters of the Orange Order, a Protestant political society in favour of continued union with Britain. Their name comes from the wearing of orange badges as a symbol of adherence to King William III, who defeated the Catholic James II at the Battle of the Boyne in 1690. William was also known as William of Orange, a town in southern France which was the home of the ancestors of the Dutch royal house.

orang-utan [L17th] The orang-utan provides one of the few contributions of the Malay language to English. It comes from Malay *orang huan* meaning 'forest person'.

orb [LME] The Latin word *orbis* 'ring' is the ancestor of orb and **orbit** [M16th]. During the Middle Ages an orb was a sphere or circle. In the early 17th century it developed the particular sense of a golden globe surmounted by a cross, forming part of the royal regalia. Orbit was originally a term for the eye socket, but the astronomical sense of the regular course of a celestial body was used as early as 1670.

orc [OE] In J.R.R. Tolkien's *The Lord of the Rings* the orcs are ugly, malevolent, goblin-like creatures that attack in hordes and sometimes ride wolves. The word was not invented by Tolkien, and had been used by the Anglo-Saxons, to whom an *orc* was 'a demon'. It had died out by AD 1000, but came back into English in the 17th century from Italian *orco* 'man-eating giant'. The source in both cases was *Orcus*, the name of a Roman god of the underworld which was also the root of **ogre** [E18th]. When Tolkien was writing in the 1930s orc had become rare, and he revived the word—as a noted scholar he would have been aware of the earlier Old English use.

orchard [OE] In Old English orchard was simply a name for a garden. The first part of the word probably comes from Latin *hortus* 'garden'. The second part is *YARD.

order [ME] An early meaning of order, which comes from Latin *ordo* 'row, series, rank', was an institution founded by a ruler to honour people. The **Order of the Garter**, the highest order of English knighthood, was established by Edward III in around 1344. According to tradition, the garter was that of the Countess of Salisbury, which fell off while she was dancing with the king. To spare her blushes he promptly picked up the garter and put it on his own leg, saying '*Honi soit qui mal y pense*' (shame be to him who thinks evil of it), which was adopted as the motto of the order. Order was also used to mean a rank, such as priest or bishop, in the Christian Church, which gave us the expression **take orders** for someone who becomes a priest. In the 16th century **out of order** meant 'not in normal sequence'. The meaning was gradually extended to mean 'not in a settled condition', and by the 18th century to 'not in good health'. Finally it came to be used of machinery that was not working, or behaviour that was seen as unacceptable. The sense of the word to mean 'a statement telling someone to do something' is found from the 16th century. By the 18th century **doctor's orders** had established itself as a term for an instruction from your doctor that had to be obeyed. Charles Dickens, in a letter of January 1841, wrote that: 'I have been obliged to make up my mind—on the doctor's orders—to stay at home this evening.'

The Latin word *ordo* also gave us **ordinary** [LME] originally 'orderly', **ordain** [ME], **ordinance** [ME] 'an authoritative order', and **ordnance** [LME]. In the army now ordnance refers to mounted guns or artillery, but in earlier days it was also used for the official body responsible for the supply of military equipment. In 1791 the official in charge, known as the **Master-General of the Ordnance**, was told to organize an official survey of the south coast of England to the scale of an inch to a mile, in anticipation of a French invasion. This grew into a series covering the whole of Great Britain and Ireland and was the origin of the **Ordnance Survey**, which today prepares large-scale detailed maps of the United Kingdom.

ore *see* IRON

organ [OE] The word organ came via Latin from Greek *organon* 'tool, instrument, sense organ', also found in **organize** [LME]. Organ was first adopted in the 'musical instrument' sense. **Organic** [LME] has been used meaning 'produced without the use of artificial chemicals' from the mid 19th century.

orgy [M16th] The word orgy goes back to Greek *orgia* 'secret rites or revels'. In the classical world these were part of the worship of Bacchus, the god of fertility and wine, in the annual festivals held in his honour, which were celebrated with extravagant dancing, singing, and drinking.

Orient [LME] Since the Middle Ages the countries of the East have been referred to as the Orient—the first recorded use of the term appears in Geoffrey Chaucer's *Canterbury Tales*. The name goes back to Latin *oriri* 'to rise', also the source of **original** [LME] and refers to the rising of the sun. The opposite is **Occident**, a name for the countries of the West which comes from Latin *occidere* 'to go down, set', and refers to the setting of the sun. The English football club Orient (later known as Clapton Orient, and now as Leyton Orient) was founded in 1881. The name was suggested by a player who worked for the Orient shipping line, and was appropriate, as the club is based in the East End of London. **Disorient** [M17th] was originally 'to turn from the east'.

origami *see* JAPANESE WORD PANEL

original *see* ORIENT

orthodox *see* PARADOX

ostracize [M17th] In ancient Athens the people of the city would gather together every year to vote on whether an unpopular citizen should be expelled for ten years. They wrote the name of the person they wanted to send into exile on an *ostrakon*, a

orchard order ore organ orgy Orient

shell or fragment of pottery, and somebody who was exiled in this way was said to have been ostracized. Today a person who is ostracized is excluded from a society or group. *See also* OYSTER

ostrich [ME] The first part of this word comes from Latin *avis* 'bird', but the second part goes back to the Greek name for a very different bird—*strouthos* 'sparrow'. The fuller term in ancient Greek was *megas strouthos* 'large sparrow'. It was also called *strouthokamelos* or 'sparrow camel', perhaps in recognition of its long neck. There was a traditional belief that hunted ostriches would bury their heads in the sand, thinking that this would hide them from view. From this we get the use of 'ostrich' to mean a person who refuses to face reality or accept facts, and also the phrase **to bury your head in the sand**.

otiose *see* NEGOTIATE

OTT *see* TOP

otter *see* WATER

ottoman *see* DIVAN

ounce [ME] The unit of weight goes back to Latin *uncia*, where it meant 'twelfth part'. In imperial measurement this would have been the twelfth part of a pound, but it is also the basis of *INCH as the twelfth part of a foot. Ounce is also another name for the snow leopard. This is a quite different word, which originally had an extra letter. In medieval French it was *lonce*, but the 'l' was misunderstood as representing *le*, the French for 'the'. The word actually goes back to Latin *lynx*, the root of **lynx** [ME].

out *see* CLOSET

oval [M16th] When we say that something is oval, we are calling it 'egg-shaped'. The word goes back to Latin *ovum* 'egg', also the source of **ovary** [M17th]. **The Oval** is an oval cricket ground in Kennington, south London, opened in 1846, the home ground of Surrey County Cricket Club. The **Oval Office** is the informal name for the oval-shaped private office of the

president of the United States, used since the 1960s.

overblown *sees* BLOOM

overboard *see* BOARD

owl [OE] The name of the owl probably comes from an imitation of its call. The bird was traditionally taken as a symbol of wisdom—in classical times it was associated with the Greek goddess Athene— and to call someone **owlish** [L16th] suggests that they look solemn or wise. It is a nocturnal bird, and its name is also used for someone, a 'night owl', who habitually goes to bed late and feels more lively in the evening. The opposite is a *LARK. In the 17th century **owling** was the term for smuggling wool or sheep out of England, to avoid paying tax. Although possibly a different word, it may also come from the bird's nocturnal habits, since such smuggling would have been done at night.

ox *see* BEEF

oyez [LME] This call asking for people's attention made by a public crier or by a court officer is from Old French *oiez!, oiez!* 'hear!'.

oyster [OE] This goes back ultimately to Greek *ostreon*, which was related to *ostrakon* 'shell or tile' and is linked to *OSTRACIZE. The possibility that on opening an oyster you might find a pearl has given us an expression that goes back to Shakespeare. In *The Merry Wives of Windsor* the boastful Pistol brags to Falstaff, 'Why then, the world's mine oyster, which I with sword will open.'

oy vey *see* YIDDISH WORD PANEL

ozone [M19th] Today the usual association of ozone is with the **ozone layer**, a layer in the earth's stratosphere that absorbs most of the harmful ultraviolet radiation reaching the earth from the sun, and which is under threat from atmospheric pollutants. Ozone is a strong-smelling, poisonous form of oxygen

ostrich otiose OTT otter ottoman ounce out

whose name goes back to Greek *ozein* 'to smell'. It was originally believed to have a tonic effect and to be present in fresh air, especially at the seaside. In Penelope Mortimer's autobiographical *About Time* (1987) she writes: 'An important part of our middle-class Englishness was the seaside holiday—no baking on a Mediterranean beach, but lungfuls of ozone, gales, hard sand.'

owl   ox   oyez   oyster   oy vey   ozone

Pp

pace [ME] The word pace comes via Old French *pas* from Latin *passus* 'stretch (of the leg)'. As well as stepping, it also meant 'journey, route' in early examples. To be **put through your paces** arose in the mid 18th century from horse-riding. The notion of 'tempo' as in **change of pace** is from the 1950s while **pace yourself** is only found from the 1970s. Other words from the same root are **pass** in the sense to go by, **passage** [ME]; **passenger** [ME] the 'n' added to conform with words like 'messenger'; and **expand**, literally to stretch out. The Old French form of expand, *espandre,* has the special sense of 'to shed, spill, pour out' and is the origin of to **spawn** [LME].

pacific, pacify *see* PEACE

pack [ME] The word pack for a container or group as in a pack of wolves is from noun *pak* found in both Middle Dutch and Middle Low German. Where they got the word from is not known. The related words **packet** (originally a little pack), and **package** developed in the 16th century. The phrase **package holiday** dates from the 1960s.

pact *see* COMPACT

pad [M16th] A word of unknown origin, although the sense 'underpart of an animal's foot' may be related to Low German *pad* 'sole of the foot. The first recorded sense was 'bundle of straw to lie on' which developed into a slang term for a bed in the early 18th century. By the 20th century this had become underworld slang for a place to take drugs or where a prostitute worked. This moved up in the world in the 1970s to become a general term for a place to live. Pad as in **notepad**, [M19th] may not be from

the same source. The verb meaning 'to tread, walk' came into English in the 16th century from Low German *padden*, which may have come from the sound made. It was originally underworld slang, and is also the source of **footpad** [L17th]. *Padden* could also mean 'to wade', hence to **paddle** [E16]. The other sense of paddle, 'oar' is found from the 15th century in the sense of a small spade-like implement and is also of unknown meaning.

paddy [E17th] The paddy of paddy field is from Malay *pādī* meaning 'rice in the straw'. Paddy meaning 'fit of anger' [L19th] is from the given name Paddy, associated with obsolete *paddywhack* meaning 'an Irishman (given to brawling)'. The name Paddy is an Irish pet-form of Padraig or Patrick and was used colloquially as a term for an Irishman from the early 18th century, but is now considered offensive.

paediatrics, paedophile *see* PAGE

paella *see* SPANISH WORD PANEL

pagan [LME] In Latin *paganus* originally meant 'of the country, rustic', and also 'civilian, non-military'. Around the 4th century AD, it developed the sense 'non-Christian, heathen'. One theory is that belief in the ancient gods lingered on in the rural villages after Christianity had been generally accepted in the towns and cities of the Roman Empire; another focuses on the 'civilian' sense, and points out that early Christians called themselves 'soldiers of Christ', making non-Christians into 'civilians'. A third view compares heathens to people outside the civilized world of towns and cities, belonging to the countryside. Curiously, it was not uncommon to find Pagan as a given name, a custom that has recently been revived. The Latin root *paganus* came from *pagus* 'country district', which is also the source of **peasant**. **Heathen** is similar in meaning and development, coming from a word meaning 'inhabiting open country' which is related to **heath**. Both these words are

pace pacific pacify pack pact pad paddy

Germanic and were already in use in Old English.

page [L16th] The page of a book goes back to Latin *pagina* 'page', from *pangere* 'to fasten'. The connection between fastening and the page of a book is probably because *pagina* was originally used of a scroll, made up of strips of papyrus glued together, and then transferred to the page of a book when books replaced scrolls. Before the 16th century older forms, such as *pagne*, were in use. The other page [ME] is first found in the sense 'youth, male of uncouth manners' and comes via Old French from Greek *paidíon* 'boy, lad'. **Page boys** at a wedding date from the late 19th century. *Paidíon* is also the source of the word-element *paed-* or *ped* found in words such as **paediatrics** 'the medical care of children' [M19], **paedophile** 'child-lover' [M20], and **pedagogue** [LME] formed from the Greek words for 'child' and 'leader', which was the word in ancient Greece for the slave who took a child to school, but became a term for a teacher in Latin. The Italian *pedante* 'teacher', which entered the language in the late 16th century as **pedant** may be from pedagogue. *See also* ENCYCLOPEDIA, PAGEANT

pageant [LME] This word had two meanings in Middle English, either a religious play or the moveable platform on which it was performed. It seems to have come via Anglo-Norman from Latin *pagina*, the source of *PAGE, but there is some debate as to how the meaning has changed. It may be from the idea that a play is performed from something written in a manuscript, or it may go back to the Latin source of *pagina*, *pangere* 'to fasten', referring to the putting together of the temporary stage. The modern sense of a showy parade is not found before the early 19th century.

pain [ME] This goes back to Latin *poena* which originally meant 'penalty' and later came to mean 'pain', and is also the source of to **pine** [OE] 'to long for', but originally meaning 'to suffer'; **penal;** and **penalty** [both LME]. **Punish** [ME] comes from the related verb *punire*. **Pain in the neck** dates from the 1920s; from this, **a pain** for an

annoying person developed in the 1930s. Although the phrase **no pain, no gain** is associated with exercise classes from the 1980s, the two words have been associated since the 16th century and 'No Pains, No Gains' is the title of a 1648 poem by Robert Herrick.

paint [ME] Paint is from Old French *peint* 'painted', from Latin *pingere* 'to paint'. To **paint the town red** dates from the late 19th century. It is first found in the USA which puts in doubt the story that it comes from an occasion in 1837 when Marquis of Waterford and some young friends ran riot in the Leicestershire town of Melton Mowbray and painted some of the buildings red. An alternative interpretation is that revellers were thought of as having such a wild time that they treated the entire town like a red light district. **Paint yourself into a corner**, from the image of someone painting a floor and forgetting to start near a doorway to avoid crossing the wet paint, arose in the 1970s. **Painter** [ME] goes back to Latin *pictor* which also gives us **picturesque** [E18th] the spelling changed to fit with *PICTURE.

pair [ME] Pair comes from Latin *paria* 'equal things', formed from *par* 'equal'. Latin *par* also lies behind **compare** [LME] 'to pair with, bring together'; **disparage** [ME] originally 'a mis-pairing especially in marriage', later 'to discredit'; **nonpareil** [LME] 'not equalled' (taken directly from the French); **par** [L16th] 'equal', a golfing term from L19th; **parity** [L16] 'equalness'; **peer** [ME] 'equal'; and **umpire** [ME] originally *noumpere*, from the same source as nonpareil, because an umpire is above all the players. *A noumpere* was later re-interpreted as 'an umpire' and the initial 'n' was lost.

pal *see* ROMANY WORLD PANEL

palace [ME] The Roman emperors had their imperial residence on the Palatine hill, one of the seven hills on which the city of Rome is built. In Latin the name of the hill was *Palatium*, which came to refer to the emperor's home and then to any vast and luxurious building housing the powerful. Our word palace derives from this, as does Italian *palazzo*, a large mansion of an Italian noble family. From the 1830s lavish places of entertainment were also called palaces, as in **gin palace** for a gaudily decorated pub. **Paladin**, for a noble knight, comes from the same source: Latin *palatinus* 'palace official' became Old French *paladin* 'warrior', and was adopted into English in the late 16th century.

palate [LME] The word palate is from Latin *palatum* 'roof of the mouth'. It came into English in this sense and rapidly developed the meaning 'sense of taste', but use of the word for wine tasting dates only from the 1970s.

palaver [M18th] When early Portuguese traders in West Africa had disputes or misunderstandings with the locals they used the Portuguese word *palavra*, literally 'word, speech', to mean 'a talk between local people and traders'. The Africans picked up the term from them, and in time passed it on to English sailors. In English palaver first meant a prolonged and tedious discussion, then in the late 19th century a fuss, commotion, or rigmarole. The Portuguese *palavra* developed from Latin *parabola* '*PARABLE'.

pale [ME] The word for a 'stake' is from Old French *pal*, from Latin *palus* 'stake', which ultimately goes back to the same root found in *PAGE and *PAGEANT as well as **paling** [LME]. The Pale was a name given to the part of Ireland under English jurisdiction before the 16th century. The earliest reference to the Pale in Ireland, from the modestly titled *Introduction to Knowledge* of 1547, stated that Ireland was divided into two parts, one being the English Pale and the other being 'the wild Irish'. Many people believe that this enclosed English part of Ireland was the source of the expression **beyond the pale** but this is extremely unlikely, as the phrase is not recorded until the 18th century, and its origin remains something of a mystery. The Latin also gives us **palisade** [E17th], and **impale** [M16th] first found in the sense

'surround with a pale, fortify', with 'thrust a stake though' recorded from the late 17th century. The adjective meaning 'light' comes via Old French *pale* from Latin *pallidus*, with the same meaning, and also the source of **pallor** [LME] and **pallid** [L16th], and has been in the language since the Middle Ages.

Palestine *see* PHILISTINE

palfrey [ME] A palfrey is literally an 'extra horse' but came to be used for an ordinary horse for riding as opposed to a warhorse. It goes back via Old French *palefrei*, to late Latin *paraveredus*, from Greek *para* 'extra' and Latin *veredus* 'light horse'. This word was of Gaulish origin, and was used for the fast horses used by couriers, who might well have had an extra horse to ride when the first tired.

palisade *see* PALE

pallet [LME] The first sense recorded for this was 'a flat wooden blade with a handle' used to shape clay or plaster: it comes from French *palette* 'little blade', from Latin *pala* 'spade' (related to *palus* 'stake', *see* PALE). The pallet used with a forklift truck is from the early 20th century. The French form was adopted directly in the early 17th century for the flat artist's **palette** on which to mix colours, with the sense of 'range of colours' developing in the late 18th century.

pallid *see* PALE

pall-mall *see* MALL

palm [OE] Although most dictionaries regard them as separate English words, palm meaning 'a tropical tree', and palm 'the inner surface of the hand' are from the same root, Latin *palma* 'palm of the hand', which is related to *planus* 'flat' (*see* PLAIN). In ancient Rome a leaf or branch of a palm tree would be placed in the hands of the victor in a contest, from which the tree got its name. The sense 'conceal' dates from the late 17th century and comes from cheats who would **palm a card** to hide it from other players. **Pelmet** [E20th] is probably an alteration of French *palmette*, literally 'small

palate   palaver   pale   Palestine   palfrey

palm', formerly a conventional ornament on window cornices.

palomino [E20th] This term for a light-coloured horse comes via Latin American Spanish from Spanish *palomino* 'young pigeon' used to describe the colour.

palpable [LME] This word is from late Latin *palpabilis*, from Latin *palpare* 'feel, touch gently', the source too of the medical term **palpate** [M19th] 'examine by touch'. When Osric says in *Hamlet* 'A hit, a very palpable hit' (Act 5, scene 2) he is using 'very palpable' in a literal sense, 'truly feelable', but the sense of a feeling that is so strong that it is almost touchable was already found in late Latin and is also in late Middle English. Latin *palpare* also developed the variant *palpitare* literally 'to touch gently repeatedly', but used for 'to tremble, throb', source of our words **palpitate** [E17th] and **palpitation** [LME].

palsy *see* PARALYSIS

pamper [LME] The early sense of pamper was 'cram with food', developing the sense' to indulge, spoil' in the mid 16th century. It is probably of Low German or Dutch origin and associated with German dialect *pampfen* 'cram, gorge'. It may be related to **pap** [LME] probably based on Latin *pappare* 'to eat', describing bland, soft, or semi-liquid food. The old sense of pap for a woman's breast could be from Latin *pappilla* 'nipple' but is more likely from a Scandinavian root imitating the sound of a baby sucking.

pamphlet [LME] The anonymous 12th-century Latin love poem *Pamphilus, seu de Amore* ('Pamphilius, or About Love') was popular in the Middle Ages and was translated into many languages, including English. Its popular name was *Pamphilet*, which became pamphlet, meaning 'a short handwritten work of several pages fastened together', and lived on long after the original poem was forgotten. Pamphlets have been associated with political theories or campaigns since as early as the end of the 16th century.

pan [OE] The word pan in the sense of something you cook with is a common West Germanic word, which may have been an early borrowing from Latin *patina* 'dish'. The same Latin word is the source, via Italian, of **patina** [E18th], perhaps because of the green film that appears on old copper dishes. The verb to **pan out** [M19th] comes from the use of a shallow pan to get gold from river sand. *See also* PANIC, PANORAMA

panacea [M16th] This word for a 'remedy to heal all diseases' came via Latin from Greek *panakeia*, from *panakēs* 'all-healing' formed from *pan* 'all' and *akos* 'remedy'. The sense 'solution for all problems' dates from the early 17th century.

panache [M16th] Soldiers in the 16th century would often wear a tuft or plume of feathers in their helmets. This tuft or plume was the original panache, a word that goes back to Latin *pinnaculum* 'little feather' from *pinna* 'feather, wing, pointed peak'. Men trying to give an impression of elegance or swagger would imitate the fashion, whose stylish associations gave rise to the modern sense, 'flamboyant confidence', in the late 19th century. *Pinnaculum* is also the source of **pinnacle** [ME], and *pinna* of a bird's **pinion** [LME], and of *PEN and *PIN.

pandemonium [M17th] John Milton's epic poem *Paradise Lost*, first printed in 1667, tells the story of the Fall of Man. In Book I the angels who rebelled against God build Satan's new palace and capital, Pandemonium. Milton coined the name, meaning 'the place of all the demons', from Greek *pan* 'all' and *daimōn* 'demon'. From the mid 18th century the word came to refer to other places that were centres of wickedness and then to noisy, disorderly places. In the early 19th century it developed its usual modern sense of 'noisy disorder, *BEDLAM, *CHAOS'.

pander [LME] The early use of pander was from *Pandare*, the name of a character in Chaucer's *Troilus and Criseyde* who acted as a lovers' go-between. Chaucer took the story from the 14th-century Italian writer

palomino palpable palsy pamper pamphlet

Boccaccio. The sense 'to indulge' does not appear until the 19th century.

pane [LME] A pane was originally a section or piece of something, such as a fence or strip of cloth. The word comes from Old French *pan*, from Latin *pannus* 'piece of cloth'. The sense 'division of a window' is found from the mid 15th century. **Panel** [ME] comes from the same root. The early sense 'piece of parchment' was extended to mean 'list', particularly a jury; this led to the notion 'advisory group'.

pang *see* PRONG

panic [E17th] Pan was the Greek god of flocks and herds, usually represented with the horns, ears, and legs of a goat on a man's body. His sudden appearance was supposed to cause terror similar to that of a frightened and stampeding herd. In Greek his name probably originally meant 'the feeder' referring to his role as god of flocks, but it was early on interpreted as from *pan* meaning 'all' and he was identified as a god of nature or the universe. **Panic button** originated in the US Air Force. Second World War bombers had an emergency bell system that was used if the aircraft was so badly damaged by fighters or flak that it had to be abandoned—the pilot gave a 'prepare-to-abandon' ring and then a ring meaning 'jump'.

panjandrum [M18th] This term for a pompous person is one of the few words we can say when, how, and by whom it was invented. It was coined in 1755 by the English actor and playwright Samuel Foote (1720–77) in response to the actor Charles Macklin's claim that he could memorize and repeat anything said to him. The word was part of a string of nonsense that went 'And there were present the Picninnies, and the Joblillies, and the Garyulies, and the Grand Panjandrum himself, with the little round button at top'.

pannier *see* COMPANION

panorama [L18th] In 1787 the painter Robert Barker invented the panorama, a spectacular method for presenting a large painting of a landscape or other scene. It could either be arranged on the inside of a cylinder and viewed from the inside, or be unrolled and made to pass in front of the viewer to show the various parts in succession. The first such picture was of a view of Edinburgh. By the early 1800s panorama had come into wider use as 'a complete and comprehensive survey or presentation of a subject', and 'an unbroken view of the whole region surrounding an observer'. Barker formed the word from Greek *pan* 'all' and *horama* 'view'. The cinematic term **pan** for a shot following someone or showing surrounding views is a shortening of panorama.

pansy *see* PENSIVE

pant¹ *see* FANCY

pant² *see* FANTASTIC

pantaloons [L16th] In Italian *Pantalone*, was one of the stock characters in the Italian theatre called the *commedia dell'arte*, which was popular from the 16th to the 18th centuries, and later in English *PANTOMIME. In the Italian tradition he was a foolish old man in a predominantly red costume that included long close-fitting trousers that covered the feet. These trousers must have made an impression, as from the 17th century the name pantaloons was given to a succession of styles, including that worn by Pantaloon himself. In the USA from the mid 19th century pantaloons was a name for any trousers, hence the modern term **pants** [M19th]. *See* ZANY

pantheon *see* ENTHUSIASM

panther [ME] Panther is from Latin *panthera*, from Greek *panthēr*. Greek *pardos*, Latin *pardus* 'leopard' existed alongside *panthera*. The two terms led to confusion, for while a panther is actually a black leopard, until the mid 19th century many experts thought the panther and the leopard were separate species. **Pard** [ME], from *pardus* was a standard word for *LEOPARD from the Middle Ages, still kept alive by Shakespeare's 'bearded like a pard' (*As You Like It* Act 2 scene 7) and Shelley's

pane   pang   panic   panjandrum   pannier

'pard-like Spirit beautiful and swift'
(*Adonais* (1821)), the now standard leopard
(Greek *leopardos*) was also used from the
Middle Ages.

pantomime [L16th] This word comes
from Greek *pantomimos* 'imitator of all'. In
Latin *pantomimus* was used for an actor
using mime. This later developed into a
comic dramatization with the stock
characters of Clown, Pantaloon (*see*
PANTALOONS), Harlequin, and Columbine.
The familiar **panto** based on fairy tales such
as Mother Goose or Cinderella and
involving music, topical jokes, and slapstick
comedy developed in the 19th century, with
a new set of conventional characters
including the dame, the principal boy, and
the pantomime horse. **Mime** [E17th] and
mimic [L16th] come from the same root.

pantry *see* COMPANION

pants *see* PANTALOONS

pap *see* PAMPER

papa *see* BABY, POPE

papacy, papal *see* POPE

paparazzi [1960s] Paparazzo was the
name of a society photographer in Frederico
Fellini's 1960 film *La Dolce Vita* (*see* ITALIAN
WORD PANEL). By the following year
paparazzo was appearing as a general name
in English for a press photographer, and it
had acquired a plural **paparazzi**, which is
how it most commonly appears nowadays.

paper [ME] The words paper and **papyrus**
are both from Greek *papuros*. Paper passed
through Latin *papyrus* and Anglo-Norman
papir, while papyrus was taken directly from
Latin, appearing as the name of the reed in
Middle English, but only in the 18th century
as the material that the ancient Egyptians
prepared from the pithy stems of the
plant.

We have the German statesman Otto von
Bismarck (1815–98) to thank for **paper over
the cracks**, 'to disguise a problem rather
than try to resolve it'. Bismarck used the
German equivalent in a letter written in

1865, referring to a convention between
Austria and Prussia. Tension had been rising
since their combined victory over Denmark
in the previous year had given control of
Schleswig to Austria and of Holstein to
Prussia, but neither was quite ready to go to
war. The convention gave a semblance of
order to the situation, while in fact giving
time for both to make preparations for an
inevitable conflict. **Paper tiger** for a person
or thing that appears threatening but is
ineffectual is a Chinese expression first
found in an English translation in 1836. It
came to wider attention through a 1946
interview with the Chinese Communist
leader Mao Zedong, in which he expressed
the view that 'all reactionaries are paper
tigers'.

par *see* PAIR

parable [ME] The word parable is from
an ecclesiastical Latin sense 'discourse,
allegory' of Latin *parabola* 'comparison'.
The source is Greek *parabolē* 'placing side
by side, application', from *para-* 'beside' and
bolē 'a throw'. The Latin **parabola** came to
be used for the symmetrical curve in the
late 16th century, and the same Latin root
lies behind **parley** and **parole** [both LME].
See also PALAVER, PARLIAMENT, BALLISTIC

parachute [L18th] This was originally a
French coinage from the combining form
para- 'protection against' and French *chute*
'fall'.

paradise [OE] Paradise goes back to the
ancient Iranian language Avestan, in which
the sacred texts of the Zoroastrian religion
were written in the 4th century AD.
Pairidaēza then meant 'an enclosure, park'.
Via Greek *paradeisos* 'royal (enclosed) park'
it was then used in the sense paradise in the
Greek translation of the Bible, and through
Latin entered Old English, where it meant
'the Garden of Eden' before coming to refer
to the *HEAVEN of Judaism, Christianity, and
Islam.

paradox [M16th] Originally a paradox
was a statement contrary to accepted
opinion. It came into English via late Latin

pantomime pantry pants pap papa papacy

from Greek *paradoxon* 'contrary (opinion)', formed from elements *para-* 'distinct from' and *doxa* 'opinion', found also in **orthodox** [LME], where it is combined with *orthos* 'straight, right'.

paraffin [M19th] This word first appeared in 1830 in German, coined by the chemist Karl Reichenbach from the Latin *parum* 'little' and *affinis* 'related' (also the source of **affinity** [ME]) because of its low chemical reactivity. It was in use in English within five years.

paragon [M16th] A paragon 'a person or thing regarded as a perfect example' is from an obsolete French word, from Italian *paragone* a 'touchstone to try good gold from bad', which came from Medieval Greek *parakonē* 'whetstone'.

parakeet *see* PARROT

parallel [M16th] Parallel goes back to Greek *parallēlos*, from *para-* 'alongside' and *allēlos* 'one another'.

paralysis [OE] This is a Latin word, formed from Greek *paraluesthai* 'be disabled at the side', formed from *para* 'beside' and *luein* 'loosen'. **Paralytic** is late Middle English, and comes via French from the same source. The sense 'extremely drunk' dates from the late 19th century. **Palsy** [ME] is from Old French *paralisie*, which was an alteration of Latin *paralysis*. The Greek *luein* is also found in **analysis** [L16th] literally a 'loosening up'.

paramount *see* MOUNTAIN

paranoia [E19th] This word is modern Latin, from Greek *paranoos* 'distracted', from *para* 'irregular' and *noos* 'mind'.

parapet [L16th] Parapet is from French, or from Italian *parapetto* 'breast-high wall', from *para-* 'protecting' and *petto* 'breast' (from Latin *pectus*). It was originally to screen and protect troops from the enemy.

paraphernalia [M17] Until the Married Women's Property Acts in the late 19th century a husband became the owner of all his wife's property when the couple married. A partial exception to this was her purely personal belongings such as clothes and jewellery, which she could keep after her husband's death. These were her paraphernalia—the word derives from Greek *parapherna* 'property apart from a dowry'. Outside the strict confines of the law, the word came to refer to a person's bits and pieces in the mid 18th century, and then to the items needed for or associated with a particular activity.

parasite [M16th] The word parasite came via Latin from Greek *parasitos* '(person) eating at another's table', from *para-* 'alongside' and *sitos* 'food', and originally came into the language as a term for a hanger-on or sponger. Its use as a term in biology dates from the early 18th century.

parasol *see* SOLAR

parcel [LME] Latin *particula* 'small part', from *pars* source of *PART, has given us parcel. In early use it shared with part the notion of something forming a section of a larger whole, as in a parcel of land. This survives in contexts such as **part and parcel** [16th], and to **parcel out**. The modern sense developed in the 17th century and initially concentrated on its contents, which would usually be a quantity of a substance or a number of goods wrapped up in a single package.

parchment [ME] This comes from Old French *parchemin*, a blend of late Latin *pergamina* 'writing material from Pergamum' and *Parthica pellis* 'Parthian skin' (a kind of scarlet leather). The use of treated animal skin as a writing material, when papyrus was the usual material (*see* PAPER), was traditionally said to have been invented by King Eumenes II of Pergamum (*r*.197–158 BC).

pard *see* LEOPARD, PANTHER

pardon [ME] This comes from medieval Latin *perdonare* 'concede, remit' from *per-* 'completely' and *donare* 'give'. Use of the word in **I beg your pardon** dates from the late 17th century; the shortened usage

paraffin   paragon   parakeet   parallel

pardon meaning 'excuse me' is found from the late 19th century.

pare *see* APPARATUS

parent *see* VIPER

pariah [E17th] This comes from the southern Indian languages Tamil and Malayalam, and literally means 'hereditary drummer' from the word meaning 'large drum'. The original pariahs were a people in southern India who acted as sorcerers and ceremonial drummers and also as labourers and servants. They were a tribal people outside the traditional Hindu caste system, and came to be regarded as 'untouchables' who did all the insanitary jobs. From there the sense 'a social outcast' developed in the early 19th century.

parity *see* PAIR

park [ME] Park is from Old French *parc*, from medieval Latin *parricus*. It is probably of Germanic origin, related to German *Pferch* 'pen, fold', which is also the source of **paddock** [M16th]. The word was originally a legal term for land held by royal grant for the keeping of game animals: the area was enclosed and therefore distinct from a *FOREST or chase, and (also unlike a forest) had no special laws or officers. A military sense 'space occupied by artillery, wagons, and stores, in an encampment' [L17th] is the origin of the verb 'to park' [M19th]. The British slang term **parky**, 'cold', dates from the 1890s. It probably comes from **perky**, 'lively, sharp' (*see* PERK).

parley *see* PARABLE

parliament [ME] A parliament is historically just a talking shop. It originates from French *parler* 'to talk', which goes back to Latin *parabola* 'word' (*see* PARABLE). **Parlour** [ME], originally a place for speaking, comes from the same root.

parody [L16th] This came via late Latin from Greek *parōidia* 'burlesque poem', from *para-* 'mock-' and *ōidē* 'ode'. The sense 'feeble imitation' dates from the early 19th century.

parole *see* PARABLE

parrot [E16th] The original English term for a parrot was **popinjay**. This came from French *papingay* which came, via Spanish, from Arabic *babbaga*, which may have been formed in imitation of the bird's cry. The ending of the French word was altered to resemble the name of the bird, the jay. The change to a term for a conceited, vain person came in the early 16th century. The origin of the word parrot may lie in the tendency to give pet birds human names. The word, recorded in the early 16th century, could represent French *Pierrot*, a pet form of *Pierre* 'Peter'. People often address a pet bird as 'Pretty Polly', and the name **Polly** has been used to mean 'a parrot' since the early 19th century, while **Poll** is first recorded as a parrot's name in 1600. The word **parakeet** [M16th] may be a similar formation based on the Spanish given name *Pedro*, also 'Peter'. Alternatively it may have come via Italian from a word meaning 'little wig', referring to the bird's head plumage. *See also* MOON

parsnip [LME] Parsnip is from Old French *pasnaie*, from Latin *pastinaca*, which is related to *pastinare* 'dig and trench the ground'. The change in the ending was due to association with **neep**, a Scots and northern English word for 'turnip' (Old English, from Latin *napus*). The form **turnip** appeared M16th, but the origin of the first syllable is not known.

parson *see* PERSON

part [OE] This is from Latin *pars*, *part-* 'part', the same Latin source that gave us **depart** [ME]; **particle** [LME]; **particular** [LME] 'small part' with the sense 'attentive to detail' developing E17th; **participate** 'take part in' [E16th]; **partisan** [M16th] 'one who takes the part of'; **partition** [LME] 'something that divides into parts'; and **party** [ME]. This last was originally used in the sense of a political party, and only developed the social gathering sense in the early 18th century. Latin *a parte* 'at the side' gives us **apart** [LME] and, via French, **apartment** [M17th], while Latin *impartare*

pare　parent　pariah　parity　park　parley

'give a share of' gives us **impart** [LME] and **impartial** [L16th].

partner [ME] The word partner is an alteration of *parcener* 'partner, joint heir', from Anglo-Norman French *parcener*, based on the Latin for partition, and thus related to the group of words at *PART. The change from 'c' to 't' was to match part. Partner for a spouse dates from the early 17th century; the term came to be commonly applied to each person of an unmarried couple sharing a home towards the end of the 20th century. **Partner in crime** dates from the early 19th century.

party *see* PART

pass, passage, passenger *see* PACE

passion [OE] The word passion comes via Old French from Latin *pati* 'to suffer'. **The Passion** refers to the suffering of Jesus Christ. The sexual sense dates from the late 16th century. **Passionate** in late Middle English included the senses 'easily moved to passion' and 'enraged'. **Passive** [LME] comes from the sense of 'being acted upon', and **compassion** [ME] is literally 'suffering with' someone, while **compatible** [LME] comes from the Latin for 'fit to suffer with'.

paste [ME] Italian pasta still retains a sophistication that the humble British **pasty** does not have, yet **pasta** [L19th], **pasty** [ME], and paste all go back through Latin to Greek *pastai* 'barley porridge' from *pastos* 'to sprinkle, to salt'. The earliest use of paste in English was to mean 'pastry'; pastry took over the sense in the 15th century. The sense 'glue' emerged in the later Middle Ages from the use of flour and water as an adhesive. Other words from the same root are **pastel** [M17th]; **patty** [M17th]; and the French equivalent *paté* [M18th]. Italian developed the form *pasticcio* for 'pie', which was also used as a term for a 'hotchpotch, mixture' and came into English via French as **pastiche** in the late 19th century. **Pastrami** [E20th] may be a more distant relative (*see* YIDDISH WORD PANEL).

pastille *see* COMPANION

pastor, pastoral *see* PASTURE

pastrami *see* PASTE, YIDDISH WORD PANEL

pastry *see* PASTE

pasture [ME] The word pasture comes via Old French from late Latin *pastura* 'grazing', from the verb *pascere* 'to graze'. A clergyman is seen as the shepherd of his flock, and **pastor** [LME] is the Latin for 'shepherd, feeder'. Late Middle English **pastoral** is from Latin *pastoralis* 'relating to a shepherd'. Its use in literary, art, and musical contexts dates from the late 16th century.

pasty *see* PASTE

pat [LME] First recorded for a blow with something flat, pat is probably imitative of the noise. The late 16th-century pat meaning 'readily' and in phrases such as to **have off pat**, 'to have memorized perfectly', were probably originally the same word. In early use it often appears as to **hit pat**, as if with the hand. In the early 20th-century Australian expression **on your pat**, 'on your own', pat is a shortening of rhyming slang **Pat Malone**, although there is no record of a particular person referred to. The English mid 20th-century equivalent, **on your tod**, however, comes from the name of the American jockey Tod Sloan (1874–1933). One sense of **patter** [E17th] developed from pat. **The patter of little feet**, is from Longfellow's 'The Children's Hour' (1860) 'I hear in the chamber above me The patter of little feet, The sound of a door that is opened, And the voices soft and sweet.' *See also* PATTER

patch *see* CROSS

paté *see* PASTE

patella *see* SPANISH WORD PANEL

patent [LME] The word patent comes via Old French from the Latin 'lying open' from the verb *patere*. In early use it was found in the phrase **letters patent**, an open document issued by a monarch to record a contract or confer a privilege. It also meant more generally 'open to view'. Use of the

partner party pass passage passenger

word to denote a licence to manufacture a commodity dates from the late 16th century.

paternal *see* PLEBEIAN

pathetic [L16th] 'Affecting the emotions' was the early sense of pathetic which came via late Latin from Greek *pathētikos* 'sensitive', based on *pathos* 'suffering' (M17th in English). **Apathy** [E17th] is from *apathēs* 'without feeling', and **empathy** (from *em-* 'in' and *pathos* 'feeling') was coined by physiologists in the early 20th century. *See also* SYMPATHY

patience [ME] Hospital patients have to have patience, and they sometimes suffer, so it is not surprising that the Latin word *pati* 'to suffer' is the root of both **patience** and **patient** [ME]. People have maintained that **patience is a virtue** since the 14th century, though a Latin equivalent is recorded much earlier. As a card game **patience** dates from the early 19th century—the earlier name, still used in the USA, is **solitaire** (*see* SOLE).

patina *see* PAN

patio *see* SPANISH WORD PANEL

patrician *see* PLEBEIAN

patriot, patriotic *see* POPE

patrol [M17th] The unpleasant side of military life is brought to the fore by patrol. It comes, via German, from French *patrouille*, from *patrouiller* 'paddle in mud'. This in turn was formed from *patte* 'paw' and dialect (*gad*)*rouille* 'dirty water'.

patron *see* PATTERN

patter [LME] This word for smooth-flowing continuous talk was first used in the sense 'recite (a prayer, charm, etc.) rapidly'. It comes from *paternoster*, literally 'Our Father', the Lord's prayer recited in Latin. The noun dates from the mid 18th century. *See also* PAT

pattern [ME] Originally pattern and **patron** were the same word. Patron comes, via French, from Latin *patronus* 'protector of clients, defender', a sense which explains J.K. Rowling's use of 'Patronus' for a spell that produces a protecting animal in the Harry Potter books. The word goes back to *pater* 'father' (*see further under* POPE). The word pattern developed from the idea of a patron giving an example to be copied. The swapping round of sounds (metathesis) of the vowel and the 'r' occurred in the 16th century, and by 1700 patron ceased to be used of things, and the two forms developed different senses.

patty *see* PASTE

paucity *see* FEW

pauper *see* POOR

pause [LME] Pause goes back to Greek *pausis*, from *pausein* 'to stop'. This is the same root as **repose** [LME], and **pose** (ME as a verb, but only E19th as a noun). The French word **poseur** was adopted in the late 19th century. *See also* PUZZLE

pavement *see* US WORD PANEL

pawn [LME] There are two separate words here. The pawn in chess came via Anglo-Norman French *poun*, from medieval Latin *pedo* 'foot soldier', from Latin *pes, ped-* 'foot' (source of **pedal** [E17th], **pedestal** [M16th], and **pedestrian** [M18th]). Figurative use 'a person used by others for their own purposes' is recorded from the late 16th century. In the sense 'to deposit an object as security for money lent', pawn entered English from French *pan* 'pledge, security' in the 15th century.

pay [ME] The original meaning of pay was 'to pacify', and it goes back to Latin *pax* 'peace' (*see* PEACE). The notion of 'payment' arose from the sense of 'pacifying' a creditor. A cartoon caption from the magazine *Punch* in 1846 was the source of **you pays your money and you takes your choice**, used to convey that there is little to choose between one alternative and another.

paternal pathetic patience patina patio

pea [M16th] You could not eat a pea until the mid 17th century. The earlier form was **pease**, which people began to think was a plural, so that if you had a handful of peas you must be able to have one pea (*compare* CHERRY). The original is recorded in Old English, and goes back to Greek *pison*; it survives in **pease pudding**, for boiled split peas mashed to a pulp. The **pea** of peacock has no connection—it derives from Latin *pavo* 'peacock', which appears as *pea* in Old English and was combined with cock 'male bird' in Middle English. Nor does a **pea jacket** have anything to do with peas. It is an early 18th-century half-hearted translation of Dutch *pijjackker* formed from *pij* 'coarse woollen cloth' (found in Middle English as *pee*) and *jekker* 'jacket'.

peace [ME] Peace is from Old French *pais*, from Latin *pax* 'peace'. The phrase **no peace for the wicked** comes from Isaiah 48:22 (There is no peace to the wicked, saith the Lord). In legal texts, the word **pacific** [M16th], from the same root, still retains its early meaning 'free from strife, peaceful'. In 1520 the Portuguese explorer Ferdinand Magellan passed through the stormy waters of the strait between what is now Tierra Del Fuego and mainland Chile. To his relief he emerged to calm seas, so called the ocean *Mar Pacifico* 'tranquil sea'. The treacherous sound he passed through is still the Strait of Magellan. **Pacify** [LME] and **pacifism** [E20th] go back to the same root, as does **appease** [ME], literally 'bring to a peaceful state'. *See also* PAY

peach [LME] Peach is from Old French *pesche*, from medieval Latin *persica*, a shortening of *persicum (malum)*, literally 'Persian apple'. Peaches are natives of China, but were introduced to Europe by way of the Middle East.

peacock *see* PEA

peak *see* PIKE

peal *see* APPEAL

pear [OE] A word adopted before the Anglo-Saxons arrived in England from the Latin *pirum*. The expression **go pear-shaped**, 'to go wrong', is from RAF slang. Although the first written examples are from the early 1980s, around the time of the Falklands War, it was probably in use several decades earlier. Some sources suggest that it may have arisen as a darkly humorous reference to the shape of a fighter plane after it has nose-dived and crashed into the ground. A more cheerful alternative theory is that it describes a novice pilot's less than successful attempts to produce a perfect circle when performing a loop in the air.

pearl [LME] Pearl is from Old French *perle* and may be based on Latin *perna* 'leg', extended to mean a leg-of-mutton-shaped water mussel (mentioned by Pliny). The Romans greatly prized fresh-water pearls, Britain's reputation as a good source of pearls being one of the motives behind their invasion. Matthew 7:6 has provided a common idiomatic expression: 'Neither cast ye your **pearls before swine**'. In Romance languages the usual word for pearl comes via Latin, from Greek *margeron*, possibly from some Eastern language. The word became *marguerite* in French, which was also used for a variety of daisy-like flowers, because they are pearly white. The word was adopted into English in the early 17th century. This is also the source of the name **Margaret**.

peasant *see* PAGAN

peck [LME] This is probably a dialect variant pick (*see* PIKE). In the 1920s researchers in animal behaviour observed that hens have a social hierarchy in which some within the flock are able to attack or threaten others without retaliation. This is the **pecking order**, soon recognized in other animal groups and also in human society. It is a translation of the original German term *Hackordnung*. The origin of **keep your pecker up**, 'stay cheerful', is unrelated to the slang use of pecker for the penis (E20th from the USA). It has been around since the 1850s, and is even used by Charles Dickens in a letter in 1857. It most probably comes from the comparison of a bird's beak to a person's nose, and is thus much the same idea as 'chin up'.

pea peace peach peacock peak peal pear

peculiar [LME] The earliest senses of peculiar in English include 'unlike others' and 'specific to a person', with the development 'strange, odd' not emerging until the early 17th century. Latin *peculium*, from which peculiar derives, meant 'private property'. It came from *pecu* 'cattle, farm animals' also the source of **pecuniary** [E16th], for 'wealth in farm animals' which developed into the sense 'money'.

pedagogue *see* PAGE

pedal *see* PAWN

pedant *see* PAGE

pedestal, pedestrian *see* PAWN

pedigree [LME] In medieval manuscripts a mark consisting of three curved lines was used to indicate a person's family descent or succession. People saw a resemblance between this mark and the claw or track of a crane, and called it 'a crane's foot'—*pé de grue* in the French spoken by the descendants of Norman settlers in England. The name, which became pedigree, then came to refer to a family tree, and from that to a person's or, from the early 17th century, animal's lineage or descent.

pediment *see* PYRAMID

peeler *see* BOB

peer *see* PAIR

peewit *see* CUCKOO

pelican [OE] The pelican has always been noted for its long bill and deep throat-pouch for scooping up fish. This distinctive feature probably gave the bird its name, which came from Greek *pelekan*, probably based on *pelekus* 'axe'. In Britain a **pelican crossing** is a road crossing with traffic lights operated by pedestrians. The name, first used in 1966, was taken from the initial letters of the formal title, *pe*destrian *li*ght *con*trolled crossing. Two other pedestrian crossings were given bird names by analogy

with the pelican, the **puffin** (from *pe*destrian *u*ser-*f*riendly *int*elligent), and **toucan crossing**. As bird names, puffin has a rather complicated history. It was used in Middle English for the Manx shearwater, probably from 'puff, puffed up', describing the shearwater's fat nestlings. As the two birds often nest together the name was then transferred to the bird we now call a puffin. Toucans, who first appeared in English in the mid 16th century, get their name from the language of the Amazonian Indians called the Tupi, and their name imitates their cry.

pellet [LME] Pellet is from Old French *pelote* 'metal ball', from a diminutive of Latin *pila* 'ball'. Latin *pila* is also the source of *PILL, originally balls of medicine, and **piles** for haemorrhoids (both LME). **Platoon** is a less obvious relative. It comes from French *peloton* 'platoon', literally 'small ball'. It captured the concept of a small body of foot soldiers acting as a closely organized unit.

pell-mell [LME] People like words that combine two almost identical forms, like **helter-skelter** [L16th], **mishmash** [LME], *NAMBY-PAMBY, and **wishy-washy** [L17th]— and **pell-mell**. Its second element represents a form of French *mesler* 'to mix' (related to *MEDLEY). The first part might be from *pelle* 'shovel', giving the sense 'mixed together with a shovel', but the simple love of rhyme may be the only explanation needed.

pelmet *see* PALM

pelt *see* PILLION

pelvis [E17th] This is a use of a Latin word meaning literally 'basin', describing the shape of the cavity.

pen [ME] The earliest pens for writing were made from a feather with its quill sharpened and split to form a nib which was dipped in ink. The origin of pen reflects this, going back to Latin *penna* 'feather'. The idea that **the pen is mightier than the sword** appeared in the works of the Latin author Cicero in the 2nd century BC. The origin of

peculiar pedagogue pedal pedant pedestal

Old English pen in the sense of an animal enclosure is not known. *See also* PANACHE, PIN

penal, penalty *see* PAIN

pencil [ME] Although it looks as if pencil should come from *PEN, the words are unrelated. A pencil once meant a fine paintbrush—Johnson's dictionary defines it as 'a small brush of hair which painters dip in their colours'. It comes from Old French *pincel*, from Latin *penicillum* 'paintbrush', from *penis* 'tail', from the tuft of hair at the end of some tails. The Latin *penis* was also used for the male organ, a use that passed into English in the late 17th century. *Penicillum* was also the source of the name of the drug **penicillin** [M20th] named from the brush-like shapes of the spore containers.

pendant [ME] This was originally a term for an architectural decoration projecting downwards. It comes from *penda(u)nt*, an Old French word meaning 'hanging', from Latin *pendere*. The word was used from late Middle English for a jewel attached to clothing but later it was applied to one attached to a necklace. Use of the word for a light fitting hanging from the ceiling dates from the mid 19th century. **Pending** [M17th] is an anglicization of French *pendant*. **Pendulum** [M17th] is taken directly from Latin, as is **pendulous** [E17th]. **Suspend** [ME] combined this root with *sub-* 'from below', and **compensation** [LME] is something that 'weighs against' something that has happened, **depend** [LME] is 'hang down', and **recompence** [LME] originally 'to weigh one thing against another'.

penguin [L16th] Penguin is a rare example of a word that is probably from Welsh, in this case from *pen gwyn* 'white head'. It is even rarer for a Welsh word to become internationally adopted for the name of a thing. Sailors and fishermen first gave the name penguin to the great auk of the seas around Newfoundland, which the penguin resembled closely, both birds being large, flightless waterfowl with black and white plumage adapted to life in freezing waters. British sailors may have mistaken penguins for great auks, or simply applied a term they knew to a previously unseen bird. Penguins have fared rather better than great auks: penguins are popular and much studied, whereas great auks were hunted to extinction, the last killed on an islet off Iceland in 1844.

penicillin *see* PEN

peninsular [M16th] A peninsula is a piece of land mostly surrounded by water or projecting out into the sea. It is almost an *ISLAND, a fact reflected in its name formed from Latin *paeninsula*, from *paene* 'almost' and *insula* 'island'.

penis *see* PEN

pennant [E17th] This word for a flag is a blend of *PENDANT and late Middle English **pennon**. The latter is a less common word for a 'flag', ultimately from Latin *penna* 'feather' (*see* PEN).

penne *see* ITALIAN WORD PANEL

pennon *see* PENNANT

penny [OE] The English word penny is related to Dutch *penning* and German *Pfennig*, but their ultimate origin is unknown. The penny, originally of pure silver, then later of copper (hence the colloquial term **coppers**), was first used in England in the 8th century. The origins of the phrase **the penny has dropped** lie in gambling arcades. The idea is of a coin-operated slot machine whirring into action when you insert a small coin. The reference to penny gives a clue as to the age of the expression, as it goes back to the 1950s. Inflation has also caught up with proverbial sayings such as **in for a penny, in for a pound**, used to express someone's intention to see an undertaking through—it dates from the late 17th century, when a penny would have been a significant investment to many. You would need at least 20p now to **spend a penny** in a British public lavatory. This phrase comes from a time when coin-operated locks were commonly found on the doors of public toilets, operated by the

penal penalty pencil pendant penguin

old, heavy pre-decimal pennies. These pennies went out of use on 5 February 1971. *See also* POUND.

pension [LME] In early use a pension was a payment, a tax, or a regular sum paid to keep someone's loyalty. The word is derived from Latin *pendere* 'to pay', the source also of **stipend** [LME]. Use of the word to describe an annuity paid to a retired employee has developed since the early 16th century.

pensive [LME] Pensive is from Old French *pensif* from *penser* 'to think': this is via Latin *pensare* 'to ponder' from *pendere* 'to weigh'. The notion is of 'weighing up' the merits of various options. **Ponder** [ME] 'to consider, weigh things up' and **ponderous** [LME] 'weighty' come from the same root. The flower name **pansy** also comes from the same source, being the English spelling of the French *pensée* 'thought'. This is because of the face-like markings on the flowers, which in old varieties looked as if they were hanging down pensively. *See* PENTHOUSE

pentagon [L16th] The Greek expertise in geometry means that many geometrical forms have Greek names. The five-sided pentagon is formed from *penta* 'five' and *gonia* 'angle', just as **polygon** [L16th] is formed from the word for 'many' plus -*gon* and **diagonal** [M16th] with *dia* 'through'. *Penta* is also found in words such as the mystic figures of the **pentangle** [LME], **pentacle** [L16th], and **pentagram** [M19th], and in the **pentathlon** [E17th], once the original five events of leaping, running, discus-throwing, spear-throwing, and wrestling of ancient Greek and Roman games. Fifty is found in **Pentecost** [OE] which came via ecclesiastical Latin from Greek *pentēkostē (hēmera)* 'fiftieth (day)'. The Jewish festival of Shavuoth is held on the fiftieth day after the second day of Passover. The Christian festival is held on the seventh Sunday after Easter commemorating the descent of the Holy Spirit on the disciples as recorded in Acts 2.

penthouse [ME] A penthouse now suggests a luxurious apartment with extensive views, but originally was much more humble—a shed, outhouse, or lean-to attached to the outside of a building, and called a **pentis**. The word came from a shortening of French *apentis*, which is from Latin *pendere* 'to hang', the source of **appendage**, *APPENDIX, and *PENDANT. In the 16th century people began to forget its origins and to associate it with French *pente* 'slope' and *HOUSE. The modern use for a flat or apartment on the top floor of a tall building began during the 1890s in the USA. At first these penthouses were not necessarily exclusive—the first reference to one talks of it as accommodation for a janitor and his family.

penultimate *see* ULTIMATE

people [ME] People is from Anglo-Norman French *poeple*, from Latin *populus* 'populace', also the source of words such as **population** [M16th]; **populace** [L16th]; and **popular** [LME] originally 'prevalent among the general public': with 'liked and admired' early 17th century. The phrase **of all people** expressing disbelief about somebody dates from the 1700s; the capitalized form in the phrase *the People* referring in US legal contexts to the State prosecution **the People versus**... dates from the early 19th century. *See also* PUBLIC

pepper [OE] The Anglo-Saxons adopted the word for this highly prized spice before they invaded England, for it is found in other West Germanic languages. The word came via Latin from Greek *peperi*, from Sanskrit *pippalī* 'berry, peppercorn'. The phrase **peppercorn rent** is from the once-common practice of stipulating the payment of a peppercorn as a nominal rent.

perceive *see* CAPABLE

perch [ME] The perch in a bird's cage is from Middle English *perch* meaning 'pole, stick' (from Old French *perche*, ultimately from Latin) which was also formerly used as a measure of length. The fish gets its name via Latin from Greek *perke* which may come from a word meaning 'speckled'.

percolate, percolator *see* PERK

pension   pensive   pentagon   penthouse

peregrinate, peregrine *see* PILGRIM

peremptory [LME] This was first used as a legal term meaning 'admitting no refusal' when used of an order or decree; it came via Anglo-Norman French from Latin *peremptorius* 'deadly, decisive', from *perimere* 'destroy, cut off'. The base elements are Latin *per-* 'completely' and *emere* 'take'.

perennial *see* ANNUAL

perfect [ME] The basic sense of perfect is 'completely made'. It is from Old French *perfet*, from Latin *perfectus*, formed from *per-* 'through, completely' and *facere* 'to do'. The early sense of the related **perfection** [ME] was 'completeness'.

perfidy [L16th] This literary word for 'deceitfulness' came via French from Latin *perfidia* 'treachery', from *perfidus* 'treacherous', based on *per-* 'to ill effect' and *fides* 'faith'. The adjective **perfidious** dates from the same period. The expression **perfidious** *ALBION is a translation of the French *perfide Albion*; the phrase appears to have been first used by the Marquis de Ximenès (1726–1817) with reference to the British joining the allies who were already fighting France in 1793, but was popularized during a recruitment campaign under Napoleon I in 1813. It was adopted into German (in its French form) during the early 19th century and had become naturalized by the time of Bismarck. It was used in German anti-British propaganda during the First World War (1914–18), and during the Second World War (1939–45) to undermine French trust in Britain as an ally.

perfume *see* FUMIGATE

pergola [M17th] This is an English use of an Italian word which came from Latin *pergula* 'projecting roof, vine arbour', from *pergere* 'to come or go forward'.

perhaps [LME] This is an unusual hybrid of French and Old Norse words. The first half is French *per* 'by' from Latin *per* 'by means of'. The second Middle English *hap* 'chance, fortune', which was adopted from

Old Norse (*see* HAPPY). The final 's' only appears about 1520.

peril [ME] The fact that trying something new can be dangerous is reflected in the history of peril. It comes via Old French, from Latin *peric(u)lum* 'danger, experiment', formed from *experiri* 'to try'.

perimeter [LME] Perimeter is simply a fancy way of saying 'the distance round' for it comes via Latin from Greek *perimetros*, based on *peri-* 'around' and *metron* 'measure'.

period [LME] When first used, period referred to the time during which something such as a disease, ran its course. It goes back to Greek *periodos* 'orbit, recurrence, course', from *peri-* 'around' and *hodos* 'way'. The sense 'portion of time' dates from the early 17th century, as does use of the word to mean 'full stop', now part of US English. *Peri* is also found in **peripatetic** [LME] now meaning 'wandering, travelling' but from Greek *peripatetikos* 'walking up and down' and originally applied to followers of the ideas of Aristotle (384–322 BC), who is said to have walked about while teaching; and **periphery** [L16th] originally the boundary of something. *Hodos*, the second part of period is also found in **episode** [L17th], literally 'coming in beside' from *epi* 'addition' and *eisodos* 'entry' (formed from *eis* 'into' and *hodos*); and **exodus**, 'departure' formed in the same way using *ex-* 'out of'. *See also* METHOD

perish [ME] To perish is literally to 'pass away' or 'go away'—that is the meaning of the source, Latin *perire*, formed from *per-* 'through, completely' and *ire* 'go'. A mischievous or awkward person, especially a child, has been a **perisher** since the end of the 19th century. For many the word is particularly associated with the comic strip *The Perishers*, about a group of children and their sheepdog Boot, which ran in the *Daily Mirror* newspaper from 1958 to 2006. Shakespeare's plays have not always been popular. From the later 17th century people preferred them in updated form, often with wholly inappropriate happy endings. In

1700 the English comic actor, dramatist, and theatre manager Colley Cibber brought out a rewritten version of Shakespeare's *Richard III*. Its only claim to fame is that it gave English **perish the thought**.

perjury *see* JURY

perk [LME] The origin of perk in to **perk up**, 'to become more lively, cheerful, or interesting', is not wholly clear, though it may be related to *PERCH, as 'perk' is an early spelling of 'perch'. A perk meaning a benefit to which you are entitled because of your job is a shortening of **perquisite** [LME], from medieval Latin *perquisitum* 'acquisition'. It is found from the early 19th century. People began to **perk** coffee in a **percolator** [M19th] around 1920. This is from **percolate** [E17th], which is based on Latin *percolare* 'to strain through'.

permanent [LME] Permanent is from Latin *permanent-* 'remaining to the end' from *per-* 'through' and *manere* 'remain'. The abbreviation **perm** in hairdressing dates from the 1920s, a shortening of 'permanent wave', a process that had been introduced only a few years earlier. Before that people had to curl their hair with hot tongs, or use the late 19th century **marcel wave**, named after François Marcel Grateau (1852–1936), the French hairdresser who invented the method.

permit [LME] This word was originally used in the sense 'commit, hand over': it is from Latin *permittere*, from *per-* 'through' and *mittere* 'send, let go'. 'Written order giving permission' is recorded from the early 18th century. **Permission** and **permissive** are also late Middle English. **Permissive society** dates from the 1970s. Latin *mittere* is the base of a number of other Latin words found in English such as **admit** with *ad* 'to'; **submit** from *sub* 'under'; **transmit** from *trans* 'across'. All are Late Middle English.

permutation *see* COMMUTE

perpendicular [LME] Those who remember school geometry lessons involving instructions to 'drop a perpendicular' may not be surprised to find that the source of this word is Latin *perpendiculum* 'plumb line', formed from *per-* 'through' and *pendere* 'to hang'. The first recorded use of the loosened sense 'very steep' is found in Shakespeare's 'That sprightly Son of Scots, Douglas, that runs a-horseback up a hill perpendicular' (*Henry IV, Part I*, Act 2 scene 5).

perquisite *see* PERK

persecute *see* SECOND

Caravanning in tiaras

What we now know as Iran was once **Persia**, *a country whose ancient empire swallowed up much of the Middle East. It had a great language to match, which has given English many familiar terms.*

TO Persians a **kiosk** was not a small hut or cubicle where you can buy items such as newspapers, but a light open pavilion or summer house. The word came via French and Turkish from Persian *kus*. The original **caravan** was quite different from the white holiday trailers that fill our roads in summer. It was a group of traders or pilgrims travelling together across a desert in Asia or North Africa, from Persian *kārwān*.

Because these people would travel heavily laden with baggage or merchandise, a caravan became a covered wagon or carriage in the late 17th century, then the travelling home of Gypsies or circus people, and in the 1930s a vehicle towed by a car and used for holidays.

Persia is the source of many words for fabrics. **Seersucker**, a light material with a crimped or puckered surface, often striped, derives from Persian *shīr o shakkar*, meaning 'milk and honey' and also 'striped cotton garment'. The first English record dates from the early 18th century. Another Persian fabric is **taffeta**, which in medieval times was a name for a kind of silk, from *tāftan* 'to shine'. A **shawl** was originally worn in the Indian subcontinent as a scarf, turban, or belt—the word is from Persian *sāl*, probably based on the name of Shaliat, a town in India. **Khaki** takes its name from its colour, coming via Urdu (a language of northern India) *kākī* 'dust-coloured' from Persian *kāk* 'dust'. The dull brownish-yellow material was first used for uniforms by British troops in India during the 1840s.

The practice among women in certain Muslim and Hindu societies of keeping out of the sight of men or strangers is known as **purdah**, from Persian *parda*, meaning 'a veil or curtain'. Much more glamorous is a **tiara**, which was originally an ancient Persian headdress, in particular a kind of turban worn by kings. The word comes ultimately from Greek. In English the use of it to refer to a jewelled coronet or headband dates from the early 18th century. *See also* ARSENIC, CHEESE, DIVAN, HAZARD, TURBAN

persist [M16th] Etymologically, someone who persists in doing something cannot be moved from their course. It comes from Latin *persistere*, formed from *per-* 'through, steadfastly' and *sistere* 'to stand'.

person [ME] When first used in English person meant 'a role or character assumed in real life or in a play' as well as 'an individual human being'. The first sense has largely been taken over by **persona**, which came directly in the mid 18th century from the source of person, Latin *persona* 'actor's mask, character in a play', and also 'human being'. The Latin term was also used by Christian writers as a term for the rector of a parish, what we would now call a **parson** [ME]. From the same source come **impersonate** [E17th] originally meaning 'personify', and **personnel** [E19th] from French and which still keeps the original stress on the final syllable normal in that language.

perspective [LME] In early use this word was a name for the science of optics: it comes from medieval Latin *perspectiva* (*ars*) 'science of optics', from *perspicere* 'look at closely'. The notion of perspective in drawings dates from the end of the 16th century. The same verb lies behind **perspicacious** [E17th] which comes from the Latin for 'seeing clearly'.

perspire *see* SPIRIT

perturb *see* TROUBLE

pervert *see* VERSE

pervious [E17th] Pervious is based on Latin *pervius* 'having a passage through' formed from combining *per-* and *via* 'way'.

pesky *see* PEST

pessimism *see* OPTIMISM

pest [LME] At first this was a term for the bubonic plague. It comes via French *peste* from Latin *pestis* 'plague'. **Pestilence** [ME] is from the same root. Pest in the sense of 'a destructive plant or animal' is not found until the mid 18th century, when fear of the Black Death has receded. The informal word **pesky** [L18th] may be related to pest perhaps via *pesty*. **Pester** [M16th], however, is not directly connected. The source is French *empestrer* 'encumber', but the English form is influenced by pest. Early use included the meanings 'overcrowd (a place)' and 'impede (a person)'. The current sense 'annoy someone with frequent requests' is an extension of an earlier use, 'infest', referring to vermin. *See also* PLAGUE

pestle *see* PISTON

pet [E16th] The word pet was first used for 'a hand-reared lamb' in Scotland and northern England, where it also meant 'a spoilt or favourite child'. It came from Scottish Gaelic *peata* 'tame animal'. By the early 18th century it had spread south to apply to any domestic or tamed animal kept for pleasure or companionship. The verb, meaning 'to stroke or pat affectionately', is found in the early 17th century, although the sense 'to engage in sexually stimulating caressing', as in **heavy petting**, is no older than the 1920s and first found in the USA.

petal [E18th] The word petal comes via modern Latin from Greek *petalon* 'leaf', formed from *petalos* 'outspread'. Since a petal is technically a modified leaf the origin is not inappropriate.

petition *see* COMPETE

petrify [LME] The original sense of petrify was 'to convert into stone', from the Latin and Greek root *petra* 'rock'. The sense 'to terrify, astonish' dates from the mid 17th century. **Petroleum** is from the same source—it is found in rocks. The second part is Latin *oleum* '*OLIVE oil' (*see* OIL).

petticoat [LME] This comes from the phrase **petty coat** which means literally 'small coat'. It was originally a masculine garment, a tight-fitting undercoat worn underneath a doublet or a padded jacket to go under armour. It seems to have been used for a similar under-garment for women. In the late 15th century it started to be fashionable for women to wear full skirts open down the front in an inverted V-shape, the gap filled with a contrasting underskirt, and the term petticoat was transferred to this under-garment.

petty [LME] This is a phonetic spelling of the pronunciation of French *petit* 'small'. The early sense recorded was 'small in size'. The sense 'of small importance' dates from the late 16th century. As well as *PETTICOAT, the word gives us **pettifogger** [M16th] for an inferior legal practitioner, from *petty* and obsolete *fogger* 'underhand dealer'. This is probably from *Fugger*, the name of a family of merchants in Augsburg, Bavaria, in the 15th and 16th centuries.

petulant *see* COMPETE

phantom *see* FANTASTIC

pharaoh [ME] Pharaoh goes back to Egyptian *pr-'o* 'great house'. Early English spellings included *Pharaon* and *Pharaoe*; the final *h* in later English spellings was influenced by the Hebrew spelling in the Bible.

pharmacy [LME] Pharmacy was originally the administration of drugs, and comes from Old French *farmacie*, via medieval Latin from Greek *pharmakeia* 'practice of the druggist', based on *pharmakon* 'drug'. **Pharmaceutical** came into English in the mid 17th century. In modern times new developments have led to word coinages based on this word such as the 1990s **pharming**, punning on 'farming', for genetically engineered plants and animals raised to produce pharmaceuticals.

phase [L17th] A phase first described an aspect of the moon, but had developed the modern sense of a distinct period by 1701. It is from French *phase*, based on Greek *phasis* 'appearance'.

pheasant [ME] An old name for the river Rion in Georgia in southeast Europe was the Phasis. The Greeks believed that the pheasant originated in that region before it spread westwards, and called it the 'bird of Phasis'. The region the Phasis flowed through was called Colchis by the Greeks, which was also said to be the land of the Golden Fleece. The modern Latin name for the common pheasant is still *Phasianus colchicus* 'the pheasant of Colchis'. The variety of autumn-flowering crocus called a **colchicum**, gets its name from the same place. It was said by ancient authors to be particularly common there, and the poison that comes from it is said to have been used by the legendary Colchican witch Medea, who helped Jason win the Golden Fleece.

phenomenon *see* FANTASTIC

phial [ME] The word phial is from Old French *fiole*, via Latin from Greek *phialē* which described a broad flat container, rather than our small, cylindrical container. **Vial** is simply a re-spelling of the same word.

philately [M19th] This is one of the few words whose origin can be pinned down precisely. A Monsieur Herpin, a keen stamp collector, proposed the French word *philatélie* in the 15 November 1864, issue of *Le Collectionneur de Timbres-poste* ('*The Stamp Collector*'). He formed it from Greek *philo-* 'loving' and *ateleia* 'exemption from payment', as a stamp shows that the price for delivery has already been paid. British stamp collectors quickly anglicized the French word to philately, which is recorded in an enthusiasts' magazine in December 1865. M. Herpin's use of *philo-* followed a well-established tradition in word formation, found in words such as **philanthropy** [E17th] from *philo-* and *anthropos* 'human being' (also found in **anthropology** [L16th], the study of mankind); **philosopher** [ME] combined with *sophos* 'wisdom' (*see further at* SOPHISTICATED), and **anglophile** [M19th].

philistine [LME] There is no reason to believe that the Philistines were philistines. In biblical times, during the 11th and 12th centuries BC, they were a people who occupied the southern coast of Palestine and who frequently came into conflict with the Israelites. The first book of Samuel tells the story of David and Goliath, a Philistine giant, and Judges relates Delilah's betrayal of Samson to the Philistines. In the late 17th century students in the university town of Jena in Germany, bearing these passages in mind, started using *Philister* (German for 'Philistine') as an insulting name for a townsperson or non-student. By the 1820s English travellers had made this German university slang familiar, and people began to use philistine for 'an uncultured person'. The word itself goes back to the same root as **Palestine**.

philosopher *see* PHILATELY

phlegmatic [ME] According to the medieval doctrine of the four humours (*see* HUMOUR) an excess of phlegm made people stolidly calm. The root of **phlegm** [ME], and so of phlegmatic, is Greek *phlegma* 'inflammation', formed from *phlegein* 'to burn'. Phlegmatic had acquired the sense 'calm and self-possessed' by the late 16th century.

phobia [L18th] This is an independent usage of the suffix -*phobia* (via Latin from Greek) meaning 'fear'. In modern times psychologists have ransacked the Greek and Latin languages to find ever more words to combine with phobia as new fears have been uncovered. These include **brontophobia** [E20th], 'fear of thunder' formed from Greek *bronte* 'thunder' also found in **brontosaurus** [L19th] literally 'thunder lizard'; **heliophobia** [L19th] formed from *helios* Greek for 'sun', also found in **heliotrope** [OE] for a plant that turns its flowers to follow the sun; and among the most recent **nomophobia**, a joking coinage of 2008 for those who feel anxious if they have no mobile phone.

phonetic [E19th] Phonetic is from modern Latin *phoneticus*, from Greek *phōnētikos*, from *phōnein* 'speak'. Other words from the same source are **gramophone** [L19th], and its reversed form **phonograph** [M19th] originally a phonetic symbol, which explains the use of the combining form—*gram* used for 'something written'; and **saxophone** [M19th] an instrument for making pleasant sounds invented by the Belgian Adolphe Sax in 1840.

phoney [L19th] The fraudulent practice of the **fawney-rig** is probably the source of phoney 'not genuine, fraudulent', which was first recorded in the USA at the end of the 19th century. In 1823 Pierce Egan, a chronicler of popular pursuits and low life in England, described how the fawney-rig worked. 'A fellow drops a brass ring, double gilt, which he picks up before the party meant to be cheated, and to whom he disposes of it for less than its supposed, and ten times more than its real, value.' The word **fawney** came from Irish *fáinne* 'a ring'. The **phoney war** was the period of comparative inaction at the beginning of the Second World War, between the German invasion of Poland in September 1939 and that of Norway in April 1940. The expression is now used of any coming confrontation, as in 'the debates on tax in the pre-election phoney war' (*Earth Matters*, 1997).

phonograph *see* PHONETIC

photograph [M19th] The original of this was French *photographie* 'photography', first recorded in 1834. The word was apparently introduced to English (along with **photographic** and **photograph**) by Sir John Herschel in a paper presented to the Royal Society on 14 March 1839. Both the French and English words were formed from Greek *photo-* 'light' (found in numerous other words) and *graphē* 'writing, drawing', as in **autograph** [M17th], something written in one's own hand, from Greek *auto* 'by oneself' and **seismograph** [M19th] combined with Greek *seismos* 'earthquake'. As early as 1860 Queen Victoria was using the short form **photo**, writing in a letter about someone 'waiting to know...about the photo'.

physician [ME] The Old English word for a medical doctor was **leech** (despite popular belief, nothing to do with the worm, but a word meaning 'a healer'). Physician arrived in the early Middle Ages, and goes back to Greek *phusis* 'nature', the root also of **physical** [LME], **physics** [LME], and numerous other English words. A **doctor** [ME] was originally not a physician but any learned person able to give an authoritative opinion, especially one of the early Christian theologians. The word started referring specifically to a medical expert at the start of the 15th century. It comes from *doctor*, the Latin for 'teacher', also found in words such as **docile** [LME] 'willing to learn'; **document** [LME] 'official paper, proof'; and **doctrine** [LME], originally the action of teaching.

piano [M18th] Before the mid 18th century the usual musical instrument in comfortable European households was the harpsichord. Its strings are plucked by quills, and the player has little or no control over the length of notes or volume. From the 18th century the **pianoforte** or **fortepiano** was developed, with strings struck by hammers, dampers to stop vibration when the keys are released and pedals to regulate the length and volume of notes. The names came from Italian *piano* 'soft' and *forte* 'loud', referring to the innovation of volume control. Soon the shortened form piano appeared, and nowadays pianoforte is a rather formal term for a piano, whereas fortepiano tends to refer to early forms of the instrument. The **harpsichord** [E17th] got its name from Late Latin *harpa* 'harp' and *chorda* 'string'.

piazza *see* PLACE

pick *see* PIKE

picnic [M18th] A picnic was originally a fashionable social event at which each guest contributed food, something like the American pot luck supper, but it fairly rapidly became a term for an outdoor meal. Both senses are found in the French original *pique-nique*. This was probably formed from *piquer* 'to pick' and *nique* 'nothing whatsoever'.

picture [LME] The word picture goes back to a form of Latin *pingere* 'to paint', from which *PAINT and **pigment** [OE] also derive. Doan's Backache Kidney Pills, claiming to cure everything from rheumatism to diabetes, were promoted with the advertising slogan **every picture tells a story**. The first known advertisement using it appeared in the *Daily Mail* of 26 February 1904. The novelist Charlotte Brontë had anticipated the advertising copy, though: in 1847 she wrote in *Jane Eyre*, 'The letter-press…I cared little for…Each picture told a story.' A caption in the magazine *Printer's Ink* for 8 December 1927, read: 'Chinese proverb. One picture is worth ten thousand words.' There is no evidence at all that it is Chinese, but **a picture is worth a thousand words** has certainly gone on to be a modern English proverb. **Depict** [LME] is from the verb *depingere* 'portray', from *de-* 'completely' and *pingere*.

picturesque *see* PAINT

pidgin [E19th] A pidgin is nothing to do with a *PIGEON, but is a simplified form of a language used for communication between people not sharing a language. It originally represented a Chinese pronunciation of the English word *BUSINESS, and with the meanings 'business, occupation, or affair' became part of the simple language used between European and Chinese traders from the 1820s. By the 1850s people were also using pidgin to describe the language itself, especially in the fuller form **pidgin English**.

pie [ME] The pie that is a dish with a pastry crust is the same as the pie in names of birds such as the magpie, which until the late 16th century was simply called a pie (the mag part comes from the name Margaret. It seems to have been quite common to give birds' names, as in the *ROBIN). The various ingredients in a pie may have suggested the objects randomly collected by the 'thieving magpie'. The word itself comes from Latin *pica* 'magpie'.

Originally **pied** [LME] meant 'black and white like a magpie' and referred to the robes of some friars. Now it chiefly refers to birds, such as the pied wagtail. Mammals such as horses are described as **piebald** [L16th], which also means 'black and white': the second part is *BALD in the old sense 'streaked with white'. The expression **pie in the sky**, 'something pleasant to contemplate but very unlikely to be realized', was originally American and comes from a song written in 1911 by Joe Hill, one of the leaders of an organization called the Industrial Workers of the World (also known as the Wobblies). Along with their union card, each member would receive a songbook containing parodies of popular songs and hymns of the day, with the motto 'To Fan the Flames of Discontent' on the cover. The song from which this phrase comes is called 'The Preacher and the Slave'. It parodies a Salvation Army hymn, 'In the Sweet Bye and Bye', which promised those suffering on earth a better life in heaven. In response to the slave asking the preacher for some food, the chorus of the parody goes: 'Work and pray, live on hay, / You'll get pie in the sky when you die.'

piecemeal *see* MEAL

piety *see* PITY

piffle *see* POPPYCOCK

pig [OE] The word pig appears in Old English only once, the usual word being **swine**. In the Middle Ages pig at first meant specifically 'a young pig', as it still does in North America. Observations such as **pigs might fly** had a 17th-century parallel in **pigs fly with their tails forward**. An early user of the modern form was Lewis Carroll in 1865 in *Alice's Adventures in Wonderland*: ' "I've a right to think," said Alice sharply… "Just about as much right," said the Duchess, "as pigs have to fly." ' In **a pig in a poke**, **poke** [ME] means 'a small sack or bag', now found mainly in Scottish English. The British phrase to **make a pig's ear out of**, 'to handle ineptly', probably derives from the proverb **you can't make a silk purse out of a sow's ear**, recorded from the 16th century. In the

picture picturesque pidgin pie piecemeal

children's game **pig** (or **piggy**) **in the middle**, first recorded in the *Folk-Lore Journal* of 1887, two people throw a ball to each other while a third tries to intercept it. This is behind the use of **pig in the middle** for a person who is in an awkward situation between two others. **Piggyback** has been around since the mid 16th century, but the origin of the expression has been lost. Early forms tend to be something like 'pick-a-pack' which seems to have been changed by folk etymology to the form we now have. *See also* HOG

pigeon [LME] The name of the pigeon comes from French *pijon*, a word for a young bird, especially a young dove. It is an alteration of Latin *pipio*, which imitates the piping or cheeping of a nestling. The phrase to **be someone's pigeon**, 'to be someone's concern or responsibility', has nothing to do with homing pigeons going astray, or indeed anything involving the bird: pigeon here is a respelling of *PIDGIN and thus means 'business'. The pigeon's distinctive walk gave us **pigeon-toed**, meaning 'having the toes or feet turned inwards', and **pigeon-chested** or **pigeon-breasted**, 'having a protruding chest', from the end of the 18th century.

piggyback *see* PIG

pigment *see* PICTURE

pike [OE] The earliest recorded meaning of pike is for a pickaxe, **pick** simply being a variant form of pike. The freshwater fish the pike gets its name from the resemblance of its long pointed jaw to the old infantry weapon called a pike, which has a pointed steel or iron head on a long shaft. While basically the same word as Old English pike, this came into English during the 16th century from French *piquer* 'to pierce'. In dialect piked 'pointed' became picked and then peaked, and this is probably the origin of the word **peak** [LME] for the pointed top of something such as a mountain. The Australian and New Zealand expressions to **pike out**, 'to withdraw or go back on a plan or agreement', and to **pike on**, 'to let someone down', go back to a 15th- and 16th-

century use to **pike yourself** 'to provide yourself with a pilgrim's pike or staff', and so 'to depart, leave'. *See also* PLAIN

pile [OE] Three different Latin words lie behind three different types of pile. Pile meaning 'heap' comes via Old French, from Latin *pila* '*PILLAR, pier'. The association with money in **make one's pile** is from the phrase 'pile of wealth' (Shakespeare *Henry VIII*: What piles of wealth hath he accumulated To his own portion?). Pile meaning a 'heavy post' driven into the ground to support a superstructure was *pīl* 'dart, arrow', and 'pointed stake' in Old English. It was adopted early into Germanic languages from Latin *pilum* '(heavy) javelin'. The pile of a carpet was first recorded in the sense 'downy feather'. It comes from Latin *pilus* 'hair', found also in **depilatory** [E17th]. The current sense of pile dates from the mid 16th century.

piles *see* PELLET

pilgrim [ME] This is one of the earliest words that came into English from French, just after the Norman Conquest in 1066. It goes back to Latin *peregrinus*, 'foreign, alien', the source of **peregrinate** 'to wander from place to place', and of **peregrine**. The peregrine falcon was called the 'pilgrim falcon' because falconers caught individuals fully grown on migration rather than taking them from the nest. The Pilgrim Fathers were the English Puritans who sailed across the Atlantic in the *Mayflower* and founded the colony of Plymouth, Massachusetts, in 1620.

pill [LME] In the past physicians would cover bitter pills thinly with gold to make them easier to swallow. This gave rise to the early 17th-century phrase **gild the pill**, 'to make an unpleasant or painful necessity more palatable'. As the practice of sugar-coating superseded gilding pills, the more familiar version **sugar the pill** took over from the end of the 18th century. Pill itself goes back to Latin *pilula* 'little ball' from *pila* 'ball'. **The Pill** as a name for a contraceptive dates from the 1950s. *See also* PELLET

pigeon piggyback pigment pike pile piles

pillage *see* CATERPILLAR

pillar [ME] The Latin word *pila* 'pillar, pier' is the source of pillar and also *PILE. People were shunted from post to pillar, 'from one place to another', back in the early 15th century, but for some reason the version **from pillar to post** came into use in the middle of the following century and soon became the favoured choice. Its origins lie in the sport of real tennis, played in an enclosed court (a bit like the one used for squash, only much larger) with sectioned walls and buttresses off which the ball can rebound. These are the 'posts' and 'pillars' of the expression. The game developed from one played by 11th-century monks in the cloisters of monasteries.

pillion [LME] The first people to ride pillion on horses were not necessarily sharing their mount. In the 15th century a pillion was a light saddle, especially one used by women. Pillion is one of the earliest words to have entered English from Gaelic, coming from Scottish Gaelic *pillean* and Irish *pillín* 'small cushion', the root of which is Latin *pellis* 'skin', the source also of **pelt** [ME]. The sense 'seat behind a motorcyclist' dates from the late 19th century

pillory [ME] This is from Old French *pilori*, probably from Provençal *espilori*, associated by some with a Catalan word meaning 'peephole', of uncertain origin. A pillory was made up of two boards brought together leaving holes for the head and hands; in Great Britain this punishment was abolished except for the crime of perjury in 1815 and totally in 1837. Its use continued in the States until 1905.

pilot [LME] The aerial pilot appears earlier than expected, with the person flying a balloon being called a pilot in the 1830s. The ultimate root is Greek *pēdon* 'oar, rudder'. To **drop the pilot** is to abandon a trustworthy adviser. 'Dropping the pilot' was the caption of a famous cartoon by John Tenniel, published in Punch on 20 March 1890. It depicted Kaiser Wilhelm II's dismissal of Otto von Bismarck as German Chancellor, who had guided the country for many years.

pin [OE] Pin is one of the words adopted from Latin by the Anglo-Saxons before they invaded Britain. Its source is Latin *pinna* 'feather', which could also mean 'point, tip, edge', and from that developed the sense 'peg', the earliest sense of the word in English and still found in mechanics. The sense of pin 'thin metal fastener' had developed by 1250. Use of the word to mean 'skittle' (as in **ninepins**) dates from the late 16th century. A pinafore [L18th] was originally an apron with a bib pinned *afore* or on the front of a dress. The pin in **pin money** was the decorative kind that women used to fasten their hair or clothing. The phrase, dating from the end of the 17th century, first referred to an allowance made to a woman by her husband for personal expenses such as clothing. *See also* PANACHE, PEN

pinch [ME] Pinch is from a variant of Old French *pincier* 'to pinch', which is the source of **pincers** [ME]. Use of the word to mean 'hardship' dates from the early 17th century (Shakespeare *King Lear*: 'Necessity's sharp pinch'); this sense found in the phrase **feel the pinch**. The transferred slang sense 'steal' dates from the mid 17th century.

pineapple [LME] The Latin *pinus* 'pine tree' had given the word for a **pine** tree to Old English, and originally a pine apple was the fruit of the pine tree, what we would now call a pine-cone. When the pineapple fruit was introduced in the early 17th century the overall shape and the segmented skin was felt to resemble a pine-cone and the name was transferred to it. *See also* GRENADE, PAIN

ping [M19th] This word imitates the noise. The game **ping-pong** got its name in the early 20th century from the sound of a bat striking a ball.

pinion *see* PANACHE

pink [M16th] A pink (Dianthus) is a plant with sweet-smelling flowers which are usually various shades of pink, purple, or white. The use of pink for the colour beloved by little girls actually comes from the flower, rather than the other way round. Similarly, several other languages use the *ROSE as their source for the colour, and since the early 20th century **fuchsia** (named after the 16th-century German botanist Leonhart Fuchs) has been used for a distinctive shade of deep pink. Shakespeare uses the pink flower to signify the supreme example of something in *Romeo and Juliet*: 'I am the very pink of courtesy.' Here he was probably making a pun on the expression **the flower of**, meaning 'the finest part or example'. This Shakespearean phrase led to the development of the expression **in the pink of condition**, which by the early 18th century was shortened to simply **in the pink** 'in very good health and spirits'. The plant name appeared in the mid 16th century, but its origin is not known for certain. It may be short for **pink eye** 'small or half-shut eye', which would make the name like its French equivalent *oeillet*, which means 'little eye'. Pink in the sense of the sort of sound an engine makes when cooling dates only from the early 20th century and imitates the sound.

pinnacle see PANACH

pious see PITY

pip [L18th] The name for the small hard seed in a fruit is a shortening of **pippin**, an apple grown from seed. English adopted the word from French, but its ultimate origin is unknown. The British politician Sir Eric Geddes was the first to use the expression **squeeze until the pips squeak**, 'to extract the maximum amount of money from', in a 1918 speech about the compensation to be paid by Germany after the First World War: 'The Germans . . . are going to pay every penny; they are going to be squeezed as a lemon is squeezed . . . until the pips squeak.' Another **pip** is an unpleasant disease of chickens and other birds which is documented as far back as medieval times. From the late 15th century various human diseases and ailments also came to be called **the pip**, though the precise symptoms are rarely specified: today's equivalent would probably be **the dreaded lurgy** (*see* LURGY). Whatever the nature of the disease, the sufferer would probably be in a foul mood,

hence **the pip** became 'bad temper' and to **give someone the pip** was to irritate or depress them. The name came from medieval Dutch *pippe*, which was probably based on Latin *pituita* 'slime, phlegm', found also in **pituitary gland** [E17th].

pipe [OE] The Old English word pipe goes back to Latin *pipare* 'to chirp, squeak'. It first referred to a simple tube-shaped wind instrument, from which came the meanings 'a tube used to convey water or other fluid' [OE] and, when tobacco was first brought to Europe in the mid 16th century, 'a device for smoking tobacco'. People have been told to **put that in your pipe and smoke it**, or accept what has been done, since the 1820s, and Charles Dickens used the phrase in *The Pickwick Papers* (1837). In **piping hot**, 'very hot', piping refers to the hissing and sizzling of food just taken from the oven or off a fire. This phenomenon has been remarked on down the centuries, with the earliest recorded example being in *The Miller's Tale* by Geoffrey Chaucer. **Pipe dream** meaning 'fanciful hope' dates from the late 19th century referring to a dream experienced when smoking an opium pipe.

pippin see PIP

pirate [ME] The key idea behind pirates is that they are people who attack you. It comes from Latin *pirata*, which went back to Greek *peirein* 'to attempt, attack'.

pissabed see DANDELION

pistil see PISTON

pistol [M16th] Pistol is a rare example of an early borrowing from Czech, from *pišt'ala*, 'whistle, pipe'. The Hussite Wars in the 15th century were the first wars in which hand-held guns were of significance, and it is at this time that *pišt'ala* was used to describe a type of gun with a clear-sounding shot. The word rapidly spread through Europe and arrived in English via French.

piston [E18th] The Latin *pistullum* meant **pestle** [ME] and is the source of the botanical **pistil** [E18th] from its similar shape. From the same source Italian formed *pestone* for a large pestle or rammer, and this, via French, is the source of piston.

pit [OE] The pit that is a large hole in the ground is based on Latin *puteus* 'well shaft'. As a North American term for the stone of a fruit, pit seems to have been taken from Dutch in the 19th century, and is related to Old English **pith**. Since the 1960s people have used **pits** as an informal shortened term for **armpits** [LME]. These often have a tendency to be damp and smelly and so it was but a small linguistic leap to have them symbolize the worst example of something. That is one explanation of to **be the pits**, 'to be extremely bad'. A more refined interpretation connects the bottom of a deep, dark hole with the lowest possible rank or class. The verb meaning 'to test in a conflict or competition', as in **pit your wits**, comes from the former practice of setting animals such as cocks or dogs to fight each other. The creatures were 'pitted' or put together in a pit or other enclosure (literally a *COCKPIT), a sense used from the mid 18th century.

pitch [OE] Of the two pitch words in English, one is simple in its meaning and history and the other complex and obscure. The name of the sticky dark substance goes back to Latin *pix*. The other pitch has senses ranging from 'the quality of a sound' through 'an area of ground for a game' to 'to aim at a target'. The ultimate origin is unknown and historical development unclear. In the original military sense a **pitched battle** [M16th as 'pitched (battle) field']is one fought between large formations of troops which is more or less confined to one location, as contrasted with a chance skirmish or a running battle, and seems to be a development of the sense 'fixed' as in 'pitched tent'.

pith *see* PIT

pittance *see* PITY

pituitary *see* PIP

pity [ME] Latin *pius* meant '**pious**'[LME] but had a wider range of meanings than the word does in modern English, to include a wide range of moral qualities from being dutiful to your parents to being loyal, affectionate, compassionate, and kind. The Latin noun was *pietas*, and this, via French, became both pity and **piety** (originally used in the same sense as 'pity'), both Middle English. *Pietas* also developed a medieval Latin form *pitantia*, which meant 'a charitable donation' and the meagre daily dole of food given out to monks and also to paupers. From this comes Middle English **pittance**.

pizza *see* ITALIAN WORD PANEL

place [OE] If you have been to Italy or Spain you have probably visited the **piazza** or **plaza** of a town. These words have the same origin as English **place** and French *place* '(public) square', namely Latin *platea* 'open space', from Greek *plateia hodos* 'broad way'. From the early Middle Ages, when it was adopted from French, place superseded **stow** (found in place names such as Stow on the Wold and Padstow) and **stead**, as in Wanstead. The sense 'a space that can be occupied' developed in Middle English from this. The orderly person's mantra **a place for everything and everything in its place** goes back to the 17th century, but the modern formulation first appears in the 1840s in Captain Frederick Marryat's nautical yarn *Masterman Ready*: 'In a well-conducted man-of-war...every thing in its place, and there is a place for every thing.' In 1897 the German Chancellor Prince Bernhard von Bülow, made a speech in the Reichstag in which he declared, 'we desire to throw no one into the shade [in East Asia], but we also demand our place in the sun'. As a result the expression **a place in the sun**, 'a position of favour or advantage', has been associated with German nationalism. However, it is recorded much earlier, and is traceable back to the writings of the 17th-century French mathematician and philosopher Blaise Pascal.

placebo [L18th] In Latin *placebo* means 'I shall be acceptable or pleasing'. Doctors have probably always prescribed some drugs just to keep a patient happy, and used the term placebo for these as far back as the

pit pitch pith pittance pituitary pity pizza

late 18th century. Researchers testing new drugs give some participants substances with no therapeutic effect to compare their reactions to those who have genuinely been treated: such a substance is also a **placebo**. Results may be confused, though, by the **placebo effect**, first identified in the early 1950s, in which the person's belief in the treatment brings about beneficial effects that have nothing to do with the properties of the placebo they have taken. **Placid** [E17th] comes from the same Latin root, along with words under *PLEASE.

plagiarism [E17th] This term for taking someone's ideas and passing them off as one's own is from Latin *plagiarius* 'kidnapper'. The Latin poet Martial (AD 40–*c*.102) used the term in one of his poems for a literary thief.

plague [LME] The late 14th-century translation of the Bible supervised by John Wyclif introduced the word plague to English. Its root is Latin *plaga* 'a stroke, wound', and 'a blow' was one of its first English senses. It was also used in reference to **the ten plagues of Egypt**, described in Exodus. Although these included boils and the death of cattle and, finally, firstborn children, they were mainly not medical conditions, but afflictions like hordes of frogs and swarms of locusts. Nevertheless, by the late 15th century people were applying plague specifically to infectious diseases and epidemics, such as **bubonic plague** (from the inflamed swellings in the armpit or groin called 'buboes' from the Greek word for the groin or a swelling there). The Black Death that reached England in 1348 is thought to have been bubonic plague. To **avoid like the plague** is not medieval, but dates from the end of the 17th century, when the Great Plague of 1665–66 was fresh in people's memories. *See also* PEST

plaid *see* SCOTTISH WORD PANEL

plain [ME] The source of both plain and plane is Latin *planus* 'flat'. Mathematicians introduced the spelling plane in the early 17th century to distinguish the geometrical

uses of plain from senses such as 'ordinary' and 'simple'. The sort of plane used to make wood flat is from the same source. Plane meaning 'an aircraft' is unconnected, and is a shortening of *AEROPLANE. Also unconnected is the **plane tree** [LME], which is not flat but 'broad', the meaning of its Greek source *platus*. The **plan** of a building [M17th], which involves putting something three-dimensional on a flat surface, is, however, related. The earlier version of the expression **as plain as a pikestaff**, 'very obvious', was **as plain as a packstaff**, which gives a small clue as to its origins. A packstaff was a long stick which a peddler used to carry his pack of goods for sale, which would probably have been obvious from a distance as the peddler trudged along the road. By the late part of the 16th century people had started to use the current version with pikestaff, and a hundred years later it had more or less taken over. A pikestaff was a walking stick with a pointed metal tip, which possibly replaced packstaff because it sounded similar and peddlers were becoming a less familiar sight. The phrase **plain sailing**, 'smooth and easy progress', probably represents a use of **plane sailing**, referring to the practice of determining a ship's position on the theoretical assumption that it is moving on a plane. **Plain Jane** first appears in 1912, in *Carnival* by Compton Mackenzie. There was probably no real Jane behind the phrase, just a fortunate rhyme.

plaintive [LME] Plaintive comes via Old French *plainte* 'lamentation', from Latin *plangere* 'to beat, lament'. The legal **plaintiff** [LME] is the same word used as a noun. *Plangere* also gives us Late Middle English **complain** (the *com-* being emphatic), and **plangent** [E19th].

plait *see* PLIGHT

plan, plane *see* PLAIN

planet [ME] Early Greek astronomers observed certain heavenly bodies moving around the night sky in contrast to the stars, which stayed permanently in a fixed position in relation to one another. This is

plagiarism plague plaid plain plaintive

why they are called planets, from Greek *planētēs* 'wanderer'. The Sun and the Moon were once thought of as planets too. **Plankton**, the term for small and microscopic organisms floating in the sea, comes via German from the related Greek word *planktos*, 'wandering or drifting'. *See also* AEROPLANE

plangent *see* PLAINTIVE

plank [ME] The word plank ultimately comes from Latin *planca* 'a board or slab'. Britons have been calling less bright people **planks** since the early 1980s, from the phrase **as thick as two planks** or **two short planks**, recorded from the previous decade. **Walking the plank** is a method of execution associated with pirates although there is little evidence that this was done regularly, and most pirates probably just threw their victims overboard.

plankton *see* PLANET

plant [OE] Old English *plante* meant 'seedling' from Latin *planta* 'sprout, cutting'. Use of the word in the phrase **plant yourself somewhere** dates from the early 18th century. Later that century plant came to be used for 'things installed', such as machinery or large pieces of apparatus. The related **plantation** [LME] described the action of planting seeds. It came to be an 'estate for the cultivation of crops such as coffee or tobacco' [E18th], then 'the settling of people in a conquered or dominated country': in the late 19th century it described the establishment of English landowners in Ireland.

plaque [M19th] This word comes via French, from Dutch *plak* 'tablet', from *plakken* 'to stick'. The notion of 'sticking' is often at the word's core, whether referring to an ornamental plaque attached to a wall [M19th], dental plaque clinging to teeth [L19th], or in medicine a fatty deposit on an artery wall [L19th].

plash *see* FLASH

plastic [M17th] The Greek word *plastikos* meant 'able to be moulded into different

shapes', and came from *plassein* 'to mould'. When plastic entered English in the 17th century it had a similar meaning, but its main modern sense is for synthetic compounds developed in the early 20th century. This sense was first used in print in 1909 by the Belgian-born scientist Leo Baekeland, inventor of Bakelite. **Plastic surgery** refers to the shaping or transferring of tissue, and the first mention of the use of plastic surgery in treating injury was in 1837. **Plaster** [OE] comes from the same root. An early plaster was a bandage spread with a curative substance which usually became adhesive at body temperature. Use of the word to mean a soft mixture of lime mixed with sand or cement and water dates from late Middle English. **Plasma** [E18th] also comes from *plassein*. Its use in medical contexts, for the material from which blood is moulded or made, dates from the mid 19th century, with the ionized gas dating from the early 20th.

plate [ME] A plate first described a flat, thin sheet, usually made of metal. It goes back, via medieval Latin *plata* 'plate armour', to Greek *platus* 'flat'. Plate as in dinner plate is from the Old French form, *plat* which meant both **platter** (ME from the same source) 'large dish', and 'dish of meat'. **Plateau** [L18th] is from Old French *platel*, a 'little plate'. **Platform** [M16th] is from French *plateforme* 'ground plan' (literally 'flat shape'), and **platitude** [E19th] is from *plat* in the sense of a dull, flat form of expression. Early explorers of Australia found they had to find names for many new animals. They turned to local languages for some names (*see* KANGAROO), but for others they invented new Latin and Greek terms as in the duck-billed **platypus**. The name given to the animal by George Shaw in 1799 in his *Naturalist's Miscellany* and is a Latinate form of the Greek *platupous* 'flat-footed' formed from *platus* and *pous* 'foot', describing the shape of its large, webbed feet. *See also* PLAIN

platoon *see* PELLET

platter, platypus *see* PLATE

plangent   plank   plankton   plant   plaque

plaudit [E17th] You receive plaudits when you are praised for something good you have done. The source is Latin *plaudite* 'applaud!', which is what Roman actors used to ask the audience to do at the end of a play. This comes from *plaudere* 'to applaud or clap', as does **applaud** itself. **Plausible**, also ultimately from *plaudere*, was at one time used to mean 'deserving applause or approval'. *See also* EXPLODE

play [OE] In Old English *plegan* or *plegian* meant 'to exercise', while *plega* meant 'brisk movement or activity', and could also be used to describe a dramatic performance on stage. These are the first uses of play. Today terms such as **swordplay** and **gunplay** preserve the old 'brisk movement' sense of the noun. To **play with fire** is to take foolish risks with something potentially dangerous. The proverb **if you play with fire you get burned** dates from the late 19th century, though a similar sentiment is expressed by the poet Henry Vaughan in 1655: 'I played with fire, did counsel spurn . . . But never thought that fire would burn / Or that a soul could ache.' **Play it again, Sam** is a popular misquotation from the film *Casablanca* (1942). Although these precise words are never actually spoken in the film, Humphrey Bogart does say 'If she can stand it, I can. Play it!', and earlier in the film Ingrid Bergman says 'Play it, Sam. Play "As Time Goes By"'. The US magazine *Playboy* was founded in 1953 by Hugh Hefner. A **playboy** was at first, back in 1616, a boy actor. The modern sense, 'an irresponsible pleasure-seeking man', started in Ireland, and is first recorded in the 1820s.

plaza *see* PLACE

please [ME] A word that comes via Old French *plaisir* 'to please' from Latin *placere*, found also in **implacable** [LME]. Phrases like **yes, please** were originally short for 'may it please you' or 'let it please you'. Please on its own, as used today, was not known to Shakespeare, who used *please you*: 'Will you hear the letter?—So please you, for I never heard it yet' (*As You Like It*). The proverbs **you can't please everyone** and **little things please little minds** are both old

and can be traced back to the late 15th and late 16th centuries. Something **pleasant** [ME] was originally something 'pleasing', the meaning of the word in its French source. If you were **complacent** [M17th] you were originally willing to go along with what pleases others.

pleat *see* PLIGHT

plebeian [M16th] This is based on Latin *plebeius*, from *plebs*, 'the common people', as opposed to the more aristocratic **patricians** who were the 'fathers of their country', getting their name from Latin *pater* 'father' (source of other words such as **paternal** [LME]). The same base is shared by **plebiscite** from the same period.

pledge *see* PLIGHT

plenty [ME] 'Fullness' and 'perfection' were the early senses of plenty which goes back to Latin *plenus* 'full'. The Greek equivalent *plēthōrē* is the source of **plethora**. This was first used as a medical term for an excess of fluid. The sense 'excess' dates from the early 18th century.

plight [OE] In the traditional marriage ceremony the bride and groom each say 'I plight thee my troth', meaning 'I pledge my word'. Plight means 'to promise solemnly', and **pledge** [ME] is probably a distant relative. **Troth** is an old variant of *TRUTH, meaning 'giving your word' and still preserved in **betroth** [ME]. The other meaning of plight, 'a predicament', is from Old French *plit* 'fold', suggesting the idea of a difficult or complicated situation. Other words from *plit* include Middle English **pliant** [LME] literally 'foldable'; and **pliable** [LME]; **pliers** [M16th] tools for bending things; and **ply** [LME] in the sense of 'thickness' as in **plywood** [E20th]. (The other ply as in ply with drink, is simply a shortening of apply, *see* APPLIANCE). **Pleat** and **plait** [ME] are further relatives. **Compliant** [M17th] looks as if it should be a relative, but its immediate source, to **comply** [E17th], originally came from Latin *complere* 'to fulfil, accomplish', although compliant later developed senses influenced by its similarity to pliant.

plimsoll [L19th] Use of plimsoll for a light rubber-soled canvas shoe, is probably because the strip covering the join between sole and upper resembles a **Plimsoll line** on the side of the ship, marking the safe limit for loading. This got its name from Samuel Plimsoll (1824–98), the English politician who fought to introduce the Merchant Shipping Act of 1876, which ended the practice of sending overloaded and heavily insured old ships to sea, from which the owners profited if they sank.

plonk [L19th] There are two different plonks. One, as in 'to plonk something down', was originally a northern English word meaning 'to hit or strike with a heavy thud', and probably comes from the sound. The other **plonk** [1930s], describing cheap wine, started out in Australia. It is probably humorous form of *blanc* in the French phrase *vin blanc* 'white wine', though some suggest that it might be meant to imitate the sound of a cork being taken out of a bottle. **Plonker**, meaning 'an idiot', dates from the 1960s but was popularized by the 1980s BBC television sitcom *Only Fools and Horses*. It is based on the first plonk and was first used to mean 'something large or substantial' and also 'penis'.

plot [OE] The first meaning of plot was 'a small piece of ground'. The sense 'secret plan' dates from the late 16th century and was probably developed out of the sense 'map, plan' influenced by Old French *complot* 'dense crowd, secret project'. Guy Fawkes' Gunpowder Plot of 1605 is thought to have spread the use of this sense. From another sense of plot, 'the main sequence of events in a play, novel, or film', comes the expression **the plot thickens**. The person to thank for it is George Villiers, the 2nd Duke of Buckingham, whose satirical drama *The Rehearsal* (1671) includes the line 'Ay, now the plot thickens very much upon us.'

plough [OE] The spelling plough did not become common until the 18th century. Before that only the noun was normally spelled this way, and the verb was **plow**, which is still the US spelling for both noun and verb. A staple of the pub lunchtime menu is the **ploughman's lunch**, a cold meal consisting of bread and cheese usually served with pickle and salad. This is not the traditional rural snack it might seem. The first recorded use of the term can be traced back only to 1960, though two years before that the same kind of thing was being given a similar name in *The Times*: 'In a certain inn today you have only to say, "Ploughboy's Lunch, please," and for a shilling there is bread and cheese and pickled onions to go with your pint'. And over a century earlier we find this curious pre-echo: 'The surprised poet swung forth to join them, with an extemporized sandwich, that looked like a ploughman's luncheon, in his hand' (John Lockhart, *Memoirs of the Life of Sir Walter Scott*, 1837).

pluck *see* PULL

plum [OE] Latin *prunum* is the source of both plum and **prune** [LME], a plum preserved by drying. The change from *pr-* to *pl-* is not an unusual one. The 'l' and 'r' are made in very similar parts of the mouth, and some languages do not distinguish between the two sounds. **Plum pudding** [M17th] was originally made with plums. The use of plum to refer to something highly desirable, 'the pick of the bunch', probably arose from the idea of picking the tastiest bits out of a plum pudding. Upper-class people are sometimes said to have **a plum in the mouth**, or to speak with a **plummy** voice. The idea of having a plum in the mouth goes right back to the 1530s, though at first it meant that the speech was indistinct rather than posh.

plumb [ME] You can say that something which is not quite perpendicular is **out of plumb**. This draws on the original meaning of plumb, a ball of lead attached to a string to determine a vertical line, or a **plumb line**. Another early use was as a term for a sounding lead used for measuring the depth of water. To plumb a body of water was to measure its depth in this way, and is the source of the phrase **plumb the depths**. The

plimsoll   plonk   plot   plough   pluck   plum

source of plumb is Latin *plumbum* 'lead', also the root of **plumber**. Medieval plumbers dealt in and worked with lead, and it was not until the 19th century that the word was applied solely to people trained in fitting and repairing water pipes, which were initially all made of lead. The Latin word *plumbum* is also the basis of **plummet**, which came into medieval English from Old French and then referred to a plumb line. The use of plummet as a verb meaning 'to drop straight down rapidly, to plunge' is more recent, first recorded in the 1850s. An early use of the verb was 'to let a vertical line fall by means of a plummet', and the modern sense developed from this. To do something with **aplomb** [L18th] comes from the French phrase *à plomb*, 'straight as a plumb line'. **Plunge** [LME] also comes from *plumbum*, this time via Old French *plungier* 'to thrust down'. The phrase **take the plunge** dates from the mid 19th century.

plume [LME] Plume and plumage come via French from Latin *pluma* 'down, soft feather'. The Latin was borrowed at an early date into many Germanic languages, probably because from Roman times there was an important trade between these northern lands and the south in warm, soft goose down for stuffing pillows and duvets. From the late 16th century plume was used to describe various objects resembling a feather such as a plume of smoke.

plummet, plunge *see* PLUMB

plus [M16th] This is an English use of a Latin word meaning literally 'more'. The garment **plus fours** (1920s) associated with golf, derive their name from the overhang at the knee requiring an extra 10cm (4in) of material. **Plural** [LME] from Latin *Pluralis* 'relating to more than one' formed from *plus*.

plus ça change *see* FRENCH WORD PANEL

ply *see* PLIGHT

pneumatic [M17th] This comes from Greek *pneumatikos*, from *pneuma* 'wind'. Greek *pnein* 'breathe' is the base. Because the Greeks felt there was a strong association between breath and the soul the pneumatic is used in New Testament Greek to mean 'spiritual', and this is the sense first recorded in English. It came to be used for things inflated with air in the middle of the 19th century, and this opened the way to the development of pneumatic to describe a well-rounded female form. Rather surprisingly, T.S. Eliot is the first recorded user of this sense: 'Uncorseted her friendly bust Gives promise of pneumatic bliss' (*Whispers of Immortality* 1919).

poach *see* POCKET

pocket [ME] The first sense recorded for pocket was a 'bag, sack'. It comes from Anglo-Norman French *poket(e)*, a little poke or pouch (*see* PIG). This also lies behind **poach**. Poaching eggs and poaching game may seem vastly different activities, but they are both probably connected with the Old French word *pochier* or French *pocher*, 'to enclose in a bag'. When you poach an egg you can think of the white of the egg as forming a pocket or bag for the yolk to cook in. The second poach first meant 'to push together in a heap', and acquired the 'steal game' sense in the early 17th century. The connection with the source word comes from the pocket or bag into which a poacher would stuff his ill-gotten gains. **Pucker** [L16th] is probably from the same source, with the little gatherings being seen as small pockets.

poet [ME] A poet is literally 'a maker', a term that was also used to mean a poet in the Middle Ages, coming from Greek *poētēs*, 'maker, poet'. When someone experiences a fitting or deserved retribution for their actions, you can say that it is **poetic justice**. Alexander Pope used the phrase in his satire *The Dunciad* (1742), where he depicts 'Poetic Justice, with her lifted scale'. *See also* LAUREL

po-faced [1930s] The po in po-faced, 'humourless and disapproving', probably

plume plummet plunge plus plus ça change

comes from the use of po to mean 'chamber pot', though it might also have been influenced by the exclamation '**poh!**', used to reject something contemptuously. In any event, the phrase is likely to be modelled on the expression **poker-faced** [E20th]. This comes from the need to keep a deadpan face when playing poker. The game, first recorded in the 1830s in the USA probably gets its name from the German word *pochen* 'to brag'.

poignant [LME] Something that makes you feel a keen sense of sadness or regret can be described as poignant. This comes from an Old French word that meant 'pricking' and derived from Latin *pungere*, 'to prick'. Back in the Middle Ages you could describe a weapon as poignant, meaning that it had a sharp point. The word could also be applied to sharp tastes or smells, as in 'a poignant sauce' or 'a poignant scent'. This sense is now covered by the related word **pungent** [L16th], which originally meant 'very painful or distressing' and at one time could also mean 'telling or convincing', as in Samuel Pepys's reference to 'a very good and pungent sermon'. The slim dagger called a **poinard** [M16th] may look as if it should be related, particularly as it is often spelt with a 'g' in early texts. However, this illustrates the danger of jumping to conclusions in etymologies. It gets its name from the fact that it is held in the fist, from Latin *pugnus* 'fist'. This is also the source, via *pugnare* 'to fight', of **pugnacious** [M17th]. *See also* POINT

point [ME] Most senses of point ultimately derive from Latin *punctum* 'a small hole made by pricking', giving rise to the meanings 'unit, mark, point in space or time', from *pungere* 'to pierce or prick'. From the same source are **punctuation** [M16th] which makes small marks on the text; **punctual** [LME] arriving at the right point in time; **punctilious** [M17th] attending to the small points in behaviour; and **puncture** [LME] a small hole. A boxer **wins on points** [L19th] when he wins because the referee and judges have awarded him more points than his opponent, rather than by a knockout. The **point of no return** [M20th] is the point in a flight at which it is impossible for an aircraft to return to its point of departure because of lack of fuel and so it has no choice but to continue. Thus it can also be the point at which you are committed to a course of action and must continue to the end. To refuse or ask about something **point-blank** [L16th] is to do so directly or abruptly and without explanation. The phrase literally describes a shot or bullet fired from very close to its target, blank being used here in the old sense of 'the white spot in the centre of a target'. If you aim or point a gun directly at the centre of the target, you need to be sufficiently close for the bullet still to be travelling horizontally (rather than starting to follow a downward trajectory) as it hits the spot. The more general meaning arose as far back as the 1650s. *See also* POIGNANT

poise [LME] The word poise originally meant 'weight', and came via Old French *pois* from Latin *pensum* 'a weight'. This gave rise to the idea of 'equal weight, balance, equilibrium', of something being equally weighted on both sides, from which developed in the late 18th century the modern senses of 'composure' and 'elegant deportment'.

poison [ME] A poison does not necessarily need to be in liquid form, but in early use the word meant a drink or medicine, specifically a potion with a harmful or dangerous ingredient. The source was Old French *poison* 'magic potion', from Latin *potio*, also the source of **potion** [ME]. The saying **one man's meat is another man's poison** has been around for centuries and was being described as long ago as 1604 as 'that old moth-eaten proverb'. A similar idea is found in the work of the Roman poet and philosopher Lucretius (*c*.94–55 BC): 'What is food to one person may be bitter poison to others.' A **chalice** [ME] from Latin *calix*, 'cup', also the source of the botanical **calix**) is a large cup or goblet, and a **poisoned chalice** something that seems attractive but is likely to be a source of problems. A poisoned chalice

po-faced   poignant   point   poise   poison

features in Shakespeare's *Macbeth*, and is the source of our expression.

poke *see* PIG

poker *see* PO-FACED

pole [OE] The Old English word from which we get pole, as in 'flag pole' or 'telegraph pole', meant 'stake' and is ultimately from the same source as *PALE. To be **in pole position** is to be in a leading or dominant position, from motor racing, where it describes the first place on the starting grid, on the front row, and on the inside of the first bend, but it comes from horse racing. On 19th-century racecourses a pole marked the starting position closest to the inside boundary rails, a favourable position in a race. Pole as in North Pole is from Latin *polus* 'end of an axis', from Greek *polos* 'pivot, axis, sky'. The adjective **polar** dates from the mid 16th century and is from medieval Latin *polaris* 'heavenly', from *polus*. The Pole Star, or Polaris, is the star around which the stars appear to rotate. *Polos* is also the probable source of pulley [ME].

police [LME] In the 15th century police, which came from medieval Latin *politia* 'citizenship, government', was another word for **policy**, from the same source. Over time the word came to mean 'civil administration' and then 'maintenance of public order'. The first people to be called **police** in the current sense was the Marine Police, a force set up around 1798 to protect merchant shipping in the Port of London. The police force established for London in 1829 was for some time known as the New Police. *See also* CONSTABLE, COPPER. Latin *politia* had been borrowed from Greek *polis* 'city, state', also found in **metropolis** [LME] 'mother city' in Greek; **acropolis** [M17th] 'high city'; **cosmopolitan** [M17th] from *kosmos*, 'world'; and **politics**. We have the ancient Greek philosopher Aristotle to thank for **politics**. Aristotle, a pupil of Plato and tutor to Alexander the Great, wrote a treatise called *ta politika*, or '*The Affairs of State*', which gave us our word. The concept of **political correctness** originated in the USA during the 1980s but the expression

dates back a lot longer. It is recorded in 1840 in the USA, and **politically correct** goes back even further, to 1793, in the records of the US Supreme Court. Originally both terms referred to people conforming to the prevailing political views of the time.

polish *see* POLITE

polite [LME] Latin *politus* 'polished, made smooth' is the source of polite, with **polish** [ME] coming from the same root via French. Polite was originally used to mean 'polished', with the sense of something that is carefully finished and maintained being transferred to language and behaviour around 1500.

political, politics *see* POLICE

pollen [E16th] This is the Latin word for 'fine powder or flour'. It was originally used in the Latin sense, and adopted for botanical use in the mid 18th century.

pollute [LME] Pollute is from Latin *polluere* 'to soil, defile', formed from *lutum* 'mud'.

polo [L19th] The name for this game (originally played in the East) is from a Balti Tibetan word meaning 'ball'.

poltergeist [M19th] This is a German word formed from *poltern* 'create a disturbance' and *Geist* 'ghost'.

poltroon [E16th] French *poltroon* came from Italian *poltrone*, a term for either a coward or a lazy person which was possibly based on the Italian word for a bed or couch, *poltro* or else is from *pullus* 'young animal' (*see* PONY). A story once widely believed was that the word related to archers shirking military service by cutting off their right thumbs, a self-inflicted wound which would make them incapable of drawing a longbow. Poltroon was supposed to be a corruption of Latin *pollice truncus*, 'maimed or mutilated in the thumb', but there is no foundation for this colourful story.

polygon *see* PENTAGON

poke poker pole police polish polite political

pom *see* AUSTRALIAN WORD PANEL

pomegranate [ME] Our name for this fruit comes from Old French *pome grenate*, from *pome* 'apple' and *grenate*, which meant 'pomegranate' but was based on Latin *granatum*, 'having many seeds'. Similarly, **pomander** [LME] for a perforated container of sweet-smelling substances is from Old French *pome d'embre*, from medieval Latin *pomum de ambra* 'apple of ambergris'. Apples are again found in **pommel** [ME]. This once described a decorative ball or finial at the top point of something. It is from Old French *pomel* 'little apple'. *See also* GRENADE, AUSTRALIAN WORD PANEL

ponder, ponderous *see* PENSIVE

pontiff [L17th] Referring to the pope, this word is from French *pontife*, from Latin *pontifex* meaning literally 'bridge-maker' but used in ancient Rome as a term for a member of the principal college of priests. This also gives us **pontificate** [LME]. The use 'express opinions in a pompous way' dates from the early 19th century. The same *pont-* 'bridge' element is found in **pontoon** [L16th]. *See also at* PUNT

pony [M17th] Different as they seem, **pony** and **poultry** [ME] have the same starting point. Latin *pullus* meant 'young animal', but it tended to be applied specifically to young horses and young chickens. The 'young horse' strand became Old French *poulain* 'a foal', and the diminutive form of this, *poulenet*, was adopted into Scots in the early 18th century as *powny*, coming into general English usage as pony. The 'young chicken' strand is the source of Old French *pouletrie*, from which we get poultry. *See also* MONKEY

poodle *see* PUDDLE, GERMAN WORD PANEL

pool *see* PUDDLE

poop *see* NINCOMPOOP

poor [ME] The Latin word for 'poor' *pauper*, is the base of **pauper** [E16th], **poverty** [ME], and poor. The phrase **poor as a church mouse**, or 'extremely poor', comes from the notion that a church mouse must be particularly deprived as it does not have the opportunity to find pickings from a kitchen or larder, and there are few crumbs to be found in a well-swept church. You sometimes hear a wealthy young person whose money appears to bring them no happiness described as **poor little rich girl** (or **boy**). Though he did not coin the phrase, Noël Coward certainly popularized it with his 1925 song 'Poor Little Rich Girl'.

pop [LME] Like **splash** [E17th], **crack** [OE], and *BANG [M16th], pop imitates the sound it describes. It was first used to refer to a blow or knock, the 'abrupt explosive noise' meaning coming later. The phrase **pop the question**, meaning 'to propose marriage', is first recorded in the early 18th century. The fizzy pop that you drink gets its name from the sound made when the cork is pulled out. It was first mentioned at the beginning of the 19th century. To **pop your clogs** is to die. Pop here is used in the sense 'to pawn' [M18th], the idea being that a person who has just died no longer has any need of their shoes or clogs and so they can be pawned. The phrase is recorded only from the 1970s, which is surprisingly recent—it may have been made up as an 'imitation' dialect expression, or be an example of a folk expression that existed for generations without being recorded in print. In reference to music, pop is short for **popular** (*see* PEOPLE). The first mention of this pop was in 1910—'a pop vaudeville house'—and **pop songs** were mentioned in *Variety* magazine during 1921. An issue of *Melody Maker* from 7 April 1956, gives us the first recorded mention of **Top of the Pops**, the best-selling recorded song or piece of music at a given time, although the first British singles chart was published in the 14 November 1952 edition of the *New Musical Express*. The BBC pop music programme *Top of the Pops* ran for 42 years from 1964 to 2006.

pope [OE] The word pope came via ecclesiastical Latin from ecclesiastical Greek *papas* 'bishop, patriarch', a variant of Greek *pappas* 'father'. From the same root came Late Middle English **papal** and

papacy, and mid 16th-century **papist.**
Patriarch [ME] is from Old French
patriarche, via ecclesiastical Latin from
Greek *patriarkhēs*: formed from *patria*
'family' and *arkhēs* 'ruling'. **Patriot** [L16th]
and **patriotic** [M17th] go back to a related
Greek *patris* 'fatherland'. These are
connected with English **papa** [L17th] for
'father' and *MUM, all being based on the
early babbling sounds produced by infants,
as is **daddy** [LME]. *See also* PATTERN

popinjay *see* PARROT

poppet *see* PUP, DOLL

poppycock [M19th] The English
language has any number of curious words
for 'nonsense', such as **balderdash** [L16th]
of unknown origins, and *CODSWALLOP,
claptrap—first used in the modern sense by
Lord Byron, and **piffle** [M19th] from the
sound. Poppycock was originally Dutch,
and comes from *pappekak*, which meant
either 'soft dung' or 'doll's excrement'
Another such term is **bosh**, a Turkish word
meaning 'empty, worthless' which was
popularized by its frequent use in James
Morier's highly successful 1834 novel
A*yesha, the Maid of Kar.*

populace, popular, population *see*
PEOPLE

porcupine [ME] An early form of
porcupine was *porke despyne*, which
possibly came from Latin *porcus spinosus*
'prickly pig'. The word appeared in many
forms between the 15th and 17th centuries,
including *portepyn, porkpen, porkenpick,*
and *porpoynt.* Shakespeare knew the animal
as a porpentine and it appears in this form
in his plays, often as the name of an inn. The
ghost of Hamlet's father tells Hamlet that his
story could make his son's hairs 'stand on
end, / Like quills upon the fretful
porpentine'.

porphyry *see* PURPLE

porridge [M16th] At first porridge was a
soup thickened with barley. The word is a
16th-century alteration of **pottage** [ME],
which in turn comes from Old French

potage 'something put in a pot'. The
porridge we are familiar with, consisting
of oatmeal boiled in water or milk, is
mentioned in the 1640s. The informal use
of porridge to mean 'prison' dates from the
1950s. It probably derives from porridge as
a typical prison food, though it might be
based on a pun involving two meanings of
stir, one as in 'stir the porridge' and the
other a slang term for 'prison', which is
perhaps from Romany *sturbin* 'jail'. The
term was immortalized by the BBC comedy
series *Porridge* of the 1970s, which starred
Ronnie Barker as Norman Stanley Fletcher,
a cynical but good-hearted old convict.

port [OE] Latin *portus* 'haven or harbour'
is the source of our word port. Its nautical
use to refer to the left side of a ship, the
opposite of **starboard** (OE from 'steer
board'—early ships were steered with a
paddle over the right side), dates from the
mid 16th century and probably comes from
the idea that this was the side of the ship
where the loading hatch was fitted and was
turned towards the quay when the ship was
in port. It replaced an older word **larboard**,
hardly surprising given the potential for
confusion between the similar-sounding
'starboard!' and 'larboard!' when shouted
into the teeth of a gale. While the second
half of larboard is 'board', the origin of the
first part is not known. The drink port is a
shortened form of Oporto in Portugal, from
which the wine was shipped. *See also*
PORTER

porter [ME] The porter who acts as a
doorman at the entrance of a hotel and the
one who carries luggage are completely
different words. The former comes from
porta, the Latin word for a gate or a door
which is also the source of **portal** [LME] and
porthole [M16th], as well as of **port** [OE] in
the sense of 'socket' as in a computer port.
The other comes from Latin *portare* 'to
carry', and so is related to words like
portable [LME], and **portfolio** [E18th],
adopted from Italian *portafogli*, from
portare 'carry', and *foglio* 'leaf, sheet of
paper'. **Portmanteau** [M16th] for a
travelling bag is from French *portemanteau*,
from *porter* 'carry' and *manteau* 'mantle'.

popinjay poppet poppycock populace popular

The drink porter, a dark brown bitter beer, was originally made for porters and others whose work involved carrying loads.

portrait *see* ABSTRACT

pose, poseur *see* PAUSE

posh [E20th] One of the more frequently repeated explanations of the origin of a word is the story that **posh**, comes from the initials of 'port out, starboard home'. This is supposed to refer to the location of the more desirable cabins—on the port side on the outward trip and on the starboard side on the return—on passenger ships between Britain and India in the 19th century. Such cabins would be sheltered from the heat of the sun or benefit from cooling breezes, and so were reserved by wealthy passengers. Sadly, there is no evidence to support this neat and ingenious explanation. The P&O steamship company is supposed to have stamped tickets with the letters P.O.S.H., but no tickets like this have ever been found. A more likely explanation is that the word comes from a 19th-century slang term for a dandy, from thieves' slang for 'money'. The first recorded example of posh is from a 1915 issue of *Blackwood's Magazine*.

positive [LME] At the core of positive is the idea of placing something firmly, and the ultimate source is Latin *ponere* 'to place'. In the 14th century the English word was used to refer to laws as being formally laid down. From this developed the more general meaning 'explicitly laid down and admitting no question' (as in **proof positive**), and later 'very sure, convinced'. **Position** [LME] comes from the same root, as does **postpone** [L15th] literally 'place after'. *See also* COMPOST, POST

posse [M17th] The word posse calls to mind the image, familiar from Westerns, of a body of men being recruited by a sheriff and saddling up to pursue outlaws or other wrongdoers. The key element in its meaning is not the pursuing, though, but the fact that the sheriff has empowered this group of people to enforce the law. In medieval Latin *posse* meant 'power', and came from Latin *posse* 'to be able'. Posse pre-dated the widespread colonization of the USA, and was first used in Britain during the mid 17th century to mean 'an assembled force or band' and specifically 'the population of local able-bodied men summoned by a sheriff to stop a riot or pursue criminals'. *See also* POWER. **Possible** [LME] comes from the same root, while Latin *potentia* 'power' formed from *posse*, gives us words such as **potent**, **potentate,** and **potential** (all LME).

possum [E17th] An informal American term for the **opossum**, a marsupial whose name comes from a Native American word meaning 'white dog'. This animal feigns death when it is threatened or attacked, which is why **playing possum**, an expression recorded from the early 19th century in the USA, is pretending to be asleep or unconscious when threatened. In Australia, to **stir the possum** is to stir up controversy or liven things up. The Australian possum is also a marsupial but is a different animal from its American counterpart. *See also* NATIVE AMERICAN AND AUSTRALIAN WORD PANELS

post [OE] English has three words spelled post. The one meaning 'a long, sturdy piece of wood', and 'to display a notice in a public place' (from fastening it to a post) is from Latin *postis* 'doorpost'. The other two, 'the official service or system that delivers letters and parcels', and 'a position of paid employment', are both from Latin *ponere* 'to place'. The 'delivering letters' sense arose from its application to each of a series of mounted couriers who were stationed at suitable places along a route and carried important letters and despatches on to the next post **post-haste** [M16th]. A fourth post is found in terms like *POSTHUMOUS, **post mortem,** and **post-war**. This comes from Latin *post* 'after'. In American English to **go postal** is to become irrational and violent, especially as a result of stress. This dates from the 1990s, and arose as a result of several cases involving employees of the US postal service running amok and shooting down their colleagues. The phrase can also be used to mean 'to get very angry, to fly into a rage'. *See also* MAIL, POSITIVE

portrait pose poseur posh positive posse

posthumous [E17th] In English posthumous means 'happening after a person's death'. Latin *postumus*, on which it is based, meant 'last'. A baby born posthumously (the most common use of the word), after the death of its father, would be the father's last child. The *h* was added to the spelling of the English word because of the influence of *humus* 'ground, earth', or *humare* 'to bury', both words that relate to the idea of death. The French near relative of *postumus* was *puisne*, formed from *puis* 'afterwards' and *né* 'born'. This originally meant a younger person, and is the source of our **puny** [M16th].

postpone *see* POSITIVE

postscript [M16th] The source of this word is Latin *postscriptum* from *postscribere* 'write under or in front of, add' (source of **proscribe** [LME] via the sense of 'writing publicly'). The base elements are Latin *post* 'after, later' and *scribere* 'write'. The sense 'sequel' dates from the late 19th century.

posture *see* COMPOSE

pot [OE] This originally referred to any cylindrical container. A number of words and expressions are based on the idea pot used to cook food. A **potboiler** is so called because writers dash off such books simply to earn a living, to 'keep the pot boiling'. **Potshot** comes from the idea of shooting an animal 'for the pot', purely for food rather than for display. You can say that something has **gone to pot** when it has deteriorated through neglect. This expression dates back to the 1530s and used to mean 'to be ruined or destroyed'. It is based on the image of chopping ingredients up into small pieces and putting them in a pot ready for cooking. So to go to pot is to go to pieces. You can talk about **the pot calling the kettle black** when someone makes criticisms about someone else which could equally well apply to themselves. A version of this saying, 'The pot calls the pan burnt-arse', is included in a 1639 collection of proverbs by John Clarke. **A watched pot never boils** dates from the 19th century. According to a comic strip in the *Washington Post* in April 2002, 'Whoever said "A watched pot never boils" obviously didn't own a microwave.' Pot meaning 'cannabis' is a different word, recorded from the 1930s in the USA. It is probably from Mexican Spanish *potiguaya* 'marijuana leaves'.

potato [M16th] 'Let the sky rain potatoes', says Falstaff in Shakespeare's play *The Merry Wives of Windsor*. A bizarre wish, you would think, until you know that he is referring to sweet potatoes, believed in the 16th and 17th centuries to have aphrodisiac qualities. Falstaff is in fact praying for erotic prowess. The first vegetable referred to as a potato in English was the sweet potato, introduced to Europe before the common white potato that we are most familiar with today. By the late 16th century, when white potatoes had appeared in England from America, the word was being applied to the new arrival. It comes from Spanish *patata*, a variant of an old Caribbean word *batata* 'sweet potato'. *See also* CRISP

potent, potentate, potential *see* POSSE

potion *see* POISON

pottage *see* PORRIDGE

poultry *see* PONY

pound [OE] This goes back to Latin *libra pondo*, a Roman weight equivalent to 12 ounces—*libra* meant 'scales, balance' and *pondo* was 'by weight'. *Libra* gives the 'L' in the old £sd , for 'pound, shillings, and pence' (the *d.* for *denarius*, the Latin word for an ancient Roman silver coin, *see* PENNY). The money sense, also Old English, arose because the first pound was literally a pound of silver. Pound meaning 'to beat, strike heavily' is a different Old English word, as is pound in the sense 'an enclosure'. In Shakespeare's play *The Merchant of Venice* the moneylender Shylock lends the merchant Antonio money on condition that if he fails to repay it on time he must forfeit a pound of his flesh. When Antonio is unable to pay, Shylock insists on holding him to the agreement, but is foiled by the clever pleading of Portia, who argues that if the flesh is taken it must be done without spilling any blood in the process, as the deed specifies flesh only. To demand **your pound of flesh** has come to mean 'ruthlessly demand something you are owed'.

poverty *see* POOR

powder [ME] Latin *pulvis* 'dust' is the source of **pulverize** [LME] as well as powder, which came into English via Old French *poudre*. If someone tells you to **keep your powder dry** they mean that you should be ready for action. Popular tradition attributes the advice **put your trust in God, and keep your powder dry** to the English statesman and general Oliver Cromwell (1599–1658). The combination of spiritual encouragement and practical measures is typical of him, but the line did not appear until the mid 19th century, nearly 300 years after his death, in an Irish ballad. In American English to **take a powder** is to depart quickly, especially in order to avoid a difficult situation. This may be based on the idea of a person fleeing down a road and raising dust as they go. Another theory is that it relates to a person taking a laxative powder and so having to rush to the toilet. A more genteel toilet-related expression is the euphemistic **powder your nose**, recorded since the 1920s.

power [ME] Like *POSSE, power can be traced back to Latin *posse* 'to be able'. 'We know that power does corrupt, and that we cannot trust kings to have loving hearts', wrote Anthony Trollope in *The Prime Minister* (1876). But **power corrupts** got into the language through the slightly later quotation from Lord Acton: 'Power tends to corrupt, and absolute power corrupts absolutely. Great men are almost always bad men, even when they exercise influence and not authority' (letter to Bishop Mandell Creighton, 1887). Whoever the authorities or people in control are in a particular situation can be referred to as **the powers that be**, a phrase that comes from the Bible: 'For there is no power but of God: the powers that be are ordained of God' (Epistle to the Romans).

powwow *see* AMERICAN WORD PANEL

practise [LME] The rule that in English English (but not US) the verb practise is spelled with an 's' and the noun with a 'c' is drilled into schoolchildren, but has only been standardized since the 18th century. The 's' of the verb comes from Old French *practiser*, the noun keeping the original 'c', on the pattern of pairs such as *advise*, *advice*. The source is Latin *practica* 'practice', from Greek *praktikē* 'concerned with action'.

prairie [L18th] This is an adoption of a French word, formed from Latin *pratum* 'meadow'.

praise *see* PRICE

praline [E18th] This chocolate filling is named after the French Marshal de Plessis-Praslin (1598–1675), soldier, diplomat, and politician, whose cook, Lassagne, is credited with having invented it. It is said that the delicious results were influential in his diplomatic successes.

prank [E16th] A prank was once more serious than it is now, not a practical joke nor a piece of mischief but rather some wicked or malicious act. For example, the 17th-century biblical commentator John Trapp described a person's murder of their brother and sister as 'lewd pranks'. The origin of the word is unknown.

prawn *see* RAW

prayer *see* PRECARIOUS

precarious [M17th] This is from Latin *precarius* 'obtained by entreaty', from *prex*, *prec-* 'prayer'. The notion is one of something being dependent on the good grace of somebody else (needing entreaty), and therefore uncertain. **Prayer** [ME] is from the same word.

precede *see* CEDE

precinct [LME] This first described an administrative district; it is from medieval Latin *praecinctum*, from *praecingere*

poverty   powder   power   powwow   practise

'encircle'. The term **shopping precinct** dates from the middle of the 20th century.

precious *see* PRICE

precipice [L16th] The original meaning of precipice was 'a headlong fall'. It was not long, though, before precipice was being used in its modern sense, describing a steep cliff or mountainside. The ultimate source is Latin *praeceps* 'steep or headlong', also the origin of **precipitation** [E17th] which originally meant the action of falling or throwing down, rather than rainfall or snow.

precise *see* DECIDE

precocious *see* APRICOT

precursor *see* CURSOR

predatory *see* PRISON

predecessor *see* CEDE

predict *see* VERDICT

predominant *see* DANGER

pre-eminent *see* EMINENT

pre-empt [M19th] It you pre-empt someone, you get there first. The original Latin came from *prae* 'in advance' and *emere* 'buy'. **Pre-emption** [E17th] was the earliest form of the word, pre-empt being formed from it. The same root lies behind **premium** [E17th].

prefer [LME] If you prefer something you make it your first choice, a sense found in the original Latin *praeferre* formed from *prae* 'before' and *ferre* 'to carry'. *See also* REFER

preggers *see* RUGBY

prehensile *see* PRISON

premium *see* PRE-EMPT

prepare *see* APPARATUS

preposition *see* COMPOST

preposterous [M16th] The Latin word *praeposterus* meant both 'reversed, back to front', and 'absurd', combining *prae* 'before' and *posterus* 'coming after'. When the English word entered the language it had a pair of meanings that mirrored those in the Latin. One of these, 'having last what should be first', is very rare now. But the other, describing anything that seems contrary to reason or absurd, is still going strong.

prequel *see* SEQUEL

presbyter, Presbyterian *see* PRIEST

present [ME] Latin *praeesse* 'to be at hand' was formed from *prae* 'before' and *esse* 'be'. This was the source of **presence** [ME], present both in the time sense and 'to give', and, via the Latin variant *praesentare* 'place before', of the sense 'a gift'.

presently *see* SOON

preserve *see* CONSERVE

press [ME] Both press and **print** [ME] can be traced back to Latin *premere*, 'to press', as can **pressure** [LME]. Journalists and the newspaper industry have been known as **the press**, in reference to printing presses, since the late 18th century, although before that a press was a printing house or publisher. Another name for journalists, used since the 1830s or 1840s, is **the fourth** *ESTATE. It was originally used of the then unrepresented mass of people: Henry Fielding wrote in 1752 'None of our political writers...take notice of any more than three estates, namely, Kings, Lords, and Commons...passing by in silence that very large and powerful body which form the fourth estate in this community...The Mob.' By the middle of the 19th century it was firmly established for the press. Carlyle wrote in 1841 'Burke said there were three Estates in Parliament, but in the Reporters' Gallery...there sat a fourth Estate more important far than they all.' Burke has been credited with the term, but no evidence beyond Carlyle has yet been found. **Press the flesh** is US slang from the 1920s meaning 'to shake hands'. These days it is generally used of celebrities or politicians

precious precipice precise precocious prefer

greeting crowds by shaking hands with random people. The heyday of the **press gang**, a group employed to force men to join the navy, was the 18th and early 19th centuries, but the first record of the term comes before 1500. Press-ganging people was really a form of arbitrary **conscription**, a word that appears in Late Middle English in the literal sense of 'writing down together' from Latin *con* 'with' and *scribere* 'write', but which was only introduced in the modern sense of compulsory enlistment in Britain in 1916, during the First World War, although the word was first recorded in 1800. **Depress** [LME] has the basic sense of 'press down'.

prestige [M17th] The 2006 film *The Prestige* was about a rivalry between two stage magicians in Edwardian London, reviving an early meaning of the word, 'an illusion or conjuring trick'. Prestige came into English in the mid 17th century, borrowed from a French word meaning 'illusion, glamour' which came from Latin *praestigium* 'illusion'. The modern meaning, 'widespread respect and admiration', developed by way of the sense 'dazzling influence, glamour'. The idea is that the glamour of a person's past achievements can blind people to any possible faults they might have. The related adjective **prestigious** is an older word which originally described the skilful use of your hands when performing conjuring tricks. It only came to mean 'inspiring admiration' in the early 20th century. Magicians often say **hey presto!** to announce the climax of a trick. **Presto** is borrowed from Italian, in which it means 'quick or quickly', and comes ultimately from Latin *praestus*, 'ready'. **Presto, be gone** seems to have been a common feature of the patter of 17th-century conjurors and jugglers, and hey presto became popular in the following century. *See also* ABRACADABRA

presume *see* ASSUME

pretend [LME] The basic idea behind pretend is that you claim to be something that you are not. It comes from Latin

praetendere 'to claim, put forward', from *prae* 'before' and *tendere* 'stretch, hold out'.

pretty [OE] In his diary entry for 11 May 1660, Samuel Pepys mentions 'Dr Clerke, who I found to be a very pretty man and very knowing'. Pepys meant that the doctor was admirable, 'a fine fellow'. This is merely one of the many senses that pretty, a word that comes from a root meaning 'trick', has had over the centuries. The first was 'cunning, crafty', which was followed by 'clever, skilful', 'brave', and 'admirable, pleasing' before the main modern sense, 'attractive' appeared in the 15th century, each step in itself easily followed, even if the modern sense has come a long way from the original. Around that time the meaning 'considerable, great' also developed, which is now only found in **a pretty penny**. Pretty has been used as an adverb in the sense 'fairly, moderately', since the mid 16th century. **Sitting pretty**, 'comfortably placed or well situated', is originally American, and is first recorded in 1915.

prevent [LME] People originally used prevent to mean 'to act in anticipation of or in preparation for something', as in the 17th-century poet George Herbert's lines 'Thus we prevent the last great day, / And judge our selves.' Similarly, you could once talk about preventing someone's wishes or desires, for anticipating them. The word comes from Latin *praevenire* 'to precede or hinder'. In time to prevent something was to thwart someone's plans, from which developed the idea of stopping something from happening. **Prevention is better than cure** dates from the 17th century. An early example comes from 1618: 'Prevention is so much better than healing, because it saves the labour of being sick.'

prey *see* PRISON.

price [ME] The medieval word *pris*, which was from Old French, meant not only 'price' but also 'prize' and 'praise'. Over time these three meanings split into three different words. *Pris* became price, and the meaning 'praise' started to be spelled *preise* and then praise. Originally simply an alternative way of spelling price, prize too became a separate word. The Latin original of the French was *pretiem* 'price' which also lies behind **appreciate** [M18th], and the related **appraise** [M16th] and **apprize** [M16th], all with the basic sense of 'set a price to'; **depreciate** [M17th]; and **precious** [ME].

pride [OE] In Old English *pryde* was 'excessive self-esteem', and from medieval times pride was regarded as the first of the Seven Deadly Sins. Also medieval is its use to mean 'a social group of lions', although it died out only to be revived in the 19th century. As lions are the kings of beasts, the term was presumably felt to be appropriate for them. **Pride goes** (or **comes**) **before a fall** is a reworded version of a sentence from the biblical Book of Proverbs: 'Pride goeth before destruction, and an haughty spirit before a fall.' **Pride of place** is associated with falconry, referring to the high position from which a falcon swoops down on its prey. It is first recorded in Shakespeare's play *Macbeth*, in a passage suggesting how the natural order of things has been reversed following the killing of Duncan: 'A falcon, tow'ring in her pride of place, / Was by a mousing owl hawk'd at and kill'd.' Your **pride and joy** is the thing you are most proud of; the expression is recorded only from the beginning of the 20th century, but since the Middle Ages something a person is very proud of has been their 'pride'. Pride and joy may have been suggested from the poem *Rokeby* (1813) by Sir Walter Scott: 'See yon pale stripling! when a boy, / A mother's pride, a father's joy!'

priest [OE] The Greek *presbuteros* 'elder' was used in the New Testament for 'elder of the church, priest' and became *presbyter* in Latin, which passed into Old English as *preost*, modern 'priest'. Presbyter is also the source of **presbytery** [LME] and **Presbyterian** [M17th]. The usual Latin word for priest was *sacerdos* from *sacer* 'holy', which is the source of many words including **sacrament** [ME], **sacred** [LME], **sacrifice** [ME], and the opposite **execrate** [M16th] 'to curse'. The related **sacrilege** comes from Latin *sacrilegus* 'stealer of holy things'. *See also* SAINT

prig [M16th] A prig is a self-righteously moralistic person who behaves as if they are superior to others. Perhaps they would feel less superior if they knew that a prig in the 16th century was a tinker or a petty thief. As time went on the word came to be applied to anyone who was disliked, and by the end of the 17th century it was used specifically to describe someone who was affectedly and self-consciously precise.

prime [E16th] At the start of the 16th century to prime was 'to fill or load', especially a gun for firing. It was probably based on Latin *primus* 'first', also the source of the adjective prime [LME], since priming something is the first operation you perform before using it. **Priming the pump** of business refers to pouring a small amount of water into a mechanical pump to establish suction so that it can begin to work properly. *Primus* is also the source of **primary** [LME]; **primeval** (M17th from *primus* and *aevum* 'age'); and **primitive** [LME]. It is probably also the source of **prim** [L17th], via a Provençal variant *prin* meaning 'excellent, delicate'. Prim blended with sissy gives **prissy** [L19th].

prince [ME] The Latin word *princeps*, 'first, chief, sovereign', is the source of prince, and also of both **principal** [ME] meaning 'chief' and **principle** [LME] 'a rule or theory on which something is based'. A prince was originally a ruler of a smaller state, as in the **Prince of Wales**, a title that since the reign of Edward III has been given to the eldest son of the king or queen of England. At first this was the only use in England, but over time the term has been extended to include other members of the royal family. In the reign of James I it was applied to all the sons of the sovereign, and later, under Queen Victoria, to all the grandsons too. **Prince Charming** is the traditional name of the young prince who marries the heroine in a pantomime or fairy tale such as *Cinderella* or *Sleeping Beauty*. He first appeared as *Le roi Charmant*, or 'King Charming', in the French fairy story *The Blue Bird* (1698), and made his English debut in a play of 1851.

price   pride   priest   prig   prime   prince

print *see* PRESS

prison [OE] This comes via Old French
from Latin *prehendere* 'to seize'. *Prehendere*
is a rich source of English words, being
found, amongst many, in **apprehend**
[L16th], **comprehend** [L16th]; **prehensile**
[L18th]; and **reprehensible** [LME].
A shortening of *prehendere* lies behind
praedari 'plunder' and *praeda* 'booty',
which lie behind **depredation** [LME];
predatory [L16]; and **prey** [ME].

prissy *see* PRIME

private [LME] Someone who is private
has literally 'withdrawn from public life' and
is acting as an ordinary citizen—that is the
meaning of the Latin root, from *privare* 'to
bereave, deprive' from *privus* 'single,
individual'. It is also the root of **deprive**
[ME], **privilege** [ME], and **privation** [ME]. In
the army privates are ordinary soldiers as
opposed to officers. They were originally,
from the 1570s, **private soldiers**. Privates
meaning 'the genitals' is first recorded in
around 1450. Back in the 13th century **privy**,
which is from the same root, meant
'belonging to your own private circle'. The
meaning 'a lavatory' is as old and comes
from the idea of this being a private place.

prix fixe *see* FRENCH WORD PANEL

prize *see* PRICE

probate, probation, probe *see* PROOF

problem [LME] A problem was initially a
riddle or puzzle, or a question put forward
for academic discussion. 'Put forward' are
the key words here, as the ancestor of the
English word is the Greek verb *proballein*,
'to throw out or put forth'. This Greek word
is based on *pro* 'forward' and *ballein* 'to
throw', also the source of *BALLISTIC.

proceed *see* CEDE

procrastinate [L16th] To procrastinate
is to put off doing something. The Latin
word it comes from, *procrastinare*, had the
sense 'to put off till the morning', with the
cras part meaning 'tomorrow'. The saying

procrastination is the thief of time
originates in the poem *Night Thoughts*
(1742–45) by Edward Young:
'Procrastination is the Thief of Time; / Year
after year it steals, till all are fled.' *See*
mañana in SPANISH WORD PANEL

prodigy [LME] A prodigy initially was
something extraordinary considered to be
an omen. It comes from Latin *prodigium*
'portent'. It came to be applied to a person
possessing an amazing quality or talent in
the mid 17th century. Similarly **prodigious**
[LME] only developed the sense 'very large'
in the mid 17th century.

produce *see* DUCT

profane [LME] The early sense of this
was 'heathen' from Latin *profanus* 'outside
the temple, not sacred' from Latin *pro-*
'before' and *fanum* 'temple'.

profound *see* FOUND

progress [LME] Latin *progressus* 'an
advance', was formed from *pro-* 'forward'
and *gradi* 'to walk, proceed'. *Gradi* is also
found in **regress** [LME] 'walk backwards',
aggression [E17th] originally 'an attack' by
way of 'proceeding towards', and
ingredients [LME] 'things that enter into
something'.

project *see* JET

prologue *see* LOGIC

prominent *see* EMINENT

promiscuous *see* MISCELLANY

pronounce *see* ANNOUNCE

proof [ME] This came via Old French
proeve from Latin *probare*, 'to test or prove'.
Proof spirit or 100 per cent proof spirit was
originally defined as a solution of alcohol
that will ignite when mixed with
gunpowder—in Britain this meant an
alcohol content of 57.07 per cent. In the
expression **the proof of the pudding is in
the eating**, proof is used in the sense 'test'
rather than 'verification, proving to be true'.

print prison prissy private prix fixe prize

Probare is also the source of **prove** [ME], **probe** [LME], **probate** [LME] where you have to prove the will in law, and **probation** [LME] which is a form of testing.

propaganda [L17th] Today propaganda has negative connotations, with implications of bias and deception, but these date only from the mid 19th century. In 1622 Pope Gregory XV set up the *Congregatio de Propaganda Fide*, the 'Congregation for Propagation of the Faith' responsible for spreading the word of Christianity by missions around the world. **Propagate**, from the same Latin word, was already well established, having arrived in the 16th century.

propel *see* APPEAL

property [ME] Latin *proprius*, 'one's own, special, particular', source of **proper** [ME], developed an abstract noun *proprietas* 'ownership' which is not only the source of property, but of **proprietary** [LME], **proprietor** [M16th], and **propriety** [LME]. **Appropriate**, from a Latin word using *ad-* 'to', here in the sense 'making [one's own]' is from the same root.

prophet *see* EUPHEMISM

proprietary, propriety *see* PROPERTY

proscribe *see* POSTSCRIPT

prosody *see* ACCENT

prostitute *see* CONSTITUTION

protagonist *see* AGONY

protein *see* FIRST

protest *see* TESTICLE

prototype *see* FIRST

protract *see* ABSTRACT

prove *see* PROOF

proverb *see* WORD

provide *see* VISION

provoke *see* VOICE

prude [E18th] The old French word *prudefemme*, which was applied to a modest and respectable woman, was the source of prude in the early 18th century. This was the female equivalent of French *prud'homme* 'a good man and true'. The English word was used in a more negative sense than the French one, describing an excessively prim and demure woman, and is now applied to either sex.

prune *see* PLUM

Prussian *see* SPRUCE, ULTRAMARINE

psyche [M17th] We associate psyche with things of the mind, but to the Greek s*psukhē* meant 'breath, life, soul', which then developed into the idea of 'self'. This base is involved in the first element of the science terms **psychology** [late 17th], and **psychiatry** (mid 19th century from Greek *psukhē* and *iatreia* 'healing'). **Psychedelic** was coined in the 1950s from *psyche* and Greek *delos* 'clear, manifest'. The tale of Cupid and Psyche, a folk tale turned into an allegory of love and the soul, dates from the 2nd century AD, but probably has an earlier source. *See also* PNEUMATIC

pterodactyl *see* HELICOPTER

puberty [LME] Puberty is from Latin *pubertas*, from *puber* 'adult', related to *pubes* 'genitals' (source of **pubic** [E19th]).

public [LME] The root of public, Latin *publicus*, is shared by **publish** [ME] 'to make public' and **republic** [L16th] Latin *res public* 'the business of the people', and is related to *PEOPLE. People have been able to go to a **public house** for a drink since the 1650s, and to the abbreviated **pub** since around 1800. In Australia they could also stay the night—there a pub can also be a hotel. The first **publicans** were collectors of taxes (collectors of the public revenue), not sellers of drinks. This explains the disparaging references to them in various biblical passages, such as: 'And when the Pharisees saw it, they said unto his disciples, Why eateth your Master with publicans and sinners?' (Gospel of Matthew). The use of the term to refer to a person who manages a pub dates from the early 18th century. In North America and elsewhere **public schools** are schools supported by public funds and open to all, and people often wonder why English public schools, which are private, fee-paying, and independent, are so called. In England a public school, a term first recorded in 1580, was originally a grammar school founded for the benefit of the public, as opposed to a **private school** run for the profit of its owner. Such schools were open to all and took resident students from beyond their local neighbourhood. The passing of the Public Schools Act in 1868 to regulate the large, long-established schools of Eton, Winchester, Westminster, Harrow, Rugby, Charterhouse, Shrewsbury, Merchant Taylors', and St Paul's, led to the term becoming a prestigious one which was also applied to newer schools. The source of the saying **any publicity is good publicity** appears to be a passage by Raymond Chandler, in the *Black Mask* (1933): 'Rhonda Farr said: "Publicity, darling. Just publicity. Any kind is better than none at all." ' An alternative form is **there's no such thing as bad publicity**.

puce [L18th] This colour term is from a French word for 'flea'.

pucker *see* POCKET

pudding [ME] 'Black pudding' preserves the original meaning of pudding, 'a kind of sausage'. The link between this and the modern meaning is the idea of putting a filling into a casing, as is done when making sausages. The word was subsequently applied to various dishes made by tying ingredients up in a bag and cooking them. Puddings could be savoury, like a steak and kidney pudding, or sweet, like a Christmas pudding, but by the end of the 19th century a sweet pudding was a popular way to end a meal, and had become the word's dominant meaning. Pudding comes from Old French *boudin* 'black pudding', from Latin *botellus* 'sausage, small intestine'. When someone goes too far in doing or embellishing something, they are said to **over-egg the**

pudding. The idea is of using too many eggs in making a pudding, so that it does not set or cook properly or is too rich. *See also* BOWEL, PROOF

puddle [ME] Old English had a word *pudd* 'ditch, furrow', and a puddle was originally a small one of these. **Pool**, 'standing water' goes back to the same West Germanic root. The common Germanic heritage comes out in German *Pudel(hund)* the origin of the **poodle** [L18th]—*see* GERMAN WORD PANEL. Poodle sometimes has the sense 'lackey', introduced when Lloyd George called Lord Balfour a poodle in Parliament in 1907. The colloquial verb poodle meaning 'go around in a leisurely manner' is found from the 1930s.

puerile [L16th] 'Like a boy' was the early meaning. It comes from French *puéril* or Latin *puerilis*, from *puer* 'boy'. The sense 'childish behaviour' arose in the late 17th century.

puffin *see* PELICAN

pugnacious *see* POIGNANT

puke [L16th] This is probably imitative and was first recorded in Shakespeare's *As You Like It* 'At first the infant, mewling, and puking in the nurse's arms'.

pukka *see* RAJ WORD PANEL

pull [OE] A word that originally expressed a short sharp action, more like **pluck** [OE] or **snatch** [ME], all words with obscure origins. To **pull the plug** is to prevent something from happening or continuing. Nowadays this probably brings to mind the image of someone disconnecting an electrical device by pulling out the plug from the socket, but the plug referred to here is one found in a forerunner of the flushing toilet, used from the mid 18th century. To flush it you had to pull a stopper or plug. To **pull someone's leg**, or tease them, has been used since the late 19th century, but the idea probably goes back to the 16th century, when you might **pull someone by the ear**, **nose** or **sleeve** to insult or make fun of them. If you **pull out all the stops** you make a very great effort to

puce pucker pudding puddle puerile puffin

achieve something. The stops in this expression are the knobs or levers on a church organ which control the pipes. Pulling out all the stops will obviously result in the maximum volume possible.

pulley *see* POLE

pulse *see* APPEAL

pulverize *see* POWDER

punch [LME] The punch that means 'to strike' was first used in the sense 'to puncture or prod', which is probably where the term for a tool for making holes comes from. Ultimately, the word goes back to the same source as *POINT and *POIGNANT. A person doing something that might be thought to be beyond their capacity or ability can be said to be **punching above their weight**. This is a boxing metaphor—contests are generally arranged between opponents of nearly equal weight. The drink punch, first mentioned in English in 1600, has a completely different source. It seems to come, via Hindi, from Sanskrit *pañca* 'five, five kinds of'. The drink originally had five ingredients—strong alcohol, water, fruit juices, spices, and sugar. Finally, there is the Punch that appears in the early 19th-century expression **pleased as Punch** (or **proud as Punch**), referring to the gleeful self-satisfaction of the grotesque hook-nosed male character of the *Punch and Judy Show*. Punch was originally a dialect term for a short, fat person and is a short form of Punchinello, the name of a stout hook-nosed character in traditional Italian theatre.

punctilious, punctual, punctuation, puncture *see* POINT

pundit [L17th] A modern pundit is an expert in a particular subject called on to give their opinions about it to the public. The source of the word is Sanskrit *pandita* 'learned', used to describe a learned man versed in Sanskrit law, philosophy, and religion. The 'learned expert or authority' sense dates from the early 19th century.

pungent *see* POIGNANT

punish *see* PAIN

punk [L17th] Long before the days of Johnny Rotten and the Sex Pistols, all sorts of people found themselves labelled as punks. In the past the word has been used as a term for a prostitute, a male homosexual, and in show business for a youth or young animal. In American English it has been used since the early 20th century as a disparaging word for a person and in particular a young hooligan or petty criminal. In the film *Dirty Harry* (1971) Clint Eastwood says to a crook: 'I know what you're thinking. "Did he fire six shots or only five?" Well, to tell you the truth, in all this excitement I kind of lost track myself…You've got to ask yourself a question: Do I feel lucky? Well, do ya, punk?' Since the 1970s the word has been applied to admirers or players of **punk rock**, a loud, fast-moving, aggressive form of rock music: the first US mention of punk rock comes in 1971, five years before the first British punk record, 'New Rose' by the Damned. The original punk was not a person at all, but, in 17th-century North America, a term for soft crumbly wood that has been attacked by fungus. This was used as tinder as it caught fire easily. Its ultimate origin is not known, although it probably related to **spunk** [M16th], which originally meant a spark, a fire or tinder, before developing the senses 'courage and determination' [L18th], and 'semen' [L19th] which is itself of uncertain origin.

punt [OE] A flat-bottomed boat, a long kick, and a bet have little in common, and most dictionaries class punt as three separate words. The kind of boat you propel with a long pole is from Latin *ponto*, which meant 'flat-bottomed ferry boat' and is also the source of **pontoon**, a vessel used to support a temporary bridge or landing stage (*see also* PONTIFF). The punt that is a bet is a much later word, from the early 18th century and coming from French *ponte* or Spanish *ponto* 'point'. In English it first referred to a person playing a card game. **Punter**, 'a person who gambles', is from this word—the sense 'a customer or client' first appeared as recently as the 1960s. Punt meaning 'a long kick' is first recorded in the rules of football at Rugby School, home of rugby, in 1845, only 20 or so years after the game was invented. It may be from the local dialect word punt, meaning 'to push or kick'.

puny *see* POSTHUMOUS

pup [M16th] The word pup is a shortening of **puppy** [LME], from Old French *poupee* 'doll, plaything', which is related to **poppet** [LME] and **puppet** [M16th]. To **sell someone a pup** is to swindle them, especially by selling them something that is worth far less than they expect. This dates from the early 20th century and was presumably based on the idea of dishonestly selling someone a young and inexperienced dog when they were expecting an older, trained animal.

pupil [LME] The two words spelled pupil have entered English by different routes and acquired very different meanings, but they share a root, Latin *pupa*, which meant both 'doll' and 'girl'. The first pupil was originally an orphan or ward under the care of a guardian, from which emerged the idea of someone taught by another. It came into English via Old French from Latin *pupus* 'boy' and *pupa* 'girl'. The other pupil, the round opening in the centre of your eye, comes from the 'doll' meaning of *pupa*. People must have noticed the tiny images of themselves reflected in another person's eyes and thought they resembled little dolls (a similar idea is behind an old use of *BABY). In the 18th century *pupa* was borrowed directly from Latin as a term for an insect in its inactive immature form, between larva and adult.

puppet *see* PUP, DOLL

puppy *see* PUP

purdah *see* PERSIAN WORD PANEL

purple [OE] Just as *CRIMSON is named after an insect, so purple is named after a shellfish, and at one time these two words described the same colour. The first thing to be described as purple was a crimson dye obtained from some molluscs, called *porphyra* in Greek, the source also of the name of the purple stone called **porphyry** [LME]. The dye was rare and expensive and was used for colouring the robes of Roman emperors and magistrates. The actual colour of the dye varied widely, and over time the word came to mean the colour between red and blue that we now call purple. From the late 16th century purple has been used to mean 'striking' or 'ornate' in phrases such as **purple prose** or **a purple patch**. The latter term, describing an over-elaborate passage in a literary composition, is a translation of Latin *purpureus pannus* and comes from the Roman poet Horace's *Ars Poetica*: 'Works of serious purpose and grand promise often have a purple patch or two stitched on, to shine far and wide'.

purse [OE] A purse gets its name from its traditional material, leather. The word came into English some time in the 11th or 12th centuries from Latin *bursa*, which meant 'money bag' and also 'leather, animal skin'. *Bursa* is the source of **bursar** [L16th], **disburse** [M16th], and **reimburse** [E17th]. Despite the difference in spelling, it is also the root of **sporran**, a small pouch worn around the waist by Scotsmen as part of Highland dress. The Latin word developed into Irish *sparán* 'purse' and then Scottish Gaelic *sporan*, and was first used in English by the Scottish novelist Sir Walter Scott in the early 19th century.

pus *see* FOUL

push *see* APPEAL

putrid *see* FOUL

putz *see* YIDDISH WORD PANEL

puzzle [L16th] The word puzzle is a puzzle. Some have suggested that it is derived from **pose** (*see* PAUSE), just as **nuzzle** came from **nose**. Although pose did at one time mean 'to perplex someone or put them at a loss', the evidence for a connection between the two words is not strong and it is likely that they arose independently.

pyjamas *see* RAJ WORD PANEL

pyramid [LME] The word pyramid was first used in English in the geometrical sense. It came via Latin from Greek *puramis*, which also meant a type of cake. This is taken by some to be the earlier sense, the geometrical sense arising from a resemblance in shape. An Egyptian origin is now generally rejected. **Pediment** [L16th] for the triangular upper part of a building was formerly written as *periment* and may be an alteration of pyramid.

pyre, pyromaniac *see* FIRE

python [LME] A python's name comes from Greek *Puthōn*, the name of a huge serpent or monster killed by Apollo in Greek legend. Poets in the 17th and 18th centuries sometimes described any monster or plague as a python. Python was only used as a generic term for a snake that crushes its prey from the early 19th century. The BBC comedy series ***Monty Python's Flying Circus*** was first shown on 5 October 1969. The name was deliberately chosen to have no real meaning—it was the winning candidate from a list of absurd titles such as *Gwen Dibley's Flying Circus*, *Vaseline Review,* and *Owl-Stretching Time*. After a slow start the programme became so popular and influential that in 1975 it gave the language a new word, **Pythonesque**, to describe surreal humour.

pyx *see* BOX

pyjamas pyramid pyre pyromaniac python

Qq

Q-boat *see* DECOY

quack [M16th] 'If it looks like a duck, walks like a duck, and quacks like a duck, then it just may be a duck.' was the comment made by the US union leader Walter Reuther about the alleged communists investigated by Senator Joseph McCarthy in the early 1950s. The quack of a duck, recorded from the mid 16th century, is just an imitation of the bird's characteristic sound. The kind of quack who dishonestly claims to have medical skills was originally a **quacksalver**, a 17th-century word from Dutch *quacken* 'to talk foolishly' and *salf* the same word as '**salve**' [OE] from a Germanic base meaning 'clarified butter'.

quadrangle [LME] Latin *quattuor* 'four' and *angulus* 'corner, angle' are the base elements of quadrangle. The *quadri-* and *quadru-* in many English words also mean 'four' as in **quadrant** [ME], and from mid 17th century come **quadratic**; **quadrilateral**; and **quadruped**.

quaint [ME] In the Middle Ages quaint meant 'wise, clever', and 'ingenious, cunningly designed, or skilfully made'. Another early sense was 'beautiful or elegant'. Over time these meanings led to the more general notion of 'out of the ordinary'. The current use, describing something interestingly unusual or old-fashioned, is found from the late 18th century—before this, the word had become quite rare. It comes from Old French *cointe*, from Latin *cognoscere* 'to know', which is the root of words such as **acquaint** [ME], literally 'to make known to'; **cognoscenti** [L18th] from Italian for 'those who know'; *INCOGNITO; and *RECOGNIZE.

quality [ME] The early senses of this were 'character, disposition', and 'particular property or feature'. It comes from Latin *qualis* 'of what kind, of such a kind'. **Qualify** [LME] from the same root, was originally 'to describe (something) in a particular way'.

quango [1970s] Originally a US term, quango is an acronym from *quasi* (or *quasi-autonomous*) *non-government(al) organization*.

quantum [M16] Although you will often come across a sentence like 'This product represents a quantum leap forward in telecommunications technology', the curious thing about the term **quantum leap** is that, strictly speaking, it does not describe a large change at all, but a tiny one. Quantum comes from Latin *quantus*, 'how big?' or 'how much?', and originally meant 'a quantity or amount'. In physics a quantum (a term introduced by the physicist Max Planck around 1900) is a very small amount of energy, the minimum amount of energy that can exist in a given situation, and a **quantum jump** is the abrupt change of an electron or atom from one energy state to another. Although this is a tiny jump in terms of size, it is an instantaneous and dramatic one, which explains why the term came into general usage from around 1970 to describe a sudden large increase or major advance. **Quantity** [LME] comes from the same root as quantum.

quarantine [LME] Literally meaning '40 days', quarantine comes from Italian *quarantina*, from *quaranta* '40'. In the early 16th century this was the number of days during which a widow had the right to remain in her deceased husband's house. A more familiar meaning refers to a period of isolation imposed on a person or animal to test that they are not carrying a contagious disease. This was first used in English in the mid 17th century, though the practice dates back to the 14th century, when the ports of Venice and Ragusa (now Dubrovnik) required ships from plague-stricken countries to lie at anchor for 40 days before they were allowed to enter the ports.

quark [M20th] In physics a quark is a type of subatomic particle believed to be one of the basic constituents of matter. The name was coined in the 1960s by the American physicist Murray Gell-Mann, who initially spelt it *quork* but changed this to quark after he came across the line 'Three quarks for Muster Mark' in James Joyce's *Finnegans Wake* (1939). Joyce's word is meant to suggest the cawing sound seagulls make. It appealed to Gell-Mann, as at the time only three varieties of quark (known as up, down, and strange quarks) were believed to exist.

quarry [ME] The quarry that yields stone comes ultimately from Latin *quadrum* 'a square'. This is based on the idea that a quarry is a place where stones are squared, or cut into regular shapes, to make them ready for use in building. The other quarry, 'a pursued animal', is from Old French *cuiree* and based on Latin *cor* 'heart' (*see* CORDIAL). In medieval deer-hunting the term referred to the deer's entrails, which were placed on the hide and given as a reward to the hounds. It could also be used to refer to a heap of deer carcasses piled up after a hunt, and so to a pile of dead bodies: 'Then went they in haste to the quarry of the dead, but by no means could find the body of the King' (John Speed, *The History of Great Britain*, 1611).

quart [ME] Quart as a unit of capacity measuring a quarter of a gallon is from Old French *quarte*, from Latin *quarta* (*pars*) 'fourth (part)', from *quattuor* 'four'. The same base is shared by Middle English **quarter** and early 17th century **quartet** 'set of four'.

quartz [M18th] Quartz, a hard mineral consisting of silica, comes via German from Polish dialect *kwardy*, corresponding to Czech *tvrdý* 'hard'.

quay [LME] One of those words that seems designed to trip up poor spellers, this word was originally spelt as it is pronounced, *key*. It comes from Old French *kay*, of Celtic origin. The change of spelling occurred in the late 17th century, influenced by the modern French spelling *quai*. **Cay** or **key** for a sand bar is the same word.

queen [OE] The Old English spelling of queen was *cwēn*. This originally meant 'a wife', specifically that of a king or some other important man. Related to *cwēn* was Old English *cwene* 'woman', which became the archaic **quean**, 'a bold or impudent woman', sometimes encountered in Shakespeare's work. In the 16th and 17th centuries it was also a term for a prostitute. Because the two words came to be pronounced in the same way the derogatory sense dropped out of use as too confusing. The sense of queen 'an effeminate gay man' dates from the beginning of the 20th century.

queer [E16th] There is some doubt as to the origin of queer, but it may come from German *quer* 'oblique, perverse'. 'Eccentric' and 'strange' were early senses, though there was also the notion 'of questionable character, dubious'. The meaning 'unwell, ill' dates from the late 18th century, although it is often avoided now because of the potential confusion with the derogatory sense 'homosexual', recorded from the late 19th century.

A rather old-fashioned way of saying that someone is in difficulty, especially by being in debt, is to say that they are **in Queer Street**. This was an imaginary street where people in difficulties were supposed to live. Since the early 19th century the phrase has suggested various kinds of misfortune, though mainly financial difficulty: 'Queer Street is full of lodgers just at present' (Charles Dickens, *Our Mutual Friend*, 1865). To **queer someone's pitch** is to spoil their chances of doing something, especially secretly or maliciously. This started out as 19th-century slang. The 'pitch' in question was probably the spot where street performers stationed themselves or the site of a market trader's stall. **There's nowt so queer as folk** is first recorded in 1905, though it is described as an 'old saying'. **Nowt** is a Northern English variant of **nought**, 'nothing'.

quell *see* KILL

query *see* QUESTION

que sera sera *see* SPANISH WORD PANEL

question [LME] This comes via Old French from Latin *quaerere* 'ask, seek'. Also from *quaerere* are **query** [M17th] an anglicized form of the Latin *quaere*, 'Ask!' used in the 16th century in English as a verb in the sense 'enquire'; **quest** [LME]; and *INQUEST.

queue [L16th] Think of a long queue of people stretching back from a ticket office or bus stop. It looks a bit like an animal's tail, and this is the literal meaning of the word, which comes from French and was based on Latin *cauda* 'tail'. Queue was originally used as a heraldic term for the tail of an animal. In the 18th and 19th centuries it also referred to a pigtail, sometimes spelt cue, and source of the long thin rod **cue** [M16th] used in snooker. It came to describe a line of people in the mid 19th century.

quibble [E17th] A quibble was originally a pun or play on words. It probably comes from Latin *quibus*, meaning 'for which' or 'for whom', a word that often appeared in legal documents and so was associated with subtle distinctions or verbal niceties. The idea of a pun led to that of basing an argument on some likeness or difference between words or their meanings, and from this arose the notion of a petty objection or a trivial point of criticism.

quick [OE] The original meaning of quick in Old English was 'living' or 'alive', contrasting with something dead or inanimate. This early sense still survives in the expression **the quick and the dead**, meaning 'the living and the dead', which comes from the Apostles' Creed in the *Book of Common Prayer* (1662): 'From thence he shall come to judge the quick and the dead.' **Quicksand** [OE] is so called because it moves—and swallows things up—as if it were alive. The original 'alive' sense of quick also led to the use of the word to refer to the soft, tender flesh below the growing part of a fingernail or hoof. Nervous people might bite their nails right down 'to the quick'. This area is well supplied with nerves and is very

sensitive to touch or injury (and so seems more 'alive' than other parts of the skin). So **to cut someone to the quick** is to upset them very much by saying or doing something hurtful. It was a simple step in the word's history to go from 'alive' to senses such as 'lively' and 'vigorous' and, from the late 16th century, 'fast'. MERCURY was formerly known as **quicksilver**—the silver substance moves in such an unpredictable way that it seems to be alive.

quid [L17th] Nowadays quid is an informal word for one pound sterling, but it formerly referred specifically to a sovereign, a gold coin worth a pound. Its origin is unknown. In Australian English someone who is **not the full quid** is not very intelligent—in Britain the equivalent is **not the full shilling**. To be **quids in** is to be in luck or in a fortunate position, an expression that dates from the First World War.

quiet *see* QUIT

quintessence [LME] Classical and medieval philosophers believed that there were four elements that made up everything that existed in the world (*see* HUMOUR). In addition, they thought that there was a fifth substance hidden in all things, of which the heavenly bodies were composed. This they called the quintessence, from medieval Latin *quinta essentia* 'fifth *ESSENCE'. Later the word came to mean 'the most typical or perfect example or form of something', as in Sir Walter Scott's remark in a letter written in 1823, 'You have escaped the quintessence of bores.'

quisling [M20th] A quisling is a traitor who collaborates with an enemy force occupying their country. The original quisling was Major Vidkun Quisling, an army officer who ruled Norway on behalf of the German occupying forces during the Second World War. After the war he was charged with treason and executed.

quit [ME] An Old French word from the same root as **quiet**, Latin *quietus* 'quiet, still, resting'. The first meanings of quit were 'to

query   que sera sera   question   queue

pay off a debt', 'to repay a service or favour', and 'to set free'. It also meant 'to declare a person not guilty', a meaning for which we would now use the related word **acquit**. The modern meanings, 'to leave, go away', and 'to stop doing something', are from the 17th century. To **call it quits** is to agree that terms are now equal, especially in the settlement of a debt, or to decide to abandon what you are doing in order to cut your losses. It dates back only to the 1890s and is a fairly informal expression, but an earlier version, **cry quits**, is recorded from the 1630s and comes from the world of officialdom. Church records of accounts from the late 15th century use the word quits to indicate that money owing to someone has been paid in full. Church business was usually conducted in Latin, and so quits probably arose from a scribe's shortening of the medieval Latin word *quittus*, meaning 'discharged', written on receipts to indicate that the goods had been paid for. **Quite**, found from the Middle Ages in the sense 'completely, fully' is probably from quit. The sense 'fairly' does not develop until the 19th century.

quixotic [L18th] A quixotic person is idealistic, unrealistic, and impractical, like the hero of the Spanish novel *Don Quixote* (1605–15) by Miguel de Cervantes. Don Quixote is a middle-aged country gentleman obsessed with tales of chivalry who decides to become a knight and rides out with his squire Sancho Panza in search of adventure. *See also* TILT

quiz [L18th] The credit for inventing the word quiz is sometimes given to a late 18th-century Dublin theatre proprietor called Daly. He is said to have made a bet that he could introduce a new word into the language within 48 hours, and to have hired a number of street urchins to chalk the nonsensical quiz on walls all over the city. The next day all Dublin was talking about this new word. Unfortunately, there is no evidence to support this story. What we do know is that quiz was first used to mean either 'an odd or eccentric person', or 'an odd-looking thing', as in 'Where did you get that quiz of a hat?' (Jane Austen, *Northanger Abbey*, 1798). As a verb it originally meant 'to mock or make fun of someone'. The use of the word for a test of knowledge came later, in the 1860s, and might have been influenced by the word **inquisitive**. *See also* MILLION

quorum [LME] This originally referred to justices of the peace whose presence was needed to constitute a deciding body. It was used in commissions for committee members to attend, in the Latin phrase *quorum vos...unum* (*duos*, etc.) *esse volumus* meaning 'of whom we wish that you...be one (two, etc.)'.

quote [LME] This comes from medieval Latin *quotare*, from *quot* 'how many', source also of LME **quota**. The original sense was 'mark a book with numbers, or with marginal references'; later it came to mean 'give a reference by page or chapter' which led in the late 16th century to 'cite a text or person'. **Quotation** (apart from a rare appearance in Middle English meaning 'a numbering') dates from the mid 16th century when it was 'a marginal reference to a passage of text'. **Quotient** for the result of dividing one quantity by another comes from Latin *quotiens* 'how many times', from *quot*.

quoth *see* BEQUEATH

quit quixotic quiz quorum quote quoth

R r

rabbit [LME] We think of rabbits as being as much part of the language as of the countryside, but the rabbit was introduced to Britain by the Normans in the 12th century to provide meat and fur. The name is not recorded until the late 14th century, when it meant particularly a young animal of this kind. Before that, rabbits were known as **conies**. In 16th-century slang a coney was what we would now call a mark—someone to cheat or rob, and doing so was known as 'coney-catching'. We are not sure where rabbit comes from, but it seems to have come into English from Old French, related to French dialect *rabotte* meaning 'young rabbit'. It may be of Dutch origin and have a link with Flemish *robbei* 'rabbit'. To **breed like rabbits** is to reproduce prolifically, like the animal itself. This view of rabbits is of quite long standing. In 1868 Queen Victoria explained why she could not be too excited by acquiring a fourteenth grandchild. 'It seems to me' she wrote to her eldest daughter 'to go on like the rabbits in Windsor Park!' A person who chatters incessantly is sometimes said to 'rabbit on'. This expression comes from mid 20th-century rhyming slang, in which **rabbit and pork** means 'talk'. *See also* BUNNY

rabid, rabies *see* RAGE

raccoon *see* NATIVE AMERICAN PANEL

race [OE] The earliest sense of race was of rapid forward movement. It was originally a word from northern English, which entered the general language around the middle of the 16th century. It comes from Old Norse *rás* 'current'. Senses that developed at this period were 'contest of speed' and 'channel, path', as in **mill race** or 'mill stream'. The idea of **a race against time** as a situation in which you try to do or complete something in a given time or before something else happens is found from the mid 19th century. Race with the meaning 'a division of humankind' dates from the 16th century, and is a quite different word. It probably comes from an Italian word, *razza*, of unknown origin. *See also* RAT

rack [ME] The rack is the name of a medieval instrument of torture. It consisted of a frame on which a victim was stretched by turning rollers to which their wrists and ankles were tied. To rack someone was to torture them on this device, and from this we get **rack your brains** [L16th] to mean 'to make a great effort to think of or remember something'. The rack [ME] that you stand things on is related, and both come from German *rek* 'horizontal bar or shelf'. This is not, however, the origin of winemaking rack meaning 'draw off the sediment' [LME]. This is from Provençal *arracar*, from *raca* 'stems and husks of grapes, dregs'. Another use of rack [L16th] represents yet another word. When something deteriorates through neglect we may say that it is **going to rack and ruin**. Rack here is a variant spelling of **wrack**, meaning 'destruction' and is related to *WRECK.

racket [LME] In Middle English this is a game a bit like modern squash or real tennis (*see* PILLAR), only appearing as the bat used to hit the ball around 1500. The word comes from a French and Italian term for 'palm of the hand', for the ball was originally hit with the hand. The noisy sort of racket is a separate word, which appeared in the mid 16th century, perhaps in imitation of the noise. The sort of racket practised by a **racketeer** [E20th] seems to have evolved from this.

radar [M20] This system for detecting objects by sending out radio waves which are reflected back was developed in the 1930s. The name comes from the opening letters of **ra**dio **d**etection **a**nd **r**anging, and was coined in 1941. Police started using **radar traps** to detect speeding motorists in the early 1960s. In the Second World War the myth that pilots ate lots of carrots to help them see in the dark was spread to explain how they could detect enemy planes, as radar was still a secret. Other words have been coined on the pattern of radar, such as **lidar** [M20th], which works like radar, but uses light from lasers [M20th]—**laser** itself being an acronym from 'light amplification by the stimulated emission of radiation'.

radiation see RAY

radical [LME] The earliest sense of radical is 'having to do with the basic nature of something, fundamental', and it goes back to Latin *radix* 'root', the source also of **eradicate** [LME] 'to root out' and **radish** [OE], and related to *ROOT. In political terms, a radical is someone who wants complete political or social reform—to be achieved by going to the root of the problem. In the 1970s, the American writer Tom Wolfe coined **radical chic** for a fashionable affectation of radical left-wing views.

radio, radius see RAY

raft [LME] In the Middle Ages a raft was a beam or **rafter** (OE from the same root). The source was Old Norse *raptr* 'rafter'. Politicians of today often talk about their party having **a whole raft of** policies. Raft meaning 'a large amount' appears in the 19th century. It represents an alteration of a dialect word *raff* meaning 'abundance', probably by association with the earlier raft 'floating mass'.

rag [ME] A Scandinavian word for 'tufted' probably lies behind rag. In **lose your rag** [E20th] 'to lose your temper', rag is probably an old slang term for the tongue—the phrase was originally **get your rag out**. This sense of rag may well be behind the student rag or prank, found from the early 19th century, and the dated verb meaning 'to tease, play a joke on'. **From rags to riches** describes someone's rise from a state of extreme poverty to great wealth, as in a fairytale like Cinderella. The concept is ancient, but the phrase was not recorded until the late 19th century, when a play

called *From Rags to Riches* was mentioned in a US newspaper. A group of people regarded as disreputable or undesirable may be described as **ragtag and bobtail**. **Bobtail** [E17th] was an established term for a horse or dog with a docked tail, but rag and **tag** (LME of unknown origin) were separate words conveying the same meaning of 'tattered or ragged clothes'. Putting them together gives you the literal sense of 'people in ragged clothes together with their dogs and horses'. In one traditional folk song a lady leaves her house, land, and 'new-wedded lord' to run away with 'the raggle-taggle gypsies'. **Raggle-taggle** [L19th] here is an elaboration of **ragtag**. Similarly **ragamuffin** is probably an elaboration of rag. The word is found once *c.*1400 as the name of a devil, but then not until 1586. The 1990s term **ragga** for a style of dance music is taken from ragamuffin, because of the style of clothing worn by its fans. **Rug** [M16th], once a name for a type of coarse woollen cloth, is probably from the same root. The sense 'small carpet' dates from the early 19th century. So too is **rugged** [ME]. 'Shaggy' was an early sense of *rugged* as was 'rough-coated' (in descriptions of horses).

ragamuffin see RAG

rage [ME] In medieval times rage could also mean 'madness'. It goes back ultimately to Latin *rabere* 'to rave', which is also the source of **rabies**, and early 17th-century **rabid** of which the early sense was 'furious, madly violent' (Dickens *Dombey and Son*: 'He was made so rabid by the gout'). The sense 'affected with rabies' arose in the early 19th century. Since the late 18th century something that is the subject of a widespread temporary enthusiasm or fashion has been described as **the rage** or **all the rage** to mean 'very popular or fashionable'. In 1811 the poet Lord Byron wrote that he was to hear his fellow poet Samuel Taylor Coleridge, 'who is a kind of rage at present'. Bad drivers have always caused annoyance, but with increasing traffic and pace of life some people are now provoked into **road rage**. The phrase is first recorded in 1988, since when many other

radiation radical radio radius raft rag

kinds of rage have been reported, among them **air rage**, **trolley rage** in a supermarket, and even **golf rage**. Enrage dates from the late 15th century.

ragga, raggle-taggle *see* RAG

Ragnarök *see* TWILIGHT

rail [ME] You might think that trains have no link to the classical world, but the word rail goes back to Latin *regula* 'straight stick', the source also of *RULE. The first rails that vehicles ran along—pulled then by horses— are described in the account of an English colliery at the end of the 16th century. Before that a rail was a fixed bar forming part of a fence, which in due course gave us both **railings** [LME] and the rails of a racecourse. References to **railways** begin in the late 17th century, followed a little later by **railroad**, now the American term but at first used in Britain interchangeably with railway. Someone whose behaviour is out of control may be said to have **gone off the rails**. The phrase is first recorded in 1848, when railways and trains would have been a novelty. Someone who complains bitterly is sometimes said to rail [LME]. This is a completely different word, and goes back ultimately to Latin *rugire* 'to roar' (*see also* RUT).

rain [OE] The word rain, spelt *regn* in Old English, features in a number of sayings and common expressions. The phrase it is **raining cats and dogs** is first found in the 18th century, but the alternative **rain dogs and polecats** goes back a further hundred years. That in the past, gullible people might have believed that drowned dogs and cats seen floating in flooded streets had fallen from the skies during the previous heavy downpour is the best that has been found by way of explanation. Someone concerned about a future period of financial need might talk about saving for a **rainy day**. This may go back to the days when farm labourers working on a casual basis needed to save a proportion of their wages for times when bad weather stopped them working and earning money. One way of politely refusing an offer is to imply that you might take it up at a later date, or **take a rain check**. In the USA a rain check is a ticket given to spectators at a sporting event. If the event is cancelled because of rain—or 'rained off'—they can then claim a refund.

rainbow *see* BOW

raise *see* RETRO

raj *see* RAJ WORD PANEL

Proper pukka

*Early in the 17th century Britain began to take an interest in India, and the impact of its languages on English goes back almost as far. But it was the **Raj**—the British colonial rule—that fixed many Indian words in the language.*

SOME terms were consciously borrowed. In the 18th century a wealthy man who had made his fortune in India might be called a **nabob**, a word that came ultimately from Urdu (a language of northern India which took many words from Persian), and was originally the name for a Muslim official under the Mogul empire. **Sahib** was a polite title for a man in British India, and **memsahib** for a woman—sahib came via Urdu from

Arabic *sāhib* 'friend, lord', while the *mem-* in **memsahib** was an Indian pronunciation of **ma'am**.

Other words have become so much part of the language that it is easy to forget their Indian origin. Living in a **bungalow** may seem completely part of the British scene, but the first 'bungalows' were cottages built in Bengal for early European settlers there, and the name comes from a Hindi word meaning 'belonging to Bengal'. If you make out a **chit** for someone's expenses, you are using a term that comes from Hindi *citthī* 'a note or pass'.

British chef Jamie Oliver gleefully introduced **pukka** to millions of TV viewers in the slang sense 'excellent', but the word was being used in India as far back as the middle of the 17th century. Its first sense was 'of full weight', which gradually evolved into 'certain, reliable' and 'genuine, authentic', then 'top-quality, impeccable', and 'socially acceptable, well brought up'. Jamie's sense is of early 1990s vintage. The word is from Hindi *pakkā*, meaning 'cooked, ripe, or substantial'. And Indian cuisine has contributed other familiar terms, including **curry**, from a Tamil word adopted in the late 16th century, and **kedgeree**, from Hindi *khichri*, originally a dish of rice and pulses. Things first got **cushy** during the First World War. It was originally an Anglo-Indian word from Urdu *kushi* 'pleasure', going back to Persian *kus*. As well as describing an easy job or post, cushy could also be used in connection with a wound that was not dangerous or serious.

Riders have been wearing **jodhpurs** since the late 19th century. The word comes from Jodhpur, a city in western India where similar garments are worn by men as a part of everyday dress. The **gymkhana**, a children's event with races and other competitions on horseback, is now a staple of every pony club, but in Victorian India it was a public place with facilities for sports. The English form of the word, which comes from the Urdu term *gendkhāna*, meaning 'racket court', has been influenced by the spelling of **gymnastic**. The **pyjamas** we put on at night are literally 'leg clothing'—the word is from Urdu *pāy* 'leg' and *jāma* 'clothing'. They were originally loose silk or cotton trousers that both men and women wore in such countries as Turkey, Iran, and India, until Europeans living in these places started wearing them for bed. A man might wear a **cummerbund**, a kind of sash, around his waist as part of evening dress for a smart party, but it was first worn in the Indian subcontinent by domestic staff and office workers of low status. The word is from Urdu *kamar-band*, from *kamar* 'waist or groin' and *bandi* 'band'.

Some Indian-based words may look misleadingly as though they come from familiar English words. **Shampoo**, for example, has nothing to do with **sham**, or with **poo**. English speakers first came across the term in the 18th century in Turkish baths, where the original use was 'to give a massage to'. The word itself is from Hindi *cāmpo!*, an instruction to a masseur to 'press!'. The 1930s slang word of approval, **tickety-boo**, has no association with **tick** or **ticket**, but probably comes from a Hindi expression *thīk hai* 'all right'.

The British rule of India as a Crown possession from 1858 to 1947 is known as the **Raj**, from the Hindi word *rāj* 'reign'. The Raj itself has long since passed into history, but the term is still with us. Evidence of its lasting impact on the language came in 2005, when the journalist Jeremy Paxman reached for it to describe the number of Scottish politicians at Westminster. 'We live', he said, 'under a sort of Scottish Raj.'

See also HORDE, INDIAN, JUGGERNAUT, JUNGLE, LOOT, THUG, VINDALOO

rake [OE] The rake used by gardeners to smooth soil or gather leaves in autumn is an Old English word, from a root meaning 'heap up'. **Thin as a rake** is a comparison used since Geoffrey Chaucer's day. The phrases **rake over old coals** and **rake over the ashes** come from the idea of searching through a dead or dying fire to see if a spark remains. For reviving memories the expression came into use in the USA in the mid 19th century. A fashionable, rich but immoral man can also be known as a rake. This is an abbreviation of the old word **rakehell** [M16th], which had the same meaning: the original idea was of the kind of sinful person likely to be found if you searched through Hell with a rake. A **rake's progress** is a progressive deterioration, especially through self-indulgence—*A Rake's Progress* was a series of engravings by the 18th-century artist William Hogarth, which depicted the progression of the rake from wealthy and privileged origins to debt, despair, and death on the gallows.

rampant [ME] Something rampant flourishes or spreads in an uncontrolled way. This is a development of the original use in heraldry, which described an animal, like the **lion rampant** of Scotland, rearing up on its left hind foot with its forefeet in the air. Its origins are much less vigorous, going back to French *ramper*, which means 'to creep, crawl', or 'to climb'. **Rampage** [L17th], originally a Scottish word, comes from the same root, as does the **ramp**, used in Middle English to mean 'to rear up', and as a slope to get you up to another level from the late 18th century

ramshackle [E19th] A shaky building or a car with its bumper tied on with string might

be called ramshackle, but it has nothing to do with rams or shackles. The word was originally a dialect term meaning 'irregular, disorderly', and is related to *RANSACK.

ranch [E19th] The ranch featuring in many Westerns appears in American sources from the early 19th century and comes from Spanish *rancho*, 'a group of people eating together'. The phrase **meanwhile back at the ranch** was originally used in cowboy stories to introduce a subsidiary plot.

rancid [E17th] Latin *rancidus* which means 'stinking' is the source of rancid in English. The related *rancor* 'rankness' gives us **rancour** [ME].

random [ME] In early use random referred to an 'impetuous headlong rush'. It comes from Old French *randon* 'great speed', from a Germanic root.

rank [OE] In relation to position in a hierarchy, rank has the same root as *RING, and has been part of the language since medieval times, when it came into English from Old French. When we talk about the **rank and file** of an organization we mean the ordinary members as distinct from the leaders. This goes back to the idea of rows and columns of soldiers in military formation, drawn up 'in rank and file', the ranks being the rows and the files the columns. If you fail to maintain solidarity with your fellows you **break ranks**, and if you unite to defend a common interest you **close ranks**. In the armed forces **the ranks** are those who are not commissioned officers: if you work your way up from a lowly position to one of seniority you may be said to have **risen from the ranks**. Rank

rake rampant ramshackle ranch rancid

as an adjective is a different word, which dates back to Old English. Early senses included 'fully grown' and 'luxuriant', but later meanings involve the idea of disagreeable excess: a rank smell is extremely unpleasant, and rank grass grows too thickly.

ransack [ME] This is a word which is still very close in meaning to its original 14th-century sense. The Old Norse word *rannsaka* from which it comes, made up of *rann* 'house' and a second element related to 'seek', was a legal term referring to the searching of property for stolen goods. *See also* RAMSHACKLE

ransom [ME] In medieval times a captured enemy might be released if a sum of money, or ransom, was paid, and if you held them captive and demanded such a payment you were said to **hold them to ransom**. The word comes from the same Latin root as **redeem** [LME], and **redemption** [ME] *redimere* 'buy back'. *See also* KING

rap [ME] The word rap, in the sense of a blow, is of Scandinavian origin and is probably like **clap** [LME] and **flap** [ME], meant to imitate the sound. Since the end of the 18th century rap has been associated with rebuke and punishment, as in the phrase **a rap on the knuckles** for a sharp criticism. In early 20th-century American English the word developed the further meanings of 'a criminal charge' and 'a prison sentence'. If you were acquitted you were said to **beat the rap**. To **take the rap** was to be punished or blamed, especially for something where other people were wholly or partly responsible. Performers of rap music tend to have a dangerous, bad-boy image, but the root of the term is not the 'criminal charge' or 'prison' senses but the old northern English sense 'conversation, chat'. This was carried over the Atlantic, and rap in the sense 'a talk or discussion' is now an American use. The first reference to rap music comes in 1979.

rape [LME] This originally referred to the violent seizure of property, and later to the carrying off of a woman by force. It comes via Anglo-Norman French from Latin *rapere* 'seize', also the source of the word **rapacious** and **rapid** [both M17th], and of **rapt** [LME] and **rapture** [L16th], when you are carried away by your feelings. In Old French *repere* was changed to *ravir*, source of **ravish** [ME]. The plant name, rape, originally referred to the turnip. It is from Latin *rapum, rapa* 'turnip'.

rapid, rapt, rapture *see* RAPE

raspberry [E17th] A raspberry was originally a *rasp* or a *raspis*, but the ultimate origin of all these words is unknown. To **blow a raspberry** is to make a derisive or contemptuous sound with your lips. The expression comes from rhyming slang, where **raspberry tart** means 'fart'. *See also* CHEER

rastafarian *see* REGGAE

rat [OE] The rat has been part of our language since Anglo-Saxon times, but its ultimate origin is not known. It probably goes back to the time when the creature first came to Europe from Asia. The term **rat race** has been used since the mid 20th century. The image behind this is of rats struggling with each other to move forward in a confined space, rather than of the ordered world of a race track. Sailing ships would traditionally have been infested with rats, which would try to escape en masse from a vessel that was in trouble. This gave rise to **rats deserting a sinking ship**.
A person has been a rat since the 1760s, and 50 or so years later to rat started to mean 'to desert a cause, become a traitor' and then 'to inform on'. Someone who suspects a trick is said to **smell a rat**—a phrase which in the 18th century is found as part of an elaborate mixed metaphor attributed to an Irish politician, Boyle Roche: 'Mr Speaker, I smell a rat; I see him forming in the air and darkening the sky; but I'll nip him in the bud.'

ration [M16th] The words **ratio** [M16], ration, and **rational** [LME] all come from the Latin root, *ratio* 'reckoning, reason'. The

ransack   ransom   rap   rape   rapid   rapt

use of ration for 'a fixed allowance' became particularly associated with official control of scarce food supplies, or **rationing**, at the time of the First World War. Before that it was used in the armed forces for a soldier's daily share of the provisions.

ravel *see* UNRAVEL

ravish *see* RAPE

raw [OE] This Old English word shares an ancient root with Greek *kreas* 'raw flesh'. In Australian English a stupid person can be referred to as a **prawn** (ME of unknown origin), and to **come the raw prawn** is to attempt to deceive someone, presumably by pretending that you are too simple to cheat.

ray [ME] The ray that means 'beam of light' is a medieval word going back to Latin *radius* 'spoke, ray', the source of **radiate** [L16th], **radio** [E20th], and **radius** [L16th]. The term **ray of sunshine** for someone who brings happiness into the lives of others, dating back to the early 20th century, is often used ironically for someone who in fact spreads little cheer. **Ray** as a name for a fish is a different word, from Latin *raia*.

razzle, razzmatazz *see* DAZE

read [OE] Alfred the Great, king of Wessex between 871 and 899, did much to promote education in his kingdom, and the word read is first found in his writings. The word goes back to a Germanic root meaning 'advise, guess, interpret', and Old English **riddle** comes from the same root. **The three Rs** [E19th] have been 'reading, (w)riting, and (a)rithmetic', regarded as the fundamentals of elementary education. The expression is said to have originated as a toast proposed by the banker and politician Sir William Curtis (1752–1829). **Read my lips** was most famously used by the first President Bush in 1998. In making a campaign pledge not to raise taxes, he said 'Read my lips: no new taxes.' If you want to give someone a severe warning or reprimand, you may **read the riot act** to them. The Riot Act was passed by the British government in 1715 to prevent civil disorder in the wake of the Jacobite rebellion of that year. The Act made it an

offence for a group of twelve or more people to refuse to disperse within an hour of being ordered to do so, after a magistrate had read a particular section of the Act to them. This created something of a problem, as reading legal language aloud is not the easiest thing to do in the middle of a genuine riot—and defendants might claim later that they had not heard the key words. The Act failed to prevent a number of major disturbances over the years, but was not repealed until 1967. **Riot** [ME] originally meant dissolute living and comes from an Old French word meaning 'to quarrel'.

real [LME] Latin *res* 'thing' lies behind real. It developed a form *realis* 'relating to things' which came into English via French as a legal term which still survives in the expressions **real property** and **real estate**. Real estate is so-called because it is immovable property such as land and houses, the opposite of personal property. **Realize** [E17th] was originally used to mean 'to make real' as in **to realize your plans**. The sense 'become aware' started in American English in the late 18th century; it was often condemned by English writers in the middle of the 19th century.

ream [LME] The term ream for 500 sheets of paper goes back ultimately to Arabic *rizma* 'bundle'. In the later 16th century it came to mean a large quantity of paper, without reference to the specific number of sheets—in 1814 Sir Walter Scott referred to 'whole reams of modern plays'. In turn this gave us the general use of **reams of** to mean 'a large quantity of', which is found from the beginning of the 20th century.

reap [OE] Reap is something of a mystery. We do not know its origin, and it has no matching words in related languages. A person who seems unwilling to face up to the consequences of their actions may be told that **you reap what you sow**. This proverbial saying goes back to a verse in the biblical Epistle to the Galatians: 'Be not deceived; God is not mocked: for whatsoever a man soweth, that shall he also reap.' *See also* GRIM

ravel ravish raw ray razzle razzmatazz

rear *see* RETRO

reason [ME] The ultimate source of reason is Latin *reri* 'to consider', which is also the root of *RATION and associated words. **Theirs not to reason why** comes from Lord Tennyson's poem 'The Charge of the Light Brigade' (1854). This describes a notorious incident in the Crimean War, when British cavalry unhesitatingly obeyed a suicidal order to ride straight at the Russian guns. *See also* RHYME

reaver *see* ROB

rebel [ME] The Latin word *rebellis* was originally used in reference to someone making a fresh declaration of war after being defeated. The root was *bellum* 'war', as in **bellicose** [LME] or 'warlike', combined with *re-* 'again'. A person who is deeply dissatisfied by society in general but does not have a specific aim to fight for might be described as **a rebel without a cause**. The first such person was James Dean, star of the 1955 film *Rebel Without a Cause*. **Revel** [LME] comes from the French equivalent, which developed the sense 'to make a noise' from the basic sense 'to rise in rebellion'.

rebound *see* BOUND

rebuke [ME] Someone who has been rebuked or told off may feel cut down to size—its source is medieval French *rebuker*, which originally meant 'to cut down wood'.

recalcitrant [M19th] This word is from Latin *recalcitrare* 'kick out with the heels', based on *calx* 'heel'.

recall *see* CALL

recede *see* CEDE

receive *see* CAPABLE

recite [LME] This was first used as a legal term in the sense 'state (a fact) in a document', but the sense 'repeat aloud something learned by heart' soon followed. It comes via French from Latin *recitare* 'read out', from *re-* (a sense intensifier here) and *citare* 'cite',

source of **cite** [LME] which originally meant to summon someone to court.

reclaim *see* CLAIM

recline *see* LEAN

recluse *see* CLOSET

recognize [LME] To recognize someone is literally to know them again, from Latin *recognoscere*, from *re-* 'again' and *cognoscere* 'to know'. Already in Latin this had developed logical extensions to the senses such as 'examine, acknowledge, certify'. It was in these legal senses that the word first entered English, alongside **recognition**. Its use to mean 'know by some distinctive feature' dates only from the early 18th century. **Reconnaissance** [E19th] and **reconnoitre** [E18th] both come from the French form of the word, *reconnoître*. *See* QUAINT

recoil [ME] This word first meant the act of retreating. It is from Old French *reculer* 'move back', based on Latin *culus* 'buttocks'. The sense 'spring back in horror' dates from the early 16th century.

recollect *see* COLLECT

recommend *see* COMMANDO

recompense *see* PENDANT

reconnaissance, reconnoitre *see* RECOGNIZE

recount *see* COUNT

recover [ME] This was originally with reference to health, with the modern sense appearing soon after. It comes from Anglo-Norman French *recoverer*, from Latin *recuperare* 'get again', from which the similar **recuperate** [M16th] was taken directly.

recreation *see* CREATURE

recriminate *see* CRIME

rectangle [L16th] A rectangle is a shape made up of four right angles, and both English and the Latin source of the word use

rear reason reaver rebel rebound rebuke

the same image, for rectangle comes from *rectus* 'right, straight' combined with *angulus* 'angle', also found in *ANGLE itself. *Rectus* is the source of a number of words in English including **direct** [LME] 'in a straight line', **rectify** [LME] 'put right', **rectitude** [LME] 'straightness', and **rectum** [M16th] from the Latin *rectum intestinum* 'straight intestine'

rector *see* REGENCY, VICAR

rectum *see* RECTANGLE

recuperate *see* RECOVER

recur *see* CURSOR

red [OE] An Old English word which shares an ancient root with Latin *rufus*, Greek *eruthros*, and Sanskrit *rudhira* 'red'. The colour red has traditionally been associated with radical political views, and from the 19th century particularly Communists. During the Cold War, when Americans feared **reds under the bed** or Communist sympathizers, the expression **better dead than red** was used to mean that the prospect of nuclear annihilation was preferable to that of a Communist society. The slogan was reversed by nuclear disarmament campaigners of the late 1950s as 'better red than dead'. Something involving savage or merciless competition might be described as **red in tooth and claw**. The phrase came from Lord Tennyson's poem 'In Memoriam' (1854): 'Nature, red in tooth and claw'. In Church calendars a saint's day or Church festival was distinguished by being written in red letters. This gives us a **red letter day** [E18th] for a pleasantly memorable, fortunate, or happy day. A less cheering use of red ink was customarily made to enter debit items and balances in accounts —which gives us **in the red** [E20th] to mean in debt or overdrawn.

The colour red is supposed to provoke a bull, and is the colour of the cape used by matadors in bullfighting. From this we say that something will be like a **red rag to a bull** [L19th]. A **red herring** is something, especially a clue, which misleads or distracts you. Red herrings have been around since the 15th century and got their colour from being heavily smoked to preserve them. The pungent scent was formerly used to lay a trail when training hounds to follow a scent. The **red light district** of a town is one with a lot of businesses concerned with sex. The phrase is from the red light traditionally used as the sign of a brothel. *See also* PAINT. People have been complaining about **red tape**, or excessive bureaucracy, since the 1730s. Real red or pinkish-red tape is used to bind together legal and official documents. Americans sometimes talk of not having a **red cent** to their name. Red got attached to the cent in the mid 19th century and refers to the colour of the copper used to make the one cent coin. **Ruddy** is from Old English *rud*, a variant form of 'red'. The word's use as a euphemism for *bloody* dates from the early 20th century.

redeem, redemption *see* RANSOM

redstart *see* NAKED

reduce *see* DUCT

reef [L16th] A coral reef is often curved in the shape of a rib, which is the origin of the word, as it comes from Old Norse *rif* 'rib, reef'.

reek [OE] We think of a reek today as an unpleasant smell, but in Old English the word meant 'smoke'. This gave us the traditional name, used since at least the beginning of the 19th century, of **Auld Reekie** ('Old Smoky') for Edinburgh.

refer [LME] Refer comes from Latin *referre* 'carry back', from *re-* 'back' and *ferre* 'bring'. **Referee** dates from the early 17th century, but did not appear in sports contexts until the mid 19th century. *Referre* is also the source of mid 19th-century **referendum** from the Latin for 'referring'. *Ferre* is the source of numerous words in English including **confer** 'bring together'; **defer** 'put to one side or away', which shares an origin with **differ**; **fertile** 'bearing'; and **transfer**

'carry across', all of which came into the language in the Late Middle English period.

reference *see* RESPECT

refine *see* FINANCE

reform *see* FORM

refrigerate, refrigerator *see* FRIGID

refuge, refugee *see* FEVER

refusenik *see* YIDDISH WORD PANEL

regal *see* REGENCY

regard *see* REWARD

regency [LME] Between 1811 and 1820 George, Prince of Wales was **regent** [LME] for his father King George III, who was suffering from a long-term mental illness. The prince was known for his fun-loving lifestyle and support for the arts, and the period of **the Regency** was noted for its distinctive fashions and architecture—such as, for example, the wildly exotic Brighton Pavilion designed by John Nash. The balls and parties held by the aristocracy of the time are imagined in the romantic historical novels set in this period and called **Regency romances**. The source of regency is Latin *regere* 'to govern, rule', which means it is related to words like **regal** [LME] 'like a ruler'; **rector** [LME] 'governor'(*see* VICAR); **regime** [LME] 'rule or regulation'; **regiment** [LME] which originally had the same sense as regime; **region** [ME] an area governed; **regular** [LME] originally 'governed by a rule'; *ROYAL; and *RULE.

reggae [1960s] This word for a popular style of music with a strongly accented subsidiary beat may be related to Jamaican English *rege-rege* 'quarrel, row'. At one time reggae was strongly associated with **Rastafarians** [M20th]. They got their name from their belief that Ras Tafari, another name for the Emperor Haile Selassie of Ethopia (1892–1975), was God Incarnate. This word has been a model for new coinages, of which the best known is the **trustafarian**—young people who can spend

their time having fun because they have an income from a trust fund.

regime, regiment, region *see* REGENCY

regress *see* PROGRESS

regular *see* REGENCY

regurgitate [L16th] This comes from medieval Latin *regurgitare*, formed from Latin re- 'again, back' and *gurges* 'whirlpool'. It was first applied to fluids or gases to mean 'gush, pour back again'. It was only in the mid 18th century that it came to mean vomit.

reimburse *see* PURSE

reiver *see* ROB

rejoice *see* JOY

rejuvenate *see* YOUNG

relax, relay, release *see* LANGUISH

relieve *see* ELEVATE

relinquish *see* DERELICT

relish [ME] The word relish is an alteration of obsolete *reles* which comes from Old French *reles* 'remainder'. The early noun sense was 'odour, taste', something that is left behind. This gave rise in the mid 17th century to 'appetizing flavour, piquant taste', leading to its use as a term for 'condiment' in the late 18th century.

reluctant [M17th] This is a word that has lost much of its strength. The early sense was 'writhing, offering opposition' as in Milton's *Paradise Lost*: 'Down he fell A Monstrous Serpent on his Belly prone, Reluctant, but in vain' (1667). It is from Latin *reluctari* 'struggle against'.

rely [ME] The word rely is from Old French *relier* 'bind together', from Latin *ligare* 'bind'. The original sense was 'gather together', later 'turn to, associate with', which then led to 'depend upon with confidence'. The same Latin root gives us

reference refine reform refrigerate

liable [1642] originally meaning 'bound by law', **ligament** [L16th], and **ligature** [ME], both originally used for anything that ties.

remain *see* MANSION

remand *see* COMMANDO

remember, remind, reminisce *see* MEMORY

remonstrate *see* MUSTER

remorse [LME] The idea behind remorse is of regret or guilt that eats away at you, prompting you to repent. The word goes back to Latin *remordere* 'to annoy, trouble'. The first part of the word, *re-*, adds intensity, and the second is *mordere* 'to bite'. As *re-* most often means 'again' in a word, remorse was literally translated in Middle English as 'again-bite'. There is a famous English religious work called *Agenbite of Inwyt* ('Remorse of Conscience') written *c*.1340. James Joyce used the expression in *Ulysses* (1922), thereby introducing it to a wider audience.

Renaissance [M19th] The Renaissance of the 14th to 16th centuries was literally a 'rebirth' of culture after what was regarded as the uncivilized period of the Middle Ages. It began in Florence, where there was a revival of interest in classical antiquity, and spread to Venice, Rome, and then throughout Europe. Renaissance is a French word derived from Latin *nasci* 'to be born' (*see* NATION), which was not used in English until the 1840s—before that it was known as the **Revival of Learning**. A **Renaissance man** has many talents and interests, like the great Renaissance figure Leonardo da Vinci, who was a notable painter, scientist, inventor, and engineer. An ideal gentleman of the time was expected to have many accomplishments and a broad education in both the arts and the sciences.

renounce *see* ANNOUNCE

renovate *see* NEW

repeat *see* COMPETE

repel *see* APPEAL

repertory [M16th] A repertory was once an index or catalogue. It comes from late Latin *repertorium*, from Latin *reperire* 'find, discover'.

report [LME] Report is from Latin *reportare* 'bring back'. The sense 'give an account' gave rise to 'submit a formal report', hence 'inform an authority of one's presence' [19th]. The sense 'resounding noise' (report of a gun) is found from the late 16th century.

repose *see* PAUSE

reprehensible *see* PRISON

reprieve [LME] Some words have not just changed their meaning, but reversed it. When reprieve came into English from Old French, based on Latin *reprehendere* 'to seize, take back', it meant 'to take back to prison'. In the mid 16th century it referred to postponing or delaying a legal process, before developing into the current sense of cancelling an impending punishment.

reptile [LME] A mention of reptiles today conjures up a picture of snakes and lizards, but in the 14th century the word included other creatures. It comes from Latin *repere* 'to crawl' and was originally used for any creeping or crawling animal. The first use of reptile as an insulting term for a person is found in Henry Fielding's *Tom Jones* (1749) 'For a little reptile of a critic to presume to find fault with any of its parts . . . is a most presumptuous absurdity.'

republic *see* PUBLIC

requiem [ME] This is from Latin *requies* 'rest', the first word of the Mass for the Dead, said or sung for the repose of their souls: *Requiem aeternam dona eis, Domine* 'Grant them, O Lord, eternal rest'. The Latin word goes back to *quietus* 'quiet', which is the source of *QUIT, **requite** [E16th], and **tranquil** [E17th] and, via the French for *QUIET, **coy** [ME].

remain   remand   remember   remind

rescue [ME] Rescue is from Old French *rescoure* based on Latin *excutere* 'shake out, discard'. The prefix *re-* intensifies the sense. The notion here is of 'shaking out' a captive from the hands of an enemy.

research *see* SEARCH

resemble *see* SIMILAR

resent [L16th] The word resent is from obsolete French *resentir*, from *re-* serving as an intensifier and *sentir* 'to feel', from Latin *sentire*. The early sense was 'experience (an emotion or sensation)' which later developed into 'feel deeply', giving rise to 'feel aggrieved by'.

reserve *see* CONSERVE

resign *see* SIGN

resilient [M17th] This is from Latin *resilire* 'leap back'. The first senses recorded were 'returning to the original position' and 'looking back'; the prime current sense, for someone who bounces back under pressure dates from the early 19th century. **Result** [LME] developed from a closely related Latin verb *resultare* 'to spring back'.

resist *see* CONSIST

resolve *see* SOLVE

resonant *see* SOUND

resort [LME] A resort was initially 'something to turn to for assistance' from Old French *resortir*, from *re-* 'again' and *sortir* 'come or go out'. The sense 'place frequently visited' (as in holiday resort) dates from the mid 18th century.

resound *see* SOUND

rest [OE] In the sense 'to stop working or moving', rest is an Old English word from a root meaning 'league' or 'mile'—the reference was to a distance after which a person rested. The rest that means 'the remaining part' comes from Latin *restare* 'to remain', also the source of to **arrest** someone [LME], which you do by stopping them, and **restive** [L16th]. Like *REPRIEVE,

restive is a word whose meaning has been reversed. Its original meaning was 'inclined to stay still, inert'. It was then applied particularly to a horse which remained stubbornly still or shifted from side to side instead of moving on. From this came the current meaning of 'restless, fidgety'.

restaurant *see* RESTORE

restitution *see* CONSTITUTION

restive *see* REST

restore [ME] This is from Old French *restorer*, from Latin *restaurare* 'rebuild, restore'. This can also mean 'to provide food for' from its restorative effects, which is the source of **restaurant** [E19th].

result *see* RESILIENT

resume *see* ASSUME

resurrect, resurrection *see* SURGE

retail [LME] Retail is from an Anglo-Norman French use of Old French *retaille* 'a piece cut off', from *tailler* 'to cut', from selling in small quantities, as opposed to the large quantities of **wholesale** [LME]. *See also* ENGROSS

retire [M16th] This was first used in the sense 'withdraw (to a place of safety or seclusion)'. French *retirer* is the source, from *re-* 'back' and *tirer* 'draw'. The sense 'withdraw from a job' is late 17th century.

retort *see* TORCH

retract, retreat *see* ABSTRACT

retribution *see* TRIBUTE

retro [1960s] The fashion term retro is from French *rétro*, an abbreviation of *rétrograde* '**retrograde**' [LME]. This was originally a term in astronomy referring to planets appearing to move in a direction from east to west. It comes from Latin *retrogradus*, from *retro* 'backwards' and *gradus* 'step'. Retro- is also the source of words such as **retrospect** [E17th] from Latin *retrospicere* 'look back' and **rear** 'back part'.

rescue   research   resemble   resent   reserve

This was first used as a military term from French *arrière* 'behind', which came from *retro*. The phrase *th'arrear* 'the back' was mis-analysed as 'the rear' and the 'a' at the beginning of the word dropped. It was used colloquially to mean 'buttocks' from the late 18th century. The other **rear**,' to raise up' and its close relative **rise**, both Old English, come from an Germanic root, with **raise**, a Middle English introduction from Old Norse coming from the same source.

rev *see* REVOLVE

revamp *see* VAMP

reveal *see* VEIL

revel *see* REBEL

revenge [LME] 'Revenge', said the 17th-century courtier and scholar Francis Bacon, 'is a kind of wild justice.' The idea that wrongs can be most successfully avenged by someone who has taken the time to plan their response is formulated in the proverb first recorded in the late 19th century, **revenge is a dish best eaten cold**. The word is from Old French *revencher*, which was from Latin *vindicare* 'to claim, avenge'—the root of **vindicate** [E17th] and **avenge** [LME].

revenue [LME] The word revenue is from Old French *revenu(e)* meaning 'returned', from Latin *revenire* 'return', from *re-* 'back' and *venire* 'come'. An obsolete and rare use was 'return to a place'; it was more commonly 'yield from lands and property', what would today be called a return on your investment. **Venue** [L16th] is an obvious relative. It was first used as a term for 'an attack or 'a thrust' in fencing and as a legal term meaning 'the county or district within which a criminal or civil case must be heard'. The sense of a place for entertainment only dates from the 1960s. **Avenue** [E17th] which at first meant 'way of approaching a problem' is another relative. It then developed a mainly military sense of a way to access a place, and from that a formal approach to a country house. Only in the middle of the 19th century did it become a term for a wide street.

reverberate [LME] The early sense was 'drive or beat back'. Latin *reverberare* 'strike again' is the source, from *re-* 'back' and *verberare* 'to lash'.

review *see* VIEW

revise *see* VISION

revive *see* SURVIVE

revoke *see* VOICE

revolt, revolution *see* REVOLVE

revolve [LME] The Latin verb *volvere* had the sense 'to turn round, roll, tumble'; add *re-* in front and you get meaning such as 'turn back, turn round'. This is the basic idea behind revolve and its offshoots: **revolution** [LME] which only came to mean the overthrow of a government in 1600, and which developed the form **rev** for the turning over of a motor in the early 20th century; and **revolt** [M16th] initially used politically, and developing the sense 'to make someone turn away in disgust' in the mid 18th century. The sense 'roll, tumble' of *volvere* developed into **vault**, both for the sense 'leap' [M16th] which came via Old French *volter* 'to turn (a horse), gambol', and for the arch that springs up to form a roof [ME]. The turning sense is found in **voluble** [ME] initially used to mean 'turning', but was used for words rolling out of the mouth by the late 16th century, and in **volume** [LME] originally a rolled scroll rather than a book, but with the sense 'quantity' coming from an obsolete meaning 'size or extent (of a book)' by the early 16th century. **Convoluted** [L18th] comes from *convolvere* 'rolled together, intertwined' (the plant **convolvulus**, from the same root, that climbs by turning its stem around a support already existed as a word in Latin, where it could also mean a caterpillar that rolls itself up in a leaf); while **devolve** [LME] comes from its opposite *devolvere* 'to unroll, roll down'; and **involve** [LME] from *involvere* 'to roll in'.

reward [ME] This comes from a variant of Old French *reguard* '**regard**, heed', also an early sense of the English word (*compare* GUARD and ward). The notion of payment, showing your regard, was also early; found as money offered for the capture of a criminal or for the return of lost property from the late 16th century

rhapsody [M16th] Rhapsody comes from Greek *rhaptein* 'to stitch', and its earliest sense carries the idea of words woven together. In the 16th century a rhapsody was a long poem, like Homer's *Odyssey* or *Iliad*, suitable for recitation. From this developed first the idea of a medley or collection, and then the sense of pleasure and approval expressed with enthusiasm rather than careful thought. The musical sense developed in the late 19th century.

rheumatism [ME] People have been **rheumatic** in the sense of suffering from too much rheum, or watery discharge since the Middle Ages but doctors have only been diagnosing rheumatism in their patients since the 17th century. The disease was originally supposed to be caused by watery fluids in the body, and the word comes from Greek *rheumatizein* 'to snuffle', from *rheuma* 'stream'.

rhinoceros [LME] It is the look of the rhinoceros that provides its name, which comes from Greek *rhino-* 'nose' and *keras* 'horn'. The animal has been known in English since the end of the 14th century, but the first reference to it calls it a kind of unicorn. *Rhino-* will be familiar to gardeners from the **antirrhinum** [M16th], the alternative name for the snapdragon, whose name means 'counterfeiting a nose' from its appearance, while *keras* appears in **keratin** [M19th], the substance from which horn is made.

rhizome *see* LIQUORICE

rhododendron [E17th] Rhododendron means 'rose tree' from Greek *rhodos* 'rose', also found in the name Rhoda, and *dendron* 'tree' found in many plant names as well as in **dendrochronology** [E20th], the science of dating things through tree rings.

Rhododendron was originally used of the rose-flowered oleander which explains its name, and only transferred to the modern plant in the mid 17th century.

rhubarb [LME] English speakers have been eating rhubarb since medieval times. It came originally from China and Tibet, and the name reflects its exotic origins, going back to Greek *rhabarbarum*, the second part of which comes from *barbaros* 'foreign' (*see* BARBARIAN). It was originally a medicinal plant and the variety used as part of a meal only appears in 1650. Actors who wanted to give the impression of indistinct background conversation on stage traditionally achieved this by repeating 'rhubarb, rhubarb', leading to the word becoming a verb in the mid 20th century.

rhyme [ME] Both rhyme and **rhythm** come from the same source, Greek *rhuthmos*. Before it referred to a musical beat rhythm meant 'rhyme'. Since the 16th century a person wanting to complain that something completely lacked logical explanation might say that there was no **rhyme or reason** to it.

ribald [ME] This was first used as a noun for a 'lowly retainer' or a 'licentious or irreverent person'. It comes from Old French *ribauld*, from *riber* 'indulge in licentious pleasures', from a Germanic base meaning 'prostitute'. It became an adjective in the early 16th century.

rich [OE] The Anglo-Saxons would probably have understood the US novelist F. Scott Fitzgerald's remark to Ernest Hemingway: 'Let me tell you about the very rich. They are different from you and me.' In Old English rich meant both 'powerful' and 'wealthy'. The idea of unlimited wealth led to an association of 'given without restraint', and in the 18th century rich began to mean 'outrageous, beyond acceptable limits', which gave us **a bit rich** in reference to something causing ironic amusement or exasperation. Riches for 'wealth' is strictly speaking not a plural of rich, but from French *richesse* 'wealth'.

reward   rhapsody   rheumatism   rhinoceros

rickety [late 17th century] Rickety is based on mid 17th-century **rickets**, a disease in children due to vitamin D deficiency, causing bow legs, a name with an obscure origin.

riddle see READ

ride [OE] A word related to *ROAD, from a time when horses were the usual means of transport. When people in Yorkshire refer to the **East Riding**, **North Riding**, or **West Riding** they are not making any reference to horses. The word for each of the county's three former administrative divisions goes back to Old Norse *thrithjungr* 'third part', from *thrithi* 'third'. Over the years the initial 'th' was lost, so that the east, north or west 'third part' of the county became a **riding**. A person who behaves in a reckless or arrogant way that invites defeat or failure is sometimes said to **ride for a fall**. The phrase comes from 19th-century descriptions of hunters riding in a way likely to lead to an accident. To **ride herd on** someone is to keep watch over them. This North American expression comes from the idea of cowboys guarding or controlling a herd of cattle by riding round its edge. People who achieve a happy conclusion may be said to **ride off into the sunset**, a reference to the traditional closing scene of a Western, when the main characters ride off towards the setting sun after everything has been satisfactorily resolved. The proverb **he who rides a tiger is afraid to dismount**, meaning that once a dangerous or troublesome venture is begun the safest course is to carry it through to the end, is recorded from the 19th century. Winston Churchill used it with ominous effect in 1937: 'Dictators ride to and fro upon tigers which they dare not dismount. And the tigers are getting hungry.'

ridiculous [M16th] This comes from Latin *ridiculus* 'laughable', from *ridere* 'to laugh'. **Ridicule** dates from the late 17th century. **Derision** [LME] and its later relatives such as **deride** [M16th] come from the same root.

riff-raff see RIFLE

rifle [ME] The Old French *rifler* meant both 'to plunder' and to 'to scratch'. The plunder sense developed via 'search for valuables' into 'to search thoroughly' [M17th]. The word was then re-borrowed from French in the 'scratch' sense for the making of grooves in the barrel of a gun [M17th]. These rifled guns then became known as **rifles** [M18th]. **Riff-raff** [ME], formerly written as *riff and raff*, is probably also from *rifler* combined with *raffler* 'to carry off'. The sense 'disreputable person' would have developed in much the same way as *VULGAR and *HOI POLOI.

right [OE] The root meaning of right is not a turn or side but movement in a straight line—the first senses were 'straight, not curved' and 'direct, straight to the destination' as well as 'morally good, just' and 'true, correct'. Right as in the opposite of *LEFT is a later meaning that dates from the 13th century. The political application originated in the French National Assembly of 1789, in which the nobles as a body took the position of honour on the president's right, and the Third Estate—the French bourgeoisie and working class—sat on his left. A person who holds right-wing views of the most extreme kind can be described as being **somewhere to the right of Genghis Khan**. This expression uses Genghis Khan (1162–1227), the founder of the Mongol Empire, as a supreme example of a repressive and tyrannical ruler. The name of the early 5th-century warlord Attila the Hun, an equally dominant and brutal figure, is sometimes substituted for Genghis. See also DEXTER, RECTANGLE, SINISTER

rile [E19th] Rile 'to anger' and **roil** 'to anger or to churn' [L16th] are both the same word probably from Old French *ruiler* 'mix mortar'.

rind [OE] In Old English rind is the word for the bark of a tree, developing the sense outer part of fruit in the Middle Ages.

ring [OE] In Anglo-Saxon times a gold ring was worn as an indication of wealth and status—the word comes from the same root as *RANK. In some traditional legends, such as the one told in Wagner's opera cycle *The Ring of the Nibelungen*, a ring is also an object of power, an idea reinforced by J.R.R. Tolkien's fantasy *The Lord of the Rings* which draws on the tradition. The singing game **ring-a-ring o'roses** is commonly interpreted as referring to the bubonic plague which swept through England in 1665–66, with the 'ring o'roses' the rash symptomatic of the disease, the 'pocketful of posies' herbs carried to ward off infection, and the final 'falling down' part symbolizing death. This is unlikely, as the song first appeared in print only in 1881. The use of ring to mean 'give out a clear sound' is also recorded from Old English, but is a quite different word, probably representing an imitation of the sound. The phrase **ring the changes**, meaning 'to vary the ways of arranging or doing something', comes from bell-ringing. The 'changes' here are the different sequences in which a peal of church bells can be rung. The idea that something vaguely remembered might **ring a bell** in your head is a common one, but the expression goes back only to the 1930s.

rink [LME] In medieval Scotland jousting knights not skaters took to a rink. It was only in the 18th century that a rink became a stretch of ice set aside for the sport of curling, and the word remained a Scottish one until the end of the following century.

riot *see* READ

RIP *see* LATIN WORD PANEL

rise *see* RETRO

risqué *see* FRENCH WORD PANEL

ritzy *see* GLITTER

rival [L16th] A rival was originally someone with whom you had to share your water supply. Recorded in English from the late 16th century, the word goes back to Latin *rivalis*, which originally meant 'person living on the opposite bank and using the same stream as another'. It comes via Latin *rivus* 'stream' from *ripus* *RIVER. **Derive** [LME] was originally 'draw a fluid through

or into a channel' and comes from *de-* 'down, away' and *rivus*.

river [ME] River comes from the same root at *RIVAL. To **sell someone down the river** is to betray them, especially to benefit yourself. The expression refers to the slave-owning period of American history. It was the custom to sell troublesome slaves to owners of sugar-cane plantations on the lower Mississippi, where conditions were harsher than those in the more northerly slave-owning states. The first recorded use is in 1851 by the American writer Harriet Beecher Stowe, whose best-known work is the anti-slavery novel *Uncle Tom's Cabin* (1852). The 'betray' sense did not emerge until much later, in the 1920s, perhaps because the subject was too sensitive to be used casually. In the USA someone who has been sent **up the river** is in prison. The phrase originally referred to Sing Sing prison, which is situated up the Hudson River from the city of New York.

roach *see* COCKROACH

road [OE] In Old English road meant 'a journey on horseback', and the word is related to *RIDE. The sense of 'a wide track to travel on', the equivalent of *STREET, did not appear until the end of the 16th century. The **middle of the road** has been the place for moderate views since the 1890s, originally in the context of US politics. The phrase has referred to easy-listening music since the late 1950s. **The road less travelled** to refer to an unconventional or unusual course of action comes from the poem 'The Road Not Taken' (1916) by Robert Frost: 'Two roads diverged in a wood, and I— / I took the one less travelled by, /And that has made all the difference'. *See also* HELL, RAGE

roast [ME] The word roast is from Old French *rostir*, of West Germanic origin. Roast originally meant to cook before a fire while *BAKE meant 'cook in an oven'; but now that we rarely use an open fire the distinction between roast and bake refers to the type of food. The colloquial sense 'ridicule, criticize' dates from the early 18th century. A **roster** [E18th] was originally a list

rink riot RIP rise risqué ritzy rival river

of duties and leave for military personnel. It comes from Dutch *rooster* 'list', earlier 'gridiron', from *roosten* 'to roast', with reference to its parallel lines.

rob [ME] The words rob and **robe** come from the same ancient root, a word meaning 'booty'—clothing would have been the kind of property stolen in a raid. To **rob Peter to pay Paul** is to take something away from one person to pay another. The expression probably refers to the apostles St Peter and St Paul, who in Christian art are often shown together as equals. Although the earliest examples feature robbery, other versions have cropped up over the centuries, such as **unclothe Peter to pay Paul** and **borrow from Peter to pay Paul**. The last example probably helped in the additional meaning 'to pay off one debt only to incur another'. The Scottish and English **reavers** or **reivers**, who plundered each other across the border got their name from 'to **reave**', another form of the original word, and those who are **bereaved** [OE] have also been robbed of something precious—**bereft** is the old form of the word. A **rover** [ME] was originally another form of the word, but to **rove** [LME] is a different word: it was originally a term in archery meaning 'shoot at a casual mark of undetermined range'. This may be from dialect *rave* 'to stray', probably of Scandinavian origin.

robin [LME] People seem to like giving birds names (*see* PIE and PARROT). Just as we might call a parrot Polly, so the bird known as a redbreast, from its distinctive colouring was called 'Robin Redbreast'. The nickname gradually ousted the original part of the name, so that today robin is the normal term.

robot [1920s] This is one of the few English words to have come from Czech—from *robota* 'forced labour'. The term was coined in Karel Čapek's play *R.U.R.*, or *Rossum's Universal Robots* (1920), when it described an artificial man or woman.

robust *see* CORROBORATE

rock [OE] The hard rock that makes up much of the earth came into medieval English from Old French *rocque*, which can be traced back to medieval Latin *rocca* but no further. The classical Latin word was *petra*, the source of *PETRIFY. People have been **caught between a rock and a hard place** since the 1920s, first of all in Arizona and California. Also American is **on the rocks** meaning a drink 'on ice', first recorded in 1946, while the slang term for a precious stone is 1920s. In France the modern form of the word, *roc* developed the form *rocaille* to describe the decoration using shells and pebbles fashionable in the 18th century. In the 19th century this was changed by French workmen to *rococo*, originally to mean something old-fashioned, but now used to describe the art of the 18th century. **Rock** meaning 'to move to and fro' is an Old English word. **Rock music** was originally **rock and roll**, which is first found in 1951, although a song called 'Rock and Roll' came out in 1934. Rock and roll combined black rhythm and blues and white country or 'hillbilly' music. Elvis Presley's first single, 'That's All Right Mama' and Bill Haley's 'Rock Around the Clock', both released in 1954, are often considered the first rock and roll records, but similar-sounding music was produced in the 1930s and 1940s by black performers like Big Joe Turner and Fats Domino.

If you are **off your rocker** you are mad or crazy. A **rocker** here is a curved piece of wood or metal placed under a chair or cradle so that it can rock backwards and forwards. In the early 1960s rockers were also youths who liked rock music, leather clothing, and motorcycles, and were the sworn enemies of the **mods** (short for **modernists**), who were noted for their smart appearance, motor scooters, and fondness for soul music.

rocket [E17th] Rocket comes ultimately from Italian *rocca* 'a distaff', the stick or spindle on which wool was wound for spinning. Like the firework, it was cylindrical in shape. The development of rockets for space travel after the Second World War gave rise to the expression **not rocket science** to suggest that something is

rob   robin   robot   robust   rock   rocket

not really very difficult. Rocket meaning 'a reprimand', as in to **give** or **get a rocket**, is Second World War military slang—the first recorded example is **stop a rocket**. The salad vegetable **rocket** is a totally different word, which came via French *roquette* from Latin *eruca*, meaning a kind of cabbage.

rococo *see* ROCK

rod [OE] In Old English rod meant 'slender shoot growing on or cut from a tree' but also 'straight stick or bundle of twigs used to inflict punishment', and phrases linked with it tend to evoke traditional, and severe, ideas of discipline. If you exert control over someone strictly or harshly you may be said to **rule them with a rod of iron**. The expression goes back to the Bible, to Psalms: 'Thou shalt break them with a rod of iron; thou shalt dash them in pieces like a potter's vessel.' The proverb **spare the rod and spoil the child**, meaning that if children are not physically punished when they do wrong their personal development will suffer, is found from Anglo-Saxon times. It too has a biblical origin, from Proverbs: 'He that spareth his rod, hateth his son.' *See also* KISS

rodent [M19th] The teeth of rodents such as rats and mice grow continuously and must be kept worn down by gnawing, a fact that gives a clue about the origin of the term rodent. The word comes from Latin *rodere* 'to gnaw', which is related to **erode** [E17th], *CORRODE, *ROOT, and *ROSTRUM. The original sense of the word is preserved in that unpleasant affliction the rodent ulcer.

roil *see* RILE

roll [ME] Roll goes back ultimately to Latin *rotula* 'little wheel' and is related to an actor's part or **role** in a play or film, which entered English from French *roule* 'roll', referring to the roll of paper on which the part would originally have been written. **Enrol** [LME] originally referred to the names being written on the roll. If you **roll with the punches** [M20th] you adapt yourself to difficult circumstances. The image here is of a boxer moving their body away from an opponent's blows so as to lessen the impact.

A **rolling stone** is someone who does not settle in one place for long. The expression comes from the proverb which has been around in various languages from at least the 15th century, that **a rolling stone gathers no moss.** The Rolling Stones took their name not directly from the proverb but from a song by the US blues musician Muddy Waters.

rollicking *see* BOLLOCKS

romance [ME] The Romance languages are the European languages descended from Latin, and the word romance came via Old French from Latin *Romanicus* 'Roman'. A romance became a medieval narrative in the local language that described the adventures of a hero of chivalry. These adventures tended to be so wild and improbable that the word came to be associated with any work of fiction depicting events remote from everyday life or, because love was often a subject, dealing with love. The senses 'idealized or sentimental love' and 'a love affair' are Victorian. **Romantic** is a more recent word from the mid 17th century. At the end of the 18th century the **Romantic movement** arose, exemplified by the writers Wordsworth, Coleridge, Byron, Shelley, and Keats and painters such as William Blake, J.M.W. Turner, and Goya.

Romany *see* ROMANY WORD PANEL

Rome For centuries Rome, known as **the Eternal City**, was the heart of a great empire. It is not surprising, then, that it became a byword for power and features in a number of common phrases. The proverb **all roads lead to Rome** [LME] echoes a Latin saying which reflected the power and prestige of Rome. The city was built up gradually from humble beginnings, a fact which gave us the practical warning against expecting results too quickly, **Rome was not built in a day** [M16th]. **When in Rome do as the Romans do**, often shortened to **when in Rome . . .**, refers to a comment by St Ambrose, 4th-century Bishop of Milan. Writing to St Augustine, he explained that when he was in Rome he followed the local custom of

Travellers broaden the mind

Gypsies probably originated in the Indian subcontinent, and their language, **Romany***, is related to the Indian languages Hindi and Sanskrit. It has given English some colourful slang words, along with terms relating to Gypsy life.*

THE word **Romany** itself comes from *Rom*, which means 'a male Gypsy' in Romany—the plural of Rom, *Roma*, is another name for the Gypsy people. A **rye** is 'a man or gentleman', while a **Romany rye** is a man who is not a Gypsy but who associates with them. You might find him in a **vardo**, 'a caravan', but that would be no place for a **gorgio**, 'a non-Gypsy'.

Probably the best-known English expression to come from Romany is **pal**, which is first recorded in the late 17th century and can be traced back through Turkish and Transylvanian Romany to ancient Sanskrit. Pals were originally accomplices in crime, but now they are simply friends. Older people might refer to a pal as a decent **cove**, a word meaning 'a man' which is probably from Romany *kova* 'thing or person', and goes back as far as the 1560s. Another friendly word from Romany is **mush** (pronounced like *push*), which is British slang for a person's mouth or face, and is also a form of address. In Romany the word simply means 'man'.

Cushty, meaning 'very good', has been around since the 1920s, but was popularized by the TV comedy *Only Fools and Horses* in the 1980s. It derives from Romany *kushto* or *kushti* 'good'—the spelling was probably influenced by **cushy**, meaning 'easy, undemanding'. Another word familiar to Del Boy and Rodney in *Only Fools and Horses* is **wonga**, 'money', from Romany *wongar*, which means 'coal' as well as 'money'.

Some Romany terms reflect the traditionally marginalized status of Gypsies. **Dick** meaning 'detective' may be from the old slang word *dick*, 'look', which was a Romany expression. **Stir** or 'jail' dates from around 1850, and is probably from Romany *sturbin*, also meaning 'jail', and a **chiv** or **shiv** is a knife or razor used as a weapon, from *chiv* 'blade'.

See also BLOW, CHAV, NARK

fasting on a Saturday, although at home in Milan he did not do this. *See also* FIDDLE

room [OE] In Old English room meant 'the amount of space occupied by something', and did not mean 'an interior division of a building' until the 14th century. The majority of houses then would have had only one room. Sometimes political negotiation is described as having taken place **in a smoke-filled room**, meaning that it has been conducted privately rather than more openly. The expression comes from a 1920s news report about the selection of the Republican presidential candidate, Warren Harding, who in 1921 became the 29th

romance   Romany   Rome   room

president of the United States. According to the report he was 'chosen by a group of men in a smoke-filled room'. Harding was at the time something of a dark horse, and a lack of openness and democracy was associated with his selection. **Room at the top** is a way of describing the opportunity to join the higher ranks of an organization. The phrase is attributed to the American politician Daniel Webster (1782–1852), who was warned against attempting to enter the overcrowded legal profession. He is said to have replied, 'There is always room at the top.' The phrase was taken up in the early 20th century and was used as the title of John Braine's first novel, published in 1957, about an ambitious young man in an industrial town in the north of England which was filmed in 1959. An **elephant in the room** is an obvious, major problem or controversial issue that is being studiously avoided as a subject for discussion. The phrase was originally American, and seems to have been first used in the early 1980s, in the language of therapists treating people addicted to drink or drugs. An alternative is a **moose on the table**. *See also* CAT

root [OE] This is an Old English word related to Latin *radix* (*see* RADICAL) and **wort**, which is used in the names of plants such as St John's wort. **Root and branch**, used to emphasize how thoroughly something is dealt with, goes back to the biblical book of Malachi: 'The day cometh that shall burn them up...that it shall leave them neither root nor branch.' *See also* MONEY. Root used of an animal turning up the ground with its snout in search of food is a completely different word, that may ultimately be linked to Latin *rodere* 'gnaw' (*see* RODENT). Someone backing a candidate for a post may be said to be **rooting for** them—perhaps with the idea of trying to dig up further support through their efforts.

rope [OE] This is one of the oldest English words, recorded as early as AD 725. A way of dealing with a person who is causing problems is to **give them enough rope**—in full **give a man enough rope and he will hang himself**. **On the ropes** is from boxing, and conjures up the picture of a losing contestant forced back by his opponent against the ropes that mark the sides of the ring. To **show someone the ropes** is to teach them the established way of doing things. The origins of this expression go back to the mid 19th century and the days of sailing ships. Skill in handling ropes and tying knots was essential for any sailor, and the idea was soon extended to other walks of life. A range of variations on the theme developed, including **learn the ropes** and the more familiar **know the ropes**. **Ropy** meaning 'not very good' is RAF slang, dating from the early 1940s. It probably derives from the phrase **money for old rope** (*see* MONEY), although another idea links it to the old biplanes, festooned with 'ropes' or supporting wires, that were then being replaced by modern Spitfires and Hurricanes.

rose [OE] The rose (from Latin *rosa*) is beautiful but prickly, and the proverbial saying **no rose without a thorn** goes back to medieval times. There is nothing spiky about an **English rose**, an attractive, fair-skinned English girl. A person who takes an unduly indulgent or optimistic view of things is said to be looking through **rose-coloured spectacles**. The idea here is that everything you look at is bathed in warm flattering light. Charles Dickens talked of living 'in a rose-colored mist' in *Little Dorrit* (1857), but the first example of the full phrase is from *Tom Brown at Oxford* (1861) by Thomas Hughes. The decorative quality of the rose is taken up in **rosette** 'a little rose' borrowed from French in the mid 18th century. A **rosary** means 'a rose garden' and appears in this sense in Middle English. There was a medieval Latin term for a prayer book *hortulus animae* 'little garden of the soul' and the idea of calling a series of prayers a rose garden [M16th] probably came from this. **Rosemary** [LME] originally had no connection with 'rose' or 'Mary', although these have influenced the form the word now takes. The plant was Latin *ros marinus* 'dew of the sea'. The plant grows wild by the sea in southern Europe, and the leaves have a misty blue cast. *See also* RING

roster *see* ROAST

root rope rose rosette rosemary roster

rostrum [M16th] A rostrum is now a raised platform on which a person stands to make a speech, but it was originally part of a ship. It is an English use of a Latin word meaning 'beak', which came from *rodere* 'to gnaw'. In the days of the Roman Empire the part of the Forum in Rome which was used as a platform for public speakers was decorated with the 'beaks' or pointed prows of captured enemy warships. *See also* RODENT, ROOT

rotation [M16th] The Latin *rota* 'wheel' and the verb from it *rotare* 'to turn' is the source of rotation and related words. These include **rotund** [L15th] for something well rounded, and **rotunda** [E17th] for a round building or room. It is an alteration of Italian *rotonda* (*camera*) 'round (chamber)'. **Round** [ME] comes from the same source via French. The worldwide charitable society of business people formed in 1905 known as **Rotary International** owes its name to the fact that its members hosted events in rotation.

rout, route, routine *see* RUT

rove, rover *see* ROB

row [OE] The sense 'an orderly line' is recorded from Old English. Row meaning 'to propel with oars' is also Old English, but is a different word that goes back to a root shared also by Latin *remus* 'oar'. The kind of row that results from a heated argument is a different word again, with a different pronunciation. It turned up in English from an unknown source in the middle of the 18th century, when it was considered to be slang or 'low' speech.

rowdy *see* US WORD PANEL

royal *see* RULE

rub [ME] The origin of this word is unknown. If you want to impress the consequences of a mistake on someone you may be tempted to **rub their nose in it**. This comes from house-training puppies or kittens: literally rubbing their noses in any deposit they may make in the house in an attempt to dissuade them from repeating

the offence. To **rub someone up the wrong way**, or irritate them, is another pet-related image, from the idea of stroking a cat against the lie of its fur. Someone pointing out a particular difficulty may say **there's the rub**. The expression comes from Shakespeare's *Hamlet*, when Hamlet says: 'To sleep: perchance to dream: ay, there's the rub.' In the game of bowls a rub is an impediment that prevents a bowl running smoothly. The same idea is found in **the rub of the green**, which in golf is an accidental interference with the flight or roll of the ball, such as hitting a tree. More broadly it is also luck or fortune, especially in sport. **Rubber**, recorded from the mid 16th century, is based on the verb *rub*. The original sense was 'an implement (such as a hard brush) used for rubbing and cleaning'. Because an early use of the elastic substance once known as *caoutchouc* was to rub out pencil marks, rubber acquired the sense 'eraser' in the late 18th century. The meaning was subsequently generalized in the mid 19th century to refer to the substance in any form or use, at first often differentiated as **India rubber**.

rubbish [LME] This is from Anglo-Norman French *rubbous*; it may be related to Old French *robe* 'spoils' (*see* ROB). The change in the ending was due to association with words ending in *-ish*. The verb meaning 'denigrate', found from the 1950s, was originally Australian and New Zealand slang. **Rubble** [LME] may also be an alteration *robe*.

ruby [ME] This is the English form of *rubinus*, the Latin name of the precious stone. This comes from *rubeus* 'red'. This is also the source of **rubric** [LME] which goes back to Latin *rubrica* (*terra*) 'red (earth or ochre as writing material)', from the fact that rubrics were originally written in red ink.

rucksack [M19th] This is an adoption of a German word, from *rucken* (a dialect variant of *Rücken* 'back') and *Sack* 'bag, sack'.

ruddy *see* RED

rude [ME] Many a schoolchild has sniggered at old books or hymns that mention 'rude dwellings'. Especially for children, the dominant sense of rude is now 'referring to a subject such as sex in an embarrassing or offensive way', yet this is a recent development, being recorded only from the early 1960s, a development of an old sense 'bad-mannered, rough'. The word came via Old French from Latin *rudis*, 'unfinished, roughly made, uncultivated', and in medieval times meant 'uneducated, ignorant, uncultivated', and 'roughly made' as well as 'impolite'. *See also* MECHANICAL. In Jamaica a **rude boy** is a poor, lawless urban youth. The expression became more widely known in the late 1970s with the popularity of bands playing 'ska' (a kind of speeded-up *REGGAE) many of whose songs mentioned rude boys.

ruffian [LME] This is from Old French *ruffian*, from Italian *ruffiano*, perhaps from dialect *rofia* 'scab, scurf', of Germanic origin.

rug *see* RED

rugby [M19th] The game of rugby is named after Rugby School in Warwickshire, England, the public school where it was first played. According to tradition, in a school football match in 1823 a boy named William Webb Ellis first took the ball in his arms and ran with it, so originating the game. The informal name **rugger** was invented at Oxford University in, it seems, 1893. At the time there was a student craze for adding –er to the end of words, which gave us words such as *SOCCER, **brekkers** (for 'breakfast'), and **preggers** (for 'pregnant'), as well as some that lasted only for a year or so, like **Pragger-Wagger** for the Prince of Wales, and even **wagger-pagger-bagger** for 'wastepaper basket'. Ironically, the craze started at Rugby School, home of rugby.

rugged *see* RED

rugger *see* RUGBY

rule [ME] We think of rules as giving us lines to follow, and the word goes back to Latin *regula* 'straight stick', and beyond that

to *regere* 'to rule', the source of *REGENCY and **royal** [LME]. To **rule the roost** is to be in complete control. The original form of the phrase was **rule the roast**, from the end of the 15th century, which may imply that it referred to the most important person at a banquet or feast. **Roast** changed to **roost** in the 18th century when people started thinking about a cockerel asserting itself over the other roosting birds in the farmyard. The rule in **run the rule over**, 'to examine quickly', is a measuring stick or ruler. It has the same meaning in **rule of thumb**, 'a broadly accurate guide based on practice rather than theory'. This expression, recorded from 1692, is probably from the ancient use of parts of the body, such as the *FOOT and the hand, as units of measurement. The first joint of a man's thumb is about an inch long, and so is useful for making rough measurements when you have mislaid your ruler. *See also* RAIL

run [OE] An important little Anglo-Saxon word found in many common phrases. If you come into conflict with someone you have **run foul** of them. This nautical expression refers to a ship which had collided or become entangled with another vessel or with an obstacle. If people are angry public feeling may **run high**, which is another nautical phrase, from waves or tides rising about their normal height, especially in stormy conditions. Both of these phrases appeared around 1700. An ordinary or undistinguished person might be described as a **run-of-the-mill** type. Here the run is the material produced from a mill before it has been sorted or inspected for quality. When you find someone after a long search you may feel that at last you have **run them to earth**. The earth is a fox's home, and the literal meaning is 'to chase a hunted animal to its lair and corner it there'. A confrontation that has gone on for a long time is sometimes called a **running battle**. The idea reaches back into the history of warfare. Literally, a running battle is one that constantly changes its location, the opposite of a **pitched battle** (*see* PITCH). The expression is first recorded in the late 17th century as **running fight** and described a naval engagement that continued even as one side was fleeing. The current version was not recorded until the 20th century, but is now the more common. *See also* GAUNTLET

rural [LME] This comes from late Latin *ruralis*, from *rus* 'country'. In early use little difference exists between rural and **rustic** [LME], but later usage shows rural in connection with locality and country scenes, with rustic being reserved for the primitive qualities of country life. The use of rustic for 'unsophisticated; plain and simple' dates from the beginning of the 17th century

ruse [LME] In hunting terminology a ruse was a turn or detour or other trick made by a hunted animal to escape the hounds. The word came from Old French *ruser*, which meant 'to use trickery' and which in another sense, 'to drive back', was also the origin of **rush**. The plant name rush is Old English

russet [ME] Russet comes via Anglo-Norman French from Latin *russus* 'red'. It was originally a name for a coarse homespun woollen cloth that was reddish-brown, grey, or neutral in colour, used formerly for making clothing for land workers. When is came to be used for a colour in the 15th century it was usually

applied to cloth. The type of apple, named from its colour appears in the early 18th century. **Rust** [OE] is more closely related to the Old English word for 'red' although they both go back to the same Indo-European root.

rustic *see* RURAL

rut [LME] In the days of horse-drawn vehicles a cartwheel travelling many times along the same track would carve out a deep groove or rut. The deeper the rut became, the more difficult it would be to follow any other route. Someone following a fixed, and probably rather tedious, pattern of behaviour is **in a rut**. Rut in this sense is probably from Old French *rute*, also the source of **route** [ME] which both go back to Latin *rupta* (*via*) 'broken (way)'. Route is also the origin of **routine** [L17th] for something that is like travelling the same road again. *Rupta* is the source of **rout** [ME] for a decisive defeat, from the idea of a broken army. The **rut** of male deer is a different word. In the breeding season stags challenge one another by roaring calls, when they are **in rut**: here rut probably comes from Latin *rugire* 'to roar' (*see also* RAIL).

rye *see* ROMANY WORD PANEL

run rural ruse russet rustic rut rye

sabbath [OE] The sabbath is the day of rest—Saturday for Jews, Sunday for Christians. The Hebrew word *sabat*, 'to rest', is the ultimate source. The Law of Moses dictated that every seventh year should be observed as a 'sabbath', during which the land lay fallow. In the late 19th century US universities extended the idea of this **sabbatical year** to give professors and other academic staff every seventh year free to research or travel. Nowadays a sabbatical may come at other intervals of time, and members of other occupations also use the term for paid leave for professional development.

sabotage [E20th] French peasants and other workers traditionally wore *sabots*, wooden clogs. When French workmen took action against the introduction of new technology by destroying machines and tools in the 19th century, people looked at them and called the action sabotage. The word first appeared in English in the first decade of the 20th century, referring to a court case in Paris. By 1916 the *Sydney Morning Herald* could report a labourer on an Australian sheep farm threatening sabotage against politicians and employers.

sabre [L17] We think of curved swords as typically oriental, and the sabre is no exception. It probably comes from some unknown oriental language and passed into English by a long route that took it from Hungarian *szablya* via German and French. The extinct **sabre-toothed** tiger was first described in 1849. *See also* RATTLE

sack [OE] When it refers to a bag, sack is related to Dutch *zak* and German *Sack*, and goes back to Semitic, the family of languages that includes Hebrew and Arabic. The word passed through Greek and Latin into the language of the Continental Anglo-Saxons, who brought it with them to England, leaving us with the interesting question of what words were being used for an object that these cultures must have had before the borrowing, and why they felt the need to borrow it. Latin *saccus* is the source of the biological **sac** [M18th] and, via French, of **sachet** [M19th] and **satchel** [OE]

both 'a little sack'. The sack meaning 'to plunder or pillage a town or city' came in the mid 16th century from French, where the phrase was *mettre à sac*, 'to put to the sack'. This may have originally referred to filling a sack with plunder, so the two words would ultimately be the same.

People in employment have been **given the sack** since the early 19th century, probably echoing a French phrase. In ancient Rome **the sack** was much more serious than losing a job—it was being sewn into a sack and drowned as a punishment for killing a parent or other near relative. Sacks were made of a coarse rough fabric woven from flax and hemp, called **sackcloth**. The Gospel of St Matthew describes the wearing of sackcloth and the sprinkling of ashes on your head as signs of repentance and mourning, and people experiencing these emotions can still be **in sackcloth and ashes**.

sacrament, sacred, sacrifice, sacrilege *see* PRIEST

sad [OE] The original meaning of sad in Old English was 'having no more appetite, weary'. The word comes from the same root as Latin *satis* 'enough', the source of **satiated**, **satisfactory,** and **satisfy** (all LME), and the idea was similar to our expression **fed up** [E20th]—of being unhappy through being too 'full' of something. The word then developed through 'firm, constant' and 'dignified, sober' to our modern sense of 'unhappy' in the medieval period. In the 1990s 'You're so sad!' became the refrain of every teenager in the land, often to their parents. This use, meaning 'pathetically inadequate or unfashionable', was not completely new, and had been around since the 1930s. *See also* MELANCHOLY

saddle *see* SALOON

sadism [L19th] During several periods of imprisonment in the later 18th and early 19th centuries, French writer and soldier the Marquis de Sade (1740–1814) wrote pornographic books. One sexual perversion in particular fascinated him, arousal from inflicting pain on others. The French named it *sadisme* after him, and English adopted the word as sadism in the 1880s. *See also* MASOCHISM

safety [ME] Like **safe**, this ultimately comes from Latin *salvus* 'uninjured, safe', also the source of **salvage** [L17th] originally payment for saving a ship, *SALVER, **salvation** [ME], and *SAVE. The proverb **there is safety in numbers** has echoes in the biblical Proverbs: 'In the multitude of counsellors there is safety'. The first to use the modern phrasing was Jane Austen in her novel *Emma*, published in 1814: 'She determined to call upon them and seek safety in numbers.'

saffron *see* ARABIC WORD PANEL

saga [E18th] The original medieval sagas told traditional stories of the families of Iceland and the kings of Norway. No one in Britain paid much attention to them until the 18th century, at the same time as the word saga entered the language. Its old Icelandic original is the equivalent of English **saw** in **old saw**, an old proverb or maxim, and meant 'a narrative, a story'. From the mid 19th century saga came also to apply to stories of heroic achievement and then to novels tracing families through several generations. The 1990s gave us the **Aga saga**, a novel by a writer such as Joanna Trollope set in a rural location and concerning the emotional lives of characters who set great store by their Aga, a stove invented in Sweden. Aga [M20th] gets its name from the initial letters of Svenska Aktiebolaget Gasackumulator, Swedish Gas Accumulator Company, the original manufacturers.

sahib *see* RAJ WORD PANEL

saint [ME] Saint comes via Old French, from Latin *sanctus* 'holy'. The word has been used in the names of many diseases such as **St Vitus' dance** [E17th] with the supposition that the associated saint would ward off the illness. Also based on *sanctus* are **sanctify** [LME], **sanctity** [LME], **sanctimonious** [E17th] originally meaning 'holy in character', and **sanctuary** [ME] originally a holy place where you were safe from attack or arrest. A **sanction** [LME] was originally an ecclesiastical decree and comes from Latin *sancere* which meant both 'to make holy' and 'to decree'.

sake [OE] Old English *sacu* 'contention, crime' is from a Germanic source, from a base meaning 'affair, legal action, thing'. The phrase **for the sake of** was not in Old English and may be from Old Norse. It was originally a legal expression. Sake remains hidden in the language in the words **forsake** [OE], which originally meant 'renounce, refuse'; **keepsake** [L18th] something kept for the sake of the giver; and **namesake** [M17th] which may be a shortening of 'for one's name sake'. The Japanese rice wine **sake**, pronounced with two syllables, is simply the Japanese word for 'alcohol'. *See also* SEIZE

salacious *see* SALIENT

salad [LME] One of many words that go back to Latin *sal* *SALT. The root implies that it was the dressing or seasoning that originally characterized a salad, and not the vegetables. The expression **your salad days**, 'the time when you are young and inexperienced', is one of Shakespeare's inventions, occurring in *Antony and Cleopatra*. The idea behind the phrase becomes clearer when you read the full line spoken by Cleopatra: 'My salad days, When I was green in judgement'. Shakespeare used the word salad in a play on *GREEN, which is still used today in the sense 'inexperienced or naïve'. The expression was made better known by the success of Julian Slade's 1956 musical *Salad Days* about some students starting out in the adult world.

salami, salary *see* SALT

sale *see* SELL

salient [M16th] This was first used as a heraldic term meaning 'leaping'. It comes from Latin *salire* 'to leap'. The sense 'outstanding, significant' as in salient point is found from the mid 19th century. *Salire* is behind many other English words including **assail** and **assault** [ME] 'jumping on' people; **exult** [L16th] 'jump up'; *INSULT; and **result** [LME] originally meaning 'to jump back'. **Salacious** [M17th] 'undue interest in sexual matters' is based on Latin *salax*, from *salire*. Its basic sense is 'fond of leaping', but as the word was used of stud animals it came to mean 'lustful'. From the French form of *salire* come to **sally out** [M16th] and **sauté** [E19th].

saline *see* SALT

sally *see* SALIENT

saloon [E18th] Along with gunfights between goodies in white Stetsons and baddies in black ones, the saloon or bar is an important feature of Westerns. Like many an outlaw in the American West, people may sometimes have to **drink at the last chance saloon**, 'take one final chance to get something right'. The name, sometimes expanded to First and Last Chance Saloon, was used in the US from about 1890 for the name of a saloon on the edge of town. The name was introduced to a wider public as the place that Frenchie, played by Marlene Dietrich, ran in the 1939 Western *Destry Rides Again*. Saloons (the word comes via French from Italian, from *sala* 'hall') were originally much more genteel than those on the wild frontier—the word at first applied to a large reception room or an elegant drawing room, as did **salon** [L17th], which has exactly the same source. Until many pubs were remodelled in the 1980s, most had a **saloon bar**, a separate area that was more luxuriously furnished and where drinks were more expensive than in the **public bar**. During the 19th century a saloon was a luxurious railway carriage used as a lounge or restaurant or for a private party. As the age of the car followed that of the train, a closed car with a separate boot came to be a **saloon car** in Britain. The American name, found from 1912 in this sense, is **sedan**, which was an Italian dialect word from Latin *sella* 'seat', also the source of **saddle** [OE].

salsa *see* SAUCE

salt [OE] The root of salt is Latin *sal*, from which words such as *SALAD, **salami** [M20th], **saline** [LME], and *SAUCE derive. A person who is **the salt of the earth** is kind, reliable, and honest. The phrase comes from St Matthew's Gospel: 'Ye are the salt of the earth: but if the salt have lost his savour, wherewith shall it be salted?' The expression **sit below the salt**, 'to be of lower social standing', goes back to the days when formal dinners were more common and when a person's rank determined where they sat at the table. Long dining tables running the length of the room were the norm, and those of the highest rank sat at the top end of the table, with the others arranged in descending order of status along the remaining length. The salt cellar was usually placed halfway down, and so anyone sitting below it knew they were socially inferior. **Salt cellar** itself has nothing to do with dark underground storage places. The second element was originally **saler**, which meant 'salt box' on its own. It came through Old French from Latin *salarium*, which also gave us **salary**—a *salarium* was originally a Roman soldier's allowance of money to buy salt (*see also* JAPANESE WORD PANEL). As early as the 15th century people did not fully understand saler and added salt in front of it. Finally it became a complete mystery, and they substituted the familiar cellar (*see* CELL). Before the invention of the refrigerator food was salted, or treated with salt, to preserve it. This is the idea behind **salting away** money for future use, an expression that dates from the 1840s.

saltimbocca *see* ITALIAN WORD PANEL

salute [LME] Salute is from Latin *salutare* 'greet, pay one's respects to', from *salus*, 'health, welfare, greeting' as greetings usually involve wishing someone good health. The same root gives us **salutary** [LME] originally 'conducive to health' and **salubrious** [M16th] 'healthful'. **Salvo** [L16th] comes, via Italian, from the Roman greeting *salve*, from *salutare*, and *SAFETY, *SALVER, and *SAVE also go back to the same root.

salvage, salvation *see* SAFETY

salve *see* QUACK

salver [M17th]
Early Spanish kings were afraid of being poisoned, so they employed servants to taste their food and drink before touching it themselves. The taster would put items that had been checked on a tray or salver for presenting to the monarch—anything on the tray was free from danger. Spanish *salva* 'the sampling of food' came from *salvar* 'to make safe' and goes back to Latin *salvus* 'uninjured, safe', the root also of *SAFETY, *SALUTE, and *SAVE.

salvo *see* SALUTE

sample *see* EXAMPLE

samurai *see* JAPANESE WORD PANEL

sanctify, sanctimonious, sanction, sanctity, sanctuary *see* SAINT

sandalwood [E16th]
The name of this Indian tree and its fragrant timber and oil has no connection with sweaty feet and **sandals**. It is based on *candana*, a word in Sanskrit, the ancient language of India, which passed into Latin as *sandalum*. Our word **sandal** came instead from Greek *sandalon* 'wooden shoe'.

sandwich [M18th]
John Montagu, the 4th Earl of Sandwich, was a notorious gambler. So that he did not have to leave the gaming table to eat, he had cold beef put between slices of bread and brought to him. This was the first sandwich, whose earliest mention comes in 1762, although it is hard to believe that no one had eaten them before this.

sane *see* SANITY

sangria *see* SPANISH WORD PANEL

sanguine [ME]
According to the medieval doctrine of the four humours (*see* HUMOUR), having a constitution in which blood predominated over the other three gave people a cheerfully optimistic or sanguine disposition, as well as a florid complexion. The root of sanguine is Latin *sanguis* 'blood'.

sanity [LME]
Latin *sanus* meant 'healthy' which is the first recorded sense of sanity in English. Current meanings date from the early 17th century when **sane** was first recorded, although **insane** dates from the mid 16th century. **Sanitary, sanitation,** and **sanatorium** where you go to recover your health, all 19th century, come from the same root.

sap [OE]
Old English *sæp* 'vital fluid' is probably of Germanic origin. The verb (as in sapped his energy) dating from the mid 18th century is often interpreted as a figurative use of the notion 'drain the sap from' but is unrelated. It comes originally from the late 16th-century verb sap 'dig a tunnel or covered trench' thus meaning 'undermine'. The latter is from French *saper*, from Italian *zappa* 'spade, spadework', probably from Arabic *sarab* 'underground passage', or *sabora* 'probe a wound, explore'. This is where the military engineers called **sappers** get their name.

sapphic *see* LESBIAN

sarcasm [M16th]
The words of a sarcastic person are 'biting', and it is the idea of biting into the flesh that is behind sarcasm. The word came into English in the mid 16th century from French, and is based on Greek *sarkazein* 'to tear flesh', which also came to mean 'to gnash the teeth, speak bitterly'. **Sarcophagus** [LME] has a similar history. The original Greek meant 'flesh-eating', and was formed from *sarx* 'flesh', the root also of **sarcoma** [M17th], and *-phagos* 'eating'. Sarcophagi were originally made of a type of stone that the ancient Greeks believed consumed the flesh of any dead body in contact with it.

salvage salvation salve salver salvo sample

sardonic [M17th] The Greek epic poet Homer, of the 8th century BC, used the word *sardanios* to describe bitter, scornful laughter. Later Greeks and Romans did not really understand the reason for this word and decided it must be *sardonios* 'Sardinian' and refer to a 'Sardinian plant' which produced facial convulsions resembling horrible laughter, usually followed by death. English adopted sardonic in the mid 17th century to refer to grimly mocking or cynical smiles, grins, and looks as well as to laughter. The island of Sardinia also gave us the name of the **sardine** [LME], the small fish which was once common off its shores—the Latin source of the word, *sarda*, is probably from the Greek name for the island *Sardō*.

sash [L16th] A sash is now worn over one shoulder or around the waist, but it was originally wrapped round the head. Between the late 16th and early 18th centuries a sash was a length of fine fabric twisted round the head as a turban, as in some Middle Eastern countries—the word is from Arabic. The sash in **sash window** is an alteration of **chassis**, which means 'frame' in French, based on Latin *capsa* 'box'. Originally both French and English people pronounced the final -*s* of **chassis**. English-speakers then took this as a plural form and shortened it to form a new singular which became sash. Chassis was readopted from French in the early 20th century to mean 'the base frame of a vehicle'. *See also* SCARF

Sassenach *see* SCOTTISH WORD PANEL

Satan [OE] This has been used as a name for the Devil since Anglo-Saxon times, and goes back to Hebrew *sātān*, which literally meant 'adversary'. William Blake's great poem 'Jerusalem', which is part of *Milton* (1804–1808) and later became a popular hymn, is the source of the phrase **dark satanic mills**. 'Jerusalem' also gave us 'England's green and pleasant land'.

satchel *see* SACK

sateen *see* SATIN

satellite [M16th] In 1611 the German astronomer Johannes Kepler, writing in Latin, gave the name *satellites* to the moons of Jupiter, which Galileo had recently discovered. An English publication referred to 'a Satellite of Jupiter' in 1665. In Latin *satelles*, of which *satellites* is the plural, meant 'an attendant or guard', a use occasionally found in English from the mid 16th century, usually with overtones of subservience or fawning attentiveness. Until the 1930s the only satellites in space were natural bodies such as planets and moons, but in 1936 the word was first applied to a man-made object (at that point just a theoretical one) put into orbit around the earth. The first artificial satellite to be launched was the Russian Sputnik 1, in 1957, and in 1962 the Telstar satellite relayed the first **satellite television** signal. **Sputnik** means 'fellow traveller' in Russian, while **Telstar** got its name because it was built by Bell Telephone Laboratories and used for telecommunications.

satiated *see* SAD

satin [LME] The word satin came via Old French from Arabic *zaytūnī* 'of Tsinkiang' which refers to a town in China. In the past satin was a silk fabric and China the main and at one time only source of silk. Late 19th-century **sateen** is an alteration of satin, on the pattern of velveteen. *See also* SILK

satire *see* SATURNINE

satisfactory, satisfy *see* SAD

saturnine [LME] In medieval astrology the planet Saturn represented lead, and those born under its influence could expect to be gloomy, sluggish, and cold. Belief in planetary influence may no longer be scientific, but the description saturnine lives on. The planet takes its name from the Roman god Saturn, the equivalent of Greek Cronus or Kronos, who had been the supreme god until Zeus dethroned him. **Saturday** [OE] was 'the day of Saturn' in Roman times. **Satire** [E16th] has no connection with Saturn, nor with satyrs. It comes from Latin *satura* 'poetic medley'

sardonic   sash   Sassenach   Satan   satchel

later used in the modern sense, while where the Greeks got the term for the goatish **satyrs** [LME] is not known. *See also* JOVIAL.

sauce [ME] This is another word that goes back to Latin *sal* *SALT, along with **sausage** [LME], and **salsa** [M19th], which is simply the Spanish word for 'sauce'. The Latin American dance the salsa [L20th] is so named because it is 'saucy'. The expression **what's sauce for the goose is sauce for the gander** implies that both sexes should be able to behave in the same way. John Ray, who recorded the saying in his *English Proverbs* of 1670, remarked that 'This is a woman's Proverb'. Cups now sit on saucers, but in the Middle Ages a **saucer** was used for holding condiments or sauces, and was usually made of metal. The description **saucy** originally simply meant 'savoury, flavoured with a sauce'. In the early 16th century it began to refer to people and behaviour, meaning at first 'impudent, presumptuous', mellowing into 'cheeky', then taking on suggestive overtones.

saurian *see* DINOSAUR

sausage *see* SAUCE

sauté *see* SALIENT

savage [ME] According to the origin of the name, savages live in woods. Savage derives from Latin *silva* 'a wood', the source also of the literary word **sylvan** [M16th], and perhaps of **sylph** [M17th], an imaginary spirit of the air. The overtones of savage are usually negative, suggesting violence and cruelty, but in the later 18th century the French writer and philosopher Jean-Jacques Rousseau (1712–78) conceived the idea of the **noble savage**, an idealized being without the corrupting influence of civilization, showing the natural goodness of humankind.

save [ME] A medieval word that is based on Latin *salvus* 'uninjured, safe' (*see* SAFETY). The idea of **saving someone's skin** goes back to the late 16th century, a century before **save someone's neck** is recorded. *See also* BACON. A boxer in imminent danger of being knocked or counted out may be **saved**

by the bell [M20th] for the end of the round and be able to go back to his corner for a rest. Goalkeepers in soccer have **saved shots** since the 1880s, but before that the word was used in cricket when a fielder prevented a run being scored.

savour *see* FLAVOUR

saw *see* SAGA

saxophone *see* PHONETIC

say [OE] Old English *secgan* is of Germanic origin, related to Dutch *zeggen* and German *sagen*. Say, *SPEAK, and *TELL are near-synonyms but say is usually followed by the words or statement actually said, giving the verb the sense 'utter, declare'. **When all is said and done** dates from the mid 16th century; to **say it with flowers** was an early 20th century advertising slogan of the Society of American Florists. **You can say that again** was originally a US usage from the 1940s. The phrase **I say, I say, I say** to introduce a joke is first recorded from the 1960s.

scab [ME] This comes from Old Norse, going back to a Germanic root meaning 'itch'. The sense 'contemptible person' dating from the late 16th century was probably influenced by Middle Dutch *schabbe* 'slut'. It was used to refer to a blackleg in a strike from the mid 18th century, originally in the USA. **Shabby** [M17th] comes from a dialect variant of the source of scab. Dr Johnson wrote that shabby was: 'A word that has crept into conversation and low writing, but ought not to be admitted into the language'.

scald [ME] To scald comes from Anglo-Norman French *escalder*, from late Latin *excaldare* 'wash in hot water' formed from Latin *ex-* 'thoroughly' and *calidus* 'hot'.

scale [ME] English has three main words scale, two of which share an ancestry. The scale of fishes and reptiles has the same root as the scale used for weighing, and both are related to *SHELL. The first scale is the one in **the scales fall from someone's eyes**, 'someone is no longer deceived'. In the biblical Acts of the Apostles the expression describes how St Paul, blinded by his vision on the road to Damascus, was given his sight back by God. The weighing scale had the early sense 'drinking cup' (a meaning which survives in South African English) which probably transferred to the pans of the scales. It comes from Old Norse *skál* 'bowl', also source of the drinking toast **skol**. The scale in music and measuring derives from Latin *scala* 'ladder', from the root of *scandere* 'to climb', an element in **ascend, descend,** and **condescend,** all Late Middle English. *See also* ECHELON, SCAN

scamp [M18th] Nowadays most scamps are children but in the 18th century a scamp was a much more serious proposition—a highwayman. In the 19th century the original sense moderated into 'a swindler, cheat', a derogatory use still in existence in Caribbean English. The word probably derives from early Dutch *schampen* 'to slip away'. This may also be the source of **scamper** [L17th] although Italian *scampare* 'decamp' is an alternative source. The first recorded sense was 'run away'. It was very common between 1687 and 1700, and may have been military slang.

scan [LME] This was first used as a verb in the sense 'analyse the metre (of verse)'. The source is Latin *scandere* 'climb' by comparison with the raising and lowering of one's foot when marking rhythm. From this the sense developed into 'estimate the correctness of' and 'examine minutely', which in turn led to 'look at searchingly' in the late 18th century. *See also* SCALE

scandal [ME] The words scandal and **slander** [ME] are closely related. Both go back to Latin *scandalum* 'cause of offence', from Greek *skandalon* 'snare, stumbling block'. Originally scandal was a term restricted to the Christian Church. It referred to behaviour by a religious person that might bring discredit on their beliefs, and then, going back to the idea of a 'stumbling block', something that hinders faith. Our modern sense of an event causing general public outrage dates from the late 16th century and is first recorded in

Shakespeare's *Comedy of Errors*: 'I wonder much That you would put me to this shame and trouble, And not without some scandal to your self, With circumstance and oaths, so to deny this chain, which now you wear so openly'. *See* LIBEL

scapegoat [M16th] In the biblical Book of Leviticus God tells Moses that the Jewish people should take two goats and cast lots to determine their fate—the chief priest is to lay the sins of the people on one before driving it out into the wilderness, while the other is to be sacrificed. The animal driven away is the scapegoat. This was the only context in which the word appeared until the early 19th century, when it extended its meaning to 'a person who is blamed for the wrongdoings of others'. The first part, **scape**, is a shortening of **escape**, as the goat escapes death by sacrifice.

scarecrow *see* DARE

scarf [M16th] While a *SASH was once a head covering, a scarf was once what we would now call a sash. Worn chiefly by officials or soldiers it served for carrying things. It is likely that it is based on Old Northern French *escarpe*, probably identical with Old French *escharpe* 'pilgrim's bag or pouch'.

scarlet [ME] Scarlet originally referred to an expensive type of cloth. Since good strong colours, particularly a fast bright red, were expensive they were only used on high-quality cloth and the word was associated with the colour rather than the cloth by the 15th century. It is a shortening of Old French *escarlate*, from medieval Latin *scarlata*: this came via Arabic and medieval Greek from late Latin *sigillatus* 'decorated with small images', from *sigillum* 'small image', which must originally have referred to embroidered or damasked cloth. The sense 'red with shame or indignation' dates from the mid 19th century. The phrase **scarlet woman** arose in the early 19th century, originally applied (as scarlet lady), with reference to Revelation 17, to the Roman Catholic Church, by those who perceived it as devoted to showy ritual.

scamp   scan   scandal   scapegoat   scarecrow

scarper [M19th] This is probably from Italian *scappare* 'to escape', influenced by the rhyming slang Scapa Flow 'go'.

scavenger [M16th] The earliest form of scavenger was *scavager*, an official who collected **scavage**, a toll on foreign merchants' goods, found from the 15th century. Scavagers eventually also acquired the duty of keeping the streets of their town clean. In the mid 16th century people began to insert an -*n*- in the word and scavenger was born, in the same way as **messenger** and **passenger**, both also words that started out life without an -*n*-. In time the municipal officials lost their more important duties and a scavenger became simply a street cleaner and then a person who collects anything usable from discarded waste.

scene [M16th] The scenes in **behind the scenes**, 'in private', are the pieces of scenery on a theatre stage. This reflects the origin of scene, which is ultimately from Greek *skēnē* 'tent, stage', source also of **scenario** [L19th], **scenery** [M18th], and **scenic** [M17th]. The theatrical associations of scene gave us the meaning 'a public display of emotion or anger', which is from the middle of the 18th century.

scent [LME] Before it was perfume, scent was a hunting term for a hound's sense of smell. From there it became an odour picked up by a hound, and then in the 15th century a pleasant smell. The word came into medieval English through Old French from Latin *sentire* 'to feel or perceive', from which **sensation** [E17th], **sense** [LME], **sensible** [LME], **sensitive** [LME], **sensory** [M18th], **sentence** [ME] originally a way of perceiving, and numerous other words without a -*c*- derive. People started spelling scent with a -*c*- in the 17th century, but no one knows exactly why.

sceptic [L16th] This word comes from Greek *skeptikos*, from *skepsis* 'inquiry, doubt' and was first used to refer to a philosopher denying the possibility of knowledge in a certain sphere; the leading ancient sceptic was Pyrrho (*c*.360–270 BC)

whose followers at the Academy vigorously opposed Stoicism.

sceptre [ME] The sceptre carried by modern rulers on ceremonial occasions is generally a short ornamented stick, but the word's origin shows that it was originally longer. The word came into medieval English from Old French *ceptron*, but goes back to Greek *skēptron*, from *skēptein* 'to lean on'. Ancient Greek vase paintings show kings holding tall sceptres long enough to lean on. **This sceptred isle** is Britain. The term comes from John of Gaunt's description of the island in Shakespeare's *Richard II*: 'This royal throne of kings, this sceptred isle...This precious stone set in the silver sea.'

schadenfreude *see* GERMAN WORD PANEL

schedule [LME] An early schedule was a 'scroll, explanatory note, appendix'. It comes via Old French from late Latin *schedula* 'slip of paper' from Greek *skhedē* 'papyrus leaf'. The sense 'timetable' is found from the mid 19th century in US usage. The British pronounce the word with an initial 'sh' sound but Americans with a 'sk'. This prompted Dorothy Parker (1893–1967) to say to the British actor Herbert Marshal who had annoyed her by repeated references to his busy 'shedule' 'I think you're full of skit'.

scheme [M16th] This was originally a term in rhetoric for 'a figure of speech'. It comes from Latin *schema*, from Greek. An early sense in English was 'diagram of the position of celestial objects', giving rise to 'diagram, outline', which led to the current senses.

schism [LME] This goes back to Greek *skhisma* 'cleft' from *skhizein* 'to split'. This is also the origin of **schizophrenia** [E20th] combining *skhizein* with *phren* 'mind', and of the rock called **schist** [L18th] which splits easily into layers.

schlep *see* SLAP, YIDDISH WORD PANEL

schlock, schmaltz, schmooze, schmuck, schnozz *see* YIDDISH WORD PANEL

school [OE] The school that children go to derives from Greek *skholē* 'leisure, philosophy, place for lectures', the source also of **scholar** [OE]. Many ancient Greeks clearly spent their leisure time in intellectual pursuits rather than physical recreation. This is not the same **school** that large groups of fish or sea mammals congregate in. Here the word comes from early German and Dutch *schōle*, 'a troop, multitude', and comes from the same root as **shoal** [OE] and is related to **shallow** [LME].

schtick, schtum *see* YIDDISH WORD PANEL

science [ME] Originally science was knowledge in general, or any branch of knowledge, including the arts, and the word is from Latin *scire* 'to know' (also found in **conscience** [ME] 'inner knowledge' and *NICE). The restricted modern sense of science, concentrating on the physical and natural world, dates from the 18th century. **Science fiction** was first mentioned in 1851, but this was an isolated use, and the term did not become common until the end of the 1920s, when US 'pulp' magazines (so called because of the cheap paper they were printed on) like *Astounding Stories* carried tales of space adventure. Before science fiction was coined the stories of writers such as Jules Verne were called **scientific fiction** or **scientifiction**.

scintillate *see* TINSEL

scissors [LME] Scissors is from Old French *cisoires*, from late Latin *cisoria*, the plural of *cisorium* 'cutting instrument'. The prefix *cis-* here is a variant of *caes-*, from *caedere* 'to cut', a variant also found in **chisel** [LME]. The spelling with *sc-* occurred in the 16th century by association with the Latin *sciss-* from *scinder* 'to cut'.

scold [ME] This is probably from Old Norse *skáld* 'poet'; there may have been an intermediate sense 'lampooner'. In early use in English the word often referred to a woman using ribald language; and the verb had gained the sense 'chide' by the early 18th century.

scone [E16th] Until the 19th century the scone was known only in Scotland. The novels of Sir Walter Scott probably helped bring the word to wider notice, and Robert Louis Stevenson wrote in 1886 in *Kidnapped*: 'We lay on the bare top of a rock, like scones upon a girdle.' The first scones were large round cakes made of wheat or barley and often cut into four quarters. The word is probably from early Dutch *scoon broot*, 'fine bread'. **Scone** can be pronounced to rhyme with either gone or tone. In the US the pronunciation rhyming with tone is more common, whereas in British English the two pronunciations traditionally have different regional and class associations. The first tends to be associated with the north of England, while the second is associated with the south and is thought of as more 'refined'.

scoop *see* SHAPE

scope *see* KALEIDOSCOPE

score *see* SCOTCH

scorn [ME] Scorn is a shortening of Old French *escarn*, of Germanic origin. The phrase **hell hath no fury like a woman scorned** is a version of a line in William Congreve's 1697 play *The Mourning Bride*: 'Heav'n has no Rage, like Love to Hatred turn'd, Nor Hell a Fury, like a Woman scorn'd'.

scotch [E17th] To scotch or decisively put an end to something derives from an old use of the word for a wedge placed under a wheel to prevent its moving or slipping. Another use of scotch, 'to make something temporarily harmless', goes back to a line from Shakespeare's *Macbeth*: 'We have scotched the snake, not killed it.' This is not what originally appeared in Shakespeare's

schlock schmaltz schmooze schmuck

text, where the word first used was 'scorched', meaning 'slashed with a knife'. This was an alteration of **score** but was short-lived, and later editors wondered what on earth burning the skin of a snake had to do with it, assuming that 'scorched' must be a printer's error. The origin of scotch itself is unknown, but score [OE] comes from Old Norse 'to make a cut or notch'. The term for twenty comes from counting by cutting notches in a piece of wood called a tally, with the word for the notch transferred to the number.

scot-free [ME] The people of Scotland are fond of freedom, but they play no part in this expression, which means 'without suffering any punishment or injury'. The scot here is a payment corresponding to a modern tax or property rate, so scot-free was 'tax-free'. The word came from old Scandinavian in the Anglo-Saxon period, and is the equivalent of Old English *shot*. The first **Scots** were an ancient Gaelic-speaking people that migrated from Ireland to the northwest of Britain around the end of the 5th century. The name appears in Latin around AD 400, and then in Old English, originally referring to Irishmen, then to the Scots in northern Britain. There is no original person called Scott in the exclamation **Great Scott!**, which is recorded from the 1880s. It was simply a way to avoid saying 'God'. Other similar expressions of the time were **Great Caesar!** and **Great Sun!**.

For auld lang syne

Scotland *has given English many words—some from the Gaelic language, some from Scots, and others reflecting links to further shores. The Scots poet Robert Burns (1759–96) has also weighed in with memorable expressions.*

A FTER a history marked by conflict, the Scottish and English nations were joined by the Act of Union in 1707, but tensions still sometimes surface. When a Scot calls an Englishman a **Sassenach** he is reaching back into history, as the word is a Gaelic version of Latin *Saxones* 'Saxons'.

Anyone who has ever been to a New Year's Eve party will have linked arms to the song 'Auld Lang Syne', but probably not known what the expression means. *Auld lang syne* is literally 'times long past', and **for auld lang syne** is 'for old times' sake'. The phrase was popularized as the title and refrain of a 1788 song by Robert Burns. *Syne* is an old Scottish and northern English spelling of 'since'.

Wee, 'small', was originally a noun meaning 'a little or young thing, a child' and 'a small quantity'. It is from Old English *wēg* or *wēge*, which was connected with *WEIGH. The word is particularly associated with the opening of Burns's poem 'To a Mouse' (1786): 'Wee, sleekit, cowrin', tim'rous beastie / O what a panic's in thy breastie!' **Sleekit** or **sleeked** means 'having smooth, glossy skin or fur'.

Scotland is known as the Land of Cakes, but the phrase refers to oatcakes rather than to sweet treats. It is also famous for a dish addressed by Burns as

scope   score   scorn   scotch   scot-free

'Great chieftain o' the puddin'-race'. This was not a dessert, though, but the haggis. Scots have been eating a dish called **haggis**, consisting of chopped offal with suet and oatmeal boiled in a casing (traditionally a sheep's stomach), since the late Middle Ages. The word probably comes from **hag** 'to hack, cut', a Scottish and northern English equivalent of **hew**.

Burns is also responsible for the name of the **tam-o-shanter**, a woollen cap of a kind originally worn by ploughmen and other workers in Scotland. It is named after the hero of the poem 'Tam o' Shanter' (1790), a farmer who, returning home late after a long evening in the pub, came upon witches dancing in a churchyard and was chased by them over a bridge, escaping only because his horse's tail came off as the leading witch grasped it. Contemporary illustrations of the poem often showed Tam in this kind of cap.

Many Scots words refer to distinctive clothing. Nothing could be more Scottish than **tartan**, a woollen cloth woven in a pattern of coloured checks and intersecting lines, but the word is probably from Old French *tertaine*, a kind of cloth that may have got its name because it was imported from the distant east through Tartary, a region that included what are now Siberia, Turkestan, and Mongolia.

The origins of the **kilt** are less distant. In medieval English **kilt** was a verb meaning 'to tuck up the skirt around the body' that came from Scandinavia. As an item of male Highland dress it is not recorded until around 1750.

You are most likely to see a **plaid** as part of the ceremonial dress of the pipe band of a Scottish regiment—it is a piece of tartan worn over the shoulder. Although people now associate it with the Scottish Highlands, the plaid was formerly also worn as a shawl or cloak in other parts of Scotland and in the north of England. In the Highlands it was often a person's principal, if not only, garment. The word may come from Scottish Gaelic *plaide* 'blanket', though it is possible that **plaid** is an early form of **plied**: to **ply** originally meant 'to fold'.

A **brogue** was originally a crude kind of shoe worn by the inhabitants of the wilder parts of Ireland and the Scottish Highlands. The word comes from Gaelic, though in origin it is Scandinavian and related to **breeches**. In the early 20th century the brogue emerged as a stout shoe for outdoor pursuits. The use of **brogue** to mean an Irish or Scottish accent may come from the way that those who wore brogues spoke.

See also MULL, PILLION, SLOGAN, TROUSERS, WHISKY

---

scourge [ME] Scourge is a shortening of Old French *escorgier*, from Latin *ex-* 'thoroughly' and *corrigia* 'thong, whip'. It is a word used most often figuratively as in the **Scourge of God** for an instrument of divine chastisement, the title given by historians to Attila the Hun in the 5th century.

Scouse [M19th] The success of the Beatles and other Liverpool groups and singers in the 1960s focused attention on their native city, and the words Scouse and **Scouser** became widely familiar in Britain. They represent shortenings of **lobscouse**, a stew made with meat, vegetables, and ship's biscuit formerly eaten by sailors and so a staple food in the thriving port of Liverpool. Lobscouse is recorded from the early 18th century, but its origin is unknown. Before the 1960s **Scouse** meaning 'Liverpudlian' appeared in print only in a 1945 report of a trial, where a witness used the word and a puzzled judge asked for an explanation, although it was recorded 100 years earlier for the food.

scout [LME] Scouts go ahead of a main force to gather information about an enemy's position and strength. The root of the word scout implies that the first scouts used their ears to pick up clues rather than making visual observations, as it is Latin *auscultare* 'to listen to'. The English soldier Lord Baden-Powell admired the skills and resilience of these military scouts, and had also seen the successful use of boys as scouts by the Boers in southern Africa. In the summer of 1907 he organized a camp for boys on Brownsea Island in Dorset, and the following year founded **the Scout Association** to develop boys' characters by training them in self-sufficiency and survival techniques. The organization now exists worldwide, and has admitted girls since 1990. **Scout's honour** is the oath members take that they will stand by a promise or tell the truth.

scrabble [M16th] In the game **Scrabble** players build up words from small lettered squares or tiles. The name was registered as a trademark in January 1950, but the word **scrabble** dates from the mid 16th century, and came from early Dutch *schrabben* 'to scrape'. The original meaning was 'to scrawl or scribble', followed by 'to scratch or grope about' in the late 16th century.

scramble [L16th] This is an imitative word comparable to the dialect words *scamble* meaning 'stumble' and *cramble* meaning 'crawl'. The word **scram** which appeared in the early 20th century is probably from the verb *scramble*.

scrape [OE] Old English *scrapian* meant 'scratch with the fingernails'. The sense 'awkward predicament' (**got himself into a scrape**) dates from the early 18th century

and is probably from the notion of being 'scraped', making one's way along a narrow passage. This sense may be behind the use of **scrap** [L17th] for 'to fight', while scrap [LME] for small piece originally referred to food, and comes from the Old Norse equivalent of scrape.

scratch [LME] Two English dialect words with the same meaning, **scrat** and **cratch**, probably combined to form **scratch** in the medieval period. The origins of **from scratch**, 'from the very beginning, without making use of any previous work', lie in the sporting world. In the past certain sports such as cycling and running sometimes used a particular handicap system. A line or mark, known as the scratch, was drawn to indicate the starting position for all competitors except those who had been awarded an advantage: they were allowed to start a little way in front. So a competitor starting from scratch would start from a position without any advantage. The expression **up to scratch**, meaning 'up to the required standard', also comes from this practice, as originally it referred to someone who was good enough to start from the scratch line. Napoleon had bad experiences in Russia. In 1812 the severity of the Russian winter and the resistance of the Russian people forced his retreat from Moscow. Of the Russians Napoleon is reported to have said 'scratch the Russian and you will find the Tartar'. Whether or not this is true, from 1823 the saying is referred to in English, and people began to use the formula **scratch X and find Y** of other nationalities and persons. George Bernard Shaw wrote in *St Joan* in 1924: 'Scratch an Englishman, and find a Protestant', while Dorothy Parker wrote in 1937 'Scratch a lover, and find a foe'.

screw [LME] Pigs have curly tails like corkscrews, and the ultimate source of **screw** is Latin *scrofa* 'a sow', source also of **scrofula** [LME], a disease people thought breeding sows were particularly susceptible to. Scrofula was also called the **King's Evil**, because kings were traditionally thought to be able to cure it. *Scrofa* changed its meaning to 'screw' in Latin, and then

scout   scrabble   scramble   scrape   scratch

altered its form as it passed through French and arrived in English in the late medieval period. The slang sense 'to have sex', dating from the early 18th century, is probably the source of **screw up** meaning 'to mess up', which started off in the Second World War. It was a US euphemism for **f— up**.

scripture [ME] Latin *scribere* 'to write' is the source of scripture, literally 'writings', of **scribe** [ME] and **inscribe** [LME]; **script** [LME] 'something written' and **scribble** [LME] 'little writing'.

scrofula *see* SCREW

Scrooge [M19th] The transformation of the bad-tempered, miserly Ebenezer Scrooge into a kind and philanthropic old gentleman is the theme of Charles Dickens's *A Christmas Carol*, published in 1843. On Christmas Eve the ghost of Marley, his former business partner, shows him visions of the past, present, and future, including what his own death will be like if he does not mend his ways. On Christmas Day Scrooge sends a turkey to his abused clerk Bob Cratchit, subscribes willingly to charities, and is generally genial to all. The book became an instant Christmas classic, and since the mid 20th century any miserly killjoy has been a **Scrooge**.

scruff [E16th] As an insult for a person with a dirty or untidy appearance, scruff is an alteration of **scurf** [OE], meaning dandruff or a similar skin condition, which comes from the same root as Old English words meaning 'to gnaw' and 'to shred'. The reversal of letters from **scurf** to **scruff** is also seen in *BIRD and *DIRT, originally *brid* and *drit*. The **scruff of the neck** was originally the **scuff**—the word is recorded from the late 18th century, but its origin is obscure.

scrutiny *see* INSCRUTABLE

scud *see* SCUTTLE

scuff *see* SCRUFF

scupper [L19th] This was first used as military slang in the sense 'kill, especially in an ambush'. The origin is uncertain. It may

be from scupper in the sense of the opening on a ship to allow water to drain, with the idea that a fallen sailor would roll into the scuppers, but since we do not know the origin of this word, we do not get much further. The sense 'sink' dates from the 1970s, perhaps through confusion with *SCUTTLE.

scurf *see* SCRUFF

scurrilous [L16th] This word meaning 'spreading scandal' is based on Latin *scurrilus* which comes from *scurra* 'buffoon'.

scuttle [OE] There are three main scuttles in English. The one you keep coal in meant a dish in Old English and comes via Old Norse from Latin *scutella* 'dish'. The one for moving is probably from dialect *scuddle* from **scud** [M16th] 'move quickly', which may have come from **scut** [LME] originally meaning a hare, but now better known as the tail of a hare or rabbit. This would give scud an original meaning similar to the modern informal 'to hare along' for to move quickly. The scuttle of a ship is first found as a noun meaning 'hatchway' at the end of the 15th century, and only as a verb 'to sink' from the mid 17th. It may come, via French, from Spanish *escotilla* 'hatchway'.

sea [OE] An Old English word, related to Dutch *zee* and German *See*. A person who is **at sea** or **all at sea** is confused or unable to decide what to do—they are being likened to a ship out of the sight of land which has lost its bearings. The term **sea change** for a profound or notable transformation comes from the song 'Full fathom five' in Shakespeare's *The Tempest*: 'Nothing of him that doth fade, / But doth suffer a sea change / Into something rich and strange.'

seagull *see* GULLIBLE

seal [OE] Rather than signing their name, people formerly stamped a personal seal in wax on a completed letter or other document. The expressions **put the seal on**, 'to put the finishing touch to something', and **set your seal to**, 'to mark something with your own distinctive character', both derive from this. To **seal something off**

scripture scrofula Scrooge scruff scrutiny

reflects the use of seals to check that something has not been opened or disturbed. In these and related uses, seal goes back to Latin *sigillum* 'small picture', from *signum* 'a sign', the source of **design** [L16th], **designate** [M17th], **ensign** [LME], **insignia** [M17th], **sign** [ME], **signal** [LME], *SCARLET, and numerous other English words. This seal dates from Middle English. The name of the animal seal derives from Old English *seolh*, the source also of the **selkie** or **silkie** [M16th], the mysterious seal woman of folklore.

search [ME] This is from the Old French verb *cerchier* from late Latin *circare* 'go round', from Latin *circus* 'circle'. The main semantic strands are 'explore thoroughly' (**search the premises**) and 'try to find' (**search out the truth**), both of which have been present from the start. In **research** [L16th] the prefix *re-* is an intensifier of the meaning. The Old English equivalent **seek** is unconnected, going back to an Indo-European root shared by Latin *sagire* 'perceive by scent'.

season [ME] This is from Old French *seson*, from a Latin term which initially meant 'sowing' but which later came to mean 'time of sowing', from *serere* 'to sow'. The sense 'add savoury flavouring to (a dish)' was in early use; it comes from the primary sense in Old French which was 'to ripen, make (fruit) palatable by the influence of the seasons'.

seat [ME] An old Scandinavian word which goes back even further to the same source as Latin *sedere* 'to sit'. The Latin word is also the origin of **sedentary** [L16th], **sedative** [LME], and **sediment** [M16th], and from its past tense **session** [LME] literally an act of sitting, so settling down to deal with something. The sense 'a place where a government is based', as in **seat of government** or **power**, comes from the throne or 'seat' of a king or governor. American pilots in the 1940s were the first to use **by the seat of the pants**, meaning that they flew the plane using their instinct and experience rather than relying on the aircraft's instrument panel. An experienced

pilot could tell by a change in the vibrations of the seat if, for example, the plane was about to stall, and so take early action to rescue the situation.

seclude *see* EXCLUDE

second [ME] This comes from Latin *secundus* 'following, second', from *sequi* 'to follow', which gives its base sense. The time word [LME] is from medieval Latin *secunda* (*minuta*) 'second (minute)', referring to the 'second' operation of dividing an hour by 60. The verb [E19th] as in **seconded the motion** is from French *en second* 'in the second rank (of officers)'. The use was originally military involving the removal of an officer temporarily from his regiment to an extra-regimental appointment. **Sect** [ME], originally 'a following' is also from *sequi*, as is **persecute** [LME] 'to follow with hostility', and *SEQUEL.

secret [LME] Secret goes back to the Latin adjective *secretus* meaning 'separate, set apart'. **Secretary** [LME] originally referred to a 'person entrusted with a secret'. A *secretarius* in late Latin was a 'confidential officer'. **Secrete** [M18th] meaning 'to hide' is from the same source, but the sense secrete 'produce and discharge' (**secreting insulin**) dates from the early 18th century and was from **secretion** [M17th] which is from Latin *secretio* 'separation'.

sect *see* SECOND

section *see* INSECT

secular [ME] Use of the word in contexts where there is a contrast between religious life and civil or lay life is based on Latin *saeculum* 'generation, age'. In Christian Latin this meant 'the world' as opposed to the Church. Use of secular in astronomy or economics (**secular acceleration, secular trend**) is early 19th century, from *saecularis* 'relating to an age or period'.

secure *see* CURATE

security *see* SURE

sedan *see* SALOON

search season seat seclude second secret

sedative, sedentary, sediment *see* SEAT

seduce *see* DUCT

see [OE] The see meaning 'to perceive with the eyes' perhaps comes from the same ancient root as Latin *sequi* 'to follow', seen in *SECOND and *SEQUEL. Referring to the district of a bishop or archbishop, see goes back to Latin *sedere* 'to sit' (*see* SEAT). In the 1927 film *The Jazz Singer* Al Jolson uttered the aside 'You ain't heard nothing yet'. This became the model for similar phrases, notably **you ain't seen nothing yet**. The computer slogan **what you see is what you get**—abbreviated as **WYSIWYG**—began life in the USA; the first recorded example is from the *New York Times* in 1971. It refers to the representation of text on screen in a form exactly corresponding to its appearance on a printout. 'Why don't you **come up and see me sometime?'** will be forever associated with the vampish actress Mae West. What she actually said in the film *She Done Him Wrong* (1933) was 'Why don't you come up sometime, and see me?'. Mae West is remembered for a number of saucy quips, among them 'Is that a gun in your pocket, or are you just glad to see me?' and 'It's not the men in my life that counts—it's the life in my men', while her buxom figure led to the inflatable life jacket issued to RAF personnel during the Second World War being called a **Mae West**. *See also* EVIL

seed *see* SOW

seek *see* SEARCH

seersucker *see* PERSIAN WORD PANEL

seethe [OE] Old English *sēothan* meant 'make or keep boiling'. The sense 'be in a state of inner turmoil' dates from the early 17th century and has parallels in words like stew, which only developed the sense of 'fret, worry' in the early 20th century, although **stew in your own juice** is found from the mid 17th.

segment *see* INSECT

segregation *see* CONGREGATE

segue *see* SEQUEL

seismograph *see* PHOTOGRAPH

seize [ME] Seize goes back to the customs of feudal times. It is from Old French *seizir* 'give seisin' (legal possession), from medieval Latin *ad proprium sacire* 'claim as one's own', from a Germanic base meaning 'procedure' going back to the same root as *SAKE. The sense 'jam, cease to function' in mechanical contexts dates from the late 19th century. *See also* LATIN WORD PANEL

selkie *see* SEAL

sell [OE] An Old English word that originally meant 'to give, hand over in response to a request'. The longer version of the expression **sell your soul**, 'to do absolutely anything to achieve your objective', is **sell your soul to the devil**. Over the centuries various people reputedly agreed to give their soul to the devil if in return he would grant them all their heart's desires in this life. The most famous person alleged to have made such a pact was the 16th-century German astronomer and necromancer Faust, whose story inspired Christopher Marlowe's play *Doctor Faustus*, and gives us the expression Faustian [L19th] as in **Faustian pact**. **Sale** [OE] comes via Old Norse from the same Germanic root as sell. Use of the word for selling goods at a lower price than before dates from the mid 19th century.

semblance *see* SIMILAR

semen *see* SOW

senate [ME] Senate and senator are from Latin *senatus*, from *senex* 'old man'. Use in modern times was taken from the Roman Senate, and elected body which was originally believed to have been a council of the elders of the tribes, chosen for their wisdom. *See also* SIR

senile *see* SIR

sensation, sense, sensible, sensitive, sensory, sentence *see* SCENT

sedative sedentary sediment seduce see

separate *see* APPARATUS

seppuku *see* JAPANESE WORD PANEL

September, septet *see* SEVEN

septic [E17th] Septic came via Latin from Greek *sēptikos*, from *sēpein* 'make rotten'.

sequel [LME] The earliest use of sequel was 'a band of followers'. Latin *sequi* 'to follow' is the source, seen also in **consequence** [LME] and **sequence** [LME], and perhaps in the root of *SEE. Sequel developed the senses 'what happens afterwards' and 'the remaining part of a story' in the early 16th century. In the 1970s it inspired the **prequel**, which portrays events that precede those of an existing completed work. From music comes **segue** [M18] from Italian *seguire* from *sequi*. It was originally an instruction in classical music to continue to the next movement without a break, but is now more often found used of moving from one recorded song to another without a break.

sequin *see* ARABIC WORD PANEL

serenade [M17th] A serenade conjures up an image of a young man singing or playing to his beloved under her window or balcony at night. The word's origins imply none of these things, requiring only that the performance be 'serene'. It goes back through French and Italian to Latin *serenus* 'calm, clear, fair'. The idea of serenading by night may derive from association with *sera*, the Italian word for 'night'. *Serenus* is also the source of **serene** and **serenity** [both LME].

serendipity [M18th] The delightful word serendipity, meaning 'the occurrence of events by chance in a beneficial way', was invented by the writer and politician Horace Walpole before or at the beginning of 1754, from **Serendip**, an old name for Sri Lanka. Walpole was a prolific letter writer, and he explained to one of his main correspondents that he had based the word on the title of a fairy tale, *The Three Princes of Serendip*, the heroes of which 'were

always making discoveries, by accidents and sagacity, of things they were not in quest of'.

serene, serenity *see* SERENADE

sergeant [ME] Sergeant is from Old French *sergent*, from Latin *servire* 'serve'. Early use was as a term meaning 'attendant, servant' and 'common soldier'; the term was later applied to specific official roles. The Middle English word **serjeant** is a variant commonly used in legal contexts.

series [E17th] This is an English use of a Latin word meaning literally 'row, chain'.

serpent *see* SNAKE

serrated [E18th] This is based on late Latin *serratus*, from Latin *serra* 'saw'.

sesame [LME] One of the stories told in the *Arabian Nights* is that of 'Ali Baba and the Forty Thieves'. Ali Baba gains access to the robbers' cave by saying the magic words 'open sesame!', at which the door flies open. This and the other Arabic tales in the collection were published in French in the early 18th century and were quickly translated into English. This gave a new lease of life to, and fixed the form of, sesame as the name of a plant with oil-rich seeds, which had appeared occasionally since the later Middle Ages in a variety of spellings. The word itself is recorded in Greek as *sēsamon* or *sēsamē*, but is probably connected to Arabic *simsim*. Since the early 19th century **an open sesame** has meant an easy way of securing access to what would normally be inaccessible.

session *see* SEAT

set [OE] Old English *settan* is from a Germanic source and is related to Dutch *zetten*, German *setzen*, and English **sit** [OE]. Confusion between *set* and *sit* began as early as the 14th century from similarity of certain past forms and certain senses. Meanings branch into: 'cause to sit' (**set them upon the camel's back**); 'sink' (**the sun has set**); 'put in a definite place' (**sleeves set into the shirt**); 'appoint, establish' (**set a boundary**);

'arrange, adjust' (**set a snare**); 'place mentally' (**set at naught**); 'come into a settled condition' (**her face set in a sulky stare**); and 'cause to take a certain direction' (**set our course at north north-east**). The word for a group or collection is partly from Latin *secta* ('*SECT', and partly from set 'fix, place.'

seven [OE] Seven days of the week, seven deadly sins, seven dwarfs, seven wonders of the world, the Magnificent Seven . . . the number seven crops up again and again in history and culture. The word is from the same ancient root as Latin *septem* and Greek *hepta* 'seven'—*septem* is the source of **September** [OE], originally the seventh month of the Roman year, and of **septet** [E19th], whereas *hepta* is found in words such as **heptagon** [L16th] 'seven angled', and **heptathlon** [1970s] combined with *athlon* 'contest'. The **seven-year itch** was originally a semi-proverbial medical condition, dating from the middle of the 19th century, but these days is a supposed tendency to infidelity after seven years of marriage. The phrase originated in the USA, and *The Seven Year Itch*, a 1955 comedy written and directed by Billy Wilder and starring Marilyn Monroe, introduced it to a wider audience.

severe [M16th] This comes from Latin *severus* 'strict harsh' the earliest sense of the word in English. The sense 'sober, austerely plain' (**severe dress**) dates from the mid 17th century; the first example of severe weather dates from the late 17th century.

sewer [ME] This initially meant a watercourse to drain marshy land. The source is Old Northern French *seuwiere* 'channel to drain the overflow from a fish pond', based on Latin *ex-* 'out of' and *aqua* 'water'. **Sewage**, developed from sewer in the mid 19th century.

sex [LME] Sex entered the language in medieval times from Latin *sexus*, and first referred to the two genders. Women have been **the fair** or **the fairer sex** since the middle of the 17th century, when men were

sometimes called **the better** or **the sterner sex**. In reference to hanky-panky, sex has only been used since the early part of the 20th century, with D.H. Lawrence being among the first to talk of 'having sex'. To **sex up** has been around as an expression since the 1940s, meaning 'to make more sexy'. A new use hit the headlines in 2003 when a BBC journalist claimed that the British Labour government had knowingly 'sexed up' a report on whether Iraq possessed weapons of mass destruction. People or things have been **sexy** in the literal sense since the 1920s. The sense 'very exciting or appealing' appeared in the 1950s, and has led to some odd phrases, like this from the *New York Magazine* in 2003: 'Sexy flat-panel screen, woofer, and remote control included'.

sextet, sextuple *see* SIX

shabby *see* SCAB

shack [L19th] A word from the USA, shack is perhaps from Mexican *jacal*, Nahuatl *xacatli* 'wooden hut'.

shade [OE] The Old English word shade is related to **shadow,** both going back to the same Indo-European root. Late 16th-century **shady** is based on *shade*; colloquial use meaning 'questionable, disreputable' arose in the mid 19th century perhaps from university slang. The origins of **shades of—**, used to suggest that one thing is reminiscent of another, have nothing to do with colour, but go back to an old use of shade to mean 'a ghost'. The idea behind the phrase is that the person or event either resembles or calls to mind someone or something from the past. By the late 19th century the meaning 'ghost' was more or less restricted to works of literature, so it is odd that it should have been revived in this phrase in the mid 20th century. An example from the American magazine *Town & Country* reflects its popularity: 'Shades of Jackie O, the Duke and Duchess, Capote, and an era when classic French cuisine, spacious luxury, and swizzle sticks were *de rigueur*.'

seven severe sewer sex sextet sextuple

shag [OE] Shag as in **shag pile carpet** was *sceacga* 'rough matted hair' in Old English. Of Germanic origin, it is related to Old Norse *skegg* 'beard'. The mid 16th-century bird name shag is perhaps a specific use of the word, with reference to the bird's 'shaggy' crest. The use of the verb to mean sexual intercourse is first recorded in 1788, but is probably older. It may go back to an older verb meaning 'shake' (which may be the origin of shag) which is recorded between the 14th and 16th centuries.

shah *see* CHECK

shake [OE] Early examples of shake, an Old English word, include not only the senses 'to tremble' and 'to make something vibrate' but also the poetical sense 'to depart or flee'. The **Shakers** are members of a US religious sect, properly called the United Society of Believers in Christ's Second Coming, which split off from the Quakers (properly called the Religious Society of Friends) in the mid 18th century. Participants in the group's services engaged in wild ecstatic movements, and people called them the **Shaking Quakers**. They were persecuted for their radicalism, and in 1774 left for America, where they lived frugally in celibate communities and made furniture noted for its simplicity and elegance. People sometimes think of the spy James Bond as being **shaken not stirred**, but the phrase refers to his drink, not to his temperament. In *Dr No* (1958) by Ian Fleming, Bond gave instructions on how he wanted his favourite tipple: 'A medium vodka dry Martini—with a slice of lemon peel. Shaken and not stirred.' Although Bond is usually described as being **licensed to kill**, the phrase does not occur in any of the original novels by Ian Fleming. 'The licence to kill for the Secret Service, the double-0 prefix, was a great honour', again from *Dr No*, was the closest approximation. In the 1962 film version it became 'If you carry a 00 number it means you're licensed to kill, not get killed.' **No great shakes**, meaning 'not very good', dates from the early 19th century. It probably comes from the shaking of dice, where an unlucky throw would be 'no great shakes'

shallow *see* SCHOOL

shambles [LME] 'He was felled like an ox in the butcher's shambles', writes Charles Dickens in *Barnaby Rudge* (1841). The writer is referring not to a state of chaos but to a slaughterhouse. Over the period of a thousand years shambles, from Latin *scamnum* 'a bench', has moved from being 'a stool' and 'a counter for displaying goods for sale', to 'a state of total disorder'. The link lies in covered butchers' stalls in market places, a use which in Britain survives in street names, notably the Shambles in York, a narrow winding medieval street. In the mid 16th century a shambles became also 'a place for slaughtering animals for meat', and later in the same century 'a place of carnage'. The less bloody modern sense did not appear until the 20th century, in the USA. As a description of ungainly movement, to shamble may derive from **shamble legs**, a description of misshapen legs that probably refers to the splayed legs of the trestles of a butcher's stall

shampoo *see* RAJ WORD PANEL

Shank's pony [L18th] To go somewhere on Shank's pony is to go on foot. The expression is based on a pun with the surname Shanks and the now informal term **shanks** meaning 'legs', which originally came from an Old English word meaning 'shin bone'. It was first used by the Scottish poet Robert Fergusson in 1785 in the version **shanks-nag**. Another alternative is **on Shanks's mare**, now common in North America. The phrase is typically a wry observation regarding a person's inability to afford any means of transport other than their own two feet.

shanty [E19th] The **sea shanty**, the song to which sailors hauled ropes, probably comes from French *chantez!*, an order to 'sing!' It is recorded from the mid 19th century. A slightly earlier shanty appeared in North America for a small, crudely built shack and may come from Canadian French *chantier* 'lumberjack's cabin, logging camp', a specialized used of the word which usually means 'building site' in France. This shanty

shag   shah   shake   shallow   shambles

gave the world the **shanty town**, such as the **favela** in Rio de Janeiro and other Brazilian cities. This word, from the Portuguese equivalent of shanty is first recorded in 1961.

shape [OE] An Old English word related to **scoop** [ME] that originally meant 'to create'. The origins of to **lick into shape** go back to early medieval animal lore which claimed that bear cubs were born as formless lumps and were licked into shape by their mother. This belief seems to have persisted for some time, as the current use does not appear until the early 17th century. In Shakespeare's *Henry VI, Part 3* Gloucester (later Richard III) compares his deformed body to 'an unlick'd bear-whelp That carries no impression like the dam'. Since then other versions including to **knock** and **whip someone into shape** have come into use, possibly reflecting the former popularity of corporal punishment as a parenting tool.

shark [L16th] We do not know where the name for the fish comes from, but it is thought that the shark as in **loan shark** may be from German *Schurke* 'worthless rogue', influenced by the zoological term. **Shirk** [M17th] originally meaning a scrounger, may be from the same German word. The sense 'avoid work' dates from the late 18th century.

shawl *see* PERSIAN WORD PANEL

shed *see* WATER

sheep [ME] We have had sheep in the language since Anglo-Saxon times, but perhaps surprisingly people did not start using the word to mean 'someone too easily influenced or led' until the 16th century. The expression to **separate the sheep from the goats**, 'to divide people or things into superior and inferior groups', is a biblical reference to the account of the Last Judgement in the Gospel of Matthew. There the apostle describes how all the nations of the world will be gathered before God and how 'He shall separate them one from another, as a shepherd divideth his sheep from the goats: And he shall set the sheep on his right hand, but the goats on his left.'

sheet [OE] English dictionaries usually recognize two words spelled sheet. The first, referring to items including bed coverings, paper, and glass, shares an ancient root with **shoot**, one sense of which was 'to project'. Sheet could be used for something giving protection or an awning, which links the two senses. The second is nautical, and was distinct from the first in Old English, though they are ultimately related. Sheets are the ropes attached to the corners of a ship's sail, used for controlling the extent and direction of the sail. If they are hanging loose in the wind, the vessel is likely to be out of control or taking an erratic course. This is the situation referred to in **three sheets to the wind**, meaning 'very drunk'.

Sheila *see* AUSTRALIAN WORD PANEL

shelf [ME] Shelf is from Middle Low German *schelf*; related forms are Old English *scylfe* 'partition', *scylf* 'crag'. The late 16th-century verb **shelve** had the sense 'project like a shelf', first found in Shakespeare's *Two Gentlemen of Verona*: 'Her chamber is aloft. And built so shelving, that one cannot climb it'. The form is from shelves, the plural of shelf.

shell [OE] The Old English *scell* is Germanic in origin, related to Dutch *schel* 'scale, shell' and English *SCALE. Use of the word as a term for an explosive projectile dates from the mid 17th century, suggested by the metal protective casing for the powder. **Shell shock** dates from the First World War. The notion of a shell as a place to which to withdraw (**go into one's shell**) dates from the early 19th century.

shelve *see* SHELF

sherbet [E17th] The words sherbet and **sorbet** [L16th] are essentially the same, and are closely related to **syrup** [LME] and **shrub** [M18th], a drink made with sweetened fruit juice and rum or brandy. All go back to a group of words centring on Arabic *sariba* 'to drink'. The sharp-tasting powdered sweet sherbet was originally used to make a fizzy drink, from the 1850s.

sherry *see* SPANISH WORD PANEL

shape   shark   shawl   shed   sheep   sheet

shibboleth [M17th] The people of Gilead, east of the river Jordan, and members of the Hebrew tribe of Ephraim did not speak the same dialect, and neither were they the best of friends. The Book of Judges recounts a battle between them, in which Jephthah told his men, the Gileadites, to identify defeated Ephraimites by asking them to say 'shibboleth', a Hebrew word meaning 'ear of corn' or 'stream in flood'. Ephraimites had difficulty in pronouncing *sh*, and if a soldier said 'sibboleth' then he was killed as an enemy. Since the mid 17th century English speakers have used shibboleth for 'a word used to detect foreigners or strangers', and in the early 19th century extended this to 'a custom, principle, or belief that distinguishes a particular class or group'. It now especially refers to a long-standing belief regarded as outmoded or no longer important.

shilly-shally [M18th] People unable to make up their minds whether to do something are likely to ask themselves 'Shall I?' repeatedly. With the rhyming impulse also seen in **dilly-dally** [E17th] (dally came from the French for 'to chat' in the Middle Ages) and *WILLY-NILLY, people in the 18th century mocked this tendency by expanding it to 'shill I, shall I?', and so shilly-shally was born.

shingle [ME] With the meaning 'a rectangular wooden tile used on walls or roofs', shingle probably goes back to Latin *scandula* 'split piece of wood'. In the early 19th century the word developed the meaning 'a piece of board', and in the USA in particular 'a small signboard'. To **hang out your shingle**, an American expression for 'to begin to practise a profession', refers to a doctor or lawyer hanging up a sign outside their office advertising their professional services. The shingle on a seashore is a different word, whose origin is unknown, and the painful medical condition **shingles** is different again. Its origin is medieval Latin *cingulus* 'belt, girdle', a reference to the blisters that appear in a band around the body.

ship [OE] An Old English word related to Dutch *schip* and German *Schiff*. The expression **when someone's ship comes in**, 'when someone's fortune is made', is recorded from the mid 19th century. The safe arrival of a ship carrying a valuable cargo meant an instant financial reward for the owner and any others with shares in the enterprise. *See also* BRISTOL, HALF

shipboard *see* BOARD

shipwright *see* WORK

shirk *see* SHARK

shirt [OE] The garments shirt and **skirt** [ME] share an ancient root, which is also that of **short**, the basic sense probably being 'short garment'. The idea behind **shirty** [M19th], 'bad-tempered or annoyed', is the same as that behind **keep your shirt on**, 'don't lose your temper, stay calm'. The offended or riled person is about to take his shirt off ready for a fight. In **lose your shirt** or **put your shirt on** the shirt is seen as the very last possession that you could use to bet with.

shiv *see* ROMANY WORD PANEL

shiver [ME] The Middle English spelling of this word was *chivere*, which is perhaps an alteration of dialect *chavele* 'to chatter', from Old English *ceafl* 'jaw', from the teeth chattering due to the cold. The sense meaning 'to break' or 'small piece' is from a Germanic root with the base idea of 'slit, splinter'. **Skewer** [L17th] may be related.

Shoah *see* HOLOCAUST

shoal *see* SCHOOL

shock [M16th] The shock that now means 'a sudden upsetting event or experience' came from French *choc* in the mid 16th century with the sense 'an encounter between two charging forces or jousters', and in English it started life as a military term. **Shocking** meaning 'very bad' is first found at the end of the 18th century, in a collection of letters called *The Paget Papers*: 'Shocking Weather since you left'. A modern **short, sharp shock** is likely to be a brief but harsh custodial sentence imposed on

shibboleth   shilly-shally   shingle   ship

offenders in an attempt to discourage them from committing further offences. At the Conservative Party Conference in 1979 the then Home Secretary William Whitelaw had proposed this as a form of corrective treatment for young offenders. He was quoting from *The Mikado* (1885) by Gilbert and Sullivan: 'Awaiting the sensation of a short, sharp shock, / From a cheap and chippy chopper on a big black block.' An unkempt or thick shock of hair probably did not get its name from its shock value. The word originally referred to a dog with long shaggy hair—the poodle was a typical **shock dog**, though the term is long obsolete. It may be the same as earlier **shough**, a lapdog said to have originated in Iceland. Shakespeare in *Macbeth* wrote of 'spaniels, curs, shoughs'.

shoot *see* SHEET, SHUT

shop [ME] The earliest shops were small stalls or booths, like the ones you might see today in a market or used by a pavement trader. Shop came into English as a medieval shortening of early French *eschoppe* 'lean-to booth'. The activity of **shopping** dates from the 1760s. The slang sense 'to inform on' is earlier, dating from 1583—the original implication was of causing someone to be locked up. A slang dictionary of 1874 first recorded **all over the shop** as 'pugilistic [boxing] slang'—to inflict severe punishment on an opponent was 'to knock him all over the shop'. Nowadays it means 'everywhere, in all directions', or 'wildly or erratically'.

shopaholic *see* WORK

short *see* SHIRT

shrapnel [E19th] During the Peninsular War in Spain and Portugal (1808–14), General Henry Shrapnel invented a shell that contained bullets and a small bursting charge, which, when fired by the time fuse, burst the shell and scattered the bullets in a shower. Those firing the projectile gave it the name **Shrapnel shell**—the bullets were **Shrapnel shot**, or simply shrapnel. During the Second World War shrapnel acquired its modern sense, 'fragments of a bomb, shell, or other object thrown out by an explosion'. The sense 'coins, loose change' started life as New Zealand military slang around the time of the First World War.

shred *see* SHROUD

shrew [OE] Old English *scrēawa* is from a Germanic source related to words with senses such as 'dwarf', 'devil', or 'fox'. No one knows for certain whether a bad-tempered woman is a shrew because people compared her to the mouse-like animal or whether the animal is a shrew because it was considered venomous and dangerous, like an aggressively assertive woman. When **shrewd** first appeared it shared these negative associations, but as connection with the shrew and belief in the shrew's evil weakened, it developed the sense 'cunning' and then the modern positive meaning 'having sharp powers of judgement, astute'.

shrift [OE] To give someone **short shrift** is to treat them in a curt and dismissive way. The phrase originally referred to the short time that a condemned criminal was allowed to make their confession to a priest and be **shriven**, prescribed a penance, and absolved of their sins, before being executed. Its first use in the literal sense comes in Shakespeare's *Richard III*: 'Make a short shrift, he longs to see your head.' The **Shrove** in **Shrove Tuesday** is a form of shriven. As the day before the start of Lent, it is marked by feasting and celebration before the Lent fast begins. In Britain people eat pancakes on the day, giving the alternative name **Pancake Day** or **Pancake Tuesday**. Other countries celebrate it as the carnival of **Mardi Gras**, French for 'Fat Tuesday'. *See also* CARNIVAL

shrine [OE] Old English *scrīn* was a 'cabinet, chest, reliquary'. Its ultimate source is Latin *scrinium* 'chest for books'.

shrink [OE] Old English *scrincan*, of Germanic origin, is related to Swedish *skrynka* 'to wrinkle'. The sense 'draw back' in an action of recoiling in abhorrence or timidity dates from the early 16th century. **Shrivel** [M16th] comes from a related Scandinavian word. In the informal sense 'a psychiatrist' shrink is a shortening of **headshrinker**. The longer form appeared in print in 1950, and **shrink** itself in 1966. A headshrinker was originally a head-hunter who preserved and shrank human heads.

shrive *see* SHRIFT

shrivel *see* SHRINK

shriven *see* SHRIFT

shroud [OE] Late Old English *scrūd* meant 'garment, clothing' and is from a Germanic source from a base meaning 'cut'; **shred** [OE] is related. An early sense of to shroud in Middle English was 'cover so as to protect'. Use for the sheet in which a corpse is laid out, dates from the late 16th century.

Shrove Tuesday *see* SHRIFT

shrub *see* SHERBET

shufti *see* ARABIC WORD PANEL

shut [OE] Old English *scyttan* 'put (a bolt) in position to hold fast' is West Germanic in origin, related to Dutch *schutten* 'shut up, obstruct' and English **shoot**. The phrase **get shut of** for to 'get rid of' is found from around 1500. The colloquial **shut up!** is recorded from the mid 19th century.

shuttle [OE] Old English *scytel* meant 'dart, missile' and is from a Germanic source; Old Norse *skutill* 'harpoon' is related. The use for a form of transport going backwards and forwards between two fixed places stems from association with the movement of the shuttle used in weaving going from one side of the loom to the other. The word's use in space travel is from the 1960s.

shuttlecock *see* BADMINTON

shy [OE] Old English *scēoh* was applied to horses meaning 'easily frightened'. The word's application to people is seen from the start of the 17th century. The shy

meaning 'fling, throw' of **coconut shy** is a late 18th-century word of unknown origin.

shyster [M19th] An American story goes that there was once an unscrupulous lawyer called Scheuster who gave his name to the shyster, but no record of him has ever been found. It is more likely that German *Scheisser* 'worthless person' formed from *Scheisse* 'excrement', is the word's origin, since it first appeared in New York, home to many German-speaking immigrants, as a term for an unqualified lawyer who preyed on inmates of the notorious prison called the Tombs. Shyster was first recorded in 1843, and soon took on the sense of an unscrupulous lawyer rather than a fake one.

sibling *see* GOSSIP

sick [OE] The Old English word sick was the usual way of referring to someone physically unwell before *ILL arrived in the Middle Ages, and is still normal use in the USA. A variety of animals have cropped up over the centuries in phrases emphasizing how ill someone is feeling. The first was the *DOG, back in the early 18th century. Other comparisons include the *HORSE, the *PIG, and the *CAT, the latter well known for its problems with hairballs, and so common a comparison that 'to cat' was 19th-century schoolboy slang for 'to vomit'. All these phrases refer to physical sickness, whereas being **as sick as a parrot** is a mental state, to do with feeling depressed. This goes back to the 1970s and is particularly associated with despondent footballers and managers being interviewed after a defeat. The phrase may have been suggested by the Dead Parrot sketch in the television comedy series *Monty Python's Flying Circus*. The opposite is **over the moon**—*see* MOON.

Tsar Nicholas I of Russia reportedly said of the Sultan of Turkey in 1853: 'I am not so eager about what shall be done when the sick man dies, as I am to determine with England what shall not be done upon that event taking place.' His remarks reflected the precarious state of the Ottoman Empire and its slow but inevitable disintegration. Political commentators exploited this view and started to refer to Turkey as **the sick**

shrink   shrive   shrivel   shriven   shroud

man of Europe. The expression **the sick man of—** was applied to other countries over the following decades, and now often refers to factors other than economics or politics.

sideburns [L19th] The 19th-century American general Ambrose E. Burnside sported muttonchop whiskers and a moustache, with a clean-shaven chin. By the 1870s people were calling this style a **Burnside**; then changing fashion did away with the moustache and **burnsides** became the strips of hair down the face in front of a man's ears. Fame fades fast, and the general's name must have puzzled many, though they understood the 'side' part. In the 1880s the elements reversed order to form **sideburns**, though this still left 'burns' as a puzzle, and the more familiar **sideboards** was sometimes substituted as an alternative.

sidewalk *see* US WORD PANEL

siesta *see* SPANISH WORD PANEL

sight [OE] An Old English word related to *SEE. Shooting has given us the expression **in your sights** from the device on a gun which helps you aim more precisely. The implication is that you are firmly focused on achieving your ambition. The same idea is found in to **raise** (or **lower**) **your sights**, meaning 'to become more (or less) ambitious', and to **set your sights on**, meaning 'to have something as an ambition'.

sign [ME] Sign comes via Old French from Latin *signum* 'mark, token'. From the same source come **signal** [LME], **significant** [L16th], **signet** [LME] 'small seal' with which you make your mark, and mid 16th-century **signature**, which was first used as a Scots legal term for a document presented by a writer for royal approval and seal. **Resign** [LME] is from Latin *resignare* 'unseal, cancel' *See also* SEAL

silence [ME] Both silence and **silent** [LME] came from Latin *silere*, 'to be silent'. The fuller form of **silence is golden** is **speech is silver but silence is golden**. Both

are recorded from the 19th century. Originally **the silent majority** were the dead. In the 20th century they became those who hold moderate opinions but rarely express them. Richard Nixon brought the phrase to prominence by claiming to speak for this section of society in his 1968 presidential campaign.

silhouette [L18th] Étienne de Silhouette (1709–67) was an French author and politician. Why he gave his name to the dark outline of something against a brighter background remains obscure. One account says that the word ridiculed the petty economies Silhouette introduced while holding the office of Controller General, while another refers to the shortness of his occupancy of that post. A scholarly French dictionary suggested that Silhouette himself made outline portraits with which he decorated the walls of his château at Bry-sur-Marne. More than two centuries on, we shall probably never know the truth.

silk [OE] In the ancient world silk came overland to Europe from China and Tibet. The Greeks and Romans called the inhabitants of these far-away and unknown lands **Seres**, and from this word **silk** developed. The observation that **you can't make a silk purse out of a sow's ear** has been proverbial since the late 16th century. There was an earlier version featuring 'a goat's fleece' rather than 'a sow's ear'. A silk is a senior lawyer who has been made a Queen's (or King's) Counsel. The name comes from the silk robes they are entitled to wear—they are also said to **take silk** when they reach this rank. *See also* SATIN

silkie *see* SEAL

silly [LME] A medieval Englishman would have been pleased if you described him as silly—you would have been saying he was happy or lucky. The word is an alteration of earlier *seely*, from an ancient root meaning 'luck, happiness'. The Old English sense of *seely* was 'happy, fortunate, blessed by God'. This subsequently developed into 'holy', then 'innocent, defenceless, deserving of pity', at which point, in the later Middle

Ages, silly largely took over. Cynical people often regard goodness and simplicity as showing a lack of intelligence, and since the late 16th century the primary sense has been 'foolish'. In cricket, silly is used in the names of fielding positions such as **silly mid-off** and **silly point**, to indicate that the fielder is positioned closer than usual to the batsman. What makes such positions 'silly' is that the fielder is required to stand perilously close to the bat. In high summer wealthy and important people deserted Victorian London while Parliament and the law courts were in recess. Since the mid 19th century the months of July and August have been **the silly season**, when British newspapers often print trivia because of a lack of important news. The first **silly billy** was either William Frederick, the Duke of Gloucester (1776–1834), or King William IV (1765–1837). William IV, the predecessor of Queen Victoria, became unpopular when he intervened in politics by imposing the Conservative Robert Peel as prime minister, despite a Whig majority in Parliament.

similar [L16th] This was also originally a term in anatomy meaning 'homogeneous'. It comes from Latin *similis* 'like'. The literary device **simile** for drawing comparisons [LME] is from the same source; as are **simulate** [M17th], **resemble** [ME], and **semblance** [ME].

sine *see* INSINUATE

sing *see* SONG

sinister [LME] In Latin *sinister* meant 'left' or 'left-hand', but apart from terms in heraldry such as **bend sinister**, a broad diagonal stripe from top right to bottom left of a shield which is a supposed sign of illegitimacy, sinister in English has never meant the physical left-hand side. Instead it reflects deep-rooted prejudices against left-handedness, which had associations of evil, malice, or dishonesty. *See also* AMBIDEXTROUS, DEXTEROUS

sinuous, sinus *see* INSINUATE

sip *see* SOP

sir [ME] A shortened form of **sire** that has been a title for a knight since the Middle Ages. Kings were formerly addressed as sire, though now the term is more often used for the male parent of an animal. Sire is from Latin *senior* [LME] 'older, older man', related to *senex* 'old, old man', from which *SENATE and **senile** [M17th] also derive. In languages descended from Latin, words based on *senior* often became the way of addressing a man, for example **señor** in Spanish, **signor** in Italian, and the second element of **monsieur** in French. *See also* SENATE

siren [ME] In classical mythology the Sirens were bird-women whose beautiful singing lured sailors to their doom on submerged rocks. People hear a **siren song** or **siren call** when they are attracted to something that is both alluring and potentially harmful or dangerous. In 1819 the French engineer and physicist Charles Cagniard de la Tour used siren as the name for his invention of an acoustic instrument for producing musical tones. Later in the century steamships began to use a much larger instrument on the same lines as a foghorn or warning device, and in the Second World War sirens sent people scurrying to bomb-shelters for protection from air raids. The phrase **siren suit** from the 1930s was from its use as a one-piece garment for women in air-raid shelters.

sirloin [M16th] The name sirloin for a choice cut of beef dates from the late Middle Ages. It came from French, and the first element is from French *sur* 'above', because it is the upper part of the loin. The later spelling with *sir*- has led to false associations with *SIR and various accounts of a king knighting the roast for its excellence, dubbing it 'Sir Loin'. A mid 17th-century source mentions a tradition that the monarch in question was Henry VIII. Jonathan Swift, on the other hand, names James I, while yet another account attributes the action to Charles II. We can be reasonably certain that it was none of them.

sissy [M19th] This was originally a pet form of **sister** [OE] but soon came to be used in the sense 'effeminate person, coward'.

sit *see* NEST, SET

six [ME] The number six is Old English, but comes from the same ancient root as Latin *sex* and Greek *hexa* 'six'. These gave us **sextet** [M19th], **sextuple** [M16th], **hexagon** [L16th], and similar words (*compare* SEVEN). In cricket a six is a hit that sends the ball clear over to the boundary without first striking the ground, scoring six runs. The ball needs to be struck hard to go that far, and this is the image behind the expression to **knock for six**, 'to utterly surprise or overcome', recorded from the beginning of the 20th century. A form of the phrase also occurs as to **hit for six**, which tends to have the slightly different meaning of 'to affect very severely'. The origins of **at sixes and sevens**, 'in a state of total confusion and disarray', lie in gambling with dice. The phrase first occurs in Geoffrey Chaucer's poem *Troilus and Criseyde*, in the version to **set on six and seven**. It is most likely that the phrase was an alteration of the Old French words for five and six, *cinque* and *sice*, these being the highest numbers on a dice. The 'inflation' of the numbers probably came about either because people who did not know French misheard the words, or as a jokey exaggeration. The idea was that betting on the possibility of these two numbers coming up was the height of recklessness, and could result in your whole world falling apart. A man's **six-pack** is his toned midriff—the abdominal muscle is crossed by three bands of fibre which look like a set of six separate muscles if the person is slim and fit. The original six-pack is associated more with couch-potatoes, as it is a pack of six cans of beer held together with a plastic fastener.

size [ME] Early use of the word was as a synonym for **assize**, of which it is a shortening. This came from French *assise*, from Latin *assidere* 'sit by' which developed the sense 'to sit down in judgement, **assess**' of which it is also the source. The notion of fixing an amount led to the word's use to express magnitude and bulk. The phrase

size up appeared in the late 19th century. The history of the size [ME] used in painting is not clear. *See also* SEAT

skate [M17th] Skate as in **ice skates** was originally written as the plural *scates*. It comes from Dutch *schaats* (a singular form but interpreted as plural), from Old French *eschasse* 'stilt'. The phrase **get one's skates on** 'hurry up' was originally military slang in the late 19th century.

skeleton [L16th] This is modern Latin, from the Greek *skeletos* 'dried up'. The general sense 'supporting framework' is found from the mid 17th century.

skewer *see* SHIVER

ski *see* SKID

skid [L17th] This was first used in the sense 'supporting beam'; it may be related to Old Norse *skíth* 'billet, snowshoe' (which also gave English **ski** in the mid 18th century via Norwegian). The verb was first used meaning 'fasten a skid to (a wheel) to slow its motion', later coming to mean 'slip'. To **hit the skids**, 'to begin a rapid decline or deterioration', and the similar to **put the skids under someone** or **something** both originated in the USA. This skid is a North American term for a wooden roller that is used as part of a set to move logs or other heavy objects. Once a log is on the skids it can be slid forward very easily, gathering momentum until it reaches the end of the rollers and comes to an abrupt halt. **Skid row**, meaning 'a run-down part of town frequented by tramps and alcoholics', is also connected with logging. It originated as **skid road** in the late 19th century, and at first simply described a part of town frequented by loggers.

skin [OE] Old Scandinavian gave us skin in the later Old English period—the word used until then was *HIDE. The expression **by the skin of your teeth** arose from a misquotation from the biblical book of Job: 'I am escaped with the skin of my teeth.' The implication is 'and nothing else'. *See also* BEAUTY. The **skinhead** is associated with the Britain of the 1970s, but the first skinheads

sit six size skate skeleton skewer ski skid

were American. In the 1950s recruits to the US Marines were known as skinheads because of the severe way their hair was cropped when they joined up. The colloquial word **skint** first found in the 1920s is a variant of colloquial *skinned* used in the same sense.

skint *see* SKIN

skirt *see* SHIRT

skol *see* SCALE

skunk *see* NATIVE AMERICAN WORD PANEL

sky *see* LOFT

skylark *see* LARK

slack *see* SLAKE

slag [mid 16th century] Slag is from Middle Low German *slagge*, perhaps from *slagen* 'strike', with reference to fragments formed by hammering. From the sense of refuse developed a slang use meaning 'worthless person' in the late 18th century, which only developed the modern dominant sense 'promiscuous woman' in the mid 20th century. The verb sense 'criticize' as in **slagged off**, dates from the 1970s.

slake [OE] Slake and **slack** [OE] share a Germanic root, slake originally meaning 'to become less eager' in general, before it was restricted to words such as thirst. Slack originally meant 'lazy, unhurried'. Both words are more distantly related to Latin *laxus* 'loose', *see* LANGUISH

slander *see* SCANDAL

slap [LME] When slap first came into English it was probably meant to imitate the sound of a blow with the palm of the hand. **Slap and tickle**, playful sexual activity, dates from the early 20th century. To create the sound of a blow in the theatre or circus, pantomime actors and clowns use a device consisting of two flexible pieces of wood

joined together at one end. This is a **slapstick**, so called since the late 19th century. Since then it has also been the term for comedy based on deliberately clumsy actions and embarrassing events. **Slaphead** is British slang for a bald man, recorded from the late 1980s. It could be a reference to a long-running routine of the comedian Benny Hill, in which Hill slapped his short, bald sidekick Jackie Wright repeatedly on the head. Another 1980s British slang term of uncertain origin is **slapper**, 'an unattractive woman'. It may be from a woman 'slapping on' a large amount of make-up, or could be connected with Yiddish *schlepper* 'scruffy person' (*see* YIDDISH WORD PANEL). From this source comes to **schlep**. Originally meaning 'to haul', and first recorded in this sense in James Joyce's *Ulysses* (1922) 'She trudges, schlepps, trains, drags . . . her load', but now more often found in the sense 'traipse, trudge'.

slate [ME] This is from the Old French *esclat* 'a piece broken off'. **Slat** [LME] is a variant which meant 'roofing slate' until it developed the current sense in the mid 18th century. Schoolchildren formerly used flat pieces of slate for writing on in chalk, and shops and bars used the same materials for keeping a record of what a customer owed. This is the origin of the expression **on the slate**, 'to be paid for later, on credit'. The related French *esclice* 'splinter' gives us **slice** [ME] and their common Germanic source also gives us **slit** [OE]. In the sense 'to criticize', dating from the mid 19th century, slate is probably a different word. It might derive from the slightly earlier Irish sense 'to beat, beat up' and be related to a Scots use of slate meaning 'to set a dog on', which is from Old Norse.

slaughter [ME] Slaughter is from Old Norse *slátr* 'butcher's meat'. **Slay** [OE] is related.

slaughterhouse *see* BATED

slave [ME] Our word slave was shortened from early French *esclave* in the Middle Ages. In medieval Latin the equivalent form *sclavus* is identical with *Sclavus*, the source of **Slav**. The Slavic peoples of eastern and central Europe had been conquered and reduced to a servile state during the 9th century. **Wage slaves** is a term used in the English translation of the *Communist Manifesto* by Karl Marx and Friedrich Engels.

slay *see* SLAUGHTER, SLEDGE

sleazy [M17th] It was originally thin or flimsy fabrics that were sleazy, not nightclubs or bars. The familiar modern senses 'squalid and seedy' and 'sordid, corrupt, or immoral' did not develop until the 1940s, from the idea of cloth being cheap and poor-quality. The corresponding noun **sleaze** was created from sleazy in the 1960s.

sledge [OE] The sledge that is a vehicle used on snow and ice came in the late 16th century from Dutch and is related to **sled** [ME], **sleigh** [E18th], **slide** [OE], and **slither** [ME]. Sleigh is from Dutch, and was originally adopted in North America. To **take for a sleigh ride** is a dated slang phrase meaning 'to mislead', from the use of sleigh ride for an implausible or false story or a hoax. A sleigh ride could also mean 'a drug-induced high'—this went with the use of **snow** for cocaine in white powder form, an early 20th-century use for this Old English word. As a name for what we would now more usually call a **sledgehammer**, the other sledge is recorded in Old English and goes back to a root meaning 'to strike' and related to **slay**. A sledgehammer is a large, heavy hammer used for jobs such as breaking rocks and driving in fence posts, so to **take a sledgehammer to crack a nut** is to use a disproportionately forceful means to achieve a simple objective. The expression is recorded in the 1930s, but a decade earlier an American version **use a sledgehammer to kill a gnat** appears. In the 1970s Australian cricketers started **sledging**, or making offensive or needling remarks to opposing batsmen in an attempt to break their concentration. The idea behind the term is the crudity and lack of subtlety involved in using a sledge or sledgehammer.

sleek *see* SLICK

sleep [OE] A word first recorded around AD 800. The modern-sounding phrase **sleep with**, meaning 'to have sex with', is almost as old, and was used by the Anglo-Saxons. **Sleep like a log**, meaning 'to sleep very soundly', is not recorded before the 1880s, but the earlier version **sleep like a top** was used in the 17th century—the top here was a wooden toy that spun when whipped by a child, but was otherwise still and lifeless. The modern form of the proverb **let sleeping dogs lie** appears first in Sir Walter Scott's 1824 novel *Redgauntlet*. Long before that, in the 14th century, Geoffrey Chaucer advised in *Troilus and Criseyde* that 'it is not good a sleeping hound to wake'.

sleigh *see* SLEDGE

sleight *see* SLY

sleuth [ME] A sleuth was first a **sleuth-hound**, a type of bloodhound employed in medieval Scotland for pursuing game or tracking fugitives. A tracker or detective has been a sleuth-hound since the mid 19th century, and shortly after that in the USA a simple sleuth. The word sleuth itself derives from Scandinavian, and its earliest meaning was 'the track or trail of a person or animal'.

slice *see* SLATE

slick [ME] Although it is not recorded until after the Norman Conquest, slick, originally meaning 'glossy' was probably in Old English as it is a Germanic word. The sense 'plausible' dates from the late 16th century; 'skilful, adroit' dates from the early 19th century. **Sleek** [LME] is a later variant of slick. **Slight** [ME] is related, for it originally meant 'smooth' although negative senses also exist in related languages. The sense 'treat with disrespect' is found from the late 16th century, from the earlier sense of 'to level'. For **sleekit** *see* SCOTTISH WORD PANEL

slide *see* SLEDGE

slight *see* SLICK

slay sleazy sledge sleek sleep sleigh sleight

slim [M17th] Slim may now be something we aspire to be, but it comes from a Low German or Dutch base meaning 'slanting, cross, bad'. The pejorative sense found in Dutch and German existed originally in the English noun slim 'lazy or worthless person' and South African usage still reflects the meaning 'crafty, sly'. While it came into English in the sense 'gracefully thin', it has reflected the sense 'poor, slight' as in **slim chance** [L17th].

sling [ME] When referring to a loop used as a support or weapon, sling is probably from Dutch. The expression **slings and arrows**, 'adverse factors or circumstances', comes from the 'To be or not to be' speech in Shakespeare's *Hamlet*: 'Whether 'tis nobler in the mind to suffer / The slings and arrows of outrageous fortune, / Or to take arms against a sea of troubles, / And by opposing end them.'

slink *see* SNAKE

slip [ME] English has several words spelled slip. The one meaning 'to lose your footing' or 'to move out of position or someone's grasp' is probably Germanic, from a root that also gave us **slippery** [LME]. This is the slip in **slipper** [LME], and in **slipshod** [L16th], which originally meant 'wearing slippers or loose shoes'. In phrases such as **a slip of a girl**, meaning a small, slim person, slip is the same word that means 'a small piece of paper' and 'a cutting taken from a plant'. It dates from the later medieval period and probably comes from early Dutch and German *slippe* 'a cut, strip'. The saying **there's many a slip 'twixt cup and lip**—in other words, many things can go wrong between the start of something and its completion—dates back to the mid 16th century. A similar idea was expressed by the Roman statesman and orator Cato the Elder: 'I have often heard that many things can come between mouth and morsel'.

slit *see* SLATE

slither *see* SLIDE

Sloane [1975] We have one person to credit for calling upper-class young women Sloanes or **Sloane Rangers**. In 1975 Peter York, style editor on the magazine *Harpers & Queen*, identified the cultural stereotype of the wealthy, fashionable, but conventional-minded London girls and began writing about them, eventually co-authoring the book *The Official Sloane Ranger Handbook* in 1982. He coined the name by combining Sloane Square in west London, their home territory, with the masked cowboy hero the Lone Ranger. Her male equivalent is the **Hooray Henry**, a loud but harmless young upper-class man. He is first mentioned in a story by the US writer Damon Runyon in 1936, as a Hoorah Henry.

slobber [LME] This is probably from Middle Dutch *slobberen* meaning both 'walk through mud' and 'feed noisily', imitative of the noise.

slog *see* SLUG

slogan [E16th] The first slogan was not in the world of advertising or politics, but was the Scottish Gaelic word for a battle cry or war cry, *sluagh-ghairm*, from *sluagh* 'army' and *gairm* 'shout'. For Scottish Highlanders the slogan would often be someone's surname or a place name. For three centuries the word was confined to the work of Scottish writers, but in the early 19th century it gained a wider popularity in the novels of Sir Walter Scott, and later in the century came to mean a short memorable motto or phrase. An early attempt to anglicize *sluagh-ghairm* produced the spelling *slughorn*. This was misinterpreted as some kind of military musical instrument, most famously in Robert Browning's atmospheric poem of 1855 *Childe Roland to the Dark Tower Came* 'Dauntless the slug-horn to my lips I set, And blew.'

sloop *see* DUTCH WORD PANEL

slosh *see* SLUSH

slough [OE] A slough is a swamp (*slōh* in Old English), and a **slough of despond** a condition of despondency, hopelessness, and gloom. The phrase comes from John Bunyan's *The Pilgrim's Progress* (1678),

slim sling slink slip slit slither Sloane

where it is the name of a deep boggy place between the City of Destruction and the gate at the beginning of Christian's journey. **Slump** [L17th] originally meant to fall in a bog and probably came from the sound that would be made. The economic sense is late 19th century. Slough in southern England also takes its name from Old English *slōh*, not the most appealing of origins. To add to the unglamorous town's image problems, the English poet John Betjeman wrote of it in 1937: 'Come, friendly bombs, and fall on Slough! / It isn't fit for humans now.' The slough meaning the skin shed by a snake is Middle English and originally meant 'skin' in English. It may be related to Low German *sluwe* 'husk, peel'.

slug [LME] In medieval times a slug was a slow-moving lazy person, and over time the word came to describe any slow-moving animal or vehicle. For example, the big-game hunter William Baldwin, writing in 1863, described one of his horses as 'an incorrigible slug'. It has been the term for a slimy snail-like creature since the early 18th century. A slug of whisky, or of lead, is probably the same word, but to slug someone is not, and is related to **slog** [E19th], and we do not know the origin of either. **Sluggard** is based on the rare verb slug, 'to be lazy or slow', which may be Scandinavian in origin and which is probably also the source of sluggish, 'slow and lazy'.

sluice *see* EXCLUDE

slump *see* SLOUGH

slur [E17th] The medieval English word slur meant 'thin, fluid mud'. Early senses of the verb were 'to smear' and then 'to criticize'—you can see the same metaphor at work in the phrase 'mud-slinging' and in the history of the word *ASPERSION. Later on it came to mean 'to gloss over a fault', and from this developed the idea of speaking indistinctly. **Slurry** [LME] also comes from medieval *slur*, and here the connection with mud is much clearer.

slush [M17th] Slush and **sludge** [E17th] probably both imitate the sound made by walking through them, with **slosh** [E19th] being a variant of slush. Slush was also used by sailors for the accumulated fat which was left in the pot after meat was boiled for the crew. This could be sold off for use as a lubricant or fuel and the money used to buy luxuries for the crew. This was the original **slush fund** [M19th], which had come to mean money used as a bribe by the late 19th century.

sly [ME] Early use of sly, which comes from Old Norse *slœgr* 'cunning', included the sense 'dexterous, skilful'. The phrase **on the sly** is recorded in use from the early 19th century. **Sleight** [ME] is from the same source, and passed from the sense 'cunning' to 'sleight of hand' in the late 16th century.

smack [OE] English has many smacks. Smack as in 'it smacks of fish' is based on Old English *smaec* 'flavour or smell'. The one meaning both 'to part your lips noisily' and 'to strike someone', arrived from Dutch *smacken* in the mid 16th century. Initially people smacked their lips in the context of eating and drinking and, later, kissing, but by the early 19th century the word was being used in the sense of hitting someone. The smack that is a kind of sailing vessel is also Dutch, while the slang word for 'heroin' is probably from Yiddish *schmeck*, 'a sniff, a smell', from the same Germanic root as the Old English smack. *See also* DUTCH AND YIDDISH WORD PANELS

small [OE] A word recorded since around AD 700. In Old English it could refer to something slender or narrow as well as something more generally of less than usual size. From the 16th century **small beer** was a term for weaker beer, the sort that people drank for breakfast when water supplies were unsafe. In *Macbeth* Iago dismisses women as fit only to 'chronicle small beer', and from this sort of use developed the sense of something insignificant. **Small potatoes** started out as a phrase in American English, usually in the fuller form **small potatoes and few in the hill**—an expression used by Davy Crockett in 1836.

slug   sluice   slump   slur   slush   sly

The phrase **small is beautiful**, suggesting that something small-scale is better than a large-scale equivalent, comes from the title of a book by E.F. Schumacher, published in 1973. It is perhaps best known as a slogan adopted by environmentalists.

smart [OE] The first English use of smart was as a verb meaning 'be painful', which survives in the verb meaning 'to feel a sharp, stinging pain in a part of the body'—its root is probably related to Latin *mordere* 'to bite'. The original meaning of the adjective was 'causing sharp pain', which led to 'keen or brisk' and developed into the current senses of 'mentally sharp, clever' and 'neat, well turned out'. We probably call an irritating person who always has a clever answer a **smart alec** after Alex Hoag, a notorious thief and conman in New York in the 1840s, who earned the nickname Smart Alex from his reputation for not getting caught. In the late 17th century **smart money** was money paid to sailors and soldiers to compensate them for wounds. Smart here meant 'physical pain'. Modern usage, from around 1900, refers to money bet by people with expert knowledge, with smart meaning 'quick-witted'. The sugar-coated chocolate sweets called **Smarties** were launched in 1937. Because of their similar appearance to pills, doctors are sometimes accused of handing out drugs 'like Smarties'.

smear [OE] Old English *smeoru* meant 'ointment, grease'. Figurative use meaning 'to attempting to discredit' dates from the mid 16th century.

smell [ME] No one is sure where smell comes from—there is no related word in other languages. To **come up smelling of roses** is to make a lucky escape from a difficult or unpleasant situation with your reputation intact. Rose bushes thrive on plenty of manure, and the image here is of someone falling into a freshly fertilized rose bed. Dating from the 1930s and American in origin, is **stop and smell the roses**, or take time to fully appreciate life's pleasures. If someone tells you to **wake up and smell the coffee**, on the other hand, they are urging you to be less relaxed, and to become more realistic or alert. The phrase was popularized by the US advice columnist Ann Landers from the mid 1950s.

smile [ME] Smile may be of Scandinavian origin and related to Old English **smirk**. Smirk's early sense was 'to smile' but it later gained a notion of smugness or silliness.

smithereens [E19th] This word for tiny fragments into which something is broken was first recorded in the early 19th century. It probably comes from Irish *smidirín* from *smiodar* 'fragment'.

smock [OE] In Old English *smūgan* meant 'to creep'. Just as today we can talk about, say, wriggling into a pair of jeans or slipping into a dress, so the Anglo-Saxons used the word as a way of describing putting on a piece of clothing. This is why the related word *smoc*, which became **smock**, was applied to a woman's loose-fitting undergarment. It was not until the 19th century that the word was used for a piece of clothing worn by agricultural workers decorated with **smocking**, and only since the 20th that it has described a loose dress or blouse, or the loose garment that artists wear to keep their clothes clean.

smoke [OE] The Old English word smoke is around a thousand years old, and people are first recorded as smoking tobacco at the start of the 17th century. A big city has been called **the Smoke** or **the Big Smoke** since the 1840s—the first examples refer not to London but to Australian towns. A piece of indisputable and incriminating evidence can be described as **a smoking gun**. This conjures up the image of someone standing holding a smoking gun next to a corpse with gunshot wounds. The natural assumption is that they are the guilty party. The phrase came to prominence during the Watergate scandal in the early 1970s. An incriminating tape revealed President Nixon's wish to limit the FBI's involvement in the investigation, prompting Republican congressman Barber T. Conable to observe: 'I guess we have found the smoking pistol, haven't we?' **There's no smoke without fire**, suggests that there is always some reason for a

smart   smear   smell   smile   smithereens

rumour. The English version dates back at least to the 15th century, though the same idea appears in the work of the Roman comic dramatist Plautus—'the flame is right next to the smoke'—and in a 13th-century French proverb. The phrase **smoke and mirrors** refers to the illusion created by conjuring tricks and can be traced back to the US political columnist Jimmy Breslin, writing in 1975: 'All political power is primarily an illusion ... Mirrors and blue smoke, beautiful blue smoke rolling over the surface of highly polished mirrors ... If somebody tells you how to look, there can be seen in the smoke great, magnificent shapes, castles and kingdoms, and maybe they can be yours.'

smug [M16th] No one likes a smug person, but in the mid 16th century they were popular. The word comes from German *smuk* 'pretty' and originally meant 'neat or spruce' when describing men. Not much later it was being applied to women and girls too, as in 'She is indeed a good smug lass', a line from a play by Thomas Otway in 1677. Another early meaning was 'smooth', hence Shakespeare's reference to 'the smug and silver Trent'. Exactly when smug began to suggest complacency is difficult to pinpoint.

snack [ME] The early sense recorded was 'snap, bite', from Middle Dutch *snac(k)*, from *snacken* 'to bite', a variant of *snappen*, source of late Middle English **snap**. Senses relating to food date from the late 17th century; use of the word to mean 'light incidental meal' dates from the mid 18th century. Since **snatch** [ME] originally meant 'snap suddenly' it is probably related.

snake [OE] Snakes take their name from the fact that they have no legs and crawl along the ground. The ancestor of snake is an ancient Germanic word that meant 'to crawl or creep'. **Serpent** [ME] has a similar origin—it comes from Latin *serpere*, which also meant 'to crawl or creep'. Yet another word with this original sense was Old English **slink**. You can describe a treacherous person as **a snake in the grass**, with the idea of a lurking danger. Snakes are

associated with treachery not only in Genesis but in the 6th century BC fables of the Greek storyteller Aesop. In one of his stories a man finds a snake frozen with cold and puts it close to his chest to warm it up. As soon as the snake revives it bites him (*see also* VIPER). Before the 17th century the equivalent phrase had featured toads, which were at one time thought to be poisonous— a treacherous person was called **a pad in the straw** (*pad* is an old dialect word for a toad). The current expression may have originated from a Latin poem by the Roman poet Virgil. The children's game **Snakes and Ladders**, called in the USA **Chutes and Ladders**, was first played at the end of the 19th century. It may be based on an ancient Indian game called *Moksha Patamu*, which was used to teach children about the Hindu religion— the good squares allowed a player to go to a higher level of life, whereas the evil 'snakes' sent them back through reincarnation to lower tiers of life.

snap, snatch *see* SNACK

sneeze [ME] When we get a cold we should really start *fneezing* rather than **sneezing**. This is because the word comes from medieval English *fnese*. People were not used to seeing the *fn-* combination at the beginning of a word by then, and someone must have mistaken f for the long medieval s, which looked like an f without a cross bar, and written it down as *sn-* instead.

snitch *see* NARK

snob [L18th] There is a long-standing belief that snob has some connection with Latin *sine nobilitate* 'without nobility', abbreviated to *s-nob*, which then became snob. It is an ingenious theory but highly unlikely, as a snob was first recorded in the late 18th century as a shoemaker or cobbler. The word soon came to be used for any person of humble status or rank— Cambridge undergraduates used the term to mean 'someone from the town, not a member of the university', and this in turn led to the broader sense 'a lower-class person, or a person lacking in good

smug　snack　snake　snap　snatch　sneeze

breeding, or good taste'. In time the word came to describe someone who seeks to imitate or give exaggerated respect to people they perceive as superior in social standing or wealth.

snook *see* COCK

snooker [L19th] Both the game and the word snooker originated among British army officers serving in India in the 1870s. Colonel Sir Neville Chamberlain (not the future British prime minister) is said to have coined the name for a fast-moving version of billiards that he and his associates in the officers' mess had devised. Snooker was already army slang for 'a newly joined cadet', and the choice of name may have been intended to refer to the inept play of a fellow officer.

snout [OE] Think how many words to do with noses begin with the letters *sn-*. Most are medieval. There is snout, which in early use could describe not only the projecting part of an animal's face but also an elephant's trunk, and a bird's beak. A variant of snout was **snoot** [M19th], which is where **snooty** [E20th] comes from—snooty people have their noses stuck in the air. **Snot** [LME] and **snotty** [L16th] are also based on snout. **Snuff** [E16th] used to mean 'to inhale through the nostrils' before it became a term for powdered tobacco that you inhale through your nostrils. **Snuffle** [L16th] is related. **Snivel** [ME] originally referred to mucus. **Snore** [ME] and **snort** [LME] once had each other's meanings— **snore** meant 'a snort' and **snort** meant 'to snore', and both probably imitated the sound.

snow *see* SLEDGE

snuff, snuffle *see* SNOUT

snug [L16th] The first use of snug was as a sailors' term, probably from German or Dutch, that meant 'shipshape, properly prepared for bad weather': 'Captain Read...ordered the Carpenters to cut down our Quarter Deck to make the Ship snug and the fitter for Sailing' (William Dampier,

A New Voyage Around the World, 1697). A small, comfortable room in a pub was known as a snug from the 1830s, but the original name was a **snuggery**—in *The Pickwick Papers* (1837) Charles Dickens refers to 'the snuggery inside the bar'. There used to be a verb snug that meant 'to lie or nestle closely', and from this we get **snuggle** [L17th].

soak *see* SUCK

soar [LME] Soar is a shortening of Old French *essorer*, 'to rise into the air' based on the Latin elements *ex-* 'out of, from' and *aura* 'breeze'.

sober *see* JUDGE

soccer [L19th] This is a shortening of **Association football**, the official name given in the late 19th century to the game, to distinguish it from rugby football. The word was formed by the same process that gave us rugger for *RUGBY.

social [LME] Latin *socius* 'companion' is the base of social and **society** [M16th]; while **associate** [LME] comes from closely related *associare* 'to unite'. The early history of the word **socialism** is obscure. The word made its appearance in 1832 in France contrasted with *personnalité*; three or four years later the modern political sense was attributed to a use by either Leroux or Reybaud in their writings. However, the source has also been attributed to an English use in 1835 during the discussions of a society founded by Robert Owen.

sock [OE] Old English *socc* was a 'light shoe'. It goes back ultimately to Latin *soccus* 'comic actor's shoe, light low-heeled slipper', from Greek *sukkhos*. The phrase **knock the socks off** was originally US English from the early 19th century; **pull one's socks up** arose in the late 19th century; **put a sock in it** is early 20th century.

socket [ME] Early use was as a term for the 'head of a spear, resembling a ploughshare'. It comes from a diminutive of Old French *soc* 'ploughshare', probably of

snook snooker snout snow snuff snuffle

Celtic origin. The notion of a hollow part in a cylindrical shape for fitting together with another part dates from the 15th century.

soil [ME] You might think that soil meaning 'earth' and soil meaning 'to make dirty' are linked, but they are quite distinct words. When you use the noun to refer to 'home soil' or 'foreign soil' you are using the word in its original sense. It came from Old French and once referred to a land or country: 'The man who with undaunted toils / Sails unknown seas, to unknown soils' (John Gay, 1727). It could also refer to the ground, and later to the layer of earth that plants grow in. The verb soil, 'to make dirty', comes from Old French *soiller*, which was based on Latin *sucula* 'a little pig'. Pigs are not as dirty as their reputation suggests, but there is presumably the idea of making a place into a pigsty behind the use of the English word.

solar [LME] This is from Latin *solaris*, from *sol* 'sun', a base shared by mid 19th-century **solarium**, a use of a Latin word meaning both 'sundial' and 'place for sunning oneself'. From the same source comes **solstice** [ME], the second half of which comes from Latin *sistere* 'to stop'; and from Italian, based on Latin, **parasol** from *parasole*, formed from *para-* 'protecting against' and *sole* 'sun'. Old English *SUN is from the same Indo-European root.

soldier [ME] Soldiers take their name not from the fact that they are trained to fight but because they are paid to do so. The word entered English in the 13th century, from Old French *soldier*, from *soulde* 'pay, especially army pay'. The ultimate source is Latin *solidus*, the name of a gold coin that the Romans used. **Don't come** (or **play**) **the old soldier** is something you might say to a person who tries to use their greater age or experience of life to deceive you or to shirk a duty. An old soldier, someone who has been around and knows all the tricks, has been a proverbial figure since the 1720s.

sole [ME] There are three different words 'sole' in English. The two nouns are connected: the word for the under part of

the foot comes via French from Latin *solea* 'sandal, sill', from *solum* 'ground, sole'. The word was re-borrowed for the flat-fish, because its shape is reminiscent of a sole. The adjective for 'only' comes from Latin *solus* 'alone', source of **solitary** [ME], **desolate** [LME], and the musical **solo** [L17th]. **Solitaire** [E18th], both the single stone in its setting and the card game played by yourself, comes from the same source.

sol-fa *see* GAMUT

solitaire, solitary, solo *see* SOLE

solstice *see* SOLAR

soluble, solution *see* SOLVE

solve [LME] The early senses of solve were 'loosen, dissolve, untie'; the source is Latin *solvere* 'loosen, unfasten'. Other words sharing this base are late Middle English **soluble** and **solution,** and mid 17th century **solvent**. From the same Latin root come **absolve** [LME] 'loosen from'; **dissolve** [LME] 'loosen apart'; **dissolute** [LME] of loose morals; and **resolve** [LME] 'thoroughly loosen'.

sombre [M18th] If you are in a sombre mood you can be thought of as being under a shadow, rather like those cartoons showing a dark cloud hanging over a person's head. The word came into English from French in the middle of the 18th century but was based on Latin *sub* 'under' and *umbra* 'shade or shadow'. **Sombrero**, the broad-brimmed hat, is a Spanish word with a similar origin. *See also* UMBRELLA

somersault [M16th] This word is from Old French *sombresault*, from Provençal *sobresaut*, from *sobre* 'above' and *saut* 'leap'

somnolent [LME] 'Causing sleepiness' rather than 'sleep' was the early meaning of this. It goes back to Latin *somnus* 'sleep', which also provides the first element of **somnambulist** [L18th] (with *ambulare* 'to walk' the second element), and the second element of **insomnia** [E17th] 'lack of sleep'.

soil   solar   soldier   sole   sol-fa   solitaire

son [OE] An Old English word, which goes back to an Indo-European root with the idea of 'birth'. When we call someone a **son of a gun** we are using a term that probably came from naval history. The gun was one of the guns carried on board ships, and the phrase is supposed to have been applied to babies born at sea to women allowed to accompany their husbands. If the father was not known, the child was described in the ship's log as a 'son of a gun'. **Sonny Jim**, now a slightly disparaging address for a man or boy, was originally **Sunny Jim**. Jim was an energetic boy used to advertise a brand of breakfast cereal called Force in the early years of the 20th century. He was the winning entry in a competition run by the company to find a suitable character to promote the cereal. One slogan ran: 'High o'er the fence leaps Sunny Jim / "Force" is the food that raises him.'

sonar *see* SOUND

song [OE] The Old English words **sing** and **song** are from the same ancient root. The phrase to **sing for your supper**, 'to derive a benefit or favour by providing a service in return', derives from the nursery rhyme *Little Tommy Tucker*: 'Little Tommy Tucker / Sings for his supper; / What shall we give him? / White bread and butter.' If something is on sale **for a song** it is being sold very cheaply. This expression may come from the old practice of selling written copies of ballads at fairs. You could also say **for an old song**, perhaps because you would be likely to pay much less for an old ballad sheet than for a recent one. The phrase was popularized in the 1970s when *Going for a Song* was used as the title of a television quiz show in which teams had to guess the date and value of antiques. If you **make a song and dance about** something you cause a fuss or commotion or, in American English, give a long explanation that is deliberately misleading or confusing. In 17th-century America a 'song and dance' referred to a form of entertainment later applied to a vaudeville act. The modern senses developed around the turn of the 20th century. *See also* ALL

sonorous *see* SOUND

soon [OE] Over the centuries soon has become less urgent. In Anglo-Saxon times it meant 'immediately, without delay'. A similar case is **presently**, which also used to mean 'immediately' and now means 'soon'. The same thing is happening today with expressions like **directly**, **just a moment**, and **in a minute**. The idiomatic phrase **sooner you than me** is recorded from the 15th century; **as soon** meaning 'rather' dates from the late 16th century; (Irish poet W.B. Yeats *Hour-Glass*: 'I'd as soon listen to dried peas in a bladder as listen to your thoughts').

soothe [OE] In Anglo-Saxon times to soothe was to show or prove that something is true. The first part of **soothsayer** [ME], 'someone who can foresee the future', is based on the same word and originally described someone who speaks the truth, while the archaic **forsooth** is simply another way of saying 'in truth'. During the 16th century the meaning of **soothe** moved from 'to corroborate a statement, back someone up in what they are saying', to 'humour or flatter someone by agreeing with them'. This finally led to the meaning 'to calm, comfort, or placate' which we are familiar with today.

sop [OE] The Old English word sop first meant 'to dip bread in liquid'—Chaucer says of his Franklin 'Wel loved he in the morn a sop in wyn'—but nowadays a sop is something you do or offer as a concession to appease someone. This was originally used in the phrase **a sop to Cerberus**, referring to the monstrous three-headed watchdog which, in Greek mythology, guarded the entrance of Hades. In the *Aeneid* Virgil describes how the witch guiding Aeneas to the underworld threw a drugged cake to Cerberus, which allowed the hero to pass the monster in safety. When **soppy**, which comes from **sop**, first appeared in English in the early 19th century it meant 'soaked with water', not tears, as you might expect today from a feeble, sentimental soppy person. The writer H.G. Wells was one of the first to use the word in this sense. **Soup** [ME] comes from the French form of the same word. The American **from soup to nuts** for 'from beginning to end' dates from the early 20th century, while **in the soup**, also originally

American and a variant of being in hot water is slightly earlier. **Sip** [OE], **sup** [OE], and **supper** [ME] go back to the same root.

sophisticated [E17th] If you describe someone as sophisticated you probably mean that they are worldly-wise, discriminating and cultured—all positive traits. But when the word was first used it had a much more negative meaning, 'corrupted' or 'adulterated', especially referring to food and drink. Over time it shifted in sense and acquired associations of a lack of naturalness or simplicity, as in this example from Leslie Stephen's *The Playground of Europe* in 1871: 'The mountains...are a standing protest against the sophisticated modern taste.' This in turn led to the modern sense. The root was Greek *sophos*, 'wise'. **Sophist** [M16th], originally a term for a paid teacher of philosophy in the Classical world, but which came to mean someone who reasons with clever but false arguments of **sophistry** [ME] comes from the same root. So, too, does the US **sophomore** [L17th] for a second-year student, which comes from obsolete *sophumer* 'arguer'.

soprano *see* ITALIAN WORD PANEL

sorbet *see* SHERBET

sorcerer [LME] A sorcerer was originally a *sorser*. The word comes via Old French *sorcier* from Latin *sors* 'lot, fortune', the root of **sort** [LME]. The Latin relates to the use of oracles and the casting of lots to foretell the future. A **sorcerer's apprentice** is a person who starts a process but is then unable to control it without help. This is the translation of the French *L'apprenti sorcier*, the title of an 1897 symphonic poem by Paul Dukas based on *Der Zauberlehrling*, a ballad written in 1797 by the German poet and dramatist Goethe. In this ballad the apprentice's use of magic spells when his master is absent sets in motion a series of events which he cannot control.

sorry [OE] In the Anglo-Saxon period to be sorry was to be pained or distressed,

full of grief or sorrow—the meaning gradually weakened to become 'sad through sympathy with someone else's misfortune', 'full of regret', and then simply an expression of apology. The source was **sore**, which originally had the meaning 'causing intense pain, grievous' (*see also* PAIN). **Sorrow** is also Old English, but is not closely related to the other two words. The expression **more in sorrow than in anger** is taken from Shakespeare's *Hamlet*. When Hamlet asks Horatio to describe the expression on the face of his father's ghost, Horatio replies, 'a countenance more in sorrow than in anger'.

sort *see* SORCERER

sotto voce *see* ITALIAN WORD PANEL

sound [OE] There are four different 'sounds' in English. The one relating to noise is from Latin *sonus*. Related words are **dissonance** [LME] 'inharmonious'; **resonance** [LME] 'echo, resound'; **resonant** [L16th]; **resound** [LME]; and **sonorous** [E17th]. **Sonar**, however, is an acronym formed from **So**und **Na**vigation and **R**anging on the pattern of *RADAR. Sound, meaning 'in good condition, not damaged or diseased', is from Old English *gesund*. In Middle English the prominent sense was 'uninjured, unwounded'. Use of sound to mean 'having well-grounded opinions' dates from the early 16th century; the phrase **as sound as a bell** appeared in the late 16th century. This puns on the first meaning of sound, and also on the fact that a cracked bell will not ring true. The third sound [LME] 'ascertain the depth of water' is from Old French *sonder*, based on Latin *sub-* 'below' and *unda* 'wave'. The final one for a narrow stretch of water is Middle English from Old Norse *sund* 'swimming, strait', related to *SWIM.

soup *see* SOP **source** *see* FOUNTAIN

south *see* WEST

Meerkats on a tickey

South Africa *has eleven official languages, among them English and the native Zulu and Xhosa. European settlement began with the Dutch in the 17th century, and the language of their descendents, Afrikaans, has given South African English many words.*

FIRST of those in any dictionary is the **aardvark**, a badger-sized burrowing mammal whose name comes from *aarde* 'earth' and *vark* 'pig'. The **meerkat**, star of natural history programmes, has a complex history. The word is Dutch and may come from *meer* 'sea' and *kat* 'cat', perhaps with the idea of a cat-like creature from overseas, or it could be an alteration of Hindi *markata* 'ape'. Meerkats are agile creatures, able to turn **on a tickey**, or in a very small area. The expression goes back to the period before South African coinage was decimalized, when a **tickey** was a tiny silver coin worth three pennies. The equivalent British phrase is **on a sixpence**.

The most athletic person would not be able to emulate a meerkat, even when wearing **tackies**, or plimsolls. There may be a connection here with the English word **tacky** meaning 'slightly sticky', perhaps to do with the effect of extreme heat on the plimsolls' rubber soles. Wherever the name comes from, it has provided a number of phrases. The essential worthlessness of an old plimsoll gives us **a piece of old tackie** for an easy task that presents no problems, and to **tread tackie** is to drive or accelerate, with the idea of putting your foot down on the accelerator.

Dutch settlers in South Africa came to be known in English as **Boers**, from the Dutch word for 'farmer'. In 1835 many of them set out northwards on **the Great Trek** (*see* TREK) to find and settle new territory. On overnight stops they formed their wagons into a **laager** or circular encampment, which has given us **laager mentality** for an entrenched viewpoint.

In the TV comedy series *Fawlty Towers* Basil Fawlty crushes an expectant hotel guest by asking sarcastically if she was expecting to see 'herds of wildebeest sweeping majestically' out of a Torquay window. He was using the Afrikaans word for a creature better known as the **gnu**, a name from the indigenous African languages Khoikhoi and San, which probably imitates the sound the animal makes. *See also* BOOR, COMMANDO

sovereign [ME] Latin *super* 'above' as in *SUPERIOR was used to form Old French *soverain*. The ending was then altered in the 15th century so that it looked as if the word was associated with *reign*. The word was used as a term for a gold coin minted in England from the time of Henry VII to Charles I; it was originally worth 22s. 6d. The sovereign was revived in 1817 with a value of one pound.

sow [OE] Sow, in the sense to plant is Old English and had the sense 'disseminate' from early on. The image of **disseminate** [LME] is the same, for it comes from Latin **semen** [LME] meaning 'seed'. **Seed** [OE] in turn comes from the same Germanic root as sow. The differently pronounced sow that is the female pig is also Old English, and goes back to an Indo-European root shared by Latis *sus* and Greek *hus* which suggests they were on the menu for our early ancestors.

spade [OE] A spade for digging is related to Greek *spathē* 'blade or paddle' and has been in the language since Anglo-Saxon times, while the spade that appears on a playing card dates from the 16th century. The latter is based on Italian *spada* 'a broad-bladed sword', though the design (a black upside-down heart shape with a stalk) looks more like a pointed spade than a sword. To **call a spade a spade**, 'to speak plainly, without avoiding unpleasant or embarrassing issues', dates from the mid 16th century. In *The Importance of Being Earnest* (1895), Oscar Wilde has the nicely brought up Miss Gwendolen Fairfax respond to this: 'I am glad to say that I have never seen a spade'. A tongue-in-cheek variation, dating from the early 20th century, is **call a spade a shovel**. In spades means 'to a very high degree', or 'as much as or more than could be desired', and comes from the card game bridge, in which spades are the highest-ranking suit.

span [OE] Span as a measure of distance was originally a 'distance between the tips of the thumb and little finger'. Of Germanic origin, it was rare in Old English but was reinforced from 1300 by Old French version *espan*. The meaning 'a short space of time' (mortal span) dates from the late 16th century. The word was applied to the 'arch of a bridge' only from the early 19th century.

spaniel [LME] The Spanish origin of this breed is shown in the name, which is a form of Old French *espaigneul* 'Spanish [dog]'. The breed had long had a reputation for its submissive nature, and is first found used as an adjective in Shakespeare's *Julius Caesar* 'Low-crooked-curtsies, and base

Spaniell fawning.' This sense is most often found today in the expression **Spaniel eyes**.

spanner [L18th] The word spanner is based on German *spannen* 'draw tight'.

spare [OE] In the senses 'left over, extra', and 'to avoid harming', spare is an Old English word, but the **spare** in **spare ribs** is quite different. **Spare ribs** probably comes from the old German word *ribbesper*, which meant 'pickled pork ribs roasted on a spit'. Once English speakers started using the German term in the 16th century they soon swapped the two parts round to make it sound more like an English word (*compare* SIDEBURNS). The title of the British feminist magazine *Spare Rib*, first published in 1972, is a pun on the 'spare' rib that God took from Adam's body to create the first woman, Eve.

spartan [LME] A spartan place or lifestyle is one lacking comfort or luxury. The word is a tribute to the Spartans of ancient Greece, traditional foes of Athens, who left weak or sickly babies out on a cold mountain slope at night to die and forced all children to live in military 'boarding schools' from the age of about seven. Their terse speech also gave us the word *LACONIC.

spawn *see* PACE

speak [OE] The close relationship between speak and **speech** is clearer in the original Old English, where they are *sprecan* and *sprēc*, the 'r' dropping out of the words early on. 'I speak as I find', first appears in Shakespeare's *The Taming of the Shrew*: 'Mistake me not; I speak but as I find.' **Never speak ill of the dead** has an even longer history. 'Speak no evil of the dead' is attributed to the Spartan magistrate Chilon as far back as the 6th century BC, and a later Latin proverb, *de mortuis nil nisi bonum*, can be translated as 'say nothing of the dead but what is good'. The English version of the proverb is first recorded in the 16th century, originally in the form 'rail not upon him that is dead'. **Speakeasy** [L19th] an American term for an unlicensed drinking establishment, gets its name for 'speak' and 'easy' in the sense 'gently, softly' from the

sow   spade   span   spaniel   spanner   spare

need to be discreet when talking about it. *See also* ACHE

species [LME] The connection may not be immediately obvious, but species is based on Latin *specere* 'to look'. The Latin root is reflected in some of the early uses of the word, such as 'the outward look or appearance of something', or 'an image or reflection'. Over time this idea of the visible form of something developed into the more general notion of a thing's 'type' or 'kind'. *See also* FEMALE. Other English words based on Latin *specere* or the related verb *spectare* include **special** [ME]; **spectator** [L16th]; **spectre** [E17th] (literally 'an appearance'); **specimen** [E17th]; and **spy** [ME]. Another is **spectacle** (ME in the sense 'a show')—a spectacle, originally used in the singular, was a term for a device to assist eyesight as far back as the 15th century. In one of his sermons written in 1628, the poet and preacher John Donne thanked the man 'that assists me with a Spectacle when my sight grows old'.

speech *see* SPEAK

speed [OE] The Germanic root of this Old English word had a basic sense of 'prosper, succeed', which still survives in expressions as **God speed!** and **more haste less speed**. The link between this and 'rapidity' is probably our tendency to equate doing something well with doing it quickly. Speed has been a slang term for amphetamines since the 1960s.

spell [OE] In Old English *spel* meant 'story, speech', a sense still hidden in the word *GOSPEL. By the late 16th century this had become the right speech to use when invoking magic powers, via the late Middle English *nightspell*, special words to protect you at night. Meanwhile the verb had developed from 'speak, tell' to read out loud with difficulty, or 'spell out' words, and from this the sense to use the right letters in a word.

spend *see* EXPENSE

spick and span [L16th] 'My Lady Batten walking through the dirty lane with new

spick and span white shoes', writes Samuel Pepys in his diary in 1665. He was not saying that her shoes were clean or neat, but that they were brand new, which is what spick and span meant in the 17th century. It was based on the earlier phrase **spick and span new**, a more emphatic version of the dialect **span new**, which came from Old Norse *spán-nýr*, 'as new as a freshly cut wooden chip'. The spick part was influenced by Dutch *spiksplinternieuw*, literally 'splinter new'.

spider *see* SPINSTER

spike [ME] In the noun sense 'a sharp-pointed piece of metal or wood' spike derived from Dutch or German. The verb came later, in the early 17th century. To **spike someone's guns** is to thwart their plans. This expression refers to the practice of disabling cannons captured from the enemy. A spike was driven into the small hole through which the charge was ignited, making it impossible to fire the gun. To **spike someone's drink**, first recorded in the late 19th century, is based on the idea of making a drink 'sharper'. *See also* SPOKE

spill [OE] Old English *spillan* meant 'kill, destroy', a sense that was common until about 1600, and 'shed (blood)'. The sense 'allow liquid to pour out or over' arose from the latter in late Middle English.

spin [OE] An Old English word that originally meant 'to draw out and twist fibre'. The expression to **spin a yarn**, 'to tell a long, far-fetched story', is nautical in origin. An important job on board ship was making and repairing ropes, a task which involved twisting together a number of long threads or 'yarns'. The image of this process and the reputation sailors had for telling tall tales of fabulous far-flung lands combined to produce the phrase we know today. Tony Blair's Labour government in Britain, elected in 1997, gained a reputation for its use of **spin** and **spin doctors**, but spin meaning 'the presentation of information in a particular way, a slant' started in the USA. It was first recorded in 1977 in the *Washington Post*, with spin doctor following

species speech speed spell spend spider

Paella on the patio

*Spain is a popular choice for Brits holidaying or moving abroad. This is hardly surprising when you see how many **Spanish** words in English are connected with relaxation and enjoyment.*

SPANISH **paella** and **tapas** are perfect for outdoor dining on a **patio**, originally the name for an inner courtyard in a Spanish house. The dish of rice with chicken and shellfish, cooked in a large shallow pan, goes back to Latin *patella* 'a small shallow dish'—so the plate of food balanced on your knee has a close connection with **patella** as the anatomical name for the kneecap. **Tapas**, small savoury dishes served with drinks at a bar, used to come free, and were traditionally served on a dish balanced atop a glass. This was the origin of the name, since the word literally means 'cover' or 'lid'.

Sangria, a mixture of red wine, carbonated water, and a sweetener, would be just the drink for a patio meal. Its colour is the source of the name, which in Spanish means 'bleeding'. Although **sherry** has a typically British feel to it, the name comes from *vino de Xerez* or 'wine of Xerez'—the original name of Jerez in southern Spain, from which the drink came. After all this eating and drinking, a **siesta** or nap might be welcome. This Spanish word for a rest taken at the hottest time of the day goes back to Latin *sexta hora* 'sixth hour of the day'.

Certainly *not* relaxing, but traditionally Spanish, is a bullfight. A mounted bullfighter is called a **toreador**, from *toro* 'bull', and the bullfighter whose task is to kill the bull is the **matador**, a word which means literally 'killer'. It goes back ultimately to Persian *māt* 'dead', the origin of the *-mate* part of **checkmate** (*see* CHECK). An English proverb warns us not to put off till tomorrow what we can do today, but the relaxed Spanish have given us **mañana**, 'tomorrow', to express a more easy-going attitude to pressing schedules. You could respond to any protests about slackness with **que sera sera**, which indicates that you have no control over the future. The Spanish phrase, meaning 'what will be, will be', was popularized in English by the 1956 song '*Que Sera, Sera*', sung by Doris Day.

See also AMATEUR, CASTLE, FLAMINGO, SOMBRE

in 1984. **Spindle** [OE], originally *spinel*, comes from 'spin'.

spinach [ME] Persian *aspanak* is the ultimate source of the word. It passed from Persian into Arabic and then into Latin. From there it took various forms in many European languages, and probably came into English via French or possibly Dutch.

spindle *see* SPIN

spine [LME] Spine is from Latin *spina* 'thorn, prickle, backbone'. The word has

spike spill spin spinach spindle spine

been used to denote the back of a book from the 1920s. **Spinney** [L16th] is a shortening of Old French *espinei*, from an alteration of Latin *spinetum* 'thicket', from *spina*.

spinster [LME] A spinster was originally a woman who spun, something that many unmarried women used to do at home to earn their living. The word was often added after the name of a woman to describe her occupation, and in time became the official description of an unmarried woman. Today it has a dated feel and alludes to a stereotypical figure of an older woman who is unmarried, childless, and prim or repressed. The word could also once refer to another kind of spinner, a spider, and **spider** itself is descended from Old English *spithra*, from *spinnan* 'to spin'. *See also* COBWEB

spire [OE] Old English *spīr* was a 'tall slender stem of a plant', related to German *Spier* 'tip of a blade of grass'. The word came to be used in the late 16th century for a slender structure such as a spire of rock or a church spire. Dreaming spires comes from Matthew Arnold, writing of Oxford in *Thyrsis* (1865) 'And that sweet city with her dreaming spires . . . Lovely all times she lies, lovely to-night'. Spire has no connection with **spiral** [M16th] which comes from Latin *spira* 'coil'.

spirit [ME] Our word spirit is based on Latin *spiritus* 'breath or spirit', from *spirare* 'to breathe'—the ancient Romans believed that the human soul had been 'breathed' into the body—the image is the same as 'the breath of life'. The sense 'strong distilled alcoholic drink' comes from the use in alchemy of spirit to mean 'a liquid essence extracted from some substance'. People sometimes say **the spirit is willing but the flesh is weak** when they have good intentions but yield to temptation and fail to live up to them. The source is the New Testament, where Jesus uses the phrase after finding his disciples asleep in the Garden of Gethsemane despite telling them that they should stay awake. *Spirare* forms the basis of numerous English words including **aspire** [M16th] from *adspirare* 'to breath upon, seek to reach'; **conspire** [LME]

from *conspirare* 'to breath together, agree'; **expire** [L16th] 'to breath out'; **inspire** [LME] 'breath into' from the idea that a divine or outside power has inspired you; and **perspire** [M17th] 'to breath through'; and **transpire** [LME] 'breath across. In English spirit was shortened to **sprite** [ME] which in turn developed **sprightly** [L16th].

spit [OE] The root of the Old English word spit imitated the sound of someone spitting out saliva from their mouth. Spit in the sense of **spit-roast** is from another Old English word meaning 'thin, pointed rod', and the spit of land came from this. When we notice that someone looks exactly like someone else we can say that they are **the spit of** or **the spitting image** of the other person. This last phrase is an altered form of an earlier version, **spit and image**, early examples of which, from the 1600s, describe a man as being so like another that he could have been spat out of the latter's mouth. Another explanation is based on the idea of a person apparently being formed, perhaps by witchcraft, from the spit of another, so great is the similarity between them. Easier to explain is the expression **spit and sawdust**, used to describe an old-fashioned or unpretentious pub. This recalls the former practice of sprinkling the floor of the pub with a layer of sawdust, to soak up spillages in general and customers' spit in particular. **Spout** [ME] shares a root.

spite *see* DESPISE

splash *see* FLASH, POP

splay *see* DISPLAY

splendid [E17th] Early 17th-century examples of splendid, which comes ultimately from Latin *splendere* 'to shine brightly', describe a grand place or occasion. The phrase **splendid isolation** was first used at the end of the 19th century to refer to the diplomatic and commercial non-involvement of Great Britain in Europe.

split [L16th] This was originally used in the sense 'break up (a ship)', describing the force of a storm or rock; it was borrowed from Middle Dutch *splitten*. The idiom **split**

hairs dates from the late 17th century; **split the difference** arose in the early 18th century; **split the atom** is recorded from the early 20th century.

spoke [OE] In the sense 'a bar or rod connecting the centre of a wheel to its edge', spoke is an Old English word, related to *SPIKE. It appears in the slightly puzzling expression **put a spoke in someone's wheel**. This means 'to prevent someone from carrying out a plan', but since wheels are supposed to have spokes it does not appear to make a lot of sense. It is probably a mistranslation of Dutch *een spaak in 'twiel steeken*, 'to put a bar in the wheel'—the image that should come to mind is of a bar being stuck into a wheel to stop it turning properly.

spoof [L19th] An example of a word made up by a specific person, the English comedian Arthur Roberts (1852–1933). He invented a card game involving bluff, which he called Spoof. The word subsequently came to be applied to a hoax or swindle, and to a parody.

spoon [OE] In Old English a spoon was a chip of wood or a splinter, from the same Germanic root that gives us the span of *SPICK AND SPAN. The 'eating utensil' sense came in the Middle Ages, probably from the fact that spoons were most often carved out of wood or horn. The team that comes last in a competition can be said to **win the wooden spoon**. The original winner, back in the early 19th century, was the candidate coming last in the final examination in mathematics at Cambridge University. As a symbol of his 'wooden-headedness' or stupidity he would be presented with a wooden spoon. **Spooning** is an old slang word meaning 'to behave in an amorous way, kiss and cuddle', first recorded in the 1830s and in vogue until the middle of the next century. It probably comes from the use of spoon to mean 'a foolish person', which developed into **being spoons about** someone, or **having the spoons for** them— being infatuated with them.

spoonerism [E20th] A spoonerism is a verbal error in which you accidentally swap round the initial parts of two words, as in 'Our queer old dean' instead of 'Our dear old queen'. The term comes from the name of the Reverend William Archibald Spooner (1844–1930), an Oxford academic who was reputedly prone to such slips of the tongue, although there is no hard evidence he said many of the things attributed to him. A classic 'spoonerism' associated with him was 'You have tasted your worm, you have hissed my mystery lectures, and you must leave by the first town drain', supposedly said to an idle student.

sporadic [L17th] This came via medieval Latin from Greek *sporadikos* 'scattered'. It is related to *speirein* 'to sow', the source, too, of mid 19th-century **spore**. The scattering of Greek islands known as the Sporades get their name from the same source.

sporran *see* PURSE

sport [LME] Sport comes from a shortening of **disport** [ME], formed, via French, from Latin *dis* 'away' and *portare* 'carry' used in much the same way as the expression 'to take someone out of themselves'. Sport meant any kind of entertainment, and only started to be used in the modern sense of physical activities with set rules in the late 18th century. **The sport of kings** [M17th] once referred to war-making but was later applied to hunting and horse-racing.

spout *see* SPIT

sprightly *see* SPIRIT

spring [OE] An Old English word that originally referred to the source of a well or stream, the place where a flow of water rises naturally from the earth. People soon started using spring in the context of the first sign or beginning of something— expressions such as 'the spring of the day', 'the spring of the dawn', and 'the spring of the year' were commonly used from around 1380 to 1600. From the middle of the 16th century the last of these expressions became shortened to spring as the name of

spoke   spoof   spoon   spoonerism   sporadic

the first season of the year. Before that this season of new growth had been known as **Lent**, a word now only used in a religious context to refer to the period of fasting and repentance between Ash Wednesday and Easter, an Old English term of obscure origin. The kind of spring that is a metal coil is also the same word. This meaning was suggested by the verb sense 'to come out or jump up suddenly'. Someone who is **no spring chicken** is not as young as they used to be, a phrase recorded from the early years of the 20th century. Spring chickens were birds born in spring and eaten when they were about 10–15 weeks old.

sprite *see* SPIRIT

spritzer *see* GERMAN WORD PANEL

spruce [L16th] Prussia was a former kingdom that covered much of modern northeast Germany and Poland. Between the 14th and 17th centuries it was also known in English as both **Pruce** and **Spruce**, and these words could also be used to mean 'Prussian'. **Spruce** was in time used as the name of a type of fir tree grown in Prussia. It was also used in the phrase **spruce leather**, a fashionable type of leather imported in the 16th century from Prussia and used especially for jerkins. It is probably from this that the sense 'neat or smart in dress or appearance' developed.

spunk *see* PUNK

spurious [L16th] 'Born out of wedlock, bastard' was the early sense of spurious based on Latin *spurius* 'false'. The sense became generalized to 'of doubtful origin' by the beginning of the 17th century.

spurt *see* FLIRT

sputnik *see* SATELLITE

spy *see* SPECIES

square [ME] A word that comes via Old French *esquare* from Latin *quadra* 'square'. **Squad** [M17th] and **squadron** [M16th], which originally meant a group of soldiers in square formation, come via French from the Italian form *squadra*. The rather odd term **a square meal** is sometimes said to derive from the square wooden platters on which meals were served on board ship. More likely, though, is that (as with 'square deal' and 'fair and square') square simply suggests something that is 'honest', 'straightforward', or 'right', with the additional idea that it has been solidly or properly constructed. The word was used since the 17th century to mean 'honourable, upright', which gave us the square person who is old-fashioned or boringly conventional. To **square the circle** is to do something impossible. The phrase refers to the mathematical problem of constructing a square equal in area to a given circle, a problem which cannot be solved by purely geometrical means, though this has not stopped mathematicians from the ancient Greeks onwards from trying to solve the puzzle. The use of **square up** in reference to a person about to fight comes from the typical posture adopted, with the shoulders back and the fists held out at right angles. It is first found in the 1820s.

squire *see* ESQUIRE

squirrel [LME] A squirrel is literally a 'shadow-tail', an appropriate description if you picture the animal holding its long bushy tail over its back like a sunshade. The Greeks called it *skiouros*, based on *skia* 'a shadow' and *oura* 'a tail', and the English name evolved from this.

stable [ME] The French word *estable*, from which we get stable, could refer to a shelter for pigs as well as one for horses, and in English a stable originally housed any domestic animal. Stable meaning 'firmly fixed' is a quite different word, that goes back to Latin *stare* 'to stand'. The saying **shut (or lock) the stable door after the horse has bolted**—take preventive measures too late, once the damage has already been done—dates back to medieval times, though until the late 19th century it specifically referred to horse-stealing and was used in the form **shut the stable door after the steed is stolen**, as in Robert Louis Stevenson's novel *Kidnapped* (1886): 'A guinea-piece . . . fell . . . into the sea . . . I now saw there must be a hole, and clapped my hand to the place . . . But this was to lock the stable door after the steed was stolen.' *See also* CONSTABLE

stadium *see* FURLONG

staff *see* STAVE

staid *see* STATIONER

stain *see* TINCTURE

stake [OE] In the sense 'a thick pointed stick driven into the ground', stake is related to *STICK. The gambling sense might relate to the idea of an object being placed as a wager on a post or stake, though there is no definite evidence of the existence of this custom. If you **stake a claim** you declare or assert your right to something. This expression originated in America at the time of the California gold rush of 1849. Prospectors would register their claim to a particular plot of land by marking out the boundary with wooden stakes that they drove into the ground, thus 'staking a claim'. Also American in origin is the phrase **pull up stakes**, meaning 'to move or go to live elsewhere'. The stakes being referred to here are pegs or posts for securing a tent or making a fence around a temporary settlement.

stalactite [L17th] Stalactites hang down from the roof of a cave. The name comes from Greek *stalaktos* 'dropping or dripping'. **Stalagmites** [L17th], on the other hand, rise up from the floor of a cave, formed from the evaporated dripping from above. Greek *stalagma* 'a drop or drip' is the source this time.

stale [ME] Stale ale may not have much appeal, but beer is what stale originally described—not beer that has gone off, but beer that has been standing long enough for it to clear and perhaps improve in strength. The word was applied to food from the early 16th century.

stalk *see* STEAL

stand *see* STEAD

standard [ME] A standard, from Old French *estendre* 'to extend', was originally a flag raised on a pole as a rallying point for soldiers, and typically carrying the distinctive badge of a leader, nation, or city. The word appears first in English with reference to the Battle of the Standard in 1138, between the English and the Scots. The 'standard' in question was apparently the mast of a ship with flags at the top, mounted on a wagon brought on to the battlefield. In later use the idea of the royal flag or 'standard' came to represent a source of authority, the centre from which commands are issued. This led to its modern use in connection with the setting of a fixed scale of weights and measures, and indeed of any established level of quality or quantity.

star [OE] The Latin word *stella* 'star', which gave us star **constellation** [ME] and **stellar** [M17th], was related to the two Greek equivalents, *astēr* and *astron*, the source of words such as *ASTERISK and **astrology** [LME]. The latter is the source of expressions such as **thank your lucky stars** found from the late 16th century. Star did not apply to famous or talented entertainers until the beginning of the 19th century. Eventually a star was not big or glittering enough, and **superstar** was coined around 1925, followed by **megastar** in 1976. *See also* HITCH

starboard *see* PORT

starch, stark, starkers *see* NAKED

start [OE] Old English *styrtan* meant 'to caper, leap'. From the sense 'sudden movement' arose the meaning 'initiation of movement, setting out on a journey', which then gave 'beginning (of a process, etc.)'. **Startle** [OE] comes from the same root. *See also* NAKED

starve [OE] In Anglo-Saxon times starve simply meant 'to die', especially a lingering death from hunger, cold, disease, or grief. People continued to use the word in this way for many centuries, and in northern

stadium staff staid stain stake stalactite

English dialect starve can still mean 'to die of cold'. The origin of the word is probably an ancient Germanic base that meant 'to be rigid'. This rigid/dead connection is preserved in the modern slang use of *STIFF to refer to a dead body.

state *see* ESTATE

stationer [ME] In the Middle Ages stationers sold not **stationery**, writing materials but books. The word comes from medieval Latin *stationarius*, referring to a tradesman who had a shop or stall at a fixed location, as opposed to one who travelled around selling their wares. The ultimate source is Latin *statio* 'standing', which is also the root of **stationary** with an *a*, 'not moving' and **station** [ME]. In medieval England selling parchment, paper, pens, and ink was a branch of the bookseller's trade, and in due course booksellers became known as stationers. **Statue** [ME] and related words come from the same Latin root as do **stature** [ME] which originally meant 'height when standing', **status** [L18th] 'legal standing', and **statute** [ME], a law that had been set up. The verb to **stay** [LME] is yet another word from the root. **Staid** [L16th] is an archaic past of stay, describing a character that is fixed in its ways.

statistic [L18th] This is from the German adjective *statistisch*, and the noun *Statistik*. This German noun was used by a German writer called Aschenwall in 1748 as a name for the area of knowledge dealing with the constitutions and resources of the various states of the world. French writers of the 18th century refer to Aschenwall as having introduced the word, which then gave rise to French *statistique*. In English the word was first found in the phrase **statistic science** (a collection of numerical facts to do with economic conditions) in the late 18th century.

statue, stature, status *see* STATIONER

statute *see* CONSTITUTION, STATIONER

stave [ME] Old English *staff* 'walking stick' had a plural staves, which with the -s

dropped became stave—the sort of stick from which you could built a barrel. Use as a musical term for a set of lines for musical notation dates from the early 19th century. Current senses of the verb date from the early 17th century, with **stave off**—fend off as if with a staff—found from the same date.

stay *see* STATIONER

stead [OE] Old English *stede* meant 'place'. From a Germanic source, it is related to Dutch *stad* 'town', German *Statt* 'place', from an Indo-European root shared by the verb **stand**. **Instead** [ME] is simply 'in stead, in place of' run together. The adjective **steadfast** [Old English] is literally 'standing firm'; a **homestead** [OE] is your 'home place'; while if you are **steady** [ME] you are not easily moved from your place. *See also* PLACE

steal [OE] Steal has two basic but connected senses: 'take dishonestly' and 'go secretly'. If someone **steals your thunder** they win attention for themselves by pre-empting your attempt to impress. The source of this expression is surprisingly literal. The English dramatist John Dennis (1657–1734) invented a new method of simulating the sound of thunder as a theatrical sound effect and used it in his unsuccessful play *Appius and Virginia*. Shortly after he heard the same thunder effects used at a performance of Shakespeare's *Macbeth*. Dennis was understandably furious. 'Damn them!', he fumed, 'they will not let my play run, but they steal my thunder!' **Stealth** [ME] is closely connected and originally meant 'theft', and the phrase **by stealth** meant 'by theft' in late medieval English. The modern meaning of stealth evolved by homing in on all the furtiveness and secrecy associated with stealing. **Stalk** [LOE] as in 'to stalk game' is another relative, originally meaning 'walk cautiously or stealthily'. The stalk of a plant [ME] is unconnected and may be a form of dialect *stale* 'rung of a ladder, long handle'.

steam [OE] In Old English steam was any kind of hot vapour or gas, and did not settle into the modern meaning until the 15th century. The phrase **let off steam**, meaning 'to get rid of pent-up energy or strong emotion', originated in the context of steam engines in the early 19th century. The literal meaning is 'to release excess steam from a steam engine through a valve', vital in preventing the engine from blowing up. The meaning which is familiar today arose in the 1830s in the alternative version **blow off steam**. There is a related image in **have steam coming out of your ears**, meaning 'to be very angry'. Other phrases that recall the days of steam engines include **get up** (or **pick up**) **steam**, **run out of steam,** and **under your own steam**.

steeplechase [L18th] A steeplechase was originally a horse race across country over hedges, walls, and ditches. The term dates from the late 18th century and comes from the idea of using a distant church steeple to mark the finishing point of the race, which you have to reach by clearing any intervening obstacles. Steeple comes from the same root as the adjective **steep** (both Old English).

steeplejack *see* JACK

stellar *see* ASTERISK

stench *see* STINK

stevedore *see* STIFF

stew [ME] When stew entered the language it referred to a cauldron or large cooking pot, not to what was being cooked in it. The source was Old French *estuve*, probably based on Greek *tuphos* 'smoke or steam', which is also where the fevers **typhus** [L18th] and **typhoid** [E19th] come from, because they create the kind of stupor that is associated with smoke inhalation. The verb 'to stew' originally referred to bathing in a hot bath or steam bath. It was not long before the idea of heating people in a bath had changed to heating food in an oven, specifically cooking a dish of meat and vegetables by simmering it slowly in a closed vessel. **Stifle** [LME] probably comes from the same Old French root, and **stove**

[ME], originally a 'sweating room' in a steam bath, may be related. *See also* SEETHE

stick [OE] The two English words spelled stick are both Old English. The noun, 'a thin piece of wood', and the verb, meaning 'to push something pointed into' and 'to cling, adhere', are probably connected, with the basic idea being one of piercing or pricking. If a person **comes to a sticky end** they meet a nasty death or other fate. The phrase is first found in a 1904 account of a US baseball game, and by 1916 had made its way to Britain. *See also* WICKET, WRONG

stickler [M16th] A stickler is a person who insists on a certain quality or type of behaviour. The first recorded sense, in the 1530s, was 'referee or umpire', and the word was based on the now obsolete term *stickle*, meaning 'to be an umpire': 'There had been blood-shed, if I had not stickled', wrote the English dramatist William Cartwright in 1643.

stiff [OE] An Old English word, stiff goes back to a Germanic root meaning 'inflexible' and shares an Indo-European ancestry with Latin *stipare* 'press, pack' source of **constipate** [LME] and via Spanish the **stevedore** [L18th] who packs away cargo. As a noun meaning 'a dead body' it dates back to the USA of the 1850s. **The stiffs**, meaning the reserve team of a sports club, is a 1950s use. *See also* STARVE.

The **stiff upper lip**, a quality of uncomplaining stoicism so often thought of as peculiarly British is apparently North American in origin. The earliest recorded example is from the US writer John Neal's novel *The Down Easters* (1833): 'What's the use o' boo-hooin'? . . . Keep a stiff upper lip; no bones broke.'

stifle *see* STEW

still [OE] In the sense 'not moving' still is Old English. The kind of still used to make whisky and other spirits is a different word, from **distil** [LME], which itself is based on Latin *stilla* 'a drop'. The **still small voice** for a person's conscience, is biblical in origin. The prophet Elijah hid in a cave but was told to come out and hear the word of God. A great wind come first, then an earthquake, and finally a fire: 'And after the earthquake a fire; but the Lord was not in the fire: and after the fire a still small voice.' Going back at least to the 15th century is the expression **still waters run deep**, suggesting that a quiet or placid manner may conceal a passionate or subtle nature. A 1616 version is 'Where rivers run most stilly, they are the deepest.'

stilted [E17th] Stilted is first found in the literal sense of 'having **stilts**', a medieval word of Germanic origin with a probable base meaning of 'walk stiffly'. It is first found used about language, originally meaning 'unnaturally elevated' in a letter written by Byron in 1820 'You are taken in by that false, stilted, trashy style'.

stimulate [M16th] The early sense of this was 'sting, afflict'; it is from Latin *stimulare* 'urge', 'goad'. **Stimulus** is a late 17th-century use of a Latin word meaning 'goad, spur, incentive'.

stink [OE] Old English *stincan* 'stink and its close relative *stenc* 'smell' source of **stench** both go back to a common Germanic root.

stipend *see* PENSION

stir *see* PORRIDGE, ROMANY WORD PANEL

stitch [OE] In Anglo-Saxon times stitch was used to describe any sharp stabbing pain rather than just a pain in the side caused by strenuous exercise. The word is related to *STICK. Shakespeare seems to have been the first to mention a stitch brought on by laughing. In *Twelfth Night* Maria invites her fellow conspirators to observe the lovelorn Malvolio, saying: 'If you ... will laugh yourselves into stitches, follow me.' The sewing sense of stitch arose in the Middle Ages. According to the 18th-century proverb, **a stitch in time saves nine**. In other words, if you sort out a problem immediately, it may save a lot of extra work later. There does not seem to be any particular significance in the choice of the number nine aside from its similarity in

sound to the word 'time'. **Stitch up**, meaning 'to frame or betray someone', is recorded only from the 1970s. It was probably suggested by the betrayal being as neat and conclusive as an invisible repair to an item of clothing.

stoic [LME] Today a child who falls over but does not cry might be described as stoic—a long way from the original Stoics (3rd century BC) of ancient Athens. They were the followers of a school of philosophy which taught that wise men should live in harmony with Fate or Providence, and be indifferent to the ups and downs of life and to pleasure and pain. From there stoic or **stoical** came to mean 'enduring pain and hardship without complaint'. The word is from the *Stoa Poikilē*, or 'Painted Porch', where the school's founder, Zeno, taught. *See also* CYNIC, EPICURE

stomach [ME] The ultimate source of our word stomach is Greek *stomakhos* 'gullet', from *stoma* 'mouth', source of the anatomical term [L17th]. A common saying is **the way to a man's heart is through his stomach**. The earliest expression of these sentiments is by John Adams, the second American president, in a letter he wrote in 1814: 'The shortest road to men's hearts is down their throats'. *See also* NATION

stone [OE] An Old English word first found in the writings of Alfred the Great (849–99). The imperial unit of weight, recorded from the 14th century, is now equivalent to 14 pounds but formerly varied, and would originally have been just the weight of a particular rock used as a local measure. To **cast** (or **throw**) **the first stone** is to be the first to accuse or criticize. The phrase comes from St John's Gospel. A group of men preparing to stone to death a woman who had committed adultery were addressed by Jesus with the words: 'He that is without sin among you, let him first cast a stone at her.' Drug takers have been **stoned** since the 1950s, originally in the USA—the image is of someone so dazed they seem to have been hit by a large stone. If something is **set** (or **carved**) **in stone** it is fixed and unchangeable. This refers to another

stilted stimulate stink stipend stir stitch

biblical story, of Moses and the Ten Commandments. According to the Book of Genesis God wrote the Commandments on tablets of stone and handed them down to Moses on Mount Sinai.

stool [OE] In Anglo-Saxon times a stool was any kind of seat for one person, and in particular a throne. Among the other types of seat it came to refer to was one enclosing a chamber pot, and so a privy or lavatory. Then the word was transferred to the act of going to the toilet itself, which is how it ended up as a term for faeces. The Groom of the Stool was formerly a high officer of the royal household, in medieval times responsible for the royal commode or privy. To **fall between two stools** is to fail to take either of two satisfactory alternatives. This comes from the old proverb **between two stools one falls to the ground**, which was first referred to in English by the medieval writer John Gower around 1390: 'Thou farest as he between two stools That would sit and goes to ground.' The first **stool pigeon** [L19th] is often said to have been a pigeon fixed to a stool as a decoy for wildfowl, but in reality it probably had nothing to do with a small chair. It is more likely to come from the old term **stale**, from Old French *estale*, applied to a pigeon used to entice a hawk into a net. It came to be applied to a person employed by gamblers or criminals as a decoy, and later (on the other side of the law) to a police informer. *See also* NARK

storey *see* STORY

stork *see* NAKED

story [ME] Both **storey** and **story** (and indeed *HISTORY) come from Latin *historia* 'history, story'. A story was initially a historical account or representation, usually involving passages of bible history and legends of the saints. From the 1500s the word was used in connection with fictitious events for the entertainment of people. As for **storey**, which is essentially the same word, there may have originally been a reference to tiers of painted windows or sculptures used to decorate the front of a building, each one representing a historical

subject. So each tier was a different 'story' or, once the spelling changed, 'storey'. Eventually the word came to refer to a level or floor of a building. At some time in the 1930s or before, someone told a long, rambling anecdote about a dog with shaggy hair. It must have caught the public imagination, as ever since then any long rambling story or joke that is only amusing because it is absurdly inconsequential or pointless has been a **shaggy-dog story**.

stove *see* STEW

stow *see* PLACE

strafe [early 20th century] This term for 'to attack from low-flying aircraft' was a humorous adaptation of the German First World War catchphrase *Gott strafe England* 'may God punish England'.

straight [ME] The word straight is the old past form of Old English **stretch**, and originally meant 'extended at full length'. The sense relating to an alcoholic drink, 'undiluted', is the American equivalent of *NEAT and dates from the middle of the 19th century. **The straight and narrow** is the honest and morally acceptable way of living. The earliest example of this expression was the longer **the straight and narrow path** (or **way**). It arose through a misunderstanding of the meaning of a word in this passage from the Gospel of Matthew: 'Because strait is the gate, and narrow is the way, which leadeth unto life, and few there be that find it'. Strait [LME] here simply means 'narrow', from the same source as *STRICT, a sense which only really survives today in the noun meaning 'a narrow passage of water connecting two seas', as in the Straits of Gibraltar. The confusion probably came about because crooked, the opposite of straight, had long been used to mean 'dishonest'.

strand [OE] The strand meaning 'leave aground' is the same as that meaning 'land bordering water'. The strand of thread is unrelated and of uncertain history.

strange [ME] Strange is a shortening of Old French *estrange*, from Latin *extraneus*

stool   storey   stork   story   stove   stow   strafe

'external, strange', also the source of **stranger** [LME].

straw [OE] An Old English word related to **strew** that shares an ancient ancestor with Latin *sternere* 'to lay flat'. Straws crop up in various common English expressions. The person who ends up being chosen to perform an unpleasant task can be said to **draw the short straw**, from drawing lots by holding several straws of varying lengths with one end concealed in your hand and then inviting people to take one each. A person in danger of drowning would try to grab hold of anything to keep afloat, the source of the old proverb **a drowning man will clutch at a straw**, recorded in various forms since the mid 16th century. Nowadays, you are more likely to come across the abbreviated version **to clutch** (or **grasp**) **at straws**. Another old proverb provides **the last** (or **final**) **straw**, referring to a final minor difficulty or annoyance that, coming on top of a whole series of others, makes a situation unbearable. The full version is **it is the last straw that breaks the camel's back**. Earlier variations included **the last feather breaks the horse's back**, which dates back to the mid 17th century. No one is really sure what **strawberries** have got to do with straw. One possible explanation is that a strawberry's runners reminded people of straw strewn on floors. Or perhaps the name of the fruit refers to the small seeds scattered over its surface, which resemble tiny pieces of straw or chaff.

street [OE] A street is literally a road with a paved surface, based on Latin *strata via* 'paved way'. Some ancient Roman roads in Britain preserve this usage in their names, such as Watling Street (from Dover to Wroxeter) and Ermine Street (from London to Lincoln and York). The modern use, referring to a public road in a city, town, or village that runs between lines of houses and buildings, goes back to Anglo-Saxon times. We have used the phrase **the man on the street** to refer to an ordinary person in contrast to an expert since the early 19th century. *See also* MAN, QUEER

stress *see* DISTRICT

stretch *see* STRAIGHT

strew *see* STRAW

strict [LME] People first used strict to mean 'restricted in space or extent'. The 17th-century philosopher Richard Burthogge wrote in 1675: 'I am apt to think that Hell is of a Vast Extent, and that the bounds and limits of it, are not so strict and narrow, as the most imagine.' Other early meanings included 'tight' and 'stretched taut' before the meaning 'imposing severe discipline' developed in the late 16th century. The source is Latin *strictus*, based on *stringere* 'to tighten or draw tight'. **Stringent** [M17th] and its variant **astringent** [M16th] are from the same source. *See also* DISTRICT

strident [M17th] This is from Latin *stridere* 'to creak'.

strife *see* STRIVE

strike [OE] In Anglo-Saxon times to strike was 'to go or flow' or 'to rub lightly', close in meaning to the related word **stroke** which shares a Germanic root. By the Middle Ages striking had become more forceful, and the word was being used in the familiar sense 'hit'. To **strike while the iron is hot** is a metaphor from the blacksmith's forge, where iron can only be hammered into shape while it is hot. The proverb is quoted by Geoffrey Chaucer in 1386 and used in a slightly modified form by Shakespeare in *Henry VI Part 3*: 'Strike now, or else the iron cools.' The sort of strike that involves stopping work as a protest was first heard of in 1810, but the verb, meaning 'to go on strike', was earlier. This quote from the *Annual Register* of 1768 could be the source of the term: 'A body of sailors...proceeded...to Sunderland...and went on board the several ships in that harbour, and struck [lowered] their yards [spars], in order to prevent them from proceeding to sea'. In the 1980s legislation was passed in some states of the USA known as the **three strikes** law or rule. It makes an offender's third felony punishable by life imprisonment or other severe sentence. The term comes from baseball—if a batter has

straw street stress stretch strew strict

three 'strikes', or unsuccessful attempts to hit a pitched ball, they 'strike out' or are out.

string [OE] The Germanic root of the Old English word string is related to **strong**, and in early use it could refer to a rope or cord of any thickness. If you **have many strings to your bow** you have a wide range of resources, just as an archer ought to have spare strings. A different kind of string lies behind the expression **have someone on a string**, meaning 'to have someone under your control or influence'. The idea behind this 16th-century phrase is of a puppeteer manipulating a puppet by its strings. An opportunity or offer with **no strings attached** has no special conditions or restrictions that apply. This is a relatively recent expression, first used in the 1950s, though it is based on an earlier US use of string meaning 'a limitation or condition'.

stringent *see* STRICT

strive [ME] Strive and **strife** both come from shortened forms of Old French *estriver* 'strive'. As well as expressing conflict, the word in early examples meant 'striving together'.

stroke *see* STRIKE

stroll [E17th] 'You had a foolish itch to be an actor, / And may stroll where you please', wrote Philip Massinger in his play *The Picture* (1629). If you **strolled** in the early 17th century you were wandering from place to place, especially as a vagrant, a use now obsolete, although the phrase 'strolling player' is still used. The sense of walking in a leisurely way only appeared towards the end of the 17th century. Stroll may come from a German word for 'a vagabond'.

strong *see* STRING

stub [OE] A stub was originally a tree stump. From this developed the general idea of a portion being left behind when something has been removed, such as a counterfoil in a chequebook or a cigarette butt. The verb was initially used in the sense 'to dig up a plant by the roots'. The meaning 'to accidentally strike', as in 'I stubbed my

toe', was first used in the USA in the mid 19th century. **Stubborn** may be based on stub, though this is by no means certain. A stub or tree stump is difficult to remove, so there may be a connection. Stubborn originally meant 'untameable or ruthless' before the modern meaning, 'obstinate', emerged.

stuff [ME] Stuff originally meant the material for making clothes. It is a shortening of Old French *estoffe* 'material or furniture', which is related to *estoffer* 'to equip, furnish', the source of the verb stuff. **Do your stuff** is first recorded in 1663 in the journal of George Fox, founder of the Quakers: 'A while after, when the priest had done his stuff, they came to the friends again.' **Stuff and nonsense**, first found in *Tom Jones* (1749) by Henry Fielding, is really 'nonsense and nonsense'—stuff is used in the 16th-century sense 'nonsense, rubbish'.

stump [ME] One sense of stump refers to part of a limb remaining after an amputation, and this was the original meaning of the noun. The verb was initially 'to stumble over an obstacle', especially over a tree stump. The sense 'to baffle', was first used in American English in the early 19th century and probably arose from the idea of coming across stumps in ploughing which obstruct the progress of the plough. The Australian phrase **beyond the black stump** means 'beyond the limits of settled, and therefore civilized, life'. It comes from the custom of using a fire-blackened stump of wood as a marker when giving directions to travellers. To be **on the stump** is to go about the country making political speeches, a usage that originated in rural America in the late 18th century, when a person making a speech would often use a tree stump as an impromptu platform. The Democratic politician Adlai Stevenson said of Richard Nixon that he was 'the kind of politician who would cut down a redwood tree, and then mount the stump, and make a speech on conservation'. To **stump up** a tree is to dig it up by the roots. This gives the meaning 'to pay up, especially reluctantly', from the image of digging deep into your pocket.

stun see ASTONISH

stunt see US WORD PANEL

stupid [M16th] Our word stupid comes from French *stupide* or Latin *stupidus*, from *stupere* 'to be amazed or stunned', also the source of **stupor** [LME] and **stupendous** [M16th]. The 'slow-witted, foolish' sense dates from a similar period and eventually became established as the main meaning.

sturdy [ME] 'Reckless, violent' and 'rebellious, obstinate' were the early meanings of sturdy, which comes from Old French *esturdi* 'stunned or dazed'. This may be based on Latin *turdus* 'a thrush', a bird that used to be associated with drunkenness, probably because it was once common to see thrushes tottering around unsteadily after eating partly fermented grapes—there is a French expression *soûl comme une grive*, which means 'drunk as a thrush'.

suave [LME] The early sense of this was 'gracious, agreeable'. It is from Latin *suavis* 'agreeable'. The current sense dates from the mid 19th century.

subdue see DUCT

subject see JET

sublime [L16th] Originally sublime meant 'dignified or aloof'—the source is Latin *sublimis* 'in a high position, lofty', probably from *sub-* 'up to' and *limen* 'threshold or lintel'. The modern sense of 'outstandingly beautiful or grand' arose in the 17th century. **Sublimate**, from the same source, had been used by medieval alchemists as a chemical term. The expression **from the sublime to the ridiculous** is a shortening of the saying **from the sublime to the ridiculous is only a step**, a remark attributed to Napoleon Bonaparte, following the retreat from Moscow in 1812. Napoleon was not the first to express such an idea, though. The English political writer Thomas Paine wrote in *The Age of Reason* (1794): 'The sublime and the ridiculous are often so nearly related, that it is difficult to class them separately. One step above the sublime, makes the ridiculous; and one step above the ridiculous, makes the sublime again.'

submit see PERMIT

subordinate see COORDINATE

subscribe see UNDERWRITE

substance [ME] This word was first used to refer to the essential nature of something. It comes from Old French, from Latin *substantia* 'being, essence', from the verb *substare* 'stand firm'. The word was used to refer to a 'solid thing' from the late 16th century.

substitute see CONSTITUTION

subterranean see TERRACE

subtle [ME] 'Not easily understood' was an early sense of subtle, via Old French *sotil* from Latin *subtilis* meaning 'fine, delicate'.

suburb, suburban see URBANE

succeed see CEDE

suck [OE] The Old English verb *sūcan* is from an Indo-European root imitating the sound; Old English **soak** is related. The phrase **suck up to** was originally schoolboys' slang of the mid 19th century. Late Middle English **suckle** was probably formed from the slightly earlier **suckling** from suck. The word **suction** made its appearance in the early 17th century from the related Latin *sugere* 'suck'. A **sucker** [LME] was originally a young mammal before it was weaned, or a baby feeding at its mother's breast. The notion of a naïve and innocent baby led, in the 19th century, to that of a gullible person or an easy victim. *See also* EVEN

sudoku see JAPANESE WORD PANEL

suffer [ME] The root of suffer is Latin *sufferre*, from *sub-* 'from below, under' and *ferre* 'to bear'. As well as 'to undergo or endure', it can mean 'to tolerate', and this is the sense you are using when you say that

stun stunt stupid sturdy suave subdue

someone **does not suffer fools gladly**. The expression is biblical, from the second Epistle to the Corinthians: 'For ye suffer fools gladly, seeing ye yourselves are wise.' For related words *see* REFER

suffrage [LME] The Latin *suffragium* meant both 'support' and 'right to vote', and was formed from *suf-* 'under, near' and *fragor* 'din, shout of approval'. In medieval Latin, when democracy was not relevant, the 'support' sense was strongest, and suffrage first came into English in the sense of prayers for the departed and of intercession. The sense of a vote reappeared in the mid 16th century, with the sense 'a right to vote' first appearing in the United States Constitution of 1787. **Suffragette**, for a female campaigner for suffrage, was an initially mocking coinage of the early 20th century.

sugar *see* ARABIC WORD PANEL

suggestion [ME] Suggestion entered English as 'an incitement to evil', but the use soon became generalized to 'proposal, thought put forward'. The word came from Latin *suggerere* 'suggest, prompt', the source, too, of early 16th-century **suggest**.

sullen [ME] To be sullen originally related to the idea of being on your own. The source is Old French *sulein*, from *sol* 'sole, alone', which came ultimately from Latin *solus* 'alone'. Early meanings were 'single', 'solitary', and 'unusual'. There is obviously a link between being solitary and being averse to company or unsociable, and such associations led in the late 14th century to a shift in sense as the word came to describe someone who is silently gloomy, resentful, and moody.

sum [ME] The sums you did at school and the **summing up** of a judge are linked by the fact they both come from Latin *summa* which meant both 'main part' and 'total', formed from *summus* 'highest'. **Summary** [LME] and **summit** [LME] are from the same source.

summon [ME] The source of summon is Latin *summonere*, originally meaning 'give a

hint' but later used in the sense 'call, summon'. It was formed from *sub-* 'secretly' and *monere* 'warn'.

sump *see* SWAMP

sumptuous [LME] The early sense of this was 'costly' rather than 'rich'. It comes from Latin *sumptuosus*, from *sumptus* 'expenditure'. As costly things are often magnificent it had gained this sense by the mid 16th century.

sun [OE] An Old English word whose root was related to the Latin and Greek words for sun, *sol* (*see* SOLAR) and *hēlios*. People say **the sun is over the yardarm** when they think that the time of day has been reached when it is socially acceptable to drink alcohol. This is an old nautical expression which goes back to the late 19th century. A yardarm is the end section of a yard, a thick tapering pole slung across a ship's mast for a sail to hang from. At certain times of year the sun rises far enough up the sky to show above the topmost yardarm. In summer in the north Atlantic, where the phrase seems to have originated, this would have been at about 11 a.m., which was the time of the first rum issue of the day—not 6 in the evening, as is often thought. The earliest known example of the phrase comes from a series of travel articles by Rudyard Kipling, published under the title *From Sea to Sea* (1899): 'The American does not drink at meals as a sensible man should … Also he has no decent notions about the sun being over the yard-arm or below the horizon.' A **sundowner** is a different matter altogether. In colonial days, especially in South Africa, it was a drink taken at sunset, whereas in Australia it was a tramp who arrived at a sheep station around sundown and pretended to be seeking work, to get food and a night's lodging. The phrase **there is nothing new under the sun** is biblical, from the Book of Ecclesiastes: 'The thing that hath been, it is that which shall be; and that which is done is that which shall be done: and there is no new thing under the sun.' People only seem to have **sunbathed** since the 1940s—before that the usual term was

sunbath or, in Australia and New Zealand, **sunbake**. *See also* SON

sundae [L19th] The origin of the ice-cream dessert, originally from the USA, is unclear. It could be an alteration of **Sunday**—either because the dish was made with ice cream left over from Sunday and sold cheaply on the Monday, or, some claim, because it was sold only on Sundays to get round Sunday trading restrictions. The spelling may have been changed out of deference to religious people's feelings.

sup *see* SOP

superb [M16th] The first things described as superb were buildings and monuments. Later the word could describe a proud or haughty person, as in John Aubrey's 1697 assessment of William Oughtred, the English mathematician and inventor of the slide rule: 'Before he died he burned a world of papers, and said that the world was not worthy of them; he was so superb.' From the early 18th century people started using superb in the sense 'very fine, excellent'. It comes from Latin *superbus* 'proud, magnificent'.

supercilious [E16th] A supercilious person has an air of contemptuous superiority. One way they might show this is by raising their eyebrows in disdain—a clue to the word's origin. *Supercilium*, the Latin source of the English word, means 'eyebrow'.

superficial [LME] This is from Latin *superficies* 'surface', and was at first used in the literal sense. The word came to be applied to people meaning 'shallow' in the early 17th century (Shakespeare *Measure for Measure*: 'A very superficial, ignorant, unweighing fellow'). **Surface** [E17th] was a 16th-century French coinage based on the Latin.

superfluous *see* AFFLUENT

superintendent *see* INTEND

superior [LME] This came via Old French from Latin *superior* 'that is higher', from

super 'above'. The noun use meaning 'person of higher rank' is recorded from the late 15th century. **Supreme** [LME] is one step higher, from *supremus* 'highest'.

superstar *see* STAR

superstition [LME] The Latin word *superstitio* comes from *super-* 'over' and *stare* 'to stand'. The idea seems to have been of 'standing over' something in amazement or awe. By the time superstition first appeared in English at the beginning of the 15th century it referred to an irrational religious belief based on fear, or ignorance or to a religious belief considered false or pagan. The more general 'irrational or unfounded belief' sense is first recorded in the 1790s.

supervise *see* ADVICE

supper *see* SOP

supplant [ME] This is from Old French *supplanter* or Latin *supplantare* 'trip up', from *sub-* 'from below' and *planta* 'sole of the foot'. Initially the word could be used both in the modern sense and in the original Latin sense. Milton, in *Paradise Lost* was one of the last to do this 'His Armes clung to his Ribs, his Leggs entwining Each other, till supplanted down he fell A monstrous Serpent.'

supple [ME] This word, which originally meant 'of yielding consistency', is from Old French *souple*, from Latin *supplex* 'submissive'

suppose *see* COMPOST

supreme *see* SUPERIOR

sure [ME] This is from Old French *sur*, from Latin *securus* 'free from care'. The same Latin word gives us **security** [LME], the legal **surety** [ME], and **insecure** [M17th] 'not free from care', as well as **assure** [LME]. *See* CURATE

surface *see* SUPERFICIAL

sundae sup superb supercilious superficial

surge [LME] Early examples of surge mean a fountain or stream, with the verb meaning 'rise and fall on the waves', and 'swell with great force'. The word comes from Latin *surgere* 'to rise', found also in **resurrection** [ME] 'to rise again', and **insurrection** [LME] 'to rise up'.

surgeon [ME] The key thing about surgeons in terms of word history is that they work with their hands, using manual skill to cure or treat people rather than giving them drugs. Surgeon is a shortening of Old French *serurgian*, which came via Latin *chirurgia* from Greek *kheirourgia* 'handiwork', from *kheir* 'hand' and *ergon* 'work'. *See also* WORK

surly [M16th] Surly was originally *sirly*, a clue to its early meaning. In medieval times *sirly* meant 'in the manner of a *SIR or lord', and surly was originally used in the sense 'lordly, haughty, arrogant'. The 'bad-tempered and unfriendly' meaning emerged late in the 16th century.

surprise [LME] From the 15th century a surprise was a sudden unexpected attack or seizure of a place. You could also use the word to talk about simply taking a place by force, whether unexpected or not, as in 'the surprise of Troy', even after a siege of ten years. Over time the suggestion of force faded away and the sense of something being unexpected came to the fore. The source was medieval Latin *superprehendere* 'to seize', from *prehendere* source of words listed at *PRISON.

surround [LME] 'Overflow' was the early meaning of surround. It came via Old French, from late Latin *superundare*; formed from the elements *super-* 'over' and *undare* 'to flow'. The meaning altered under the influence of 'round'. Military use ('enclose on all sides so as to cut off') arose in the mid 17th century. *See also* WATER

surveillance *see* VIGIL

survive [LME] Survive entered English via Old French from Latin *supervivere*, based on *vivere* 'to live', as in **revive** [LME], **vivacious** [M17th], and **vivid** [M17th]. According to

Charles Darwin's theory of evolution, those animals and plants which tend to survive and produce more offspring are the ones best adapted to their environment, while those less well adapted become extinct. The idea is summed up in the phrase **the survival of the fittest**, which was coined by the English philosopher and sociologist Herbert Spencer in *Principles of Biology* (1865). Darwin himself had originally used the term **natural selection**, but approved of Spencer's version. Beyond its technical use the phrase is often used loosely to suggest that the strongest or most ruthless will succeed at the expense of others, though this is a distortion of the original Darwinian notion.

susceptible *see* CAPABLE

suspect [ME] The Latin source of suspect is *suspicere* 'mistrust', formed from *sub-* 'from below' and *specere* 'to look' also the source of **suspicion** [ME].

suspend *see* PENDANT

suspicion *see* SUSPECT

Svengali *see* TRILBY

swab [M17th] A swab was initially a 'mop for cleaning the decks'. It was formed from **swabber** 'a sailor detailed to swab decks': this derives from early modern Dutch *zwabber*, from a Germanic base meaning 'splash' or 'sway'. The medical sense dates from the mid 19th century.

swagger [E16th] A bulging bag is the link between swagger and **swag** [ME]. This is what swag originally meant, and it later led to the word being used as a verb in the sense 'to make something sway or sag'. Swagger appears to have developed from this, expressing the idea of walking or behaving arrogantly or self-importantly. By the late 18th century the 'bulging bag' meaning of swag had come to be applied to a thief's booty. It also came to refer to a bundle of personal belongings carried by a traveller in the Australian bush.

swain *see* COX

surge   surgeon   surly   surprise   surround

swallow [OE] A swallow is popularly regarded as a sign of summer. According to the proverb **one swallow does not make a summer**—a single fortunate event does not mean that what follows will also be good. The proverb is recorded from the 16th century: 'It is not one swallow that bringeth in summer. It is not one good quality that maketh a man good.' Charles Dickens has an expanded version in *Martin Chuzzlewit* (1844): 'One foul wind no more makes a winter, than one swallow makes a summer.' The bird's name and the verb meaning 'to allow food or drink to pass down the throat' are unrelated, though both are Old English words.

swamp [E17th] Swamp is first found in the compound 'swampwater' and probably goes back to a Germanic root with the senses 'sponge, fungus'. **Sump** [ME] is probably related, as it is first found with the meaning 'swamp'.

swan [OE] The bird's name and the verb swan, meaning 'to go about in a casual or ostentatious way', are the same word. The verb originated as military slang as recently as the 1940s, referring to the free movement of armoured vehicles. A **swansong** [E19th] or final public performance or work is based on German *Schwanengesang*, which refers to the classical legend that the normally mute swan is supposed to sing just before its death. The legend is also behind the long association of bards and poets with swans, hence Shakespeare's title **the Swan of Avon**.

swap [ME] This word was originally used in the sense 'throw forcibly'. It is probably imitative of a resounding blow. Current senses have arisen from an early use meaning 'strike hands as a token of agreement'.

swear [OE] This first meant 'to make a solemn declaration'. The use of swear in connection with bad language came later, around the 15th century, as an extension of the idea of using a sacred name in an oath. Someone who swears a lot can be said to **swear like a trooper**. A trooper was originally a private soldier in a cavalry unit.

By the 18th century these soldiers had developed a reputation for coarse behaviour and bad language. In his novel *Pamela* (1739–40), Samuel Richardson wrote: 'She curses and storms at me like a Trooper.' **Answer** [OE] comes from the same root, and originally meant to rebut an accusation.

sweat *see* SWOT

sweet [OE] The original use of this was for the taste, the 'dessert', and 'confectionery' senses only dating from the 19th century. The slang use **sweet on**, 'infatuated with', dates from the mid 18th century, while the meaning 'fine, good' was originally Australian, from the 1890s. The Fanny Adams in **sweet Fanny Adams**, 'absolutely nothing at all', really existed. She was the unfortunate young victim in a brutal murder of 1867, whose body was mutilated and cut up by her killer. By the end of the century sailors in the Royal Navy were using her name, with gruesome black humour, as a slang term for a type of tinned meat or stew. The current meaning arose in the early 20th century and is sometimes shortened to **sweet FA**. People often translate *FA* here as standing for *F— All*, but this was not the expression's origin. The phrase **sweetness and light** was first used by Jonathan Swift in *The Battle of the Books* (1704). Both are produced by bees: 'Instead of dirt and poison, we have rather chosen to fill our hives with honey and wax, thus furnishing mankind with the two noblest things, which are sweetness and light.' Later the phrase was taken up by Matthew Arnold in *Culture and Anarchy* (1869), where he used it with aesthetic and moral reference: 'The pursuit of perfection, then, is the pursuit of sweetness and light.'

sweetheart *see* TART

sweetmeat *see* MEAT

swim [OE] The Old English epic poem *Beowulf*, probably written in the 8th century, is the first recorded source of swim. To **sink or swim**, 'to fail or succeed entirely by your own efforts', refers to the ducking of a woman suspected of witchcraft. It was not

swallow   swamp   swan   swap   swear   sweat

an attractive choice—either the woman sank and was drowned or she floated on the surface of the water and was therefore proven to be a witch. **In the swim**, meaning 'in tune with the fashion', first appeared in the late 19th century.

swindler [L18th] This is from German *Schwindler* 'extravagant maker of schemes, swindler': this comes from German *schwindeln* meaning both 'be giddy' and 'tell lies'. The early 20th-century word **swizzle** is probably an alteration of *swindle*.

swine see PIG

swing [OE] Our word swing meant both 'to beat or whip' and 'to rush, to fling yourself' in Old English. The 'playground swing' sense of the noun dates from the late 17th century. The saying **what you lose on the swings you gain on the roundabouts** [E20th], usually shortened to **swings and roundabouts** is a metaphor not from the playground but from the fairground. To **swing the lead** is nautical. Swinging the lead was the job of lowering a lump of lead on a rope to ascertain the depth of water, a task which in itself was quite important but which sailors perhaps sometimes deliberately did as slowly as possible to avoid being assigned a more strenuous duty. Swing [L19th] is an easy flowing but vigorous rhythm, especially in jazz. 'It don't mean a thing / If it ain't got that swing' is from the song 'It Don't Mean a Thing' (1932), by Duke Ellington and Irving Mills. In the 1930s a **swinger** was a jazz musician who played with 'swing'. The 1960s saw the swinger become a lively, fashionable person, and also someone who was into partner-swapping or group sex—known as **swinging**.

swirl [LME] Swirl was originally Scots in the sense 'whirlpool'. The word may be Low German or Dutch in origin, related to Dutch *zwirrelen* 'to whirl'.

swizzle see SWINDLE

sword [OE] As with *swim, *Beowulf* gives us the first example of sword. The notion of devoting resources to peaceful rather than aggressive or warlike ends is sometimes expressed as **beating** (or **turning**) **swords into ploughshares**, a reference to the biblical image of God's peaceful rule: 'they shall beat their swords into ploughshares, and their spears into pruning hooks' (Book of Isaiah). Also biblical is the expression **he who lives by the sword dies by the sword**—in the Gospel of Matthew, when men came to arrest Jesus in the Garden of Gethsemane one of his disciples drew his sword and cut off the ear of 'the servant of the high priest', earning a rebuke from Jesus: 'All they that take the sword shall perish with the sword.' *See also* THREAD

swot [M19th] A variation of **sweat** [OE] that started life as army slang. Swot was first 'studying, school, or college work', and referred especially to mathematics. This led to its use to describe someone who studies hard or excessively.

sycophant [M16th] This is a story of figs and flattery. The Greek word *sukophantēs* meant 'informer'. It was based on *sukon* 'fig' (also the root of **sycamore** [ME] and originally used for a fig tree) and *phainein* 'to show', and so literally meant 'a person who shows the fig'. Some people have suggested that this related to the practice of informing against people who illegally exported figs from ancient Athens, as recorded by the Greek biographer Plutarch. A more likely explanation is that the term referred to an obscene gesture known as 'showing (or making) the fig'. When sycophant entered the English language in the 1530s it meant 'an informer', and soon also 'a person who tells tales or spreads malicious reports about someone'. The modern sense of 'a servile flatterer' probably comes from the notion that you can ingratiate yourself with someone in authority either by slandering others or by flattering the person in question.

syllable [LME] Syllable comes via Old French and Latin from Greek *sullabē*, from *sun-* 'together' and *lambanein* 'take'. A syllable is basically a group of sounds 'taken together' and uttered with a single effort.

swindler swine swing swirl swizzle sword

syllabus [M17th] An early syllabus was a 'concise table of headings of a text'. From modern Latin, it was originally a misreading of Latin *sittybas*, from Greek *sittuba* 'title slip, label'. Use of the word in educational contexts for a programme of study is recorded from the late 19th century.

sylph, sylvan *see* SAVAGE

symbol [LME] This comes from Latin *symbolum* 'symbol, creed (as the mark of a Christian)'; it was first used in English to refer to the Apostles' Creed. The source is Greek *sumbolon* 'mark, token'. It had come to be used in non-religious senses by the late 16th century.

sympathy [L16th] This was first used to express 'understanding between people'; it came via Latin from Greek *sumpathēs* (from *sun-* 'with' and *pathos* 'feeling'). The word **sympathize** is from the same period in the sense 'suffer with another person'. In the mid 17th century the adjective **sympathetic** (on the pattern of *pathetic*) joined this group of related words and meant 'relating to a paranormal influence'; the phrase **sympathetic magic** illustrates its use in the context of magical ritual involving objects associated with an event.

symphony *see* CACOPHONY

synagogue [ME] Despite its strong Jewish associations, this came via Old French and late Latin from Greek *sunagōgē* 'meeting', from *sun-* 'together' and *agein* 'bring'.

synchronize *see* ANACHRONISM

syncopate [E17th] This comes from late Latin *syncopare* 'to swoon'. The notion of temporary loss of consciousness led to associations of weakening and strengthening of musical beats or omission of sounds.

syndicate [E17th] A syndicate was initially a committee of syndics (government officials). It comes from late Latin *syndicus* 'delegate of a corporation'. Current verb senses such as 'control by a syndicate' date from the late 19th century.

syndrome [M16th] This is a modern Latin word, from Greek *sundromē*, from *sun-* 'together' and *dramein* 'to run'. Other words formed from *sun* include **synopsis** [E17th] from *sun-* 'together' *opsis* 'seeing', and **synthesis** [E17th] from *suntithenai* 'place together'.

syrup *see* SHERBET

system [E17th] This word comes to us via Latin from Greek *sustēma*, of which the base elements are *sun-* 'with' and *histanai* 'set up'.

T One way of saying that something is an exact fit is to say that it fits **to a T** (or **to a tee**). Various ideas as to what the **T** stands for range from a golfer's tee to a builder's T-square, but none is totally convincing. It may have originated from the action of completing a letter T with the horizontal stroke, as in **dot the i's and cross the t's**, meaning 'to make sure all the details are correct'. The problem with all these explanations is that this 17th-century expression is found earlier than the proposed sources. One historically possible suggestion is that it is a shortened version of the early 17th-century phrase **to a tittle**, which has the same meaning as **to a T**. A **tittle** was a small stroke in writing or printing, such as the crossbar of a *T* or the dot of an *i*, which fits the idea perfectly. *See also* JOT. The **T-shirt** is so called because it is shaped like a T when spread out flat. The term was first recorded in 1920.

tab *see* TAG

tabby [L16th] A striped tabby cat is said to get its name from a kind of silk which was originally striped, although later tabby was used for silk with a watered finish. The word goes back to the name of the quarter of Baghdad where the material was manufactured, al-Attābiyya.

table [OE] The earliest examples of the word, from Latin *tabula*, referred to a flat board, slab, or surface, and it did not grow legs until around 1300. One of the first meanings was a gaming board—in the case of backgammon the plural **tables** was used, because its board has two folding halves. Although this meaning had died out by the mid 18th century it is preserved in the expression **turn the tables**, which arose from the common practice of turning the board round between games so that a player had to play from what had previously been their opponent's position. The early sense of table is also found in **tablet** [ME] for a small slab of stone. The notion of a compressed drug or confection in the shape of a lozenge dates from the late 16th century. The word **tabloid** [L19th], based on tablet, was originally the proprietary name of a

medicine sold in tablets; the term then came to denote any small medicinal tablet of any brand. The application of tabloid to a newspaper (early 20th century) is from the notion of the stories being concentrated into an easily digestible form. **Table d'hôte** adopted from French in the early 17th century is literally 'host's table'. The term originally described a table in a hotel or restaurant where all guests ate together, which led to its use for a meal served there at a stated time and for a fixed price. *See also* CARPET

taboo [L18th] There are not many words in English which come from the Polynesian language of Tongan, but taboo is one of them. It was introduced into English by the explorer Captain James Cook in 1777 in the narrative of his voyages. He wrote: 'Not one of them would sit down, or eat a bit of any thing...they were all *taboo*.' He went on to explain that the word was generally used to mean 'forbidden'. *See also* TATTOO

tack *see* TACKY

tackie *see* SOUTH AFRICAN WORD PANEL

tacky [L18th] The origin of tacky in the sense 'sticky' is from the word **tack** [ME] 'to fasten lightly', or for an object that does that job. The origin of this word is obscure. The sense of tacky meaning 'in poor taste, cheap' is different, but equally obscure. It was first found at the beginning of the 19th century in the USA meaning a weedy horse. By the late 19th century it was applied to a poor white in some southern states, and had also acquired its modern sense. The shortening tack did not happen until the

T tab tabby table taboo tack tackie tacky

1980s. The sense tack for horses equipment is a shortening of tackle.

tact [M17th] Tact in early examples referred to the sense of touch. It comes from Latin *tactus* 'touch, sense of touch', from *tangere* 'to touch'. The word developed a notion of 'sensitivity' and in the late 18th century gained its modern sense 'delicacy in dealing with others'. The Latin source also gave the English word **tactile** which in the early 17th century meant 'perceptible by touch', and **tangible** [L16th]. **Tangent** [L16th], first used in geometry to mean 'touching', is also from *tangere*.

tactile *see* TACT

taffeta *see* PERSIAN WORD PANEL

taffy *see* TOFF

tag [LME] When first recorded, this word referred to a narrow hanging section of a skirt slashed as a decorative feature. It is of unknown origin but may be related to late Middle English **dag** (*see* AUSTRALIAN WORD PANEL). Use of tag for a label indicating ownership began in US English in the mid 19th century. **Tab** [LME] may be related. It originally described a small flap or strip. In American English in the late 19th century it developed the sense 'an account', commonly reflected in the idiom **keep tabs on** meaning 'keep a regular check on' someone. This is the same word used to mean 'bill' in a restaurant.

Taig *see* TYKE

taikonaut *see* CHINESE WORD PANEL

tail [OE] The base of the Old English word tail meant 'hair' or 'hairy tail'. The opposite side of a coin to heads has been tails since the 1680s or thereabouts—it is so called because it is the 'reverse' or 'rear' of the main or front side. A dog's tail is a good indicator of its mood, and this has given us various expressions. Someone who appears ashamed or dejected has been described since the Middle Ages as having their **tail between their legs**. Alternatively, someone **with their tail up** is in a confident or cheerful mood. Sometimes the usual roles in an organization are reversed, and a less important part dictates what is going to happen. When that occurs, someone may comment that **the tail is wagging the dog**. As a verb [E16th] the original sense was 'fasten to the back of something', with the meaning 'follow closely' developing from this at the beginning of the 20th century.

tailor [ME] A tailor's work is indicated in the source of the word, which goes back to Latin *taliare* 'to cut'.

tale *see* TALK

talent [OE] This came ultimately from Greek *talanton*, and referred originally to a unit of weight used by the Babylonians, Assyrians, Romans, and Greeks. The use of talent to mean 'natural aptitude or skill' comes from the biblical parable of the talents in the Gospel of Matthew. In this story a master gives one, two, and ten talents of silver to each of three servants. Two of them use their talents well and double the value of what they have been given, but the third buries his coin and fails to benefit from it. **Talent scouts** and **talent shows** have searched for new talent since the 1930s. Another kind of talent is the local talent, or the good-looking people of an area—an expression used since the 1940s, and probably originating among British servicemen.

talk [ME] Talk is from the same root as **tale** [OE] and *TELL. A person who talks incessantly is sometimes said to be able to **talk the hind leg off a donkey**. Versions of this expression go back to the 19th century but the animal may vary—*Cobbett's Weekly Political Register* for 1808 has 'talking a horse's hind leg off', and in 1879 the novelist Anthony Trollope mentioned **talk the hind legs off a dog** as an Australian variant. Another way of saying that someone chatters constantly is to accuse them of **talking nineteen to the dozen**. Presumably the idea is that the person is talking so quickly that they get in 19 words in the time it would take someone else to say a dozen. Nobody seems to know why 19 is the

tact   tactile   taffeta   taffy   tag   Taig

traditional number here, but the phrase has been in this form ever since it was first written down in the late 18th century. The term **talking head** for a television reporter who is viewed in close-up addressing the camera, is first recorded in the 1960s in the USA. Also American, also from the 1960s, is **talk show**, a programme in which the presenter talks informally to celebrities.

tall [LME] Some words have undergone remarkable changes in meaning over the centuries. One such is tall. In medieval times it was used in such senses as 'quick', 'handsome', and 'good at fighting', as in Sir Walter Scott's reference to 'the ' "tall men", or champions, of Wales'. Only in the 16th century did the sense 'of more than average height' appear. A privileged or distinguished person may be referred to as **a tall poppy**. This goes back to a story about the Roman tyrant Tarquin, who is said to have struck off the heads of a row of poppies in a gruesomely graphic demonstration of the way in which the important men of a captured city should be treated. Since the early 1980s, originally in Australia, the expression **tall poppy syndrome** has been used for the tendency to criticize people who have become rich, famous, or socially prominent.

tamagotchi *see* JAPANESE WORD PANEL

tam-o-shanter *see* SCOTTISH WORD PANEL

tamper [M16th] An alteration of *TEMPER whose origin may lie in the idea of working with or 'tempering' clay. Tamper was first used in the mid 16th century to mean 'to busy yourself for a particular purpose', but quickly developed the negative associations of meddling or interfering damagingly with something.

tan [OE] The original sense of tan is to convert skins into leather. The sense of the colour that the skin acquires after exposure to the sun dates only to the middle of the 18th century. Tan probably comes directly from Latin *tannare*, but may ultimately go back to a Celtic word for an oak tree. This reflects the process of tanning, whereby the

crushed bark of an oak was steeped in water in which skins and hides were then immersed. Oak bark was used because it is rich in **tannins** [E19th], compounds which will tan. The related word **tawny** [ME] comes from Old French *tauné*, 'tanned'.

tandem [L18th] In Latin *tandem* means 'after a long time' or 'at length'. It first came into English as a slang term for a carriage drawn by two horses harnessed one behind the other—a 'long' set-up which inspired a pun on 'at length'. A tandem is now a bicycle for two riders, one behind the other. The expression **in tandem** is still used today to mean 'one behind another', but is more common in the sense 'together as a team'.

tang [ME] In medieval times a tang was the forked tongue of a snake, which was believed to be its 'sting'. The word goes back to Old Norse *tangi* 'the point of a knife'. The idea of a piercing point lies behind the modern sense of 'a penetrating flavour'.

tangent, tangible *see* TACT

tangle [ME] Scandinavia is probably the origin of tangle, which is probably related to Swedish *taggla* 'to disarrange'. A **tangled web** is a complex and difficult situation. The expression comes directly from Sir Walter Scott's epic poem *Marmion* (1808): 'Oh what a tangled web we weave / When first we practise to deceive.' *See* TOGGLE

tango [L19th] In Latin *tango* means 'I touch', which would seem to be an appropriate origin for the sensual South American dance the tango, but the word has quite a different origin. It is from Latin American Spanish, and is perhaps ultimately of African origin. **It takes two to tango** has become a modern-day proverb meaning 'both parties involved in a situation are equally responsible for it'. It started life as the title of a song written in 1952 by Al Hoffman and Dick Manning.

tank [E17th] In early 17th-century English, tank was the name given to a pool in India, going back to Sanskrit *tadāga* 'pond' and probably also influenced by the Portuguese word for 'pond', *tangue*. It was being used for a domestic container of liquid in the modern way by the end of the century. In 1915 tank was used as a secret code word for the armoured military vehicles that were first being made. A *Times* column of September 1916 remarked: 'The name has the evident official advantage of being quite undescriptive.' A sleeveless **tank top** is not so called because it was worn by the driver of a tank, but because it resembles the top part of a one-piece swimsuit known as a **tank suit**, worn in 'swimming tanks' or swimming pools. A drunk person has been **tanked up** since the 1890s. The comparison is with a vehicle filled with water or fuel from a tank.

tannin *see* TAN

tantalize [L16th] In Greek mythology Tantalus was a king of Lydia (modern-day Turkey) who killed his son Pelops, and served him in a stew to the gods. His punishment was to be forced to stand for eternity up to his chin in water which receded whenever he tried to drink it and under branches of fruit that drew back when he tried to reach them. Tantalize is based on his name. The same story is reflected in **tantalus** [L19], a stand in which decanters of whisky, brandy, and other spirits are locked out of reach but remain visible. In the early 19th century a newly discovered metal was named tantalum because its inability to absorb acid was similar to Tantalus' inability to absorb water. **Tannoy** [1920s] is a contraction of *tantalum alloy* which is used as a rectifier in this sound reproduction and amplification system. Tannoy was originally a proprietary name.

tantamount [M17th] This comes from the Italian *tanto montare* 'to amount to as much'.

tap [OE] A tap was originally a stopper for a cask. It controlled the flow of liquid, so the same word came to be used for the fitting which controlled the flow of water elsewhere. Drink from a cask that was ready for immediate consumption was **on tap**. From the 1860s tap began to be used in reference to listening in secretly to a

telegraph and then a telephone, from the idea of 'siphoning off' information. Tap in the sense of 'strike lightly' is a completely different word, which probably represents an imitation of the action in its sound.

tapas *see* SPANISH WORD PANEL

taper [OE] In Anglo-Saxon times a taper was a wax candle. The name comes, with a change of *p* to *t*, from the Latin word *papyrus*, because the pith of the papyrus plant was used for candle wicks. The verb was first used in the 16th century to describe the action of rising like a flame, and this picture led to the further idea of something 'tapering away' from a broad base to a narrow point.

tapestry [LME] Tapestry comes from French *tapis* 'carpet', easier to understand if you know that in the past carpets were far too valuable to walk on and were used for wall hangings and to cover tables.

tar [OE] In the past tar was mainly distilled from wood, and the word tar may ultimately be related to *TREE. **Tar** or **Jack tar** has been a name for a sailor since the 17th century. It is perhaps an abbreviation of **tarpaulin** [E17th], which was also a nickname for a sailor. As well as being the name of a waterproof cloth of tarred canvas, a tarpaulin was a kind of hat worn by sailors. The expression **tar with the same brush** comes originally from the practice of shepherds using tar to cover any wounds suffered by their sheep, to prevent infection. (*see* HALF). To **tar and feather** someone was to smear them with tar and then cover them with feathers as a punishment. The practice was introduced into Britain in 1198, when Richard I decreed that it should be the punishment for members of the navy found guilty of theft. Since then it has sometimes been inflicted by a mob on an unpopular individual, notably against customs officials in the War of American Independence (1775–83), and by the IRA against people suspected of collaborating with the British.

tarantula [M15th] The Italian seaport of Taranto gave its name to the tarantula, a large black spider found in southern Europe. Its bite was formerly thought to cause **tarantism**, a psychological illness marked by an extreme impulse to dance, which affected many people in Italy from the 15th to the 17th century. The rapid whirling **tarantella** [L18th] dance gets its name from the same source, as it was believed to be a cure for tarantism, with people dancing the tarantella until exhausted.

tariff [L16th] A tariff once referred to an arithmetical table. It came via French from Italian *tariffa*, based on Arabic *'arrafa* 'notify'. The word came to be used for a list of customs duties, but it was not until around 1890 that the sense 'classified list of charges' in a hotel or other business came into common English use (although more frequent earlier in Europe and the US). *See also* ARABIC WORD PANEL

tarnish [LME] Silver that is not polished will tarnish, losing its lustre. The word goes back to French *terne* 'dark, dull'. The metaphorical use, 'to make less valuable or respected', has been established since the 17th century. In 1805, on the eve of the Battle of Trafalgar, Lord Nelson prayed that God might grant them 'a great and glorious victory; and may no misconduct in anyone tarnish it'.

tart [LME] Today a tart is likely to be filled with jam or fruit, but in medieval times it was a savoury pie. In mid 19th-century slang it was an affectionate word for a woman (perhaps as an abbreviation of **sweetheart**), but by the end of the century it was being applied disparagingly to a prostitute or promiscuous woman. **Tart up**, 'to dress up ostentatiously', came from this use in the 1930s. Tart meaning 'sharp to the taste', also found in medieval English, is a different word. It goes back to Old English and originally meant 'harsh, severe', especially in reference to punishment.

tartan *see* SCOTTISH WORD PANEL

task *see* TAX

taste [ME] When first found, the word taste also had the sense 'touch'. The noun comes from Old French *tast*, the verb from Old French *taster* 'touch, try, taste'. This may be a blend of Latin *tangere* 'to touch' and *gustare* 'to taste'.

tattered [ME] Like *TAG, tattered is first found relating to the medieval fashion for slashed clothing, in the sense 'dressed in decoratively slashed or jagged clothing'. **Tatter** 'scrap of cloth' comes from Old Norse *tǫtrar* 'rags'. **Tatty** [E16th], originally Scots for 'tangled, matted, shaggy', is related, and was shortened to **tat** 'worthless articles in the mid 19th century.

tattoo [M17th] The military tattoo sounded by a drum or bugle to recall soldiers to their quarters in the evening was originally written **tap-too**. It comes from Dutch *doe den tap toe*, which meant literally 'close the tap'. The *TAP was on a cask, closing it signalled the time for drinking was over and soldiers should go home. Tattoos on the skin are a different word, which came into English in the 18th century from the Polynesian languages of the Pacific Islands—Captain Cook's journals are the first to record the word. *See also* TABOO

tatty *see* TATTERED

taunt [E16th] Taunt is probably from French *tant pour tant* 'like for like, tit for tat', from *tant* 'so much'. An early use of the verb was 'exchange banter, retort with banter'.

taut *see* TOUGH

tavern *see* INN

tawdry [E17th] Tawdry was originally short for **tawdry lace**, a fine silk lace or ribbon worn as a necklace in the 16th and 17th centuries, a contraction of the original term **St Audrey's lace**. Audrey was a Latinized form of Etheldreda, name of the 7th-century patron saint of Ely, who was said to have worn many showy necklaces in her youth, before she became a nun. When she became terminally ill with a throat tumour she saw her illness as retribution for her vanity. Tawdry laces, along with other

tariff   tarnish   tart   tartan   task   tatty

finery, were traditionally sold at St Etheldreda's Fair in Ely, and their cheapness and poor quality led to the modern associations of tawdry.

tawny *see* TAN

tax [ME] Tax and **task**—the earliest sense of which was to impose a tax on—both go back to Latin *taxare* 'to censure, charge, compute'. Task in the general sense 'something that has to be done' is found from the late 16th century.

tea [M17th] No drink could be more British than tea, but it did not enter the language or the country until the 17th century. The word goes back to Mandarin Chinese *chá*. A 'nice cup of tea' might be offered to someone feeling shocked and distressed, and **tea and sympathy**, used as the title of a play in 1953 and a film in 1956, has become a general phrase for comforting behaviour towards someone who is upset or in trouble. Tea became a meal in the mid 18th century, at first afternoon tea but then sometimes, especially in northern England, Australia, and New Zealand, an evening meal. **A storm in a teacup**, meaning 'a great deal of anxiety or excitement over a trivial matter', dates from the 19th century, but with different wording, such as **a storm in a cream bowl**, the idea goes back at least to the 1670s. A **tempest in a teapot** is the US equivalent. *See also* CHINESE WORD PANEL

teach [OE] In Anglo-Saxon times to teach was at first 'to present' or 'to point out', although the idea of instructing someone soon developed. The word shares an ancient root with *TOKEN. The proverb **don't teach your grandmother to suck eggs** has been in use since the 18th century as a caution against offering advice to someone wiser and more experienced than yourself. Sucking eggs was something thieves did on a farm, as to suck the centre from an egg on the spot is the quickest and safest way to eat it surreptitiously. Many similar expressions have been invented down the years, such as **don't teach your grandmother how to steal sheep**, with the shared idea that an older person knows a lot more about cunning

dodges than you do. The assumption here is that the longer experience of the older person brings wisdom, but the saying **you can't teach an old dog new tricks** associates the knowledge of years with rigidity, and an inability to take new things on board.

team [OE] The original Anglo-Saxon meaning of team was 'the bearing of children'. From there it became 'a brood of young animals', and then 'a set of draught animals working together', which gave us the modern idea of a group of people or set of sports players in the 16th century. In the sense 'to be full of' **teem** [OE] is linked to team, but teem [ME] as in 'teeming with rain' is a different word altogether, which comes from Old Norse *tómr* 'empty'—the original sense was 'to drain liquid from', the same image as in 'its pouring with rain'.

tear [OE] The word tear meaning 'to pull apart' is found in Old English. To **tear someone off a strip**, or rebuke them angrily as if by pulling off a strip of their skin, was originally RAF slang, and is recorded from the 1940s. The tear that you shed in distress is a different word, still Old English. The expression **without tears**, for learning, first appears in the title of a book for children published in 1857 *Reading without Tears or, A pleasant method of learning to read*. Terence Rattigan borrowed the phrase for the title of his 1937 play *French Without Tears*. The person whose works were first called **tearjerkers**, in 1921, was James Whitcomb Riley, a US writer known for sentimental poems such as 'Little Orphan Annie'. *See also* CROCODILE

tease [OE] When you tease someone you may 'rub them up the wrong way'. This looks back to the original meaning of the word, since in Old English tease meant 'to comb wool in preparation for spinning'. We still use the same idea when we talk of **teasing out** tangles in hair. The process was sometimes carried out using a dried, prickly flower head, which is where the plant the **teasel** [OE] gets its name.

teat *see* TIT

tawny tax tea teach team tear tease teat

technology [E17th] This is from Greek *tekhnologia* 'systematic treatment', from *tekhnē* 'art' and *-logia* 'speaking, discourse'. Early 19th-century **technique**, comes via French.

teddy [E20th] Theodore 'Teddy' Roosevelt, US president from 1901 to 1909, was a keen bear-hunter, a fact celebrated in a comic poem published in the *New York Times* of 7 January 1906, concerning the adventures of two bears called 'Teddy B' and 'Teddy G'. These names were then given to two bears presented to the Bronx Zoo later in the year, and toy manufacturers saw an opening. Toy 'teddy bears' or 'Roosevelt bears' were imported from Germany, and became an instant success in America. **Teddy boys** or **Teds** owe their name to Teddy as a pet form of Edward. In the mid 1950s some youths began to favour a style featuring drainpipe trousers, long velvet-collared jackets, bootlace ties, and hair slicked up in a quiff. The style was based on the fashions current in the early years of the 20th century in Britain during the reign of Edward VII.

teem *see* TEAM

teepee *see* NATIVE AMERICAN WORD PANEL

teetotal [M19th] The first part of teetotal has nothing to do with *TEA, but is actually a way of emphasizing total, by reproducing its first letter. It was apparently first used by Richard Turner, a member of the temperance movement from Preston, in a speech made in 1833. Early temperance reformers had limited themselves to suggesting abstinence from spirits, but this was an appeal to them to avoid all alcohol.

telegraph [L18th] The name telegraph was first used for a semaphore signalling device, consisting of an upright post with movable arms, invented in 1792 by the French engineer and cleric Claude Chappe. The word was based on Greek *tēle* 'far off' (source of words like *TELEVISION and **telephone** [M19th] from Greek *phōnē* 'sound, voice') and *graphein* 'to write'. The first practical electric telegraphs were those of Sir Charles Wheatstone in Britain in 1839

and of Samuel Morse in the USA. A **bush telegraph** is a rapid informal network by which information or gossip is spread. The expression originated in the Australian outback in the late 19th century. Bushrangers, outlaws who lived in the bush to avoid the authorities, used to rely on a network of informers, nicknamed the bush telegraph, to warn them about the movements of the police in their vicinity. *See also* GRAPEVINE

television [E20th] Television was first demonstrated in 1926 by the Scottish inventor John Logie Baird, but the word was thought up before the design was perfected, in 1907. The first part of television means 'at a distance', and comes ultimately from Greek *tēle* 'far off'. The second part goes back to Latin *videre* 'to see'. C.P. Scott, a journalist and editor of the *Manchester Guardian* from 1872 to 1929, was unhappy about the formation, and perhaps about the invention: '*Television*? The word is half Greek, half Latin. No good can come of it.' It was first shortened to **TV** just after the Second World War.

tell [OE] In Old English tell meant 'to count', a sense that is still seen in the term **teller** [ME] for a bank official. The meaning 'to disclose, reveal' does not appear until medieval times. To **tell tales out of school** is to gossip or reveal secrets about the wrongdoing or faults of someone else. In Old English **untold** meant 'not counted, unspecified'. In late Middle English this became 'not able to be counted' (untold suffering). *See also* MARINE, TALK

Telstar *see* SATELLITE

temper [OE] The first sense of temper was 'a person's state of mind', either angry or calm. The word goes back ultimately to Latin *temperare* 'to mingle', and in medieval times the noun referred to the right balance in a mixture of elements or qualities, still used of metals. It was particularly associated with the thought of the combination of the four bodily humours (*see* HUMOUR) believed to control whether you were naturally calm, optimistic,

technology   teddy   teem   teepee   teetotal

melancholy, or irritable. This dictated what kind of **temperament** you had, a Late Middle English term from the Latin for 'correct mixture'.

temperature [LME] This is from Latin *temperatura*, from *temperare* 'restrain'. The word originally described 'the state of being tempered or mixed', later becoming synonymous with temperament as a combination of bodily humours or a state of mind. The modern sense in the context of heat intensity dates from the late 17th century.

temple [OE] Temple comes from Latin *templum* 'open or consecrated space'. The temple which is part of your forehead is a different word, going back to Latin *tempus*, whose main meaning was 'time'. *Tempus* is the source of several words in English, such as **contemporary** [M17th] 'of a time with', grammatical **tense** [ME], and **temporary** [M16th]. **Tempo** [E18th], which came to English from Italian, is now a musical term, but in the 17th century was used in fencing for the timing of an attack. **Tempest** [ME] also goes back to *tempus*, via Latin *tempestas* 'season, weather, storm'.

tempt [ME] Tempt goes back to Latin *temptare* 'to test, try', which is the sense in the expression **tempt Providence**. To be unwise enough to test Providence, or your luck, is to invite misfortune. In the Middle Ages **temptation** was particularly used in relation to the biblical story, in the Gospel of Matthew, of Jesus being tempted to sin by the Devil when he spent 40 days in the wilderness. Modern temptations are generally more trivial urges to indulge yourself. In 1892 Oscar Wilde wrote: 'I can resist everything except temptation' (*Lady Windermere's Fan*). **Attempt** [LME] is from the same root.

ten [OE] The number ten goes back to an ancient root shared by Latin *decem*, the source of **decimal** [E17th] and similar words. The rules of conduct given by God to Moses on Mount Sinai, according to the biblical book of Exodus, have been known in English as the **Ten Commandments** since the Middle Ages. The common practice in schools of setting tests with ten questions has led to **ten out of ten** coming to mean 'completely right, perfect'.

tenant [ME] Tenant is from an Old French word meaning literally 'holding', which came from Latin *tenere* 'to hold'. This Latin verb also gave rise to late 16th-century **tenable**, and early 17th-century **tenacious**.

tender [ME] In the senses 'gentle and kind' and 'sensitive to pain or damage', tender goes back to Latin *tener* 'delicate'. It appears in a number of phrases relating to feeling for others. **Tender loving care** goes back to Shakespeare's *Henry VI, Part 3*: 'Go, Salisbury, and tell them all from me / I thank them for their tender loving care.' Its abbreviation **TLC** is comparatively modern, dating from the 1940s. The phrase **tender mercies** was probably originally a biblical allusion to a verse in the Book of Proverbs: 'The tender mercies of the wicked are cruel.' The tender in 'an invitation to tender' is a different word that was originally a legal term meaning 'to formally offer a plea, evidence or the money to discharge a debt'. It comes ultimately from Latin *tendere* 'to stretch, hold out', also the source of **tend** [ME], first found in the sense 'move or be inclined to move in a certain direction'.

tennis [LME] Around 1400 tennis was the name for what is now known as **real tennis**, played on an enclosed court, but since the 1870s it has referred to the outdoor game also called **lawn tennis**. The name probably comes from Old French *tenez* meaning 'take!'—presumably the server's call to an opponent. **Anyone for tennis?** is supposedly a typical entrance or exit line spoken by a young man in the kind of drawing-room comedy popular in the 1920s or 1930s, although no actual example has been traced—the closest is 'Anybody on for a game of tennis?', from *Misalliance* (1914) by George Bernard Shaw.

tenor [ME] In medieval music the tenor part was given the melody, and therefore 'held' it, reflecting its root, Latin *tenere* 'to hold'. The tenor of something, as in 'the general tenor of the debate', also goes back to Latin *tenere*, via *tenor* 'course, substance, meaning of a law'.

tense *see* TEMPLE, TENT

tent [ME] Tent goes back to Latin *tendere* 'stretch', since early tents were made of skins or cloth stretched on poles. It is also the source of **tense** [L17th] in the sense 'stretched, tight', and **tension** [M16th] first found as a medical term for the condition or feeling of being physically strained. To be **on tenterhooks** is to be in a state of nervous suspense. A **tenter**, from the same Latin root as tent, is a frame on which fabric can be held taut so that it does not shrink while drying or being manufactured, and tenterhooks were the hooks or bent nails used to fasten woollen cloth in position. This tightening procedure had obvious appeal as an image for person in difficulties or suspense, at first on tenters and later on tenterhooks. The phrase has survived long after real tenterhooks disappeared.

tentacle [M18th] This word has been anglicized from modern Latin *tentaculum*, from Latin *tentare* 'to feel, handle, try'. **Tentative** [L16th] also comes from *tentare*

tenterhooks *see* TENT

tenuous *see* THIN

tepee *see* NATIVE AMERICAN WORD PANEL

terrace [E16th] In the early 16th century a terrace was an open gallery, and later it came to mean a platform or balcony in a theatre. A terrace of houses was originally a row built slightly above the level of the road—the first terrace of houses was mentioned in the 1760s, at first in street names like Adelphi Terrace. The source was a medieval French word meaning 'rubble, platform', based on Latin *terra* 'earth', the source of many other English words such as **terrain** [E18th], **terrestrial** [LME], **territory** [LME], and **subterranean** [E17th]. A territory was originally the area surrounding a town and was subject to its laws. To say that something **goes with the territory** is to say that it is an unavoidable result of a

situation. Territory here is probably used in the sense 'the area in which a sales representative or distributor has the right to operate', which developed in the US in the early 20th century. In Arthur Miller's play *Death of a Salesman* (1949), the central character Willy Loman tells his son that a salesman has to dream: 'It comes with the territory.' *See also* KOP

terrapin *see* NATIVE AMERICAN WORD PANEL

terrestrial *see* TERRACE

terrible *see* TERROR

terrine *see* TUREEN

territory *see* TERRACE

terror [LME] Like **terrible** [LME], terror comes from Latin *terrere* 'to frighten' and goes back to medieval times. **The Terror** was the period of the French Revolution, from about March 1793 to July 1794, marked by extreme repression and bloodshed. The expression **reign of terror**, which may now be applied to any brutal exercise of power, was originally coined to describe this time. **Terrorist** also has links with this period, as the word was originally used to describe the Jacobins, the revolutionary group who were responsible for the repression and executions of the Terror. Terrible once meant 'causing terror or awe', a meaning reflected in the name of the feared 16th-century tsar of Russia Ivan the Terrible. The weakened sense 'very bad, appalling' gradually evolved from the start of the 17th century. Today parents talk of **the terrible twos**, a period in a child's development around the age of two that often involves defiant or challenging behaviour. The term is first found in the title of a film produced in 1950 for the Department of National Health and Welfare in Canada, called *The Terrible Twos and the Trusting Threes*.

terse [E17th] In the early 17th century terse meant 'polished, trim, spruce', and when applied to language 'polished, polite'. It goes back to Latin *tersus* 'wiped, polished'. The sense we have today developed from the idea of language from which everything

tense   tent   tentacle   tenterhooks   tenuous

unnecessary has been trimmed away, and which is concise and to the point—as in the historian Lord Macaulay's praise of a passage as giving 'an eminently clear, terse, and spirited summary'.

test [LME] During medieval times a test was another name for what is now called a cupel, a shallow, porous container in which gold or silver can be refined or tested. The word goes back to Latin *testu* or *testum* 'earthen pot'. The original function of the container lies behind phrases like **put to the test** and **stand the test**. *See also* ACID. The first cricket matches to be called **Test matches** seem to have been those played between Australia and the touring English team in 1861–62. The term probably arose from the idea that the matches were a test of strength between the sides. If someone reproaches an irritable friend for being **testy** they are using a word which first meant 'headstrong, impetuous' and goes back to Old French *teste* 'head'. The words are linked by the fact that *teste* (modern French *tête*) goes back to *testum*. In popular Latin 'pot' was used as a slang term for head in the way we might employ 'use your loaf' today. **Tetchy** has the same meaning but is unrelated—it is probably a variant of the old Scots word *tache* 'blotch, fault', from French.

testicle [LME] The ancient Romans felt that a man's testicles testified that he was male. They formed the word *testiculus* from Latin *testis* 'witness', the source also of **attest** [L16th]; **detest** [LME] which originally meant to denounce; **protest** [LME]; **testify** [LME]; and **intestate** [LME] 'without a witnessed will'. The testicles were the 'witnesses' of the man's virility.

testy, tetchy *see* TEST

text [LME] A text is created when words are woven together, and the term goes back ultimately to Latin *texere* 'to weave', also the source of **texture** [LME] which originally meant 'a woven fabric', **textile** [E17th], and **context** [LME]. Text is a good example of how words develop new meanings in response to changes in the world. It is associated with the most traditional forms of the written word, but technological changes have introduced **text messaging**. You might think that the verb **text** (as in 'I'll text you when I get back') has only been in the language a short time, but here is Shakespeare using the word 400 years ago in the context of inscribing something on a gravestone in large or capital letters: 'Yea and text underneath, here dwells Benedick the married man' (*Much Ado about Nothing*).

thaler *see* US WORD PANEL

thane *see* EARL

theatre [LME] The earliest theatres were the open-air theatres of the classical world, first mentioned in English in the writings of Geoffrey Chaucer. People go to the theatre to watch a play, and the word itself goes back to the Greek *theasthai* 'to look at'. A theatre for surgical operations, or **operating theatre**, gets its name, recorded from the 1660s, because early rooms of this type were arranged like theatres, with banks of seats for observers. *See also* ABSURD

theology *see* GOD

thermometer *see* WARM

Thermos, thermostat *see* WARM

thesaurus [L16th] The source of thesaurus is Greek *thēsauros* 'storehouse, *TREASURE'. In the late 16th century a thesaurus was a dictionary or encyclopedia; the current English meaning of the word comes from the title of one of the best-known works of reference, Roget's *Thesaurus of English Words and Phrases*, first published in 1852.

thespian [L17th] The dramatic poet Thespis, who lived in the 6th century BC and is traditionally regarded as the founder of Greek tragedy, gave us this word for an actor.

thick [OE] The 'slow-witted' sense of this Germanic word dates from the late 16th century. In Shakespeare's *Henry IV, Part 2*

test testicle testy tetchy text thaler thane

Falstaff says disparagingly of his companion Poins: 'His wit's as thick as Tewkesbury mustard'. A very stupid person might be as **thick as two short planks**, **thick as a plank** or **thick as a brick** – there is a play on thick in the usual sense 'deep from side to side' and the sense 'stupid'. Thick with the meaning 'very friendly', as in **thick as thieves**, comes from the sense 'very close together, tightly packed'. To go **through thick and thin** goes back to medieval times and originally probably referred to someone pushing their way both through a **thicket** (a related OE word), where trees grew closely, and 'thin wood', where the going would be easier. *See also* CALLOUS

thief *see* HONOUR

thimble *see* THUMB

thin [OE] The Old English word thin shares an ancient root with Latin *tenuis* 'thin, fine, shallow', the source of **extenuate** [M16th] and **tenuous** [L16th]. An action which is unimportant in itself, but likely to lead to more serious developments is sometimes described as **the thin end of the wedge**. The idea here is of something being levered open by the insertion of the edge of a wedge into a narrow crack to widen the opening so that the thicker part can also pass through. **The thin red line** used to be a name for the British army, in reference to the traditional scarlet uniform. The phrase first occurs in *The Times* of 24 January 1855, reporting a debate about the distribution of medals for the Crimean War in the House of Lords at which the Earl of Ellenborough who spoke of 'the services of that "thin red line" which had met and routed the Russian cavalry.' It has now become so much part of our language that the colour may be altered to change the meaning—**the thin blue line** can mean the police force.

thing [OE] Just about anything can be called a thing, but in Old English it first meant 'a meeting, an assembly' or 'a court, a council'. The word developed through 'a matter brought before a court' and 'a concern, an affair' to its more general modern senses. To **be all things to all men**

can mean either 'to attempt to please everyone' or 'to be able to be used differently by different people'. The expression probably goes back to a biblical verse in the First Epistle to the Corinthians: 'I am made all things to all men.' Odd sounds at night can be alarming, but if you are frightened you could recite 'The Cornish or West Country Litany', a traditional prayer which runs: 'From ghoulies and ghosties and long-leggety beasties / And things that go bump in the night, / Good Lord, deliver us!' This has given us the expression **things that go bump in the night** for ghosts and supernatural beings. After a certain age everyone can be struck by the gloomy thought that **things ain't what they used to be**. The phrase originated as the title of a song by Ted Persons in 1941. The idiom **do one's (own) thing** is recorded from the mid 19th century, but it did not become widespread until the 1960s during the hippie culture; **have a thing with (somebody)** dates from this same decade.

thingamabob, thingy *see* DINGUS

think [OE] The Old English word think is related to **thank** [OE] (*see also* STAR) and **thought** [OE]. Hasty words can land you in trouble, and there is a traditional saying that warns you how to avoid this. **Think first and speak afterwards** goes back to the 16th century. Another proverb, **great minds think alike**, dates from the 17th century. **They think it's all over**, used as the title of a British TV sports quiz, is an extract from one of the most famous sports commentaries ever. Towards the end of extra time in the 1966 World Cup final between England and West Germany, with England leading 3–2, some spectators spilled on to the pitch as England attacked, thinking that the final whistle had blown. The TV commentator Kenneth Wolstenholme said, 'They think it's all over', whereupon Geoff Hurst scored and he continued 'It is now!' A **think tank** is now a body of experts providing ideas, but it was originally a US slang term for the brain, recorded from 1905. A newspaper report in 1964 said that 'Truman . . . hoped to live to be 90 but only "if the old think-tank is working".' The modern sense appeared in the 1950s. The phrase **(on) second thoughts** dates from the mid 17th century; **lost in thought** is early 19th-century; **it's the thought that counts** is recorded from the 1930s.

Third World *see* WORLD

thong [OE] Thong is related to **twinge** [OE], which originally meant to pinch. In Anglo-Saxon times a thong was a shoelace. It then came to be used for any narrow strip of leather, and finally to any thin strip of material, from which came the modern use for minuscule underwear in the 1970s.

thorn [OE] One of the earliest recorded Old English words, first found before AD 700. A **thorn in the side** or **thorn in the flesh** is a source of continual annoyance or trouble. Both expressions are of biblical origin. The Old Testament book of Numbers has a verse which reads: 'Those which ye let remain of them shall be pricks in your eyes, and thorns in your sides, and shall vex you in the land wherein ye dwell.' In the New Testament the Second Epistle to the Corinthians has: 'And lest I should be exalted above measure through the abundance of the revelations, there was given to me a thorn in the flesh, the messenger of Satan to buffet me.'
See also ROSE

thorough [OE] Old English *thuruh* was an alteration of *thurh* '**through**', and the two forms were both originally used for through. The adjective 'carried out in every detail' dates from the late 15th century, a period when it also meant 'going or extending through something' surviving in late Middle English **thoroughfare** (literally 'a track going through'), and familiar from Shakespeare's 'Over hill, over dale, Thorough bush, thorough briar' in *A Midsummer Night's Dream*.

thought *see* THINK

thrash [OE] Thrash and **thresh** are variant forms of the same Old English word. The Germanic root sense was probably 'to tramp with the feet'. Thrash was used for treading out corn by men or oxen; when beating with

a flail replaced treading, thresh was restricted to producing grain, and thrash extended to more generalized notions of knocking, beating, and striking. In **threshold** [OE] the first element is related to *thresh* in the Germanic sense 'tread', but the origin of the second element remains unknown.

thread [OE] A Germanic word distantly related to *THROW. The expression **hang by a thread** goes back to the 16th century, and comes from the legend of Damocles. He was a flattering courtier of Dionysius I, ruler of Syracuse in Sicily in the 4th century BC, who constantly told his ruler that he must be the happiest of men. Eventually the king decided to give Damocles a graphic demonstration of how fragile his happiness was. Dionysius invited him to a sumptuous banquet, but then Damocles realized he had been seated under a sword suspended by a single hair right above his head. The legend has also given us the expression a **sword of Damocles** for an imminent danger or ever-present threat.

three [OE] This shares an ancient root with Latin *tres* and Greek *treis*. Three inseparable friends may be called **the three musketeers**. The original three musketeers were Athos, Porthos, and Aramis, whose motto was 'One for all, and all for one'. They appear in the 1844 novel *Les Trois Mousquetaires* by Alexandre Dumas père. The expression **the third degree** for long and harsh questioning by the police is American, recorded from the beginning of the 20th century. Perhaps in reference to the Holy Trinity, three is traditionally a lucky number, and this is reflected in **third time lucky**, used to suggest that someone should make another effort after initial failure. **Third time is the charm** is an American version of this saying. The same idea is probably present in the saying **the third time pays for all**, meaning that success after initial failure makes up for earlier disappointment. **Threescore** is an old-fashioned way of saying 'sixty'. According to the Bible, 'The days of our age are threescore years and ten.' (Psalm 90).
See also SHEET

Third World thong thorn thorough thought

thresh *see* THRASH

thrill [ME] In medieval times thrill meant 'to pierce, penetrate', and the word is related to **through** and *THOROUGH. The sense 'to affect with a sudden feeling of excitement and pleasure' dates back to the 17th century, but it was not until the early 20th century that someone delighted could say 'I'm thrilled!' The first **thrillers** were exciting plays in the 1880s.

throttle [LME] Throttle, to stop someone breathing by squeezing their throat is a development of Old English **throat**. As a mid 16th-century noun it was at first an alternative word for throat. Use of the word to refer to a valve controlling the flow of fuel dates from the early 19th century.

through *see* THOROUGH

throw [OE] A word which at first meant 'to twist' or 'to turn', and is related to *THREAD. The sense 'to give a party', dating from the 1920s, probably came from the meaning 'to perform a leap or somersault', whereas the idea of 'throwing' a game or match is likely to be short for **throw away**. When you withdraw from a contest you **throw your hand in**. The idea here is of a player in a card game throwing their hand down on the table as a signal that they are withdrawing from the game. The origins of **throw in the towel** or **throw in the sponge** lie in the boxing ring. Boxers or their trainers traditionally signal that they are conceding defeat by throwing the towel or sponge used to wipe the contestant's face into the middle of the ring. The earliest version of the phrase is **throw up the sponge**, dating from the 1860s. The idea that **those who live in glass houses should not throw stones**, dates from the 17th century. *See also* BABY

thug [E19th] In the early 19th century a thug was a member of an organization of professional robbers and assassins in India who strangled their victims, deceiving them by pretending to be fellow travellers, and gaining their confidence. The word comes from Hindi *thag* 'swindler, thief'. We meet the first British thugs or violent louts in the 1830s, in Glasgow.

thumb [OE] Like *FINGER, thumb is Old English. It shares an ancient root with Latin *tumere* 'to swell', probably because the thumb is a 'fat' or 'swollen' finger. **Thimble** is formed from thumb, in the same way that handle is formed from *HAND. The expression **thumbs up**, showing satisfaction or approval, and its opposite **thumbs down**, indicating rejection or failure, hark back to the days of Roman gladiatorial combat. The thumbs were used to signal approval or disapproval by the spectators—despite what many people believe, though, they turned their thumbs down to indicate that a beaten gladiator had performed well and should be spared, and up to call for his death. The reversal of the phrases' meaning first appeared in the early 20th century. In one of the stories from Rudyard Kipling's *Puck of Pook's Hill* (1906), a Roman centurion facing a bleak future says to his friend, 'We're finished men—thumbs down against both of us.' In Shakespeare's *Macbeth* the Second Witch says as she sees Macbeth, 'By the pricking of my thumbs, / Something wicked this way comes.' A sensation of pricking in the thumbs was believed to be a foreboding of evil or trouble. *See also* LIMB, RULE

thump *see* JUMP

Thursday *see* TUESDAY

thwart *see* TORCH

tiara *see* PERSIAN WORD PANEL

tick [ME] The tick shown as a ✓ first meant 'to pat, touch' and goes back to medieval English, where it was related to **tickle** [ME], although its history is obscure. This is also the tick used to imitate the sound of a clock, and in **ticker**, or the heart, a sense first used in the USA at the end of the 19th century. The 'bloodsucking parasite' sort of tick is a different, older word which gives us the expressions **tight as a tick** or **as full as a tick** for 'very drunk', both of which refer to the way ticks swell as they gorge themselves on blood. Both forms of the phrase have the additional meaning 'be full after eating', but the more recent tight as a tick plays on two senses of *TIGHT, which can mean both 'drunk' and 'stretched taut'. When you buy on credit or **on tick**, you are using yet another word, which is an abbreviation of *TICKET. The ticket in question is an IOU promising to pay the money due, but there is also the suggestion of a pun on the reputation of moneylenders as 'bloodsucking parasites'. Both **on tick** and **on the ticket** date back to the 17th century.

ticket [16th] This is a shortening of an Old French word *estiquette*, which is also the origin of *ETIQUETTE. A ticket was originally a 'short written note' and 'a licence or permit'— the use for a piece of paper or card giving admission or permission to travel dates from the late 17th century.

tickety-boo *see* RAJ WORD PANEL

tickey *see* SOUTH AFRICAN WORD PANEL

tickle *see* TICK

tide [OE] In Old English a tide was a period or season, a sense surviving in **Eastertide** and **Shrovetide**, and it was not used in connection with the sea until the later medieval period. The saying **time and tide wait for no man** originally referred just to time, with tide used as a repetition of the sense to add emphasis. Despite the great difference in their contemporary meanings, **tidy** [ME] is from tide. Right up to the early 18th century it meant 'timely, seasonable, opportune', and acquired its current sense via the uses 'attractive, good-looking' and 'good, pleasing' around 1700. Perhaps based on tidy is the verb **titivate** which in the early 19th century was also spelt *tidivate*.

tiger [OE] Tiger goes back via French and Latin to Greek *tigris*—the beast was formerly found in Turkey and the Middle East, and would have been known to Europeans in classical times. The tiger is a fierce and dangerous creature, and to **have a tiger by the tail** is to have embarked on a course of action which turns out to be unexpectedly difficult, but which you cannot easily abandon. Having a **tiger in your tank** means that you have energy and spirit. The expression originated as a 1960s advertising slogan for Esso petrol, 'Put a tiger in your tank.' Since the start of the

1980s the successful smaller economies of East Asia, especially those of Hong Kong, Singapore, Taiwan, and South Korea, have been called **tiger economies**. The strength of Ireland during the 1990s led to its being dubbed the **Celtic tiger**. S*ee also* RIDE, WOLF

tight [ME] In early medieval times to call someone tight meant that they were healthy or vigorous. The senses we know today came along later, and it was not until the early to mid 19th century that the informal meanings 'stingy' and 'drunk' appeared. *See also* TICK. A 'tight ship' was originally one in which ropes were tightly fastened. From this came the sense of a ship under firm discipline and control—which gives us the expression **run a tight ship**. **Tights** are predominantly a women's garment, but they started life as tight-fitting breeches worn by men in the 18th and early 19th centuries. Dancers and acrobats then favoured them, before the first references to women's tights in the 1890s.

tilt [ME] In its earliest sense, around 1300, tilt meant 'to fall, topple', and a jousting knight who **tilted at** a mounted opponent by riding with a lance levelled at his body was trying to knock him off his horse. This image of two armoured figures galloping towards each other is the source of **at full tilt**, 'with maximum energy or force'. In the mock-heroic novel *Don Quixote* (1605–15) by Miguel de Cervantes, the hero Don Quixote sees a line of windmills on the horizons and takes them for giants, which he attacks. This gave us the expression **tilt at windmills**. *See also* QUIXOTIC

timber [OE] Timber originally meant a building as well as building material. Of Germanic origin, it is related to German *Zimmer* 'room', from an Indo-European root meaning 'to build'.

time [OE] To the Anglo-Saxons time and *TIDE meant the same thing. Both **time immemorial** and its equivalent **time out of mind** were originally legal formulas. Their exact meaning was 'a time beyond legal memory', which was fixed very precisely by statute in 1276 as 1 July 1189, the beginning of the reign of Richard I. The idea was that if you could prove possession of a land or a title or right from that date there was no need to establish when or how it was originally acquired. Not surprisingly, everyone but the lawyers soon forgot the specific meaning and both phrases developed the more general sense of 'a very long time ago'. We hear a lot today about the 'money-rich but time-poor' lives of many in the West, and the expression **time is money** has a very modern ring to it. But it seems to have been coined as long ago as 1748 by the American statesman and scientist Benjamin Franklin, in a speech entitled 'Advice to Young Tradesmen'. Before that the thought had clearly occurred to many over the centuries, as 'the most costly outlay is time' is attributed to the ancient Athenian orator and politician Antiphon. *See also* MOVE

tin [OE] The metal tin appears in the writings of the Anglo-Saxon king Alfred the Great. Use of tin to mean a sealed metal container for food or drink dates from the late 18th century. Tin is not a precious metal, and a number of phrases refer to its relative lack of value. To **have a tin ear** is to be tone-deaf. The term **a little tin god** for someone regarded with unjustified respect conjures up the idea of an idol made of cheap tin instead of gold or silver. In the early 20th century a **tin Lizzie** was an affectionate nickname for a car, especially one of the early Ford models. Since the late 1980s the wood preservative manufacturer Ronseal has seen its slogan **It does exactly what it says on the tin** become a catch-all phrase for anything which unpretentiously does what it claims to.

tincture [LME] A tincture was originally a dye or pigment. It comes from Latin *tinctura* 'dyeing', from *tingere* 'to dye or colour'. Because dying involves making solutions and extracting active ingredients, it started to be used for a pharmaceutical extract in the late 17th century. The slang sense for 'an alcoholic drink' evolved from this in the early 20th century. A number of other words go back to *tingere*. **Tint** [E18th]

was originally *tinct*, and **tinge** [L15th] comes from the related verb *tingere*, 'to colour'. **Stain** [LME] goes back to *tingere* via a shortening of *distain*, from Old French *desteindre* 'tinge with a colour different from the natural one'.

tinker [ME] We do not know where the word tinker came from, but in the past tinkers played an important role travelling round mending metal utensils. They had, however, a reputation for bad language giving us the expression **not give a tinker's curse**, sometimes shortened to **not give a tinker's**. The verb meaning 'to attempt to repair or improve something in a casual way' was suggested by the improvized way that tinkers worked, and is found from the mid 17th century.

tinsel [LME] Sparkly tinsel comes from Latin *scintilla* 'a spark', which is also the source of **scintillate** [E17th]. In medieval times tinsel was fabric woven with metallic thread or spangles—it became something like our familiar shiny strips in the late 16th century. The idea of glitter was picked up during the 1970s in **Tinseltown**, a nickname for Hollywood and its cinema.

tint *see* TINCTURE

tip *see* TOP, WINK

tipple [LME] To tipple was originally to sell alcoholic liquor, not to drink it. It came in the late 15th century from earlier **tippler** 'a seller of alcohol', the source of which is unknown, though it may be related to Norwegian dialect *tipla* 'to drip slowly'. Emphasis moved to the drinker towards the end of the 16th century.

tiramisu *see* ITALIAN WORD PANEL

tire *see* TYRE

tissue [LME] An Old French word that goes back to Latin *texere* 'to weave', the source of *TEXT. Tissue was originally a rich material often interwoven with gold or silver threads. From the idea of woven material came the notion of an intricate, connected series in the phrase **a tissue of lies**. The

tin tincture tinker tinsel tint tip tipple

biological sense is from the mid 19th century. The 20th-century modern disposable paper hankie developed from **tissue paper**, which has been shortened to tissue since the late 18th century.

tit [OE] Few words in English have such snigger-inducing contrasts in meaning. In the name for small songbirds, tit is probably of Scandinavian origin and related to Icelandic *titlingur* 'sparrow'. It first appeared in English in the Middle Ages in the longer equivalent **titmouse**, though mice had nothing to do with it—the second element was originally *mose*, which also meant 'tit'. It changed to **mouse** in the 16th century, probably because of the bird's small size and quick movements. In Old English a tit was a teat or nipple—it is from the same root as **teat** [ME]. In modern English it is a term for a woman's breast, a use that arose in the USA in the early 20th century. Since the 1970s British **tits and bums** and American **tits and ass** have suggested crudely sexual images of women. As a name for a foolish person, used since the 19th century, tit may be the same word, or it may have evolved from *TWIT.

titanic [E18th] In Greek mythology the Titans were gigantic gods who were the children of Uranus (Heaven) and Gaia (Earth). Zeus, son of their leader Cronus, rose up against his father and defeated them to became chief god. They were the source of titanic, 'of exceptional strength, size, or power'. The most immediate association of the word nowadays is with the *Titanic*, the British passenger liner that was the largest ship in the world at her launch and supposedly unsinkable. She struck an iceberg in the North Atlantic on her maiden voyage in April 1912 and sank with the loss of 1,490 lives. In 1976 Rogers Morton, President Ford's campaign manager said, after losing five of the last six primaries 'I'm not going to rearrange the furniture on the deck of the *Titanic*'. Although references similar to **rearranging the deckchairs on the *Titanic*** have been recorded earlier than this, this comment popularized the concept.

titch [E20th] Harry Relph (1868–1928), was a diminutive English music-hall artist whose stage name was 'Little Tich'. He acquired the nickname as a child because of a resemblance to Arthur Orton, notorious as 'the Tichborne claimant'. Orton had returned to England from Australia in 1866 claiming to be Roger Charles Tichborne, the heir to a title and estate who had been lost at sea, but was eventually tried and imprisoned for perjury. In the First World War British soldiers began to use tich or titch as a name for a small person. **Titchy** developed from this in the mid 20th century.

titillate [E 17th] Titillate is from Latin *titillare* 'to tickle'.

titivate *see* TIDE

tittle *see* JOT, T

TLC *see* TENDER

toady [E19th] In the 17th century unscrupulous charlatans and quacks would try to sell their supposed remedies by demonstrating their powers. One technique was to have an assistant take the quack medicine and then eat, or pretend to eat, a toad—people thought that toads were poisonous and so were likely to attribute the assistant's survival to the charlatan's wares. Such an assistant was a **toad-eater**. In the 18th century the word also came to mean 'a fawning flatterer', and in the early 19th this was shortened to toady. **Toad** is an Old English word, and **toadstool** late Middle English apparently from the plant being the right size and shape to be a toad's stool.

toast [LME] There is a connection between the toast you eat and the toast you make with a raised glass. Toast is based on Latin *torrere* 'to parch, scorch, dry up', the source also of **torrid** [E17th], and **torrent** [LME] a rushing or 'boiling' flow of water. 'To parch' was the earliest meaning of the English word, and before long it was used to describe browning bread in front of a fire. Drinking toasts goes back to the late 17th century, and originated in the practice whereby a drinker would name a lady and request that all the people present drink her health. The idea was that the lady's name flavoured the drink like the pieces of spiced toast that people sometimes added to wine in those days.

tobacco [M16th] This is from Spanish *tabaco*, but where it came from before that is confused. It is said to be either from a Carib word for a tobacco pipe or from a Taino word for a primitive cigar. However, there is also an Arabic word *tabbaq* used for various herbs, and it is possible that Spaniards, influenced as they were by Moorish culture, used this old Arabic word for the new herb, or blended the different strands together.

toboggan [E19th] The origin of this word is Canadian French *tabaganne*, from the Micmac *topaĝan* 'sled'.

tod, on your see PAT

today see TOMORROW

toddy [E17th] Some palm trees have a sugary sap that is drunk in parts of Africa, South India and the Philippines, especially when fermented into an alcoholic drink. This was the original toddy. The word comes from the Indian languages Hindi and Marathi, and goes back to a Sanskrit name for an Asian palm, the palmyra. Travellers brought it back to the colder climate of Britain, and the **hot toddy** of whisky or some other spirit with hot water, sugar, and spices has soothed many a cold since the late 18th century.

toe [OE] An Old English word recorded as early as AD 700. To **toe the line**, 'to accept the authority or principles of a particular group', derives from competitors placing their toes just touching the starting line at the beginning of a race. Vagrants without proper clothing have long used rags wrapped round their feet as socks. Since the mid 19th century such a piece of improvized footwear has been a **toerag**. The term transferred to the unfortunate wearer later in the century, and nowadays toerag is an insult for anyone considered worthless or contemptible.

toff [M19th] This is perhaps an alteration of **tuft**, once a term for titled undergraduates at Oxford and Cambridge, who wore a gold tassel on their caps—social climbers and toadies were called **tuft-hunters** from the mid 18th century. The associations of the word may have influenced **toffee-nosed** or 'snobbish', which was originally military slang. Toffee seems to have been a desirable commodity to soldiers during the First World War—**not be able to do something for toffee**, or be totally incompetent at it, is first recorded in 1914 in the mouth of a British 'Tommy'. **Toffee** [E19th] is an alteration of **taffy** [E19th], now mainly used in North America for a sweet resembling toffee. The **Taffy** that is a name for a Welshman is quite different, representing a supposed Welsh pronunciation of the name David or Dafydd.

toffee see TOFF

toggle [M18th] Toggle was originally in nautical use, a term for a short pin passed through a loop of a rope to keep it in place. The origin is obscure but there is probably a relationship with *TANGLE. The word's generalization to a 'fastener' on a strap or garment dates from the late 19th century. It has been used as a term in computing since the 1980s for a command that has the opposite effect on successive occasions: the notion is one of turning through 90 degrees.

toil, toile see TOILET

toilet [M16th] A toilet was originally a cloth used as a wrapper for clothes or a covering for a dressing table, from French *toilette* 'cloth, wrapper'. From the first meaning developed a group of senses relating to dressing and washing, including 'the process of washing, dressing, and attending to your appearance', now rather dated, which is also expressed in the French form **toilette**. In the 18th century it was fashionable for a lady to receive visitors during the later stages of her 'toilet', which led to uses such as this by the dramatist Sir Richard Steele in 1703: 'You shall introduce him to Mrs Clerimont's Toilet.' People

tobacco   toboggan   tod   today   toddy   toe

started using the word for a dressing room, and, in the USA, one with washing facilities. It was not until the early 20th century that it became a particular item of plumbing, namely a lavatory. *See also* LOO. The French word was a diminutive of **toile**, used for a type of dress fabric since the late 18th century, and of **toils** [M16th] for entrapment, a figurative use of an earlier sense, 'net'. **Toil** in the sense of hard work in Middle English has had a bad reputation from the start, as it was originally used to mean 'strife, quarrel, battle', and from then came to be used for something unpleasantly hard. It comes via French from Latin *tudiculare* 'stir about'.

token [OE] 'He gave him . . . a cordial slap on the back, and some other equally gentle tokens of satisfaction', wrote the novelist Fanny Burney in 1778. She was using token in the meaning it had had since Anglo-Saxon times, 'a sign or symbol'. In the 17th and 18th centuries there was often a scarcity of small coins, and tradesmen issued their own coin-shaped pieces of metal to exchange for goods or cash. Such a disc was a token as it 'symbolized' or substituted for real money. Use of the word for a voucher, as in a **book token**, dates from the early 20th century.

Tom [ME] Like *JACK, Tom has long been used to represent an ordinary man. The expression **Tom, Dick, and Harry**, meaning 'a large number of ordinary people', first appeared in an 18th-century song: 'Farewell, Tom, Dick, and Harry. Farewell, Moll, Nell, and Sue'. During the 19th century the British army offered specimens of completed official forms using the name Thomas Atkins for the fictitious enlisted man. From the 1880s Rudyard Kipling helped popularize **Tommy** as a name for the ordinary and much-exploited British soldier. His poem 'Tommy' (1892) contained such lines as 'O it's Tommy this, an' Tommy that, an' "Tommy go away" / But it's "Thank you, Mr Atkins," when the band begins to play'. The 'tommy' in **tommy gun** is not an anonymous private soldier, but the US army officer John T. Thompson, who conceived the idea of this type of sub-

machine gun and financed its development. The designer, O.V. Payne, insisted in 1919 that it be called the **Thompson gun**, but by the late 1920s it had been domesticated as the tommy gun. In the mid 16th century a **tomboy** was actually a boy, specifically a rough or boisterous one. The word was applied to a girl who enjoys rough activities traditionally associated with boys at the end of that century. The cylindrical drum called the **tom-tom** is a different word, from Hindi *tam tam*. It came over to Britain in the 1690s.

tomorrow [ME] A word formed by the combination of **to** and **morrow** (*see* MORNING) in the 13th century, in the same way as **today** and **tonight**. Reflections on the future include **tomorrow is another day**, a 20th-century variant of **tomorrow is a new day**, recorded from the early 16th century. 'Tomorrow is another day' is remembered by many as the last line of the film *Gone With The Wind* (1939). The proverb **tomorrow never comes** was foreshadowed in 1523 when Lord Berners wrote: 'It was said every day among them, we shall fight tomorrow, the which day came never.' *See also* JAM

tom-tom *see* TOM

ton [ME] Ton is a variant of **tun**, both spellings being used for the container and the weight in the past. The senses were differentiated in the late 17th century, with tun limited to a 'cask'. A ton was originally a term for the capacity for a ship, originally the volume of space occupied by a cask or wine. The metric **tonne**—1 000 kilograms—first appears in English in the late 19th century, adopted from French. A little ton was, in French, a *tonel*, source of the word **tunnel** [LME].

tongue [OE] Despite the difference in spelling, the Old English word tongue is ultimately related to Latin *lingua*, the source of *LINGO and *LANGUAGE. In the 18th century to **put your tongue in your cheek** meant 'to speak insincerely'. This came from a contemptuous gesture which involved poking your tongue in your cheek,

token Tom tomorrow tom-tom ton tongue

and led to the expression **tongue in cheek**, 'in an ironic or insincere way'. When the disciples were filled with the Holy Spirit after the ascent of Jesus into heaven, they were given **the gift of tongues**, the power of speaking in unknown languages. Members of Pentecostal churches believe that they, like the Apostles, can **speak in tongues**.

tonight *see* TOMORROW

tooth [OE] An Old English word from an ancient root shared by Latin *dens*, the source of **dental** [L16th], **dentist** [M18th], **trident** [L16th] 'three teeth', and *INDENT. To **fight tooth and nail** was in the 16th century to **fight with tooth and nail**. Although in a real fight this would mean 'by biting and scratching', the phrase is almost always used of non-physical struggles. To **set someone's teeth on edge** is to cause them intense irritation. The expression comes from the Bible, and expresses the unpleasant sensation felt when you have bitten into something that is bitter or sour: 'Every man that hath eaten the sour grape, his teeth shall be set on edge' (Jeremiah). *See also* HEN

top [OE] Found in Old English a child's toy, related to **tip**; and from Old Norse in Middle English. The expression to **go over the top** originated in the First World War, when it described troops in the trenches charging over the parapets to attack the enemy. It gradually developed the meaning 'to do something to an excessive or exaggerated degree', possibly in reference to the huge numbers of soldiers who died in the conflict. Soon people were shortening it to simply **over the top**, and since the early 1980s it has been reduced even further to the abbreviation **OTT**, particularly when referring to acting. *See also* SLEEP

topiary [L16th] Topiary is from French *topiaire*, from Latin *topia opera* 'fancy gardening'.

topic *see* COMMONPLACE

topography *see* UTOPIA

topsy-turvy [E16th] Things have been topsy-turvy since at least 1528. The term is probably based on *TOP and **turve**, an old word meaning 'to topple over, overturn'; the extra -*ys* are similar to those in **hurly-burly** (M16th from 'hurling' meaning 'commotion') and **arsy-versy** (also M16th, from *ARSE and Latin versus, 'turned').

torch [ME] A torch in the original sense of 'something soaked in an inflammable substance used to give light' was often made of twisted hemp or other fibres. This is still the American meaning, and reflects the word's Latin origin, *torquere* 'to twist'. Only in British English can torch describe a battery-powered electric lamp, which Americans call a **flashlight**. A **torch song** is a sad or sentimental song of unrequited love, whose name, used since the 1920s, comes from the phrase **carry a torch for**, 'to love someone who does not love you in return'. The image in **pass on the torch**, 'to pass on a tradition, especially one of learning or enlightenment', is that of the runners in a relay race passing on the torch to each other, as was the custom in the ancient Greek Olympic Games. The Latin source of torch, *torquere*, is found in a large number of other English words. Most obviously it is the source of the engineer's **torque** [L19th], and the twisted Celtic neck-ring the **torc** [M19th]. Less obviously it is in **contort** [LME] 'twist together'; **distort** [LME] 'twist out of shape'; **extort** [E16th] 'twist out of'; and **retort** [LME] 'to twist back' (the chemical apparatus gets its name from its twisted shape). *Tortura* 'twisting, torment' the Latin noun formed from the verb gives us **torture** and **tortuous** (both LME), and **torment** [ME]. **Thwart** [ME] is an Old Norse word that goes back to the same Indo-European root.

toreador *see* SPANISH WORD PANEL

torment *see* TORCH

tornado [M16th] A tornado was originally a violent thunderstorm over the tropical Atlantic Ocean. The word may be an alteration of Spanish *tronada* 'thunderstorm', influenced by *tornar* 'to

tonight tooth top topiary topic topography

turn', a reference to the shape of a 'twister'.
See also TYPHOON, TSUNAMI

torpedo [E16th] Although we think of a torpedo as speeding through the water towards its target, at the heart of the word's origin is the notion of slowness and paralysis. The electric ray, a sluggish sea fish that lives at the bottom of shallow water, produces an electric shock to capture prey and for defence. Its Latin name was *torpedo*, from *torpere* 'to be numb or sluggish', source also of **torpid** [E17th], and when first used in English in the early 16th century torpedo referred to this ray. In the late 18th century the inventor of a timed explosive for detonation underwater gave it the name torpedo from the fish, and this is the ancestor of the modern self-propelled underwater missile.

torque *see* TORCH

torrent, torrid *see* TOAST

torso [L18th] Like *BUST, torso at first described sculpture, referring to the *TRUNK of a statue without the head and limbs. Charles Dickens, in *Our Mutual Friend* (1865), was one of the first to apply it to the living human body, writing of a man with 'too much torso in his waistcoat'. The word itself came from Italian, where it originally meant 'a stalk or stump'.

tortoise *see* TURTLE

tortuous, torture *see* TORCH

totem *see* NATIVE AMERICAN WORD PANEL

toucan *see* PELICAN

touch [ME] A word from Old French *tochier* 'to touch'. In modern French this is *toucher*, which is the source of **touché**, literally 'touched!', said in fencing to acknowledge a hit made by your opponent, and more generally in recognition of a good or clever point in a discussion. In the mid 19th century touch developed a number of slang meanings among criminals. It described various ways of getting money from people, either by stealing, especially

pickpocketing, or by some con trick. A **soft touch** was someone who was particularly easy to con or steal from, and even today the phrase is often used to describe someone who is always willing to lend money to a friend. Someone **touched** is slightly mad or crazy. The sense has been used since about 1700, and was probably suggested by a line of Shakespeare's, from *Measure for Measure*: 'I am touch'd with madness.'

From the 16th century a **touchstone** was a piece of jasper or other stone used for testing alloys of gold by observing the colour of the mark which they made on it. Nowadays a touchstone is usually a standard or criterion by which people judge or recognize something. **Touchy**, 'easily upset or offended', may not be directly from touch, though it has been influenced by the word. It was probably originally an alteration of **tetchy** (*see* TEST).

tough [OE] An Old English word related to **taut** [ME] the early spelling of which was *tought*. As a noun, meaning 'a rough and violent man or youth', it dates from the 1860s, in the USA. If you are **as tough as old boots** you are very sturdy or resilient. The earliest version of the phrase was **as tough as leather**. Before he became the British prime minister or even party leader, Tony Blair made a speech at the Labour Party Conference in September 1993, when he was Shadow Home Secretary. The speech brought him to public attention and included the words: 'Labour is the party of law and order in Britain today. Tough on crime and tough on the causes of crime'.

toupee [E18th century] A toupee was initially a curl or a lock of artificial hair; it is an alteration of French *toupet* 'hair-tuft', a diminutive of Old French *toup* 'tuft', distantly related to *TOP.

tour [ME] This was initially a word for a 'turn' or 'spell of work' (tour of duty) from an Old French word meaning 'turn', via Latin from Greek *tornos* 'lathe'. The notion of visiting a number of places was associated with tour from the mid 17th century. **Tournament** and **tourney** [ME] where you

torpedo torque torrent torrid torso tortoise

turn round to confront each other are from the same source.

tousle *see* HASSLE

tout [ME] The early spelling was *tute* and the meaning 'look out'. From a Germanic source, *tout* is related to Dutch *tuit* 'spout, nozzle' (from the notion of 'protruding, poking one's head out'). Later senses were 'watch, spy on' (late 17th century), and 'solicit custom' (mid 18th century). The noun is first recorded in examples from the early 18th century in the slang use 'thieves' lookout'. **Ticket tout** is first found in the mid 20th century.

tow *see* WANTON

tower [OE] This comes ultimately from Greek via Latin and French *tour*. The phrase **tower of strength** is from a use in the Book of Common Prayer: 'O Lord…be unto them a tower of strength' and originally meant 'a strong tower'. A **turret** [ME], in Old French *tourete*, is a little tower.

town [OE] This originally meant 'an enclosed piece of ground' then 'a farm or estate', and 'a collection of houses'. Town gradually grew until by around 1150 it referred to a place of the size we might recognize today as a town. Scandalous gossip has been **the talk of the town** since the 1620s. *See also* PAINT

toxic [M17th] Toxic is from medieval Latin *toxicus* 'poisoned': this comes from the Greek phrase *toxikon* (*pharmakon*) '(poison for) arrows', from *toxon* 'bow'. **Intoxicate** [LME] comes from the related *toxicum* 'a poison'. The association with alcohol is found from the late 16th century.

toy [LME] A toy was originally a funny story or remark, and later a prank, trick, or frivolous entertainment. The usual modern sense, of an object for a child to play with, dates from the late 16th century. Older women had taken up with younger men before the 1980s, but it took until then for the rhyming **toy boy** to appear. The origin of toy, like that of *BOY, is medieval but otherwise unknown.

trace *see* TRAIN

track [LME] A 15th-century word that perhaps came from the same Dutch source as *TREK. The first meaning was 'a mark or trail left by a person, animal or vehicle'—the sort of tracks used by *TRAINS was first described in 1805. The expression **the wrong side of the tracks**, 'a poor or less prestigious part of a town', originated in America from the idea of a town divided by a railroad track and dates from the early 20th century.

tract *see* TREAT

tractor *see* TRAIN

trade [LME] Trade came from German and is related to **tread** [OE]. It originally meant 'a track or way', and then 'a way of life', and 'a skilled handicraft'—the 'buying and selling' sense dates from the 16th century. A **trade wind** has nothing to do with commerce. The term arose in the mid 17th century from **blow trade** 'to blow steadily in the same direction', or along the same course or track. Sailors thought that many winds blew in this way, but as navigation technology improved they realized that there are only two belts of trade winds proper, blowing steadily towards the equator from the northeast in the northern hemisphere and from the southeast in the southern hemisphere.

tradition [LME] A tradition is something passed on and comes from Latin from *tradere* 'deliver' formed from *trans-* 'across' and *dare* 'give'. The abbreviation **trad** dates from the 1950s, usually in the context of jazz. **Traitor** [ME], someone who hands over things to the enemy, and **treason** [ME] the act of handing over, are from the same root.

traffic [E16th] Borrowed from French *traffique*, or the Spanish or Italian equivalents, this originally referred to commercial transportation of merchandise or passengers. The sense 'vehicles moving on a public highway' dates from the early 19th century. The **traffic warden** first appeared in London in 1960. **Traffic**

tousle tout tow tower town toxic toy trace

calming is a translation of German *Verkehrsberuhigung* and arrived on British roads in the late 1980s. *See also* JAM. Nowadays **trafficking** implies dealing in something illegal, especially drugs, but in the mid 16th century to traffic was a neutral term meaning 'to buy and sell, trade'. By the end of that century, though, it had started to take on negative connotations.

trail *see* TRAIN

train [ME] Before railways were invented in the early 19th century, train followed a different track. Early senses included 'a trailing part of a robe' and 'a retinue', which gave rise to 'a line of travelling people or vehicles', and later 'a connected series of things', as in **train of thought**. To train could mean 'to cause a plant to grow in a desired shape', which was the basis of the sense 'to instruct'. The word is from Latin *trahere* 'to pull, draw', and so is related to word such as **trace** [ME] originally a path someone is drawn along, **trail** [ME] originally in the sense 'to tow', **tractor** [L18th] 'something that pulls', **contract** [ME] 'draw together', and **extract** [LME] 'draw out'. Boys in particular have practised the hobby of **trainspotting** under that name since the late 1950s. Others ridicule this hobby and in Britain in the 1980s **trainspotter**, like *ANORAK, became a derogatory term for an obsessive follower of any minority interest. Irvine Welsh's 1993 novel *Trainspotting* gave a high profile to the term. The title refers to an episode in which two heroin addicts go to a disused railway station in Edinburgh and meet an old drunk in a disused railway station who asks them if they are trainspotting. There are also other overtones from the language of drugs—*TRACK is an addicts' term for a vein, **mainlining** [1930s] for injecting a drug intravenously, and train for a drug dealer. **Trainers** were originally **training shoes**, soft shoes without spikes or studs worn by athletes or sports players for training rather than the sport itself. The short form began to replace the longer one in the late 1970s.

traitor *see* TRADITION

trajectory *see* JET

tram [E16th] This is a borrowing from Dutch of a word for a shaft or beam, and was first used for the shafts of a cart or barrow, and then for barrow-like devices used in coal mines. In the early 19th century the word was used for the parallel wheel tracks used in a mine, on which the public tramway was modelled; hence the word's use for the passenger vehicle itself.

trampoline [late 18th century] This is from Italian *trampolino*, from *trampoli* 'stilts'.

trance *see* TRANSIT

tranquil *see* REQUIEM

transaction *see* ACTOR

transfer *see* REFER

transient *see* TRANSIT

transistor [1940s] Transistor was formed by blending *transfer* and *resistor*.

transit [LME] Transit initially meant 'passage from one place to another'. It is from Latin *transire* 'go across'. The grammatical term **transitive** [L16th] for verbs that 'go across' to an object is from the same source, as are **trance** [ME], and **transient** [LME].

translucent [L16th] Formed from the Latin elements *trans* 'across' and *lucere* 'to shine', this was originally used in the literal sense 'shining through'. The sense 'allowing the passage of light' dates from the late 18th century.

transmit *see* PERMIT

transpire *see* SPIRIT

transport [LME] Transport is from Latin *transportare*, from *trans-* 'across' and *portare* 'carry'. The word's use to denote 'a means of transportation' arose in the use of **transport ships** to carry soldiers or convicts, and later army supplies. **Import** [LME] and

export [LME] are the carrying of goods in and out of the country.

transvestite *see* TRAVESTY

trappings [LME] Animal **traps** [OE] have nothing to do with trappings, which go back to Latin *drappus* 'cloth', the source of **draper**, **drab** [M16] originally undyed cloth, and **drapery** [LME]. In the 14th century trappings were an ornamental harness for a horse, but now people more often use the word in contexts such as 'the trappings of success' for the outwards signs or objects associated with a particular role or job.

trash [E16th] Popular culture is often called **trashy** [E17th], and this goes right back to the beginnings of trash's history—one of the first things that the word referred to was bad literature. It was originally a word for various kinds of refuse, including cuttings from a hedge, and domestic refuse became trash at the beginning of the 20th century. People have called others trash since the early 17th century—Shakespeare wrote in *Othello* 'I do suspect this trash / To be a party in this injury'; and in the USA **white trash** [M19th] is a derogatory term for poor white people living in the southern states. The verb is first recorded in the mid 18th century in the sense 'strip (sugar canes) of their outer leaves to encourage faster ripening'; the other senses ('vandalize', 'impair the quality of something') date from the 20th century.

trauma [L17th] This is an English use of a Greek word meaning literally 'wound'. It was transferred to the notion of a 'mental wound' in the late 19th century.

travel [ME] Even today travel can be hard work, and travel comes from Middle English **travail** 'painful or laborious effort'. The two forms were once interchangeable, and originated in an instrument of torture, called *trepalium* in Latin, that consisted of three stakes. Robert Louis Stevenson, himself a keen traveller, was the first to express the view that **it is better to travel hopefully than to arrive**, in 1881. The idea that **travel broadens the mind** appeared first in 1900.

travesty [M17th] Both travesty and **transvestite** go back to Latin *trans* 'across' and *vestire* 'to clothe', and in the theatre a **travesty role** is still one designed to be played by a cross-dressing performer. The earliest use of travesty, which came through French *travesti*, 'disguised', was 'dressed to appear ridiculous'. The usual modern sense, 'a false or absurd representation of something', developed from the word's application to literary parodies and burlesques. Academic interest in sexuality developed in Germany and Austria in the late 19th and early 20th centuries, and the immediate source of transvestite, recorded from the 1920s, was German *Transvestit*. *See also* INVEST

tray [OE] Late Old English *trīg* is from the Germanic base of **tree** [OE]. The primary sense may have been 'wooden container'. **Trough** [OE] had a primary meaning of 'wooden vessel' and is related. The notion of a downturn on a graph or similar representation dates from the late 19th century in meteorology, the early 20th century in economics, and generally (peaks and troughs) from the 1930s.

treachery *see* TREAT

treacle [ME] It is now a kind of syrup, but treacle was originally an antidote against poison. When the word entered medieval English from Old French *triacle*, which went back to Greek *thērion* 'wild beast', it was a term for an ointment made with many ingredients that counteracted venom. The idea of an antidote extended into that of a remedy or medicine, and later, by way of the sugar syrup used to make a medicine more palatable, into the current sense at the end of the 17th century. Lewis Carroll played on the healing sense when he wrote about treacle wells in *Alice in Wonderland*, for he was referring to a real, ancient healing well at Binsey just outside Oxford.

tread *see* TRADE

treason *see* TRADITION

transvestite trappings trash trauma travel

treasure [ME] This came through Old French from Greek *thēsauros* 'treasure, store, storehouse', also the source of *THESAURUS. A **treasure trove** [LME] is now a collection of valuable or pleasing things that is found unexpectedly, but it originally referred to valuables of unknown ownership that were found hidden, which were the property of the Crown. The term came from Anglo-Norman French *tresor trové* meaning literally 'found treasure'.

treat [ME] Treat is first recorded with the meanings 'negotiate' and 'discuss (a subject)'. It is from Old French *traitier*, from Latin *tractare* 'handle'. The sense 'event that gives great pleasure' dates from the mid 17th century, developing via the senses 'treatment of guests' and the entertainment you put on for them. Late Middle English **treatise** is also from Old French *traitier*, while **treaty** [LME], and **tract** [LME] are related.

tree *see* TRAY

trek [M19th] The **Boers** were originally Dutch settlers in South Africa, who got their name from the Dutch for 'countryman, farmer' (*see* BOOR). Between 1835 and 1837 large numbers of Boers, discontented with British rule in the Cape area of South Africa, migrated north and eventually founded the Transvaal Republic and the Orange Free State. This was **the Great Trek**, which largely introduced the Dutch word **trek** to the English-speaking world. It came from *trekken* 'to pull, travel', from which *TRACK may also derive. During the 19th century the word was restricted to South African contexts, but during the 20th migrated into international English for any long, arduous journey. The US science-fiction television programme *Star Trek* was not a success when it was first shown in 1966 and has given us **Trekkie** as a word for a Star Trek fan. The 'pull' sense of *trekken* lies behind the thing you pull on a gun, the **trigger** [E17th].

trellis [LME] This once referred to any latticed screen. It is from Old French *trelis*, from Latin *trilix* 'three-ply', from *tri-* 'three',

and *licium* 'warp thread'. This was used in France for a strong fabric and then something woven from wire. The word is found in gardening contexts from the early 16th century.

tremendous [M17th] Tremendous goes back to Latin *tremere* 'to tremble', and had the original sense of something that makes you **tremble** [ME]. **Trepidation** [LME] and **intrepid** [L17th] are from the related *trepidare* 'tremble'.

trend [OE] Old English *trendan* had the meaning 'revolve, rotate'. Of Germanic origin, it is related to *TRUNDLE. The sense 'turn in a specified direction' dates from the late 16th century, and developed into 'show a general tendency' in the mid 19th.

trepidation *see* TREMENDOUS

trews *see* TROUSERS

triad [M16th] Triad meaning 'set of three' goes back to Greek *tres* 'three'. The Chinese secret societies are called Triads from their Chinese name *San Ho Hui* which can be translated as 'tripe union society'. **Triangle** [LME] comes from the same word. The **eternal triangle** of romance dates from the early 20th century. *Trinitas* is the Latin for 'triad' and the source of **trinity** [ME]. The musical **trio** [E18th] comes from the Italian development of *tres*. **Triple** [ME] is from the same root; and **tripod** [E17th] is a three-footed device, from *tri-* 'three' *podes* 'feet'. **Trivet** [LME] comes from the Latin form of the word.

triage [E18th] This is an English use of a French word, from *trier* 'separate out'. The medical sense dates from the 1930s, from the military system of assessing the wounded on the battle field.

trial *see* TRY

triangle *see* TRIAD

tribe [ME] In the early days of ancient Rome the people fell into three political divisions. This division into 'three' (*tri-* in Latin) may be the origin of *tribus*, from

treasure treat tree trek trellis tremendous

which tribe descended, along with **tribunal** [LME], **tribune** [LME], **tribute** [ME], and **retribution** [LME] 'paying back'. The first uses of tribe in English referred to the twelve ancient tribes of Israel claiming descent from the twelve sons of Jacob. From tribute comes **tributary**, found from the 15th century for someone paying tribute. The sense of a smaller river adding its contribution to the big one developed from this in the early 19th century.

trice [LME] Unlike most *tri-* words, trice has nothing to do with 'three'. It comes from early Dutch *trisen* 'to pull sharply, hoist', and in the Middle Ages **at a trice** meant 'at one pull or tug' rather than 'in a moment, immediately'. By the late 17th century the original form of the expression had given way to the more familiar **in a trice**.

trick [LME] A medieval word from Old French *trichier* 'to deceive or cheat', which also gave us **treachery** [ME]. A 16th-century sense of the word was 'habit', which is where the expression **up to your old tricks** comes from. Children say **trick or treat** at Halloween when they call at houses, threatening to play a trick on the householder unless a treat is produced in the form of sweets or money. The phrase did not appear until the 1930s in the USA. *See also* HAT-TRICK

tricycle *see* BICYCLE

trident *see* TOOTH

trigger *see* TREK

trike *see* BICYCLE

trilby [L19th] Trilby was the heroine of George du Maurier's novel *Trilby*, published in 1894. In the stage version the Trilby character wore a soft felt hat with a narrow brim and indented crown, which was immediately dubbed a trilby. Trilby falls under the influence of a musician called Svengali, who trains her voice by hypnotizing her and makes her into a famous singer, although she had been tone-deaf before meeting him. A person who exercises a controlling or mesmeric

influence on another is consequently sometimes called a **Svengali**.

trim [OE] The history and development of this word are obscure, and shows how dependent we are on luck for the survival of the information we need. Trim appeared in Old English in the sense 'to make firm, arrange', but there is little record of it in the medieval period. From the 16th century, though, it burst on the scene to serve many purposes, relating to fitting out ships for sea, preparing a candle wick for use, repairing something, decorating clothing, and cutting away the unwanted parts of something. A trim ship was well equipped and in good condition, which gave us the sense of a slim and fit person having a trim figure. To a sailor to **trim a sail** means 'to adjust the sail of a boat'. On land to **trim your sails** came to mean 'to make changes to suit your new circumstances', from which we get a **trimmer** [L17th] for an unscrupulous person who adapts their views to the prevailing political trends.

trinity *see* TRIAD

trip [ME] The early Dutch word *trippen* 'to skip, hop' is the source of trip. The English word was initially used to describe not only stumbling by catching your foot on something, but also dancing and nimble movement. The noun meant 'a light lively movement' before it became 'a short journey', originally a sailor's term for a short sea journey. The sense 'hallucinatory experience caused by taking a drug' was first recorded in the late 1950s. *See also* FANTASTIC

triple, tripod *see* TRIAD

trite [M16th] The idea behind trite is one of wearing something away by use and perhaps also of causing irritation through repetition. The word first appeared in English in the mid 16th century, from a form of Latin *terere* 'to rub'. An old meaning, now obsolete, was 'physically worn away or frayed'.

triumph *see* TRUMP

trice   trick   tricycle   trident   trigger   trike

trivet *see* TRIAD

trivial [LME] Latin *trivium* meant 'a place where three roads meet', and it is from this that we get our word trivial. Medieval universities offered a basic introductory course involving the study of three subjects—grammar, rhetoric, and logic—known as the *trivium*. The earliest uses of trivial relate to this basic, low-level course, with the main modern meanings, 'commonplace, ordinary' and 'unimportant, slight', developing in the late 16th century. The plural of Latin *trivium* has also entered English as **trivia**. A crossroads, a place where not three but four roads meet, has a similar metaphorical relationship with *CRUCIAL, a word which means almost the exact opposite of trivial.

troll [LME] In Scandinavian folklore, trolls are ugly giants or dwarfs that usually live in caves. The word entered English in the early 17th century, and has no connection with the much earlier troll 'to fish by trailing a baited line along behind a boat', or 'to search'. Nowadays internet users also 'troll', or send a provocative email or newsgroup posting to provoke an angry response or flame mail. The origin of this **troll** is uncertain—its original sense was 'to stroll, roll', which might be connected to old French *troller* 'to wander here and there', or early German *trollen* 'to stroll'. It is probably the origin of **trolley** [E19th], originally a kind of low cart used for transporting goods such as fruit, vegetables, or fish. The trolley in **off your trolley**, is a kind of pulley that runs along an overhead track and transmits power to drive a tram. If a tram becomes disconnected from the pulley, it is no longer under control. A similar idea is found in to **go off the rails**, meaning 'to start behaving in an uncontrolled or unacceptable way', from the image of a train leaving the tracks or being derailed.

troop [M16th] Troop is from French *troupe*, formed from *troupeau*, a diminutive of medieval Latin *troppus* 'flock', probably of Germanic origin.

trophy [LME] Both **tropic** [LME] and trophy are ultimately from Greek *trepein* 'to turn'. In ancient Greece and Rome a trophy was a pile of the weapons of a defeated army set up as a memorial of a victory. The attractive young **trophy wife** of a successful older man, is a term first used in the late 1980s. A **tropic** is a 'turning point', a point on the path through the sky that the sun can be seen to take through the year where, at the solstice, it appears to turn back again towards the equator.

tropic *see* TROPHY

troth *see* PLIGHT

trouble [ME] Our word trouble comes, by way of Old French *truble*, from Latin *turbidus* 'disturbed, turbid', source of **turbid** [E17th], and related to **disturb** [ME], **perturb** [LME], and **turbulent** [M16th]. From the start, in the 13th century, it meant 'difficulty or problems'. 'Man is born unto trouble, as the sparks fly upward' is from the biblical book of Job who was a virtuous man that God tested by sending him many troubles. Most people now think of **the Troubles** in Northern Ireland as beginning in the early 1970s, but the same term applied to the unrest around the partition of Ireland in 1921, and in an 1880 glossary of words used in Antrim and Down **the Troubles** are defined as 'the Irish rebellion of 1641'. The first **troubleshooters** had a very specific occupation. In the early years of the 20th century they mended faults on telegraph or telephone lines.

trough *see* TRAY

trousers [E17th] Scottish Highlanders and Irishmen once wore a **trouse** or **trouses**, a kind of knee-length shorts whose name came from Irish *triús* or Scottish Gaelic *triubhas*. The same words gave us **trews** [M16th], once similar to the trouse but now close-fitting tartan trousers as worn by some Scottish regiments. In the early 17th century people started calling the trouse **trousers**, on the analogy of **drawers** (probably from their being things that you pull or draw on). Until the end of the 18th

century men in Europe wore tight breeches—looser trousers were adopted by the working classes during the French Revolution, and the style imported to Britain by dandies like Beau Brummell. The dominant member of a married couple **wears the trousers** now, and has done since the 1930s, but long before that the phrase was **wear the breeches**, recorded from the 16th century.
See also PANTS, TWEEZERS

trousseau [ME] The romantic trousseau conjures up an image of a blushing bride in flowing white or smart honeymoon outfit, but the original meaning was simply a bundle or package, and it did not acquire its modern meaning until the 1830s. The word derives from French *trousse*, an earlier form of which gave us **truss** [ME] 'a supporting framework', and 'a surgical support for a hernia'.

trout [OE] Late Old English *truht* is from late Latin *tructa*, based on Greek *trōgein* 'gnaw'. Use of the derogatory **old trout** for an elderly woman is found from the late 19th century.

trove *see* TREASURE

trow *see* TRUCE

trowel [ME] The word trowel is from Old French *truele*, an alteration of Latin *trulla* 'scoop'.

truant [ME] In the 13th century a truant was someone who begged out of choice rather than necessity, what the Elizabethans called 'a sturdy beggar'. The idea of voluntary idleness led to its application in the later medieval period to children staying away from school without permission. The word came from Old French, but is probably ultimately of Celtic origin, related to Welsh *truan* and Scottish Gaelic *truaghan* 'wretched'.

truck [ME] The truck that is a large road vehicle originally meant 'a wheel or pulley', and may be a shortening of **truckle** [LME], which once had the same sense but now only refers to a small barrel-shaped cheese.

It came from Latin *trochlea* 'wheel of a pulley'. To **have** (or **want**) **no truck with**, meaning 'to avoid dealings with', has no connection with the transportation of goods; here truck is from French *troquer* 'to barter'. Since the 1920s US English truck has had the slang sense 'to move or proceed'. **Keep on truckin'** was the caption, first used in 1967, of a series of cartoons by the US artist Robert Crumb.
See also JUGGERNAUT

true [OE] From the same root as **truce** [ME] and *TRUTH, this originally meant 'loyal or steadfast'. Over time this gradually led to the idea of being reliable or honest, and then to that of truthfulness. The idea behind **many a true word is spoken in jest** is found in Geoffrey Chaucer's *Canterbury Tales* in the late 14th century, but the modern form of the proverb first appeared in print in the 17th century.

truffle [L16th] This word for a type of fungus is probably via Dutch from obsolete French *truffle*, perhaps based on Latin *tubera*, the plural of *tuber* 'hump, swelling', also the source of **tuber** [L17th]. Use of the word in confectionery dates from the 1920s. The related verb *tumere* 'to swell' is the source of **tumult** [LME]

trump [E16th] The word trump, 'a playing card of the suit chosen to rank above the others', is an alteration of triumph, which was once used in the same sense. The Latin source of **triumph** [LME] *triumphus* probably came from Greek *thriambos* 'hymn to the god Bacchus'. In ancient Rome a triumph was the grand entry of a victorious general into the city. In some card games the trump suit is chosen before each game, while in others it is the suit of the last card dealt, which is turned over to show its face. This gives rise to the phrases **come** or **turn up trumps**, 'to produce a better outcome than expected', reinforced by the fact that a hand with many trump cards is likely to be a winning hand. In the expression **the last trump**, trump is a form of **trumpet** [ME]. The instrument had strong military associations and comes ultimately from

trousseau   trout   trove   trow   trowel   truant

the same source as trump. Officers making public announcements would sometimes blow a blast on a trumpet to get people's attention. To **blow your own trumpet** comes from the idea of going out into a public space and making an announcement about yourself.

truncate, truncheon *see* TRUNK

trunk [LME] Trunk comes via Old French from Latin *truncus* 'the main stem of a tree'. The word has branched out in several directions. The meaning 'a tree's main stem' is behind the sense 'the human body' and others with the notion of a central connection, such as **trunk road**. The 'chest, box' meaning arose because early trunks were made out of tree trunks. The circular shape of a tree trunk prompted another branch referring to cylindrical hollow objects, including, in the 16th century, the elephant's trunk. In the 16th and early 17th centuries men wore **trunk-hose**, full breeches extending to the upper thighs and sometimes padded, worn over tights. The style went out of fashion, but in the theatre actors wore short light breeches over tights, which they called **trunks**. In late 19th-century America men's shorts for swimming or boxing took over the name. **Truncheon** [ME] comes from the same root. In early use this referred to a piece broken off from, for example, a spear and was also a word for a cudgel. The word came to refer to a staff carried as a symbol of office from the late 16th century and eventually (late 19th century) to a short club carried by a police officer. **Truncate** [LME] is unconnected, being from Latin *truncare* 'maim'.

truss *see* TROUSSEAU

trustafarian *see* REGGAE

truth [OE] This comes from the same root as *TRUE and also originally suggested qualities of faithfulness and loyalty. Lord Byron was the first to popularize **truth is stranger than fiction**, in his poem *Don Juan* in 1823. The first verifiable instance of **truth is the first casualty of war** is an epigraph by

the British politician Arthur Ponsonby in 1918: 'When war is declared, Truth is the first casualty.' One of the adages of the Dutch humanist and scholar Erasmus (*c*.1466–1536), writing in Latin, was *in vino veritas*, translated as **there is truth in wine**, and this English version has continued in use, though the Latin form is probably more familiar. The idea itself goes back to Greek, and is attributed to the poet Alcaeus of the 6th century BC. *See also* PLIGHT

try [ME] From Old French *trier* 'to sift', source also of **trial** [E16th]. In rugby an act of touching the ball down behind the opposing goal line has been called a try since the 1840s. It got its name because a try gives the scoring side the right to try to kick a goal. The cliché **try anything once**, dates from the 1920s. The British conductor Sir Thomas Beecham (1879–1961) is generally credited with 'You should try everything once except incest and morris dancing', but the composer Sir Arnold Bax reported a similar comment in a 1943 autobiography.

Tsar *see* CAESAR

tsunami [L19th] The tsunami of Boxing Day 2004 made this Japanese word for a huge sea wave caused by an underwater earthquake known to everyone, replacing the misleading term tidal wave. It is formed from *tsu* 'harbour' and *nami* 'wave'. *See also* TORNADO, TYPHOON

tuber *see* TRUFFLE

tucker *see* BIB

Tuesday [OE] The ancient Germanic god Tiw is the source of Tuesday. When Germanic peoples came into contact with the Romans they realized that their god Tiw was similar to Mars, the Roman god of war whose day was the third of the week (and who appears in forms such as the French *Mardi*), and started to call that day 'Tiw's day' or Tuesday. Other days of the week were formed in a similar way, with **Wednesday** being Woden's day, **Thursday** Thor's day, and **Friday** Freya's day; Woden or Odin was the supreme god of the German and Scandinavian peoples, Thor the god of thunder, and Freya or Frigga the goddess of love and fertility.

tuft, tuft-hunter *see* TOFF

tuition [LME] 'Custody, care' was the early meaning of tuition which comes via Old French from Latin *tueri* 'to watch, guard'. Current senses to do with instruction date from the late 16th century. **Tutor** is from the same root and same date. *See also* PEDAGOGUE

tulip *see* TURBAN

tumbler [ME] The early sense of this was an acrobat, one who **tumbled** [ME]. The straight-sided drinking glass comes from tumble. In the 17th century tumblers had rounded bottoms and would not stand upright, presumably so that the drinker would have to keep holding the glass and would drink more.

tumult *see* TRUFFLE

tun, tunnel *see* TON

tuppence *see* TWO

turban [M16th] The words turban and tulip are from the same source. Turkish people compared the flower of the tulip to the shape of the turban and gave the plant the same name, *tūlbend*, which they took from Persian *dulband*. The tulip made a spectacular impression, and cost a spectacular amount of money when it came from Turkey into western Europe in the 16th century. At first forms such as *tulipan* and *tulban* existed alongside **turban** as the name of the headdress, whereas the name of the flower always appeared in the -*l*- form, and eventually monopolized that spelling.

turbid, turbulent *see* TROUBLE

tureen [M18th] The original form of tureen was **terrine**, from a French word for a large earthenware pot that goes back to Latin *terra* 'earth', source of *TERRACE, *TERRITORY, and many other words. From its arrival in the early 18th century terrine

referred both to a pot and its contents, but not long after its arrival the 'cooking pot' sense began to be spelled **tureen**, perhaps influenced by the city of Turin in north-western Italy.

turf [OE] The Old English word turf goes back to a root shared by *darbha* 'tuft of grass' in Sanskrit, the ancient language of northern India. The grass surface of a racecourse has led horseracing to be **the turf** since the mid 18th century. The turf in **surf-and-turf**, a dish containing both shellfish and steak, represents the lush prairies or meadows on which beef cattle graze and the bounty of the sea. Since the 1950s criminals or street gangs have their own turf, an area of personal territory, the source also of **turf wars** [1970s].

Turk *see* YOUNG

turkey [M16th] The turkey got its name because it had been brought to England by merchants from the eastern Mediterranean, whom the English called Turkey merchants because the whole area was then part of the Turkish Ottoman Empire. The new bird was called a Turkey bird or Turkey cock. Turkeys actually came from Mexico and were first brought back from there about 1520.

turn [OE] The origin of Old English turn is Latin *tornare* 'to turn', from *tornos*, the Greek word for a lathe. The sense 'a song or other short performance' developed in the early 18th century from the meaning 'an opportunity or obligation to do something', as in 'It's your turn', which is medieval. Card games and betting combine to give us **a turn-up for the book**, 'a completely unexpected event or occurrence'. Turn-up here refers to the turning up or over of a particular card in a game, while the book is one kept by a bookie to record bets made in a race. The leaf in to **turn over a new leaf**, 'to improve your behaviour or performance', is a sheet of paper in a book, not a part of a plant or tree. A **turncoat** is a person who deserts one party to join an opposing one. The term dates from the mid

16th century and is said to be a reference to a Duke of Saxony whose land was located between the French and Saxons, who were at war with each other. The Duke wore a reversible coat, one side of which was blue (the Saxon colour) and the other side white (the French colour), so that he could change his display of allegiance quickly should the need arise.

turnip *see* PARSNIP

turret *see* TOWER

turtle [M17th] English sailors gave the turtle its name in the 1650s. They probably based it on *tortue*, an early form of **tortoise** [LME], from French *tortue* and Spanish *tortuga* 'tortoise' of uncertain origin. A boat is said to **turn turtle** when it turns upside down, because it then looks a bit like the shell of a turtle, or because it is as helpless as a turtle flipped over on its back. **Mock turtle soup**, inspiration for the Mock Turtle in Lewis Carroll's *Alice in Wonderland*, is soup made with a calf's head, in imitation of turtle soup, once an important part of grand banquets. The turtle in **turtle dove** is a completely different word whose ultimate source is Latin *turtur*, an imitation of the bird's cooing. 'The time of the singing of birds is come, and the voice of the turtle is heard in our land' is from the biblical Song of Solomon, a reference to the fact that the turtle dove is a migratory bird.

tussle *see* HASSLE

tutor *see* TUITION

tutu [E20th] The female ballerina's costume gets its name from the French nursery. In French *tutu* is a child's alteration of *cucu*, an informal term for the bottom, from *cul* 'buttocks'. The outfit originally referred to was the short classical tutu, with a skirt projecting horizontally from the waist. The **leotard** sometimes worn by dancers gets its name from that of the French trapeze artist Jules Léotard (1830–1870).

twain [OE] An old form of *TWO. The comment **never the twain shall meet**, suggesting that two things are too different to exist alongside each other, quotes from 'The Ballad of East and West' (1892) by Rudyard Kipling: 'Oh, East is East, and West is West, and never the twain shall meet.'

twee [E20th] A child's pronunciation of *SWEET, recorded from the first decade of the 20th century. Originally twee was as complimentary as sweet, now it is intended as an insult, meaning 'excessively or affectedly quaint, pretty, or sentimental'.

tweed [M19th] Tweed was originally produced in Scotland, where it was called **tweel**, a Scots form of **twill** [ME], a word based on *TWO and like **twine** [OE] indicating two-ply yarn. Around 1830 a cloth merchant misread this as tweed, a mistake perpetuated by association with the River Tweed, part of which forms the border between England and Scotland. Tweed is traditionally worn by the English country gentry, and **tweedy** has been used since the early 20th century to suggest a robust, traditional kind of Englishness.

Tweedledum and Tweedledee

[E18th] The English poet John Byrom coined Tweedledee and Tweedledum in a satire of 1725 about the composers George Frederick Handel and Giovanni Battista Bononcini, musical rivals who were both enjoying success in London at the time. To **tweedle** [L17th] is to play a succession of shrill notes or to play an instrument carelessly. Lewis Carroll picked up the names and used them for two identical characters in *Through the Looking-Glass*, and now they apply generally to any pair of people or things that are virtually indistinguishable. **Twiddle** [M16th] is a variant of tweedle, and **twiddle your thumb**s dates from the late 19th century.

tweet *see* CHAT

tweezers [M17th] In the 17th century a **tweeze** was a case of surgical instruments. It appears to be a shortened form of *etweese*, a plural of *etui* [E17th], which was a term for a small ornamental case for holding needles, cosmetics, and other articles, that came from French. In the mid 17th century tweeze was extended to tweezer, while the plural tweezes became tweezers. Trouse became *TROUSERS in much the same way. In the 1930s tweeze was re-formed from tweezers to mean 'to pluck with tweezers'.

twelve, twenty *see* TWO

twiddle *see* TWEEDLE

twilight [LME] A medieval combination of *twi-*, a form of *TWO, and *LIGHT. What significance 'two' has here is not entirely clear, though perhaps there is the idea of half-light, between day and night. In Scandinavian and German mythology **the twilight of the gods** is the destruction of the gods and the world in a final conflict with the powers of evil. English also uses the German and Old Norse equivalents *Götterdämmerung* and *Ragnarök*, the first of which is the title of the last opera in Richard Wagner's Ring cycle. Today, a **twilight zone** is primarily an urban area in a state of dilapidation or economic decline, but the term will forever be associated with the US television series *The Twilight Zone*, first shown in 1959. Each episode of the series offered a self-contained story with a science fiction or horror theme.

twill *see* TWEED

twin *see* TWO

twine *see* TWEED

twinge *see* THONG

twinkle [OE] As well as its original sense 'to sparkle, glimmer', twinkle also meant 'to wink, blink the eyes' from the 14th to the early 19th century. The meaning 'the time taken to wink or blink'—a very short time, in other words—is just as old, but it survives only as **in the twinkling of an eye**, 'very quickly'. This is probably because the phrase appears in various passages in the Bible, including Corinthians: 'In a moment, in the twinkling of an eye, at the last trump.' A similar expression containing the same idea is **in the blink of an eye**.

twit [OE] The kind of twit that is a silly or foolish person dates only from the 1930s and comes from an English dialect use that meant 'a tale-bearer'. It may come from twit in the sense 'to tease or taunt someone, especially in a good-humoured way', which is a shortening of Old English *ætwītan* 'reproach with'.

twitter *see* CHAT

two [OE] An Old English word from the same source as *TWAIN, **twelve**, **twenty**, *TWILIGHT, and **twin** (all OE), with an ancient root shared by Latin and Greek *duo*, source of **double** [ME], **duo** [L16th], **duplicate** [LME], and other words. The formula **it takes two to**...appeared in the 1850s in **it takes two to make a quarrel**, and in the 1940s in **it takes two to make a bargain** (*see also* TANGO). The saying **two's company, three's a crowd** was originally **two's company, three's none**, in the 1730s. Before the British currency was decimalized in 1971 twopence or **tuppence** was a standard sum. To **add** or **put in your twopenn'orth** is to contribute your opinion; **twopenn'orth** is a contraction of **twopennyworth** meaning 'an amount costing two pence', used also for 'a small or insignificant amount'.

tycoon [M19th] A tycoon is now a powerful businessman, but was originally a Japanese ruler, for it comes from Japanese *taikun* 'great lord'. Foreigners applied the title tycoon to the shogun, or military commander of Japan, in power between 1857 and 1868, and in the same period Americans nicknamed President Abraham Lincoln 'the Tycoon'. The word then extended to any important or dominant person, from the 1920s especially to a business magnate.

tyke [LME] The word tyke (from Old Norse *tík* 'bitch') was first a term for a dog, especially a mongrel. It quickly became a rough man and then a **Yorkshire tyke**, 'a person from Yorkshire', before being used as an affectionate term for a cheeky child. In Australia and New Zealand tyke is an offensive term for a Roman Catholic. This is an alteration of **Taig**, a Northern Ireland Protestant's insulting name for a Catholic, from the Irish name *Tadhg*, which has been used since the 17th century as a nickname for an Irishman.

typhoid *see* STEW

typhoon [L16th] The fierce tropical storm brings together two sources, Arabic *tūfān*, which may be from Greek *tuphōn* 'whirlwind', and Chinese dialect *tai fung* 'big wind'. The Portuguese picked up the first in the Indian oceans, while merchants and sailors in the China seas would have encountered the Chinese expression. A wide variety of spellings appeared before the word finally settled down into typhoon in the 19th century. *See also* TORNADO, TSUNAMI

typhus *see* STEW

tyrant [ME] In English a tyrant has always been a cruel and oppressive ruler, but in ancient Greece, where the word comes from, this was not originally the case. In the 6th and 7th centuries BC a tyrant, or

turannos, was simply a man who seized power unlawfully. The **tyrannosaurus** is the 'tyrant lizard'. The fossilized remains of this large carnivorous dinosaur were found in North America at the beginning of the 20th century, and the palaeontogist H.F. Osborn gave it the modern Latin name *Tyrannosaurus* in 1905, taking it from Greek *turannos* 'tyrant' and *sauros* 'lizard'. The full name, *Tyrannosaurus rex*, adds Latin *rex* 'king'.

tyre [LME] In the past wheelwrights strengthened the outside of the wheels of carts with curved pieces of iron plate called the tire, probably a shortened form of **attire** (an ME word originally meaning to put in order), because the tyre was the 'clothing' of the wheel. Originally the spellings **tire** and tyre were interchangeable, but in the 17th century **tire** became the settled spelling, which has remained the spelling in the USA. In Britain the development of the pneumatic tyre seemed to require some differentiation from the metal rim, and **tyre** was revived.

typhoid   typhoon   typhus   tyrant   tyre

über-, überbabes *see* GERMAN WORD PANEL

ubiquitous [M19th] This was formed from Latin *ubique* meaning 'everywhere', from *ubi* 'where'.

ugly [ME] The word ugly came into English in the 13th century from Old Norse *uggligr* 'to be dreaded', and had a stronger meaning than it does now, 'frightful or horrible'. In Hans Christian Andersen's fairy tale the 'ugly duckling' is a cygnet hatched by a duck that is jeered at until it turns into a graceful swan. The tale appeared in English in a translation of 1846, and **ugly duckling** was soon in use for people. The American entertainer Danny Kaye brought the idea to a wider audience when he wrote and sang 'The Ugly Duckling' in a 1952 biographical film of Andersen's life. In *Cinderella*, the heroine has two ugly and unpleasant stepsisters who make her work in the kitchen. Since the late 19th century an **ugly sister** has been an unattractive person or thing or an undesirable counterpart. More recent is the **ugly American**, the American who behaves offensively abroad. The original context of the phrase is that of Americans who adversely affect the lives of the people they live among in southeast Asia. It comes from the title of a 1958 book by William Lederer and Eugene Burdick, which was released as a film starring Marlon Brando in 1963.

ukulele [L19th] The ukulele is a development of a Portuguese instrument called the *machete* that appeared in Hawaii in the late 1870s. Around that time a British army officer, Edward Purvis, acted as vice-chamberlain of the court of King Kalakaua. According to the story, local Hawaiians gave Purvis, a small, energetic, and agile man, the nickname *ukulele* 'jumping flea'. When he took up the instrument he played with typical liveliness and with such success that they started to use his nickname as the name of the instrument.

ulna *see* BOW

ultimate [M17th] Ultimate is from Latin *ultimus* 'last'. **The ultimate** meaning 'the last word' (**the ultimate in fashion**) dates from the late 17th century. **Penultimate** [L17th] is *paene* 'almost' and *ultimus*.

ultramarine [M17th] The brilliant bright blue pigment ultramarine originally came from lapis lazuli, a rock brought from Afghanistan that was more precious than gold. Latin *ultramarinus* meant 'beyond the sea', and forms descended from it became the name for the pigment in most European languages. It was not until the early 18th century that a reliably fast, and much cheaper, alternative deep blue was discovered by accident by a man called Diesbach who lived in Berlin. This was then the capital of Prussia, and so the colour became known as **Prussian Blue**.

umbrella [E17th] An umbrella is strictly a sunshade. The word came from Italy in the early 17th century, and goes back to Latin *umbra* 'shade'. Britain's wet weather meant that not much more than twenty years after the word's first appearance an **umbrella** became something to keep the rain off. Another word from *umbra* is **umbrage** [LME], as in **take umbrage** or take offence. An early sense was 'a shadowy outline', which then gave rise to 'a ground for suspicion' and led to the current sense.

umpire *see* PAIR

umpteen [E20th] Signals regiments in the army once used **umpty** to indicate the dash in Morse code (the dot was **iddy**). One slang dictionary states that this began in India, as a way of teaching the Morse system to Indian troops. The military term may be behind the use of umpty for an indefinite large number, recorded from the late 19th century and developing into **umpteen**, on the model of thirteen or fourteen, in the early 1900s.

unanimous [E17th] This is based on Latin *unanimus*, from *unus* 'one' and *animus* 'mind', giving 'of one opinion'.

uncanny [L16th] The Scots originally used uncanny, just as they did its positive equivalent **canny**, 'shrewd, cautious', 'clever' or 'nice, pleasant'. Uncanny has always had overtones of the occult, and originally implied 'malignant or malicious', but during the 19th century the word left Scotland to develop its usual modern meaning 'mysterious, weird, strange'.

uncle [ME] Both uncle and **avuncular** [M19th] came through Old French from Latin *avunculus* 'uncle on the mother's side'. In the late 16th century people started misinterpreting an uncle as a **nuncle**, and **uncle** developed a parallel form **nuncle**— the opposite of the process seen in *ADDER, *APRON, and umpire (*see* PAIR). In Shakespeare's *King Lear* the Fool addresses his employer Lear as 'nuncle'. The expression **Uncle Tom Cobley and all** comes from an old song called 'Widdicombe Fair', dating from around 1800. The song lists the men's names, ending with 'Uncle Tom Cobley and all'. The independent use of the phrase itself did not develop until around a century later, in the 1930s. **Uncle Sam** has personified the government or people of the USA since the early 19th century. The name is probably based on the initials US. Since the 1920s **Uncle Tom** has been an insulting and offensive name for a black man considered to be excessively obedient or servile to whites. The original 'Uncle Tom' was an elderly slave who was the central figure of Harriet Beecher Stowe's 1852 anti-slavery novel *Uncle Tom's Cabin*. *See also* DUTCH

uncouth [OE] A word that originally meant 'unknown'. For much of the history of uncouth, most people would not have used or understood its opposite, **couth**. This originally meant 'known' but was later only used in Scottish English, for 'kind' or

'comfortable'. **Uncouth**, though, developed a fully independent life. It came to refer to unsophisticated language or style in the late 17th century, and then to uncultured or ill-mannered people or behaviour. In 1896 the English essayist and critic Max Beerbohm (1872–1956) was the first to use couth as a deliberate opposite of uncouth meaning 'cultured, well-mannered'. **Ungainly** [E17th] developed in a similar way. There is a word **gainly**, but it has never been common and its original meaning, 'suitable, fitting', now occurs only in Scottish dialect. Gainly came from the old word **gain**, which was used especially in the senses 'kindly' and 'convenient', and is of Scandinavian origin.

unction [LME] This is from Latin *unctio*, from *unguere* 'anoint', also the source of **unguent** [LME], and via French of **anoint** [ME] and **ointment** [ME]. The phrase **extreme unction** in the Roman Catholic Church refers to a final anointing of a sick person in danger of death. **Unctuous** had the early sense 'greasy; like an ointment', which rapidly developed into 'rich'. The sense 'having spiritual unction' developed in the mid 18th century, but rapidly developed the sense that this was hypocritical.

underwrite [LME] This is first recorded in the literal sense 'sign at the bottom of a document', what an insurer would do at the bottom or end of an insurance document. Nowadays the important thing is that they are guaranteeing to pay a certain sum if something is damaged or lost. In business contexts like these, underwrite was probably a direct translation of Latin *subscribere* 'to write underneath', the source of **subscribe** [LME], which people originally used in the same way.

undulate *see* WATER

ungainly *see* UNCOUTH

unguent *see* UNCTION

uni *see* UNIVERSITY

unicycle *see* BICYCLE

unanimous uncanny uncle uncouth unction

uniformity [LME] This is from Latin *uniformis* 'of one form'. **Uniform** [M16th] had the same meaning, until the modern sense of clothing of a fixed style worn by each member of a group developed in the mid 18th century.

Union Jack *see* JACK

unique, unison, unity *see* ONE

unkempt [LME] People have only **combed** their hair since around 1400; before that they would have kembed it and their hair would have been **kempt**. These are forms of the old word kemb, which was eventually replaced by the related word **comb**, an Old English word which may have the underlying sense of 'tooth'. The term has survived, though, sometimes in the form kempt but especially in **unkempt**, which has come to mean 'untidy or *DISHEVELLED' rather than 'uncombed'.

unravel [E17th] The Dutch were the first to **ravel**, which originally meant both 'to entangle' and 'to disentangle'. In the early 17th century **unravel** added to the existing complexity. You might think that ravel would then have settled down as its opposite, 'to entangle', but that is not what happened, and ravel and unravel usually have the same meaning.

untold *see* TELL

unwieldy [LME] The early meaning recorded was 'lacking strength, infirm'. The word is composed of the prefix *un-* 'not' and *wieldy* in the obsolete sense 'active', from the Old English **wield** 'rule, direct'. Unwieldy has meant 'huge and awkward in shape' since the late 16th century.

upbraid [OE] Late Old English *upbrēdan* meant 'allege (something) as a basis for censure', based on braid in the obsolete sense 'brandish' thus giving a notion of holding something up for disapproval. The current sense 'find fault with' is Middle English.

uproar [E16th] The origins of uproar have no connection with roaring. It came from

Dutch, from *up* 'up' and *roer* 'confusion'. It sounded as though it could be a native English form, and people associated the second element with roar, shifting the meaning from its original sense of 'rebellion, uprising' to 'loud confused noise'.

uranium [L18th] A rare radioactive metal, uranium is found in the mineral pitchblende. The German chemist Martin Klaproth isolated the metal and called it uranium after the planet **Uranus**, which the astronomer Sir William Herschel had discovered less than a decade before, in 1781.

urbane [M16th] This word was first used in the sense 'urban'; it comes from Latin *urbanus* 'belonging to the city', from *urbs* 'city', the source of **urban** [E17th] and **conurbation** [E20th]. **Suburban** appears in the early 17th century used literally for 'relating to a **suburb**' (an LME word meaning 'outside the city'). The disparaging sense appears in 1817 with Byron's 'vulgar, dowdyish, and suburban'.

urchin [ME] An urchin was originally a hedgehog, and the name, based on Latin *hericius* 'hedgehog', is still used in some English dialects. People started applying urchin to poor, raggedly dressed children in the mid 16th century, though this did not become common until more than 200 years later. As a name for a marine invertebrate **sea urchin** comes from the original sense, referring to the spines on its shell.

Urdu *see* HORDE

urgent [LME] This word comes via Old French, from Latin *urgere* 'press, drive', which also gave us **urge** [M16th].

usher [LME] The primary function of an usher was originally to be a doorkeeper, and the word is based on Latin *ostium* 'door'. The duties of an usher extended to showing people to their seats, as ushers in a cinema still do, and from the mid 16th century into the 19th an usher could also be an assistant schoolmaster. The use of usher for someone assisting people

Crossing the pond

*New words and phrases have been slipping into English from the USA
almost since the birth of the nation more than two hundred years ago.
Purists may bemoan Americanisms, but **US** culture, particularly through
business and entertainment, continues to enliven the language.*

I N 1935 the BBC correspondent Alistair Cooke (1908–2004) remarked in
his weekly *Letter from America* broadcast that the average Briton uses
dozens of Americanisms every day. Some American expressions have
been in English for much longer than that. In the early 19th century a
blizzard was 'a sharp blow or knock' or 'a shot' in the USA, and probably
arose as an imitation of the sound of a blow. The sense 'a severe snowstorm'
followed in the 1850s. At the start of the same century a **rowdy** was a rough,
lawless man living out in the backwoods, the remote forests beyond settled
areas. The modern meaning 'noisy and disorderly' came about in the 1840s
as a description of these people's typical manner.

You say **sidewalk**, we say **pavement**, you say *DIAPER, we say **nappy**—and
as for *BUM and **fanny**, 'don't even go there'. British and US often have
different words for the same thing, and in many cases the US words actually
originated in Britain. One example is **fall** for *AUTUMN, and another is
faucet, a medieval word from French *fausset* which has fallen out of use in
Britain but is the usual US term for a *TAP.

From *JAZZ and blues to rock, *PUNK and *RAP, practically all the terms for
popular music are American, as is the language of films. Americans rejected
the French word *CINEMA in favour of the more straightforward **movies**,
recorded from 1903, and **picture house** or **movie theatre**.

Students are fond of a **stunt**, a word that originated as US college slang
towards the end of the 19th century. The students first used it to mean 'a
daring or athletic feat', but it is not clear where they got it from. In British
English the word was first used by soldiers to mean 'an attack or advance',
and by airmen in reference to aerobatics.

Word-watchers in the USA noted **burger** in the late 1930s and 1940s. It
must have been used mainly in speech and on menus, as examples of it in
print do not appear until the 1960s. It is a shortening of **hamburger**,
recorded since the 1880s, which was originally a **Hamburger steak**, named
after the German city of Hamburg. The association with Hamburg began
to be lost, and as early as 1940 ham had given way to beef, with the
beefburger leaving no doubt as to its main ingredient. The development
of **burger** as a separate word was probably influenced by the need to
combat the restrictions on meat-eating imposed by rationing in 1943. This
led to recipes for liver burgers, lamb burgers, veal burgers, and even
potato burgers being published in articles and advertisements of that year.
The accompanying chips are another source of confusion, as chips in the

USA are what the British would call crisps, and chips are French fries to the Americans.

Yankee appeared first as an individual's nickname in the late 17th century, and may be from Dutch *Janke*, a pet form of *Jan* 'John'. In the mid 18th century it became a general name for a person from New England or any of the northern states, and during the Civil War Confederate soldiers applied it to their Federal opponents. Outside the USA people use **Yankee** or **Yank** indiscriminately for any American.

A **dollar** was originally a German silver coin, one that historians now call a **thaler**. The name comes from German *Thaler* or *Taler*, short for *Joachimsthaler*, which was a coin from the silver mine of Joachimsthal ('Joachim's valley'), now called Jáchymov, in the Czech Republic. People later applied the term to a coin used in the Spanish American colonies and also traded widely in British North America at the time of the American War of Independence. The new nation adopted **dollar** as the name of its monetary unit after achieving independence. Inflation is to blame for **the sixty-four thousand dollar question**—it was originally **the sixty-four dollar question**. The top prize in the 1940s quiz show *Take It or Leave It* was at first $64, but by the 1950s had increased to $64,000. Nowadays, something which is not known and on which a great deal depends is the sixty-four thousand dollar question.

See also BLUE, GERRYMANDER, MACARONI, OK, ROCK, SILVER, NATIVE AMERICAN WORD PANEL

at a wedding was originally American, from the late 19th century.

usual [ME] The English words **use** and usual are both medieval and derived from Latin *usus* 'a use'. People have used drugs or been drug **users** since the late 1920s, although they could equally be said to **abuse** [LME], 'use in the wrong way', them. **User-friendly** is recorded since 1977. **The Usual Suspects** is the title of a film released in 1995. It comes from a line in the Humphrey Bogart film *Casablanca* (1942): 'Major Strasser has been shot. Round up the usual suspects.' **Utility** [LME] is from the same root.

utmost [OE] Old English *ūt(e)mest* meant 'outermost'. The phrase **one's utmost** meaning 'one's very best' dates from the early 17th century. *See* UTTER

utopia [M16th] The English scholar and statesman Sir Thomas More wrote *Utopia* in Latin in 1516, depicting an imaginary island enjoying a perfect social, legal, and political system. The name implies that such an ideal place exists 'nowhere', as More created it from Greek *ou* 'not', and *topos* 'place' the source of terms such as **topography** [M17th], the arrangement of the physical features of an area. In the 17th century other writers started using utopia for other imaginary places where everything is perfect. The opposite of a utopia is a **dystopia** where everything is as bad as possible, a word formed in the late 18th century from Greek *dus-* 'bad', as if More had formed the word from Greek *eu-* 'good'. **Cacotopia** or **kakotopia** [E19th] are less popular alternatives to dystopia. *Topia* has recently come to be used as a combining form for new words such as **ecotopia**, an ideal ecological world; **motopia**, a slightly misleading term as it means an ideal world where the use of cars is limited; **pornotopia**, the ideal setting for pornography; **queuetopia**, a far from ideal world of long

urchin   Urdu   urgent   usher   usual

queues; and **subtopia**, the ideal suburban world.

utter [OE] There are two utters in English. Old English, *ūttra* meaning 'outer', is the comparative of *ūt* 'out', just as **inner** is of **in**; it was in very frequent use in this sense from around 1400 to 1620 (Milton *Paradise Lost*: 'Drive them out From all Heav'ns bounds into the utter Deep'). The sense 'extreme, complete' became very common from around 1515 (Shakespeare *Henry VI, Part 1*: 'The utter losse of all the Realme'). The other utter is from Middle Dutch. An early, now obsolete use, was 'put (goods) on to the market, sell'; later meaning 'circulate (money) as legal tender' and 'publish'. The basic notion is one of 'put forth' which is carried over into the meaning 'declare, speak'.

utility   utmost   utopia   utter

vacation [LME] People did not really have holidays in the Middle Ages, and vacation was freedom or rest from work or occupation. The root of the word is Latin *vacare* 'to be unoccupied', source also of **vacancy** [L16th], **vacant** [ME], and **vacate** [M17th]. The vacation then became the fixed time between terms when lawyers and university teachers vacate their premises and are free from formal duties. In North America it is the usual word for a holiday, a sense first used in the 1870s; a holiday is normally a specific national holiday such as Thanksgiving.

vaccine [L18th] The English physician Edward Jenner (1749–1823) knew the folk tradition that milkmaids did not catch smallpox, and speculated that this might be because they had come into contact with the virus causing cowpox, a disease whose effect on humans resembles mild smallpox. In 1796 he deliberately infected an eight-year-old boy, James Phipps, with small amounts of cowpox, and when the medical world rejected the successful result he repeated the experiment on several other children, including his own baby son. In 1798, writing in Latin, Jenner referred to cowpox as *variolae vaccinae*, from *vaccus* 'cow', and the beginning of the 19th century saw the words vaccine, **vaccinate**, **vaccination,** and the beginning of the end of a deadly and disfiguring disease.

vacuum [M16th] This modern Latin word is from Latin *vacuus* 'empty', a base shared by mid 17th-century **vacuous** meaning, in early examples, 'empty of matter'. 'Unintelligent' became one of the word's meanings in the mid 19th century.

vagabond, vagary *see* VAGUE

vagina *see* VANILLA

vague [M16th] A number of English words descend from Latin *vagari* 'to wander' and *vagus* 'wandering'. In the 16th century vague applied the idea of a 'wandering' mind to someone who cannot think or communicate clearly. A **vagabond** [ME] was originally just a **vagrant** [LME], someone who roams from place to place

without a settled home, until it acquired the additional suggestion of 'an unprincipled or dishonest man'. Before it came to refer to impulsive changes or whims, as in 'the vagaries of fashion', **vagary** [L16th] was used to mean 'to wander'.

vain *see* VANITY

valentine [LME] Valentine was the name of two early Italian martyrs, whose feasts were celebrated on St Valentine's Day, 14 February. It became associated with lovers in the Middle Ages, perhaps because of an old belief that birds mate on that day, perhaps a survival of the pagan fertility festival of Lupercalia celebrated on the 15th.

valet [LME] Rich men who could afford to employ a valet to look after their clothes had to be careful that he was also not a **varlet** [M16th], 'an unprincipled man', as the words are essentially the same. French *valet* 'attendant' and its early variant *varlet* are related to **vassal** [LME], from medieval Latin *vassallus* 'retainer', which derived from a Celtic word. The first valets were 15th-century footmen who acted as attendants on a horseman.

valiant [ME] Early senses included 'robust' and well-built'. The source is Old French *vailant*, based on Latin *valere* 'be strong'. The sense 'courage' came in late Middle English. The same Latin source gives **valour** [LME] which at first referred to 'worth derived from personal qualities or rank' and later (towards the end of the 16th century) to 'courage', and **valid** [L16th]. Via French *valoir* 'be worth' we also get **value** [ME].

valve [LME] Latin *valva* meant a leaf of a door and valve entered the language with this sense. Towards the end of the 18th century it was used to describe a door or flap controlling the flow of water and modern senses developed from this.

vamoose [M19th] The word vamoose used as an informal word for 'depart' is from Spanish *vamos* 'let us go'.

vamp [ME] From around 1200 the vamp was the part of a stocking that covered the foot and ankle, and from the 17th century the upper front part of a boot or shoe. The word comes from an early form of French *avantpied*, from *avant* 'before' and *pied* 'foot' (*compare* **vanguard** at CARAVAN). One of the cobbler's regular tasks was to replace vamps, and from the late 16th century the job could be described as **vamping** boots and shoes (revamp is only found from the mid 19th century). This cobbling work gave rise to a general sense 'to improvise' and to **vamp up**, 'to repair or improve'. The 'improvise' sense survives in jazz and popular music, where to vamp is to repeat a short, simple passage of music. The vamp who uses her sexual attraction to exploit men is an early 20th-century shortening of *VAMPIRE.

vampire [M18th] The best-known vampire is Count Dracula in *Dracula* by Bram Stoker, but these blood-sucking corpses of folklore had caught the public imagination long before the book was published in 1897. They had appeared in English since the mid 18th century, and in 1819 *The Vampyre* by John William Polidori had been a huge popular success. The word is from Hungarian *vampir*, perhaps from Turkish *uber* 'witch'. The 20th-century film industry gave vampires and vampirism a great publicity boost, as well as introducing the *VAMP or **vampish** heroine.

van *see* CARAVAN

vandal [M16th] In the 4th and 5th centuries AD the Vandals were a Teutonic people who ravaged Gaul, Spain, and North Africa, and sacked Rome in 455. In Latin the name for a Vandal was *Vandalus*, which is

also behind **Andalusia**, the southernmost region of Spain. The Romans overthrew the Vandals in 533 at the battle of Tricamarum, and like most victors set about discrediting their opponents, with the result that the Vandals were branded as destroyers of anything beautiful or worthy of preservation. Our modern sense evolved in the 17th century, and **vandalism** in the 18th. The Goths suffered the opposite fate. They were another Germanic tribe who invaded other parts of Europe in the same period. When **Gothic** was applied to medieval architecture in the mid 17th century it was often used disparagingly, but once the style came back into fashion it became approving.

vane [LME] This word for a 'broad blade (driven by the wind)' is a dialect variant of obsolete *fane* 'banner', of Germanic origin.

vanguard *see* CARAVAN

vanilla [M17th] This word for a flavouring is from Spanish *vainilla* 'pod', a diminutive of *vaina* 'sheath, pod', from Latin *vagina* 'sheath', also source of **vagina** [L17th]. The spelling change was due to association with French *vanille*. Since the 1970s the word has been used to mean 'plain, basic, conventional' from the popular perception of vanilla as the basic or usual flavour of ice-cream.

vanish *see* VANITY

vanity [ME] In early use vanity meant 'futility, worthlessness', with the idea of being conceited recorded a century later. This is the quality condemned in 'Vanity of vanities; all is vanity' from the biblical book of Ecclesiastes. The source of the word is Latin *vanus* 'empty, without substance', also the source of **vain** [ME] and **vanish** [ME]. In *The Pilgrim's Progress* by John Bunyan, published in 1678, **Vanity Fair** is held in the town of Vanity, through which pilgrims pass on their way to the Eternal City. All kinds of 'vanity', things of no real value, were on sale at the fair. The 19th century took the name Vanity Fair to represent the world as a place of frivolity and idle amusement, most notably in Thackeray's novel *Vanity Fair* (1847–48). *Vanity Fair* has been the title of four magazines since the 1850s, in particular the current US one founded in 1914. From its earliest appearance in around 1300 vain has meant 'lacking real worth, worthless'. To **take someone's name in vain**, 'to use someone's name in a way that shows disrespect', echoes the third of the biblical Ten Commandments: 'Thou shalt not take the name of the Lord thy God in vain.' Since the late 17th century vain has also described someone who has a high opinion of their own appearance.

vanquish *see* VICTORY

vapour [LME] This comes from Latin *vapor* 'steam, heat'. **Evaporate** [LME] comes from the Latin for 'to change into vapour', *evaporare*. Latin *Vapidus* 'savourless', source of **vapid** [M17th], is probably related. *See also* HYSTERIA

vardo *see* ROMANY WORD PANEL

variety [LME] Latin *varius* 'diverse' was the source not only of variety, in the late 15th century, but also of **variable** [LME], **variegated** [M17th], **various** [LME], and **vary** [ME]. The **variety show** that consists of a series of different types of act is particularly associated with the British music halls, but the first examples of the term are from the USA where variety was first performed in saloons in front of a heavy-drinking male clientele, but when cleaned up and staged in more legitimate theatres it was transformed into *VAUDEVILLE. We have the 18th-century English poet William Cowper to thank for the familiar proverb **variety is the spice of life**. His poem 'The Task' contains the line: 'Variety's the very spice of life, / That gives it all its flavour.' The dramatist Aphra Behn, who had a similar idea around a century earlier, might possibly have inspired him. Her version, from the play *The Rover*, reads: 'Variety is the very soul of pleasure.'

varlet *see* VALET

varmint *see* VERMILION

varnish [ME] Varnish is from Old French *vernis*, from medieval Latin *veronix* 'fragrant resin,' which comes from medieval Greek *berenikē* from *Berenice*, the name of a town in Cyrenaica, a region of Libya.

vary *see* VARIETY

vassal *see* VALET

vaudeville [M18th] Olivier Basselin was a 15th-century Frenchman from Vau de Vire, Normandy, who composed songs reputedly given the name *chansons du Vau de Vire*, or 'songs of the valley of Vire'. This was adapted to French *ville* 'town' and became *vau de ville* and later *vaudeville*, which was applied to a light popular song sung on the stage, the first meaning of vaudeville in English in the mid 18th century.

vault *see* REVOLVE

veer *see* GYRATE

vegetable [LME] The early use was adjectival in the sense 'growing as a plant', from late Latin *vegetabilis* 'animating'. The noun dates from the late 16th century. Related words include **vegetative** [LME]; **vegetation** [M16th]; and **vegetate** [E17th]. The slang use **veg out** meaning 'pass the time in mindless activity' arose in the 1980s. **Vegetarian** is an irregular formation of the mid 19th century; the abbreviation **veggie** dates from the 1970s.

vehicle [E17th] Vehicle is from Latin *vehiculum*, from *vehere* 'carry'.

veil [ME] Our word veil is from Latin *vela*, plural of *velum* 'sail, covering, veil'. The first uses refer to the headdress of a nun, and **take the veil**, or become a nun, appears about a hundred years later. Christian brides have worn veils since around the 3rd century, taking the custom from ancient Rome. The expression **beyond the veil**, 'in a mysterious or hidden state or place', comes from the Bible. In ancient times the veil was the piece of precious cloth separating the innermost sanctuary from the rest of the Jewish Temple in Jerusalem. The idea soon

vanquish   vapour   vardo   variety   varlet

developed of this cloth representing a barrier between this life and the unknown state of existence after death, giving rise to the current phrase. To **draw a veil over** something dates from the early 18th century, and is the opposite of **reveal** [LME] which comes from Latin *revelare* 'lay bare' in the sense of 'lifting the veil'.

velocipede *see* BICYCLE

velvet [ME] Velvet is noted for its smoothness and softness. Latin *villus*, 'tuft, down', is the source of it and of **velour** [E18th]. **An iron fist in a velvet glove**, meaning 'firmness or ruthlessness cloaked in outward gentleness', has been current in English since the 1830s when it appeared as a saying of Napoleon's. People gave the name **velvet revolution** to the relatively smooth change from Communism to a Western-style democracy in Czechoslovakia at the end of 1989. The similarly trouble-free division of that country into Slovakia and the Czech Republic in 1992 was the **velvet divorce**.

venal [M17th] This adjective meaning 'motivated by susceptibility to bribery' was initially used in the sense 'available for purchase', referring to merchandise or a favour. Latin *venalis* is the source, from *venum* 'thing for sale'.

vendetta [M19th] Corsicans and Sicilians were the first to pursue vendettas. The word is Italian, and goes back to Latin *vindicare* 'to claim, avenge', the source *REVENGE.

vendor [L16th] Vendor and **vend** [E17th] go back to Latin *vendere* 'sell'. The first **vending machines** appeared at the end of the 19th century.

veneer [E18th] The earliest form of veneer was *fineer*. It came into English through German *furnieren* from Old French *furnir* 'to furnish', and so is related to **furnish** [LME] and **furniture** [E16th]. The idea behind it is that of 'furnishing' a piece of furniture with a thin surface.

vent, ventilate *see* WIND

ventriloquist [M17th] Ventriloquists speak with their belly—the word is based on Latin *venter* 'belly' and *loqui* 'to speak', from which **elocution** [E16th], **eloquent** [LME], and **loquacious** [L17th] also derive. Originally a ventriloquist was a person appearing to speak from their abdomen because of spiritual possession. For someone who practises the skill for public entertainment it dates from just before 1800.

venue *see* REVENUE

veranda [E18th] This is from Hindi *varaṇḍā*, which was borrowed from Portuguese *varanda* 'railing, balustrade'.

verb, verbal *see* WORD

verboten *see* GERMAN WORD PANEL

verb sap *see* WORD

verderer *see* FOREST

verdict [ME] After the Norman Conquest, French became the language of the law in England and many French legal terms made their way into English. Verdict came immediately from French, but goes back to Latin *verus* 'true', source also of **verify** [ME], **veritable** [LME], and **very** [ME], and *dicere* 'to say', from which **addict** [M16th] originally 'assigned by decree' and so bound to something; **condition** [ME] speaking with, agreement; **contradiction** [LME] 'speaking against'; **dictate** [E17th]; **predict** [L16th] 'speaking in advance'; and numerous other words derive.

verge [LME] Verge came via Old French from Latin *virga* 'rod', and its first meaning in medieval English was 'penis'. This sense soon dropped out of use, and was replaced by 'a rod or sceptre as a symbol of office', and 'a boundary or margin', probably from the idea of a rod used as a boundary marker. The modern senses 'an edge or border' and 'a limit beyond which something will happen', as in 'she was on the verge of tears', are from the 17th century. The church **verger** first took his name from the role of carrying a rod or similar symbol of office in front of a bishop or other official. Since the

velocipede   velvet   venal   vendetta   vendor

early 18th century a verger has also been a church caretaker and attendant. Verge with the sense 'incline towards' is early 17th century, and had the early sense 'descend (to the horizon)' (Sir Walter Scott *Talisman*: 'The light was now verging low, yet served the knight still to discern that they two were no longer alone in the forest'). The source is Latin *vergere* 'to bend, incline'.

verify, veritable *see* VERDICT

vermicelli ITALIAN WORD PANEL

vermilion [ME] The name for this brilliant red colour and pigment goes back to Latin *vermis* 'a worm', source also of **vermin** [ME], and its variant **varmint** [M16th]. The reason for the unlikely connection probably lies in the red colours *CRIMSON and **carmine** [E18th], which were originally extracted from the body of the kermes insect. People mistakenly thought that vermilion was also derived from an insect or worm, although its main early source was in fact cinnabar, a bright red mineral.

vermouth [E19th] One of the common ingredients of the aromatic wine vermouth is wormwood, a bitter-tasting shrub. Their names go back to the same source: vermouth came through French from German *Wermut* 'wormwood', which corresponds exactly to Old English *wermōd*. People in the late Middle Ages modified this to **wormwood**, as if the word had in fact been formed by putting together two more familiar words **worm** and **wood**.

verse [OE] In his poem 'Digging' (1966), Seamus Heaney resolves to carry on the family tradition of digging the soil by 'digging' himself, not with a spade like his father and grandfather, but with a pen. The link between agriculture and writing poetry goes all the way back to the origin of the word verse, as Latin *versus* meant both 'a turn of the plough, furrow' and 'a line of writing'. The idea here is that of a plough turning and marking another straight line or furrow. *Versus* is also the source of **versatile** [E17th] and **version** [LME], and it is based

on Latin *vertere* 'to turn', from which **vertebra** [E17th], **vertical** [M16th], **vertigo** [LME], and many other words such as **adverse** [LME], **convert** [LME], and **pervert** [LME] 'turn bad'. **Vortex** [M17th] is closely related. **Versed** [E17th], as in **well versed in**, is different, coming from Latin *versari* 'be engaged in'.

vertebra, vertical, vertigo *see* VERSE

verve [L17th] Verve started out meaning 'special talent in writing'. It is from a French word for 'vigour', and before that 'form of expression', from Latin *verba* 'words'. The word came to be used in the generalized sense 'energy, vigour' in the middle of the 19th century.

very *see* VERDICT

Vespa *see* WASP

vespers *see* WEST

vest *see* INVEST

vestige [LME] This word meaning 'trace' comes via French from Latin *vestigium* 'footprint'. **Investigation** [LME] was formed from the related verb meaning 'to track, to follow the traces of'.

veteran [E16th] Veteran comes via French from Latin *vetus* 'old', also the source of **inveterate** [LME] 'long-standing'. **Vet**, the abbreviation, is recorded from the mid 19th century. The other kind of vet, also mid 19th-century, is a shortening of **veterinary** [18th] from Latin *veterinarius*, from *veterinae* 'cattle'.

veto [E17th] The common people in ancient Rome elected tribunes of the people to protect their interests. When these officials opposed measures of the Senate or actions of magistrates they said *veto*, Latin for 'I forbid'.

vex [LME] Vex and **vexation** come via Old French from Latin *vexare* 'shake, disturb'.

via [L18th] The Latin word *via* meant 'way, road'. It survives in the names of major

verify   veritable   vermicelli   vermilion   very

Roman roads, such as **Via Appia**. The Christian Church also uses it in terms such as the **Via Dolorosa**, the route Jesus is believed to have taken to crucifixion and meaning 'the painful path'. A **deviation** [LME] is literally a turning away from the path as is behaviour that is **devious** [L16th]. **Viaduct** was formed from via in the early 19th century on the model of **aqueduct** (*see* DUCT). An **envoy** [M17th] is someone sent on their way, formed from French *envoyé* 'sent', while **obvious** [L16th] comes from Latin *ob viam* 'in the way'.

viable [E19th] This is based on French *vie* 'life', from Latin *vita*. The literal sense is 'able to live'; the sense 'workable, practicable' arose in the mid 19th century.

viaduct *see* VIA

vial *see* PHIAL

vicar [ME] The original **vicar** was a person who stood in for another; at first, around 1300, as an earthly representative of God or Christ (the pope), and then for an absent parson or rector. From there the vicar became the minister in charge of a parish where tithes or taxes passed to a monastery or other religious house, who paid the vicar as their 'representative'—a **rector** (LME from the Latin for 'rule'), on the other hand, kept the tithes for himself. These meanings reflected the root, Latin *vicarius* 'a substitute', from which **vicarious** [M17th], 'experienced in the imagination through the actions of another person', also derives.

vice [ME] In the sense of immorality vice is from Latin *vitium* 'vice', also the source of **vicious** [ME]. This originally meant 'showing vice' but was extended to mean 'savage' in descriptions of bad-tempered horses [E18th], and later [E19th] to mean 'spiteful'. The tool sense was originally a word for a screw or winch that comes via Old French *vis*, from Latin *vitis* 'vine' from the spiral growth of the vine's tendrils.

vice versa [E17th] This is an English use of a Latin phrase meaning literally 'the position being reversed'.

vicious *see* VICE

victim [LME] Latin *victima*, the source of this word, originally meant an animal killed as a religious sacrifice. Use of a person who is harmed by another is mid 17th century.

victory [ME] A medieval word that goes back to Latin *victoria* 'victory'. The ultimate root was Latin *vincere* 'to conquer', also the source of **convince** [M16th], **convict** [LME], **evict** [E16th], and **vanquish** [ME]. **Dig for Victory** was a British slogan of the Second World War which urged people to grow their own food to make up for the loss of imports. A **Pyrrhic victory** is a victory won at too great a cost. It comes from Pyrrhus, a king of Epirus, part of present-day Greece. Pyrrhus invaded Italy in 280 BC and defeated the Romans at the battle of Asculum, though only after such heavy losses that after the battle he is said to have exclaimed: 'One more such victory and we are lost.' Queen Victoria, whose name is the Latin for 'victory', and whose long reign lasted from 1837 to 1901, gave her name to the **Victorian** era. A support for **Victorian values**, often summed up as hard work, social responsibility, and strict morality, is associated with former British Prime Minister Margaret Thatcher, who said in 1983: 'I was asked whether I was trying to restore Victorian values. I said straight out I was. And I am.'

video *see* VIEW

view [ME] View goes back to Latin *videre* 'to see'. **Review** [LME], first recorded as a noun denoting a formal inspection of military or naval forces, is literally a re-viewing. **Video** [1930s] is the Latin for 'I see' just as **audio** is the Latin for 'I hear'. **Visa** [M19th], evidence that your right to enter a country has been checked, is a shortening of Latin *charta visa* literally 'seen paper'.

vigil [ME] Vigil comes from Latin *vigilia* 'wakefulness', from *vigil* 'awake'. It was first used for the night before a religious festival, when people might stay wakeful all night in prayer. Related words include **vigilant** [LME]; **vigilance** [L16th]; and **vigilante** [M19th] adopted from a Spanish word with

viable viaduct vial vicar vice vice versa

the literal meaning 'vigilant'. **Surveillance** [E19th] is from the same root and is literally watching over something, also found when someone **invigilate**s [M16th] an exam.

vignette [ME] In French a vignette is a 'little vine', and the word was once an architectural term for a carved representation of a vine, while in design and book production it referred to decorative depictions of foliage. From the mid 18th century a vignette became a design that shaded off into the background without a definite border. Restriction to visual features ended in the late 19th century, when the word assumed its usual modern sense, 'a brief evocative description, account or episode'.

vigour [ME] Vigour and **vigorous** [ME] are from Latin *vigor*, from *vigere* 'be lively', also found in **invigorate** [M17th].

Viking [E19th] The Vikings were seafaring pirates and traders from Scandinavia who raided and settled in many parts of north-western Europe from the 8th to the 11th century. Scholars formerly assumed that the name came from Scandinavian *vík* 'creek, inlet', and referred to their setting out from the inlets of the sea, but it may well derive from Old English *wīc* 'camp', since formation of temporary encampments was a prominent feature of Viking raids. The situation is complicated by the fact that it is not an old word in English, but borrowed from Icelandic in the early 19th century, although there was an equivalent Old English word *wicing*.

villa, village *see* VILLAIN

villain [ME] In medieval England a villain was a feudal tenant who was entirely subject to a lord or manor—now usually spelled **villein**. People began to use villain as an insult implying someone was a low-born rustic, and the meaning deteriorated even further to 'a person guilty of a crime, a criminal'. A bad character in a book was a villain from the 1820s. The word came from French and goes back to Latin *villa* 'country house with an estate or farm', from which

villa [E17th] itself and **village** [LME] also derive.

vindaloo [L19th] The vindaloo is one of the hottest curries in the British Indian restaurant's repertoire, but in origin the word was not Indian and did not imply spiciness. It probably derives from Portuguese *vin d'alho* 'wine and garlic sauce'. A recipe for vindaloo is recorded in English in 1888, which describes it as a Portuguese curry, but it did not become familiar until Indian restaurants spread widely in the 1960s.

vindicate *see* REVENGE

vine, vinegar, vintage, vinyl *see* WINE

viper [E16th] Some vipers give birth to live young which have hatched from eggs within the parent's body, whereas the eggs of most snakes are laid before they hatch. The name viper derives from the fact they are **viviparous** ('producing live young' M17th), coming from Latin *vivus* 'alive', as in **vivisection** [E18th], and *parere* 'to bring forth', the source of **parent** [LME]. The phrase **a viper in your bosom**, 'a person you have helped but who has behaved treacherously towards you', comes from one of Aesop's fables in which a viper reared close to a person's chest eventually bites its nurturer. *See also* ADDER, SNAKE

virago [OE] The second chapter of the Book of Genesis describes the creation of Eve: 'And Adam said, This is now bone of my bones, and flesh of my flesh: she shall be called Woman, because she was taken out of Man.' In the Latin version of the Bible known as the Vulgate, the word Adam uses for Eve is *Virago*. This is not the insult it appears to be now. *Virago* meant 'heroic woman, female warrior' in Latin and derived from *vir* 'man', the source of **virile** [LME] and **virtue** [ME] originally meaning 'manliness'. Virago first appeared in English with reference to Eve, but medieval man started using it in the disparaging sense 'a domineering, violent, or bad-tempered woman' that survives today.

vignette vigour Viking villa village villain

virile, virtue *see* VIRAGO

virulent *see* VIRUS

virus [LME] A virus was originally the venom of a snake, and was an English borrowing of a Latin word meaning 'slimy liquid' or 'poison', that is also the source of **virulent** [LME]. Early medical practitioners used the word for a substance produced in the body as the result of disease. The modern meaning dates from the late 19th century. The **computer virus** dates from the early 1970s.

visa *see* VIEW

viscous [LME] Viscous comes via Anglo-Norman French from Latin *viscum* 'birdlime', the sticky substance used to trap birds.

vision [ME] A vision initially referred to a 'supernatural apparition'; it comes via Old French from Latin from *videre* 'to see'. **Revise** [M16th] originally 'look again or repeatedly (at)' is from the same source, as is **provide** [LME]. **Visit** [ME] is from *visare* 'view' formed from *videre* while **visual** [LME] is from *visus* 'sight', again from *videre*. *See also* ADVICE

vital [LME] Latin *vita* 'life' is the source of vital and also of *VITAMIN. Medieval senses relate to the force or energy that is in all living things. A later meaning 'essential to life' evolved for anything regarded as essential, such as the vital organs, also known as **the vitals** from the early 17th century. **Vital statistics** are usually understood now as the measurements of a woman's bust, waist, and hips. This meaning has only been around since the 1950s, and for more than a hundred years before that vital statistics were just the numbers of births, marriages, and deaths in a population. *See also* ARTERY

vivacious, vivid *see* SURVIVE

viviparous, vivisection *see* VIPER

vixen *see* FOX

vocabulary, vocal, vocation, vociferous *see* VOICE

vodka [E19th] The name of the clear, strong alcoholic spirit claims that it is just 'water'—it is a diminutive form of Russian *voda* 'water'. Travellers to Russia brought the word back to Britain in the early 19th century. *See also* WATER, WHISKY

vogue [L16th] Fashion and rowing may not appear to have much in common, but Italian *voga*, from which vogue came derives from *vogare* 'to row, go well'. During the 17th century vogue was definitely in vogue, developing most of its current meanings. In the 1980s dancers in clubs began to vogue, imitating the characteristic poses struck by a model on a catwalk—the word here refers to the glossy fashion magazine *Vogue*, which started life as a weekly New York society paper before the US publisher Condé Nast bought it and transformed it from 1909.

voice [ME] A word derived from Latin *vox* 'voice' and is related to **vocabulary** [M16th], **vocal** [ME], **vocation** [LME], and **vociferous** [E17th], while the verb *vocare* 'to call' appears in **convoke** [L16th] 'call together'; **equivocate** [LME] literally 'call by the same name'; **evoke** [E17th] 'call out'; **invoke** [LME] 'call upon'; **provoke** [LME] 'call forth'; **revoke** [LME] 'call back'; and **vouch** [ME] and **voucher** [E16th]. **Vowel** [ME] is from Old French *vouel*, from Latin *vocalis (littera)* 'vocal (letter)'. The Latin root survives in **vox pop**, 'an informal survey of people's opinion', which is short for Latin *vox populi* or 'voice of the people'. When people refer to an ignored advocate of reform as a **voice in the wilderness** they are echoing the words of John the Baptist proclaiming the coming of the Messiah: 'I am the voice of one crying in the wilderness.'

volatile [ME] This was first used as a noun meaning a 'creature that flies', and it was also a collective word for 'birds'. It derives from Old French *volatil* from Latin *volare* 'to fly'. The association of the word with temperament is found from the mid 17th century, and with liquids that

virile virtue virulent virus visa viscous

evaporate quickly by the later 17th. The flying shot called a **volley** [L16th] comes from the same source.

volcano [E17th] In Roman mythology Vulcan was the god of fire, and a metalworker. A conical mountain with erupting lava, rock fragments, hot vapour, or gas must have suggested his forge or smithy, and Italians named such a feature *volcano* or *vulcano* after him.

volley *see* VOLATILE

voluble, volume *see* REVOLVE

voluntary [LME] Voluntary goes back to Latin *voluntas* 'will'. The related word **volunteer** dates from the late 16th century as a military term.

voluptuous [LME] Voluptuous is from Latin *voluptas* 'pleasure'. The word became associated with fullness of form suggesting sensuous pleasure from the early 19th century.

vortex *see* VERSE

vote [LME] Vote is from Latin *votum* 'a vow, wish', from *vovere* 'to vow'. The verb dates from the mid 16th century. The word **votive** [L16th] meaning 'offered in

fulfilment of a vow' is from *votum* as are **vow** [ME], **devout** [ME], and **devotion** [ME].

vouch, voucher *see* VOICE

vow *see* VOTE

vowel, vox pop *see* VOICE

voyage [ME] Voyage was first used for a journey by sea or by land. It is from Old French *voiage*, from Latin *viaticum* initially meaning 'provisions for a journey' and, in late Latin, 'journey'.

vulgar [LME] Latin *vulgus* 'the common people' is the source of vulgar. The original senses, from the late Middle Ages, were 'used in ordinary calculations', which survives in **vulgar fraction**, and 'in ordinary use, used by the people', which survives in **vulgar tongue**. The sense 'coarse, uncultured' dates from the mid 17th century. **Divulge** [LME] is from the same root, from Latin *divulgare* 'to spread among the people', hence to make generally known.

vulnerable [E17th] This comes from late Latin *vulnerabilis*, from *vulnus* 'wound'. The word appeared later than its opposite **invulnerable** which is late 16th century.

Ww

wafer *see* WAFFLE

waffle [L17th] Someone who waffles now talks on and on in a vague or trivial way, but in the 17th century to waffle was 'to yap or yelp', and then 'to dither'. It came from the English dialect term *waff* 'to yelp' (the same word as **woof** [E19th], both imitating the sound), and seems to have been used mainly in northern England until the modern meaning developed at the start of the 20th century. Waffle meaning 'a small crisp batter cake' is quite different: it comes from Dutch *wafel*, and before that Old French *gaufre*, the root of **wafer** [ME]. *Gaufre* also meant 'honeycomb', and this is probably the basic idea—the criss-cross indentations on a waffle or wafer look like a honeycomb.

wag [ME] The sort of wagging done by dogs is from the Old English word *wagian* 'to sway', source also of **waggle** [L16th]. **Wangle** [L19th] is first recorded as printers' slang. The origin is unknown but is perhaps based on *waggle*. Wag meaning 'a joker' is a different word, dating from the 16th century, which first meant 'a mischievous boy or lively young man', and was often used as a fond name for a child. Showing the grim gallows humour of the times, it probably comes from *waghalter*, 'a person likely to be hanged'. In the 2006 World Cup a new meaning of wag suddenly became popular. The **WAGs** were the **W**ives **a**nd **G**irlfriends of the England players. The term had already been used in the 2004 European Championship.

wage *see* ENGAGE

wagon [LME] The Dutch word *wagen* is the source of our wagon. It is related to **wain**
[OE], an old word for 'wagon' that is now mainly encountered in the name of a star formation **Charles's Wain**, now more commonly called the Plough. **Wainscot** [ME] is from Middle Low German *wagenschot*, apparently from *wagen* 'wagon' and *schot*, probably meaning 'partition'. If you are **on the wagon** you are avoiding alcohol. The original version of this expression was **on the water wagon**, which first appeared in America in the early 20th century. A water wagon was a sort of barrel on wheels which was used to water dusty streets. These vehicles had been around since the early 18th century at least, but it may have been the increasing popularity of the temperance movement in the latter part of the 19th century that gave rise to the phrase. *See also* HITCH

waif [LME] In the 1990s a new look became popular for fashion models—the very thin, childlike girls were called waifs or **superwaifs**. The word waif can be traced back to medieval law, where it was a term for a piece of property found without an owner, which belonged to the lord of the manor if it was not claimed—**waifs and strays** was an overall term for lost property and stray animals. It was not until the 1600s that waif first referred to a homeless or neglected person. The word is from Old French *gaif*, and before that was probably Scandinavian.

wain, wainscot *see* WAGON

waist *see* WAX

wake *see* WATCH

Wales *see* WALNUT

walk [OE] An Old English word that originally meant 'to roll, toss' and 'to wander', and did not start to mean 'walk' until about 1300. The odd expression **walk of life**, meaning 'a person's occupation or position within society', probably derives from the use of walk to refer to the round or circuit of a travelling tradesman or official. In Australian English a **walkabout** is a journey into the bush that an Aboriginal makes to re-establish contact with traditions and spiritual sources—to **go walkabout** is to go on such a journey. Since around 1970 the term has also been used of the informal strolls among welcoming crowds favoured by members of the royal family and visiting dignitaries. It can also mean 'to go missing, disappear', especially in the context of small objects such as pens, car keys, and television remote controls. The Sony **Walkman**, a type of personal stereo using cassette tapes, was trademarked in 1981 became a generic term for 'personal stereo'. *See also* BLOOD

wall [OE] Wall comes from Latin *vallum* 'rampart', from *vallus* 'stake', which implies that the earliest walls were defensive ones around a town or camp. To **go to the wall** is now to fail commercially but originally meant 'give way' or 'be beaten in a battle or fight'. The idea may be that of a hard-pressed fighter retreating until he had a wall behind him and he could retreat no more—until he had his **back against the wall**. There may also be a link to the proverb **the weakest go to the wall**, which dates back to the end of the 15th century, and is usually said to derive from the installation of seating round the walls in churches of the late Middle Ages. Someone who is **off the wall** is unconventional or crazy. This is a quite recent phrase, first recorded in the mid 1960s, in the USA. One suggestion is that it refers to the way that a ball sometimes bounces off a wall at an unexpected angle. The proverb **walls have ears** dates back to the early 17th century. A more rural version is **fields have eyes, and woods have ears**, which is first recorded some 400 years earlier. Saying that **the writing is on the wall** is a biblical allusion to the description of Belshazzar's feast in the Book of Daniel. In this account Belshazzar was the king of Babylon whose death was foretold by a mysterious hand which wrote on the palace wall at a banquet.

wallet [LME] A wallet was originally a bag, pouch, or knapsack. Medieval pilgrims would carry them, and the earliest recorded use of the word is by Geoffrey Chaucer, in the prologue to the *Canterbury Tales*. The modern meaning did not turn up until the 1840s, in the USA. The word is from Old French, and is related to *WELL, in the water sense.

wallop [ME] The original meaning of wallop was 'to gallop', and the Old French sources of **gallop** [E16th] and wallop, *galoper* and *waloper*, are related. It seems that there is something gratifying about the way wallop sounds that makes people use it in lively ways. The next sense to develop was 'to boil violently', and then 'to move in a heavy or clumsy way', and 'to flop about, dangle, flap'. The modern sense, 'to hit very hard', appeared in the early 19th century. *See also* CODSWALLOP

wally [1960s] You can say that wally, meaning 'a silly or inept person', is short for the name Walter, and that it was first used in the 1960s—beyond that nothing is certain. The most popular theory about its origin connects it with an incident at a pop festival where a chap called Wally became separated from his companions: his name was announced many times over the loudspeaker and was taken up as a chant by the crowd. In the 1970s hippies would certainly shout out 'Wally!' in an exuberant and random fashion, and there was even a rock band at the time called Wally.

walnut [OE] For the Anglo-Saxons and other ancient peoples of northern Europe the walnut was the 'foreign nut'. The nut they knew was the hazelnut, and walnuts would have been exotic imports from the Roman world of the south. The *wal-* part comes from *Volcae*, the Latin name for a particular Celtic tribe that the Germanic peoples came to use for all Celts (it is where **Welsh** [OE] and **Wales** come from) and eventually for anyone not of Germanic stock.

walrus [E18th] The Anglo-Saxons seem to have thought the walrus looked a bit like a horse, for they called it the *horschwæl*, 'horse-whale'. We owe our name for the creature to the Dutch, who took the same idea but reversed it: the *wal-* bit is 'whale' and *-rus* is probably 'horse'.

wall wallet wallop wally walnut walrus

waltz [L18th] This word is from German *Walzer*, from *walzen* 'revolve'. The transferred verb use 'move nimbly' (**waltzed off down the road**) arose in the mid 19th century. *See also* AUSTRALIAN WORD PANEL

wan [OE] This is an example of a colour word that has reversed in meaning, like *AUBURN. Until AD 700 wan meant 'dark, black', and it did not start to mean 'pale' until around 1300. As well as 'dark' it originally meant 'of an unhealthy greyish colour', particularly of the face of a person who was dead or affected by disease, and this notion of unhealthiness could have provided the connection with 'pale'.

wand [ME] A word from Old Norse, and related to **wend** [OE] and **wind** [OE] 'to move in a twisting way'—the basic idea seems to be of a supple, flexible stick. Wand did not have any connection with wizards and spells until about 1400, some 200 years after it was first used. **Wander** [OE], 'to move in a leisurely or aimless way', comes from a similar root.

wander *see* WAND

wane *see* WAX

wangle *see* WAG

wanton [ME] The spelling in Middle English was *wantowen* 'rebellious, lacking discipline', from *wan-* 'badly' and Old English *togen* 'trained' (related to *TEAM and **tow** [OE]).

war [ME] Before the mid 12th century there was no English word exactly meaning war, nor did any of their Germanic relatives have one despite their warlike reputation. The word came over from Old French *guerre* and is related to **worse** [OE]. The *Guerre* itself is of Germanic origin, and originally meant 'confusion, discord'.

ward, warden, wardrobe *see* GUARD

warlock [OE] A warlock is not connected with war or locks, and was not originally anything to do with magic. To the Anglo-Saxons a warlock was 'an evil person,

traitor', 'monster, savage', and 'the Devil'. The sense 'sorcerer, wizard' was originally Scottish, and only became more widely known when it was used by the novelist Sir Walter Scott in the early 19th century. It comes from Old English words meaning 'agreement, promise' and 'deny'. *See also* WITCH

warm [OE] Warm is an Old English word but can be traced right back to a root that was also the source of Greek *thermos* 'hot', which gave us **thermometer** [M17th], **thermostat** [M19th], and the **Thermos** flask [E20th]. **Cold hands, warm heart** is a proverb first found in the early 20th century.

warp [OE] This is from a Germanic source with a basic sense of 'to throw, twist'. Early verb senses included 'throw', 'fling open', and 'hit (with a missile)'; the sense 'bend' dates from late Middle English. The noun was originally a term in weaving, reflecting the way threads go backwards and forwards.

warrant, warranty *see* GUARANTEE

wart [OE] The Anglo-Saxons suffered from warts—the word is first recorded around AD 700, and we have an Old English charm for getting rid of them. The expression **warts and all**, meaning 'including features or qualities that are not appealing or attractive', dates back to the mid 19th century. The source of the phrase can be traced back to Horace Walpole's *Anecdotes of Painting in England* (1763), in which he recounts a request supposedly made by Oliver Cromwell to the portrait painter Peter Lely: 'Remark all these roughnesses, pimples, warts, and everything as you see me; otherwise I will never pay a farthing for it.'

wary *see* AWARE

wash [OE] An Old English word that is related to *WATER. Someone who is **washed up** is no longer effective or successful—they are like something thrown up on to a beach. The first example of the expression, from the 1920s in the USA, states that it is stage slang. Similarly ineffective or disappointing is a **wash-out**, recorded from around 1900,

waltz wan wand wander wane wangle

which in RAF slang was specifically a person who failed a training course. To **wash your hands** is a euphemism for going to the lavatory—a male equivalent of **powdering your nose**, used since the 1930s. To **wash your hands of**, or disclaim responsibility for, is a biblical allusion to the Gospel of Matthew. Pontius Pilate, the Roman governor of Judaea who presided at the trial of Jesus, was unwilling to authorize his crucifixion, but saw that the crowd were intent on his death. 'He [Pilate] took water, and washed his hands before the multitude, saying, I am innocent of the blood of this just person.'

wasp [OE] Our distant linguistic ancestors had a word wasp which can be traced back to an ancient root that also produced the Latin word for 'wasp', *vespa*. The ultimate origin may be a word that meant 'to weave', the connection being the way that wasps chew up wood into a papery substance that they use to construct their nests. The Latin word *vespa* was carried forward into Italian and used as the name for the **Vespa**, the little motor scooter beloved by Italians, named for its hyperactive buzzing.

wassail [ME] In the Middle Ages wassail was a drinking toast that literally meant 'Be in good health'. The polite reply was **drinkhail**, 'Drink good health'. Both words come from Old Norse, and were probably introduced by Danish-speaking inhabitants of England. By the 12th century they were considered by the Normans to be characteristic of Englishmen: in a work of 1190 the English students at the university of Paris are praised for generosity and other virtues, but are said to be too much addicted to 'wassail' and 'drinkhail'. The second half of each toast is related to the Old English words **hale** [OE], as in **hale and hearty**, **hail** [ME] to greet', and **whole** [OE].

waste [ME] This is from Old French *waster*, based on Latin *vastus* 'unoccupied, uncultivated'. The idiomatic phrase **lay waste** dates from the early 16th century; waste in the sense 'refuse' is found from the late 17th century.

watch [OE] In Old English watch meant 'to be or remain awake', and it is from the same root as **wake** [OE] and **awake** [OE]. The connection with timepieces arose because in the 15th century the first watches were alarm clocks of some kind, whose function was to wake you up. **The watches of the night** are the hours of night, especially as a time when you cannot sleep. This watch was one of the periods into which the night was divided for the purposes of guard duty. The link with insomnia first appears in the writings of Sir Walter Scott, who wrote in his journal for January 1826: 'The watches of the night pass wearily when disturbed by fruitless regrets.'

water [OE] The people living around the Black Sea more than 5 000 years ago had a word for water. We do not know exactly what it was, but it was probably the source for the words used for 'water' in many European languages, past and present. In Old English it was *wæter*. The Greek was *hudōr*, the source of words like **hydraulic** [M17th] and **hydrotherapy** [L19th]. The same root led to the formation of Latin *unda* 'wave', as in **inundate** [L18th], **abound** [ME] (from Latin *abundare* 'overflow'), and **undulate** [M17th], Russian *voda* (the source of **VODKA*), German *Wasser*, and the English words **wet** [OE] and **otter** [OE]. **Of the first water** means 'unsurpassed'. The three highest grades into which diamonds or pearls could be classified used to be called waters, but only **first water**, the top one, is found today, describing a completely flawless gem. An equivalent term is found in many European languages, and all are thought to come from the Arabic word for water, *mā*, which also meant 'shine or splendour', presumably from the appearance of very pure water. People and things other than gems began to be described as **of the first water** in the 1820s. Nowadays the phrase is rarely used as a compliment: in a letter written in 1950, P.G. Wodehouse commented disparagingly on J.M. Barrie's play *The Admirable Crichton*: 'I remember being entranced with it in 1904 or whenever it was, but now it seems like a turkey of the first water.' If you study a duck shaking its wings after diving for food you will see the point of **water off a duck's back**, used since the 1820s of a potentially hurtful remark that has no apparent effect. The water forms into beads and simply slides off the bird's waterproof feathers, leaving the duck dry. **Water under the bridge** refers to events that are in the past and should no longer to be regarded as important. Similar phrases are recorded since the beginning of the 20th century. A North American variant is **water over the dam**. The first uses of **waterlogged**, in the late 18th century, referred to ships that were so flooded with water that they became heavy and unmanageable, and no better than a log floating in the sea. A **watershed**, a ridge of land that separates waters flowing to different rivers or seas, has nothing to do with garden sheds but means 'ridge of high ground' and is connected with **shed** [OE] meaning 'discard'.

wave, waver *see* WOBBLE

wax [OE] An old English verb *weaxan* 'grow, increase' is now restricted to only a few contexts. We use it to mean 'become' in expressions such as 'he **waxed lyrical**', and we use it for 'to grow' when we talk of the moon **waxing and waning**. It is possible that the wax that bees make comes from the same root, in the sense of what grows in the hive, but no one is certain. **Waist** [LME] seems to come from the same root, perhaps with reference to childbirth. **Wane** [OE] is from Old English *wanian* 'lessen'.

weald *see* WILD

wealth *see* WELL

wear *see* INVEST

weasel [OE] The sneaky characteristics of this animal were not transferred to people until the late 16th century. Its bad reputation comes from the belief that weasels creep into birds' nests and suck the contents out of their eggs, leaving the empty shell behind. This lies behind the originally US phrase **weasel words** [E20th] for words used to reduce the force of a concept being expressed; the more general verb sense

'extricate' (**weaselled his way out of doing the chores**) arose in the 1950s.

weather *see* WITHER

weave [OE] English has two words spelled weave. The one meaning 'twist from side to side' probably comes from Old Norse *veifa* 'to wave, brandish'. The other one is Old English and comes from an ancient root shared by Sanskrit *ūrnavābhi* 'spider', or literally 'wool-weaver'. **Web** is a related word, first recorded in about AD 725. The **World Wide Web** was first mentioned in writing in 1990, in a paper by Tim Berners-Lee and Robert Cailliau, who are credited with its invention.

web *see* WEAVE

wedding *see* ENGAGE, MARRY

Wednesday *see* TUESDAY

wee *see* SCOTTISH WORD PANEL

week [OE] An Old English word that is probably from a root meaning 'sequence, series'. The seven-day week used in the Hebrew and then the Christian calendar corresponds to the biblical creation story, in which God created the universe in six days then rested on the seventh. The Romans, who adopted it in AD 321, would have brought this week over to Britain. 'A **week is a long time in politics**' was first said by Harold Wilson, the British Labour prime minister, at the time of the 1964 sterling crisis. Wilson came up with a number of memorable phrases, including 'the **gnomes of Zurich**', to describe Swiss financiers (1956), 'the **university of the air**' (1963) as a name for the Open University, which his government founded, and 'the pound here in Britain, in your pocket, or purse, or bank' (1967), which is often quoted as 'the **pound in your pocket**'. *See also* TUESDAY

weep [OE] A Germanic word in origin, Old English *wēpan* is probably imitative of the sound of moaning and sobbing, although in modern use the verb indicates the more or less silent shedding of tears. Weep is now normally restricted to literary use.

wave waver wax weald wealth wear weasel

weigh [OE] The word weigh can be traced back to an ancient root that also gave us Latin *vehere* 'to carry', the source of *VEHICLE. Early senses of weigh that are no longer used included 'to transport from one place to another' and 'to raise up', still in **weigh the anchor** of a boat or ship. The modern meaning probably comes from the idea of lifting something up on a pair of scales or similar device to weigh it. **Weight** is not directly related, but Old English *gewiht* was re-formed under the influence of weigh.

weird [OE] To the Anglo-Saxons weird was a noun, spelled *wyrd* and meaning 'fate, destiny'. The Weirds were the *FATES, the three Greek goddesses who presided over the birth and life of humans. The adjective originally meant 'having the power to control destiny', and was used especially from the Middle Ages in **the Weird Sisters**, for the Fates, and later also the witches in Shakespeare's *Macbeth*. The modern use, 'very strange, bizarre', as in **weird and wonderful**, dates from the early 19th century.

welcome, welfare *see* WELL

welkin *see* LOFT

well [OE] The well meaning 'in a good way' and well 'shaft giving access to water' are different Old English words. The first provides the first half of **welfare** [ME]. The start of **welcome** [OE], on the other hand, is from another Old English element, *wil-* meaning 'pleasure'—welcome originally meant 'a person whose arrival is pleasing'. **Wealth** [ME] has a basic sense of 'well-being', being formed from well in the same way that **health** [OE] is formed from hale (*see* WASSAIL). The title of Shakespeare's comedy *All's Well that Ends Well* was already an old saying when he wrote the play at the beginning of the 17th century. The first record of the proverb is as early as 1250. People have been **well endowed** only since the 1950s, but men could be **well-hung** in the early 17th century. At this time it meant 'having large ears' as well as 'having a large penis'. The well you get water from is Old English *wella* 'spring of water', of Germanic

origin, from a base meaning 'boil, bubble up'.

wellington [E19th] The wellington boot is named after Arthur Wellesley, the first Duke of Wellington, whose army defeated Napoleon at the Battle of Waterloo in 1815. The first wellington boots were long leather ones, as worn by the great general—rubber **wellies** [1960s] do not seem to have caught on until the beginning of the 20th century.

Welsh *see* WALNUT

weltanschauung *see* GERMAN WORD PANEL

wench [ME] Wench is an abbreviation of obsolete *wenchel* 'child, servant, prostitute'; it is perhaps related to Old English *wancol* 'unsteady, inconstant'.

wend *see* WAND

Wendy house [M20th] The name for a toy house large enough for children to play in comes from J.M. Barrie's play *Peter Pan* (1904). In the play, which Barrie turned into the novel *Peter Pan and Wendy* in 1911, Peter and the Lost Boys build a small structure for Wendy to live in following their flight to Neverland, where she keeps house for them.

werewolf *see* WOLF

west [OE] All of the words for compass points are Old English. West can be traced back to an ancient root that also produced Latin *vesper* 'evening', also the source of the church service **vespers** [LME], the connection being that the sun sets in the west. **Go west**, meaning 'be killed', comes from the idea of the sun setting in the west at the end of the day, and became common during the First World War. The expression is also used more generally in the sense 'be lost or broken', and this is the meaning found in the American equivalent **go south**. The choice of a different compass point is possibly connected with the idea of something being on a downward trend, or perhaps go west sounded too positive, given the hopeful promise of the American West

weigh weird welcome welfare welkin well

represented in the exhortation 'Go west, young man! Go west!', recorded from 1851. The lawless western frontier of the USA during the period when settlers were migrating from the inhabited east was known as **the Wild West** from the 1840s, and was the setting for **Westerns** featuring cowboys, Indians, and cattle rustlers from about 1910. *See also* TWAIN

wet *see* WATER

whammy [M20th] A whammy is an evil influence or hex (*see* HAG), formed from **wham**, which itself is an imitation of the sound of a forcible impact and has only been around since the 1920s. Whammy has been used since the 1940s but is particularly associated with the 1950s cartoon strip 'Li'l Abner', in which the hillbilly Evil-Eye Fleegle could shoot a **single whammy** to put a curse on somebody by pointing a finger with one eye open, and a **double whammy** with both eyes open.

wheat [OE] An Anglo-Saxon word, wheat is related to *WHITE, presumably on account of its pale colour. To **separate the wheat from the chaff**, meaning 'to distinguish the valuable from the worthless' is a biblical concept. In the Gospels of Matthew and Luke, John the Baptist tells the people that a being mightier than him will soon come and gather in the wheat, or good people, but ruthlessly burn the chaff. In several other passages God's anger is spoken of as driving away the wicked just as the wind blows away chaff. The first part of the name of the **wheatear**, a small songbird with a white rump, is from white rather than wheat. The second part seems odd, as birds do not have ears—it is actually from *ARSE, in reference to the bird's rump.

wheel [OE] The wheel was probably invented some time around 4000 BC in Mesopotamia (present-day Iraq). Its name, probably based on a word meaning 'to turn', moved east to India, where it produced Sanskrit *cakra* 'wheel, circle', source of the **chakra** [L19th] of yoga, and west, where it gave rise to Greek *kuklos* 'circle', the source of **cycle** [LME] and **cyclone** [M19th]. It is

recorded in Anglo-Saxon English from about AD 900. To **reinvent the wheel** is a 20th-century expression. **Wheels within wheels** is an allusion to a biblical quotation from the Old Testament book of Ezekiel. The prophet Ezekiel sees a vision in which four cherubs appear: 'And as for their appearances, they four had one likeness, as if a wheel had been in the midst of a wheel'.

wheelwright *see* WORK

wheeze [LME] Wheeze is probably from Old Norse *hvæsa* 'to hiss'.

whimper *see* WIMP

whimsy [17th] The first sense of this was 'a sudden fancy, a whim'. The word comes from **whim-wham**, first recorded in the 1520s and meaning 'a decorative object, a trinket', and 'an odd notion or fancy'. **Whim**, which first meant 'a pun or play on words', also came from whim-wham in the 17th century.

whine [OE] Old English *hwīnan* meant 'whistle through the air'; it is related to late Old English **whinge** (*hwinsian*) and German *winseln*.

whip [ME] A word that came into English from old German and Dutch *wippen* 'to swing, leap, dance'. The parliamentary whip, responsible for ensuring that party members turn up and vote in debates, was originally a **whipper-in**. This is a term in hunting, where the whipper-in uses his whip to keep the hounds from straying. The short form is first found in 1850. A **whip-round**, or collection of contributions of money, is related, coming in the 1860s from whip in the sense 'a notice from a whip requiring MPs to attend a vote'. Since the late 17th century a **whippersnapper** has been a young person who is presumptuous or overconfident. It is literally 'a person who cracks a whip'—the connection was probably making a lot of noise but achieving little. A **whipping boy** is a person who is blamed for the faults of others. Originally it was a boy who was educated with a young prince and, because it

wet whammy wheat wheel wheelwright

would not be right for a commoner to beat a royal person, punished instead of him.

whisker [LME] A whisker was originally a bundle of twigs used to **whisk** with. It was used for facial hair, particularly a moustache from about 1600, presumably because of some perceived similarity, and only used of animals at the end of the 17th century. **Cat's whisker** was used for the wire used to tune an early crystal radio set at the start of the 20th century. The card game **whist** was originally called whisk when it came in during the mid 17th century.

whisky [E18th] The root of whisky is the Gaelic word *uisgebeatha*, literally 'water of life'. The spelling whisky is first recorded in 1715, but more Gaelic forms like *usquebaugh* and *usquebae* were used from the 16th century. Today whisky is the usual spelling for Scotch, and **whiskey** for Irish whiskey. The sense is found elsewhere—two terms for brandy also mean 'water of life', Latin *aqua vitae* and French *eau de vie*, whereas *VODKA is a diminutive form of 'water' in Russian.

whisper *see* WHISTLE

whistle [OE] The first meaning of whistle was 'a small pipe or flute'. Its origin seems to lie in imitation, for it mimics the physical process of whistling. **Whisper** [OE] comes from the same root. In **wet your whistle**, or have a drink, the whistle is your mouth or throat. The first example of its use is by Geoffrey Chaucer in *The Reeve's Tale*. To **blow the whistle on** someone responsible for doing something wrong is to inform on them. The expression comes from a referee blowing a whistle to indicate that a player has broken the rules. When first used in the 1930s it meant 'bring to an abrupt halt', but by the 1970s it had come to refer specifically to people exposing wrongdoing in government or industry. In the 1930s a **whistle-stop** was a small American town on a railway. If a passenger wanted to get off the conductor would sound a whistle to tell the driver he had to stop. A **whistle-stop tour** was one made by a politician before an election that took in even these obscure places.

white [OE] The Old English word white, related to *WHEAT, is used in many English phrases. A **white elephant** is a useless or unwanted possession, especially one that's expensive to maintain. The originals were real albino animals regarded as holy in some Asian countries, especially Siam (present-day Thailand). The story goes that it was the custom for a king of Siam to give one of these elephants to a courtier he particularly disliked: the unfortunate recipient could neither refuse the gift nor give it away later for fear of causing offence, and would end up financially ruined by the costs of looking after the animal. A **whited sepulchre** is a hypocrite. The phrase comes from Jesus's condemnation of the Pharisees in the Gospel of Matthew: he likens them to whited sepulchres, or whitewashed tombs, 'which indeed appear beautiful outward, but are within full of dead mens' bones, and of all uncleanness'. **The white heat of technology** is a phrase usually credited to Harold Wilson. What he actually said in a 1963 speech was, 'The Britain that is going to be forged in the white heat of this revolution will be no place for restrictive practices or for outdated methods on either side of industry.' **The white man's burden**, the task of imposing Western civilization on the inhabitants of colonies, comes from a poem by Rudyard Kipling, published in 1899. Called 'The White Man's Burden: The United States and The Philippine Islands', it urged the USA to take up the burden of empire following its acquisition of the Philippines after the Spanish-American War. The festival **Whit Sunday** or **Whitsuntide** also comes from white. It is a reference to the white robes worn by early Christians who were baptized at this time. **White feather** [L18th] as a sign of cowardice refers to a white feather in the tail of a fighting cock, seen as a sign of bad breeding. **White-knuckle ride** [1970s] refers to the effect caused by gripping tightly to side rails of a fairground ride. *See also* BLACKMAIL, BLUE

whole *see* HOLY, WASSAIL

whisker   whisky   whisper   whistle   white

wholesale *see* RETAIL

whore [OE] Late Old English *hōre*, of Germanic origin, is related to Dutch *hoer* and German *Hure*, from an Indo-European root shared by Latin *carus* 'dear'.

wicca *see* WITCH

wicked [ME] This comes from Old English *wicca* '*WITCH*'. Wicked is one of those words, like *BAD, which has completely reversed its meaning in the slang sense 'excellent, very good', first used in the 1920s. **No peace for the wicked** is a biblical allusion, to the Book of Isaiah: 'There is no peace, saith the Lord, unto the wicked.' *See also* THUMB

widget [1930s] The widget is first recorded in the 1920s in the USA, in the general sense 'a small gadget', and is probably an alteration of GADGET. In the early 1990s a widget became a specific sort of device used in some beer cans to introduce nitrogen into the beer, giving it a creamy head.

widow [OE] Widow is descended from an ancient root meaning 'to be empty', which may also be the source of *DIVIDE. A **grass widow** is now a woman whose husband is away often or for a prolonged period, but originally it was an unmarried woman who had been the mistress of more than one man: the term may have come from the idea of a couple having lain on the grass instead of in bed. **Widow's weeds** dating from the early 18th century was expressed earlier as mourning weeds: here weeds is in the obsolete general sense 'garments' from Old English *wǣd(e)*.

wield *see* UNWIELDY

wife [OE] The original meaning of wife was simply 'woman', a sense still used in Scotland and in terms such as **fishwife** [E16th] and *MIDWIFE. **All the world and his wife**, meaning 'everyone' or 'a great many people', is first recorded in Jonathan Swift's *Polite Conversation* (1738). *See also* CAESAR, WOMAN

wigwam *see* NATIVE AMERICAN WORD PANEL

wiki [L20th] Wiki, for a web page that can be edited by its users, comes from Hawaiian *wikiwiki* 'very quick'. The WikiWikiWeb was the first such site founded in 1995, which was named after the Wiki Wiki shuttle bus that runs between Honolulu Airport terminals. This has since been eclipsed by the collaborative encyclopedia Wikipedia founded in 2001. Wiki is sometimes explained as from 'What I Know Is' but this is what has been christened a backronym—an acronym formed to explain an extant word.

wild [OE] Both wild and **wilderness** are Old English words. The first sense of wild was 'not tame or domesticated', and wilderness means literally 'land inhabited only by wild animals'—it comes from Old English *wild dēor* 'wild deer'. This is the sense in *The **Call of the Wild*** (1903), a novella by the American writer Jack London about a pet sold as a sled dog that returns to the wild to lead a pack of wolves. To the Anglo-Saxons **wildfire** was originally a raging, destructive fire caused by a lightning strike. It was also a mixture of highly flammable substances used in warfare, and a term for various skin diseases that spread quickly over the body. Use of **spread like wildfire** was suggested by Shakespeare's line in his poem *The Rape of Lucrece*: 'Whose words like wild fire burnt the shining glorie / Of rich-built Illion [Troy]'. A **wild goose chase** does not come from hunting. Early examples, dating from the late 16th century, refer to a popular sport of the time in which each of a line of riders had to follow accurately the course of the leader, like a flight of wild geese. The wooded uplands know as **wolds** [OE], as in Cotswolds, or **wealds** are probably from the same root. *See also* DEER, VOICE, WEST, WOOL

wildebeest *see* SOUTH AFRICAN WORD PANEL

will-o'-the-wisp *see* JACK

willy-nilly [E17th] This was originally **will I, nill I**, meaning 'I am willing, I am unwilling'. It dates from the early 17th century. *SHILLY-SHALLY was formed in a similar way from 'shill I, shall I?', where 'shill' is just a variation on 'shall'.

wimp [1920s] Wimp seems to have originated in the USA in the 1920s, although it was not really used much until the 1960s. There was an earlier slang term wimp which meant 'woman', used at Oxford University in the early years of the 20th century: this could be the origin, or wimp could simply be an alteration of **whimper**. Like bonk, drum, and hoot, **whimper** is another of those words suggested by the sound it represents. 'This is the way the world ends / **Not with a bang but a whimper**' is from '*The Hollow Men*' (1925) by T.S. Eliot.

wind [OE] A word from an Indo-European root that also gave us Latin *ventus*, the source of **vent** [LME] and **ventilate** [LME]. **Winnow**, *windwian* in Old English, is to use the wind to separate grain and chaff. To **get wind of** something comes from the idea of hunted animal picking up the scent of a hunter. The phrase **wind of change** was used by Harold Macmillan, British prime minister 1957–63, during a speech he made in Cape Town in 1960: 'The wind of change is blowing through this continent, and, whether we like it or not, this growth of [African] national consciousness is a political fact.' *See also* ILL. For the differently pronounced verb *see* WAND

windbag *see* FOOL

window [ME] Window is from Old Norse *vindauga*, which literally meant 'wind eye'. Before that the Anglo-Saxons words were *éagthyrl* and *éagduru*, 'eye hole' and 'eye door'. Early windows would generally have been just openings in a wall, sometimes with shutters or curtains. The computing sense 'a framed area on a screen for viewing information' was first recorded in 1974, and in 1985 Microsoft released the first version of its Windows operating system. *See also* EYE

wine [OE] At heart wine is the same word as **vine** [ME]. Both can be traced back to

Latin *vinum*, 'wine', which also gave us **vinegar** [ME] formed from Latin *vinus acer* 'sour wine'; **vintage** [LME] via French *vendage*, from Latin *vindemia* 'wine removal'; and **vinyl**—in technical use vinyl is a plastic created from a derivative of ethylene, which is a naturally occurring gas given off by ripening fruit. **Wine, women, and song** [L19th] was suggested by 'Wine and women will make men of understanding to fall away' from the biblical book of Ecclesiasticus, which is probably behind 'Who loves not wine, woman, and song, / He is a fool his whole life long', a translation of an anonymous German fragment of poetry. The original German *Wein, Weib, and Gesang* was first popularized as the title of an 1869 Strauss waltz, and the translation became a generic term for this kind of music. *See also* TRUTH

wing [ME] Before wing came into English from Old Norse *vængr*, the term used was **feathers**, an Old English word from a Germanic root. In a theatre the wings are where actors wait for their cue to come on stage: someone **waiting in the wings** is ready to do something at the appropriate time. To **wing it**, or do something without preparation, is originally theatrical slang, which meant 'to play a role without properly knowing the text', either by relying on a prompter in the wings or by studying the part in the wings between scenes. It was used in this sense from the late 19th century, but did not acquire its more general meaning of 'improvise' until the 1950s. **On a wing and a prayer**, 'with only the slightest chance of success', is from the title of a 1943 song by the American songwriter Harold Adamson, 'Comin' in on a Wing and a Pray'r'. He took it from a comment made by a wartime pilot speaking to ground control just before he made an emergency landing in his damaged plane.

wink [OE] Today someone who winks closes and opens an eye quickly. In Anglo-Saxon times to wink was simply to close the eyes. **Hoodwink**, meaning 'to trick or deceive', harks back to this original meaning. To hoodwink someone in the 16th century was to blindfold with a hood, before

wimp wind windbag window wine wing

an execution or while attacking them. The modern metaphorical sense developed early the next century. To **tip someone the wink** is an example of old underworld slang or 'rogues' cant' recorded from the 17th century. It is probably the source of **tip** in the sense of 'a useful piece of advice'. Tip here means simply 'to give, allow to have'—its use in sentences like 'tip me a shilling' led to the modern sense of tip, 'a sum of money given as a reward for good service', found from the mid 18th century. *See also* NOD

winnow *see* WIND

winter [OE] The word winter is probably related to **wet** (*see* WATER), with the basic idea being 'the wet season'. *Richard III*: 'Now is the winter of our discontent / Made glorious summer by this sun of York' gave us **The winter of discontent** of 1978–79 in Britain, when widespread strikes forced the Labour government out of power.

wire [OE] The base of wire probably meant 'to plait or weave'. In the 1850s people started taking or sending a message **by wire**, or by telegraph. If a situation goes **down to the wire** its outcome is not decided until the very last minute. This expression originated in the USA in the late 19th century and comes from the world of horse racing. Racecourses there have a wire stretched across and above the finishing line: a race that goes **down to the wire** is one in which the horses are neck and *NECK right to the finish.

wise [OE] Both wise and **wisdom** [OE] are related to **wit**, and the three words share an ancient root meaning 'to know'. The *-wise* in **clockwise** [LME] and **lengthwise** [L16th] means 'way, manner', but is ultimately related to the other wise. Of the many proverbs and sayings relating to wisdom, **it is easy to be wise after the event** originated in the early 17th century, whereas **the price of wisdom is above rubies** comes from the biblical book of Job. In the USA a **wise guy** is a person who makes sarcastic or cheeky remarks to show how clever they are. Since the 1970s it has also been a term for a

member of the Mafia. *See also* EARLY, HISTORY, IGNORANCE, MAGIC, MONKEY, WORD

wishy-washy *see* PELL MELL

wit *see* HISTORY, WISE

witch [OE] In Anglo-Saxon times witches were of both sexes. The masculine form was *wicca*, which is the source of WICKED, and has also been revived in recent times by modern pagans as the name of their religion, **Wicca**. A female witch was a *wicce*. A male witch would now be called a **wizard** [LME], a word that comes from *WISE—in the Middle Ages wizards were wise men or sages, only becoming magicians in the mid 16th century. *See also* WARLOCK. **The witching hour** is midnight, the time when witches are active. The phrase is from Shakespeare's *Hamlet*. Hamlet himself declares: Tis now the very witching time of night, / When churchyards yawn, and hell itself breathes out / Contagion to this world.' George Orwell was the first to use **witch-hunt** to mean 'a campaign directed at people holding views considered unorthodox or a threat to society', in reference to Communists being persecuted in the Spanish Civil War (1936–39). Before that a witch-hunt was a real hunt for witches, though the term is recorded first in novels from the 19th century, long after witches had stopped being burned at the stake.

wither [LME] Wither and **weather** [OE] seem to be the same word, the different forms coming to be used for different senses. Weather itself is from a Germanic root linked to *WIND. The phrase **wither away** originated in early 20th century tracts about Marxist philosophy describing the decline of the state after a dictatorship has effected changes in society such that the state's domination is no longer necessary.

wizard *see* WITCH

wobble [M17th] A German word first used in English in the mid 17th century. Wobble is related to **wave** [OE] and **waver** [ME] which come from Old Norse, and until the mid 19th century was generally spelled *wabble.* To **throw a wobbly** is to have a fit of temper or panic. This is a recent expression recorded only from the 1960s, first of all in New Zealand, although **throw a wobbler** appears in the 1930s, in a US dictionary of underworld and prison slang. **Wave** did not come to be used for hair until the mid 19th century and the expression to **make waves** dates only from the 1960s. **Mexican wave** describing a wavelike effect when spectators stand, raise their arms, and sit again in successive crowd sections, originated at the World Cup football competition held in Mexico City in 1986.

woe [OE] Many ancient languages, including Old English, Latin, and Greek, had woe or a similar word—a natural exclamation made by someone unhappy or in distress. The medieval word betide, meaning 'to happen', comes from the same source as *TIDE, and these days is mainly found in the phrase **woe betide**, a light-hearted warning that a person will be in trouble if they do a particular thing.

wold *see* WILD

wolf [OE] The Indo-European root of wolf also gave rise to Greek *lukos* and Latin *lupus*, the source of **lupine** [M17th], 'like a wolf'. The Greek word gave us **lycanthropy** [M16th], the mythical transformation of a person into a wolf or **werewolf** [OE]: the were- part of werewolf is probably from *wer*, the Old English word for 'man' or 'person', just as the second half of the Greek comes from *anthropos* 'man' (*see* WORLD).

The story of the shepherd boy who thought it would be funny to cause a panic by falsely **crying 'wolf!'** is one of the fables of Aesop, the Greek storyteller of the 6th century BC. To **keep the wolf from the door** is to have enough money to avoid starvation: the phrase has been used since the 15th century. To **throw someone to the wolves**, or leave them to be roughly treated, is surprisingly recent though, being recorded only from the 1920s. The image here is of travellers on a sledge who are set upon by a pack of wolves, and decide to throw out one of their number to lighten the load and allow themselves to make their escape. A **wolf in sheep's clothing** is a person or thing that appears friendly or harmless but is really hostile. This comes from the Sermon on the Mount, as recounted in the Gospel of Matthew, when Jesus says: 'Beware of false prophets, which come to you in sheep's cloth, but inwardly they are ravening wolves.'

woman [OE] In Old English the spelling of **woman** was *wifmon* or *wifman*, a combination of *WIFE (which then meant simply 'woman') and *MAN (which meant 'person'), so a woman was a 'female person'. **A woman's work is never done** and **a woman's place is in the home** reflect the traditional view of the sexes. The former was first recorded in 1570, as 'Some respite to husbands the weather doth send, but housewives' affairs have never no end'. In response to such ideas, during the 1970s and 1980s some feminists decided that the usual plural of woman, **women**, had to be changed, because it contained men. They used **womyn** or **wimmin**, neither of which really caught on. The saying 'A woman without a man is like a fish without a bicycle' is sometimes credited to the American feminist Gloria Steinem but was probably just an anonymous piece of graffiti.

wonga *see* ROMANY WORD PANEL

wood [OE] The first meaning of wood was 'a tree', although the sense 'small forest' was found soon after. People **touch wood** (or in North America **knock on wood**) to ward off bad luck. The expression is recorded only since 1849. **Be unable to see the wood from the trees** is older, dating from the mid 16th century. Another phrase relating to the 'small forest' sense is **out of the woods**, meaning 'out of danger or difficulty'. This probably comes from the 18th-century proverb **don't halloo** [shout for joy] **till you are out of the wood**. *See also* NASTY, NECK, SPOON

woof *see* WAFFLE

wool [OE] Wool is first recorded in Old English around AD 700 and can be traced

woe wold wolf woman wonga wood woof

back to a root shared by Latin *lana* 'wool', found in **lanolin** [L19th], literally 'oil from wool'. The first person mentioned as trying to **pull the wool over someone's eyes** is an attorney, or American lawyer, in the mid 19th century, which implies that the 'wool' referred to is a lawyer's curly wig. The phrase may also be connected with the expression to **wool someone**, meaning to pull their hair or 'wool' as a joke or insult. Someone **wild and woolly**, or rough and uncouth, is so called in reference to cowboys in the Wild West who wore shaggy sheepskin garments with the wool on the outside. Woolly in the sense 'vague or confused' is early 19th century and draws on the idea of something woolly having a fuzzy, indistinct outline.

word [OE] Word is ultimately related to Latin *verbum*, the source of **verb** [LME], **proverb** [ME] the 'pro' here having the sense 'put forth', and **verbal** [LME]. '**In the beginning was the Word**, and the Word was with God, and the Word was God' are the first words of the Gospel of John, which continues: 'And the Word was made flesh, and dwelt among us...full of grace and truth.' To **eat your words** is first found in a 1571 translation of a work by the French Protestant theologian John Calvin: 'God eateth not his word when he hath once spoken.' **A word in your ear** is of similar vintage, coming from Shakespeare's *Much Ado About Nothing*: 'Come you hither sirra, a word in your ear, sir'. People sometimes say **a word to the wise** or **a word to the wise is enough** to imply that only a hint or brief explanation is required. The wording of the first English use, at the start of the 16th century, was 'Few words may serve the wise', although the concept was expressed much earlier than that in the Latin saying *verbum sapienti sat est*, sometimes shortened to *verb sap*.

work [OE] Work is connected with the Greek word *ergon*, which is the source of **energy** [L16th], **ergonomic** [1950s], and *SURGEON. **Wrought**, meaning 'made in a particular way' and found in **wrought iron** [E18th], is the old past form of work, which people used where we now use **worked**.

Wright, a common surname that means 'maker' and is found in words such as **shipwright** [OE] and **wheelwright** [ME], is also closely related to work. The first **workaholic** was mentioned in 1968. Since then we have had **chocaholics** and **shopaholics**, but the first word to be formed in this way from **alcoholic** was **foodaholic**, in 1965. The dictum 'Work expands so as to fill the time available' is known as Parkinson's law. It was first expressed by Professor C. Northcote Parkinson in 1955. Much older is the proverb **All work and no play makes Jack a dull boy**, which is first found in 1659. *See also* DEVIL

world [OE] The ancient root of world meant 'age or life of man'. The first part is the same as *were-* in **werewolf** (*see* WOLF)—it means 'man'—and the second part is related to *OLD. The Anglo-Saxons first used world to mean 'human existence, life on earth' as opposed to future life in heaven or hell. America was first called **the New World** in 1555, and Europe, Asia, and Africa the **Old World** at the end of that century. **Olde worlde** is a 'fake' antiquated spelling for old-fashioned things intended to be quaint and attractive, and dates only from the 1920s. The developing countries of Asia, Africa, and Latin America were initially known as **the Third World** in the 1950s by French writers who used *tiers monde*, 'third world', to distinguish the developing countries from the capitalist and Communist blocs. The first use in English came in 1963. **The best of all worlds** or **of all possible worlds** is from *Candide* (1759) by the French writer Voltaire. It is a translation of a statement by the ever-optimistic Pangloss, 'Everything is for the best in the best of all possible worlds'. The character of Pangloss, who remained constantly cheerful despite all the disasters that happened to him and his travelling companions, is a satire on the views of the German philosopher Leibniz, who believed this philosophy. *See also* OPTIMISM, OYSTER, WHIM, WIFE

worm [OE] In Old English worm was spelled *wyrm* or *wurm*. The first meaning was 'serpent' or 'dragon', a sense still occasionally found in dialect and preserved

wild and woolly   word   work   world

in folk tales such as 'The Lambton Worm'. Worm came to mean 'crawling animal, reptile, or insect' and then, in about 1100, an earthworm or similar creature. In a **can of worms** the worms are probably maggots—think of a fisherman on a riverbank with his wriggling bait tin. **The worm has turned** means 'a meek person has retaliated after being pushed too far'. The original form, in 1546, was 'Tread a worm on the tail and it must turn again'.

worry [OE] In Old English worry was 'to strangle'. The Middle Ages saw the meanings 'to choke with a mouthful of food', 'to seize by the throat and tear', and 'to swallow greedily', and in the 16th century 'to harass'. This gave rise to 'to annoy or disturb' in the late 17th century, and then 'to cause anxiety to'. The sense 'to feel anxious or troubled' (**he worried about his son**) is not recorded until the 1860s, and was initially regarded as a rather informal use.

worse *see* WAR

worship [OE] The writings of Alfred the Great, king of Wessex from 871 to 899, are the first source of worship, which is literally 'worthship'. It initially meant 'good name, credit' and 'dignity, importance', which survives in **your worship**, used for a high-ranking person such as a magistrate or mayor. The word was not found in religious contexts until around 1300. **Hero-worship** originally referred to the ancient worship of heroes such as Hercules, regarded as semi-divine, and often the subject of myths. The historian Thomas Carlyle was partly responsible for the modern sense—his lectures *On Heroes, Hero-Worship, and the Heroic in History*, published in 1841, expounded his view that history is fundamentally the history of great men, who are worshipped as heroes.

wort *see* ROOT

wotcha *see* CHEER

wrack *see* RACK

wreak *see* WRECK

wreathe *see* WRONG

wreck [ME] When it first appeared wreck meant 'cargo or wreckage washed ashore from a wrecked or stranded vessel'. The word came into English from Old French *wrec*. The source was an Old Norse word meaning 'to drive' that was related to **wreak**, 'to cause a lot of damage or harm', and to *RACK. A person in a state of stress or emotional exhaustion has been a wreck since the 1790s and a **nervous wreck** since about 1870. **Wretch** [OE] and **wretched** [ME] are related to wreak.

wright *see* WORK

wring, wrist *see* WRONG

write [OE] The idea behind write in the ancient Germanic languages was 'to score or carve'—people in northern Europe would have written first by inscribing letters on wood. The original meaning in Old English was 'to draw or outline the shape of something'. The first person to use the phrase **nothing to write home about**, meaning 'be mediocre or unexceptional', appears to have been the comic writer Ian Hay in 1914. Hay was also a soldier who served in the First World War and was awarded the Military Cross, and the expression was probably a military one (*see also* FUN). If you say that a particular quality or feeling is **written all over someone's face**, you are echoing Shakespeare. In *Measure for Measure* Duke Vincentio says: 'There is written in your brow, Provost, honesty, and constancy.' *See also* WALL

writhe *see* WRONG

wrong [OE] An Old English word from Old Norse *rangr* 'awry, unjust', which first meant 'crooked, curved, or twisted' and is related to **wring** [OE]. Until the 17th century the *wr-* would have been pronounced, and there was obviously something about the sound that suggested the idea of twisting—many English words beginning with *wr-*, such as **wrist**, **writhe**, and **wreathe** (all OE), contain the notion. Although to **get the wrong end of the stick** now means 'to misunderstand something', the original sense seems to have been 'to come off worse'. The example in *The Swell's Night Guide*, a guide to London low life published in 1846, gives an idea of what was wrong with the 'wrong end': 'Which of us had hold of the crappy...end of the stick?' The proverb **two wrongs don't make a right** dates from the late 18th century. The Hungarian-born psychiatrist Thomas Szasz summed up the feelings of many when he said in 1973: 'Two wrongs don't make a right, but they make a good excuse.'

wrought *see* WORK

wyrm *see* WORM

WYSIWYG *see* SEE

writhe   wrong   wrought   wyrm   WYSIWYG

Xerox *see* ELIXIR

Xmas [M16th] This term for Christmas was originally only a written form, with X representing the initial letter of Greek *Khristos*, 'Christ', in the Greek alphabet. It is not possible to tell when people started pronouncing it with the sound of *x*.

xylene *see* XYLOPHONE

xylophone [M19th] This is the only common word formed from Greek *xylo-* 'wood', although it is common enough in science in words such as **xylene** [M19th] a hydrocarbon made from distilled wood, and archaeologists can describe a single lump of wood as **monoxylic** [M19th] on the model of **monolithic** [M19th] for 'single stone'.

Xerox   Xmas   xylene   xylophone

yacht *see* DUTCH WORD PANEL

yahoo [M18th] The fourth part of Jonathan Swift's satire *Gulliver's Travels*, published in 1726, describes the country of the Houyhnhnms, who were intelligent horses. Their simplicity and virtue contrasts with the disgusting brutality of the Yahoos, beasts in the shape of men. Soon yahoo was being used for a coarse person or lout. In Australia the **Yahoo** is a large, hairy man-like monster supposedly inhabiting the east of the country. The name is recorded from the mid 19th century, and may have originated in an Aboriginal word, though Swift's Yahoos influenced the form in English. In the internet site and search engine **Yahoo!**, Yahoo stands for Yet Another Hierarchical Officious Oracle, but was chosen partly because the associations of yahoo appealed to them.

Yankee *see* US WORD PANEL

yard [OE] The yard as a unit of length descends from Old English *gerd* 'twig, stick, rod', and has been the standard English unit of measure equal to three feet since the later medieval period. Since the Old English period this yard has also been a nautical term for a long spar for a square sail to hang from. *See also* SUN. The other yard derives from Old English *geard* 'building, home, enclosure' and is related to *GARDEN and *ORCHARD, and also to Russian *gorod* 'town', used in place names such as Novgorod. In Britain a yard is usually an enclosed piece of ground near a building, whereas in the USA it means the garden of a house. In Jamaican English yard means 'a house or home', and among expatriate Jamaicans **Yard** is Jamaica. This is the origin of **Yardie**, used by Jamaicans for a fellow Jamaican, but since the mid 1980s in Britain to refer to a member of a Jamaican or West Indian gang of criminals.

ye [OE] In deliberately quaint names such as Ye Olde Tea Shoppe, ye represents an imaginary old form of **the**. In the Middle Ages English used a letter called a thorn that indicated the sound of *th*. It looked rather like *y*, and came to be written in an identical way, so that **the** could be **ye**. This spelling was kept as a convenient abbreviation in handwriting down to the 19th century, and in printers' types during the 15th and 16th centuries, but it was never pronounced as 'ye'. The other ye was simply a regular old form of 'you'.

year [OE] This shares an ancient root with Greek *hōra* 'season, time', source of **horology** [LME], **horoscope** [OE], and *HOUR. The term **leap year**, used from the 14th century, probably comes from the fact that in a leap year feast days after February fall two days of the week later than in the previous year, rather than the usual one day, and could be said to have 'leaped' a day.

yellow [OE] As with other colour words such as *AUBURN and *BROWN, the root of yellow probably referred to a wider range of colours than the modern word. It shares an ancestor with gold (*see* GOLDEN), but is also related to **gall** [OE], **bile** [M17th], and the final element of *MELANCHOLY, all of which derive from the greenish colour of bile. The yellow egg **yolk** [OE], which could be spelt *yelk* into the 17th century, was also related to **yellow**. In the 17th century yellow rather than *GREEN was the colour of jealousy, possibly with the idea of a jealous person being 'jaundiced' or bitter. The word **jaundice** [ME] is from Old French *jaune* 'yellow', from the symptomatic yellowish complexion. Yellow is now associated with cowardice, a link that began in the 1850s in the USA. Since the 1920s a coward has been said to be **yellow-bellied** or a **yellow-belly**.

yen [L19th] The vocabulary of drug users entered mainstream English before modern times. The yen in to **have a yen for**, 'to long or yearn for', originally referred to the drug addict's craving for opium. The word came from Chinese *yăn* 'craving' in the 1870s. The

yacht   yahoo   Yankee   yard   ye   year

yen that is the monetary unit of Japan comes from Japanese *en* 'round'.

yeti *see* ABOMINABLE

Enough words already!

Yiddish, *based on German dialect combined with words from Hebrew and Slavic languages, was spoken by Jews in central and eastern Europe before World War Two. It is still used in Israel and parts of Europe and the USA, especially New York, and has added an extra tang to English speech.*

THE most familiar Yiddish word may be **nosh**, 'to eat greedily', used in English since the late 19th century and deriving from Yiddish *nashn*. Foods worth noshing include **bagels** (ring-shaped bread rolls), **lox** (smoked salmon), **matzos** (crisp biscuits of unleavened bread), and that staple of huge American-style sandwiches, **pastrami** (seasoned smoked beef).

The opening *sch-* is characteristic of Yiddish words, including **schlep** (to go or move with effort), **schlock** (inferior goods or material, rubbish), **schmaltz** (excessive sentimentality, literally 'dripping, lard'), **schnozz** (the nose), and **schtick** (an attention-getting routine or gimmick). Most of these date from the early or mid 20th century, although **schmooze**, 'to chat intimately and cosily', is from the 1890s.

Yiddish words often express a certain attitude—**oy vey!** (oh dear!), enough with the **kvetching** (moaning and complaining) already! This use of **already** to express impatience is influenced by Jewish speech, and is a translation of Yiddish *shoyn* 'already'. It is an example of the way Yiddish has exerted a subtle influence on English. If you say you **need something like a hole in the head** (used in English since the early 1950s), you are translating the Yiddish expression *tsu darfn vi a lokh in kop*. Other familiar idioms that are translations from Yiddish are **it's OK by me** and **get lost!**, both of which are first found in the USA.

Chutzpah is almost untranslatable—'extreme self-confidence or audacity' is probably the closest approximation. A **klutz** is clumsy, awkward, or foolish and a **nebbish** is a feeble or timid man, while a **schmuck** is foolish or contemptible—the word literally means 'penis', as does **putz**, also used to mean 'a stupid or worthless person'. On a more positive note, a **maven** is an expert or connoisseur, and a **mensch** a man of integrity and honour.s

Although Yiddish is today associated particularly with New York, it has also influenced the speech of Londoners. Cockneys tell each other to keep **schtum** or silent, and call bad things **dreck** or rubbish and good ones *KOSHER—a Hebrew word that was spread by Yiddish-speakers.

The *-nik* in words like **beatnik** is another Yiddish contribution to English. It was originally used in Russian to form words for people of a particular kind, and was taken up by Yiddish-speakers in the USA. Today we have terms such as **kibbutznik**, a member of a kibbutz or communal farm in Israel, and **refusenik**, a Jew in the Soviet Union who was refused permission to emigrate to Israel, or more generally a person who refuses to follow orders or obey the law. The beatniks were part of the subculture associated with the **beat generation** of the 1950s and early 1960s (*see* BEAT).

See also GAZUMP, GLITCH, SLAP, SMACK

yob [M19th] This is an example of back slang, in which people say words as though they were spelled backwards. It is a reverse form of boy, and originally, in the mid 19th century, simply meant 'a boy or youth'. Now a yob is a rude, noisy, or aggressive one.

yoga [M19th] The yoga that we know in the West is a simplified version of an ancient Hindu system intended to lead to union with the divine. The word's literal meaning in the Indian language Sanskrit is 'union', and it is related to **yoke** [OE], fastened over the necks of two animals to enable them to pull in unison.

yolk *see* YELLOW

yonks *see* DONKEY

young [OE] Young and **youth** [OE] are from the same ancient root as Latin *juvenis* 'young', source of **juvenile** [E17th] and **rejuvenate** [E19th]. **The good die young** is a proverb from the late 17th century, but the idea goes back to the ancient Greek playwright Menander, who wrote: 'Whom the gods love dies young.' A **young turk** is now a young person eager for radical change, a meaning that comes from the **Young Turks** who carried out the revolution of 1908 in the Ottoman Empire and deposed the sultan Abdul Hamid II.

yo-yo [E20th] Crazes for particular toys are nothing new. In the late 1920s the **yo-yo** was the latest thing. Although toys resembling yo-yos were known in ancient China and Greece, the name probably comes from the Philippines, where the yo-yo had been popular for hundreds of years.

It entered English in 1915, and became a verb meaning 'to move up and down, fluctuate' in the 1960s.

Yule [OE] It is now just another word for Christmas, but Yule comes from the Old Norse word *jól*, a pagan festival at the winter solstice that lasted for twelve days. Germanic and Scandinavian pagans celebrated it in late December or early January, and when they adopted Christianity they simply changed the nature of the festival, turning *jól* into Christmas. In Old English Yule meant 'December or January' and also 'Christmas and its festivities'. **Jolly** [ME] from Old French *jolif* 'merry, handsome, lively', may come ultimately from the same Old Norse root.

yum [L19th] Since the 1870s our natural response to eating tasty food has been represented in writing as yum or **yum-yum**, and delicious food has been described as **yummy**. In about 1993 yummy found a new use—a young, stylish, attractive, mother, particularly a celebrity photographed with her cute child, was called a **yummy mummy**.

yuppie [1980s] The 1980s saw the rise of the yuppie, the 'young urban professional' or, as people later interpreted the initials, 'young upwardly mobile professional' (or 'person'). *The Yuppie Handbook* inaugurated their era in 1984, the year when the word is first recorded. It was possibly suggested by the **yippies**, a term for members of the Youth International Party, a group of politically active hippies formed in the USA in 1966.

yob   yoga   yolk   yonks   young   yo-yo

zany [L16th] Zany was the name of one of the servants in the improvized Italian theatre, the *commedia dell'arte*, popular from the 16th to 18th centuries. The word is a Venetian form of *Gianni*, which itself is short for *Giovanni*. In its earliest uses in English a zany was a comic performer who imitated the actions of a clown or acrobat, and zany described his behaviour. *See also* PANTALOONS

zap [1920s] In comic strips of the 1920s zap often represented the sound of a ray gun, laser, or similar weapon. The sense 'to kill' has existed since the 1940s and 'to move quickly' since the 1960s. Since the early 1980s **zapping** has also meant the use of a remote control to operate a television or other piece of electronic equipment.

zeal *see* JEALOUSY

zebra [E17th] Zebra is not from an African language, as was once thought, but via Italian, Spanish, or Portuguese from Latin *equiferus* 'wild horse'—the root is *equus*, as in *EQUESTRIAN. The **zebra crossing**, named because it is marked with black and white stripes, was introduced in Britain in 1949.

zeitgeist *see* GERMAN WORD PANEL

zenith [LME] Like its opposite, **nadir** [LME], zenith was originally an astronomical term deriving from Arabic, in this case from *samt ar-ra's*, 'path over the head'. In astronomy the zenith is the point in the sky immediately above the observer, and also the highest point reached by a particular celestial object, when it is **at its zenith**. The modern general sense of this developed from the astronomical use in the early 17th century. The nadir is the point in the sky immediately below the observer, and comes from Arabic *nazīr*, meaning 'opposite [to the zenith]'. Its general sense, 'the lowest or most unsuccessful point', also developed in the early 17th century.

zilch *see* ZIP

zip [M19th] As a name for a fastener, zip dates from the 1920s. The idea of speed was already present in a 19th-century use representing the sound of something moving through the air rapidly. **Zoom** appears at the same time with the same sense. In the USA zip also means 'nothing, nil, zero'. This appeared in print in 1900, much earlier than the similar **zilch**, the first clear example of which dates from the mid 1960s, though **Mr Zilch** had been used as an indefinite name 30 or more years before. The US **zip code**, a postal code consisting of five or nine digits, is unrelated, being short for *Zone Improvement Plan*.

zodiac *see* ZOO

zombie [E19th] This is of West African origin; Kikongo *zumbi* 'fetish' is a related form. Figurative use meaning 'dull, slow-witted person' is found from the 1930s.

zone [LME] Zone is from Greek *zōnē*, 'girdle'. It was first used to refer to each of the five belts or encircling regions (differentiated by climate) into which the surface of the earth is divided by the tropics. From this early use, the word came to be applied to various areas defined by certain boundaries or subject to certain restrictions.

zoo [M19th] The first zoo was the **Zoological Gardens** in Regent's Park, London. It was established in 1828 in the gardens of the London Zoological Society,

zany zap zeal zebra zeitgeist zenith zilch

and was at first just for scientific study, but was opened to the public in 1847. Practically all English words beginning zoo-, including **zoological** [E19th] and **zoology** [M17th], go back to Greek *zōion* 'animal', source also of **zodiac** [LME] which got its name because most of the signs of the zodiac are represented by animals.

zoom *see* ZIP

zany zap zeal zebra zeitgeist zenith zilch

Glossary

Acronym: A word formed from the initial letters of other words (laser, Aids).

Anglo-Latin: The form of Latin used in England in the Middle Ages, which developed some of its own forms, often influenced by the users' own language.

Anglo-Norman (French): The form of French used in England by the Norman elite. They had brought over their own Norman dialect, and it then developed further changes in England.

Avestan: An ancient Indo-European language spoken in the area of what is now Iran, in which the sacred writings of the Zoroastrian are preserved.

Back formation: A word formed from an existing word, which looks as if it is the source of the earlier word, such as edit from editor.

Base: *see* ROOT

Combining form: A word-element that can be combined with others to form words such as the semi- of semi-detached, the trans- of transatlantic. *See* list under *Word Building*.

Comparative: In adjectives and adverbs, forms such as bigger (= more big). Usually formed by adding -er. Biggest (= most big) is called the superlative form.

Diminutive: A form of a word that shows it refers to something smaller than usual—piglet is the diminutive of pig.

Ecclesiastical Latin: The distinctive form of Latin used by the Church (particularly the Bible and in the Middle Ages) which has differences from Classical Latin or Rome.

Figurative: Language which should not be understood literally, but which sets out to create an image.

Folk etymology: *see* word entry ASPARAGUS

Gaulish: The extinct Celtic language spoken in Gaul (the equivalent of modern France), before it was replaced by Latin and then French.

Germanic: The ancestral language of Northern Europe which later developed into the modern North Germanic languages of Scandinavia and the West Germanic languages including German, Dutch, and English.

Indo-European: The group of related languages that include most of those spoken in Europe and many of the western Asian languages including those of northern India. They are all descended from a lost, ancient language called Proto-Indo-European (often shortened to Indo-European). *See* the *Introduction*

Jargon: Special terms used in the language of a profession or group which are difficult for outsiders to understand.

Late Latin: The Latin spoken AD *c*.300–700, by ordinary uneducated people into the Early Middle Ages, which often differed from the language of the educated and from Classical Latin. The term overlaps with Vulgar Latin and Popular Latin.

Low German: The dialect of much of Northern Germany, distinct from High German spoken in the south and the usual written form. It is closely related to Dutch and sometimes used to include Dutch and other related dialects.

Metathesis: The swapping round of sounds in a word, such as saying pacific instead of specific.

Middle (Dutch, Low German etc): The form of the language spoken in the Middle Ages. The exact dates covered vary from language to language.

Modern Latin: Includes the language spoken from *c*.1500 onwards. Often used of scientific coinages.

Old French: The language spoken in France from about AD 800 until Middle French developed about 1350–1400.

Romance: The group of Indo-European languages that developed from Late Latin. Modern Romance languages include French, Italian, Spanish, and Romanian.

Root: A root or base is the underlying form from which a word has been made, and from which other words descend. This may be only one or two stages back (*see* STEM) or may go all the way back to Indo-European.

Sanskrit: An ancient language of northern India, in which many Hindu scriptures are written. It provides many important clues as to the history of Indo-European.

Stem: The basic part of a word from which other parts are formed. Run is the stem of running and runner.

Synonym: A word that means the same as another.

Superlative: *see* COMPARATIVE

Variant: A different form or spelling of a word.

Vulgate: The Latin translation of the Bible made by St Jerome in the 4th century and the main version of the Bible in western Europe throughout the Middle Ages (*see* ECCLESIASTICAL LATIN).

West Germanic: *see* GERMANIC

Yiddish: A language originally spoken by Jews in central and eastern Europe. It is based on German, but has many characteristics of Hebrew and Slavic languages.